Object-Oriented Networks

Models for Architecture, Operations, and Management

Subodh Bapat

PRENTICE HALL PTR, Englewood Cliffs, New Jersey 07632

Library of Congress Cataloging-in-Publication Data

Bapat, Subodh.
    Object-oriented networks: models for architecture, operations,
  and management/Subodh Bapat.
        p.   cm.
    Includes bibliographical references and index.
    ISBN 0-13-031097-2
    1. Object-oriented programming (Computer science) 2. Computer
  networks. I. Title.
  QA76.64.B34   1994
  004.6'01'1--dc20
                                                                   93-46364
                                                                        CIP

Editorial/production supervision: *bookworks*
Acquisitions editor: *Mary Franz*
Cover designer: *Wanda Lubelska*
Copy editor: *M.E. Williams, Inc.*
Manufacturing manager: *Alexis R. Heydt*

©1994 by Prentice Hall PTR
Prentice-Hall, Inc.
A Simon & Schuster Company
Englewood Cliffs, New Jersey 07632

Eiffel is a registered trademark of Interactive Software Engineering, Inc. Ethernet is a trademark of Xerox Corporation. MS-DOS and Microsoft Windows are trademarks of Microsoft Corporation. NetWare is a trademark of Sun Microsystems, Inc. PostScript is a registered trademark of Adobe Systems, Inc. Smalltalk is a trademark of ParcPlace Systems. UNIX is a registered trademark of UNIX System Laboratories, Inc. (a wholly-owned subsidiary of Novell, Inc.) in the United States and other countries. Other designations used by manufacturers and sellers as trademarks to distinguish their products may appear in this book. In all cases where the publisher is aware of a current trademark claim, the designations have been printed in initial capitals or all capitals.

The publisher offers discounts on this book when ordered in bulk quantities. For more information, contact: Corporate Sales Department, P T R Prentice Hall, 113 Sylvan Avenue, Englewood Cliffs, NJ 07632, Phone: (201) 592-2863, FAX: (201) 592-2249

Printed in the United States of America
10   9   8   7   6   5   4   3

ISBN   0-13-031097-2

Prentice-Hall International (UK) Limited, *London*
Prentice-Hall of Australia Pty. Limited, *Sydney*
Prentice-Hall Canada Inc., *Toronto*
Prentice-Hall Hispanoamericana, S.A., *Mexico*
Prentice-Hall of India Private Limited, *New Delhi*
Prentice-Hall of Japan, Inc., *Tokyo*
Simon & Schuster Asia Pte. Ltd., *Singapore*
Editora Prentice-Hall do Brasil, Ltda., *Rio de Janeiro*

for Ai and Baba

for everything

Contents

Preface

Why This Book Was Written

The growth of networking technologies in the past few years has been explosive. Digital communication networks, once limited to moving data between computers in universities and research laboratories, now permeate almost everywhere. The existing infrastructure of the worldwide telephone network, assiduously constructed over the last hundred years to provide voice communication, is undergoing a radical transformation as digital technologies are being deployed to provide improved quality and advanced services. In the world of tomorrow, it is not inconceivable that a combination of underlying transport technologies — wireless, analog wireline, and digital fiber among them — will combine to form a worldwide network interconnecting offices, factories, residences, commercial establishments, transportation vehicles, and many other entities. Technical reachability will impose almost no limit; actual reachability will only be constrained by policy considerations such as security, confidentiality, service deployment costs, and service usage costs.

Clearly, the task of constructing communications networks of this magnitude is formidable. As with all complex systems, the best way to approach the construction task in a manner that is manageable and understandable is to decompose the system and create a model for it. Aeronautical engineers create models for aircraft and spacecraft before they are constructed; electrical engineers create models of VLSI circuits before they are manufactured. Modeling helps to understand the complexity of the system at hand. By using a model to simulate the system before it is constructed, design errors can be detected and corrected at the modeling stage itself, when they are relatively inexpensive to correct, rather than after actual construction, at which time error correction can be very expensive. In addition, the existence of a model also assists in the maintenance and management of the system after it has been constructed.

So it is with communication networks. To successfully construct the complex communication networks of tomorrow, one must first devise a sound modeling methodology. This book attempts to provide a small start in that direction: its primary objective is to demonstrate techniques for modeling communication networks. Once we can capture the description of complex networks in a formal notation, then we can analyze the networks by analyzing the notation. By manipulating the model of the network, either manually or computationally, we can understand the network, architect it, design it, simulate it, analyze it, operate it, and manage it. We can precisely communicate our knowledge of the network to others through its model. This book attempts to create such a model and demonstrate its applications.

What This Book Does

The primary objective of this book is to develop mechanisms for modeling communication networks through the use of practical examples. The specific technique chosen is object-oriented modeling, as applied to communication networks. Although there have been many books about object-oriented programming, there have been relatively few about object-orientation as a modeling technique. This book treats object-orientation as a modeling technique at the abstract, architectural level, without regard to specific programming language implementations; from this perspective, it explains the applications of object-oriented modeling techniques as applied to communication networks.

The applications and examples span a wide range of communications networking technology. Examples are drawn from the realm of data internetworking, such as networks incorporating LAN bridges, routers, and higher-level data protocols such as TCP/IP, as well as from wide-area telecommunications networks, which include standard voice telephony as well as advanced SONET, Broadband ISDN, and Intelligent Network technologies.

The book explains how such communication networks can be modeled using object-oriented techniques, and how such models can be applied to the architecture, operations, and management of these networks. The modeling techniques described in this book are not by any means complete; they are intended as guidelines, to be extended, refined and revised as more advanced techniques become available through future research.

Of the many modeling methodologies available, object-oriented modeling has proved to be especially popular in the area of modeling complex systems. Some recent books have demonstrated the application of object-orientation to complex systems, notably *Object-Oriented Analysis and Design with Applications* by Grady Booch [Booc94] and *Object-Oriented Modeling and Design* by James Rumbaugh et al [Rumb91a]. These books have developed object-orientation as a modeling methodology (rather than as a programming paradigm, which has been done by several other current books) and show the usefulness of applying it to the design of complex systems, such as aircraft engines and flight simulators. Since communication networks are becoming complex systems, they would also benefit from being analyzed under object-oriented models.

The methodology of this book uses not only conventional object-oriented modeling concepts such as inheritance but also advanced concepts from *Specialization Theory*. The specialization-theoretic methodology is adapted to make it especially suitable for communication networks. This includes mechanisms to model aspects such as ports and protocol stacks, internetworking relationships, constraints, and logic-based reasoning about networks. Moreover, the book provides a notation within which these aspects can be precisely defined. Conventional object-oriented modeling, as explained in Booch and Rumbaugh, has typically been diagrammatic rather than notational in its development of the model; furthermore, it does not cover issues such as ports and protocol stacks associated with objects, which are important in networking. This book, while making extensive use of diagrams to demonstrate the model, complements the modeling methodology with a precise and easily readable notation.

The formalism of the model is expressed in a set of special-purpose notational constructs developed specifically to express the semantics of the model. Although the word "formal" in the realm of computer systems modeling often means "knowledge arising as a consequence of *a priori* reasoning from first principles" (and frequently incorporates mathematical notation from first-order logic, predicate calculus, and set theory), that is not the sense in which we use this word. Our modeling notation is "formal" in the sense that it "considers and evaluates the existing state of the practice, and organizes current practitioner methodologies in a common framework." This will be evident throughout the book: all the modeling constructs developed arise from examples of current engineering problems in network design, and once developed, are immediately applied to other current and future network engineering issues to demonstrate their versatility.

This book demonstrates *one* syntax which can capture the semantics of the model precisely; this is the international standard Abstract Syntax Notation One (ASN.1). This syntax is sufficiently accessible to be understandable to the human reader, while at the same time precise enough to be compiled. However, there is no requirement that this specific notation be always used with the methodology; the methodology itself is syntax-independent, and any convenient sufficiently precise syntax may be chosen to express the desired semantics.

Who Should Read This Book

There has been a great surge of overall interest industry-wide in object-oriented techniques. The promises of object-oriented technology are rich in terms of its ability to enhance reuse, promote standardization, cut down product development cycles, and thereby reduce costs. The promises of communication networks are also rich, with many corporations believing that they will gain considerable competitive advantage through advanced networking technology. The confluence of the two technologies should be of great interest to many.

As networks become increasingly complex — not only in terms of their size and capacity but also in terms of their intelligence and processing power — the corporations who construct these networks and deploy services on them will turn to automated methods for network design and operation. Clearly, the imposition of a modeling methodology will be required at this point. There are at least three areas of networking in which a formal modeling methodology will be required:

- ***Network Architecture and Planning:*** Synthesizing communication networks from available components, and determining the capacities of the network and the types of services which can be deployed on it, will require a formal model as this task becomes more complicated and automated. This book explains how a model developed using object-oriented techniques can be used algorithmically in the process of network architecture and planning, including the activities of automated network synthesis and simulation.

- ***Network Operations:*** As components in the network become smarter and increase their intelligence and processing capability, much of the "higher-level" intelligence required for operating the network will devolve down to the devices used in the network. As a basis for this intelligence, and also as a basis for assuring wide interoperability with other devices, each device will be required to have some knowledge of itself and other devices to which it may be connected. This will require a model within which such knowledge can be framed.

- ***Network Management:*** The field of network management, which uses computer systems that automatically perform diagnostics, trouble-shooting, and configuration of network devices, also requires that information about the network be conveyed within some model. This book examines some of the network models developed for the Internet and OSI network management standards. In addition, it also explains how the extended object-oriented modeling methodologies demonstrated in the book can be used to add further intelligence to network management functions.

The following people are likely to benefit from reading this book:

- ***Senior Executives*** in the communications industry who would like to understand how object-oriented technology will affect their networks in terms of its capabilities and services and how deployment cycles may be reduced, thereby helping to control costs and generate service revenue as quickly as possible;

- ***Mid-level Managers*** in the networking equipment manufacturing industry who would like to understand how object-oriented techniques may allow them to deliver advanced networking equipment and software in shorter project cycles;

- ***Marketing Executives*** in the networking industry who would like to read about and understand technologies which will help them increase market share by using additional intelligence in networking devices and network management systems as a differentiating factor for products and services;

- ***Planning Architects*** working for telecommunications service providers, who will need to use advanced models for automating the task of network architecture, planning, and synthesis;

- **System Design Engineers** working for networking equipment manufacturers, in both telecommunications and data internetworking, who will need advanced architectural techniques to increase the intelligence and capabilities of these devices;

- **Software Engineers and Architects** working for networking equipment manufacturers, who will need modeling techniques with richer semantics to build smarter network management software systems.

For the reader who already has a good grounding in data internetworking or telecommunications, this book will provide an insight into how object-oriented modeling can be applied to this discipline and the benefits resulting from this approach. For the reader already familiar with object-oriented programming, this book will introduce advanced object modeling techniques and will shed some light on communication networks as an interesting application area for the object-oriented modeling paradigm. For the reader who has neither, this book contains adequate background material to serve as an introduction to both.

How This Book Explains Its Subject

An attempt has been made to keep the style of this book as informal as possible in order to reach the widest possible audience. While any realistic modeling methodology must have some degree of rigor, its explanation and exposition need not be as formal. Typically, before introducing a modeling construct, concrete examples from current network engineering design are used as the basis of informal arguments as to why such a construct is necessary. The precise modeling construct is then introduced. To explain the use of the construct in the engineering design of current and future network architectures, the informal and intuitive style is again invoked.

Because of the informal nature of the explanations, a detailed background in object-oriented techniques is not required for understanding the material in this book. The introductory chapters contain a sufficient exposition of object-oriented techniques that people unfamiliar with the methodology will quickly grasp the necessary basic concepts. Nor is an extensive background in computer networking or telecommunications required, although some familiarity with or interest in communication networks will be of help.

The general expository technique for presenting concepts of the object-oriented model used throughout the book is almost completely example-driven. This makes it easy for persons not having a background in formal modeling to grasp the concepts. Whenever a new concept is introduced, the following steps are generally taken:

1. Introduce an example to explain the problem.

2. Generalize the problem, and explain the object modeling concept which solves the problem.

3. State the concept as a formal object modeling principle.

4. Reapply this principle to other examples to reinforce the concept and refine and extend the concept as necessary.

As a result of this expository technique, all formalisms follow quite naturally from the examples; thus, they can be grasped and assimilated quite easily. In many cases, the theory flows from the examples: the theoretical basis for the formalism is explained *after* the examples are demonstrated. This "bottom-up" approach to the exposition of advanced object-oriented modeling principles is, in the opinion of the author, an easier method of making the formal concepts accessible to readers.

Although we note that too broad a usage of the term "formal" has been criticized by some standards committees, the book's emphasis on formalism should be interpreted in the context of this expository approach. One aim is to produce "formal" specifications in the sense that they are machine-processable. More importantly, the "formalism" of the methodology broadly consists of the steps of (i) studying an example problem; (ii) solving it; (iii) explaining its solution informally; (iv) abstracting the general principles from the explanation which apply to a class of similar problems; and (v) stating these principles in a rigorous manner.

The book occasionally uses anthropomorphisms in its exposition, for example, "an object knows its class" or "tools understand the model". The intent of such construction is to explain concepts succinctly yet informally. While they largely accomplish their purpose, on occasion anthropomorphisms may be counterproductive to a true understanding of the behavior of architectural elements. For this reason, we have attempted to enclose anthromorphic terminology in quotes wherever this does not distract from the expository flow.

Throughout this book, references are made to a "compiler" which supports this methodology. This refers to any software tool which may be built to interpret the formal notation used to capture the semantics of the object model. We are presently at work in the development of such tools. At the moment, this compiler does not exist as a single program; it exists as a set of related but separate software tools. Each tool is applicable to a different subset of the formal constructs of the modeling methodology; each has a different back-end for generating output suitable for different implementation environments. To keep the focus of the book on the model, rather than on the description of the many software tools that interpret the model, we will speak of a single "compiler" when necessary; the reader should understand this to mean "an appropriate software tool capable of parsing this part of the formal notation".

How This Book Is Organized

The book is organized into 30 chapters. The first few chapters deal with purely descriptive aspects of object-oriented modeling. Readers with a very elementary knowledge of object-oriented modeling will be able to follow these without much difficulty. Chapter 1 discusses the need and the utility of modeling in communication network design; Chapter 2 introduces the basic notions and terminology of object-oriented modeling. Because many readers are more familiar with object-oriented programming than with object-oriented modeling, Chapter 3 discusses the commonalities and distinctions between the two. Chapter 4 uses concrete examples from communication networks to demonstrate how object classes can be designed. Chapter 5 introduces concepts of specialization and generalization so that classes can be precisely cast within the framework of an object-oriented model. Chapter 6 introduces formal specialization principles, using examples from telecommunication network service deployment, broadband multiplexers, and IP routers. Chapter 7 uses many examples to model an aggregation hierarchy of network object classes, such as wiring hubs for networking Ethernet, Token Ring, and FDDI networks. Chapter 8 is a complete engineering example for the architecture design of a Broadband Nodal Processor, a device which can be used for LAN-WAN internetworking; the design of this nodal processor is demonstrated using the object-oriented modeling principles developed in previous chapters. Chapter 9 discusses the registration and labeling of objects in the international registration hierarchy.

Up to this point, the book is descriptive and no formal syntax is introduced. Chapter 10 introduces Information Object Classes of the OSI Abstract Syntax Notation One standard, and shows how they can be used to develop a special-purpose network modeling notation which is precise yet human-friendly. Chapter 11 introduces the detailed syntax for network object classes. Chapter 12 applies the model syntax to concrete engineering examples such as modem devices, transport-layer protocol objects, and services like file transfer and software distribution. Chapter 13 introduces Formal Description Techniques for behavior modeling, using examples from TCP/IP state machines and datagram policy routing, and Chapter 14 introduces the formal notation for use with function modeling. Chapter 15 demonstrates how protocol stacks can be modeled and uses the syntax to specify protocols in current engineering use such as data communication stacks, Signaling System Number 7, and SONET DCC stacks. Chapter 16 describes the formal notation for models of protocol entities and stacks.

From Chapter 17 onward, we introduce several new and advanced object modeling concepts. Chapter 17 enhances conventional object-oriented modeling with the addition of inter-object relationships, using examples from telecommunication network design. Chapter 18 considers virtual relationships. Chapter 19 provides the formal models for the specification of relationships. Chapter 20 continues the treatment of advanced modeling techniques with the specification of virtual attributes. Chapter 21 introduces the mechanism of virtual object classes. Chapter 22 considers the treatment of constraints as properties of object classes, while Chapter 23 shows how production rules may be incorporated within an object-oriented model. Chapter 24 introduces the formal notation for virtual attributes, virtual object classes, constraints, and rules. Chapter 25 describes the metamodel of the methodology; this may be omitted by readers intending only to apply the methodology and not to build tools to support it. Chapter 26 describes how aspects of the model may be realized in various implementation environments.

The next three chapters apply the model to various aspects of communication networks. Chapter 27 describes how object modeling techniques are useful in the process of network architecture and planning, including automated network synthesis and simulation. Chapter 28 applies the techniques to network operations, with reference to emerging standards in the area of distributed computing systems and Intelligent Network architectures. Chapter 29 considers the use of formal modeling techniques in network management. Existing network modeling techniques in current network management standards are described and compared with the methodology of this book. Finally, Chapter 30 considers future challenges in network modeling and speculates on the further development of object modeling methodologies.

How to Use This Book

This book may be used in three different ways, depending on the interests of the reader. The chapters of this book are classified in three "tracks", as explained below. The most natural progression is the sequence in which the chapters occur; however, depending on interest, readers may wish to go through the book track by track. For easy reference, the running heads in each chapter also identify its track. The terminology in each track has its own glossary at the end.

The O-Track:

The O-Track is intended for readers who wish to understand the principles of object-orientation as a general engineering modeling methodology and apply advanced concepts from specialization theory. The chapters in the O-Track, while using examples from the realm of communication networks, are actually general enough so that they can be applied to any complex engineering system. Thus, readers interested in basic and advanced object-oriented modeling principles applicable to any engineering problem requiring an object model — not necessarily a communication network — will benefit from the O-Track. The O-Track consists of the following chapters:

>   *O-Track:*   Chapters 2, 3, 4, 5, 6, 7, 17, 18, 20,
>   21, 22, 23, 25, and 26.

The N-Track:

The N-Track is intended for readers who wish to understand object-oriented methodologies for the specific purpose of modeling communication networks. This includes all the chapters of the O-Track, plus material which shows how these techniques can be applied to the areas of modeling networks for architecture, operations, and management. However, the N-Track does not use any formal syntax for expressing the semantics of a formal network model. The N-Track is useful for readers who wish to create an object-oriented model for a communication network but do not wish to use any formal notation to create a compilable version of the model (or, for readers who wish to use their own standard or proprietary formal notation as a vehicle to carry the semantics of their network model). The N-Track consists of the following chapters:

>   *N-Track*:   All chapters of the O-Track +
>   Chapters 1, 8, 9, 13, 15, 27, 28, 29, and 30.

The F-Track:

The F-Track is intended for readers who wish to apply object-oriented techniques to the modeling of communication networks and who wish to express the formal semantics of a model in a compilable notation. This book largely uses ASN.1 as the vehicle to carry the semantics of the model. Readers wishing to use this notational formalism will benefit from the F-Track, which consists of the following chapters:

>   *F-Track*:   All chapters of the N-Track +
>   Chapters 10, 11, 12, 14, 16, 19, and 24.

Who Should Be Thanked for This Book

First and foremost, Mary Franz, Executive Editor at Prentice Hall, without whose efforts the schedule for this book could never have been met. Lisa Garboski and all the people involved in the production of this book have worked hard to ensure that this book is released on time, an effort in which I have not always been most helpful.

Many persons have contributed to the technical background of this book. I would like to thank my friends in the network management community for the many productive discussions I have had with them about the formal modeling of communication networks. Also included are many friends in the object-oriented programming community, whose ideas about formalism in object techniques and knowledge representation have been carried over and applied to communication networks. In particular, the many enlightening conversations with my colleagues Jack Stephenson, Ching Kung, and V.V. Chalam were of invaluable help in my understanding of the problem domain. I owe a special debt of gratitude to Peter Schow for providing many new ideas and much useful information which kept me abreast of new developments.

Desmond D'Souza, through the concepts developed in his training course taught through Icon Computing, exposed me to many advanced notions in object modeling and knowledge representation. Dr. Bancroft Scott of Open Systems Solutions, a company providing state-of-the-art ASN.1 compilers and software, rendered invaluable assistance in the use of formal ASN.1 specifications. Dr. Haim Kilov of Bellcore provided valuable comments in his review of the material. I must especially thank my friends Uresh and Archana Vahalia for overcoming my periodic doubts about the worthiness of this undertaking; their encouragement throughout the planning of this book considerably helped my sometimes flagging enthusiasm.

Finally, I would like to thank my friend and mentor George Yates, who, many years ago in his capacity as my supervisor in the Advanced Development group at Racal Datacom, roused me out of my conviction that I had strong career growth prospects as a software hack with esoteric knowledge of obscure UNIX minutiae, and encouraged me to undertake advanced research challenges in the high-level modeling and architecture of communication networks. After reading this book George will no doubt realize the folly of his actions.

1. Introduction to Network Modeling

"Sure, we have a formal network design process. It's called the Rube Goldberg methodology."
— *anonymous network architect.*

1.1. Introduction

This chapter introduces the general concepts behind the modeling of complex systems and shows how these apply to the design of communication networks. In particular, the benefits arising from the application of formal network models to the areas of network architecture and planning, network operations, and network management are described.

1.2. Networks as Complex Systems

The last few years have seen explosive growth of communication networks. As computer systems have proliferated, there has been increasing demand for moving data between them using data communications networks; as telephone systems have become more widespread, there has been an increasing demand for advanced services from telecommunications networks. The advent of digital techniques, in both the wireline telephone networks and in the wireless communications areas such as cellular telephony and mobile radio, has blurred the line between data internetworking and telecommunications. With the use of broadband communication technologies such as fiber optics and ATM which allow the digital transmission of not only computer-generated data but also analog information such as voice and video, the distinctions between traditional industry segments have become less meaningful. The network of tomorrow will have almost unlimited reachability from the perspective of technical feasibility; actual ability to communicate will be limited largely by considerations such as policy, security, and cost.

Today, networking technology is being deployed to provide extremely wide access to a variety of information with an unprecedented degree of convenience and flexibility.

1

Traditional data networking was once limited to interconnecting office computers by means of a local area network, interconnecting that local network with mainframes or servers to provide corporate-wide client-server computing, and perhaps interconnecting multiple geographically separate sites to facilitate electronic mail. In the traditional tele-communications area, a PBX or Centrex service with perhaps a few add-ons such as a CPE-based or central-office-based voice mail system was once considered state-of-the-art.

The increasing capabilities of networking technology have caused a qualitative change in the nature of things that can be accomplished using that technology [Pool90]. Today, grocery clerks with digital bar-code scanners directly upload inventory databases in remote mainframes using wireless media; intelligent highway systems measure and coordinate traffic flow using advanced algorithms; onboard computers in ground trans-portation vehicles provide navigational assistance; passengers in airplanes read the elec-tronic mail in their office; movies are delivered on demand to residences; mobile data terminals dynamically optimize the movement of delivery vehicle fleets; surgery is con-ducted over videoteleconferences; and residential computers automatically control home security, lighting, temperature, and entertainment. The network technology enabling these capabilities is increasing its reach, its speed, and its capacity, and is doing all three simul-taneously.

As the benefits of computer-based control are exploited in almost everything imaginable from supersonic aircraft to kitchen appliances, there is increasing demand to network all these devices together by grouping them together in meaningful configura-tions. The proliferation of systems which are "intelligent" or "smart" has created a de-mand for accessing these devices remotely across a network for the convenience of op-erating and controlling them in a flexible manner.

To quote Heilmeier [Heil92]: "In the past four decades, we have seen how rapidly a new kind of power — computing power — could become decentralized, dispersed, and accessible to millions. This process is far from over, and it may be accelerating as com-puting power is packaged in smaller, less expensive, friendlier systems. It is conceivable that, in a much shorter period, the power of information networking, arising from the convergence of computing with telecommunications and video, could become at least as widely dispersed as computing power, and as easily accessible as electricity."

Most of us will be plugged into the network of tomorrow, and though we may find its capabilities fanciful today, we will learn to routinely use its facilities in our daily lives without any more thought than we put into making an everyday telephone call. If we were to find ourselves stuck in traffic coming home from work, we could use our automobile's onboard computer to query the intelligent highway for the estimated delay; we could then send video mail to our family at home, advising of our late arrival, perhaps with convinc-ing pictures of the traffic in the background; we could arrange to have this message inter-rupt our teenage child's home video game if necessary; or, we could instruct our residence controller to delay turning on all programmed kitchen appliances.

This example is intended not so much to amuse as to emphasize that, as various networks are interconnected, the overall system so created will become extraordinarily complex. With the increase in networking capability comes an increase in the products and services that network providers can offer. This opens up greater possibilities to network users, both corporate and individual. More and more essential services — fire, police, paramedics — place their reliance on the underlying networking technology, thereby imposing complex reliability requirements on the network. As with all complex systems, such a network will overwhelm our ability to design and control it, unless we approach the task using modeling techniques suited to designing systems with complexity of this magnitude.

1.3. Modeling Complex Systems

In his seminal work on the exposition of the Internet protocol family, Douglas Comer [Come91] has identified the shifting emphasis in the development of communications technology. In the 1960s, the main issue was: "How can bits be sent across a wire so that they get across without too many errors?" This led to the development of information theory, coding and modulation techniques, as well as sampling and signal processing technology. In the 1970s, the question became: "How can entire packets be sent across a medium so they get across without too many errors?" The resulting developments were the technologies of packet switching and local area networks. At around the same time, telephone companies were working on technologies to exploit the reliability of the digital transmission of voice signals [Bell91].

Networks Everywhere

In the 1980s, four related developments occurred simultaneously and independently:

- The telephone plant nationwide underwent massive overhauls to provide faster and more dependable substrates (such as optical fiber) for digitized voice and data transmission, thereby increasing the quality and reliability of *telecommunication networks*;

- Internetworking technologies emerged from the data communications field for the error-proof transmission of data between computer systems connected in various topologies, thereby fueling explosive growth of *information networks*;

- Rapid penetration of the domestic subscriber market by cable television operators made large-scale recreational programming and bidirectional communication alternatives easily available, thereby creating an infrastructure for *entertainment networks*;

- Swift advances in the technology of wireless transmission made portable and mobile communication of voice and digital packet data affordable and easily available, thereby causing the growth and development of *mobile networks*.

In the 1990s, because of the convergence and interworking requirements of telecommunication networks, information networks, entertainment networks, mobile networks, and many others, and because of the entry of major industry corporations — previously dominant in largely one area — into every other, the distinctions among these

networks have virtually disappeared. These integrated networks will be collectively referred to in this book under the umbrella term *communication networks*.

Driven by these simultaneous developments, much of the 1980s and 1990s have
been spent in answering the question: "How can useful and reliable application services
be provided over heterogeneous, interconnected networks, using a variety of underlying
transmission technologies?" As we approach the twenty-first century, networks will become so pervasive that they must become easy to use. The question will now become:
"How can we make all these interconnected networks self-realizing and self-aware, so
that they function as invisibly as possible?" The challenge for the next generation of networking technology will be to design networks which can make intelligent decisions and
inferences about their own operation, so that they function unattended and are as self-
automated as possible. Even the most advanced networking technology must eventually
be made infrastructural — it must be "driven underground" and turned into a zero-main-
tenance system as much as possible, so that its users never have to bother with its details
and can take it for granted.

Architecture and Modeling Semantics

To design systems of such complexity, it is imperative to first describe the network in
terms of a *model*. The process of modeling elevates the problem into the realm of the
abstract, where it is generally more amenable to solution; once a solution has been defined on the abstract model of the problem, it can then be translated down into concrete
actions taken on the implemented network.

In any modeling process, the first step is to identify the *universe of discourse*. A
universe of discourse is that body of knowledge which we deem interesting enough to
model. Of necessity, the universe of discourse must be circumscribed to be some subset
of some field of knowledge; it may even be restricted to particular systems in the field of
knowledge. In this book, the universe of discourse shall be all communication networks.

Modeling allows us to describe systems in the chosen universe of discourse in a
formal manner. A good modeling technique provides a mechanism for *decomposition*. By
decomposing the complex system into its parts and by decomposing those parts into subparts, we can reduce the task of constructing such a system into manageable subtasks. The
model defines clearly separated components on which we can focus our attention separately and sequentially, because our minds can only deal with a small amount of information at any given time. The overall model of the complex system describes not only the
components which result from such a decomposition but also the relationships among
these components which describe how they interact to create the entire system.

This book concentrates on the problem of modeling communication networks. A
good modeling technique should provide an overarching, comprehensive view of the
system, that is, it should be able to formally describe the *system architecture* [Rech91].
An architecture imposes an organization on the elements of a problem domain — it provides a way of recognizing the major components of a system and the parameters under
which they interoperate. A good architecture is one that not only provides a descriptive
model of reality but also indicates possible ways of operating on that model to solve
problems of interest. The modeling technique must not only provide structure but must
also suggest function. Once such an architecture has been defined, we now have a

mechanism in which we can describe the network design problem and take the first steps towards solving it.

Modeling techniques vary in their degree of formalism. Some are graphical, some use a formal notation, and many use both. Graphical techniques can be rigorous and formal as well [Rumb91a]. Whether notational or graphical, the purpose of any technique is to correctly convey *modeling semantics*. The word "semantics" stands for the connection between symbols and their intrinsic meaning; it derives from the Greek *semaino* ("to mean"). It was coined in 1900 by Michael Breal [Brea00], a linguist, who studied the changing meanings of words in expressed language. In this book, we will use a formal notation or *syntax* to convey the modeling semantics of the universe of discourse.

With easy access to computer compilation capabilities, the popularity of capturing modeling information in a formal syntax is increasing in almost all application areas, from macroeconomics to electronic component design. For example, the VHDL language allows the specification and modeling of hardware components during systems design [IEEE 1076]. For each such knowledge domain, application-specific syntaxes have been designed to create and develop "little languages", each with its corresponding "little compiler". The objective of such special-purpose programming languages is twofold: first, to express the semantics of the knowledge domain in an appropriate syntax developed specifically for that knowledge domain; and second, to compile formal specifications of models in the knowledge domain for the analysis and simulation of specific problems.

Making Faces

As an example of how a model creates multiple benefits in a given problem domain, we consider an example of a distributed network application. Although this example is purely hypothetical, it is instructive. In this application, various law-enforcement agencies nationwide decide to connect their computer systems for the purpose of exchanging information about wanted persons. The universe of discourse is the set of all criminals and suspected criminals and all associated information about them. Suppose for the sake of this example that this information is normally stored in each law-enforcement agency's local database; it is digitally transmitted across the network to other agencies as required. Each record contains information on the criminal's name, aliases, birthdate, previous offenses, notes on modus operandi, and so on. Associated with this information there is also a digital representation of the person's face. Currently this takes the form of scanned photographs or police sketches stored in raster form by digitizing the pixels of this image. Our problem is that, because of the size of each such digital image, the database is running to capacity. An associated problem is that the multicasting of these images to other agencies takes excessive time on the network.

To address this problem, suppose we decided that, instead of storing a digitized pixel representation of the criminal face, we stored a *model* of it instead. We therefore create a model for the human face and write a software program which "understands" the model — it "knows" that a face has two eyes, a nose, a mouth with two lips, and so on. Since every face is different, we represent the model of a face in terms of a number of *adjustable parameters*. After we do some analysis, we find that the very wide diversity of human faces can all be accommodated within some relatively moderate number — say

200 — of independent parameters. These parameters include things like `heightOf-Head`, `widthOfHead`, `skinColor`, `colorOfEyes`, `colorOfHair`, `lengthOf-Hair`, `distanceBetweenEyes`, `lengthOfNose`, and so on. We can also add on optional modules as required, such as a `mustache` module with its own parameters such as `mustacheLength`, `mustacheThickness`, `percentageGray`, and so on.

Our study may show that, with the parameters we have chosen for our model for a human face, we can render 99.5% of all faces to within 95.0% representational accuracy. Assume that this is within the agencies' tolerance requirements. (If not, we can increase the number of parameters in the model for greater accuracy — an approach whose benefits and drawbacks we will examine later.) We now examine each parameter for the range of its possible values. We find that, by both scaling and interpolating every parameter appropriately, all its possible values can be represented within a range of 0 to 255 — that is, each parameter can be encoded within one byte or less. By agreeing to some universal convention for the sequence in which these parameters occur in the model, we can represent the entire model of a human face with roughly 200 bytes.

We now build many software tools to support this model. Some tools are able to inspect scanned frontal and side-view photographs or artist sketches and, because they understand the model, convert the image into its 200-byte parameterized representation and store it in the database. These tools are called *encoding tools*. Other tools perform the opposite function, converting a parameterized representation from the database into an image for visual presentation; these are called *decoding* or *rendering* tools. Yet other tools take care of routine tasks such as correctly associating each parameterized image representation with data records like name and birthdate, as well as housekeeping tasks such as database storage and retrieval and responding to network requests.

The immediate benefits of this model-based representation are, of course, reduced storage requirements, because we now store each image in 200 bytes rather than the several thousand it took for the pixel-based representation. Because the model is a universal standard, we know that every law-enforcement agency which subscribes to the standard will be able to decode the model. Network transmission times are also reduced, as we can now multicast only the 200-byte representation rather than the digitized representation.

However, there are more benefits than mere compression. For example, the model-based representation, when rendered as an image, can be smoothly scaled up to arbitrarily large sizes and does not suffer the loss of granularity associated with pixel-based scale-up. We can also define a grammar for a "little language" whose statements can assign values to specific parameters in the model, and we can write a "little compiler" which translates this language into either its database representation, network-transmission-encoded representation, or its visual image representation. By using an interactive interpreter for this little language, police artists can now instantly synthesize images by pulling up individual facial features with the proper values from a "parts catalog" (e.g., "Nose number 73, eyebrows number 157"). They can adjust their sketches merely by fine-tuning numeric values on a sliding scale, rather than having to refine and redraw them every time a new witness is interrogated. Scanning and searching programs are speeded up enormously as they are essentially reduced to numeric comparators, rather than having to use expensive and slow pattern recognition and pattern comparison algorithms.

Expressive Power versus Efficiency

It is important to note that a model's representation of reality is only as good as the parametric detail we choose to build into it. For example, in our model for the human face above, we used a single parameter for `colorOfEyes`. While this may work fine 99.999% of the time, in the 0.001% of the cases where a person has eyes of different color this model will prove inadequate. To accommodate such cases, we might consider replacing the `colorOfEyes` parameter with the two parameters `colorOfLeftEye` and `colorOfRightEye`. While such a model would be slightly more *versatile*, it would also be slightly less *efficient*, because we would now have to carry around two bytes of information which, 99.999% of the time, will be the same value. We may decide that this extra overhead is not worth it and may choose to live with a single `colorOf-Eyes` parameter, even though we know that the model will be inadequate in 0.001% of the cases.

A good model is one that strikes the correct balance in this inverse correlation between the *versatility requirements* and the *efficiency requirements* of the system. Therefore, the design of the model, and the choice of the accuracy with which it represents the reality of the underlying system, is an exercise in *recognizing, evaluating, and selecting trade-offs*. A modeling technique which has greater sophistication and versatility requirements will also be more complex and expensive to implement. A modeling technique which places greater emphasis on efficiency and low implementation costs will necessarily be simpler and less powerful. There is no single "correct" balance: different modeling techniques may make different trade-offs between complexity and simplicity, depending on the requirements of the applications and the markets they serve.

The ideal modeling technique — if such a thing can exist — would be one which can be kept simple in some situations and can be extended to express complex semantics in other situations. Under circumstances where economy of implementation is important, the modeling methodology should be reducible to its bare essentials; under other circumstances where expressive power is more important, the same modeling methodology should be extensible to capture the necessary wealth of information. The complex implementation of the modeling technique should be able to interoperate with the simpler, reduced form. If necessary, a variety of different implementations of the same methodology could be created, each making a different trade-off between expressive power and implementational simplicity, with each being able to interoperate with every other at the level of the "lower" interoperating form.

All these principles apply to the digital representation of almost any application-specific model in any universe of discourse. Audio compact discs store a digital representation of musical waveforms, a model appropriate for digitizing music (within acceptable fidelity tolerances) having been agreed upon by recording studios and stereo system manufacturers. Other digital media do the same for still images, photographs, and motion-video sequences. Image digitization devices offer a range of user-selectable trade-offs between fineness of resolution on one hand and storage capacity and speed of image encoding and decoding on the other. Devices capable of rendering images in high-resolution formats are nevertheless able to decode images stored in low-resolution formats.

All manner of textual and image information, such as engineering designs, stock portfolio histories, dictionaries, encyclopedias, atlases, survey maps, genetic data, and so on, is being stored in digital form; an appropriate modeling technique must be chosen for each. A digital road atlas encoded according to a reasonably powerful model, for example, can answer questions such as "Find the shortest route from Wheeling, West Virginia, to Dealing, Nevada, which runs only along highways allowing a 55-mph or higher speed, and does not exceed elevations of 8,000 feet through the mountain states." Naturally, an atlas capable of answering this query will have a more expensive implementation and greater storage requirements than a simpler one which only provides raw route information. Further, as monomedia technologies give way to multimedia, all this information will be combined in myriad combinations to present it to its consumer in meaningful patterns. Therefore, for every universe of discourse, the creation of a well-chosen modeling technique is crucial, because eventually, *all knowledge will be digitized.*

Model Manipulation

Once the knowledge for any application domain is modeled and digitized, it can be used in simulators to exercise a variety of scenarios, both real and hypothetical. Because digital information can be easily encoded and transmitted across a network, the network can be used to operate systems within the application domain remotely. Thus, *the operation of any system can be executed by monitoring and manipulating a digital representation of a model of the system.* The supersonic fighter pilot in a flight simulator, the teenager interactively playing his home video game with his friend in the next county, the telemetry operator tracking a space shuttle in orbit, and the medical specialist at her telesurgery workstation are all monitoring and manipulating a digital representation of some model of the world they are interested in.

For any application domain, therefore, the steps required in the methodology of creating such a model are described in Figure 1-1. Many well-known special-purpose application-specific notations have used a similar methodology: a common example is the PostScript page description language, which describes layouts to display devices in terms of a structured model rather than unstructured data. In this book, the application domain we are interested in are networks themselves — that is, we will apply a methodology similar to Figure 1-1 to the study and analysis of communication networks.

1.4. Modeling in Network Architecture

The advantages of describing a complex system in terms of its model are manifold. By correlating objects in a model world based on their relevant relationships in the real world, we create a way of manipulating the system in an abstract manner. Providing that the model is reasonably accurate — that is, it closely approximates the behavior of the actual system in reality — we can then pretend to perform operations on the system by actually performing those operations on the model. Thus, a good model can provide a good simulation of the system. This lets us detect anomalies and design errors at an earlier stage in the system's life cycle. Hence, the expense of correcting these errors is drastically reduced; the expense of correcting errors after a system is actually constructed can be very high.

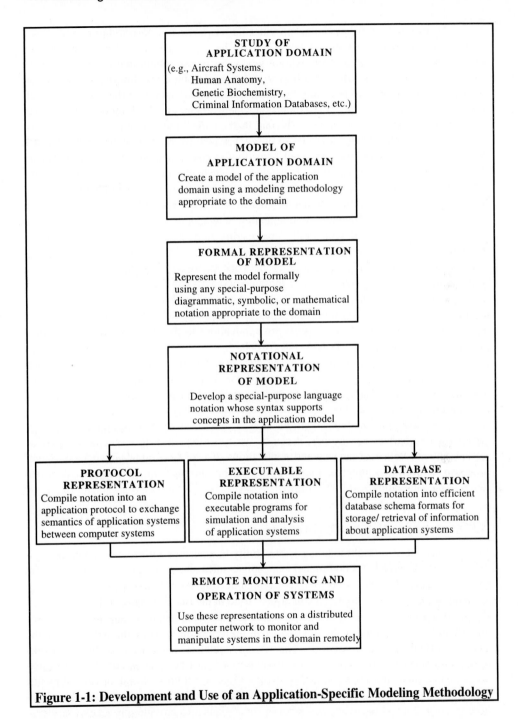

**STUDY OF
APPLICATION DOMAIN**

(e.g., Aircraft Systems,
    Human Anatomy,
    Genetic Biochemistry,
    Criminal Information Databases, etc.)

**MODEL OF
APPLICATION DOMAIN**

Create a model of the application
domain using a modeling methodology
appropriate to the domain

**FORMAL REPRESENTATION
OF MODEL**

Represent the model formally
using any special-purpose
diagrammatic, symbolic, or mathematical
notation appropriate to the domain

**NOTATIONAL
REPRESENTATION
OF MODEL**

Develop a special-purpose language
notation whose syntax supports
concepts in the application model

**PROTOCOL
REPRESENTATION**

Compile notation into an
application protocol to exchange
semantics of application systems
between computer systems

**EXECUTABLE
REPRESENTATION**

Compile notation into
executable programs for
simulation and analysis
of application systems

**DATABASE
REPRESENTATION**

Compile notation into efficient
database schema formats for
storage/ retrieval of information
about application systems

**REMOTE MONITORING AND
OPERATION OF SYSTEMS**

Use these representations on a distributed
computer network to monitor and
manipulate systems in the domain remotely

Figure 1-1: Development and Use of an Application-Specific Modeling Methodology

More importantly, modeling provides an easy way of constructing complex systems from a library of existing knowledge. By having models of a library of existing components at hand, we can then explore new ways of assembling these components together to create systems which are bigger and more complex. In almost any field of endeavor where complex systems are designed, it is a requirement that the system be modeled at first, down to a level of precision where all major ambiguities are resolved. Structural engineers have libraries of formal mathematical models of beams, girders, and trusses at hand which they assemble to create bridges. By manipulating the model of a bridge before it is actually constructed, structural engineers can answer questions about, for example, its seismic stability. If answers to such questions are unsatisfactory, the model of the bridge can be changed — designs can be altered and components can be replaced in the model — until a satisfactory match with specifications is obtained.

The task of constructing communication networks of tomorrow is perhaps no less complex than the task of structurally engineering bridges; it would, therefore, be extremely beneficial to have precise, formal models of the components constituting a communications network. This will allow the network architects to create a model using the abstract form of network components; these components can then be assembled together, manipulated, tested, replaced, reassembled, and retested in their abstract form until a satisfactory network design is obtained. Thus, a model will help in the development and operation of automated computer software applications in the areas of *network architecture, network planning,* and *systems integration.*

Figure 1-2 describes the process of *Network Design Automation.* A proposed network configuration is assembled by a *network synthesis tool,* using a library of standard devices, software, and applications from a network model information base. A *network simulation tool* then tests this configuration against a variety of possible operational scenarios. If the proposed network configuration is able to satisfy the requirements of these operational scenarios successfully, it can be used as a blueprint to create and deploy an actual network with real devices and applications. If not, a different network configuration can be proposed after the failure points in the current configuration are identified through the simulation.

1.5. Modeling in Network Operations

Another benefit of formal modeling is the ability to exchange information about the system through its model. A good model can capture sufficient information about the system very accurately. This helps not only in communicating information about the system to humans working on the project; it can also be used in the run-time system itself.

The interconnected networks of today display wide heterogeneity in terms of the underlying transport media, the devices used, the protocols used in the devices, and the services offered by each network. This is inevitable, as telecommunication networks based on copper plants, digital data networks based on fiber plants, corporate data networks based on mainframes and LANs, cable television networks based on coaxial plants, mobile data networks based on wireless media, and many other types of networks, all interconnect and interwork with each other in some manner to provide meaningful services.

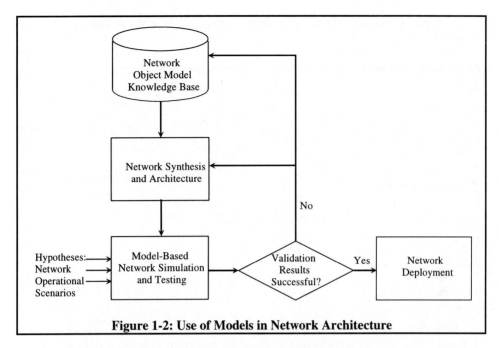

Figure 1-2: Use of Models in Network Architecture

Indeed, the technological variety will probably be so great that it will not be possible to meaningfully interconnect every network to every other. Even if protocol compatibility can be achieved, the problems of differences in equipment supplied by different vendors and differences in throughput and capacity may be sufficiently great as to preclude interoperability. And even if these could be resolved, the ultimate barrier to interoperability — human-defined interconnection policies instituted by the myriad corporate, national, and regional governmental bodies which own, operate, and regulate networks — could prove to be prohibitive.

Neglecting for the time being institutional, policy, and cost barriers to interoperability, let us assume that most networks, with sufficient attention to technological problems, could in the future be made to interoperate with each other at least in some limited fashion. The institutions who own and operate these networks will have a vested interest in accomplishing such interoperability because of the potential for generating revenue by offering a wide variety of connectivity solutions. Communication which can be performed in only one manner today will in the future be possible using many alternative technologies and providers. Each such option will create a potential market niche.

Therefore, given the financial incentive for service providers, home builders, automobile manufacturers, wireless operators, and wireline companies to work together so that all may exploit their respective margins on this revenue stream, some effort will be expended in defining standard interfaces so that their equipment can work together. The reader can doubtless think of many wonderful and interesting applications for the network of tomorrow. Aside from home automation, many other application areas will benefit from such interoperation. Manufacturing systems automation, biomedical systems automation, transportation systems automation, entertainment systems automation, and many other areas are potential applications for self-aware and self-configuring intelligent networks.

Federated Networks and Information Superhighways

Given the financial incentive, it is not unreasonable to assume that networks comprising many heterogeneous transport media, heterogeneous protocol capabilities, heterogeneous services, owned and operated by heterogeneous corporate and governmental interests, will in some manner interwork together because of user demand. Such networks are called *federated networks* [Sche90, Kim90c, Shet91].

Federated networks already exist today. A good example is the worldwide telephone network. This consists of widely disparate pieces of equipment, from crossbar switches in developing countries to sophisticated high-capacity electronic switches in developed countries, manufactured by different suppliers, operated by different corporations and governments, each with its own numbering and dialing plan and different rate charges and tariffs. Yet it is possible to place a call from any telephone terminal in the world to almost any other telephone terminal.

The Internet is another example of a federated network [Come91]. Consisting of thousands of different local data networks, each falling under separate corporate, academic, or governmental jurisdictions and interconnected by gateways using widely different wide-area transport media, it nevertheless functions together by using a common protocol suite to deliver services such as electronic mail, remote login, and file transfer.

This brings us to a key concept of how interoperability is accomplished in federated networks: *standards*. The Internet functions together in spite of its heterogeneity because its constituents agree to adhere to a common standard for transferring data — the Internet Protocol family, commonly referred to as the TCP/IP protocol suite [RFC 791, RFC 793]. The worldwide telephone network functions together in spite of its heterogeneity because its constituents agree to conform to a common family of standards, defined by the ITU-T (International Telecommunication Union, Telecommunication Standardization Sector), which, among other things, defines the interface standards for the interconnection of telephone switching equipment.

Standardization is an old activity — network standards were being defined as early as 1825 to interconnect telegraph services. With the advent of radio and telephony, the ITU was established, and was eventually co-opted as an agency of the United Nations. Many important telephony standards were defined by an organ of the ITU called the CCITT (International Telegraph and Telephone Consultative Committee). These standards were known as "CCITT Recommendations" until the CCITT ceased to exist in 1993; they are now simply "ITU-T Recommendations". Many other organizations such as the ISO (International Organization for Standardization) are also active in developing communication standards.

A federated network which can provide a combination of telecommunication, information, commercial, and entertainment services over a variety of wireline and wireless media is often called an *information superhighway*. A internetworked lattice of such information superhighways — all capable of exchanging information with each other — which is created, co-ordinated, regulated, and operated by a combination of private and public organizations is sometimes referred to as the *national information infrastructure*.

Autoconfiguration

In the traditional concept of a federated network, interoperability is accomplished by agreeing to a set of standards *a priori*. That is, equipment manufacturers, together with appropriate agencies having administrative jurisdiction over their networks, negotiate standards and interfaces among themselves before they actually interconnect their equipment with each other's networks. As any network architect knows only too well, the mere assertion of adherence to a standard interface does not guarantee that the networks actually will function together when interconnected, because of many small discrepancies between optional implementations of interfaces, but it does provide a fighting chance that they will. Negotiation of standards also provides a basis for determining which of the interconnecting parties is the offending one in case of interoperability failure and helps identify what parameters must be reconfigured to accomplish interoperability.

As network elements become more sophisticated, their capabilities increase. The more sophisticated networking devices of today are capable of supporting multiple interfaces and multiple protocol suites. As more and more such features are deployed in networking devices, their capabilities will increase, leading to a federated network which will approach "plug-and-play" capability. In a network such as this, the process of negotiating run-time communication interfaces between human agencies *a priori* will no longer be as important. The networked devices themselves will possess the intelligence necessary to perform the required handshaking and agree on a common protocol suite among themselves. The standards bodies and equipment manufacturers will continue to define new standards for delivering advanced services, but administrative agencies, service providers, and network carriers will have to be less concerned as to whether the network equipment they purchase will have the interoperability capabilities they require.

To quote McQuillan [McQu90]: "Tomorrow's broadband networks will be based on fast packet switching, which combines the best of LANs and WANs to transmit voice and data. Such networks will unite users across the entire spectrum of topologies — local, campus, city, global — at blazing speeds (an apt figure of speech, since transmission speeds will approach the speed of light). *Flexibility of configuration will be unprecedented*, far beyond anything available with today's relatively primitive services."

Such automatic flexibility of configuration will be increasingly required of a federated network as its constituent devices become sufficiently sophisticated to encompass diverse heterogeneous subnetworks. It would be a desirable feature of network devices if, on being plugged into the network, they could query each other's configurations, query each other's service capabilities, query each other's supported protocols, negotiate an acceptable protocol suite among themselves, negotiate options and parameters associated with the protocol suite, and automatically configure themselves for service — all with minimal or zero human intervention. This capability is called *autoconfiguration*.

While these capabilities would indeed be desirable, it will not be possible to accomplish this state of affairs without formal modeling. Before each network device can transmit information to other devices about its capabilities and configuration, all the devices must have agreed on a common model within which this information must be couched. Once a common model is agreed upon, engineers can then make this model available on-line, either in some accessible information base, or by embedding this knowledge within the devices themselves. It is then possible for one device to ask another: "What are you? What is your throughput? What capabilities and protocols do you support? How are you configured?" The device would then respond: "This is what I am; this is my throughput; this is how I am configured; these are the capabilities and protocols I support — which one of these protocol families would you like to use to talk to me?" Such information could be easily exchanged between devices, because both devices would share a common view of the world as defined by the model. (Clearly, there is a potential problem: what *a priori* protocol must be used to exchange information about the model itself? This is a classic bootstrapping problem and has many common solutions.) Attempts have already been made to incorporate some knowledge of the network model in a run-time network using information resource dictionary systems (IRDS) [ANSI X3-138], in new telecommunications architectures such as Bellcore's OSCA [TR 915] and INA architectures [SR 2268, SR 2282, Nata92, Rubi94], and elsewhere [ISO 10027].

With sufficiently sophisticated devices in the federated network, such capabilities would lead to networks which automatically detect the capabilities and services provided by their connected networks and automatically configure themselves in order to interoperate with them optimally, according to some predefined conception of what is optimal. Topology knowledge could be exchanged on-line. Intelligent devices could deliver advanced services by orchestrating each other's capabilities automatically. As and when necessary, networks would also detect changes in the operating conditions and topologies of their connected networks and reconfigure themselves accordingly.

The advantage of autoconfiguration capabilities can be exploited in non-federated environments as well, that is, complex networks which do not cross administrative or jurisdictional boundaries. For example, the U.S. Federal Aviation Administration's system for Air Traffic Control [Perr91a] does not function in a federated environment but is still a heterogeneous system consisting of many different computer and networking components. The U.S. military's Battlefield Information Architecture for military command, control, communication, and intelligence [Bren92] is another non-federated system which is also exceedingly complex and could benefit from autoconfiguration capabilities provided by a comprehensive network model.

Figure 1-3 demonstrates a possible mechanism for a network device which can autoconfigure its own interfaces to communicate with new devices plugged into the network. While this diagram shows a network object model knowledge base conceptually embedded within each device, this is not a prerequisite for autoconfiguration; such information could be available from external model information bases as well.

1.6. Modeling in Network Management

A special case of sharing a common world view of the network occurs in the realm of network management. In the classic network management problem, one special constituent of the network — designated a *Network Management System* or an *Operations Support System* — is required to coordinate and control the operations of other components of the network. Although the forces that traditionally drove network management were the need to troubleshoot faults in the network, today's systems perform remote configuration of network elements, assess and optimize the performance of other elements, and offer intelligent reasoning capabilities for diagnosing network faults.

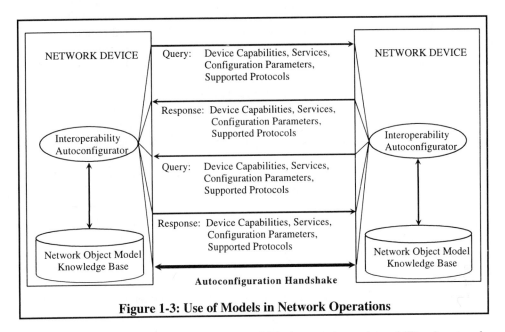

Figure 1-3: Use of Models in Network Operations

Network management systems vary widely in capacity and capability. A network management system could be a simple workstation controlling a small, homogeneous local area network, or it could be a large distributed operations support system, with many mediation devices, controlling a heterogeneous wide-area telecommunications network. Regardless of size, each network management system must be designed to accomplish its task in two steps. In the first step, a formal model of the network must be created, so that knowledge of the devices and services constituting the network can be captured precisely and formally within the model. In the second step, a protocol must be designed for conveying the semantics defined by the model. When operational information is exchanged between network devices and the network management station, each can decode the protocol and act on the information conveyed by it — information which conforms to a common model which both the management system and the network device have agreed upon. Figure 1-4 illustrates how models are typically used in network management.

Many models and many protocols exist which fulfill the requirements of the network management problem. Many of these are proprietary and therefore function only in limited, homogeneous environments and are not suitable for use in a federated network.

Among the network management protocols which have been standardized are the Internet management protocol, known as the Simple Network Management Protocol [RFC 1441, RFC 1448] and the OSI network management protocol, known as the Common Management Information Protocol [ITU-T X.711]. More interesting than the protocols, however, are the network models which have been defined for conveying the semantics of network devices. Both the Internet and OSI network modeling standards are termed the *Structure of Management Information* [RFC 1442, ITU-T X.722]. They differ widely in their modeling approaches, the sophistication of their semantics, and their ease of implementation.

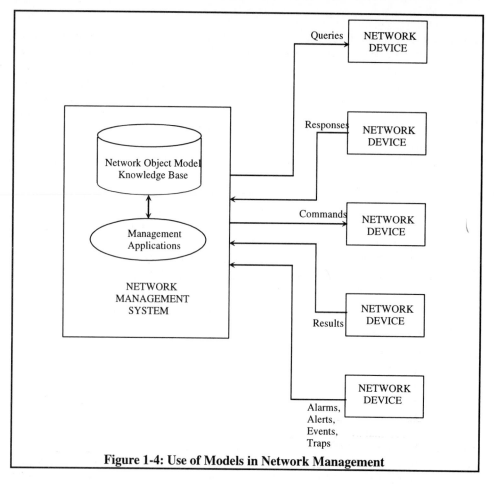

Figure 1-4: Use of Models in Network Management

Network management is perhaps the most visible area today where formal network models have achieved widespread popular success. However, the different levels of success achieved in different markets by the Internet and OSI network management approaches to modeling networks teach us some valuable lessons. The models themselves and the lessons deriving therefrom will be discussed in subsequent chapters, but one special point is worth mentioning now.

We said earlier that different modeling techniques may choose different trade-offs between sophistication and complexity on one hand and simplicity and efficiency on the other. This has already been borne out in the realm of network management. For certain network devices, particularly those being marketed in highly price-competitive markets, it is desirable to keep the overhead imposed by the network management protocol to a minimum. In such situations, the protocol itself must be implemented in the smallest possible amount of memory. This requires that the semantics conveyed by the protocol model should also be simple so that they can be easily encoded, decoded, and interpreted.

For other situations, the need to convey a great deal of network management information in complex systems outweighs the need for simplicity of protocol implementation. This typically occurs for network devices deployed in less price-conscious and more guaranteed-service intensive environments. In such markets, the sophistication of the modeling technique and its ability to capture the detailed semantics of the condition of the network are more important than the protocol overhead involved in conveying this information. Therefore, although the protocol carrying this information becomes complex to implement, the exceedingly stringent reliability requirements make sophisticated modeling techniques very important.

Network management, however, is not the focus of this book; network management is interesting because it is an important application area within which formal modeling techniques for communication networks can be applied. The primary focus of this book is to develop a single, consistent communication network modeling methodology which can be used for network synthesis and simulation (architecture and planning), in the run-time network environment (operations), and for network configuration, command, and control (management). Once such a model has been specified, many different special-purpose protocols could be defined, if necessary, for conveying the semantics of an appropriately chosen subset of the model.

1.7. The Multiparadigmatic Modeling Methodology

The methodology developed in this book uses a rigorous subset of object-oriented modeling called *specialization theory*. This book applies specialization theory to create models of communication networks suitable for network architecture (i.e., network design automation using synthesis and simulation), network operations, and network management. As we develop the methodology, we will attempt to make it sufficiently precise by expressing it in a formal syntax. The syntax in which the formalism will be demonstrated is the international standard ASN.1 [ITU-T X.680]. This syntax is one among many which can *demonstrate* the methodology; it is by no means an integral *part* of the methodology. The choice of this syntax is arbitrary; it is somewhat influenced by the existing knowledge some readers may already have of this syntax from the network management standards. However, the methodology itself is syntax-independent, and any other sufficiently precise notation may also be used to express its semantics. Readers who desire to use the methodology with a different formal syntax may skip the examples in ASN.1 notation, which have all been isolated in separate chapters.

Throughout this book, we will use the term *model information base* to indicate the conceptual repository where the constructs of the network model are persistently stored. The model information base does not necessarily imply some sort of database platform implementation, although this is certainly possible and probably likely. A model information base represents any mechanism which could be used to store and access the constructs of the modeling methodology, specified in whichever formal notation has been chosen. A subset of the model information base could be used for the process of network architecture and planning; another subset could be used for network operations, and yet another subset could be used for network management. Figure 1-5 shows how a model information base may be used.

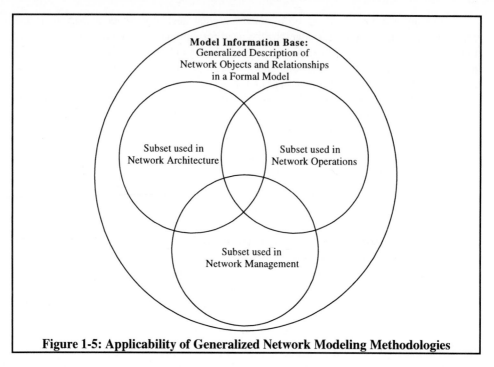

Model Information Base:
Generalized Description of
Network Objects and Relationships
in a Formal Model

Subset used in
Network Architecture

Subset used in
Network Operations

Subset used in
Network Management

Figure 1-5: Applicability of Generalized Network Modeling Methodologies

The methodology used in this book incorporates and assimilates many aspects from many emerging fields, including advanced object-oriented modeling from specialization theory, entity-relationship modeling, knowledge representation, set theory, denotational semantics, logic and inference modeling, and relational algebra. Some practitioners have referred to it as the *Multiparadigmatic Modeling Methodology* (MMM) because it embraces multiple paradigms. Throughout the book we will simply refer to it as "our methodology" or "our modeling technique".

1.8. Summary

Because communication networks must increasingly be viewed as complex systems, it is necessary to have formal modeling methodologies to understand, describe, construct, operate, and manage them. Formal models are useful in the synthesis of networks, in their run-time operations, and in their management. It would be highly desirable if a single, consistent modeling methodology could be developed for use in all these areas. A consistent generalized model must be capable of being partitioned, so that appropriate subsets of it can be used in tasks such as network synthesis and network management.

The modeling methodology must be expressive, semantically rich, and precise enough to be represented in a formal notation. At the same time, it must be flexible, so that projections of it can be taken to create submodels for use in specific economy-constrained implementations where necessary.

2. Principles of Object-Oriented Modeling

"Objects are closer than they appear."
— *mirror on anonymous motorcycle.*

2.1. Introduction

Object-oriented modeling provides a framework within which large and complex systems may be organized both in terms of their structure and their behavior. We provide in this chapter a brief introduction to the technique itself, with particular reference to examples in communication networks. This chapter describes some of the basic notions of object-oriented modeling, such as abstraction, encapsulation, classification, inheritance, extension, and evolution, and the modeling constructs that express these notions, such as attributes, functions, and classes.

2.2. Conceptual Background

Object-orientation is a *modeling paradigm*, that is, a perspective which gives rise to methodologies for creating models. Like many modeling paradigms, object-oriented modeling is a formalization of the human ability to categorize things. Much scientific knowledge is based on the fundamental ability human beings possess to recognize similarities and differences among things they encounter in their experience. The beginnings of organized knowledge stem from the ability to say that a particular object "is like" some other object we have already encountered, or that it "is unlike" it. The ability to categorize things on the basis of their likeness has led to great scientific advances. Some of the towering human intellectual achievements of the past few centuries have been the organization of biological life-forms in a hierarchy (kingdom, phylum, order, family, genus, species, subspecies, and so on) and the organization of the chemical elements into the periodic table. Both are based on the intellectual faculty of categorization, and from both these achievements have sprung very large systems of organized knowledge.

Like other modeling formalisms that have preceded it, object-oriented modeling allows us to organize knowledge by *classifying* things in terms of their similarity. We also frequently give each class a label or a name, so we can speak of its general characteristics in the abstract. When we speak of the characteristics of an entire class of objects using words such as "all mammals" and "all halogens", we are using a label to convey information about a large number of individual objects at once.

A good modeling technique allows classification based not merely on *structure* but also on *behavior*. The animal kingdom, for example, is organized not only on the basis of structure (presence of teeth, number of vertebrae, etc.) but also on the basis of behavior (means of locomotion, nature of propagation, etc.). In the periodic table of elements, structural organization is represented in the rows (number of "shells" which electrons inhabit) whereas behavioral organization is represented by columns (representing element groups, whose members resemble each other in chemical reactions). One of the reasons for the popularity of object-oriented techniques is the intellectual appeal of their ability to capture the essence of both structure and function in the single abstraction of an *object*.

In this book, we apply object-oriented modeling to communication networks. The elements comprising a communication network are complex. Modeling them in terms of both their structure and behavior requires the use of a technique which can describe both. Obviously, there are similarities and differences among the things that constitute a network: this knowledge is well understood and has been applied for years in the practice of building networks. Using object-oriented modeling techniques, we can *formalize* this knowledge in a manner amenable to computer representation and analysis.

Some modeling techniques — such as entity-attribute modeling — describe the problem domain only in structural terms. Others — such as state transition analysis — do so only in behavioral terms. Each such technique is appropriate for a certain class of problems. The analysis of communication networks falls into a class of problems which needs both. A pure structural model of a communication network would describe the nature of the elements that comprise it and their relationships with each other but would not capture behavioral aspects in terms of protocol messages and responses. A pure behavioral model would describe their function in terms of stimuli and responses but would not capture structural information.

Clearly, to properly model a communication network, we need to describe both aspects. As we shall see, object-oriented modeling allows us to merge both structural and behavior abstractions within a single comprehensive framework. The applicability of object-oriented methodologies is not restricted only to engineering systems such as communication networks; it also extends to many enterprise-modeling activities [Coad90, Jack83, Shla88, Your79, Your89].

The ability to identify a commonality of static and dynamic characteristics is essential for modeling networks. Organizing these characteristics in a knowledge *hierarchy* is an important aspect of object-oriented modeling. The process of grouping similar network objects into *classes*, by its very nature, deals in generalities — common structure and behavior are factored out, and exceptional aspects are identified.

In our object-oriented network model, we will impose a *formalism* on our design methodology. The themes of object-oriented analysis — abstraction, encapsulation, inheritance — will all find expression within the formal notation which we will adopt. Although different object-oriented formalisms differ in syntax, they are similar in their support of essentially equivalent concepts. Therefore, the transition from one formalism (such as a network model in a specification syntax) to another (such as a software implementation in a programming language) is not conceptually difficult and can be easily performed by an appropriate "model compiler".

Thus, object-oriented modeling of communication networks has a number of advantages, which makes it suitable from a number of institutional viewpoints:

- **Corporate Customer View**: Object-oriented network models provide a standard, modular mechanism which promotes a common understanding of the knowledge domain between network devices manufactured by diverse vendors, thereby assisting interoperability and integration of the corporation's network, thus reducing communication costs and improving competitive advantage.

- **Network Carrier View**: Object-oriented network models provide the ability to build upon and reuse specifications and implementation already known to the network, facilitating faster provisioning of advanced services and enhancing the revenue stream.

- **Equipment Vendor View**: Object-oriented network models assist in flexible and modular representations of network element architectures, thereby facilitating the engineering design process, speeding up product development cycles and resulting in faster time-to-market.

There are also advantages from a number of individual viewpoints:

- **Network Operator View**: Object-oriented network models provide a mechanism to perform similar operating and administrative functions on like network resources, thereby easing the process of integrating and managing diverse components of the corporate network.

- **System Designer View**: Object-oriented network models impose a very clean modular decomposition on the process of network system design, thereby reducing the development effort.

- **Implementation Manager View**: Object-oriented network models provide a vehicle for reusability of design modules, speeding up the development process and easing the evolution and maintenance of network products.

2.3. Abstraction

Abstraction is a mechanism for coping with complexity; it is a way to concentrate only on essential details of what is important for solving the specific problem at hand. Abstraction is the exercise of determining which characteristics of an object are important elements of the model and which ones are unimportant.

The process of abstraction "draws a line" around the object — it delimits it by enclosing it in a crisply defined conceptual boundary, sometimes called an *abstraction barrier*. Inside this boundary are those *essential characteristics* of the object which — from the perspective of the application domain — make it different from every other object. The characteristics chosen to be isolated inside the encapsulation barrier are called the *properties* of the object. These properties may be behavior-based, structure-based, or both. The abstraction barrier separates the characteristics of interest from those not of interest.

For example, if we choose to define the concept of a "modem" in terms of a behavior-based abstraction, we might define it as "any device which converts digital data to analog format". Clearly, this is not sufficient, as it would imply that a digital HDTV signal transmitter was a modem. If we define it in terms of structure as "any device with at least two ports, one connected to a data cable and one to an analog transmission line", then we lose the concept of the function it performs; an empty chassis thus connected might qualify as a modem.

Essential characteristics isolated inside the abstraction barrier must capture the notion of both structure-based and function-based distinctions relevant in the application domain. In our network modeling formalism, as we shall see, the essential characteristics of an object which are abstracted are its *attributes* and its *functions*. When isolated inside the abstraction barrier, these attributes and functions are the *properties* of the object.

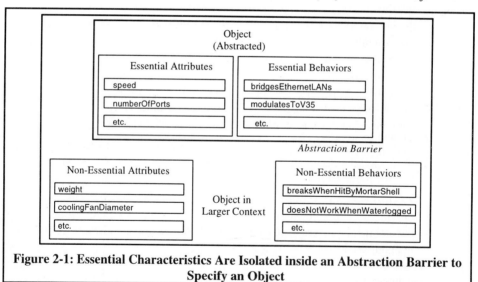

Figure 2-1: Essential Characteristics Are Isolated inside an Abstraction Barrier to Specify an Object

Figure 2-1 indicates that the process of abstraction identifies what the properties of interest are and isolates them inside an abstraction barrier to create an object. Clearly, the properties of interest depend on the application domain, that is, the perspective from which we view the object. The properties of an object that interest us as network model-ers are not the same as the properties that would interest, say, a mechanical engineer tasked with ruggedizing that object for onboard function in a combat military vehicle.

No abstraction can ever capture the complete description of an object. As we indicated in Chapter 1, a modeling methodology is only as good as the properties we invest its objects with, after evaluating the trade-offs between representational accuracy and efficiency. Objects in their totality can be extremely complicated; no single abstraction can ever suffice to completely specify the behavior, for example, of a Class 5 Central Office switch. By definition, therefore, the abstraction barrier is like a pair of blinders which we purposely choose to use to limit our vision of the universe. There is no single correct abstraction — different application domains may abstract the same object in different ways, because the crucial aspects of interest may be different.

For a given application domain, however, it is important to correctly define an abstraction, so that we may focus our attention on the real issues and not be diverted by unnecessary details. A correctly defined abstraction allows the same object model to be reused in various ways — the processes of network architecture, protocol specification, software development, database design, and even documentation and customer training may all refer back to the same model.

In our model, the notion of an *object* captures this sense of abstraction. Hereafter, when we speak of *objects*, we will do so in the very precise, narrow, technical sense of the word. An object is a representation of a network entity, abstracted for the purposes of modeling.

Generally, we will model every element of a communications network — software, hardware, circuits — as an object. Some elements which are not part of the communications network — such as sites, service providers, manufacturers, and subscribers — will also be abstracted and modeled as objects, since they are also relevant functionaries in the model. There may be other elements which are useful in operating the network — such as power surge protection equipment, battery backup packs, and fire extinguishers — that may not be of sufficient interest to us to be considered functionaries in the system model, and so we will not model them at all. Because it is an abstraction geared to our particular application domain, an object only represents a *view* of a physical or logical network element which we decide is important for our purposes.

2.4. Encapsulation

Encapsulation — sometimes referred to as *information hiding* — consists of identifying the internal implementation details of a network element and separating those from its externally visible behavior. Encapsulation suggests that, from the network modeling perspective, the internal details of how a network element is constructed are irrelevant, as long its external behavior is predictable. An object is said to be *encapsulated* if it interacts with the external world in terms of a *contractually specified interface* — thus separating this interface from its internal subsystems, which are regarded to be uninteresting. Thus, encapsulation preserves the integrity of the object — the underlying implementation may be changed, as long as the interface visible to other objects remains consistent.

Encapsulation is not unique to object-oriented analysis, but together with abstraction, gives us the ability to define clean interfaces between an object's internal and external aspects. Encapsulation and abstraction, therefore, complement each other and together provide a powerful mechanism for specifying objects in our problem domain correctly and *orthogonally* — that is, ensuring that objects are defined to be as independent of other objects as possible.

In our network model, we will sometimes refer to the demarcation of the encapsulated object from the rest of the universe of discourse as the *encapsulation barrier* — implying that the only properties of the object that are available to the outside world are those that are visible at this barrier. These visible properties are interrogated and manipulated using protocols and messages delivered to the external interfaces of the object. Indeed, any two objects with the same set of externally visible properties may have different internal implementations for each property, without being in violation of the object-oriented paradigm.

Clearly, the properties visible at the encapsulation barrier must be a subset of the properties abstracted inside the abstraction barrier. Just as the abstraction barrier separates the essential characteristics of an object (those we choose to model as properties) from the non-essential ones, the encapsulation barrier separates the externally visible characteristics (those abstracted properties we choose to make visible to other objects) from the hidden ones. The encapsulation barrier must thus lie "inside" the abstraction barrier, since encapsulated properties are a subset of abstracted properties. Usually, these two sets of properties are the same, so that in most objects the encapsulation barrier and the abstraction barrier merge. An *object* may be thus be defined as a representation of an entity, abstracted *and* encapsulated for the purposes of modeling.

The process of abstraction and encapsulation allows us to converse about network operations completely in the abstract. In the real world, for example, a Signal Transfer Point may relay a `callSetup` message to another Signal Transfer Point. In our abstract model, "an object instance has sent a message to another object instance using a mutually supported protocol stack". The change in vocabulary is not intended to make the model less accessible to the casual reader; rather, as we shall see, the abstract terminology allows us to extend the reach of the model in many ways not originally envisioned, thus giving it greater power and flexibility.

2.5. Classification

If many objects share similar properties, they are said to belong to the same *object class*. An object class (or simply *class*) is thus a *set* of objects. The common properties of the objects may be structural, behavioral, or both. The notion of a class, however, goes beyond structural and behavioral similarities into the realm of a common "teleology" — all objects in a class have the same "purpose". Two objects may support the same set of protocol stacks and yet could belong to different classes if they vary in terms of their basic networking functions.

The ability to categorize objects into classes involves recognizing the similarities between their abstract models. Thus, the process of classification, in combination with abstraction, allows us to categorize the different elements that comprise a communication network as lines, circuits, switching equipment, transmission equipment, local area network bridges, customers, users, administrators, software, services, and so on. In specialization theory, a class is a modeling construct which can also be interpreted as a *set* in the set-theoretic sense, for as we shall see, all operations on sets are also applicable to classes.

Figure 2-2 represents an unstructured collection of network objects, while Figure 2-3 represents one way of grouping them into classes. Since a class can be treated as a set, and since a Venn diagram represents set inclusions and intersections, we can use Venn diagrams to represent classes.

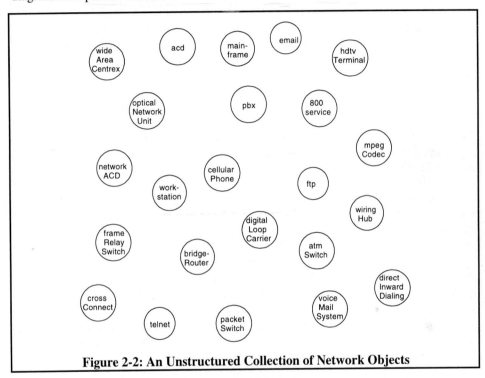

Figure 2-2: An Unstructured Collection of Network Objects

There is no unique way of categorizing objects into classes. The objects of Figure 2-3 could have been grouped into different classes had we partitioned the unstructured universe in a different way. This underscores the importance of choosing a meaningful *structuring principle* for classification. In Figure 2-3, different structuring principles were applied at different levels of the classification process to group objects together. We could have chosen other meaningful structuring principles to group the objects (for example, all objects manufactured by the same manufacturer) or some other less meaningful ones (for example, all objects of the same color). In Chapter 6, we shall see how the notion of a structuring principle can be formalized to help us correctly classify objects.

In addition to providing a grouping mechanism for objects with similar characteristics, classes also serve as templates with which to create new objects. Thus, we may add a new device to our network and introduce it to other devices as belonging to a class of objects with which they are already familiar. By merely declaring it to belong to a particu-

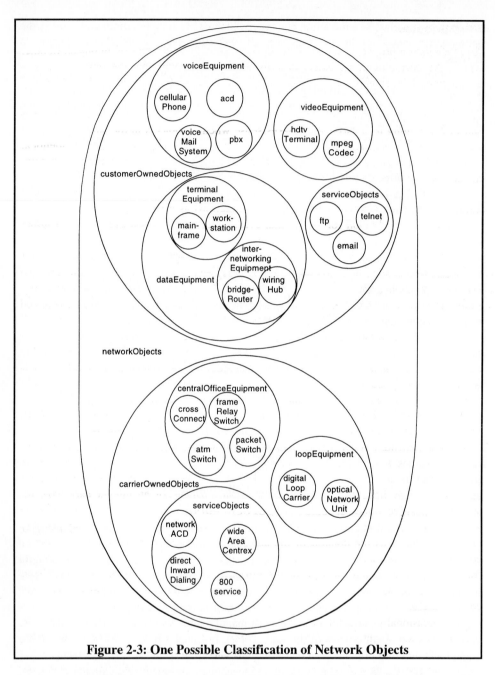

Figure 2-3: One Possible Classification of Network Objects

lar class, we in effect have conveyed to the other devices all the information they need to know about the object's properties and behavior.

2.6. Attributes

An *attribute* is a property for describing the structural characteristics of an object. In other words, the attributes of an object describe those data values that the object possesses which could conceivably be different from the data values possessed by other objects of the same class.

Although attributes are properties of objects, we will sometimes speak of attributes as belonging to a class. This makes sense when all objects in the same class share the fact they all possess the same attribute, even though they may not all possess identical values for that attribute. Since the goal of the modeling process is to identify such commonalities, we allocate the attribute to a class. Such an allocation of the attribute to the class is called a *property assignment*. A property assignment establishes a particular modeling construct (such as an attribute or a function) as a property of an object class. This is shorthand notation for saying that every object of that class possesses that property.

When we assign an attribute to a class, we say that the attribute **is-a-property-of** that class. Conversely, the class **has-as-a-property** each attribute assigned to it. We also use the equivalent terminology that the attribute **belongs-to** the class, and sometimes simply refer to it as an attribute **of** the class. The terms **is-a-property-of**, **belongs-to**, and **of** are all equivalent references to the attribute which has been assigned to the class. All these terms connote the semantic linkage between attributes and classes; they are examples of *associations*. An association establishes the semantics of a connotational coupling between two *modeling constructs* in the methodology (as opposed to a *relationship* which, as we will see in Chapter 17, establishes an operational coupling between two objects created by applying the methodology to the model of an actual network). The terms **is-a-property-of** and **has-as-a-property** are called the *property assignment associations*. In the development of our model, we will encounter many such associations.

Each attribute is said to have a *data type*. The data type defines the nature and the range of values the attribute can possess. For example, a network object may have powerStatus as an attribute of the Boolean data type, with two possible values: on and off. It may have numberOfPorts as an attribute, of an integer data type, restricted to positive values. It could have percentageUtilization as an attribute, of a positive floating-point data type. The set of all values which an attribute may possibly possess is known as the *domain* of the attribute. Attribute domains may be discrete or continuous. In our model, we will specify the data type of each attribute as we define it; this will often be called the *type of the attribute*, or simply the *attribute type*. Where meaningful, we will also specify any restriction on the domain of values the attribute could possess.

Occasionally an attribute can be specified in the model as being *unique*. This means that each object instance belonging to the class will possess a value for that attribute which no other object instance of the same class will possess. This is useful, for example, for specifying *defining attributes* of classes — items such as objectName or networkAddress which, in an appropriate context, we want to ensure can uniquely identify the object. It is also possible to have non-defining attributes which are unique.

Attributes can be simple data types, or structured types with an arbitrarily complex internal structure. In modeling, it is good practice to keep attributes, as far as possible, to model a single, indivisible characteristic of an object.

2.7. Functions

Just as an attribute describes the structural properties of an object, a *function* describes its behavioral properties. In essence, a function describes what an object *does*, rather than what it is. An object may consist of many functions, each of which could be formally described. For example, "modulate digital data arriving at an RS-232 interface to analog data in the voice frequency passband" could be a function of a `modem` object.

The complete description of a function includes a specification of its input parameters, called *arguments*, and output parameters, called *results*. Functions are of two kinds: *procedural functions* and *stream functions*. Procedural functions accept arguments and produce results which are well-defined data types — usually structured information records. Stream functions have at least one argument or one result that is not a well-defined data type but is an unstructured continuous analog or digital stream.

Stream functions make it possible to correctly and accurately describe the behavior of elements such as modulators, filters, transducers, and multiplexers which are common in multimedia networks. For example, the continuous waveform which is the input to a `pulseCodeModulation` stream function may be modeled as its argument, and the continuous bitstream which is its output may be modeled as its result. It is possible for a stream function to accept structured information arguments and produce stream results, or vice versa. For example, the function `generateTestTrafficPattern (duration = 600)` accepts a well-defined data type as an argument but produces a stream as its result; the function `computeBitErrorRate` accepts a stream as an argument but produces a data type as its result.

As we did with attributes, we will consider functions to be modeling constructs which are properties of a class. This is meaningful where all objects which are instances of the class possess that function in common. We use property assignment to allocate a function to a class: we say the function **is-a-property-of** the class, which in turn **has-as-a-property** the function. As we have already said, because of abstraction and encapsulation, the internal implementation of the function in the object is irrelevant; each object could implement the function differently for itself, as long it conforms to the same specified external behavior. Figure 2-4 illustrates the associations between attributes, functions, and object classes.

Each object may further extend the function for itself; it is allowed to "do more" than the function specification in the class. For example, one modem may use sophisticated encoding techniques to encode multiple bits per baud in differential phase shift modulation, while another may use a secondary channel to modulate additional data outside the voice frequency passband. Both of these would still qualify as belonging to the `modem` object class because they still fulfill the core functionality specified for that class.

Formal modeling of functions for network objects is an area which is at best immature and makes heavy use of pictorial techniques and textual human language descrip-

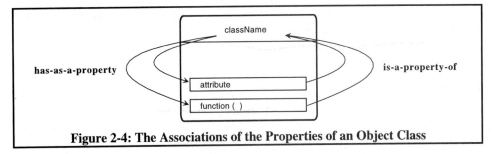

Figure 2-4: The Associations of the Properties of an Object Class

tions. There are, however, some formal description techniques which can be used to describe the behavior of certain kinds of network objects in specific, limited ways; in Chapter 13 we shall examine some of these techniques.

2.8. Inheritance and Extension

Just as classes provide a way of classifying objects, *inheritance* provides a way of *classifying classes themselves*. If we find two similar object classes sharing a subset of their properties, we abstract their common properties into a *superclass* or *parent class*. We thus have a categorization of categories. The object classes whose common properties have been thus abstracted are called *subclasses or child classes* of that superclass. It may seem counter-intuitive that *super*classes have fewer properties than *sub*classes, and actually represent a more primitive form of evolution. They are called superclasses because they are higher-order abstractions than their subclasses. Clearly, we can continue abstracting the properties of superclasses themselves and construct a complete *inheritance hierarchy* (sometimes called an *object class hierarchy*).

The inheritance hierarchy provides a *second-order abstraction*, in which common properties and behavior of classes can be isolated in yet other classes. It is thus a structuring principle which maps object classes onto other object classes. This abstraction extends the power of the model by allowing the second-order manipulation of entire classes via their superclasses, thus complementing the first-order manipulation of individual objects by their classes. This second-order abstraction is the defining characteristic of object-oriented modeling paradigms [Wegn90].

When the inheritance hierarchy is constructed to the point where no further levels of abstraction are possible, we have arrived at its *root*. For a given application domain, there is only one root of the inheritance hierarchy. In many applications, the root may be considered a pure modeling artifact, something that serves to anchor to the same tree all superclasses which cannot be abstracted further. The root is itself an object class and, by definition, has only those characteristics which are generic properties of every object of every class.

Although this description of classifying classes suggests that the inheritance hierarchy is constructed in bottom-up fashion, its power as a specification tool is best utilized in a top-down fashion. Thus, each class in the hierarchy is considered to implicitly possess the essential characteristics abstracted in its superclass. This is sometimes called a *derivation association*, in which the subclass is said to *derive-from* its superclass. The

term *ancestral classes* is used to denote all the classes above a given class in the hierarchy; the term *descendant classes* is used to denote all the classes below it. A superclass of
an object class may be equivalently defined as the ancestral class immediately above it in
the inheritance hierarchy.

Descendant classes *inherit* their properties from their ancestral classes. Thus, inheritance is also a mechanism for *implicit property assignment*: by assigning a property to
an ancestral class, it becomes available in all its descendants. When a subclass *derives-
from* a superclass, it **inherits-from** the superclass all the properties of that superclass.
Alternatively, a superclass is also sometimes said to **bequeath-to** its subclasses all its
properties; this has the same meaning. The complementary associations **inherits-from**
and **bequeaths-to** are called the *inheritance associations* between the concepts of descendant classes and ancestral classes in our model. An inheritance association is slightly
different from a derivation association, as the former applies between an object class and
all its ancestral and descendant classes, while the latter applies only between subclasses
and superclasses. The properties available in an object class through inheritance from ancestral classes are called the *inherited properties* of that object class.

In addition to inheriting characteristics from its superclass, the subclass may
choose to define additional characteristics of its own. This aspect is called *extension*.
Extension refers to the ability of the subclass to create new, semantically different entities
by specifying additional structure and behavior not present in its superclass. The properties so defined are called the *original properties* of the class, since they are not inherited
from any ancestral class. These additional characteristics will then be inherited by yet
other subclasses which derive from it. The class where a property is first defined is called
the *originating class* or simply the *origin class* for that property; the property is said to
originate in that class.

For each object class in the inheritance hierarchy, the path from the root of the
hierarchy to the class is called the *genealogy* of that class. The genealogy is an ordered
list of the names of all ancestral classes of that class. The genealogy tracks the evolution
of each class, with each step adding more detail. If classA is the ancestor of classB,
then classA must lie somewhere along the genealogy of the classB. The two classes
are then said to be *genealogically related*. If two classes anywhere in the hierarchy share a
common subset of their genealogies, this common subset can only be an initial subset. If
this common subset for any two object classes extends all the way to each class's superclass, then the two classes share a common superclass and are called *sibling* subclasses,
or simply sibling classes. Figure 2-5 illustrates superclass/subclass relationships in an inheritance hierarchy.

Inheritance and extension, therefore, are mechanisms to express the semantics of
classification and evolution. As such, they are a means of incorporating a *formalized taxonomy* within the object model itself. This implies that they create a structured organization of the universe of discourse based on our grouping objects according these principles.

Inheritance gives us an excuse to be lazy — when specifying a new object class, it
is no longer necessary to completely specify its characteristics. It is only necessary to
specify the superclass from which new object class derives and then specify only the ex-

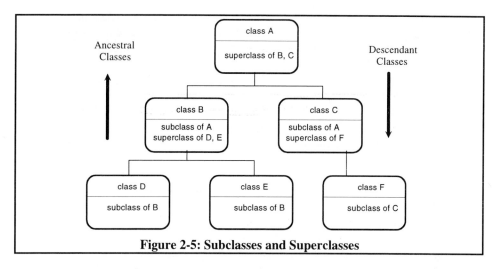

Figure 2-5: Subclasses and Superclasses

tensions, that is, the *incremental refinements* the new class makes to its inherited characteristics. Since the new class inherits its characteristics from its superclass, which in turn
inherits them from its superclass, and so on, every class in the hierarchy possesses the
characteristics of each of its ancestral classes. By merely *declaring* that one class derives
from another, we implicitly accumulate in the current class a complete assemblage of
structure and behavior imported from all its ancestral classes. Figure 2-6 demonstrates the
use of inheritance as an extension mechanism.

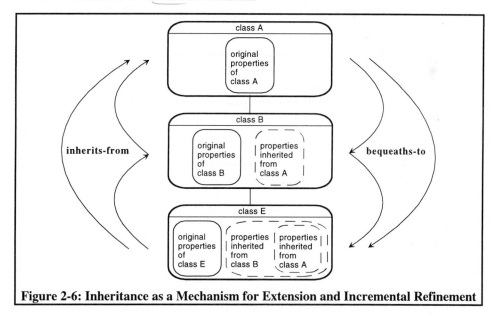

Figure 2-6: Inheritance as a Mechanism for Extension and Incremental Refinement

As we suggested before, inheritance — or the ability to declaratively refer to properties and behavior already specified elsewhere — is the defining characteristic of object-oriented modeling. It is instructive to refer to Wegner's definition of modeling paradigms [Wegn90]:

- *Object-Based Modeling*: The modeling paradigm that requires all elements of interest to be abstracted and encapsulated objects.

- *Class-Based Modeling*: The modeling paradigm that requires all objects to belong to classes.

- *Object-Oriented Modeling*: The modeling paradigm that requires all classes to support inheritance.

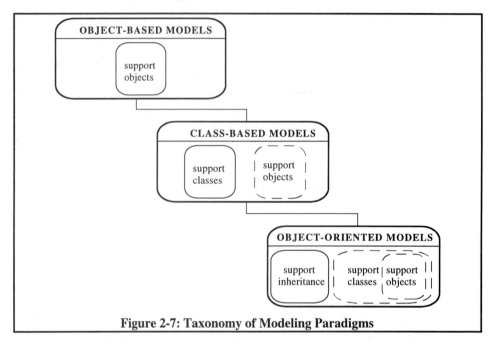

Figure 2-7: Taxonomy of Modeling Paradigms

Thus, a paradigm that supports abstraction and encapsulation is said to be *object-based*; one that, in addition, supports classification, is *class-based*; and further, if it also supports inheritance, it is said to be *object-oriented*. Figure 2-7 is a metamodel of these modeling paradigms. As we shall see in our discussion of network management standards in later chapters, some network management standards support an object-oriented model, while others are object-based. In Chapter 26, we shall see how an object-oriented model may be implemented in a reduced form as an object-based model using a technique known as *inheritance resolution*, which can be implemented by a model compiler capable of *hierarchy telescoping*. This essentially "flattens" the hierarchy into sets of scalar objects.

2.9. Instantiation

An *object instance* is a concrete object which is an example of an object class. An object instance — sometimes just called an instance — has an identity which is different from other instances of the same class; it also generally has attribute values that are different from those in other instances of the same class. The activity of creating objects as instances of a class is called *instantiation* or *exemplification*, since an instance exemplifies a class. The set of all instances of a class is called the *extent* of the class; two instances which are examples of the same object class are said to be *fellow instances* of that class.

A class which has direct instances is called a *concrete class*. Some object classes — of which the root class of the inheritance hierarchy is a good example — are never instantiated; they exist only for the purposes of modeling. Such classes are called *abstract classes*. Classes which exist at the bottom of the inheritance hierarchy and have no further descendants are called *leaf classes*. Usually, but not necessarily, leaf classes are concrete, and usually, but not necessarily, concrete classes are leaf. Classes which have further descendants are called *non-leaf classes*. Some non-leaf classes may also be concrete. If such a class has both instances and subclasses, it is a non-leaf concrete class.

On occasion, we will need to define classes which are not only themselves abstract but whose descendants (if any) are all also abstract. That is, neither the class nor any of its descendants can have instances, even if the descendants are leaf classes. Such a class is called a *fully abstract* class. Naturally, any leaf class which cannot have instances is always fully abstract; some of its ancestors may also be fully abstract. The notion of full abstraction may seem quite futile at this time, since it does not permit classes to have instances. However, as we shall see during the development of advanced modeling concepts, this notion can sometimes be very useful. Figure 2-8 illustrates some common kinds of classes.

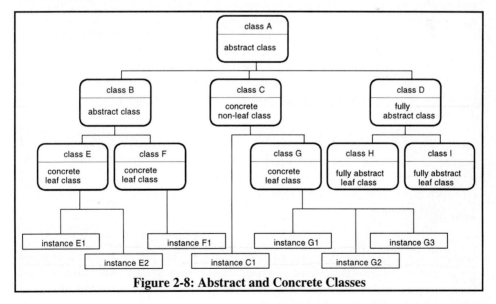

Figure 2-8: Abstract and Concrete Classes

If we could consider the organization of life-forms in the animal kingdom to be an approximately modeled object class hierarchy, it would be a good example in which only leaf classes are concrete. That is, all instantiations occur only at the lowest level of the hierarchy. There is no such thing as an instantiated generic mammal, or an instantiated generic vertebrate. All animals are instances of some species and subspecies — which are the lowest levels in the inheritance hierarchy. Thus, "Dick Whittington's cat" is an instance of *Felix Domestica*, which is a leaf class. In network modeling also, it is good practice to instantiate as close to the leaf level as possible.

(Although this example is frequently used in object-oriented modeling to illustrate inheritance, it should be borne in mind that biological taxonomies do not strictly adhere to an inheritance model. Rather, they are *polythetic* [Need75]. This means that although there are a large number of representative properties and each property is possessed by a large number of individual species, there is often no individual species that possesses every representative property. Because some exception to the set of representative properties can almost always be found — for example, mammals that lay eggs — there is no single abstract archetype which could be modeled as a superclass.)

2.10. Aggregation

Aggregation — sometimes referred to as composition — refers to the ability to construct complex objects by assembling simpler objects together in meaningful configurations. Any system of reasonable complexity is almost always an assembly of simpler components. The reason a complex system, such as an aircraft or a submarine, works is because its constituent subsystems have been designed to work together using specified interfaces.

Since we cannot mentally grasp at once the complete workings of the entire complex system, we can examine it to determine what its parts are. By examining the parts, we can determine what their subparts are. Clearly, we can continue this process until we have arrived at parts which are small enough for us to conceptualize and mentally manipulate in their entirety. If each such part is simple enough so we know how it can be constructed, we do not need to analyze it any further. At this stage, we have resolved the problem of designing the complex system into a set of subproblems, each of which we know how to solve independently. In modeling methodology, this process is known as *decomposition*.

Decomposition is neither a new concept nor is it unique to object-oriented modeling. Nevertheless, when decomposition is executed for an object-oriented model, care must be taken to ensure that it is not performed across arbitrary lines. Each part resulting from the decomposition must itself be complete enough to be treated as an object. That is, each such part should preserve encapsulation and present a well-defined set of interfaces at its object boundary.

The process of decomposition identifies component objects of a complex system. These component objects could potentially be assembled together again. Using a reassembly process, the complex system could be recreated. This process is known as *aggregation*, and the system thus created is termed an *aggregate* system. Alternatively, a different complex system could be created from the same standard components, if they are reassembled in a different valid configuration.

By examining the component parts and subparts of a complex system, we can construct an *aggregation hierarchy*. An aggregation hierarchy identifies the *part/whole* relationships between objects — that is, it specifies object classes which could possibly be components of other object classes. In a communication network, an example of a part/whole relationship would be a line card which could be contained inside a PBX.

Construction of new complex systems using known, standard parts is clearly not a revolutionary concept, having been used in manufacturing since the industrial revolution. Our network modeling methodology, however, expresses the interfaces between network objects in a formal notation, thereby allowing machine logic to determine how and where these objects can be pieced together to create complex networks.

2.11. Summary

The principles of object-oriented modeling allow us to focus our attention on only a limited subset of reality at any given time. We identify and isolate items of interest and separate those items from other items of interest. The process of abstraction captures those essential characteristics of an object which are interesting to our application domain. The process of encapsulation identifies the boundaries of the object and specifies the behavior visible at its interface. Attributes are characteristics of an object which model structural properties, while functions are characteristics which model behavioral properties.

A class is a collectivity of objects which share similar characteristics. An inheritance hierarchy is a collectivity of classes which share similar characteristics. Individual objects are said to be instances of their class. Superclasses which are pure modeling abstractions in the inheritance hierarchy and have no instances are called abstract, while classes which have instances are called concrete. It is good modeling practice to design the hierarchy such that concrete classes are leaf-level classes in the inheritance tree. An aggregation hierarchy describes part/whole relationships between complex objects and their component objects.

3. Object-Oriented Modeling versus Object-Oriented Programming

"Blessed are the meek, for they shall inherit the earth."
*— incorrect class hierarchy constructed by anonymous
early object-oriented researcher.*

3.1. Introduction

Because object-oriented programming is a more familiar topic than object-oriented modeling to most readers, we describe in this chapter some of the differences between using object-orientation for programming and for modeling. Some of the important areas covered are monotonic inheritance, the difference between subclassing and subtyping, polymorphism, referent and non-referent classes, and the distinction between object-orientation as a specification mechanism and as an implementation technique.

3.2. Conceptual Background

Specialization theory, like any modeling methodology, is used to organize our unstructured knowledge of the universe of discourse. Modeling paradigms impose an order on raw facts so that they can be meaningfully represented as a system capable of being analyzed. The nomenclature of biological life-forms and the organization of the periodic table of elements are examples of such meaningful models of knowledge.

Historically, object-oriented modeling should be seen more as an extension of existing modeling techniques which have been adapted to incorporate object-oriented concepts, rather than as an extension of object-oriented programming techniques into the realm of modeling. Many formal modeling techniques — such as entity-relationship analysis [Chen76, Nijs89] — already accommodate the concepts of decomposing the system into component entities and relationships. Other modeling methodologies

36

[Gadr87, Grie82, Gadr93, SR 1826, SR 2008] have focused on conceptual schema, information frameworks, data flows, and state transitions of system entities. The network models of this book primarily use the rigorous notions of specialization theory to create taxonomical hierarchies but retain many concepts from other methodologies where meaningful.

The emphasis in object-oriented network modeling is to understand the network in terms of its component objects, their attributes, and the relationships they bear with each other. The system must first be understood and described in an abstract form before implementation begins. Object-oriented network architects are more concerned with the "what", that is, the *specification* of the system; object-oriented programmers are more concerned with the "how", that is, the *implementation* of the system [Rumb91b].

A modeling methodology is typically applied early in the network design process, long before software implementations of the model typically occur. The conceptualization of the system using the object-oriented paradigm is independent of any programming activity which may follow. Programming languages are just one aspect of object-oriented analysis: besides serving as a basis for software construction, the object-oriented model can also serve as a basis for specification, design, and documentation. A software implementation methodology need not necessarily parallel the network modeling methodology. Indeed, it is perfectly possible to implement software for a network modeled using object-oriented techniques, in a non-object-oriented programming language. However, as we shall see, it is advantageous to use an object-oriented programming language to implement an object-oriented network model.

Many concepts and principles behind the design and construction of object-oriented software programs are already well known. The main focus of software development in this area has been the design of languages whose constructs support the object-oriented paradigm, such as C++ [Stro90, Stro91], Smalltalk [Gold83], and Eiffel [Meye88]. Of great interest to compiler developers in this area are problems such as how to create the most efficient representation of language constructs. The process of designing object-oriented languages is an extremely complex exercise, requiring many difficult design decisions and trade-offs. Designing application programs in those languages is also difficult — many low-level "how" decisions about the most optimal representation of data structures and choice of algorithms need to be made by the programmer.

Because of its different focus, many of the programming issues that arise in the construction of object-oriented software are not significant in the realm of object-oriented modeling. The following discussion will highlight some of these differences.

3.3. Reusability

Reusability is one of the more valuable and attractive facets of object-oriented programming. The mechanism for reusability is inheritance, that is, the ability to reuse implementations of classes by subclassing from them. By merely declaring a subclass to derive from an existing superclass (possibly available in some off-the-shelf class library), the programmer is saved the effort of implementing the class completely. The programmer need only specify the *incremental refinements* — that is, any additional structural or functional details — which are necessary in the subclass.

Such reusability is not a major concern in object-oriented modeling, as many network models are often done *a priori*. In object-oriented modeling, inheritance does not necessarily imply reusability of *implementations*; it only implies reusability of *specifications*. Because an inheritance hierarchy is a taxonomical mechanism, it becomes a vehicle for specification reuse: by creating new subclasses, the architect "reuses" the specifications already made for superclasses earlier in the hierarchy.

Of course, if an object-oriented network model is realized in software using an object-oriented programming language, the implementation reusability aspects of the chosen language will be of considerable benefit.

3.4. Relationships

In applying specialization theory to network modeling, the specification of *relationships* will be an important theme. Many relationships exist among objects in a network. Because modeling is largely a specification technique, it is easy to specify inter-object relationships *declaratively*.

Implementationally, however, most object-oriented programming languages do not support the explicit notion of relationships. When the semantics of the model require that relationships be represented in software, object-oriented programmers resort to conjugate pointers and other (sometimes inconvenient) practices to create inter-object relationships. Because of this, many object-oriented programmers are not enthusiastic about relationship-intensive modeling techniques, because of the belief that their software implementation in an object-oriented language compromises the notion of object encapsulation. This perceived breakdown of encapsulation — objects with a large number of internal pointers to other objects — can become especially severe in models with several many-to-many relationships. Further, as the removal of a relationship instance could require an atomic deletion of conjugate pointers from different objects simultaneously, there is danger that the system could be left in an inconsistent state.

We shall discuss these issues in considerable detail in Chapter 17 and show that inter-object relationships are crucial underpinnings of the object-oriented models of complex systems. Further, depending on the choice of implementation techniques, inter-object relationships do not necessarily compromise the encapsulation of implemented software objects in an object-oriented programming environment.

3.5. Monotonic Inheritance

As we saw in Chapter 2, inheritance is a mechanism of *incremental refinement* — every class inherits attributes and behavior from its superclass and further refines them by introducing additional attributes and behavior of its own.

Our model for communication networks uses *specialization theory*, which is a more rigorous form of object-oriented modeling. In specialization theory, refinement by cancellation is not permitted. This approach is variously called *monotonic inheritance*, *immutable inheritance*, or *strict inheritance*. Under monotonic inheritance, every subclass *must* inherit each and every attribute and function specified for its ancestral classes and may not cancel any of them. Thus, each subclass is a *monotonic extension* of its superclass. We adopt this approach because our primary use of inheritance is to create taxonomical hierarchies, rather than code reuse; the network model would become unnecessarily complicated if classes were permitted idiosyncratic behavior. As we shall see in Chapter 6, with a proper redesign of the inheritance hierarchy, exceptions can be easily accommodated and the necessity for selective inheritance can be eliminated. In practice, the monotonic inheritance requirement is not as stringent as it seems.

In conventional object-oriented software construction, the notion of *refinement by cancellation* is prevalent. Under cancellation, properties inherited from superclasses may be dropped, such that they are no longer properties of the derived class or any descendant classes thereof. This approach is sometimes called *selective inheritance*, in which the subclass may choose to selectively inherit only certain properties from the superclass. (The use of selective inheritance merely for the sake of code reuse convenience can create random behavior-sharing patterns; hence, it is sometimes called *spaghetti inheritance*.)

Of course, during the process of constructing any particular object-oriented software program, a programmer may choose to adopt a monotonic inheritance policy simply by not using any of the selective inheritance features or cancellation mechanisms provided by the language.

3.6. Multiple Inheritance

Multiple inheritance refers to the ability of an object class to derive from more than one superclass. By specifying that a subclass derives with multiple inheritance, we imbue it with the structure and behavior of more than one superclass. Thus, a multiple deriving subclass has multiple genealogies.

The need for multiple inheritance occasionally arises in modeling complex real-world situations where an object exhibits the properties of more than one superclass. Sometimes, however, programmers invoke multiple inheritance because the object class hierarchy has not been properly designed. In many cases, it can be shown that, with a proper redesign of the object class hierarchy combined with the use of aggregation, multiple inheritance can be "normalized away". Thus, each subclass need derive from only one superclass. There is, in fact, a school of thought in the object-oriented modeling community which believes that all cases of multiple inheritance are spurious and can be eliminated by a combination of normalization and aggregation [Carg92]. Others believe that the convenience of multiple inheritance justifies the expense of supporting it as a language construct.

Many object-oriented programming languages support the notion of multiple inheritance. Doing so involves some expense during the compiler design process, as algorithms must be introduced to perform resolution of possible conflicts between structure and behavior inherited from multiple superclasses.

Specialization theory permits the notion of multiple inheritance because of the semantic expressiveness it provides as a specification tool. We shall, however, rarely be required to use it. Architects using object-oriented modeling methodologies are advised to explore fully all other alternatives — such as hierarchy redesign and aggregation — to examine whether multiple inheritance is really necessary. Because of the complexities involved in multiple inheritance, it should be used with great care and only when absolutely necessary.

3.7. Overriding

Overriding is the process by which a subclass, rather than canceling inherited attributes and operations, changes them to suit itself. In object-oriented software environments, overriding is often implemented via *virtual functions*. In the modeling of communication networks, however, monotonic inheritance also implies that overriding is not allowed. If overriding were allowed in an unrestricted manner, for example, a subclass would be free to redefine an inherited function to do something entirely different. In communications network modeling, such redefinition is not meaningful.

Recall that overriding by reimplementation is not forbidden as long as the function "does the same thing". Because of encapsulation, an object class may freely reimplement inherited functions internally without changing externally observable behavior. However, overriding to change externally observable behavior is illegal in modeling, as it changes the operative meaning of an inherited function. In object-oriented programming, the subclass programmer may legally change an inherited function's implementation as long as its name is preserved.

3.8. Polymorphism

Polymorphism — literally, "many forms" — is the ability of an operation to take on different forms when applied to different objects. The idea behind polymorphism is that semantically equivalent operations should present the same interface even while being applied to different target objects.

For example, the operation `buildSpanningTree` may apply equally well to a two-port local area network bridge and to a multi-port local area network bridge. The implementation of the `buildSpanningTree` operation might be different in each bridge; the two-port bridge may use different algorithms than the multi-port bridge. However, the operation could be parameterized by the same type of arguments (e.g., manually assigned root bridge) and could return the same type of result, irrespective of which object it was applied to. Thus, the operation is said to be *polymorphic*. This means that, while it presents the same interface, its implementation is different depending on which object it is applied to.

We have already stated that, because of encapsulation, such implementation distinctions are irrelevant in network object modeling. We are only interested in the interfaces the object presents at its boundary. In object-oriented modeling, we shall consider the polymorphic implementation of functions a non-issue. We specify operations in our network model and apply them at the highest point in the inheritance hierarchy where it is meaningful to do so. The need to be concerned about whether each descendant class, or instance thereof, implements that operation most efficiently for itself does not arise in object-oriented network modeling.

Note that this only applies to *function polymorphism* and not to *signature polymorphism*. The syntax and sequence of arguments supplied to a function together constitute the *signature* of the function. In signature polymorphism — sometimes also called *parametric polymorphism* — a different implementation of a particular operation would be invoked depending on the syntax of the arguments used to invoke it. Signature polymorphism is sometimes called *overloading* in some object-oriented programming environments. In object-oriented modeling, signature polymorphism is not meaningful, because we do not alias semantically equivalent operations based on their arguments.

3.9. Dynamic Binding

In object-oriented software environments, the term *dynamic binding* refers to the ability of the system to select the most appropriate operation for the target object at run time. This implies that if an operation on an object has been redefined after the system has started execution, an invocation of the operation is able to use the latest form and apply it to the target object.

   This concept is not meaningful in the object-oriented modeling of objects which may exist in a communications network. By their very nature, network objects do not change, on the fly, the definition or internal implementation of operations which have been programmed into them. Even when new software operations and functions are downloaded into an object (for example, deploying a new service on a central-office switch), it is only done under highly controlled conditions and only after other appropriate network elements (such as operations support systems) are ready for the change. Thus, these operations may be said to be *statically bound*. Operations on network objects, therefore, are not modeled under dynamic binding. Dynamic binding is meaningful only in situations where the environment requires run-time selection between different versions of the same operation.

3.10. Delegation

Some object-based software environments support the notion of *delegation*. Delegation is behavior-sharing at the level of objects, rather than at the level of classes. Therefore, instead of having behavior specified in a hierarchy of classes, an object may choose to delegate the responsibility for performing a certain operation to another object termed a *prototype*. The prototype may, in turn, delegate the responsibility to some other prototype. Clearly, inheritance is a specialized form of delegation in which the prototype object is the superclass in the class hierarchy.

   In some delegation-based software environments, delegation is defined independently of classes, and in fact may occur in classless environments as well. For example, a method may be directly attached to an object instance, instead of to a class. Delegation would then be implemented by searching a chain of instance pointers at run time.

   The fundamental notion behind delegation — just as in inheritance — is the extension of an object to present an appearance of internalization of common operations, even though those operations may in actuality be referenced elsewhere. Like inheritance, it is a form of resource reuse. The prototype object, which is not necessarily a superclass and may in fact be an instance of another class, serves as a partial template to which operations may be referred.

Delegation is appealing to some software developers who see the requirement that every object belong to a class as too restrictive and confining; inheritance is perceived to "get in the way of" using clever programming tricks with unclassified objects at run time. Delegation, however, destroys the rich semantics in the taxonomy which we construct through inheritance. In the object-oriented modeling of communication networks, we shall not use delegation.

3.11. Visibility Control

In many object-oriented programming languages, superclasses exercise *visibility control* by reserving for themselves the right to privacy. Superclasses are allowed to choose which attributes and functions will be made visible to subclasses and other classes. Thus, a superclass may "block off" access to certain properties by its subclasses merely by declaring those properties to be so hidden. A subclass, even though it inherits these attributes, cannot modify or access them directly, except through other functions designed specifically for that purpose.

In an object-oriented model, the need for a superclass to hide its data or function members from its subclasses does not exist. Subclasses inherit the complete structure and behavior specified for the superclass and retain full visibility to all inherited class members. In addition, because subclasses may not hide or override inherited behavior due to monotonic inheritance, complete knowledge of all ancestral classes is preserved and accumulated in the leaf classes in a fully accessible form.

Visibility control is also an issue among objects of classes not related through inheritance. To enforce encapsulation, the members of an object in a software environment are not normally visible to other objects. Ordinarily, a software object can only interrogate the attributes of another object through a well-defined interface method designed for that purpose. Good program design principles require that the programmer make only that information accessible which absolutely must be known to outside modules and hide all other information that does not need to be globally available. Occasionally, however, a tactical need arises to "expose" some internal data and function attributes in an object to other trusted objects for reasons of implementation efficiency. Many object-oriented programming languages provide various mechanisms to accommodate this need.

In modeling communication networks, the issue of visibility control is not relevant. Since we use object-oriented principles only to model the system, the specification of attributes and the design of class hierarchies is a mechanism for formalizing a taxonomy. Object privacy is an issue of good software engineering practice and not a modeling concern.

3.12. Declarative Instantiation

In most object-oriented software environments, instantiation can be *declarative* — that is, having defined a class in a formal syntax, one can then instantiate variables of the class through declarations in the same syntax. In the object-oriented analysis of communication networks, as we shall see, the concept of declarative instantiation is not meaningful.

Although a formal syntax is used to define object classes, we do not actually instantiate objects during the modeling process.

In an operating network, instantiation of a new object requires that other network objects be made aware of the existence of the new object. This needs to be accomplished by the exchange of messages between objects framed in an appropriate protocol, after which each object updates an internal information base. In object-oriented programming, one instantiates an object merely by declaring a variable to a compiler.

3.13. Inter-Object Communication

The issue of *inter-object communication* in object-oriented programming is fairly straightforward: an object receives a message and responds to it. This is sometimes called "invoking a method" on an object. In an object-oriented network model, however, communication is a lot more complicated. A network object could receive different messages on different ports; furthermore, its interoperability with other network objects depends on what protocol stacks are supported on each port. We will explore this issue in much greater detail in Chapter 15, which deals with modeling ports and protocol stacks.

3.14. Non-Referent Classes

In an object-oriented network model, each class we specify has a purpose. A class definition which does not model an actual functionary in the network would be an architectural flaw. Even though many classes we specify will be abstract (i.e., without instances), they will arise from the process of generalization of concrete classes. Thus, every class in our model will have a *referent* in the actual system; these are called *referent classes*.

In object-oriented programming, however, it is possible for the programmer to create class definitions purely for the purpose of programming convenience, such as loosely collecting several primitive variables in a data structure merely in order to reduce the number of arguments to a subroutine. Classes created for such purposes do not reflect an actual object from the system model. We shall call these *non-referent classes*. (In some methodologies, referent and non-referent classes are also termed *authentic* and *synthetic* classes respectively.) In network modeling, we shall not use non-referent classes.

In object-oriented programming, non-referent classes are used not just as programming artifacts; they could also be used as vehicles for data sharing. This means classes can be instantiated and used by other objects merely as repositories for storing common data, with appropriate interface functions defined for accessing that data. Many object-oriented programmers declare and instantiate a new class when all they really need is a data structure or a record. Such classes are mere collections of data; many times they do not participate in any kind of inheritance hierarchy reflecting a system model. In our modeling methodology, this practice will not be used. When classes are instantiated, they will represent meaningful functionaries in our network model.

Even when non-referent classes belong to inheritance hierarchies, they primarily reflect hierarchies created largely for programming convenience and code reuse. For example, classes such as `list` and `queue` may participate in hierarchies so that common functions and operations (such as insertion and deletion) can be shared among different kinds of lists and queues. These are also called *standard classes* or *library classes*, as they are most often generically available from a canned class library. Generally, a library class is *applied* to an actual referent class during the development of network operations software — for example, to create a list of `router` objects or a queue of `protocol-DataUnit` objects. The library class is set up to be a *parameterized* class, so that the referent class can be specified as a parameter to the library class. While such library classes are useful and important during the implementation of a model, they are of little interest at the analysis stage itself, so we shall not consider them to be of modeling interest.

3.15. Subclasses versus Subtypes

In object-oriented programming, it is meaningful to make a distinction between subclasses and subtypes. Every class is considered a type since it may be used as a template to create instances. However, not every type is a class; for example, the built-in `integer` type is not a class in many object-oriented programming environments. Subclasses are specified by the programmer declaratively and explicitly. Because many object-oriented languages allow overriding, the programmer may arbitrarily modify or reimplement inherited behavior. Although it is good programming practice to substantially reuse ancestral behavior in subclasses, the compiler has no guarantee that the programmer in fact has done so.

The notion of *subtypes* [Scha86, Lea91, Pfen92] provides a more rigorous approach to this problem. If the syntax of an object-oriented language supports subtyping, it can provide a guarantee to the compiler that inherited behavior has not been modified. A subtype is a type derived by specifying restrictions on a supertype. Subtypes may not modify inherited behavior arbitrarily as subclasses can; they may only modify it in certain permissible ways.

The fundamental idea behind a subtype is that it should be fully substitutable everywhere its supertype can be used. This substitutability can be inferentially proved based on analytic considerations of the constraining predicates used to specify the subtype. Subclassing, on the other hand, is declarative: a subclass is a subclass only if the programmer says so. And even if the programmer says so, she may make the subclass do something entirely different than its superclass, leading to a breakdown of substitutability. By the same token, the reverse situation is also possible: the programmer may define new classes which are subtypes of (substitutable for) other classes without necessarily specifying them as subclasses.

Specialization theory depends strongly on *type theory*. Type theory is an established and well-understood subject in computer science and has foundational support in many calculi of denotational semantics. It has influenced the development of many procedural and functional programming languages [Pfen92, Jals94]. Because we use specialization theory for network modeling, we make no distinction between subclasses and subtypes. Specialization theory does not allow a subclass to override or cancel inherited operations; every subclass is a subtype of its superclass and remains fully substitutable for all its ancestral classes. In modeling methodologies that use specialization theory, the distinction between subtypes and subclasses is irrelevant, even though it may be significant in a programming language which implements the methodology.

3.16. Specification versus Implementation

An issue related to subtyping is that of the correct interpretation of inheritance. Much debate has ensued in the object-oriented programming community over whether inheritance should be considered a technique for sharing implementations, a technique for sharing specifications, both, or neither.

Since inheritance allows subclasses to use functions defined in an ancestral class, it can be used for behavior sharing. A subclass may use the same implementation of the function defined in the superclass. Yet many languages allow subclasses to override the implementation of inherited functions. In doing so, a subclass may preserve the function interface, or it may not. If a subclass reimplements the inherited function with the same interface, it has reused the specification of the function and therefore need not respecify it to other objects. It may still remain type-compatible with the superclass. In this situation, the subclass has used inheritance to acquire only the specification of the function. If the subclass reimplements the function without preserving its interface, it has not reused either the implementation or the specification.

Many designers of object-oriented programming languages have considered the approach of having two separate inheritance hierarchies, one for implementations and one for specifications. By forcing programmers to see the distinction between the two concepts, better models of real-world situations could be created. In most cases, however, languages only provide a single hierarchy for both, because separating the two concepts would complicate languages unacceptably for both users and compiler writers.

In network modeling, we will only use an inheritance hierarchy as a specification tool. Since we are not concerned with implementation of specific network objects, network designers are free to use the different implementations for the same function as long as the interface specifications are preserved.

3.17. Type Knowledge

The issue of *type knowledge* is concerned with the proper choice of location to store information about the type of each object. Some object-oriented programming languages require the programmer to keep track of an object's type at all times, as they do not allow an object to be queried for its own type at run time. In other environments, each object is assumed to be aware of its type. In object-oriented database systems, type knowledge is often typically stored in a separate data dictionary or class dictionary; it may also be stored with each object.

In object-oriented network modeling, we assume that each object conceptually possesses type knowledge, that is, it "knows" its type at all times. In a functioning network, type knowledge could be implemented inside each object, in an explicit network object dictionary, or by using any other mechanism.

Further, in a software environment, an object is sometimes required to refer to itself and its own attributes. Therefore, it needs to know its own address in memory. Many object-oriented programming languages reserve a hidden pointer in the implementation of each object containing a memory reference to itself. The object can reference this pointer when the need arises. Again, this is an issue of interest in program implementation and is not relevant at the modeling stage. We do not, in our model, imbue each object class with an attribute which is an analogous reference to its representation in memory.

3.18. Object Persistence

Many object-oriented environments are concerned with the issue of *object persistence*, that is, defining objects whose lifetime exceeds that of the program in which they were created. By merely declaring an object to be persistent, the programmer is assured that it will be retained in non-volatile storage (e.g., a disk file system) upon program exit. It can then be retrieved intact from that storage on the next invocation of the program [Bapa91b]. Declarative persistence is of great benefit to the programmer, who then does not have to define data structures for permanent storage and functions to perform reads and writes. Many object-oriented database systems have made great advances toward providing a seamless interface for persistent objects within a language environment [Kim88, Kim90a].

In modeling communication networks, we are not concerned with object persistence as such. Clearly, in a run-time implementation of the model, information about an appropriate subset of the model must be made available to every network object which requires that subset. Whether this is accomplished using persistent disk storage, non-volatile memory, or downloadable software is only an issue at the level of network element design. The ability to specify which objects should be automatically persistent is not a concern at the modeling stage.

3.19. Language Implementation Issues

In object-oriented language implementation, the issues of relevance are efficient implementation of inheritance, efficient dispatch of functions, efficient memory representation of objects, run-time resolution of polymorphic procedures based on function signatures, and so on. Other issues in language design involve assuring semantic correctness through type-checking and providing memory management via garbage collection.

The implemented form of each object also possesses certain *implementation attributes* which assist the run-time environment to keep track of the object. These are not the same as object attributes discussed earlier; they are mere artifacts arising from the need to manage the object at run time. Implementation attributes include information about the object address space, whether the object is in primary or secondary storage, how to service an object fault when an object accessed by a program is not in primary storage, location of any replicas of the object, its lock status, and the identity of the transactions owning the locks.

All of these are non-issues at the level of object-oriented network modeling. Tactical object implementation decisions in specific language environments are not of concern at the modeling stage.

3.20. Using Object-Oriented Modeling and Programming Together

Object-oriented modeling and object-oriented programming are not competing method-ologies — rather, they are complementary, each being of benefit in a different phase of the system design life cycle. Much benefit can be derived by using object-oriented net-work modeling and object-oriented programming together. The conceptual synergy be-tween an object-oriented network model and an object-oriented programming language to implement that model can be exploited to advantage. For example, the program designer need no longer expend effort for designing software classes for network objects; the ob-ject hierarchy in the model can largely be translated directly as a hierarchy of class con-structs in the syntax of the programming language.

By focusing on the abstract at the highest levels of system design, object-oriented network modeling allows the network architect to introduce more formalism and rigor in the early stages of design, filter out details, and leave the minute analyses to the network programmer. By providing programming constructs that closely approximate the system model, object-oriented languages allow the network programmer to match the implemen-tation more accurately with the system model. A network programmer using an object-oriented language need only specify declaratively what encapsulation policies (using data visibility rules) and what reusability policies (using inheritance rules) need to be en-forced; the compiler will arrange for this to be done automatically. Many such issues which were the programmer's responsibility in a non-object-oriented environment are now relegated to the compiler in an object-oriented environment.

Though the boundaries between phases in a network system development life cy-cle are not always clear (one methodology's low-level specification is another methodol-ogy's high-level pseudocode), it seems safe to say that object-oriented techniques elevate both the specification and implementation to a level closer to actual reality, as represented by the system model. Thus, by raising the focus of attention of both the system architect and the network programmer to a higher level of abstraction, the combination of object-oriented network modeling and object-oriented programming can result in considerably shortening the deployment cycles of advanced network products and services.

Figure 3-1 illustrates conventional network architecture, design, and planning methodologies, while Figure 3-2 demonstrates how these could be changed with the use of object-oriented techniques.

3.21. Summary

There is a difference in focus between object-oriented modeling and object-oriented pro-gramming. Object-oriented modeling is more abstract, less detailed, and more compre-hensive in its view of the system. It is best applied at the early stage of the network design process. Object-oriented programming is more concerned with the details of low-level system design and efficiency of implementation. It typically occurs in the later stages of the system's life cycle. An object-oriented programming language could be used to im-plement an object-oriented model. By doing so, the synergies between the modeling and implementation concepts could be exploited to considerable advantage.

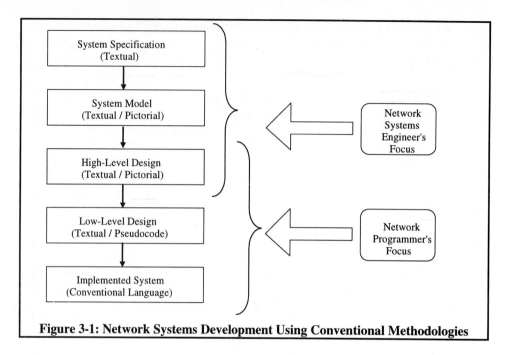

Figure 3-1: Network Systems Development Using Conventional Methodologies

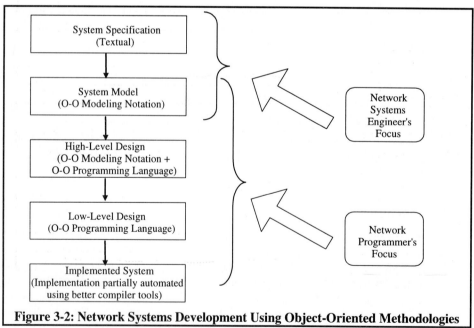

Figure 3-2: Network Systems Development Using Object-Oriented Methodologies

We shall concentrate in the remainder of this book only on object-oriented modeling as applied to communication networks, without explicit reference to any possible software implementation thereof. Table 3-1 summarizes the differences in areas of emphasis between object-oriented modeling and object-oriented programming.

FEATURES	Object-Oriented Programming	Object-Oriented Modeling
Abstraction	Yes	Yes
Encapsulation	Yes	Yes
Attributes	Yes	Yes
Functions	Yes	Yes
Classes	Yes	Yes
Inheritance	Yes	Yes
Extension	Yes	Yes
Instantiation	Declarative	System-Dependent
Aggregation	Yes	Yes
Reusability	Implementations	Specifications
Relationships	No	Yes
Monotonic Inheritance	Discretionary	Mandatory
Multiple Inheritance	Yes	Yes
Function Polymorphism	Yes	Not meaningful
Signature Polymorphism	Yes	No
Selective Inheritance	Yes	No
Dynamic Binding	Some Environments	Not meaningful
Delegation	Some Environments	No
Inheritance Visibility Control	Most Environments	No
Visibility to Other Classes	Some Environments	Not meaningful
Inter-Object Communication	Method Invocations	Protocol Messages
Non-Referent Classes	Yes	No
Subclass = Subtype	Not necessarily	Yes
Type Knowledge	Most Environments	Yes
Object Persistence	Some Environments	Not meaningful
Garbage Collection	Some Environments	Not meaningful
Type Checking	Most Environments	Not meaningful

Table 3-1: Object-Oriented Programming versus Object-Oriented Modeling

4. Designing Object Classes

"Why shouldn't I teach my object-oriented programming course from the same notes every year? I believe in reusable classes."
— *computer science professor at anonymous university.*

4.1. Introduction

In this chapter, we will examine modeling of network objects classes in greater detail. Techniques will be introduced to model collections of properties and to model optional characteristics. Examples in modeling network objects will be considered to illustrate how core characteristics and optional characteristics may be properly partitioned so that the need for multiple inheritance can be eliminated in many situations.

4.2. Specifying Object Classes

Object classes in a communication network must be defined with the proper degree of abstraction and encapsulation. Essentially, this consists of identifying attributes and functions which are relevant. There is no single correct way of defining objects — each application domain will identify different attributes and functions of interest. In our modeling, we will focus on those properties of objects which will be of interest to us in designing and architecting networks, in operating them, and in managing them. We will develop a network modeling methodology using a rigorous form of object-oriented modeling called *specialization theory*.

A meaningful object class in a network model has a referent in the actual system — that is, it models some entity in the actual system which is relevant to our purposes. Object classes need not always have a physical realization. Logical entities which are important in the network could also be modeled as object classes. Examples of typical object classes include network devices, software applications, protocol entities, network services, and so on. Other logical entities — such as sites to model geographic location and administrative domains to model jurisdictional location — can also be modeled as object classes. In addition, we will model human agencies — individual and institutional — as object classes, if they are significant to our understanding of the network. Examples of such agencies include manufacturers, service providers, and subscribers.

Every object class, irrespective of its nature, is modeled by identifying attributes and functions of interest and specifying them in a formal syntax. The class is specified as a modeling construct, and its attributes and functions are specified as independent modeling constructs which are associated with the class through property assignment. In identifying properties of interest, we will focus on two kinds of specification — *core specification* and *variant specification*. Both capture information about the essential properties of each object. Core properties are attributes and functions which are mandatory in each instance of the object class. Variant properties provide us modeling flexibility which allows us to represent options and variations on the core theme.

4.3. Core Property Specification

In specifying the core properties for an object class, we identify the characteristics which must, of necessity, be present in every instance of the class. Essentially, these properties define "what an object is". This implies that if an object were to lack any of the core properties, it would no longer be an instance of this class. Thus, core properties are considered mandatory.

Each attribute and function considered as a candidate core property must be carefully weighed. Is it absolutely necessary to specify this property? If this property were missing, would the object class no longer be useful? Is this the minimum possible definition for the property? By ensuring that each property is specified at its bare minimum level, without additional baggage, we will achieve the greatest possible generality in the class definition.

In specialization theory, attributes and functions are identified so that they are *orthogonal*. This means that there should not be a *functional dependency* of attributes or functions on other attributes or functions. That is, the value of a property should not be computable by applying some mathematical function to the values of other properties. For example, the four-channel `multiplexer` object class of Figure 4-1 may have attributes `channel1speed`, `channel2speed`, `channel3speed` and `channel4speed`. In addition, the object may also wish to use an average channel speed in certain functions. We might consider specifying `averageChannelSpeed` as an attribute of the `multiplexer` class.

We know, however, that `averageChannelSpeed` can be derived, in an algorithmic manner, from the other attributes. Therefore, we should not specify it as an independent attribute. Modeling it as an independent attribute may sometimes lead to an integrity violation: an object, not being told about the dependency between these attributes, may attempt to set them to values which are inconsistent with each other. In Chapter 15, we will show how, instead of modeling the speed of each channel as an independent attribute of the `multiplexer` object, we can instead model a single `speed` attribute for a `port` object, one or more of which is contained as a component in the aggregate `multiplexer` object. Furthermore, as we shall see in Chapter 20, characteristics such as `averageChannelSpeed` can be specified by formally modeling their functional dependency on other attributes as an *algorithm*. If such attributes are required in the model, specialization theory can model them so that they appear externally to be independent by specifying them to be *virtual attributes*.

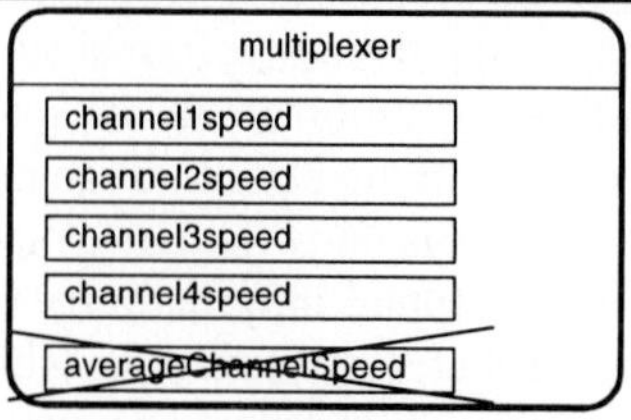

Figure 4-1: Attributes Functionally Dependent on Other Attributes Should Not Be Modeled

In specifying functions, care must be taken to ensure that only core behavior is specified for the function. Ways of specifying function arguments should be explored to reduce the number of functions that must be modeled. As a rather obvious example, when modeling a `digitalServiceUnit` object class, one would not model `fiveMinuteLoopbackTest` and `tenMinuteLoopbackTest` as two separate functions, even if they are commonly invoked differently. Since the semantics are the same, we would model a generic `loopbackTest` function and supply it with a `duration` argument.

On the other hand, it would make sense to model `carrierSideLoopbackTest` and `subscriberSideLoopbackTest` as two separate functions, because their functionality and purpose are different; it is possible to implement just one of them without implementing the other.

As we shall see in Chapter 6, an object class may derive from more than one superclass using multiple inheritance. In this situation, if its superclasses possess some properties in common, it is possible that the subclass inherits the same property from more than one superclass. If this happens, the subclass is not considered to have two "copies" of the same property; the property is considered to occur in the subclass only once.

4.4. Variant Property Specification

Network devices, protocols, and applications have many variations and options. We need a way of modeling these options in a reasonable manner. A particular network product may be available in a large number of versions, each representing a particular set of options. If there are 10 different options offered on a particular product, each of which could be independently present or absent, there are, in effect, 1024 possible versions of the product.

We might consider modeling such variations by creating subclasses. We could first define an object class to contain merely the mandatory core properties of the product. Then, we could create subclasses, each of which extended the definition of the object class with an appropriate combination of options. If we had two options, say `optionA` and `optionB`, we could create three subclasses, each extending the core behavior specified in the superclass with a different combination of optional behavior as shown in Figure 4-2.

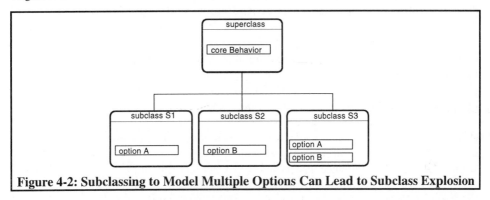

Figure 4-2: Subclassing to Model Multiple Options Can Lead to Subclass Explosion

Thus, if there are n independent options, we would have 2^n-1 subclasses from the original class. Unfortunately, such a model is not a good solution, because of the exponential growth of the number of subclasses with each option. For 10 independent options, for example, one would have to create 1023 subclasses; for 20 options, one would need over a million subclasses. The situation would quickly get out of hand and would unnecessarily complicate the object model, making it non-intuitive and hard to understand.

4.5. Capsules

To accommodate the semantics of linkage between a collection of properties, all of which may be present together or absent together as a variation on an object class, we introduce the concept of a *capsule*. A capsule is a collection of properties — attributes and functions — which are either all collectively present or are all collectively absent in a given instance of the object. The capsule may be given a name, which acts as shorthand to refer to the entire assemblage of properties it embraces.

As their heritage, capsules in specialization theory draw upon the concept of *mixin classes* in object-oriented programming. Mixin classes have been popularized in languages such as Flavors and CLOS (the Common Lisp Object System [Paep93]). A mixin class is a class that represents a collection of properties in a single assemblage but is never instantiated independently — it is only used to add a particular set of characteristics to (or to "mix in with") an instantiable class. A capsule, too, is never instantiated independently but is only used to model a particular property assemblage. As such, it acts as a mechanism to add *flexible subsets* to object classes. The entire assemblage represented by a capsule can be reproduced in an object class merely by referencing the predefined capsule.

To provide flexibility correctly, each capsule must be modeled *orthogonally* with respect to every other capsule — that is, each capsule must model a single, focused aspect of the characteristics of the network object. These characteristics should not overlap with the characteristics modeled by any other capsule, or with the core properties specified directly for (or inherited by) that object class. Once a capsule has been defined for a given class, it is inherited by subclasses that derive from it. Since different classes may share the same capsule, capsules also obviate some of the necessity to model multiple inheritance in object hierarchies.

Like a mixin class, a capsule does not have place in the inheritance hierarchy — it has no superclasses, and there are no subclasses that derive from it. Further, since a capsule models only one aspect of a network product's capabilities, it follows that a capsule may occur only once in a given network object class.

Like attributes and functions, a capsule is considered to be a property of an object class. Thus, it bears the property assignment associations — **is-a-property-of** and **has-as-a-property** — with the object classes for which it is specified. As we shall see in a later section on multiple inheritance, just as an object class may inherit the same property more than once from different superclasses, it is also possible for an object class to inherit the same capsule more than once. If this happens, then as with other properties, only one occurrence of the capsule is actually considered to be present.

A capsule provides a powerful and elegant abstraction to express variant or optional behavior. To address our original problem of modeling variations, a capsule may be specified as being a *mandatory capsule* or an *optional capsule*. Mandatory capsules are always present in every instance of the object class and in its subclasses. Optional capsules need not be present in every instance.

In specialization theory, capsules are the only mechanism to specify property subsets which must occur either collectively or not at all. They are also the only mechanism (and an adequate one) to specify any optionality at all. If an attribute or function is specified as a direct property of an object class, it is always considered mandatory. If even a single attribute of the object class needs to be optional, it must first be specified in a capsule, and then the entire capsule must be specified as optional in the object class. Though this may seem a somewhat onerous way of introducing optionality, in practice single properties are rarely optional. Almost all optional characteristics are collections of multiple related attributes and functions which occur as an assemblage, and so can be specified quite naturally as capsules.

The presence or absence of optional capsules is sometimes specified using a *flag attribute*. A flag attribute is a set-valued attribute whose value in any instance indicates which optional capsules are present in that instance. Several physical devices use such a technique — a bit mask present in a particular register represents what options have been installed with the device. Flag attributes are implementation conveniences and can usually be ignored at the modeling level. On some occasions, however, it becomes necessary to specify them at the modeling level, if they influence the subsequent development of the model.

Normally, when an optional capsule is inherited by a subclass, it remains an optional capsule — that is, the subclass may have some instances that possess that capsule and others that do not. However, the subclass may, in the process of specialization, "fix" the capsule — that is, make it mandatory in both itself and in all its descendant classes. This is known as *capsule fixing*. Later on, we will examine the specification syntax that will make this possible. Once an optional capsule is made mandatory by fixing, no descendant class may respecify it to be optional again.

If a capsule is present in a particular object instance, the attributes and functions defined in the capsule are now considered attributes and functions of the object. In other words, those attributes and functions behave no differently than the core attributes and functions defined for the object. In particular, they may be addressed and referenced the same way as any other property; the fact that they originated from an optional capsule is not of significance any more. More precisely, if an object class **has-as-a-property** a capsule which **has-as-a-property** an attribute, then the object class also **has-as-a-property** that same attribute. A capsule is a specification technique only; once it is realized in any particular instance, the "capsule coating dissolves away" and the properties it brings are internalized by the object.

Capsules can be nested, that is, an assemblage of attributes and functions could be defined in terms of assemblages of attributes and functions which have been previously defined. (However, a capsule cannot be recursively defined: it is illegal for a capsule to nest itself.) When a nested capsule occurs in an object class, all properties of all capsules are directly internalized by the object class, irrespective of the depth of capsule nesting. Further, the notion of optionality does not apply when a capsule **has-as-a-property** another nested capsule; the nested capsule is always considered to occur in the nesting capsule. Only the "outermost" capsule may be specified to be optional or mandatory by any object class that chooses to include it. A capsule "does not know" which object classes will include it as mandatory and which as optional.

An Example with Capsules

As an example, consider a situation where we are required to model internetworking devices consisting of simple MAC-layer bridges to connect local area network segments, as well as integrated bridge/routers. The LAN bridges perform simple link-layer bridging. The integrated bridge/routers examine the data-link layer frames and, if they can recognize the network-layer protocol carried within the frame, act as routers; otherwise they act just as data-link layer bridges. Assume that these objects are modeled as instances of the classes lanBridge and bridgeRouter respectively.

In our consideration of these objects, we find that certain combinations of attributes and properties occur either together or not at all. For example, we find that to specify the model of a transparent bridge we need the attributes spanningTree and forwardingDatabase. A spanningTree is a data structure which helps the transparentBridge keeps track of the topology of other bridges in the network, and a forwardingDatabase indicates which frames should be forwarded to which ports [Perl92]. Although these are complex data structures, they are attributes possessed in common by all transparent bridging functions. Together with these, spanning tree configuration attributes such as helloTime, maxAge, and forwardDelay also occur. In addition, every time we specify these attributes, we also need to specify (among other properties) the functions `buildSpanningTree` and `processDataFrame`. All of these always occur together as an assemblage, so we collectively define them to constitute the `transparentBridging` capsule, as shown in Figure 4-3.

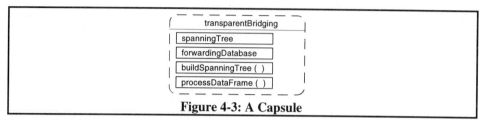

Figure 4-3: A Capsule

Similarly, we find that for bridges using source routing, we have a `process-SourceRoutedFrame` function, analogous to but different from the `processData-Frame` function in the `transparentBridging` capsule. In addition, we also have a `processRouteDiscoveryFrame` function. We collect these together in the `sourceRoutedBridging` capsule of Figure 4-4. (Clearly, there are several other functions which would be performed in both these capsules; this example has been simplified to illustrate the concept.)

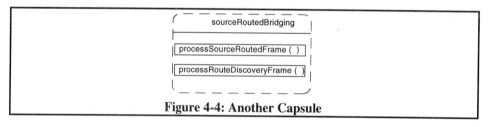

Figure 4-4: Another Capsule

Many attributes are important for specifying the `lanBridge` and `bridge-Router` object classes completely, such as `cpuType`, `manufacturerName`, and `serialNumber`, but we can assume that these are inherited from, say, an `internetworkingDevice` object class, so we do not have to specify them here. There could be, however, other core attributes which are not inherited and which we need to specify as original properties of these classes, such as `forwardingRate` and `supportedMediaTypes`. Now, if we subclassed `lanBridge` into two subclasses, say `transparentBridge` and `sourceRoutingBridge`, we could extend the general definition of a `lanBridge` in the subclass by merely referencing the capsules already defined earlier.

Further, if we wanted to specify a bridge/router with transparent bridging capability, we could simply import the `transparentBridging` capsule defined earlier, without having to respecify all its component attributes and functions. (A bridge/router would also have other properties required for network-layer routing, possibly specified in a `router` capsule.)

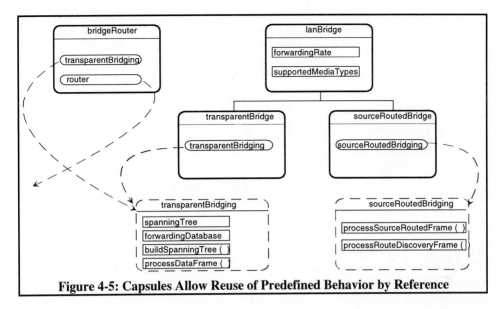

Figure 4-5: Capsules Allow Reuse of Predefined Behavior by Reference

Figure 4-5 illustrates the utility of capsules: they provide an abstract mechanism to model compartmentalized behavior, which can then be referenced as a complete assemblage wherever it is required.

Note that this compartmentalization is conceptual only and need have no correspondence with any physical implementation. Each of these modular functions may be implemented on its own card; it is also entirely possible that a transparent-Bridging capsule and a sourceRoutedBridging capsule (and indeed several other capsules) may all be implemented on the same card. If all capsules can be resident on the same physical piece of hardware, it might seem that it makes little sense to talk about them as being realizable separately. However, at the modeling stage, we are not concerned with physical implementation. In the model, each capsule represents a collection of related functionalities which is *potentially* realizable separately. We must allow sufficient flexibility in our model to cover every possible instance of lanBridge irrespective of its implementation.

In Figure 4-5, capsules are used as modeling abstractions to specify and import reusable assemblages of properties in network objects. We now demonstrate how capsules can also be used to model *optional* properties. Consider a multifunctionHub object class, which models a structured wiring device which may optionally have bridging capabilities built in. Such an object class may have as options a sourceRouted-Bridging capsule, a transparentBridging capsule, both, or neither. In this situation, we could specify both these capsules as optional in the multifunctionHub object class, as shown in Figure 4-6.

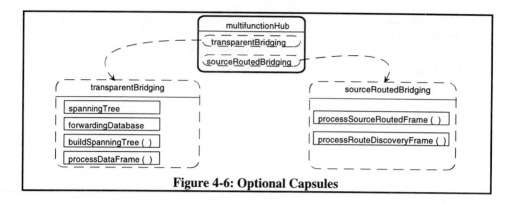

Figure 4-6: Optional Capsules

Avoiding Multiple Inheritance

A further advantage of modular construction using capsules is that, on some occasions, it helps avoid the need for multiple inheritance. For example, suppose a new model of a bridge is introduced — one that performs both source-routed bridging as well as transparent bridging and is called a source-routing transparent bridge.

One may consider modeling such an object class — say the `srtBridge` object class of Figure 4-7 — as multiply deriving from both the `sourceRoutedBridge` and `transparentBridge` object class, so that it would acquire the functionality of both its superclasses. In addition, assume that the `srtBridge` object class defines the new function `processSrtFrame`, which, based on its interrogation of the routing information indicator in each frame, then invokes either the `processDataFrame` function of the `transparentBridging` capsule, or the `processSourceRoutedFrame` function of the `sourceRoutedBridging` capsule.

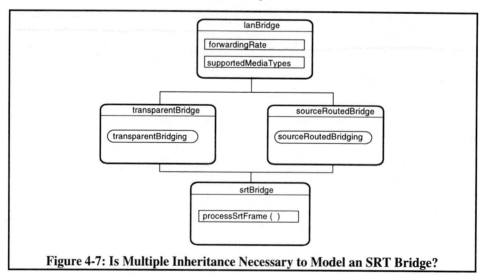

Figure 4-7: Is Multiple Inheritance Necessary to Model an SRT Bridge?

With capsules, however, multiple inheritance is not necessary; srtBridge can be subclassed directly from lanBridge. As in Figure 4-8, we need only specify both the sourceRoutedBridging and the transparentBridging capsules as mandatory capsules for this class.

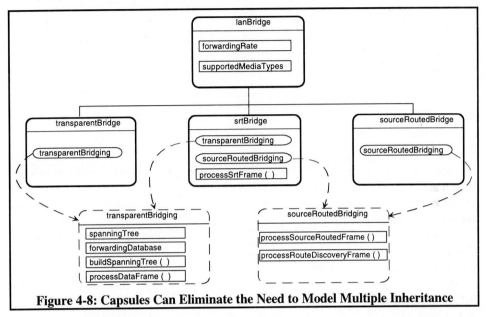

Figure 4-8: Capsules Can Eliminate the Need to Model Multiple Inheritance

In many cases, with correctly and orthogonally defined capsules and some adjustments to the inheritance hierarchy, we can eliminate the need to model multiple inheritance. This has two benefits. First, it speeds up processing in the model information base, since multiple inheritance is more expensive to compute: there are more ancestral classes in the inheritance hierarchy to traverse when performing inheritance resolution, a problem which gets worse if the two superclasses come from widely divergent branches of the hierarchies. Second and perhaps more important, it maintains precision in the taxonomical structure for assigning instances to classes.

4.10. Summary

Object classes must be specified for all meaningful functionaries — physical, logical, or human — in our network model. The core properties specified in an object class are attributes, functions, and capsules. These should be modeled orthogonally with respect to each other. Capsules are assemblages of attributes and functions grouped together so that they occur either collectively or not at all. An object class internalizes the properties of a predefined capsule by merely referencing it. To model variant behavior, capsules may be specified as optional in an object class.

5. Specialization and Generalization

"No, sir, you cannot receive calls on this in-flight phone. That's because our area code keeps changing."
— *serious explanation given by anonymous flight attendant.*

5.1. Introduction

In this chapter, we explain the semantics of specialization and generalization and the connotational associations between object classes related by inheritance. We consider how the object classes designed in Chapter 4 may be best organized an inheritance hierarchy. The exact associations between ancestral classes, descendant classes, and instances are identified and explained with respect to examples in telecommunication networks. When assigning instances to classes in the inheritance hierarchy, we consider ways of designing the hierarchy so that instances convey as much precise information as possible.

5.2. Conceptual Background

When specialization theory is applied to an engineering model, the inheritance hierarchy is primarily used as a mechanism for specifying taxonomies. In Chapter 2, we said that an inheritance hierarchy models the semantics of extension, evolution, and incremental refinement. Expanding on this theme, we also say that an inheritance hierarchy embodies the notions of *generalization* and *specialization*, with increasing generalization going up the hierarchy and increasing specialization going down the hierarchy. *Generalization* is the exercise we undertake when we construct an inheritance hierarchy in a bottom-up fashion. It involves the ability to recognize similarities between object classes, abstracting them, and elevating them to the level of a superclass.

Because a subclass not only inherits properties from its superclasses but also extends them by adding its own, it represents a "more advanced form of evolution" in the object hierarchy. Subclasses are more complicated than their superclasses in terms of structure and more sophisticated in terms of function. Because superclasses are abstractions of common properties, classes at the higher levels of the hierarchy generally represent primitive abstractions, as the number of properties common to sibling subclasses dwindles going up the hierarchy. The classes at the bottom of the hierarchy represent greater capabilities than those closer to the top. Therefore, the construction of the hierarchy in the top-down fashion — by extending superclass definitions with richer detail of structure and function — is an exercise in *specialization*. Specialization may be based either on structural refinements, behavioral refinements, or both. Its purpose is to allow us to focus on narrower and more specific aspects of the problem domain.

When organizing any universe of discourse into systematized knowledge from first principles, the first process that occurs is generalization. For example, the classification of the animal kingdom was not performed by initially postulating the *a priori* concepts of vertebrate, mammal, and so on, and then trying to assign existing species to these classes. The classification was conceived in a bottom-up fashion — by examining the commonalities among the various species (actually, instances of species) encountered in actual experience, then abstracting their similarities and giving this abstraction a label.

Once a hierarchy is constructed, specialization is useful for assigning new object classes a place in the existing hierarchy. When zoologists descended on the Galapagos Islands and discovered several new species, they assigned them places in the existing hierarchy of known life-forms. This assignment was based on how the new species were specialized from classes which were already known in the hierarchy of animals. In communication network modeling, the "discovery of new species" is analogous to the introduction of new varieties of network objects. If a manufacturer introduces a new networking product or service which is not well described by an existing class, it is possible to create a new subclass specializing from an existing class and assign the new product to it.

We will construct our hierarchies using rigorous object-oriented modeling principles embodied in *specialization theory*. Specialization theory formalizes the rules whereby subclasses can be created from existing classes. These formalized rules are known as *specialization principles*. A subclass can only be created if it arises from one or more specialization principles; other subclasses are illegal. Throughout this book, we will define all the specialization principles of specialization theory as we develop the methodology.

In specialization theory, every subclass is also a *subtype* of its superclass. The meaning of a subtype has been stated by Wegner and Zdonik [Wegn88] in their *principle of substitutability*:

> *An instance of a subtype can always be [safely] used in any context in which an instance of a supertype was expected.*

This substitutability can be mathematically proved: by analyzing the constraints on the attributes and functions in both the subclass and the superclass, it can be shown that all actions which are valid on the superclass are also valid on the subclass. Thus, an external object requesting a service from a superclass instance will receive at least the same service from a subclass instance. Of course, where the superclass is abstract, such substitutability is theoretical: the principle then implies that when some particular minimum behavior for an object is specified as a property of some abstract ancestral class, any member of that ancestral class may be used as they are all guaranteed to exhibit this minimum behavior.

The principle of substitutability guarantees only *safety*, not identical behavior. Because subclasses may extend inherited behavior, a subclass instance may exhibit *more* functionality than a superclass instance. A system in which a superclass instance has actually been replaced by a subclass instance may not behave identically but will nevertheless be compatible with the minimally required behavior. This is guaranteed by monotonic inheritance; as we develop the model, we will see how the creation of subclasses using *specialization principles* codifies Wegner and Zdonik's principle of substitutability under various circumstances.

We have mentioned before that increasing generalization leads us to a point in the hierarchy where no further abstraction is possible. We call this ultimate superclass the *root* of the inheritance hierarchy. Each application domain has only one root; its immediate descendants are called *top-level classes*. These are the classes directly below the root in Figure 5-1.

Different object-oriented methodologies have different names for this root. We will adopt the convention of referring to it by the special name genericObject. The genericObject class only captures the commonalities of the properties of every possible object modeled in the application domain. Two such properties are immediately obvious — every object has a name and every object knows its class. Aside from this, the genericObject class may be considered a pure modeling artifact, something that serves to anchor to the same tree all superclasses which cannot be abstracted further.

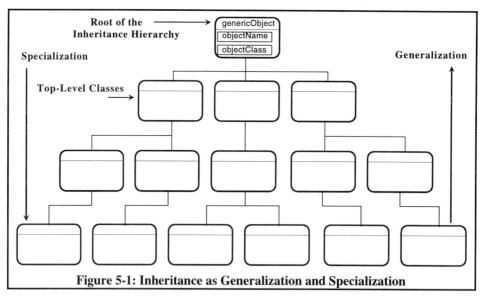

Figure 5-1: Inheritance as Generalization and Specialization

5.3. Ancestral and Descendant Classes

In traditional object-oriented modeling, a class is said to possess the connotational association **is-a** with its ancestral classes. For example, if we were to derive the class `3/1/0-crossConnect` from the class `digitalCrossConnect`, which derived from `transmissionEquipment`, we could say that a `3/1/0-crossConnect` **is-a** `digitalCrossConnect`, which in turn **is-a** `transmissionEquipment`. The **is-a** association is *transitive*, which means it is also correct to say that a `3/1/0-cross-Connect` **is-a** `transmissionEquipment`. Continuing this transitivity to the extreme, we could even say that a `3/1/0-crossConnect` is a `genericObject` (which, though true, is not very useful).

Occasionally, we will wish to refer to associations in the complementary direction. We have said that a subclass bears the **is-a** association with its superclass. Although this association is transitive, it is clearly not *symmetric*. This means the association does not work in both directions; it is meaningful only in the upward direction. It is not correct to say that a `digitalCrossConnect` **is-a** `3/1/0-crossConnect`, because a `digitalCrossConnect` could be any other kind as well [TR 170].

Specialization Associations

We will call the complementary association — that between a superclass and its subclasses — the **specializes-into** association. Thus, it is correct to say that a `transmissionEquipment` **specializes-into** a `digitalCrossConnect`, which in turn **specializes-into** a `3/1/0-crossConnect`. Just as **is-a** is transitive from a class to all its ancestral classes, **specializes-into** is also transitive from a class to all its descendant classes. Thus, it would be equally correct to say that a `transmissionEquipment` **specializes-into** a `3/1/0-crossConnect`.

When these associations are represented together on the same diagram, the inheritance hierarchy forms a directed acyclic graph which is both rooted and connected, in which every node is reachable from the root.

The **is-a** association, as it is named, conveys the semantics of subtyping, that is, the substitutability of a subclass for its superclass. The **is-a** association does not, however, impart the notions of *extension* and *incremental refinement* — that is, the notions that the subclass may contain greater detail of structure and richer capability of function than its superclass. What we would really like to convey is that the subclass not only **is-a** superclass but actually "**is-more-than**" its superclass. We will therefore also refer to the **is-a** association using the name **specializes-from**. This is the complement of the **specializes-into** association; just as we say that a `digitalCrossConnect` **specializes-into** a `3/1/0-crossConnect`, we can equivalently say that a `3/1/0-crossConnect` **specializes-from** (not just **is-a** but "is a specialized form of") a `digitalCrossConnect`. This is shown in Figure 5-2.

The associations **specializes-from** and **specializes-into** are called the *specialization associations*. They are completely equivalent to the *inheritance associations* **inherits-from** and **bequeaths-to** respectively, which we introduced in Chapter 2. This is because in specialization theory, the inheritance hierarchy is *both* a vehicle to express ex-

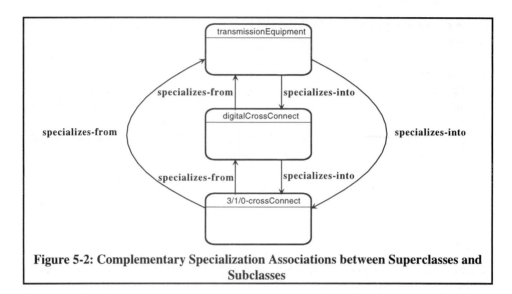

Figure 5-2: Complementary Specialization Associations between Superclasses and Subclasses

tension, evolution, and refinement, *and* a mechanism to allow reuse of specifications. (In some methodologies, it is possible for the semantics of evolution and the semantics of reuse to be embodied in *different* mechanisms.) In an expository context, we use **inherits-from** and **bequeaths-to** when talking about properties of object classes and **specializes-from** and **specializes-into** when talking about object classes themselves.

Further, the specialization association **specializes-from** is similar to the derivation association **derives-from** but not quite the same: **specializes-from** applies between a descendant and all ancestral classes, while **derives-from** applies only between a subclass and its superclass, that is, only among adjacent classes in the inheritance hierarchy. In other words, we define **specializes-from** to be transitive but not **derives-from**. Since a subclass deriving from a superclass also obviously specializes from that superclass, we consider that the **derives-from** association (the stronger form) *implies* the **specializes-from** association (the weaker form).

Although we can use the **specializes-from** to describe the association between a subclass and its superclass, it should be understood that it is not, strictly speaking, equivalent to the **is-a** association in conventional object-oriented modeling. Any descendant class may be said to **specialize-from** its ancestral classes and also bear the **is-a** association with its ancestral classes. But unlike the **specializes-from** association, **is-a** is not strictly restricted to a descendant/ancestor association alone, because a class is also allowed to bear the **is-a** association with *itself*. If **is-a** were strictly a descendant/ancestor association, it would not be the case, for example, that a printer **is-a** printer, since classes do not derive from themselves. To prevent such seeming incongruities, we permit classes to bear the **is-a** association not only with their superclasses but also with themselves. By contrast, the **specializes-from** association is strictly borne with ancestral classes only, because classes do not **specialize-from** themselves. More technically, we say that **is-a** is a *reflexive* association, whereas **specializes-from** is not. Keeping this distinction in mind, in the rest of the book we will almost exclusively use the **specializes-from** association and not **is-a**.

All object classes can be enumerated from the root class by traversing the *transitive closure* of its **specializes-into** association. Traversing the transitive closure is a term from graph theory: it means determining all nodes on the graph which are reachable, using the association, from the starting node. For example, to determine every class in the inheritance hierarchy, a class hierarchy browser may start at `genericObject`, and visit every object class which is reachable by following the chain of **specializes-into** pointers. In doing so, it will have enumerated all object classes.

We now give a precise definition of the term *descendants of a class* as the set of all classes in the transitive closure of its **specializes-into** association. Similarly, the term *ancestors of a class* is defined as the set of all classes in the transitive closure of its **specializes-from** association.

Generalization Associations

On occasion, we will refer to the semantics of generalization rather than specialization. Although the two are completely equal and opposite, one form is sometimes preferable to the other in an expository context. Thus, instead of saying that a subclass **specializes-from** its superclass, we will sometimes say that a subclass **generalizes-into** its superclass. In the complementary direction, instead of saying that a superclass **specializes-into** its subclass, we will sometimes say that a superclass **generalizes-from** its subclass. The terms **generalizes-from** and **generalizes-into** are called the *generalization associations*, and they carry completely equivalent semantics as the specialization associations in the opposite directions. Like the specialization associations, they are also transitive. Figure 5-3 illustrates these associations.

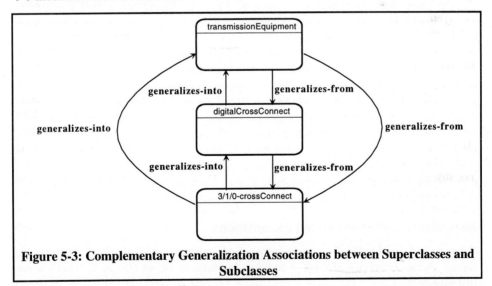

Figure 5-3: Complementary Generalization Associations between Superclasses and Subclasses

Two object classes which share a common ancestral class (other than `generic-Object`) are called *cognate object classes*. The closest common ancestor they share is called their *cognation ancestor*. The cognation ancestor must be their "lowest common ancestor"; common ancestors higher up are not considered cognation ancestors. The cognation ancestor is that ancestor at which the evolutionary characteristics of the two cognate classes began to diverge. The cognation ancestor may be as high as a top-level class; for example, if the classes `lowEndDialModem` and `highCapacityCentral-OfficeSwitch` share the common ancestor `networkDevice`, then they are cognate with respect to that ancestor. Cognation among classes implies that they have at least a few properties in common. It is a "weaker" relationship than siblinghood: all sibling classes are trivially cognate.

5.4. Classes and Instances

Instances of objects must belong to an object class somewhere in the hierarchy. It is good modeling practice to ensure that concrete classes (those having direct instances) are, as far as possible, leaf-level classes in the hierarchy. If most of our concrete classes occur at the leaf level, it means we can locate each new instance we encounter very precisely within our system of knowledge. We have successfully built a rich taxonomical structure.

For example, if we were to specify a `networkDevice` object class to abstract the notion of all networking devices, we might subclass it to derive directly from `genericObject`. Then, we could go ahead and define a direct instance of `network-Device` in the model for any one network. But such an instance would be imprecise and not very helpful, because the instance would only have the general characteristics of any `networkDevice`; we would not know exactly what purpose it serves in the network. Clearly, more meaningful classes — such as `switch`, `dialModem`, and `workstation` — can be derived from the `networkDevice` object class and will have more meaningful instantiations, as Figure 5-4 illustrates.

Non-leaf instantiations do occur, but in most cases this is a consequence of the fact that a leaf class, possessing instances, becomes a non-leaf class due the introduction of a new subclass deriving from it. For example, the existing class `dialModem` may already have several instances in the network. Now, if a manufacturer releases a new brand of modem which operates at higher speeds, we may decide to model this by deriving a new subclass of `dialModem`, called `fastDialModem`. If not all instances of `dialModem` in the network are upgraded to the new brand, the network would now have objects of two different classes: some of class `dialModem`, and some of class `fastDialModem`. The class `dialModem` of Figure 5-5 would now be a non-leaf concrete class, that is, a class with both subclasses and instances.

Instantiation and Membership Associations

An instance is said to have the **is-an-instance-of** association with its class. Thus, the instance "Acme Telecom's SONET Add-Drop Multiplexer Serial No. 987654321" **is-an-instance-of** the class `sonetADM`. Furthermore, because we treat classes as sets, an object is also considered to be a *member* of all the ancestral classes of its class. More precisely,

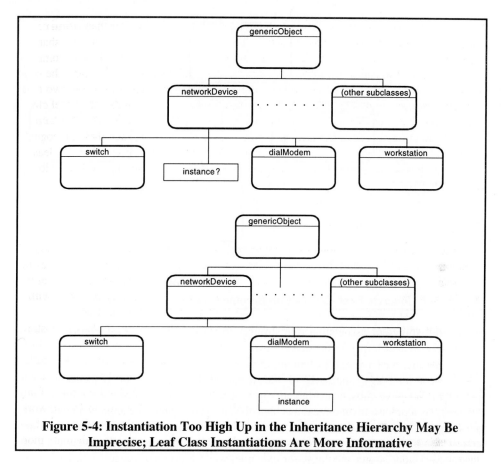

**Figure 5-4: Instantiation Too High Up in the Inheritance Hierarchy May Be
Imprecise; Leaf Class Instantiations Are More Informative**

the conjunction of the **is-an-instance-of** association between an instance and its class, with the **specializes-from** association between a class and its ancestral classes, gives us the **is-a-member-of** association between an instance and all its ancestral classes.

Thus, if the class sonetADM **derives-from** class multiplexer which in turn **derives-from** class centralOfficeEquipment, we can say (since **derives-from** implies **specializes-from** and **specializes-from** is transitive) that Acme Telecom's Unit 987654321 **is-an-instance-of** sonetADM, **is-a-member-of** multiplexer, and also **is-a-member-of** centralOfficeEquipment. The **is-a-member-of** association defines only *membership*, not instantiation; thus, while an instance is an instance of only one class, it is in fact a member of all its ancestral classes.

According to our definition of the associations above, the **is-an-instance-of** association exists between an *instance* and its *class*; the **specializes-from** association exists between the *class* and its *ancestral classes*; and so the **is-a-member-of** association exists between the *instance* and the *ancestral classes*. Thus, in specialization theory, an object **is-an-instance-of** only one class, while it **is-a-member-of** many classes (all its ancestral classes). Of course, an instance is also a member of its own class; thus we consider that

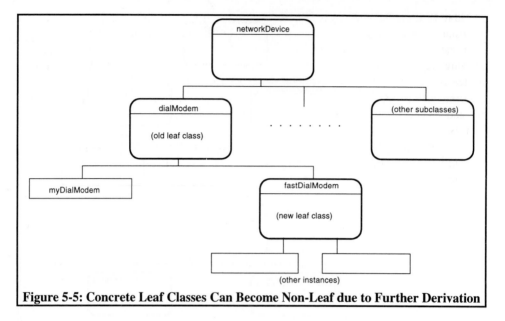

Figure 5-5: Concrete Leaf Classes Can Become Non-Leaf due to Further Derivation

the **is-an-instance-of** association (the stronger form) implies the **is-a-member-of** association (the weaker form) for the object's own class.

Because we have said that an object is only an instance of one class, we have chosen a *weak ontology* approach in the technical terminology of object-orientation [Kim90a]. We have chosen such an approach because our focus is to use the inheritance hierarchy as a precise taxonomical mechanism. The *strong ontology* approach claims that an object not only **is-an-instance-of** its own class but also **is-an-instance-of** all its ancestral classes. For us, this approach can have troubling ramifications on network configuration. Under strong ontology, for example, when a protocol request is issued to an aggregate network object to deactivate all instances of a certain class, nothing can be done, because those target instances must continue activity as they are also instances of all their ancestral classes, which have not been identified in the deactivation request. This approach is so highly counter-intuitive for our application that we consider it unacceptable.

Definitional ontological distinctions notwithstanding, when conversing about object-oriented models, we sometimes informally speak of an instance being an ancestral class object. For example, in Figure 5-5, instead of saying myDialModem **is-an-instance-of** dialModem and **is-a-member-of** networkDevice, we could informally, for succinctness, just say myDialModem **is-a** networkDevice. Although most people will understand what we mean without immediately accusing us of being strong ontologists, the precise modeling distinction between **specializes-from** (**is-a**), **is-an-instance-of**, and **is-a-member-of** is still required when specifying models to machine-based interpreters.

We will also name the complementary association between classes and instances. Just as an instance is said to bear the **is-an-instance-of** association with its class, the class is said to bear the **has-as-an-instance** association with its instances. Further, we said that an instance **is-a-member-of** all its ancestral classes; conversely, we will say that each such ancestral class **has-as-a-member** each of the instances of the concrete subclasses deriving from it. It is therefore correct to say that the class `sonetADM` **has-as-an-instance** Acme Telecom's Unit 987654321, while each of its ancestral classes `multiplexer` and `centralOfficeEquipment` **has-as-a-member** the same unit. Figure 5-6 and Figure 5-7 illustrate these complementary associations between classes and instances.

The terms **is-an-instance-of** and **has-as-an-instance** are called the *instantiation associations*, while the terms **is-a-member-of** and **has-as-a-member** are called the *membership associations*.

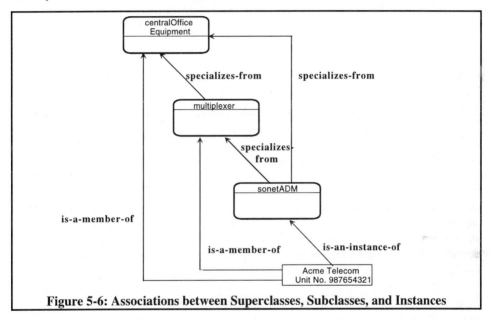

Figure 5-6: Associations between Superclasses, Subclasses, and Instances

Extent and Membership

In Chapter 2, we defined the *extent* of a class as the set of all *instances* of the class. We now define the *membership* of a class as the set of all *members* of the class. Therefore, each object which the class **has-as-a-member** belongs in its membership. More precisely, the membership of any class may be defined as the union of the extents of all its concrete descendant classes. Two objects which are members of the same ancestral class are said to be *fellow members* of that ancestral class. Naturally, if any two classes are cognate, then their instances are fellow members of their cognation ancestor.

All ancestral classes of any concrete class can have a non-null membership. As per our definition in Chapter 2, a *fully abstract* class is one which cannot have instances, and neither can any of its descendants. Thus, a fully abstract class always has a null

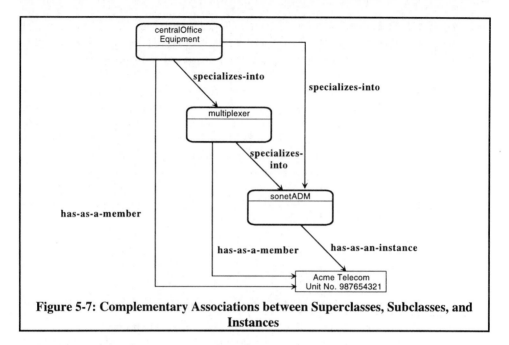

Figure 5-7: Complementary Associations between Superclasses, Subclasses, and Instances

membership. While they cannot be instantiated, fully abstract classes are important because they serve to influence the functionality and specification of other classes through *inter-class relationships*, which we shall describe in Chapter 17. (It is important to recognize the distinction between a fully abstract class, which is never instantiable, and an abstract class with concrete descendants which may not happen to have any members created in some particular network. If any class is instantiable — whether or not any objects have been assigned to it as instances — neither it nor any of its ancestors are considered full abstractions.)

Object Name and Object Class as Attributes

We model the class `genericObject`, the root of the inheritance hierarchy, with the attributes `objectName` and `objectClass`. The attribute `objectName` identifies each instance; its value is unique for every object in the universe of discourse. The attribute `objectClass` identifies the class which that object **is-an-instance-of**. Thus, each object may be said to "know" its class. In addition, the `objectClass` attribute also keeps track of the genealogy of the object; thus, each object may also be said to "remember" its ancestors. This is unlike many object-oriented programming environments, where object instances often do not "know" their class or their genealogy.

The implementation of the `objectClass` attribute is performed in a special way. In each object, the `objectClass` attribute is implemented such that it compares *equal* to every class which that object **is-a-member-of**. It is possible to compare any object's `objectClass` value to the class name of any of its *ancestors* — which are conceptually "remembered" in every object — and obtain a result of `true`. We implement the `objectClass` attribute in this manner because we consider testing it for equality with an ancestral class name as being equivalent to asking whether the object **is-a-member-of** that ancestral class. While this special implementation may appear awkward, it has considerable benefits which will become apparent in subsequent chapters.

5.5. Summary

Classes are arranged in an inheritance hierarchy with increasing generalization going up and increasing specialization going down. The root of the hierarchy is the `generic-Object` class. A class is said to possess the **specializes-from** association with its superclass and all its ancestral classes and the **specializes-into** association with all its subclasses and all descendant classes. These are also known as the equivalent associations **generalizes-into** and **generalizes-from**, respectively. A concrete object **is-an-instance-of** its class and **is-a-member-of** all its ancestral classes. The class **has-as-an-instance** the concrete object, while each of its ancestral classes **has-as-a-member** the same object. In a well-designed hierarchy, concrete classes should be leaf classes as far as possible.

6. The Object Inheritance Hierarchy

"It really opens up a whole new way of thinking about inheritance."

— anonymous genetic engineering researcher, on the discovery that the gene for myotonic dystrophy gets gradually bigger with each successive generation.

6.1. Introduction

In this chapter, we will introduce several advanced concepts about designing inheritance hierarchies. The theoretical principles underlying various modes of specialization which will serve as guidelines for organizing classes in a hierarchy will be presented. These are formalized as the principles of specialization theory, also called specialization principles. After considering these, we will conclude with a normative set of recommendations on hierarchy design.

6.2. Basis of Specialization

In specialization theory, generalization and specialization are formally described in terms of a *basis property*. This implies that, when we decide to specialize a new object class from an existing object class, we must select a *basis of specialization*. The basis of specialization acts as a distinguishing factor between subclasses; it is what makes each subclass different from its sibling subclasses. The basis of specialization can be an attribute of the superclass, or can be a function-dependent property. Most often, the basis property is an attribute of the superclass.

Because a subclass is said to be a more specialized form of its superclass, it has a greater set of capabilities than its superclass. However, because of its specialization, it effectively operates in a narrower range of the overall problem space. This narrower range of effectiveness — an increase in the specific focus of its action — arises as a result of its specialized definition. We capture this knowledge by formally indicating which basis property has been used for specialization. Specialization occurs as a result of selecting a basis property which has been given freer rein in the superclass and restricting its domain in the subclass.

If the basis property is a numerical attribute of the superclass, specialization occurs by restricting the domain of values that this attribute is allowed to possess in the subclass. This is known as a *quantitative basis of specialization*. If the basis property is an enumerable attribute of the superclass, specialization occurs by restricting the set of enumerated values this attribute can possess in the subclass. This is known as a *qualitative basis of specialization*. The examples in the following sections will clarify these concepts.

6.3. Quantitative Basis of Specialization

Assume we have defined a class of network objects called `multiplexer`. This class possesses the attribute `compositePortSpeed`, whose value indicates the speed of its composite port. It is defined as an unrestricted non-negative integer representing the speed of its composite port (or "aggregate port") in bits per second. If we decided to subclass from the class `multiplexer` choosing `compositePortSpeed` as the basis property, we might decide to have two subclasses, called `broadbandMultiplexer` and `narrowbandMultiplexer`, respectively. We might decide, as shown in Figure 6-1, that the class `broadbandMultiplexer` includes any member of `multiplexer` that operates at speeds of greater than 45 Mbps on the composite side, and all other members are considered to be `narrowbandMultiplexers`.

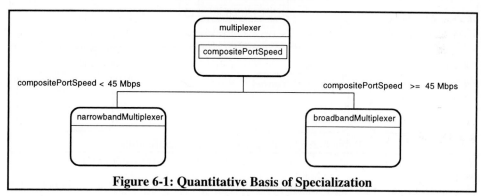

Figure 6-1: Quantitative Basis of Specialization

In Figure 6-1, specialization has occurred by choosing the `compositePort-Speed` attribute as the basis property and by *restricting its value* in the subclasses. The `compositePortSpeed` attribute, whose value was unrestricted in class `multiplexer`, now has constraints specified on the domain of values it can possess in classes `narrowbandMultiplexer` and `broadbandMultiplexer`.

6.4. Qualitative Basis of Specialization

Qualitative specialization occurs when the basis property is a superclass attribute which can possess one of an enumerated set of values. We specialize by forcing this attribute to possess fewer values (or only one value) in the subclass. As an example, assume that we have the object class customCallingService, which we have modeled with the core attributes serviceType, softwareVersionNumber, dateOfDeployment, vendorName, and so on. The serviceType is an enumerated attribute that can take on only one of a finite predefined set of values. This set might include the values such as:

```
{callWaiting, threeWayCalling, speedCalling,
 distinctiveRinging, ringWhenFree, callBlocking,
 callingNumberDelivery, callScreening, callReturn,
 anonymousCallReject, selectiveForwarding, callTracing}
```

Such an enumerated set of attributes can admittedly be very large but is still finite. Specific residential services might now be subclassed, as shown in Figure 6-2, from the generic customCallingService superclass. Naturally, each of these inherits the serviceType attribute. However, in each such subclass, the serviceType attribute is now restricted to only one value from its enumerated set; this is the value which identifies the actual service provided by the subclass object.

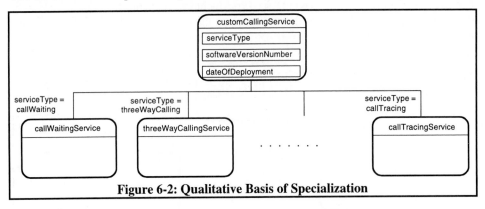

Figure 6-2: Qualitative Basis of Specialization

Thus, serviceType is now the basis of specialization. In this example, the specialization is *qualitative*: from the domain of all possible enumerated values that the basis property can possess in the superclass, each subclass selects a subset of the domain (in this case, only one value) and constrains the basis attribute to possess only those values in the subclass.

Note that the basis of specialization for subclassing can just as correctly be termed the *basis of generalization* for superclassing. If our perspective is oriented to traversing the hierarchy upward (for example, during a bottom-up construction process), then we can select a property as the *basis of generalization* to assist in abstracting and specifying each superclass from known subclasses. Generalization then occurs by *expanding* the domain of the basis property in the superclass to the *union* of its domains in the generalizing sibling subclasses.

A formal basis of specialization thus is a logical predicate which *selects* a subset of all the members of the superclass. We have said we consider the membership of the superclass (that is, all objects which are members of the superclass) to be a *set*. The subclass uses the basis of specialization as a *set-partitioning operator* to create a *subset* as the target of its own focus. In this subset, the subclass will isolate those members of the set it chooses for further refinement and evolution. In effect, basis properties are subset-selection operators, which divide the membership of the superclass into many subsets. The objects which will become members of each such partitioned subset are identified by applying the basis property criterion to every object in the membership. Each subset resulting from the partition is given the name of the newly created subclass. In Chapter 11, we shall see how the various bases of specialization may be formally specified as a logical predicate.

It is important to select a meaningful basis of specialization. In the example above, the choice of `serviceType` as the basis attribute for subclassing was a reasonable one. We could have instead conceivably chosen `dateOfDeployment`, for example, as a quantitative basis for specialization. By restricting the domain of numerical values this attribute possesses in each subclass, we could have created the subclasses of Figure 6-3, named `servicesDeployedIn1992`, `servicesDeployedIn1996`, and so on. Whether this is useful depends on the applications we intend to execute. An application that generates a network-wide report on the annual progress of deployment of services on various switches perhaps might find such a classification useful. By and large, for most qualitative specializations, using an identifying *type* attribute as the basis — one that indicates "what kind of" semantics — is the most useful way of subclassing. Nevertheless, the hierarchy designer should note that the application domain strongly influences the choice of basis of specialization.

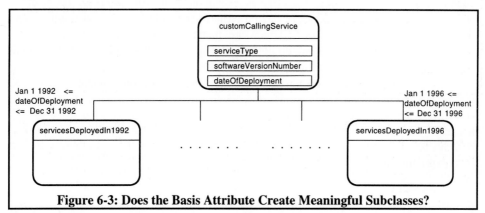

Figure 6-3: Does the Basis Attribute Create Meaningful Subclasses?

Attribute Domain Restriction

In type theory, subtypes are created by constraining the domain of the supertype to a subset of values, and the basis of specialization is also known as a *subtyping constraint*. Remember, however, that subclassing is more than a pure subtyping or set-partitioning operation, because each selected subset also undergoes extension and incremental refinement, possibly including the addition of new properties for specialized subclass function. By formally stating the logical predicate which constitutes the basis of specialization, we indicate the precise manner in which this subset was chosen for further specialization.

When the property chosen as the basis of specialization is an attribute as in the examples above, the new subset of the domain to which the attribute is restricted in each of the subclasses is explicitly indicated in the formal specification of the subclass. In specializing by restricting the domain of one or more attributes, the attributes chosen for restriction need not have originated in the superclass; they may originate in any ancestral class anywhere up the hierarchy. This mode of specialization is known as *Specialization by Attribute Domain Restriction*.

Some readers may find it instructive at this point to revisit Figure 2-3 and, as an exercise, attempt to identify what formal bases of specialization have been used at each level of classification.

6.5. Basis-Free Specialization

In addition to specialization based on restriction of a basis property, some hierarchies also use *Basis-Free Specialization*, or simply *Free Specialization*. In this situation, no single basis property is chosen as a criterion for subclassing. Specialization does not occur using domain restrictions on a basis attribute but rather occurs in a case-by-case, user-defined manner. Thus, subclasses are created as required by the application.

In specialization theory, the use of free specialization is not recommended, with a couple of notable exceptions. An obvious exception is the `genericObject` class which, having no superclass, cannot have a basis of specialization. We also admit free specialization for top-level classes which are immediate descendants of `generic-Object`. For top-level classes, we do not require that a basis of specialization be chosen as a domain restriction on an attribute of `genericObject`.

Aside from top-level classes, we recommend that every time a subclass is created, the modeler formally state what basis of specialization has been used. Experience has shown that allowing free specialization everywhere in the hierarchy soon leads to "ad hockery", with many subclasses created in an inappropriate manner. This very quickly destroys the rich taxonomical structure whose semantics we are trying to convey in our inheritance hierarchy.

6.6. Disjoint and Complete Specialization

Two important notions apply to qualitative and quantitative specialization defined using a basis attribute. One is the notion of *disjointness*. A *disjoint specialization* requires that all the subclasses of a superclass must form non-intersecting sets of objects. This implies that an object which is a member of the superclass, can be a member of *at most one* of its subclasses. If the subclasses are not disjoint, an object may then find itself overlapping into another subclass and thus be a member of more than one subclass of the specialization.

In Figure 6-1, we compelled every member of the `multiplexer` class to be either a `broadbandMultiplexer` (with `compositePortSpeed` >= 45 Mbps) or a `narrowbandMultiplexer` (with `compositePortSpeed` < 45 Mbps). By defining the domains for `compositePortSpeed` in this manner, we automatically created disjoint subclasses. We ensured that an object which was a member of the `multiplexer` class cannot be both a `broadbandMultiplexer` and `narrowbandMultiplexer`, since its `compositePortSpeed` has to be either greater than 45 Mbps or less than 45 Mbps.

Suppose we now decide to further subclass `narrowbandMultiplexer` into `t1Multiplexer` (with `compositePortSpeed` <= 1.544 Mbps), `e1-Multiplexer` (with `compositePortSpeed` <= 2.048 Mbps), and `t3-Multiplexer` (with `compositePortSpeed` between 1.544 and 45 Mbps). We now have overlapping domains, as shown in Figure 6-4. Thus, it is possible for a member of class `narrowbandMultiplexer` to be both a `t1Multiplexer` and an `e1-Multiplexer`. This is an example of *overlapping specialization*.

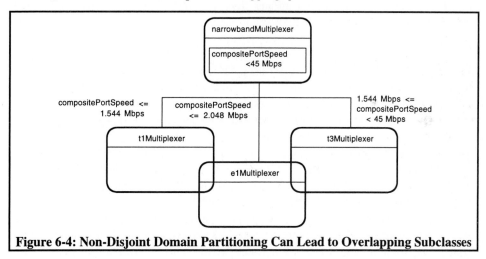

Figure 6-4: Non-Disjoint Domain Partitioning Can Lead to Overlapping Subclasses

In rare situations, it may be necessary to allow overlapping subdomains for the basis property of specialization. By and large, however, we will discourage this as a modeling practice; all attempts should be made, as far as possible, to enforce disjointness among subclasses.

In set-theoretic terms, when the basis property is used as a set-partitioning operator to create disjoint subclasses, the membership of the superclass is said to have been *framed*. Because frames cannot overlap, we will occasionally use the term *framing* as a synonym for disjoint subclassing.

A second notion which applies to specialization is that of *completeness*. A complete specialization implies that every object which is a member of the superclass, must be a member of *at least one* subclass deriving from it. In Figure 6-1, every `multiplexer` must be either a `narrowbandMultiplexer` or a `broadbandMultiplexer`, because its composite port speed must either be greater or less than 45 Mbps. In other words, we have left no "holes" in the speed subdomains which the subclasses collectively cover; the union of all subclass subdomains results in the superclass domain. This is an example of *complete specialization* or *total specialization*.

If we had left a hole in the speed domain, we would have had an example of an *incomplete* specialization. For example, if we had derived only two subclasses directly from class `multiplexer` as `t1Multiplexer` (with `compositePortSpeed <= 1.544` Mbps) and `broadbandMultiplexer` (with `compositePortSpeed > 45` Mbps), it would have been possible for a `multiplexer` operating at, say, 2.048 Mbps, to be a member of neither subclass. This situation is then said to exhibit *incomplete specialization* or *partial specialization*.

The notions of disjointness and completeness are meaningful even when the basis of specialization is qualitative. When the basis of specialization is an enumerated attribute, disjoint specialization means that, at every level of subclassing, the set of enumerated values the attribute can possess has been partitioned into non-intersecting subsets. Complete specialization means that, at every level of subclassing, every enumerated value the attribute can possess in the superclass has been repeated in at least one subclass.

As an example, consider again the class `customCallingService`. Instead of directly subclassing into individual services based on specializing the `serviceType` attribute, suppose we had specialized first into two intermediate subclasses, called `callingNumberService` and `nonCallingNumberService`, as shown in Figure 6-5. The subclass `callingNumberService` includes all the services based on the ability of the terminating switch to receive the calling party's number from the originating switch. This can be accomplished using a variety of mechanisms such as Caller ID or ANI (Automatic Number Identification). The class `callingNumberService` might constrain the `serviceType` attribute, from the original set of values it possesses in the superclass, to only the following subset of the values in the subclass:

```
{callingNumberDelivery, callReturn, callBlocking,
 anonymousCallReject, callScreening, callTracing,
 selectiveForwarding}
```

The subclass `nonCallingNumberService` might constrain it to only the following subset of enumerated values:

```
{callWaiting, threeWayCalling, speedCalling,
 distinctiveRinging, ringWhenFree}
```

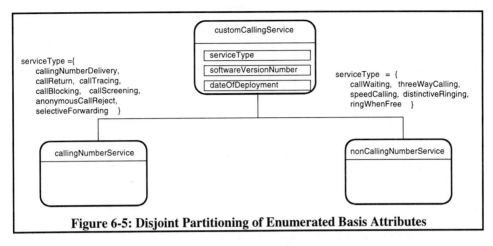

Figure 6-5: Disjoint Partitioning of Enumerated Basis Attributes

When partitioning the set of enumerated values, we ensure disjointness by making sure no value is repeated in the subsets identified for each subclass. In addition, we ensure completeness by making sure that each value enumerated for the superclass is present in at least one of the subsets enumerated for the subclasses.

Applying Disjointness and Completeness

The concepts of disjointness and completeness are independent [Elms89]. Thus, for every selected basis of specialization, we can have the four different ways of subclassing shown in Figure 6-6:

- Disjoint, complete
- Disjoint, incomplete
- Overlapping, complete
- Overlapping, incomplete

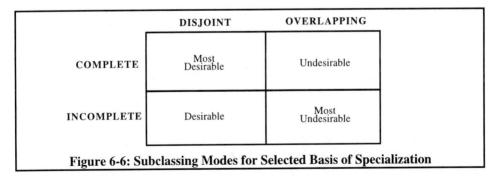

	DISJOINT	**OVERLAPPING**
COMPLETE	Most Desirable	Undesirable
INCOMPLETE	Desirable	Most Undesirable

Figure 6-6: Subclassing Modes for Selected Basis of Specialization

In applying specialization theory to network modeling, we will encourage the practice that all subclassing be disjoint and, as far as possible, complete. Disjointness assures us that each instance of a network object we encounter and place within our hierarchy can be placed in *at most* one class. It improves the richness of the taxonomical structure by removing any ambiguity and confusion with regard to where instances can be placed in the hierarchy. Completeness assures us that each instance can be placed in *at least* one class. Completeness ensures that "all bases are covered", and that we will never encounter an instance which we find we cannot properly classify because of "holes" in the hierarchy.

Locating an object class in an inheritance hierarchy constructed using disjoint and complete partitioning has been compared to playing the popular parlor game of "Twenty Questions". In this game, the questioner starts off from an extremely large and general ancestral class and, by intelligently selecting the basis of specialization with each question, skilfully partitions the domain until a very narrowly defined and highly specialized leaf class (or instance thereof) can be identified. Most good players of the game need far fewer than twenty questions to arrive at the answer. In a good object model, too, the depth of a well-designed inheritance hierarchy — with a properly chosen basis of specialization at each level — very rarely needs to exceed twenty.

If, for a given network model, subclassing at every level is done in a disjoint and complete manner and multiple inheritance is not used, the taxonomical information in the inheritance hierarchy can be reduced to a Venn diagram similar to that of Figure 2-3. In such a diagram all circles will be completely included in other circles and no two circles will intersect. Such a Venn diagram may be considered to be "a view from the top" of an inheritance hierarchy data structure. We can place an object instance in as specific a circle as we can define. (Of course, a Venn diagram is only a set-theoretic construct and does not represent the notions of evolution and extension.) Thus, a properly designed inheritance hierarchy can describe an extremely precise taxonomy of the problem space.

6.7. Compound Specialization

Occasionally, we need to use more than one basis property for the same specialization. This is known as a *compound specialization*. For example, if two different basis attributes simultaneously undergo domain restriction as part of the same specialization, we would have a compound specialization by multiple attribute domain restriction. As an example, consider our original situation where we subclassed the class `multiplexer` into `narrowbandMultiplexer` and `broadbandMultiplexer` on the basis of speed. Suppose now that we had two different brands of multiplexers in our network: one manufactured by BigTime Corporation, and another by Acme Networks Inc. Suppose that, aside from composite port speeds, there were other differences in the multiplexers depending on the brand. To help support these distinctions in our model, we may find it necessary to subclass from class `multiplexer` based on a *combined* consideration of composite port speeds *and* the brand of these devices.

Instead of two, we can now create four subclasses: `narrowbandBigTimeMultiplexer`, `broadbandBigTimeMultiplexer`, `narrowbandAcmeMultiplexer`, and `broadbandAcmeMultiplexer`. The basis of specialization is a *combination* of logical predicates, one constraining the value of the `compositePortSpeed` attribute and another constraining the value of the `brandName` attribute, as shown in Figure 6-7.

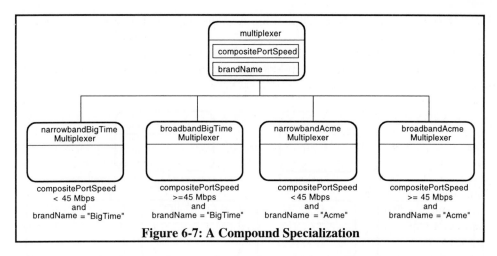

Figure 6-7: A Compound Specialization

Even though we have used a combination of two properties as the basis, there is still only one specialization — a *compound specialization* — and only one basis for the specialization. The basis just happens to be a compound logical predicate constructed of two simpler logical predicates and-ed together. By contrast, the situation in Figure 6-1 and Figure 6-2, where we used a single basis property for the specialization, is known as a *simple specialization.*

Instead of subclassing using compound specialization all at one level, we could have achieved the same effect by subclassing at two different levels using simple specializations. For example, if we had specialized based on constraining the brandName attribute at the first level and then on compositePortSpeed at the second level, we would have had the hierarchy of Figure 6-8. Or we could have reversed the order of specialization, as in Figure 6-9, to achieve the same effect.

No general recommendation can be made as to which approach is better — a compound specialization all at one level, or simple specializations at several different levels. There is no single technique which is correct in all situations. In compound specialization, we cover domains in multiple dimensions. Suppose that in the first example above, we had 10 manufacturers and had partitioned the composite port speed into, say, 4 subdomains. With compound specialization we would have had 40 subclasses all at one level. If we had stuck to simple specialization at multiple levels, we would have had 10 at the first level and 4 each at the second, or 4 at the first level and 10 each at the second. The end-result would have been the same 40 subclasses either way.

The choice between compound specialization and simple specialization really boils down to the "shape" of the inheritance hierarchy. With compound specializations, the tree tends to be rather broad and shallow; with simple specializations, narrow and deep. The proper choice at each level depends on the application domain. Compound specialization is not discouraged if it makes sense for the application domain and if the number of subclasses at each level can be kept manageable.

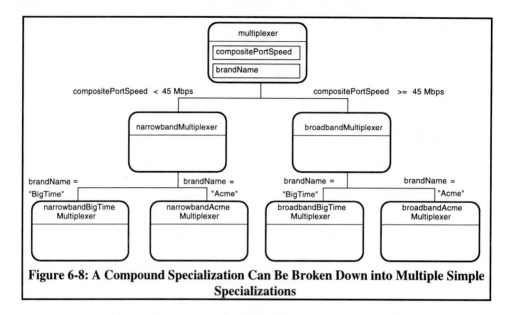

Figure 6-8: A Compound Specialization Can Be Broken Down into Multiple Simple Specializations

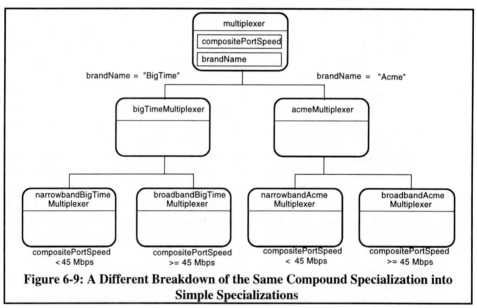

Figure 6-9: A Different Breakdown of the Same Compound Specialization into Simple Specializations

The concepts of disjointness and completeness apply to compound specialization as well. We need to consider each basis property as a separate dimension of specialization and ensure that the domain partitioning in each dimension is both disjoint and complete.

6.8. Specialization by Argument Contravariance

Another mechanism for specialization arises from the manner in which the capabilities of functions increase going down the hierarchy. Consider the example of a `router` object having the capability of routing IP (Internet Protocol [RFC 791]) datagrams. Being physically connected to a number of transmission media, part of the router's capabilities is the ability to resolve a logical network-layer IP address to an address on a physical transmission medium, such as a 48-bit Ethernet address. To accomplish this, it may use a protocol such as ARP (Address Resolution Protocol [RFC 826]), which helps to bind a network-layer address to a physical address. Suppose we model this ability to perform address resolution as a function within a `router` object class, called `resolveNetwork-Address`. Assume we model this function as accepting two arguments, an `address-Type` indicator and an actual `address`. The domains on these two arguments are restricted as follows:

```
addressType = "ipAddress"
address = {any actual IP address}
```

The `addressType` field tells the function that the next parameter is an IP address, and the `address` parameter can be any legal IP address which is to be resolved.

Now, we build a more sophisticated router. This is a multiprotocol router which can route not just IP but also OSI CLNP (Connectionless Network Protocol). In case it becomes a designated router in the local environment, it can also run OSPF and IS-IS to communicate local routing information to its peer level 2 routers in the network [Perl91]. Clearly, this represents an increase in the router's capabilities. If we subclass, say, `multiprotocolRouter` from `router`, we can invest the new subclass with functions capable of processing OSI protocols, in addition to the IP datagram processing functions it inherits from its superclass.

The `resolveNetworkAddress` function in the subclass `multiprotocol-Router` is now capable of binding not just IP addresses to physical addresses but also OSI network-layer addresses to physical addresses. It may accomplish this by running a protocol such as ES-IS (End-System to Intermediate-System) to determine the physical addresses of the end systems it can reach. Or it may perform this resolution more trivially, since some OSI addressing schemes have the SNPA (Subnetwork Point Of Attachment) actually encoded in the 6-octet ID field of their domain-specific part [Rose90].

In any event, the argument to the `resolveNetworkAddress` function, which previously was just an IP address, now can be either an IP address *or* an OSI address. The domains on the arguments to the function now are

```
addressType = "ipAddress" OR "osiAddress"
address = {any actual IP or OSI address}
```

As the subclass `multiprotocolRouter` has increased its capabilities, the domains of arguments its functions can accept have actually *expanded*. Instead of *restrict-*

ing the domain as we do for attribute bases of specialization, we have in Figure 6-10 *relaxed* the domain on the arguments of inherited functions in the subclass.

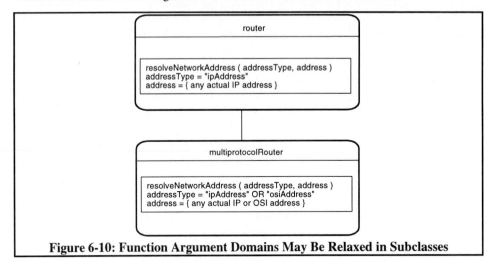

Figure 6-10: Function Argument Domains May Be Relaxed in Subclasses

       The ability of subclasses to relax the domain of arguments of inherited functions is not contradictory to the notion of specialization. We have already said that, proceeding down the hierarchy, subclasses possess greater capabilities and functions. The ability of functions in the subclass to handle a wider domain of arguments merely represents their increasing versatility. This ability is called *contravariance*. It is so named because, as subclasses become specialized and increasingly restricted in their basis properties, the arguments that their functions can handle can actually become weaker and more relaxed. Because of this seemingly inverse variation, function argument domains in subclasses are considered to be *contravariant*, that is, they vary in the opposite manner as attribute domains [Lea91, Harr91].

How Contravariance Works

Contravariance of function arguments is based on concepts in object-oriented subtyping theory. Type theory rigorously defines the circumstances when a subclass is actually also a subtype, in terms of being substitutable for its supertype. Because we are constructing modeling hierarchies under monotonic inheritance, all our subclasses are in fact subtypes. Therefore, we can use contravariance as a mode of specialization.

       Going one step further, just as a domain restriction on an inherited attribute can be used as a basis of specialization, the domain relaxation on the argument of an inherited function can also be used as a basis of specialization. We can subclass `multi-protocolRouter` from the class `router`, as in the example above, and use as a basis for specialization the increase in the domain of the argument of the `resolveNetwork-Address` function. In effect, this creates a specialized subclass based on the increased capability of one of the superclass functions. (In practice, there would probably also be a restriction in the domain of the `routerType` attribute, which would be a more likely basis for specialization.)

To better understand the notion that argument domain relaxation is actually a proper way of specializing, it may help to mentally consider the new function with the expanded domain as really consisting of *two* separate functions. The first function is the one directly inherited from the superclass with the original argument domains unchanged. The second, newer function is almost identical to the first, except that it accepts arguments in that part of the domain that the first function does not. Since we already said that a subclass may inherit superclass functions without change and may also *add* new functions, this new subclass definition is legal. Now, since the two functions perform identical operations on their arguments, all that remains is to mentally merge them back together to create a single function with an expanded argument domain.

This simple thought experiment of splitting up the expanded domain over two hypothetical functions helps to prove that argument domain relaxation in the subclass is a valid inheritance technique. As an exercise to reinforce this concept, consider the simpler example of a hypothetical `leasedLineModem` object class which accepts a domain of 0 to 60 minutes for a `duration` argument to a `loopbackTest` function. If we create a subclass `vFastModem` which accepts a domain of 0 to 120 minutes for the same function, clearly the latter represents a valid subclass with increased capability, but the argument domains are relaxed.

6.9. Specialization by Result Covariance

As a complement to the notion that a subclass may specialize by relaxing function arguments, it may also specialize by *tightening function results*. In Figure 6-1, suppose we had a function called `timeAveragedCompositePortSpeed` which reported the actual operating speed of the composite port averaged over time, after accounting for any periods during which the device may have downspeeded to operate at some sub-rate. It is clear that the values returned by this function will be significantly higher for a `broadbandMultiplexer` than for a `narrowbandMultiplexer`. By formally specifying a restricted domain for the return values of this function (e.g., "A `broadbandMultiplexer` is one which operates at a time-averaged composite port speed of 45 Mbps or more") we may in fact use this as a basis of specialization, as in Figure 6-11.

Thus, a subclass may *restrict the domain on the results* returned by a function, and such a restriction may be used as a basis for specialization. Conceptually, this is no different from restricting the domain of an attribute. This is because the reporting of any attribute's value may be internally implemented as the result returned by a function computation. For the sake of argument, it is conceivable that an architect might model the `timeAveragedCompositePortSpeed` above as an attribute and internally invoke a function computation every time the value of that attribute was interrogated. In spite of its internally resulting from a function, the domain of this attribute might, for external specification purposes, be partitioned and restricted during subclassing just like any other basis attribute. Because of encapsulation, we do not care whether an attribute is "really" a data

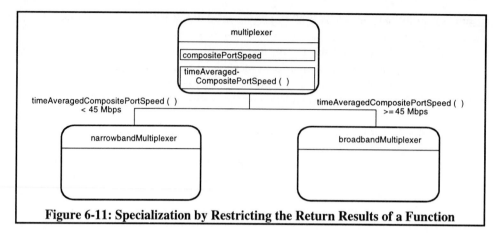

Figure 6-11: Specialization by Restricting the Return Results of a Function

item stored in a register, or the return result of a function; we are only concerned with the interface on the object boundary.

Because the results returned by a specialized function in a subclass can reside in a tighter domain, function results vary in the same way as attributes with increasing specialization. Thus, function results are said to be *covariant* with specialization. (To reduce the confusion about the covariance and contravariance of function results and arguments, practitioners who have used specialization theory have found the mnemonic WARSAW helpful: "We Allow Result Strengthening and Argument Weakening".)

6.10. Specialization by Capsule Fixing

Often, manufacturers of network products and providers of network services will allow customers to select optional features as part of their offerings. Because these features need not always be present, we might consider them variant properties and model them using optional capsules in object classes. As the products or services evolve, the manufacturer may find it necessary for competitive advantage to turn an optional feature in an older product into a standard feature in a newer product. Because this feature is no longer optional, the manufacturer often markets the newer product as a next-generation model.

As network modeling architects, it is our job to keep track of evolving object classes, even if they are only marginally specialized from existing classes. Our model must have the ability to reflect the names and options commonly used to categorize objects. If we create a subclass from an existing object class, we may find that the only difference is that a capsule which was optional in the existing class in now mandatory in the subclass. This is known as *capsule fixing*, and is shown in Figure 6-12. In our network model, we will allow the use of capsule fixing as a basis for specialization. All instances of the subclass will now possess this capsule, and it will also be mandatory for other subclasses deriving down from this point in the hierarchy.

In our formal syntax, we need to be able to express the fact that, as a basis of specialization, an optional superclass capsule has been turned into a mandatory subclass capsule. In Chapter 11, we shall see how this can be done.

Capsule fixing can also be viewed as a restriction phenomenon: the choice of *present* or *absent* for the capsule has now been restricted to *present*. Of course, this does not preclude the possibility that other extensions may appear as part of the same specialization.

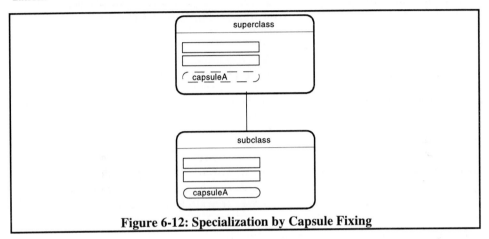

Figure 6-12: Specialization by Capsule Fixing

6.11. Specialization Principles: Addition, Restriction, and Extension

Specialization theory embodies the notions of extension and incremental refinement which we introduced in Chapter 2. As it specializes, a subclass experiences extension and incremental refinement via the processes of *addition, expansion,* and *restriction.* Because the subclass may add properties to a superclass, specialization may be viewed as an addition process (extension). Because the subclass may relax argument domains for functions (and, as we shall see in Chapter 13, increase their capabilities as well), specialization may be viewed to be an expansion process (extension). Because the domain on basis attributes and function results can be narrowed in the subclass, specialization may be viewed to be a restriction process (refinement).

In other words, to specialize a subclass from the superclass, we

- Describe it in greater detail (extension by addition of new properties);

- Expand it for richer functionality (extension by expansion of function arguments);

- Narrow it down for specific focus (refinement by restriction of attribute domains).

These meanings are not contradictory — rather, they are complementary, in that in concert they act to provide us with a powerful mechanism to model reality as we experience it.

To summarize the knowledge we have acquired so far, we will formally describe the rules of specialization theory we have learned so far. These are called *specialization principles*. A specialization principle is a rule which states how a subclass may legally **specialize-from** a superclass. We state below the principles of *attribute addition, function addition, capsule addition, attribute domain restriction, result covariance, argument contravariance*, and *capsule fixing*:

Specialization Principle:	*A descendant class may add an attribute as a new property (**Attribute Addition**).*

Specialization Principle:	*A descendant class may add a function as a new property (**Function Addition**).*

Specialization Principle:	*A descendant class may add a capsule as a new property (**Capsule Addition**).*

Specialization Principle:	*A descendant class may restrict the domain of an attribute inherited from an ancestral class (**Attribute Domain Restriction**).*

Specialization Principle:	*A descendant class may expand the domain of an argument of a function inherited from an ancestral class (**Argument Contravariance**).*

Specialization Principle:	*A descendant class may restrict the domain of a result of a function inherited from an ancestral class (**Result Covariance**).*

Specialization Principle:	*A descendant class may mandate the use of an optional capsule inherited from an ancestral class (**Capsule Fixing**).*

Notice that in every case, specialization creates extension and incremental refinement by addition to, expansion of, or restriction on inherited properties. Of course, more than one of these principles may be used simultaneously in a compound specialization. By telling us the precise rules to follow in deciding how properties can be added, what properties can be extended, and what properties can be restricted, the principles above help us in designing good hierarchies.

We will state additional principles of specialization theory which we will learn as we go along. For example, we will see how the fact that an object class participates in a relationship with another object class can also be used as a basis of specialization.

6.12. Multiple Inheritance

Multiple inheritance refers to the ability of an object class to inherit properties from more than one superclass. This is sometimes used in cases where it is found necessary in the definition of an object class to import more than one set of properties which may have been specified in separate superclasses. In this case, the class may be defined as deriving from more than one superclass. Multiple inheritance is most often considered when an ancestral class has been specialized at different times using different bases of specialization.

Consider a situation where a corporate customer has purchased a variety of networking devices, modeled as members of the class networkDevice. All these products have similar attributes, such as vendorName, manufacturerName, deviceType, and price, specified in a device object class. Suppose further that the devices are subclassed into the capitalEquipment object class, meaning all equipment that cost more than, say, $10,000, and the nonCapitalEquipment object class with everything else. Clearly, this is a quantitative specialization based on partitioning the domain of the price attribute, as shown in Figure 6-13. Further, it may also become necessary to subclass the device class in a different way, using a qualitative specialization based on restricting the deviceType attribute, as in Figure 6-14.

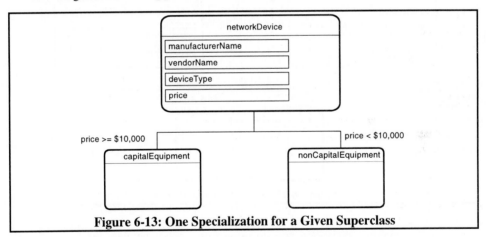

Figure 6-13: One Specialization for a Given Superclass

Now we have *multiple specializations* proceeding from the same superclass at two different times, using two different bases of specialization. This is different from *compound specialization*, where two different attributes are used in combination for the *same* specialization. In compound specialization, that combination still results in a single set of logical predicates, that is, there is still only a single specialization.

Because we have specialized from the superclass twice along two different "dimensions", every member of networkDevice will appear in both the price-based specialization and the type-based specialization. How can we now represent a file-Server object which costs more than $10,000? We may want to create a new subclass,

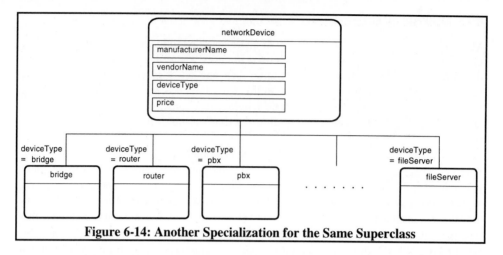

Figure 6-14: Another Specialization for the Same Superclass

called `expensiveFileServer`, shown in Figure 6-15, which derives multiply from `fileServer` and `capitalEquipment`.

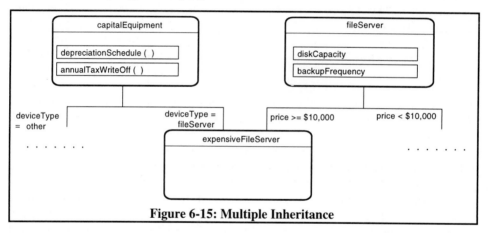

Figure 6-15: Multiple Inheritance

In this multiple derivation, we are using from each superclass the basis of specialization we did not use before: from the `fileServer` superclass we are specializing using a `price` basis, and from the `capitalEquipment` object class we are specializing using a `deviceType` basis. The new `expensiveFileServer` object class inherits the properties of the `fileServer` object class (which might be `diskCapacity` and `backupFrequency`) as well as the properties of the `capitalEquipment` object class (which might be `depreciationSchedule` and `annualTaxWriteOff`). In effect, the class has two superclasses.

A class defined using multiple inheritance possesses the **specializes-from** relationship with all its superclasses. Further descendant classes of a multiply derived class inherit all the properties of all their ancestral classes.

Multiple inheritance arises when multiple specializations have proceeded at different times from the same superclass, each using a different basis for the specialization. This partitions the set of objects along two or more different dimensions, with each specialization possibly extending the subclasses with different sets of attributes and functions. A subclass desiring to inherit the properties from all these different extensions will have to multiply inherit from the appropriate superclasses.

In specialization theory, we allow the use of multiple inheritance when required. As far as possible, though, we recommend that when subclassing, only one basis property should be selected, and all specializations should be based on this property.

Applying Multiple Inheritance

When more than one specialization proceeds from the same ancestral class, we must consider disjointness and completeness with respect to each such specialization. Each such specialization may individually be simple or compound, and each individually may be disjoint or overlapping, complete or incomplete. Furthermore, the concept of *sibling classes* applies only within a given specialization. In Figure 6-13 and Figure 6-14, the class `fileServer` is a sibling of class `pbx` but is *not* a sibling of class of `capitalEquipment`, even though `fileServer` and `capitalEquipment` have the same superclass. This is because they arise from two different specializations which use different properties as their basis of specialization. Multiple inheritance arises because such a divergence has occurred somewhere higher up in the hierarchy (perhaps even among top-level classes).

Often designers use multiple inheritance to accommodate variations on an object class. A first-generation subclass with one variation on a superclass, together with another first-generation subclass with a second variation on the same superclass, can both **specialize-into** a second-generation subclass which has both the variations and so inherits multiply from them. For example, we could have modeled the `srtBridge` object class of Figure 4-8 with multiple inheritance. But we did not need to do so, because we have the mechanism of capsules to model variations of the same object class.

When using multiple inheritance, care must be taken to avoid conflicts. As we indicated in Chapter 4, there can be cases when the subclass inherits the same property twice, once from each superclass. In this situation, we consider the subclass to have only one occurrence of the property. For example, both superclasses are descendants, at some point, of `genericObject`; each superclass has an `objectName` attribute and an `objectClass` attribute. The subclass does not possess these attributes twice; we consider that it possesses them only once.

This applies to attributes, functions, and capsules. Special care must be taken with optional capsules, however. If the superclasses have a copy of the same capsule, it may have been specified as optional in some superclasses and mandatory in others. The criteria we adopt about how a multiply inheriting subclass acquires optional capsules are as follows:

- *Capsule is mandatory in at least one superclass:*
   Capsule is mandatory in the subclass.

- *Capsule is optional in all superclasses:*
   Capsule is optional in the subclass.

Property Conflicts in Multiple Inheritance

In Chapter 2, we defined the ancestral class in which a property is first defined — that is, not inherited from any superclass — as the *origin class* for that property. When we specify our model in a formal syntax, we will see that our model compiler has the ability to perform *genealogy resolution*. Genealogy resolution involves the ability to keep track and trace back the exact origin class for each property inherited by a subclass. If there is a property conflict in a multiply inheriting subclass and if genealogy resolution shows that the property was first defined in the same origin class from which both superclasses derived, the compiler considers that there is really no conflict and the subclass receives only one copy.

On some occasions, a genuine conflict may arise. If, for example, different implementations of a function have been defined in different origin classes using the same function name, we may have to decide which function should "really" be inherited by the subclass. In the absence of any guidelines, an ambiguous situation may result.

One way to resolve such ambiguities is to allow each subclass to define a set of *precedence criteria* which will dictate which inherited version of the property will be the *dominant property* and which will be the *recessive property*. A precedence criterion can be defined as specifically or as generally as we wish. We might specify that a property originating in a class higher up in the hierarchy dominates a property originating in a class lower down in the hierarchy. We might specify the opposite. We might arbitrarily specify, for example, that after the compiler has performed genealogy resolution, a property originating in a class which was first processed by the compiler dominates a property originating in a class encountered later, or vice versa. Or, we might assign a numeric *dominance priority* to every original property of every class, so that different degrees of dominance and recessiveness can be analyzed and disambiguated should multiple inheritance conflicts arise lower down in the hierarchy.

In the absence of precedence criteria, our model compiler performs conflict resolution by *origin preservation*. This means that it simply renames each of the properties having the name conflict by prefixing each property name with its origin class name. Since the conflict arose because two different identically named properties were inherited from two different origin classes, prefixing each property name with its origin class name will disambiguate between them and allow the subclass to inherit both the versions.

This solution is awkward, inelegant, and not always workable, because it requires external objects referencing these properties to also address them with their origin-preserved name. Clearly this is not the most satisfactory situation. To avoid difficulties of this nature, we recommend that designers try to avoid using two different specializations from the same superclass. If this absolutely cannot be avoided, then one should ensure that attributes and functions are defined in a non-conflicting manner, so that no ambiguities will result in multiply inheriting subclasses.

6.13. Principles of Hierarchy Normalization

The concept of normalization helps us to target the most appropriate class in which a particular property must be placed. If we do not specify properties in their "proper" place in the hierarchy, we can run into difficulties where either certain subclasses do not have the properties they need, or certain other subclasses inherit properties they do not want. Normalization helps us define what the "proper" place for every property is.

One reason many object-oriented architects need to use *selective inheritance* is that they work with unnormalized hierarchies. In selective inheritance, the subclass may decide which properties of the superclass it wants to inherit. Selective inheritance is sometimes seen as a convenience in modeling complex real-world models, where one may find the need to create subclasses with fewer attributes than superclasses.

A Normalization Example

Suppose a manufacturer normally markets a wiring concentrator product for structured wiring for local area networks in a campus environment. Assume that every such product has a network management agent built in. We model this as the class managed-WiringHub. Suppose now that the manufacturer's marketing analysis leads it to develop and market a very price-competitive product at the low end, which does not have a network management agent built in, because it is targeted only for smaller environments not requiring the functionality. If we are using a methodology which permits selective inheritance, we may consider modeling the new object class, unmanagedWiringHub, as deriving from managedWiringHub, after dropping the property of being manageable.

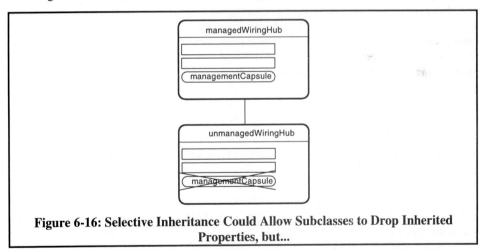

Figure 6-16: Selective Inheritance Could Allow Subclasses to Drop Inherited Properties, but...

If we normalize the model of Figure 6-16 for monotonic inheritance, we can create a new class wiringHub which does not normally possess the ability to be managed as a property. As in Figure 6-17, we can make both the classes managedWiringHub and unmanagedWiringHub derive from class wiringHub. Only managed-WiringHub now extends its inherited properties with the addition of an onboard management agent. The class `unmanagedWiringHub` can derive normally from `wiring-Hub`, without necessarily extending inherited properties. (In fact, if `unmanaged-WiringHub` is no different from `wiringHub`, there may not be any need to specify the class at all: we might be able to directly instantiate `wiringHub` as a non-leaf concrete class for the new products that do not have a management agent. If backward compatibility is not an issue and if there are no extensions in `unmanagedWiringHub`, the class may be dropped and `wiringHub` itself may be considered concrete.)

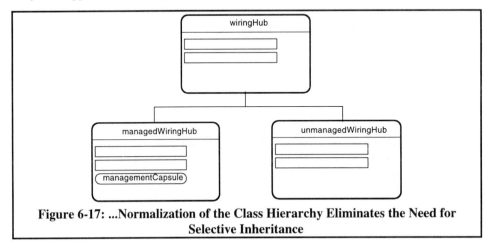

Figure 6-17: ...Normalization of the Class Hierarchy Eliminates the Need for Selective Inheritance

Thus, by normalizing the object class hierarchy, it is possible to satisfy monotonic inheritance everywhere in the object model. In specialization theory, subclass refinement is always additive; the situation where a subclass needs to drop or cancel inherited attributes need never arise after proper normalization.

Normalizing Working Hierarchies

Today, each generation of network products and services offers significant new functionality as well as faster implementations of old functionality. Clearly, these products and services represent new evolutionary patterns which extend an object class hierarchy by growth at the leaf classes. In general, however, it is a mistake to assume that the evolution of the object class hierarchy should match the chronological evolution of network objects in time. Newer network objects are not always more advanced, more sophisticated, and more highly evolved than existing ones; they could be simpler, produced in response to a low-end market need perceived later.

New classes, therefore, need not always be added to the bottom of the hierarchy; they may need to be added in the middle. In these situations, the class hierarchy needs to be adjusted for normalization, as in the example above. It is incorrect to think of the hierarchy in terms of the analogy with a botanical tree, because growth need not occur merely at the leaves. Unlike Darwinian theory, the process of specialization and evolution does not necessarily parallel the linear progress of chronological time.

The normalization of a class hierarchy may occur either at *architecture time* (when we are first defining a network model *ab initio*) or at *operations time* (when we are adjusting the model of an existing network to accommodate new products and services). At architecture time, there are no additional restrictions on performing normalization, because at the time the model is being first defined it has not been applied to any actual network. That is, there are no *instances* defined yet, and so backward compatibility is not an issue. However, there are some restrictions with respect to normalizing a class hierarchy at operations time. Because there are already instances defined in such a network, unrestricted redefinition of classes may cause instances to lose their instantiation associations with existing classes, or their membership associations with ancestral classes.

It should be noted that an inheritance hierarchy is a purely connotational data structure, and that actual objects do not really "care" what class we assign them to or how many levels down the hierarchy they are. However, once such a model is applied to an actual network and advertised to other networks, external networks and applications will use it to issue requests to objects in our network. If we are adjusting our class hierarchy after network operations have begun, then we must ensure that the *external appearance* of existing objects — as viewed by other objects or other networks — continues to be the same in the new hierarchy. Thus, objects must not change existing class memberships (though they may add memberships in new classes). The following restrictions apply to the renormalization of the class hierarchy at operations time:

- The name of any concrete class cannot change;
- The extent of a concrete class cannot change (that is, an instance of a concrete class in the old hierarchy continues to be an instance of the same concrete class in the new hierarchy);
- The name of any ancestral class of a concrete object class cannot change;
- The membership of any ancestral class of a concrete class cannot change (that is, a member of any class in the old hierarchy continues to be a member of the same class in the new hierarchy);
- The set of properties accumulating in every concrete class through inheritance cannot decrease.

The restrictions above ensure that external networks and applications still see the same set of objects enumerated when they issue a request to our network to perform a given operation on all objects of a given class. Aside from these restrictions, specialization theory permits us to perform normalization or otherwise change our model at operations time to reflect changes in the actual system. We may add new classes, redefine bases of specialization, modify derivation associations, and adjust property assignment between classes (subject, of course, to monotonic inheritance). In other words, we may make any connotational changes to *our understanding* of the model as long as it does not affect the operation of the network.

The normalization in Figure 6-17, for example, is legal both at architecture time and at operations time. The membership of the class managedWiringHub continues to be the same, and the new classes wiringHub and unmanagedWiringHub do not "take away" members from any existing class. The moment `wiringHub` is created as a superclass of `managedWiringHub`, it automatically acquires as members all the existing members of `managedWiringHub`. This is not prohibited by the restrictions above, as `wiringHub` is a newly created class.

Much work has been done on the *schema evolution* of object-oriented systems, and a rich set of rules has been articulated for the types of schema changes which can be legally applied under various circumstances [Kim87, Bane87, Penn87, Schr88, Lern90, Kim90a, Kim90b]. Many of those principles can be applied to hierarchies created using specialization theory, subject of course to other modeling restrictions such as monotonic inheritance.

Advantages of Normalization

The principles of normalization of an object class hierarchy are not as well developed as those of normalization of relational database models [Elms89, Teor94]. The process of relational database normalization concentrates on converting a schema to a desirable form (known as a *normal* form) by undertaking a series of steps. These steps result in the elimination of redundant information based on analysis of primary keys and functional dependencies between object attributes. Certain desirable states of the schema are termed the First, Second, Third, and Boyce-Codd Normal Forms [Codd70, Codd72, Ullm88]; further normal forms with stronger resolution of dependencies also exist.

Analogous principles can be applied to the design of an inheritance hierarchy. For example, if we discover that all sibling subclasses possess a common property, we can "promote" that property to their superclass and allow the subclasses to possess it through inheritance. This saves us from specifying multiple assignments for the same property in each subclass; we need only specify one property assignment for their superclass. In fact, an attribute common to any set of cognate classes can be promoted all the way up to their cognation ancestor. This process, where common attributes of classes are identified — as in Figure 6-18 — and "floated up" to the highest point of the hierarchy where they can be applied — as in Figure 6-19 — is akin to database normalization principles.

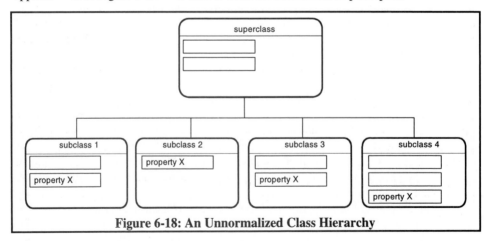

Figure 6-18: An Unnormalized Class Hierarchy

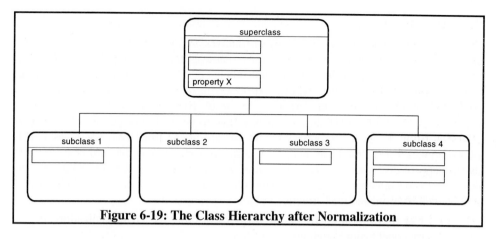

Figure 6-19: The Class Hierarchy after Normalization

If we also enforce monotonic inheritance, we can adjust the class hierarchy as we did in the `wiringHub` example, such that attributes are only added as we proceed down the hierarchy — they are never dropped or canceled. This is also analogous to database schema normalization.

A further advantage of normalization is that concrete classes tend to "sink down" to the bottom of the hierarchy; intermediate classes tend to stay abstract classes. For reasons mentioned earlier, this is a desirable feature of the object class hierarchy. Together with principles such as monotonic inheritance, normalization actually helps us design better hierarchies.

One criticism of normalization is that a class may get separated from its "natural" superclass by intervening abstract classes that arise solely as a result of modeling monotonic inheritance in the hierarchy. If too many such adjustments occur, the overall pattern of shared, referenced, and reused characteristics — which an inheritance hierarchy is supposed to convey — might become non-obvious and non-intuitive. The modeling methodology for every application domain needs to trade off the advantages of monotonic inheritance against the disadvantage of introduction of artificial abstract classes — a decision which will be influenced by the degree of idiosyncrasy among objects in the model. For example, monotonic inheritance is clearly unsuitable for hierarchies which are inherently polythetic, such as that of biological life-forms.

On the other hand, allowing unrestricted refinement by cancellation often leads to an unmanageable situation. Classes evolving at the bottom of the hierarchy, having canceled inherited properties along the way, may bear little resemblance to those at the top. Because of spaghetti inheritance, the sense of a "common purpose" is lost. This danger is prevalent especially in larger projects where different people and different project teams are responsible for specifying different branches in the hierarchy. For this reason, we will enforce monotonic inheritance in our modeling technique. Nevertheless, it should be noted that designing a class hierarchy is not always straightforward and sometimes calls for the exercise of judgment in how best to accommodate deviant characteristics among classes.

6.14. Hierarchy Design

The discussion so far indicates that many alternatives are available in the construction of an inheritance hierarchy. It is no surprise then, that even for a given application domain, there are many ways of creating classes and subclasses. Different architects may choose different bases of specialization, partition attribute domains differently, or use compound specialization, covariance, contravariance, and capsule fixing differently. Clearly, there is no one "best" way of subclassing. Decisions have to be made independently for every class as to what the most appropriate manner of subclassing from that class is, as suited for the application. To facilitate this process, the hierarchy designer should bear in mind the concepts of disjointness and completeness, which will provide valuable guidelines in building a good inheritance hierarchy. The following recommendations will help in designing well-behaved and well-structured object class hierarchies.

- *Use capsules to model minor variations* of a class and specialization to model major variations.

- *Avoid free specialization*. At every level of subclassing, select a formal basis of specialization.

- *Select only one basis of specialization* at every level of subclassing, as far as possible. This basis may be qualitative or quantitative; it may be simple or compound; it may involve property addition, attribute domain restriction, result covariance, argument contravariance, capsule fixing, or any of the specialization modes we will define in subsequent chapters. Whatever the case, ensuring that only one basis has been chosen precludes potential problems with multiple inheritance later on.

- *Ensure that each specialization is disjoint*. This will avoid ambiguous classification of objects and minimize any possible confusion with multiple inheritance later on.

- *Ensure that each specialization is complete*, as far as possible. This will ensure that all objects have a "home" somewhere in the hierarchy and will avoid the possibility of subclassing *ad hoc* in the wrong place lower down to cover a modeling "hole" higher up.

- *Push all concrete classes as far down in the hierarchy as possible*. To design a good hierarchy, try to turn as many concrete (instantiable) classes as possible into leaf classes. This will lead to a very precise categorization mechanism for objects.

- *Keep the number of subclasses manageable*. If the selected basis of specialization causes a subclass explosion, re-specify the domain subdivision of the basis property to a coarser granularity. Consider creating multiple levels in the hierarchy with fewer subclasses at each level, rather than many subclasses all at the same level.

- *Ensure that the hierarchy is normalized*, that is, each property is placed at the highest point in the hierarchy where it can be applied.

Also use normalization to ensure that subclasses do not need to drop or cancel inherited properties.

- ***Avoid multiple inheritance*** as far as possible. Explore aggregation and capsules as alternatives to multiple inheritance. If you must use multiple inheritance, ensure that there are no conflicts among multiply inherited properties.

- ***Do not create too deep a hierarchy***. Subclassing too deeply may be indicative of a need to redesign in the overall hierarchy. If you have, say, more than a dozen levels of subclassing in the hierarchy, you should re-examine your basis of specialization at each level. Remember, only 7 levels of depth are necessary to classify the entire set of known biological life-forms which contains several million species.

- ***Do not worry about the elegance of the inheritance hierarchy***. For good engineering design, you do not have to make the pictorial representation of an inheritance hierarchy look balanced or symmetric on paper. A balanced and symmetric picture of an inheritance hierarchy is only necessary when you are making a presentation of your system architecture to your Vice-President.

6.15. Summary

Classes specialize from their superclasses using a formal basis of specialization. If an attribute is used as the basis property of specialization, the subclasses created have restricted values for the domain of the attribute (Specialization by Attribute Domain Restriction). The attribute used as a basis property may be continuous-valued or discrete-valued. The domain partitioning of the basis attribute in the subclasses should be considered with respect to disjointness and completeness. Multiple properties may be simultaneously used as a compound basis of specialization.

A function may also be used as a basis of specialization. A subclass may restrict the domain on the return result of a function (Specialization by Result Covariance) or relax the domain on an argument of a function (Specialization by Argument Contravariance). Alternatively, a subclass may also fix an optional capsule as a basis of specialization (Specialization by Capsule Fixing).

The specialization principle used for each level of subclassing must be formally stated in the specification of each subclass. Multiple inheritance is permitted in the creation of subclasses but can generally be avoided through proper redesign of the inheritance hierarchy using established normalization principles.

7. The Object Aggregation Hierarchy

"A truly great network architecture is as elegant as a cathedral — you design it, and then you pray a lot."
— anonymous network architect.

7.1. Introduction

This chapter introduces the concept of *aggregate objects*, which are complex objects consisting of simpler objects. The relationships of composition and decomposition are presented, along with the modes of interaction between aggregation and inheritance. The concept of component multiplicity is introduced. Finally, additional specialization principles are inferred based on the aggregation relationships in which an object class participates.

7.2. Conceptual Background

To architect a complex network, we must find a way of breaking down the overall system in such a manner that we can deal with each piece individually. Then, we can put the pieces back together to create the complete network. If each piece is too large, it must be further decomposed into smaller pieces. The objective is to arrive at a manageable set of subproblems, each of which can be solved in a single step. We can then assemble the solutions back together in a meaningful way.

The concept of *aggregation* provides us with a way of breaking down information so that we can create complex objects by making an assembly of smaller objects act synergistically. In object-oriented modeling, as in many other modeling methodologies, this breakdown process is called *decomposition*. The reverse process, the act of assembling simpler objects together to create a complex object, is called *composition*. The object thus created is termed an *aggregate object* or *aggregate instance*.

An aggregate object is an object which, by definition, is composed of simpler objects. The specification of an aggregate indicates very clearly which and how many simpler objects are assembled together to constitute the aggregate. The simpler objects which together constitute the aggregate are known as *component objects* or *component instances*. As an example, consider an instance of the pbx object class, which has many component objects. Instances of the card object class are components of the pbx object.

Even though an aggregate object is composed of many simpler objects, it can be treated as a unit. The aggregate is considered a single object and can be referenced as such in any function. If, during network operations, we wish to execute a function on all component objects of an aggregate, we often need only specify that the function be executed once on the aggregate. Aggregation provides a powerful abstraction which facilitates the description and manipulation of entire assemblies of simpler objects together.

Aggregation Relationships

Aggregation specifies a *part-whole* relationship between object classes. The component objects are considered to be *parts* which make up the *whole* aggregate object. Therefore, the component object is said to have a *composition relationship* with its aggregate. The composition relationship is also called the is-a-part-of relationship. Clearly, the is-a-part-of relationship is not *commutative*; it does not operate in both directions. The reciprocal relationship going in the reverse direction is called the *decomposition relationship*, or the has-as-a-part relationship. It is correct to say that the aggregate object has-as-a-part each of its component objects. Figure 7-1 shows some typical composition relationships, with their complementary decomposition relationships shown in Figure 7-2.

The is-a-part-of and has-as-a-part relationships are also called *aggregation relationships*. Both these relationships are *transitive*. This means that an object which is-a-part-of an aggregate which in turn is-a-part-of a greater aggregate, is-a-part-of the greater aggregate itself. Similarly, the aggregate has-as-a-part each of the component and sub-component objects into which it can be decomposed.

While aggregation relationships are relationships among *objects*, we will speak of them as relationships between *classes*. Thus, an *aggregate class* is said to have the has-as-a-part relationship with a *component class*. This implies that each object which is a member of the aggregate class has-as-a-part some object or objects which are members of the component class. Similarly, the reverse is-a-part-of relationship also applies between a component class and an aggregate class.

Aggregation Hierarchies

Because of the transitive nature of the composition and decomposition relationships, the component breakdown of an aggregate class may be depicted in a tree-structured form. This is known as an *aggregation hierarchy*. As Figure 7-3 shows, an aggregation hierarchy is rooted at the aggregate object and proceeds downward to show its first-order components. Since each component itself may be an aggregate, we can then show its compo-

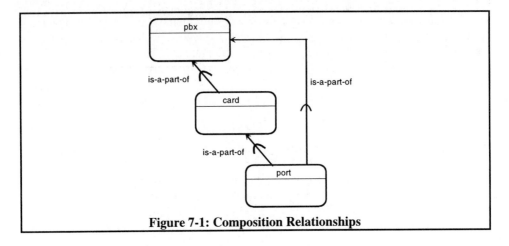

Figure 7-1: Composition Relationships

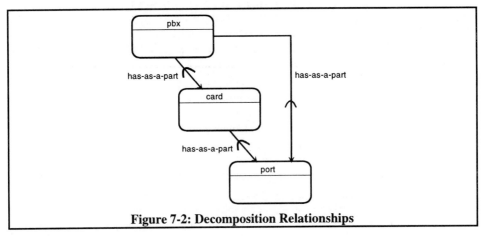

Figure 7-2: Decomposition Relationships

nents, and so on. The hierarchy terminates when the simplest objects at the bottom have no further decomposition.

Unlike an inheritance hierarchy, of which there is only one for every modeled system, more than one aggregation hierarchy may be necessary to describe the complete model of a single network. Each aggregate class can be decomposed into its separate classes and thus roots its own aggregation hierarchy. Since the component breakdown for every aggregate class is different, this gives rise to multiple aggregation hierarchies. As we shall see in the examples later in this chapter, descendants of an aggregate class can generate their own aggregation hierarchies which are specialized forms of the aggregation hierarchies of their ancestor. All these hierarchies together are necessary to describe the system.

To determine what the components of an aggregate object are, we need only find the transitive closure of its decomposition relationship. Starting at the aggregate class in the aggregation hierarchy, we visit every component node which is reachable by follow-

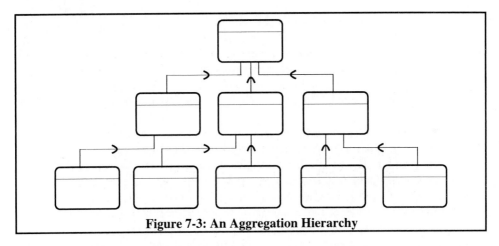

Figure 7-3: An Aggregation Hierarchy

ing the chain of `has-as-a-part` conceptual pointers. In doing so, we will enumerate the component breakdown of the aggregate.

7.3. Aggregation versus Inheritance

We cannot overemphasize the distinction between aggregation and inheritance. Many persons exposed to object-oriented modeling for the first time are sometimes confused between the two, because both arrange object classes in a hierarchy. This has often resulted in much befuddlement over the meaning of object-orientation.

In point of fact, *aggregation has nothing whatsoever to do with inheritance*. The two hierarchies convey completely different semantics. The inheritance hierarchy describes the **specializes-from** association between classes; its purpose is to specify *taxonomies* so that we can *categorize* objects. The inheritance hierarchy is a purely connotational data structure, an edifice we erect to assist our understanding of the system; how we categorize an object does not affect the operation of the object itself. By contrast, the aggregation hierarchy describes the `is-a-part-of` relationship between classes; its purpose is to define *compositions* so that we can *assemble* the objects we have categorized, or to propagate the effects of operations on one object to another. The aggregation hierarchy is operational; the composition and decomposition relationships of an object actually affect how the object operates.

Two Different Hierarchies

It is worth explicitly stating that the fact that an object class bears an operational `is-a-part-of` relationship with another object class does not mean that it bears the connotational **specializes-from** association with that class. Just because an object class `is-a-part-of` of another class does not imply that it **inherits-from** that class. For example, the fact that the `card` object class is a component of the `pbx` object class does not mean that a `card` has the characteristics of a `pbx`. The operational relationship of classes to each other in the aggregation hierarchy has nothing whatsoever to do with their connotational associations in the inheritance hierarchy. It is possible that in the inheritance hierarchy, the `card` object class may occur on a different branch than the `pbx` object class, thus having little in common with it genealogically. The position of an object class in the inheritance hierarchy depends only on the levels of specialization it has experienced. Its position in the aggregation hierarchy depends only on how deeply nested its members are within the aggregate system. There is no semantic connection or dependency between the two hierarchies.

The component and aggregate classes will all appear in both the aggregation and the inheritance hierarchies. There is, however, an important distinction. Because the same object class may be contained in many different aggregate classes (for example, a `card` object could be contained in a `pbx`, in a `crossConnect`, in an `atmSwitch`, and many other objects), the same object class may appear in *many places* in the aggregation hierarchy. By contrast, every object class occurs *exactly once* in the inheritance hierarchy.

In the inheritance hierarchy, we defined a *concrete* class as one that immediately has instances, and an *abstract* class as one that is never directly instantiated. Both concrete classes as well as abstract classes may appear in the aggregation hierarchy. If the aggregate and the component classes are concrete, it means that every object which **is-an-instance-of** the aggregate class will contain an object which **is-an-instance-of** the component class. If they are abstract, it means that every object which **is-a-member-of** the aggregate class will contain an object which **is-a-member-of** the component class.

For example, the classes `pbx` and `card` may both be abstract classes in the inheritance hierarchy. Neither might have direct instances, as they might both experience further specialization, such as `dataPbx`, `isdnPbx`, `lineCard`, and `trunkCard`. Yet, in the aggregation hierarchy, we have stated that the *abstract* superclass `pbx`, as an aggregate, possesses the *abstract* superclass `card` as a component. This means that no matter how many further descendant classes `pbx` and `card` **specialize-into**, *each object* which **is-a-member-of** class `pbx` (that is, any instance of any concrete descendant of `pbx`) will have *some object* which **is-a-member-of** class `card` (some instance of some concrete descendant of `card`) contained within it.

Using Inheritance and Aggregation Together

Neither an inheritance hierarchy nor an aggregation hierarchy by itself is sufficient to describe the schema of the entire system. They are both required together. The inheritance hierarchy helps us find the parts we need, because it has sorted and categorized them. Once we have found them, the aggregation hierarchy tells us what to do to put them together meaningfully. An inheritance hierarchy is like a hardware store — it has aisles for nails, screws, brackets, two-by-fours, and so on. Without the sorting and categorization provided by the aisles (top-level classes), shelves (intermediate classes) and bins (leaf classes), it would be difficult to find the parts we need. An aggregation hierarchy is like an assembly blueprint — once we have all the parts, it tells us how to put them together.

Part of the confusion between the inheritance and aggregation hierarchies often arises because many descriptions of object-oriented techniques tend to depict the application schema by showing both the connotational **is-a** association and the operational `is-a-part-of` relationship in the same semantic network diagram. This can be confusing

to the uninitiated, as the semantics of the two hierarchies are different. It would be difficult to understand how to construct a complex piece of machinery if the hardware catalog
were part of the same drawing as the assembly blueprint.

In applying specialization theory, we will follow the practice that a graph conveying taxonomy semantics will contain only inheritance associations and a graph conveying
composition semantics will contain only aggregation relationships. Even though we might
draw the two hierarchies together, they will not be mixed in the same graph. Our experience is that adopting the discipline of this custom eliminates much confusion, especially
among persons newly exposed to object-oriented techniques. More importantly, this helps
in the software incarnation of our model, as all graphs in our model are intended not only
for human comprehension but also as a basis for the realization of data structures in the
model information base.

To reinforce the distinction between aggregation and inheritance, in our pictorial
representation we will draw lines of aggregation with a little parabola across them open-
ing toward the component class. Even though we will not draw inheritance and aggregation hierarchies in the same graph, this convention will help distinguish an inheritance
graph from an aggregation graph.

7.4. Use of Aggregation

Aggregation hierarchies need not be concerned only with physical objects; logical objects
may also be composed in aggregation hierarchies. For example, the domain of administrative jurisdiction of a particular network provider, say a `serviceArea` object class,
may be logically broken down into `regionalArea`, `servingArea`, and so on, in
which each `servingArea` could possibly **specialize-into** either a `metropolitan-
StatisticalArea` or a `ruralStatisticalArea`.

Because an aggregate object is itself an individual object class, it has properties
(attributes, functions, and capsules) of its own. There properties are quite different from
the collection of properties of all its component objects. The `pbx` object class, as a whole,
will have attributes such as `numberOfLines` and `numberOfTrunks`, which are not
the same as the attributes of its component `card` objects.

While bearing in mind that both the aggregate and component classes have
properties, the specification of aggregation deals only with complete objects in their entirety. The definition of aggregation is not concerned with individual properties of either
the aggregate or the component objects. The properties of the individual objects involved
in the aggregation are assumed to be defined elsewhere — that is, in the class definitions
and in the inheritance hierarchy.

An aggregate may be defined in terms of other aggregates. The `pbx` object class
might contain `card` as a component, which in turn might contain `port` as a component.
Specialization theory also permits *recursive aggregation*: that is, it is possible to define
an aggregate class which contains itself as a component. We can, if we wish, define a
`network` object to be composed of other `network` objects, or possibly a `circuit`
object to be composed of other `circuit` objects. The decomposition of an aggregate

class may enumerate the same component class several times. Similarly, the same component class might appear in the decomposition of more than one aggregate class.

Exclusive and Inclusive Aggregation

When objects of both the aggregate and component classes are instantiated, two different approaches may be taken. In the first, called *exclusive aggregation*, no sharing of component instances is allowed. This means that each specific component instance can belong to only one aggregate instance. In the second, called *inclusive aggregation*, sharing of component instances is permitted: the *same* component instance may appear in more than one aggregate instance. Specialization theory permits both kinds of aggregations, as long as the nature of each aggregation relationship is identified.

Network systems exhibit both exclusive and inclusive aggregations. For example, when we say that a `hubCard` component is a part of a `wiringHub` aggregate, we intend that no other `wiringHub` object may possess that same `hubCard` component. This is an example of exclusive aggregation. On the other hand, in a distributed document processing application, suppose that a `digitalVideoClip` component object is-a-part-of a `multimediaDocument` aggregate object. This does not prevent the *same* `digitalVideoClip` object from also being a component of a *different* `multimediaDocument` object. This is an example of inclusive aggregation. When modeling inclusive aggregation, we sometimes say that the aggregate object simply `includes` the component object; this suggests that other aggregate objects are not prevented from including the same component. The roles `includes` and `is-included-in` are the same as `has-as-a-part` and `is-a-part-of`, except that they also indicate sharable components. For succinctness, we sometimes simply call an inclusive aggregation relationship an *inclusion* relationship.

Because most aggregation relationships are exclusive, in specialization theory we assume that, unless an aggregation relationship is explicitly specified to be inclusive, no component sharing is permitted. In this book, we will assume that all aggregation relationships we model are by default exclusive; inclusion relationships will be specially identified. Even when an aggregation relationship is exclusive, in Chapter 21 we shall see how its components can be made to appear *as if* they were shared through the definition of *virtual object classes*.

Propagation of Operations

The utility of aggregation as a notion in object-oriented network modeling is twofold. In the realm of network architecture, it acts as a blueprint to construct complex objects out of simpler ones. In the realm of network operations, it acts as a mechanism to perform functions on collections of objects simultaneously — for example, functions whose effects are transmitted from one object to another. Many functions performed on aggregate objects propagate down to their components. For example, if we execute a `powerOff` function on an instance of the class `pbx`, all its component `card` objects are also automatically powered off.

It should be noted, however, that not all the activities performed on an aggregate object affect its component objects. The semantics of the activity dictate whether that activity propagates down to the components. For example, changing a relationship for an instance of `pbx` — say, connecting it to an instance of class `automaticCall-Distributor` — does not imply that all its component `card` objects are also individually connected to the `automaticCallDistributor`.

When conversing about network objects, we sometimes informally speak of attributes of aggregate objects when they are really attributes of component objects. For example, a reference to a "RISC workstation" object really denotes an aggregate `work-station` object which `has-as-a-part` a `motherboard` object which `has-as-a-part` a `cpu` object, whose `architectureType` attribute possesses the value "RISC". Similarly, the "speed of this modem" really means the `speed` attribute of a `port` object component of a `card` object component of a `modem` object.

7.5. Aggregation versus Capsules

In Chapter 4, we introduced the concept of *capsules* to model predefined assemblages of behavior which can be reused in the specification of different objects and which can also be used to model variational behavior between different versions of the same object class.

When specifying objects, it is sometimes a judgment call as to whether collectively occurring assemblages of attributes and properties should be modeled as capsules, or as separate object classes which are contained in other object classes through aggregation. In the example of Chapter 4, we modeled the differences between a `sourceRoutingBridge` and a `transparentBridge` using capsules, rather than component objects. Arguably, we could have modeled that situation with both the `sourceRoutedBridging` and the `transparentBridging` capsules being separate object classes instead. We could have then modeled the bridges, bridge-routers, and hubs as aggregate objects containing one or more of these other object classes.

To assist in making judgments such as these, it should be remembered that capsules are never instantiated, whereas component objects are. Also, a class may contain more than one instance of the same component, whereas it can only contain each capsule once.

In deciding whether or not a particular assemblage of properties ought to be modeled as a capsule or as a separate object class, the following questions need to be asked:

- Does this assemblage of properties truly have a referent in the system model?

- Does this assemblage make sense if it stands alone as an instantiated object, or is it only meaningful as a variation on an existing object class?

- Could the class in which this assemblage belongs contain more than one instance of this assemblage?

- Will such an assemblage commonly be independently addressed by applications? Will external protocols issue requests to execute functions on it? If so, will it be necessary for it to have its own logical identifier?

- Do the semantics of this assemblage represent more than merely a means of putting all its properties in the same wrapper, as a convenient means of reproducing the same properties in another object class?

- Does this assemblage truly have a place in the object inheritance hierarchy? Can it derive from a superclass, and will subclasses derive from it?

If the answer to all these questions is yes, then it probably makes sense to model the assemblage as an object class. If not, it is perhaps better modeled as a capsule.

7.6. Component Multiplicity

A very important concept in the modeling of aggregate objects is the ability to specify exactly how many components are required to compose the aggregate. Sometimes, a minimum number of components is necessary in order to constitute the aggregate object. A `networkedComputer` object must have at least one `networkInterfacePort` object as a component (which may be realized on a component `networkInterface-Card` object, or directly on a component `motherboard` object). A `lanBridge` must have at least two `ports`. In specialization theory, we must specify these quantities precisely. In specifying this number, we are defining the *quantification* of the aggregation.

Aside from quantification, aggregation semantics also need to express *optionality*. A manufacturer may offer a `digitalLoopCarrier` object which may have a `tr-303-Agent` object optionally contained within it. A `wiringHub` may contain zero or more `tokenRingHubCard` objects. In specifying the composition of an aggregate object, we must also be able to specify the optionality of the components.

In specialization theory, we combine the concepts of quantification and optionality to specify the *component multiplicity* of every aggregation. The component multiplicity is a characteristic of every aggregate-component relationship. It allows us to specify the number of components which may be contained in the aggregate. The same aggregate class may have one multiplicity characteristic with one component class and a different multiplicity characteristic with another component class.

Multiplicity Interval

There are many kinds of multiplicity. The most general form of a multiplicity specification sets both a *lower limit*, N, and an *upper limit*, M, for the number of components in the aggregate. Both N and M must be non-negative integers with M greater than or equal to N. If both the limits N and M are specified, we interpret it to mean that every instance of the aggregate class must contain *at least* N and *at most* M instances of the component. This is called the *multiplicity interval* of the decomposition.

There are a number of special cases to be considered with respect to the specification of the multiplicity interval. Consideration of these special cases will provide an appreciation of the power of multiplicity as a specification tool to convey the full semantics of quantification and optionality. If the lower limit N and upper limit M are *equal*, then there is no variation permitted and the aggregate must contain *exactly* N components. If the lower limit N is 0 and the upper limit M is 1, one instance of the component is *op-*

tionally present. If N is 0 and M is greater than 1, we interpret it to mean that the aggregate may contain *zero or more up to* M of the component. If N is finite and non-zero and M is unspecified, we interpret it to mean that the aggregate is to contain *at least* N of the component. Thus, a quantification of "1 or more" may be specified by setting N to 1 and leaving M unspecified. In the complementary situation, if N is unspecified and M is finite and non-zero, we interpret it to mean that the aggregate is to contain *at most* M of the component.

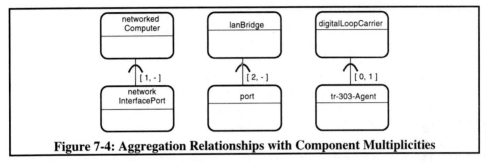

Figure 7-4: Aggregation Relationships with Component Multiplicities

In the pictorial representation of aggregation hierarchies, such as those of Figure 7-4, we represent the multiplicity along the line of aggregation toward the component class. We will adopt the following conventions with respect to the pictorial representation of multiplicity in the aggregation hierarchy:

[N,M]: N and M both specified. *The aggregate must contain at least* N *and at most* M *of the component.*

[N]: Only N specified; assume N = M. *The aggregate must contain exactly* N *of the component.*

[N,-]: N specified, M open-ended. *The aggregate must contain at least* N *of the component.*

[-,M]: N unspecified, M specified. *The aggregate must contain at most* M *of the component.*

[0,1]: Special case of [N,M]. *The component is optional.*

[0,-]: Special case of [N,-]. *The aggregate may contain zero or more of the component.*

[1,-]: Special case of [N,-]. *The aggregate may contain one or more of the component.*

none: None specified. The default is considered to be the case [1]. *The aggregate must contain exactly 1 of the component.*

If the lower bound of any component multiplicity is zero, the component is said to be *optional*; if non-zero, it is said to be *mandatory*. When we specify the syntax for aggregation, we will see how all these different cases of multiplicity may be formally specified with the object model.

7.7. Advanced Component Multiplicity Concepts

Even though the cases above cover a majority of the situations in which we need to specify component multiplicity, they are still not sufficiently complete to convey all the required semantics. Occasionally, we may encounter a situation where multiplicity is specified not in a continuous interval of integers from N to M but as discrete values or jumps; that is, the allowed multiplicity may be an enumerated list of integers.

Discrete Multiplicity Domains

Consider the situation where a telecommunications manufacturer offers a low-end SONET multiplexer with add-drop capability. The purpose of this device is to take an incoming OC-1 signal and drop a VT-1.5 tributary from it. Then it picks up an incoming VT-1.5 tributary and multiplexes it into that part of the synchronous payload envelope just vacated by the dropped tributary and emits the outgoing OC-1 signal. Assume that our hypothetical device functions only in add-drop mode and not in terminal mode. The manufacturer may offer such a device, shown in Figure 7-5, with the capability of dropping and adding 1, 2, 4, or 8 such VT-1.5 signals.

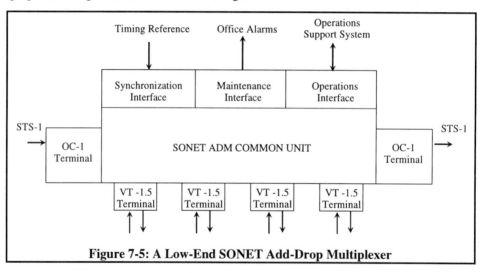

Figure 7-5: A Low-End SONET Add-Drop Multiplexer

In modeling the sonetADM as an aggregate class, we specify it to contain exactly two component sts1Port objects. In addition, for each VT-1.5 tributary added and dropped, it must contain a pair of vt-1dot5-Port objects, one for the dropped tributary and one for the added tributary. This means that it must contain either 2, 4, 8, or 16 vt-1dot5-Port components.

Our multiplicity specifications so far are not powerful enough to specify this situation. If we specify the multiplicity of the vt-1dot5-Port component in the sonetADM aggregate as [2,16], it would imply a continuous interval, and so we could legally have 3 or 7 vt-1dot5-Ports in a sonetADM. This is not true in our actual universe of discourse. We must, therefore, extend our specification to allow a *discrete set of enumerated integers* as a component multiplicity. In the pictorial representation of the hierarchy, we do this by explicitly listing the set of integers as {2,4,8,16}. The change to braces from brackets is necessary to prevent misinterpretation of [2,16] (at least 2 and at most 16) from {2,16} (either exactly 2 or exactly 16).

Attribute-Defined Multiplicity

There is yet another subtle situation in multiplicity specifications. Occasionally, the lower limit N and upper limit M of the component multiplicity are not known as integer constants in advance but need to be inferred algorithmically. The following example will clarify this concept.

Consider the situation of a wiringHub object which has a number of card slots. Each slot can potentially be filled with a card terminating a number of ports to any type of LAN interface. Each of these cards can terminate a number of coaxial Ethernet ports, or twisted-pair Ethernet ports, or unshielded twisted-pair Ethernet ports, or fast Ethernet ports, or FDDI ports, or token-ring ports, or FDDI-on-twisted-pair ports, and so on. Aside from interface cards, it may also be possible to insert function cards in the slots, such as a terminal server card, a bridge card, or a router card. In this case, we might define a generic hubCard object class which **specializes-into** a number of interface-specific card object classes or into a number of function card object classes. We might also specify that the wiringHub object class, as an aggregate, contains the hubCard object class as a component.

It is not a simple matter to specify the multiplicity of this relationship. If we specify it as [1,-] , it means that it could potentially contain an unlimited number of cards, which is not correct. Suppose we know that a particular instance of wiringHub has a maximum of 16 card slots. We could specify the multiplicity of the aggregation as [1,16]. This might be all right for the time being, but if we come across another instance of wiringHub which has 32 slots, we will not be able to accommodate it in our information model without changing the multiplicity specification in the aggregation hierarchy. In fact, we will have to change the specification of the aggregation hierarchy every time we run into a bigger instance of wiringHub.

In actuality, however, even though we might not know the multiplicity of aggregation as an integer constant, we do know that the wiringHub object class has a numberOfCardSlots attribute. For every wiringHub instance in the network, this attribute can have different values. But we know that whatever value it currently has is going to be the upper limit on its component multiplicity. Thus, even though we do not know the upper limit M for each wiringHub as an integer *constant*, we know it in terms of a *variable*: the current value of numberOfCardSlots in that wiringHub. Therefore, we extend our concept of component multiplicity to include the situation where either the lower limit, or the upper limit, or possibly both are defined in terms of the *value of an attribute in the aggregate class*. Figure 7-6 demonstrates an example of specifying a component multiplicity using such an attribute. We call such a specification an *attribute-defined expression*.

In the general case, the limit may not be equal to the value but could bear some other mathematical relation. Most generally, either limit may be some mathematical

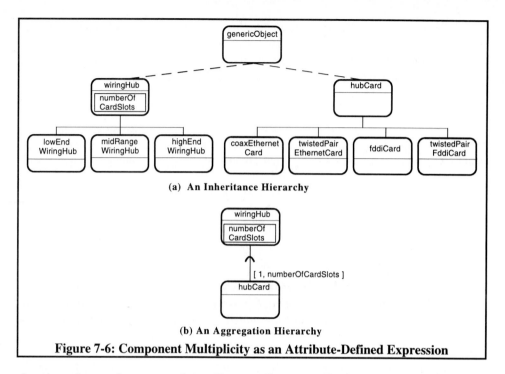

(a) **An Inheritance Hierarchy**

(b) **An Aggregation Hierarchy**

Figure 7-6: Component Multiplicity as an Attribute-Defined Expression

function of *more than one* attribute. Since reading an attribute value is conceptually no different from requesting the return result of a function, the limit may even depend on the *return result of a function* of the aggregate class. It may even depend on attribute values of other components objects contained within the object class. For example, the upper limit for multiplicity of the file object class contained within the unixFileServer object class could bear some relation to the numberOfInodes attribute of each of its fileSystem object components [Vaha93]. In most cases, the multiplicity of the component class will bear some simple relation to some *capacity-related* attribute of the aggregate class.

The ability to use aggregate object attribute values to specify component multiplicity also makes other specifications easier. In Figure 7-5, we specified the multiplicity of the vt-1dot5-Port object class in the sonetADM object class as {2,4,8,16}. For a higher-end product — say a sonetCrossConnect operating at an STS-3 signal rate — it would be impractical to specify the multiplicity as {2,4,8,16,32,64,...} which, although finite, could be very large set of enumerated integer values. We might remember, however, in modeling the sonetCross-Connect object class, we may have specified a numberOfVt-1dot5-Drops attribute. Since the domain of an attribute can be specified to take on any one of a finite set of enumerated values, we specify this attribute to contain values from the domain {1,2,4,8,...}. Now, all we have to do in the aggregation hierarchy is to specify the component multiplicity as the mathematical function {2 × numberOfVt-1dot5-Drops}.

Therefore, we extend our allowable multiplicity specifications to include the following cases:

{a,b,c,...}: *Finite set of enumerated integer constants.* The aggregate must contain a number of components which is exactly one of the numbers in the set.

{attribute-defined expression}: *Finite set of enumerated integer variables.* The aggregate must contain a number of components which is exactly one of the constants generated by plugging in the current value of the specified attribute(s) in the specified expression.

[N,attribute-defined expression]: *Upper limit attribute-defined.* The aggregate must contain a number of components which is at least N and at most the constant generated by plugging in the current value of the specified attribute(s) in the specified expression.

[attribute-defined expression,M]: *Lower limit attribute-defined.* The aggregate must contain a number of components which is at least the constant generated by plugging in the current value of the specified attribute(s) in the specified expression and at most M.

[attribute-defined expression, attribute-defined expression]: *Both limits attribute-defined.* The specified attribute(s) must be plugged into the specified expressions to obtain both the lower and upper limits of component multiplicity.

Attribute-defined expressions are based on Knuth's *attribute grammars* [Knut68]. In general, an attribute-defined expression expands according to a simple grammar allowing mathematical and logical operations on attributes. The terminal symbols of this grammar are other attributes which are required as input for the evaluation of the expression.

Although we will use the term *attribute-defined expression* throughout this book, it should be borne in mind that, generally, any element of this expression could just as well be the return result of a function instead of an attribute. If the expression involves arithmetic operators, it could use single-valued attributes or functions; if it involves set operators, it could use set-valued attributes or functions. As we have said before, reading the value of an attribute is conceptually no different from requesting the return value of a function. Because both attributes and functions could be involved in an attribute-defined expression, the term *property-defined expression* would perhaps be more appropriate. Nevertheless, we will continue to use the term *attribute-defined expression* for historical continuity, bearing in mind that function results may also be involved.

Experience has shown that using attribute-defined expressions is actually the most general and most satisfactory way of specifying multiplicity. If the aggregate class has been specified correctly, it is usually possible to select one its capacity-related attributes to specify component multiplicity. In every multiplicity specification where the network model seems to require a non-trivial integer constant for a limit, we encourage the architect to look closely for any capacity-related attribute of the aggregate class and examine it for possible use in an attribute-defined expression for the component multiplicity.

With these techniques to specify multiplicity, we now have a sufficiently powerful expressive mechanism to convey all the semantics we will encounter in formally specifying the aggregation hierarchy.

7.8. Aggregation Principles

We have said that aggregation and inheritance are different because they convey entirely different semantics. The two notions do, however, interact. In this section, we consider the modes of interaction between aggregation and inheritance. Much of the material presented below as formal concepts may already be intuitively obvious.

Both an aggregate class and its component classes have a place in the inheritance hierarchy. Therefore, each can **specialize-into** a number of descendant classes. In Figure 7-6, an instance of the `wiringHub` object class `has-as-a-part` a number of instances of the `hubCard` object class. The `hubCard` class, however, may be abstract and may itself never be instantiated. The `hubCard` **specializes-into** the concrete classes `coaxEthernetCard`, `twistedPairEthernetCard`, `fddiCard`, `twisted-PairFddiCard`, and so on. Because each of these subclasses **specializes-from** `hubCard`, it is possible that it also `is-a-part-of` the `wiringHub` object class. This is permitted in specialization theory, in spite of the fact that we have never directly specified an aggregation relationship between `wiringHub` and these concrete classes. In short, we can say that the descendants of the component `hubCard` object class have *inherited* its composition relationship with the aggregate `wiringHub` object class.

By the reverse token, the `wiringHub` class itself may never be instantiated but may **specialize-into** a number of descendant classes. We may wish to use these specializations in our model to make distinctions among different kinds of `wiringHubs`, say `lowEndWiringHub`, `midRangeWiringHub`, and `highEndWiringHub`, possibly using as a basis of specialization either its `numberOfCardSlots` attribute, its `pricePerPort` attribute, or anything else. In any event, because we have specified that the abstract superclass `wiringHub` `has-as-a-part` the class `hubCard`, it implies that each of the classes `lowEndWiringHub`, `midRangeWiringHub`, and `highEndWiringHub` also `has-as-a-part` the class `hubCard`. In other words, the descendants of the aggregate `wiringHub` object class have *inherited* its decomposition relationship with the component `hubCard` object classes.

We formalize these notions below as the *aggregation principles* of specialization theory. These principles are called *composition inheritance* and *decomposition inheritance*:

Aggregation Principle:	*A descendant of a component class inherits the composition relationship of an ancestral class with the aggregate class* (***Composition Inheritance***).
	A descendant of an aggregate class inherits the decomposition relationship of an ancestral class with the component class (***Decomposition Inheritance***).

Composition inheritance equivalently states that if an object class is-a-part-of an aggregate class, then each of its descendants also is-a-part-of the same aggregate class. Decomposition inheritance states that if an object class has-as-a-part a component class, then each of its descendants also has-as-a-part the same component class.

Looking at these principles from the inheritance viewpoint, the principles above state that descendant classes inherit the is-a-part-of and has-as-a-part relationships of an object. If an object anywhere in the inheritance hierarchy appears as either an aggregate or a component in the aggregation hierarchy, then *all its descendants in the inheritance hierarchy inherit its composition and decomposition relationships from the aggregation hierarchy*.

The principle of monotonic inheritance continues to be at work here. Recall that in specialization theory it is forbidden for a class to drop or cancel the behavior inherited from an ancestral class. This applies to composition and decomposition inheritance as well. For example, a descendant of wiringHub cannot decide that it does not wish to have any component hubCards.

Subclasses of aggregate classes not only inherit the decomposition relationships of a superclass, but they inherit its *component multiplicity* as well. We therefore get the aggregation principles of *monotonic aggregation inheritance* and *component multiplicity inheritance*:

Aggregation Principle:	*A descendant class may not cancel any composition or decomposition relationship defined for an ancestral class* (***Monotonic Aggregation Inheritance***).

Aggregation Principle:	*A descendant of an aggregate class inherits by default the component multiplicity of each decomposition relationship inherited from an ancestral class, which it may modify in permissible ways* (***Component Multiplicity Inheritance***).

Monotonic aggregation inheritance requires a class to participate in all the decomposition relationships that its ancestors do, with the same component classes. It also requires the class to participate in all the composition relationships that its ancestors do, with the same aggregate classes. Component multiplicity inheritance states that when an aggregate class specializes, each subclass of the aggregate `has-as-a-part` the same component class that its superclass had, with the same component multiplicity by default. In a later section, we will study the permissible ways in which subclasses are permitted to modify this inherited multiplicity.

It is also important to note what component multiplicity inheritance does *not* say: it does not say that, when a *component* class specializes, each subclass of the component is contained in the aggregate with the same multiplicity that the component superclass was. This in fact is not the case. The issue of what happens to the component multiplicity between an aggregate and a *subclass* of a component is somewhat complex, and we will revisit it after we study more advanced modeling principles in Chapter 17. For the time being, we will maintain that when a component class specializes, although its subclasses may be contained in the aggregate, the multiplicity with which they are contained in the aggregate is *undefined*.

Figure 7-7 explicitly demonstrates some of the additional aggregation hierarchies implied by Figure 7-6 through composition and decomposition inheritance. In specifying an actual network model, one does not have to specify these additional hierarchies explicitly; they are inferred as implicit hierarchies from those of Figure 7-6 during the compilation of the formal specification of the model.

7.9. Component and Aggregate Addition

We have said that subclasses **specialize-from** superclasses by addition, expansion, and restriction of inherited properties. It is, in fact, possible for subclasses to specialize using aggregation relationships as well. There are three important ways in which an aggregation relationship may be used for specialization, involving, respectively, the presence of new component subclasses, the component multiplicity of the aggregation, and the descendant classes of the aggregate and the component.

As we have stated, all aggregation relationships of a superclass are inherited by its subclasses. An aggregate subclass is required to participate in all the decomposition relationships of its ancestors. This does not mean that instances of the subclass are required to possess all the component instances which may be contained in the instances of its concrete superclasses. An aggregate superclass may specify an aggregation relationship with a component multiplicity of $[0,-]$. When an aggregate subclass inherits that relationship, it continues by default to have the same component multiplicity. This means the component remains optional in the aggregate subclass. An instance of the aggregate superclass could contain one instance of this optional component, while an instance of the subclass may not. As long as the aggregate subclass continues to participate in the aggregation relationship (that is, its instances could *potentially* contain the component objects) it does not violate any of our principles.

An aggregate subclass is also permitted to contain *more* component classes than its ancestral aggregate classes. This is consistent with our guideline that the functionality of an object class becomes richer and more detailed as we proceed down the inheritance

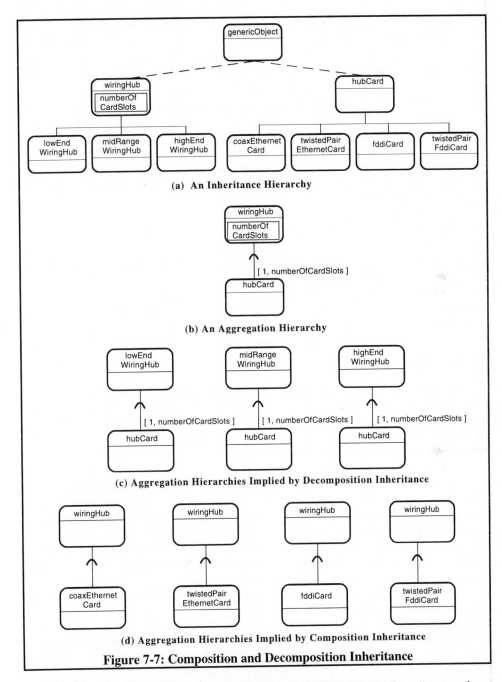

(a) An Inheritance Hierarchy

(b) An Aggregation Hierarchy

(c) Aggregation Hierarchies Implied by Decomposition Inheritance

(d) Aggregation Hierarchies Implied by Composition Inheritance

Figure 7-7: Composition and Decomposition Inheritance

hierarchy. In addition to all the decomposition relationships it inherits from its superclass, an aggregate subclass may define new decomposition relationships to add more component classes. Instances of the aggregate subclass may contain components which instances of its concrete ancestral aggregate classes do not.

Some aggregate subclasses may use the fact that they add new component classes as a basis of specialization. This is known as *Specialization by Component Addition*. This implies that the distinguishing characteristic of the subclass is that it contains more component classes (that is, participates in additional decomposition relationships) than its superclass does.

By the same token, it is permissible for the descendant of a component class to add a new aggregate. Depending on the functionality the descendant class adds, instances of a specialized component class could participate in composition relationships with more aggregates than instances of its concrete ancestral component classes. This is known as *Specialization by Aggregate Addition*.

There is, however, an important restriction: the new component classes specified in the aggregate subclass in its new decomposition relationships *cannot be the same component classes from its inherited relationships, or any of their ancestors*. This means that the new decomposition relationship which the subclass adds cannot involve a component class with which it *already* participates in an decomposition relationship. Nor can it be an *ancestor* of an existing component class. It must add a "brand-new" component class. If we permitted an aggregate subclass to define a new decomposition relationship with an existing component class (or an ancestor of an existing component class), in effect we would be permitting subclasses to arbitrarily redefine existing aggregation relationships, possibly changing multiplicities. This would violate our principles of monotonic inheritance.

Similarly, if a component class undergoes specialization, it cannot use its ability to add new composition relationships to redefine its composition relationship with an existing aggregate class, or an ancestor thereof. (Descendants of both aggregate and component classes may participate in aggregation relationship with the *descendants* of existing components or aggregates subject to certain rules, as we shall see shortly.)

We said earlier that a component of a component is also a component. This allows us to extend this principle of component addition slightly: a subclass is permitted to specialize from an aggregate superclass using component addition even if one of its *components* undergoes component addition. In other words, the new decomposition relationship need not be defined directly on the specializing subclass; it could be defined on one of its component classes. The same restriction holds: the component undergoing component addition must add a "new" component and cannot redefine any decomposition relationship it may already have with one of *its* existing components.

In specialization theory, these notions are formalized as the specialization principles of *component addition* and *aggregate addition*:

Specialization Principle:	*A descendant class may add a decomposition relationship with a new component class (**Component Addition**).*

> ***Specialization Principle:***   *A descendant class may add a composition relationship with a new aggregate class (Aggregate Addition).*

7.10. Component Multiplicity Restriction

According to the principle of component multiplicity inheritance, a subclass of an aggregate class inherits the same component multiplicity by default. It is not bound, however, to accept this default behavior. There are permissible ways for an aggregate subclass to modify the component multiplicity of an inherited decomposition relationship. Specifically, the subclass is permitted to *restrict* the inherited component multiplicity.

As a prelude to explaining why this is so, recall that we said a subclass may restrict the domain of an inherited attribute. We also said that a component multiplicity may be defined in terms of an attribute-defined expression. If the attribute used to define the component multiplicity for a particular has-as-a-part relationship in an aggregate superclass gets domain-restricted during inheritance by an aggregate subclass, it would follow that the component multiplicity in the has-as-a-part relationship inherited by subclass would have a restricted multiplicity. This is entirely reasonable and is in fact what happens.

Consider again the wiringHub object class which has-as-a-part the hub-Card object class. The multiplicity on this decomposition relationship is [1, number-OfCardSlots], where numberOfCardSlots is an attribute of the wiringHub object class. Suppose that the lowEndWiringHub subclass always has a fixed, preconfigured number — say 4 — hubCards in it. In every instance of lowEndWiringHub, exactly 4 card slots are filled. Because lowEndWiringHub **specializes-from** wiringHub, it inherits the decomposition relationship with hubCard. However, the distinguishing characteristic of lowEndWiringHub is that it has now restricted the domain of the component multiplicity from [1, numberOfCardSlots] to exactly [4]. This is shown in Figure 7-8.

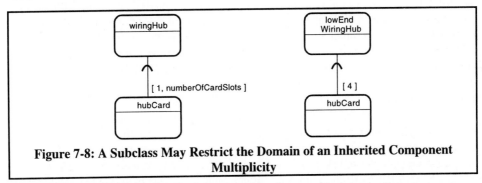

Figure 7-8: A Subclass May Restrict the Domain of an Inherited Component Multiplicity

It is, in fact, possible to use domain restriction on component multiplicity as a basis of specialization, in which case it is called *Specialization by Component Multiplicity*

Restriction. We may specify that various aggregate subclasses be created using different restrictions on the component multiplicity of a decomposition relationship of the aggregate superclass; these differences act as the distinguishing factor between the subclasses.

The domain restriction does not apply only to multiplicities with attribute-defined expressions in them; it could apply to multiplicities with constants in them as well. Consider the situation of a networked UNIX file server whose purpose is to store files for a number of networked diskless client workstations. Because its clients are diskless, all user directories are stored on the file server. The `unixFileServer` object class may have a decomposition relationship with the `userHomeDirectory` object class. The multiplicity of this decomposition may be specified as zero or more, that is, `[0,-]`.

After market segmentation analysis, the manufacturer of this product may now wish to release two different versions, a low-end product for 100 users or less and a high-end product for more than 100 users. It is now possible to subclass from `unixFileServer` and use as the basis of specialization the fact that the domain of the component multiplicity has been restricted. The class `smallUnixFileServer` could narrow the domain of its component multiplicity with `userHomeDirectory` from `[0,-]` to `[0,100]`, while the class `bigUnixFileServer` may maintain it at `[0,-]`. In fact, it may not be necessary to create a `bigUnixFileServer` subclass at all, unless there are other extensions and refinements which make it necessary to do so.

Confusion occasionally surrounds the notion of component multiplicity restriction in subclasses. A counter argument that is sometimes proposed goes as follows: "If I have a chassis in which I can insert 16 function cards and I build a bigger chassis in which I can now insert 32 cards, surely I can subclass my new box from my old one on the basis of component addition. But the multiplicity of decomposing my `chassis` object class into the `card` object class has been expanded from `[1,16]` to `[1,32]`. Does this not violate the principle that subclasses may only restrict the component multiplicity?"

This argument is specious, because the ability to add more *instances* of an existing component class does not constitute component addition. The specialization principle of component addition requires that a brand-new *class* be added as a component. Furthermore, the component multiplicity for the old chassis should never have been specified as `[1,16]` in the first place. As we said earlier, any time we need to specify either limit as a non-trivial integer constant, we should look hard to replace it using a capacity-related attribute in an attribute-defined expression. In this instance, the component multiplicity of the component `card` object class in the aggregate `chassis` object class should have been specified as `[1,numberOfCardSlots]`. Since our new box has a different value for `numberOfCardSlots`, the same specification for the domain of component multiplicity also works for the new box.

In fact, the new box can be just be another instance of the same object class; it is not necessary to create a new subclass simply to accommodate a chassis with 32 slots in our model, unless there are other reasons for doing so. If there are other reasons for doing so, it might be simpler to use as a basis of specialization the `numberOfCardSlots` as a regular inherited superclass attribute, rather than in an attribute-defined multiplicity expression. By using attribute domain restriction for the inherited `numberOfCard-`

Slots attribute, possibly from [1,-] to [1,32], we can create a subclass for the new box.

Even if the multiplicity were not specified in terms of attributes but in hard constants, it would have been incorrect to specify the component multiplicity of the chassis superclass as [1,16]. This would mean that no chassis is permitted to contain more than 16 cards, making it impossible to create a subclass of chassis which contained 32 without modifying the information model. For numerically specified component multiplicities, the upper bound for the component multiplicity in any superclass must take into account the upper bounds which will be used in all its subclasses. It is generally safer to specify component multiplicities in terms attributes of the aggregate.

For the same reason, our earlier example of a unixFileServer could be reinterpreted as simply specialization by attribute domain restriction rather than by multiplicity domain restriction. We could have specified the capacity attribute maxUsers for unixFileServer, which might have an unrestricted domain in the superclass. If the component multiplicity with userHomeDirectory is specified as [0,maxUsers], there is effectively no upper bound for the multiplicity since there is no upper bound on the value of attribute maxUsers. The subclass smallUnixFileServer could now restrict the domain of maxUsers to just the single value 100. This would mean that its component multiplicity, whose inherited definition is still [0,maxUsers], now effectively becomes [0,100]. By performing attribute domain restriction, the subclass smallUnixFileServer has *effectively* performed component multiplicity restriction, without explicitly invoking the component multiplicity restriction mechanism.

It is often the case that specialization by multiplicity domain restriction and specialization by attribute domain restriction can be interpreted interchangeably. Because multiplicity domains are often defined in terms of attributes, in many situations the model compiler analyzing the formal specification of the model may treat the two identically. In either case, the domain restriction — whether specified directly on an attribute or on a component multiplicity defined in terms of an attribute — is viewed by the compiler as a constraint which must be enforced in the subclass of the aggregate.

In specialization theory, we formalize this notion as the specialization principle of *component multiplicity restriction*:

Specialization Principle:	*A descendant class may restrict the multiplicity domain of a decomposition relationship inherited from an ancestral class (**Component Multiplicity Restriction**).*

Component multiplicity restriction also allows us to turn *optional* components into *mandatory* ones. Suppose an older-generation digitalLoopCarrier product is offered with the optional feature of having a resident tr-303-Agent [TR 57, TR 303, SR 2344]. (Note that this is an optional *component*, not an optional *capsule*, and so must be modeled as a decomposition relationship between two object classes, not as a property assignment.) In our model, the component multiplicity of the digitalLoopCarrier object class into its component tr-303-Agent object class will be [0,1].

Suppose that in the next generation of loop carriers, the manufacturer wants to turn the optional `tr-303-Agent` into a standard feature. If we create a subclass for the next-generation product, the component multiplicity for the component `tr-303-Agent` must now be narrowed from `[0,1]` to just `[1]`. This is illustrated in Figure 7-9. By specifying this new restricted domain for the component multiplicity, we can specify in our model that the optional component has now been standardized. This is analogous to specialization by capsule fixing, with the difference that we are now fixing a component class rather than the property assemblage represented by a capsule.

It is important to note that a subclass of an aggregate can only restrict the inherited component multiplicity domain, not expand it. An important consequence of this is that subclasses of an aggregate class do not have the ability to turn mandatory components into optional ones. If an aggregate class specifies the component multiplicity of a particular component class as `[1,-]`, meaning that every instance must contain at least one instance of the component, subclasses of the aggregate are not permitted to respecify the component multiplicity for the same component as `[0]`, `[0,1]` or `[0,-]`, that is, they are not permitted to make that component optional. Component multiplicity domains in the aggregate subclass with one or both endpoints being `[0]` are not subsets of the inherited domain of `[1,-]`, and hence do not represent a restriction of component multiplicity; such respecification of the domain is not permitted going down the inheritance hierarchy.

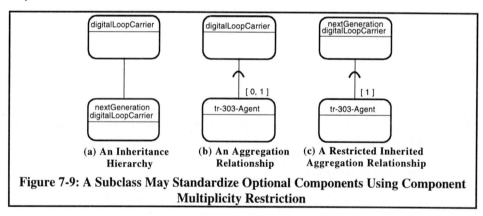

(a) An Inheritance
Hierarchy

(b) An Aggregation
Relationship

(c) A Restricted Inherited
Aggregation Relationship

**Figure 7-9: A Subclass May Standardize Optional Components Using Component
Multiplicity Restriction**

In addition, if any aggregation relationship has an optional component, it is possible for some subclass of the aggregate to choose not to contain any component at all. If the component multiplicity is `[0,-]`, then some subclass of the aggregate may legally use component multiplicity restriction to narrow this domain to `[0,0]`. This is a valid multiplicity restriction and is known as a *degenerate aggregation*. Degenerate aggregation does not violate monotonic inheritance because it uses a valid specialization mode. Because 0 was a valid value in the component multiplicity domain for the aggregate superclass, some members of the aggregate superclass were permitted not to contain any component objects. If we collect all such members in a subset, that subset can now be a subclass. Note that it is not possible for an aggregate subclass to turn an inherited aggregation relationship with a *mandatory* (i.e., at least one) component into a degenerate aggregation, because this would not be a legal domain restriction.

Based on our new knowledge of the behavior of component multiplicity under inheritance, we restate the aggregation principle of *component multiplicity inheritance* in a more refined form, as follows:

> **Aggregation Principle:** *A descendant of an aggregate class inherits by default the component multiplicity of each decomposition relationship inherited from an ancestral class, which it may restrict (**Component Multiplicity Inheritance**).*

7.11. Component and Aggregate Specialization

Aside from restricting component multiplicity, there is another way in which subclasses of aggregate objects affect their component objects. The component class contained in an aggregate may itself be an ancestor of many other descendant classes that it eventually **specializes-into**. This can also be true of the containing aggregate class. When the aggregate class **specializes-into** its subclasses, the *aggregate's descendants* can select which of the *component's descendants* they will contain.

Consider the example of a `router` object class which contains, as a software component, a `routingProtocolEntity` object class. The `router` object class may itself **specialize-into**, say, the `ipRouter`, `clnpRouter`, and `appnNetworkNode` object classes, while the `routingProtocolEntity` may **specialize-into** the `ospfProtocolEntity`, `isisProtocolEntity`, and `isrProtocolEntity` object classes. Each type of `routingProtocolEntity` is largely suited to routing a particular network-level protocol; the Open Shortest Path First (OSPF) protocol routes IP datagrams, the Intermediate-System-to-Intermediate-System (IS-IS) protocol routes CLNP PDUs, while the Intermediate Session Routing (ISR) protocol routes APPN packets.

Because of composition inheritance, each one of `router`'s descendant classes also `has-as-a-part` the `routingProtocolEntity` object class. However, the `router`'s descendants may specify which one of `routingProtocolEntity`'s *descendants* they will choose to contain. The `ipRouter` object class, for example, may choose as its component just the `ospfProtocolEntity` descendant, the `clnpRouter` may choose as its component just the `isisProtocolEntity`, while the `appnNetworkNode` may choose as its component just the `isrProtocolEntity`.

Recall that the aggregation principle of composition inheritance states that a *descendant* of an aggregate class `has-as-a-part` the same component class that the ancestral aggregate class has. If this component class itself specializes into subclasses, and if this specialization is complete, then each member of the component class is also a member of at least one of its subclasses. Thus, the descendant of the aggregate now `has-as-a-part` at least one *descendant* of the component. Not all descendants of the component may be useful to a given descendant of the aggregate; in fact, some descendants of the component may never be used as parts by the given descendant of the aggregate.

In specialization theory, this fact can indeed be used as a basis of specialization: it is called *Specialization by Component Specialization*. In effect, the *specialized aggregate is considered a specialized aggregate because it can only contain certain specialized components*.

This leads to the specialization principle of *component specialization*:

Specialization Principle:	*A descendant of an aggregate class may restrict an inherited decomposition relationship to selected descendants of the component class* ***(Component Specialization).***

A little reflection will indicate the similarity between specialization by component specialization and specialization by attribute domain restriction. If the component object had not been broken out as a separate object class, its properties would have been internalized by the aggregate class. Then, when the aggregate class **specializes-into** its descendants, these internalized properties would have undergone the same domain restrictions as they do when the component class specializes into its descendants.

Because a component of a component is also a component, this principle may be applied even when the component undergoing specialization for the aggregate subclass is not an immediate component but recursively is-a-part-of the aggregate.

By the same token, a component class may **specialize-into** a number of descendants, each one of which might be so specialized that it will not work in all descendants of the aggregate class. Rather, a component's descendants may properly work selectively in only certain descendants of the aggregate. By further categorizing the aggregate class itself into subclasses, we can identify which of the aggregate's descendants the component's specialized descendants can work in. This is called *Specialization by Aggregate Specialization*. In effect, *the specialized component is considered a specialized component because it can only work in certain specialized aggregates*.

This leads us to the specialization principle of *aggregate specialization*:

Specialization Principle:	*A descendant of a component class may restrict an inherited composition relationship to selected descendants of the aggregate class* ***(Aggregate Specialization).***

In other words, because an aggregate may specialize by having-as-a-part only certain subclasses of its component, we do not require that *all* subclasses of the component bear a composition relationship with *all* subclasses of the aggregate. If the aggregate is abstract (that is, has only subclasses, not instances), subclasses of the component satisfy composition inheritance as long as *each* is-a-part-of *some* subclass of the aggregate (or of the aggregate class itself). Symmetrically, if the component is abstract, subclasses of the aggregate satisfy decomposition inheritance as long as *each* has-as-a-part *some* subclass of the component (or of the component class itself).

Figure 7-10 describes some hierarchies for a router object; Figure 7-11 indicates the additional hierarchies implied by Figure 7-10 through component specialization and aggregate specialization.

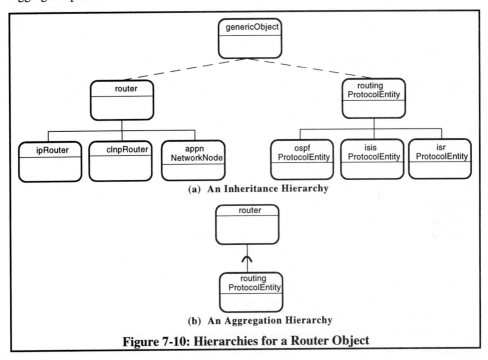

Figure 7-10: Hierarchies for a Router Object

Notice that all these specialization principles continue to refine and extend our notion of specialization as addition, expansion, and restriction, and the precept that an inheritance hierarchy assists in defining taxonomies because subclasses are "described in greater detail, narrowed down for specific focus, but expanded for richer function."

Based on our knowledge of these modes of specialization, we state the additional aggregation principles of *specialized component inheritance* and *specialized aggregate inheritance*:

Aggregation Principle:	*A descendant of an aggregate class* has-as- a-part *at least one descendant of a mandatory component class, if any specialization of the component class is complete (**Specialized Component Inheritance**).*

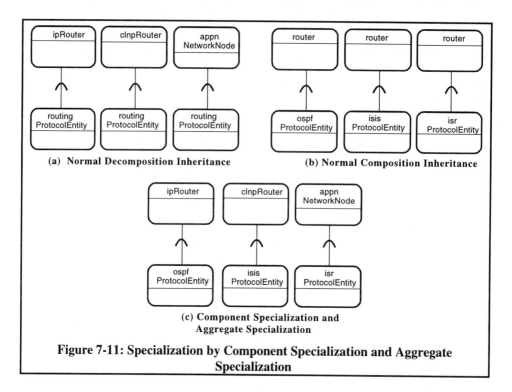

(a) **Normal Decomposition Inheritance**   (b) **Normal Composition Inheritance**

(c) **Component Specialization and
Aggregate Specialization**

**Figure 7-11: Specialization by Component Specialization and Aggregate
Specialization**

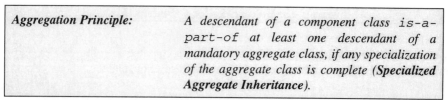

Aggregation Principle:	*A descendant of a component class* `is-a-part-of` *at least one descendant of a mandatory aggregate class, if any specialization of the aggregate class is complete (**Specialized Aggregate Inheritance**).*

The validity of specialized component inheritance can be explained in terms of instances. Since subclasses of an aggregate class inherit its decomposition relationship with the component class, every member of an aggregate *subclass* `has-as-a-part` some member of any component class which is mandatory. However, if the component class itself **specializes-into** subclasses and this specialization is complete, then every member of the component class is also a member of at least one component *subclass*. Thus, every member of the aggregate *subclass* `has-as-a-part` at least one member of a component *subclass*. We do not require that every aggregate subclass `have-as-a-part` *every* component subclass; decomposition inheritance is satisfied as long as there is at least *one*. (If the component class is optional, some aggregate subclasses might degenerate this inherited aggregation relationship, and so specialized component inheritance does not apply.) A symmetrical argument justifies specialized aggregate inheritance.

If the specialization of the component class is *not* complete, then some members of the component class might belong to none of its subclasses. As we indicated in Chapter 6, incomplete specialization leaves "holes" in the domain of the basis attribute of specialization. A member of the component may have a value for this attribute which places it in one of these holes, thus making it an instance of the component class itself, not any of its subclasses. In this case, the subclass of the aggregate which this instance `is-a-part-of` continues to enjoy its inherited decomposition relationship with the component class itself and not with any of its subclasses. The applicable aggregation principle is decomposition inheritance, not specialized component inheritance.

All of these specialization and aggregation principles help us to model the interaction of the connotational **specializes-from** and **specializes-into** associations with the operational `is-a-part-of` and `has-as-a-part` relationships, as they are defined in specialization theory. Some of these principles may seem intuitively obvious because of the commonly accepted connotations of the phrase "is a" in ordinary language. In specialization theory, however, the term **is-a** is not encouraged; we use the more sharply defined terms **specializes-from** and **specializes-into**, which, as explained in Chapter 5, have a very narrow and specific meaning implying substitutability. To implement such semantics in a machine-based algorithm which will help us to automate the tasks of network architecture, planning, and synthesis, we need to formally state all of the above principles so that they can be unambiguously programmed.

7.12. Aggregation for Naming and Addressing

The configuration of object instances as dictated by an aggregation hierarchy is sometimes used for assigning logical names and addresses. This is a convenient practice as it allows object instances to be addressed via the aggregate instances they are contained in, which in turn can be addressed via their aggregates, and so on.

Recall that an aggregation hierarchy is a specification on object classes and not on object instances. It specifies which object *classes* can *potentially* be contained in other object *classes*. It does not identify, in any given realization of a network, which object *instances* actually *are* contained in which other *instances*.

Some modeling methodologies allow an aggregate object to address a component object using a name which uniquely identifies the component among other components. Such a name is often an attribute of the component object and is called the *naming attribute*. As part of the model which specifies the aggregation, the methodology also specifies the naming attribute which will be used to uniquely identify the component object.

The issue of unambiguously addressing an object with a name is an extremely important one. In any given network realization, when information about object models and network schemas is dynamically exchanged among networks, it is necessary that they be able to logically identify individual object instances — for example, as arguments to functions. Thus, protocols exchanging autoconfiguration and interoperability information between two switches, for example, need to accommodate fields for carrying unambiguous references to the components of each switch.

Even though this aspect is important, we will not attack in this book the problem of naming and addressing of instances as an issue of modeling methodology. A network implementation using a specialization theory model may use any naming scheme which is convenient. This may include network-layer addresses, assigned global names, locally defined naming conventions, table lookups, or any of the schemes used by many networking standards. The issue of creating a logical naming scheme and the issue of modeling composition relationships are not necessarily linked; it is possible to create different structures for each.

7.13. Summary

The notion of aggregation is an abstraction which allows us to construct complex objects out of simpler objects. Aggregation relationships between object classes are either the composition relationship (is-a-part-of) or the decomposition relationship (has-as-a-part). Aggregation relationships may be graphed in an aggregation hierarchy. By applying operations to an aggregate object, we can sometimes manipulate all its component objects simultaneously.

The number of component instances which may be contained in an aggregate instance is known as the component multiplicity. The component multiplicity is specified as a domain consisting of an upper limit and a lower limit, or as an enumerated set of values. These values may be constants or variable expressions involving some capacity-related attribute of the aggregate class.

Aggregation and inheritance are semantically different concepts. Nevertheless, they do interact. A subclass inherits all the aggregation relationships from a superclass. Because of monotonic inheritance, a subclass may not cancel inherited aggregation relationships. It may, however, restrict inherited component multiplicities and may use such restriction as a basis of specialization. An aggregate subclass may restrict the components it contains to only certain subclasses of the component. A component subclass may restrict the aggregates it can be contained in to only certain subclasses of the aggregate. Such restrictions may be used as the basis of specialization.

8. Object-Oriented Architecture of a Nodal Processor

"No, those are not our flight routes. That is our network connectivity map."
— *anonymous network manager of airline corporate network.*

8.1. Introduction

In this chapter we demonstrate the practical use of many of the object-oriented concepts we have developed so far by applying the principles of inheritance and aggregation together in a complete example. We architect a *nodal processor*, a device which allows many different kinds of premises LAN traffic to be transported over a variety of WAN transport mechanisms. Many products similar to this nodal processor exist today, each performing some functions similar to those described in this chapter. Our focus will be to analyze the specification and requirements of the nodal processor and its possible options and show how practitioners can use object-oriented concepts to model the architecture of such devices.

8.2. Requirements for the Nodal Processor

Our charter is to build a nodal processor whose purpose is to act as a complete premises controller: it is to be a funneling point for many of the varieties of LAN traffic commonly found in a corporate campus environment [Mier91], and it must connect this traffic to a wide-area network provided by a telecommunications carrier. This product will be marketed to corporate end-users as customer premises equipment for concentration and distribution of data traffic at different corporate sites. A wide-area network of such nodal processors can be deployed by a corporate customer having locations in different geographical areas, connected together using lines and services provided by a WAN service provider.

The box we are required to build must have a flexible architecture so that it is potentially multipurpose [Lipp91]. It must be configurable to connect with whatever types of LAN interfaces are currently being used by the customer, of which there could be several. Also, it must be configurable to connect with whatever types of WAN interfaces are contracted for by the customer from its telecommunications provider, of which again there could be several.

In addition to just providing LAN-to-WAN access, the nodal processor must also be able to provide additional functions, both routine and intelligent. These will include local network segmentation, local bridging, remote bridging, and routing capabilities. Because it interfaces LANs to a provider's digital WAN circuits, it also serves as a demarcation point to the carrier network and must perform functions analogous to a CSU. Finally, the nodal processor needs to be network-managed.

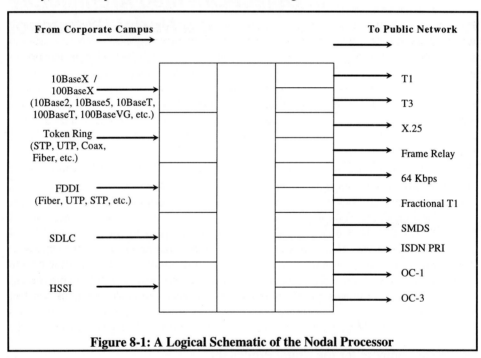

Figure 8-1: A Logical Schematic of the Nodal Processor

Figure 8-1 shows a logical schematic for the nodal processor. The product is required to support some typical interfaces to campus LANs, Front-End Processors, and LAN interconnection devices. The interfaces include, but are not limited to

- Ethernet and Fast Ethernet (10Base2, 10Base5, 10BaseT, 10BaseF, 100BaseT, and 100BaseVG interfaces)

- FDDI (Various grades of multimode fiber, STP, UTP)

- Token Ring (UTP, STP, Fiber, Coax)
- SDLC
- High-Speed Serial Interface (HSSI)

In each of these cases, we need to support standard media connection interfaces where they make sense, for example, RJ-45, DB-9, RS-232, and RS-449. Typical WAN interfaces on the nodal processor must include, but need not be limited to, the following:

• T-1	• T-3
• X.25	• Frame Relay
• 64 kbps	• Fractional T-1
• SMDS	• ISDN Primary Rate
• OC-1	• OC-3

All the LAN interfaces and all the WAN interfaces will not be present in every instance of the nodal processor. Each instance of the nodal processor will be configured with the appropriate interfaces depending on customer requirements. WAN interfaces such as T-1 and T-3 must be capable of operating in either point-to-point or networked mode.

A network of premises-based nodal processors can be deployed by corporate customers over a wide-area telecommunications network to address a variety of needs. Applications which could be provided over such a network include remote mainframe access, remote bulk data transmission, remote file server access, software distribution, LAN interconnect, private voice networks, and videoconferencing. This is shown in Figure 8-2. We will see how all these applications can be availed of as we develop the architecture of the nodal processor.

8.3. Architecture of the Nodal Processor

Our marketing department tells us that we need to split the market into a low-, middle-, and high-end. In each configuration, we will allow the customer to select a number of LAN and WAN interfaces, mixed and matched in any manner that suit their requirements. For the low-end product, the maximum number of customer-selectable interfaces is 7, for the mid-range 15, and for the high-end 31. To design the nodal processor, we turn to our crack object-oriented systems architecture task force. The task force recommends as follows.

Enclosure, Buses, and Modules

The nodal processor will be housed in an enclosure which will contain slots for various *modules*. A nodal processor could function as a single unit in a stand-alone enclosure, or several such units could be rack-mounted depending on the customer's capacity requirements. Modules will be realized on cards which can be inserted in the enclosure's card slots. Each module will provide a specific feature inside the nodal processor: these features will include LAN interfaces, WAN interfaces, and internal processing functions.

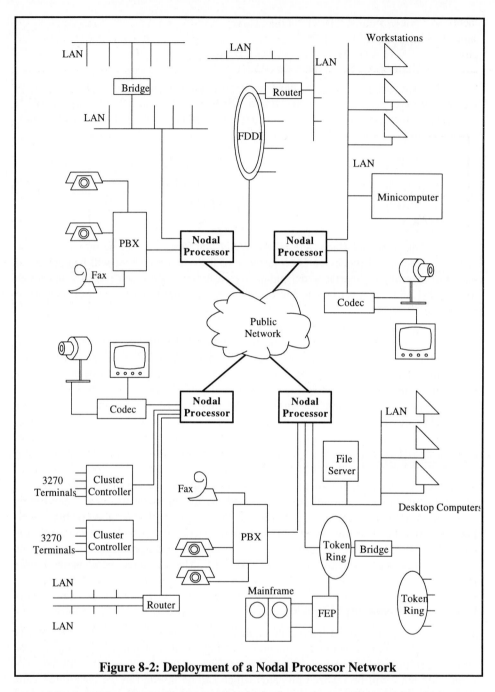

Figure 8-2: Deployment of a Nodal Processor Network

Because all modules must be housed inside the same enclosure, they will interface to the same set of buses. Of course, mechanical design issues for these modules such as form factor, power requirements, and heat dissipation will also account for co-residency in the same enclosure. The enclosure will have 8, 16, or 32 slots. A possible realization of the physical enclosure is shown in Figure 8-3.

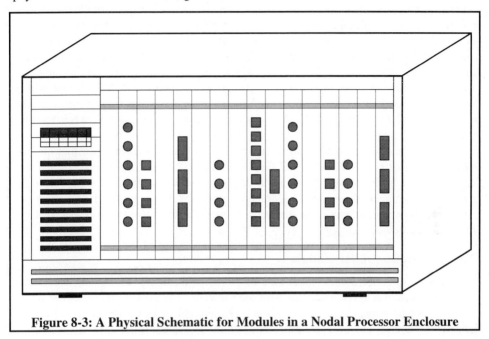

Figure 8-3: A Physical Schematic for Modules in a Nodal Processor Enclosure

All modules in the enclosure communicate over a number of *backplane buses*. The buses provide high-speed communication for intermodule traffic and ensure that there is sufficient bandwidth to prevent bottlenecks between modules. Because some configurations of the nodal processor will be required to support high-bandwidth applications, such as FDDI internetworking and OC-3 transports, the backplane will include a very high-performance proprietary bus with transfer rates suitable for these applications. This will be termed the *gigabit bus*. Further, there is also a separate, moderate-bandwidth general-purpose bus, called the *control bus*. The control bus is exclusively dedicated for control and management messages required for operating the nodal processor.

In addition to these buses, the backplane will also support a number of *media buses*, which are similar to external LAN communication fabrics except that they operate inside the nodal processor. For any given LAN segment, the shared medium can be provided on one of these media buses on the backplane. Because the nodal processor is required to provide internal segmentation and internetworking between LAN segments of similar and dissimilar types, there will be multiple media buses on the backplane. Our initial requirements call for the backplane to support up to 4 FDDI buses, 6 Token Ring buses, and 6 Ethernet buses; smaller configurations may support fewer. By supporting LAN protocols directly on these media buses, we can extend them outside the box into the campus network. Further, modules providing LAN segmentation and internetworking (such as bridge modules and router modules) can function completely internally to the nodal processor: they need have no external interfaces since they can interface with only the backplane buses.

Our initial cut at the architecture calls for four types of modules to be housed in the nodal processor. Each one of the LAN interface functions will be provided on a separate module; these will be called *access modules*. Each one of the WAN interface functions will be provided on a separate module; these will be called *transport modules*. All these modules have ports for the appropriate interfaces they are to provide. Besides interface modules, there are other modules which provide specific networking features. Examples include modules providing LAN bridging and routing functions. These will be called *resource modules*. In addition, each nodal processor will always house a *system controller module*. Figure 8-4 illustrates typical internal connections between modules and buses in the nodal processors.

Each module supports protocol functions which are appropriate for that module. Modules with external interfaces will support at least a physical-layer protocol and may support higher layers as well. Network-layer protocol entities can also be supported depending on the functions provided in the nodal processor. For example, the presence of a router resource module will imply that some network-layer protocols can be decoded and routed by the nodal processor.

The System Controller Module

The system controller module takes care of the housekeeping of the nodal processor. It uses the control bus to communicate with each module. The system controller can recognize on boot-up which modules have been installed and make decisions accordingly. It can use the control bus to orchestrate connections between specific LAN interfaces and specific WAN interfaces over the backplane buses. It can activate and deactivate the internal interfaces between specific modules and specific backplane buses. It can also arrange to multiplex several LAN interfaces onto the same WAN interface and manage the bandwidth allocation on the gigabit bus for each such connection. It can take modules offline in the event of failure, or in response to a management message.

Assuming that our buses support hot swapping, the system controller can recognize when a new module has been hot-swapped into a running nodal processor and boot the module. It monitors the system, collecting operating statistics and tracking performance information. If multiple WAN interfaces of the same type are installed, the system controller can arrange for additional WAN bandwidth on demand depending on LAN traffic load. In addition, the system controller also supports a network management agent which can act in response to external network management requests and report unfavorable operating conditions. In effect, the system controller provides centralized management and control over each of the modules in the nodal processor.

Access Modules

Each access module provides physical-layer interfaces for the appropriate type of traffic arriving at the module. Some access modules provide LAN concentration and have multiple ports for LAN end-stations, with an appropriate media connector type on each port. End-stations are directly connected to each port on a LAN access module in a point-to-

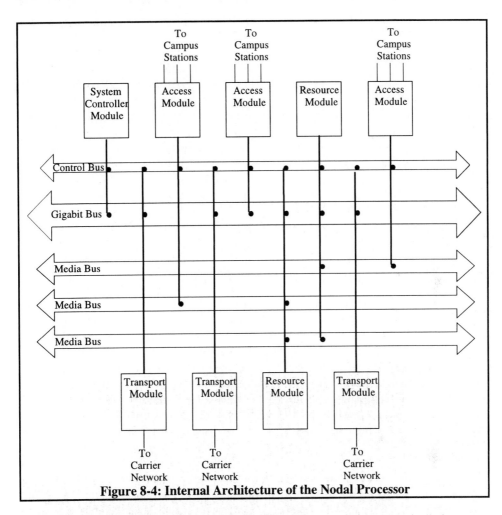

Figure 8-4: Internal Architecture of the Nodal Processor

point configuration. Each LAN access module interfaces with one of the media buses on the backplane. The media bus therefore constitutes the LAN segment whose capacity is shared among all the ports on all the LAN access modules connecting with that bus.

These LAN access modules typically provide repeater functionality and also support per-port traffic monitoring and statistics accumulation. Thus, the module transparently inspects and repeats the physical-layer traffic on each port without terminating its higher-level protocols. It supports the ability to enable and disable individual ports on the module. Depending on the number of ports on the access module, these functions may be provided under the supervision of the system controller module, or they may be provided by a small low-cost microprocessor local to the module.

Other access modules interface with external internetworking devices and provide an entry point for HSSI traffic at 50 Mbps via a Shielded Twisted-Pair physical interface. Special-purpose access modules may also be designed for interfacing with specialized external devices (e.g., video codecs).

Transport Modules

Each transport module in the nodal processor interfaces with a wide-area network provided by a public telecommunications carrier. Because different customers could subscribe to different carrier services, the nodal processor must support a variety of WAN interfaces. Our transport modules will provide most of the commonly used interfaces, including 56/64 kbps for low-bit-rate data, ISDN Primary Rate, as well as standard T-1-rate interfaces. A fractional T-1 module is also provided for those customers who only subscribe to sub-rate services and do not want to incur the expense of a full T-1-rate module. The X.25 module provides access to both switched and permanent virtual circuits in a public X.25 network.

The interface to an SMDS service from a telecommunications carrier is provided by the SMDS transport module. Over the backplane buses, the SMDS transport module accepts datagrams encoded in some known connectionless network-layer protocol. These datagrams could either originate from an external internetworking device and arrive into the nodal processor via the HSSI access module or originate at an external end-station and arrive into the nodal processor via a LAN access module onto one of the media buses, from where they could be picked up by an internal router resource module and routed to the SMDS transport module. The SMDS transport module performs the L3_PDU generation and the L2_PDU segmentation into equal-sized cells, which are then payload-mapped to a DS-1 or DS-3 frame format using the Physical-Layer Convergence Protocol. The outgoing signal is then sent out to the carrier network. We need two kinds of SMDS transport modules supporting both the DS-1 and DS-3 rates [TR 772, TR 1064].

The Frame Relay transport module provides an interface to a Frame Relay service provided by a telecommunications carrier. It accepts LAN packets over the backplane buses from the access modules, encapsulates them in LAPD frames, and relays them to the public network across the User-Network Interface. In addition to standard Frame Relay functionality, it supports global DLCI addressing, as well as multicast groups. This module provides the customer with access to a 2 Mbps Frame Relay network.

For high-bandwidth applications, the nodal processor will also support transport modules with interfaces to broadband public networks. These will include transport modules for T-3, OC-1, and OC-3 rates. These transport modules will be able to concentrate at the nodal processor multiple T-1-rate streams from existing external equipment which the customer may already possess, such as T-1 multiplexers and DSUs. The T-3 module supports C-bit parity framing. The OC-1 module has the ability to incorporate T-1 signals as locked virtual tributaries into the synchronized STS-1 signal, which can be degroomed by other nodal processors to provide easy drop-insert functionality in a multipoint network. Unsynchronized T-1 streams can also be supported as floating virtual tributaries. The OC-3 transport module allows the nodal processor to provide full internetworking of FDDI or 100BaseX traffic across a wide-area network. Customers who use the FDDI or 100BaseX media buses on the backplane and desire to internetwork them across a WAN can configure the nodal processor to payload-map a 100 Mbps stream into the 155 Mbps STS-3c synchronous envelope supported on the OC-3 transport module.

Resource Modules

Resource modules in the nodal processor provide functions other than LAN or WAN interfaces. An example of a resource module is a bridge module, which provides LAN segmentation. Many types of bridge modules can be inserted; these include bridges within a media type (such as Ethernet-to-Ethernet, Token-Ring-to-Token-Ring, and FDDI-to-FDDI) as well as bridges across dissimilar types (such as Ethernet-to-Token-Ring, Token-Ring-to-FDDI, and Ethernet-to-FDDI). These bridges typically interface to two of the media buses on the backplane.

Another example of a resource module is a router module, which functions very much like a bridge module except it provides network-layer routing between any pair of LAN segments. Local bridging and routing can be provided by having the resource module forward packets between two access modules; remote bridging and routing can be provided by having the resource module forward packets between an access module and a transport module.

Other resource modules may also be designed: for example, an RMON resource module may be added to serve as a resident network monitor and protocol analyzer for all the LAN segments in the nodal processor. This module can be inserted into one of the slots so it can interface with all the backplane buses and continuously monitor both local and remote traffic. When requested by a network management console, this module can provide traffic reports and summaries according to the RMON (Remote Network Monitoring) standard [RFC 1271].

8.4. The Nodal Processor Inheritance Hierarchy

Our architecture is not oriented toward a single product; it is flexible enough to generate a family of related products. Each productized configuration of the nodal processor will have different capabilities depending on its component objects and thus will be characterized for different application services. For example, some of the moderately priced versions may not require high-bandwidth networking and so may not contain any broadband transport cards or the gigabit bus. For deployment in environments which are not very LAN-intensive (e.g., traditional mainframe-and-terminal networks) some versions may not support all the media buses on the backplane. We shall see how, by specializing our object-oriented hierarchies appropriately, we can accommodate this entire family of products within a single architecture.

As an initial working hypothesis for the design of the nodal processor, our crack object-oriented systems architecture task force comes up with the inheritance hierarchies of Figure 8-5. We shall see how this initial working hierarchy can be refined as the design of the nodal processor is enhanced.

The `nodalProcessor` object class has attributes such as `name`, `serialNumber`, and `manufacturer`. The `bus` object class has attributes such as `speed` and, if necessary, `arbitrationMechanism`. The `module` object class has attributes such as `busesSupported`, `formFactor`, `powerRequirements`, and `powerConsumption`. Clearly, a number of functions need to be specified in each subclass of `module`, depending on what that subclass does. The `interfacePort` object class is

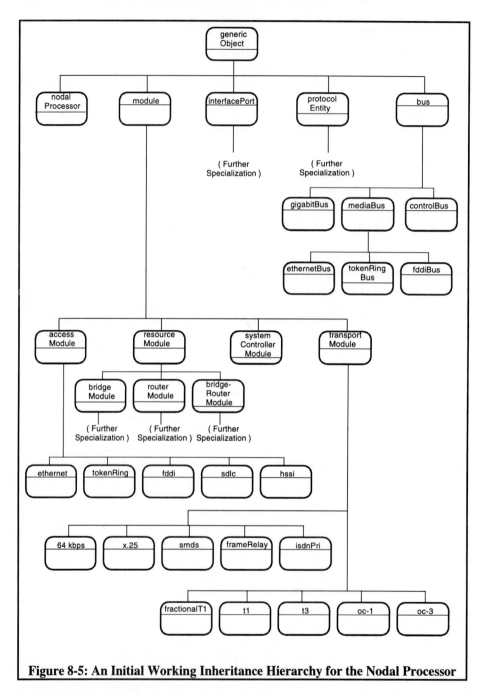

Figure 8-5: An Initial Working Inheritance Hierarchy for the Nodal Processor

characterized by attributes such as `speed`, `mediaConnectorType`, and `physical-Protocol`.

The `bus` object class **specializes-into** the `mediaBus`, `controlBus`, and `gigabitBus` object classes. The `mediaBus` object class further **specializes-into** the `ethernetBus`, `tokenRingBus`, and `fddiBus` which will be supported on the backplane. The `module` object class **specializes-into** each of the four types of modules shown in Figure 8-5. The `accessModule` class has each of the supported access module types as subclasses, while the `transportModule` class has each of the supported transport module types. The `resourceModule` class **specializes-into** the `bridge`, `router`, and `bridgeRouter` object classes. Each of these has further subclasses as there can be many different varieties of bridge and router modules depending on the combination of LAN protocols each module internetworks; these are not shown for brevity.

As a continuation of the inheritance hierarchy, the `protocolEntity` object class of Figure 8-5 further **specializes-into** a variety of subclasses. Figure 8-6 shows certain useful subclasses of the `protocolEntity` object class, with the first-level basis of specialization being the operative layer of each protocol entity.

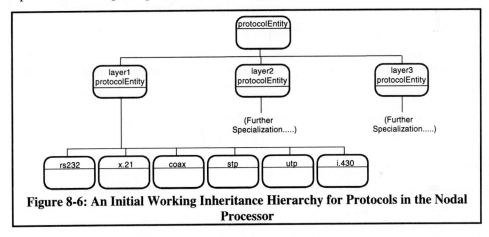

Figure 8-6: An Initial Working Inheritance Hierarchy for Protocols in the Nodal Processor

Figure 8-6 does not show all the subclasses of `protocolEntity`; in particular, certain WAN protocols (e.g., the layers of the SMDS Interface Protocol, or the frame formats for DS-1, DS-3, STS-1, and STS-3) have not been identified for brevity.

Figure 8-7 further classifies link-layer protocols. At the first level, the basis of specialization is the nature of the media on which that protocol is used — shared or dedicated. At the second level, the basis is the nature of the information conveyed by this protocol — whether user information or signaling/routing. Similarly, Figure 8-8 suggests a classification for typical network-layer protocols along the same classification lines.

The protocol classification suggested in these figures is not the only correct way of performing this specialization. Another way of classifying protocols would have been to first subclass on the basis of `sharedMediaProtocols` and `dedicatedMedia-Protocols` and then by layer. Alternatively, one could have first subclassed `protocolEntity` by `standardsFamily` and then by layer. Thus, all IEEE proto-

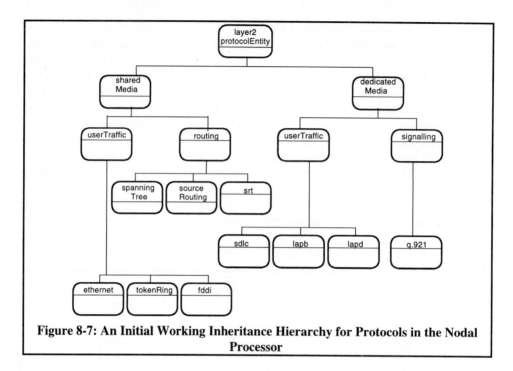

Figure 8-7: An Initial Working Inheritance Hierarchy for Protocols in the Nodal Processor

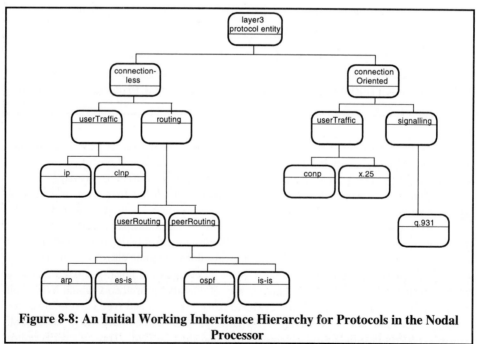

Figure 8-8: An Initial Working Inheritance Hierarchy for Protocols in the Nodal Processor

cols, for example, would have been in the same branch of the hierarchy, and all ISDN protocols would have been in another branch. Whether this is appropriate depends on which classification is most useful to the application. In general, any taxonomy which suggests the semantics of generalization and evolution — with subclasses inheriting properties from their superclasses — is acceptable, as long as such a taxonomy can be utilized to construct a system architecture.

8.5. The Nodal Processor Aggregation Hierarchies

In the aggregation hierarchy, the `nodalProcessor` object class essentially contains modules and buses; the multiplicity of each component is specified in the hierarchy. Some kinds of `module` contain `interfacePort` object classes as components. The `systemControllerModule` and the `resourceModules` do not contain any ports; an `accessModule` or a `transportModule` must contain at least one `interface-Port`. The overall aggregation hierarchy for the nodal processor is shown in Figure 8-9.

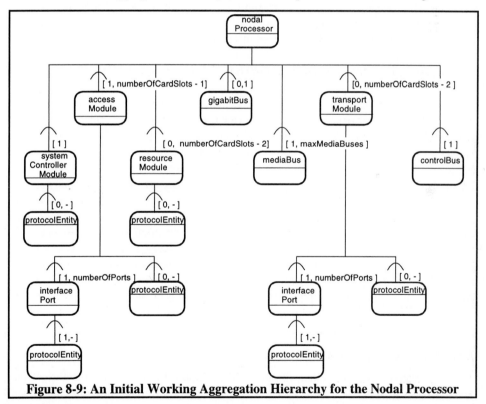

Figure 8-9: An Initial Working Aggregation Hierarchy for the Nodal Processor

Notice that the only integer constants specified as the component multiplicity in the aggregation hierarchy are trivial ones, such as 0 and 1. Any other values are always specified in terms of attribute-defined expressions, using some capacity-related attribute of the aggregate class. For example, even though we know that the `nodalProcessor` may contain up to 4 FDDI buses, 6 Token Ring buses, and 6 Ethernet buses, we do not specify the component multiplicity for the `mediaBuses` with the hard constants `[1,16]`. We prefer instead to specify the upper limit as the `maxMediaBuses` attribute of the `nodalProcessor` class. (Of course, the `maxMediaBuses` attribute happens to be equal to the sum of the `maxEthernetBuses`, `maxTokenRingBuses`, and `max-FddiBuses` attributes. When we discuss *virtual attributes* in Chapter 20, we shall see how arithmetically related attribute sets can be defined in terms of each other.)

A minimally useful `nodalProcessor` must provide at least a LAN concentration function even if it does not provide any WAN access. Therefore, an absolute minimum configuration consists of 1 system controller module and 1 access module. For this reason, the component multiplicity of `accessModule` is specified as `[1,numberOf-CardSlots-1]`, since 1 card slot will always be occupied by the system controller module. By specifying the upper limit in terms of the `numberOfCardSlots` attribute, the same multiplicity interval specification can hold whether the enclosure has 8, 16, or 32 slots. Also, because a minimal configuration could contain no transport or resource modules and because these modules can only be added on after at least 1 access module and 1 system controller module have been inserted, the component multiplicity for transport and resource modules is specified as `[0,numberOfCardSlots-2]`.

The `gigabitBus` is optional, and so has a multiplicity of `[0,1]`. Higher-layer subclasses of `protocolEntity` also need to be defined, so that we can show the `systemControllerModule` object class containing network management protocols.

Each type of `module` will have its own aggregation hierarchy, consisting of component `protocolEntity` object classes and possibly `interfacePort` object classes. Again, even if we know we will have a dozen RJ-45 ports on a `tenBaseT-EthernetAccessModule`, we model its multiplicity as `[1,numberOfPorts]` rather than `[1,12]`. All of these aggregation hierarchies are not shown; only a few samples are shown. For example, the aggregation hierarchy for the bridge module in Figure 8-10 specifies the constraints that a bridge have at least two layer-2 protocol terminations and at least one bridging function. This holds true of all bridges, irrespective of the subclass (Ethernet-to-Ethernet, Token-Ring-to-Token-Ring, Ethernet-to-Token-Ring, and so on). Each specific subclass of `bridgeModule` will further indicate exactly what it does by specifying in *its* aggregation hierarchy which specific protocols it bridges and what bridging function it uses. This will be accomplished using component specialization on its layer-2 protocol component class and its bridging function component class.

8.6. Products of the Nodal Processor Family

As we indicated earlier, the intent of our design is to use the flexible architecture of the nodal processor to create a family of related products in different configurations. Each such configuration characterizes the nodal processor for a different application. By attempting to address as many potential extensions to the product as we can possibly envision, we can exercise our proposed architecture to ensure that it possesses adequate flexibility and robustness. Testing the ability of our design to allow future migration and

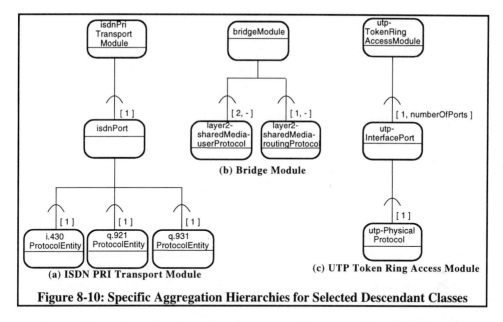

Figure 8-10: Specific Aggregation Hierarchies for Selected Descendant Classes

to accommodate new applications will ensure that we have created an architecture which is sufficiently general.

Example: Broadband Nodal Processor

In this product, we decide to offer a version of the nodal processor specifically configured for connecting to broadband carrier networks, called a Broadband Nodal Processor. The requirement for a Broadband Nodal Processor is that the product must have either a T-3, OC-1, or OC-3 WAN interface module. As a matter of engineering design, we may decide that for such a product we expect heavy bandwidth usage, and so the optional gigabit bus must be present to prevent bottlenecks inside this product.

How can we specify the semantic constraint that the presence of certain `transportModule` components requires the presence of the `gigabitBus` component? Is our current model powerful enough to specify this constraint, or do we need to create further subclasses?

Example: ATM-Based Node

In this product, we decide to offer a variation of the Broadband Nodal Processor product which, instead of using the gigabit bus for inter-module communication, uses an ATM-based switching fabric. How can the model be adjusted to accommodate this?

One way to do this is to specify a `communicationFabric` object class which, in the inheritance hierarchy, **specializes-into** either a `bus` or an `atm-SwitchingFabric` object class and, in the aggregation hierarchy, is a compo-

nent of broadbandNodalProcessor. The broadbandNodalProcessor
must contain either an atmSwitchingFabric or a gigabitBus object.
How can we specify this component multiplicity? If the atmSwitching-
Fabric is implemented on a resource module, it will use up one slot in the enclosure. How will this affect the remaining component multiplicities?

Example: Collapsed-Backbone LAN Concentrator

In this product, we offer a simpler version of the nodal processor specifically configured to act only as a LAN concentrator and repeater. This will not provide any
WAN connectivity; its purpose is simply to serve as a central wiring hub for various LAN segments using accessModules. It is required to contain at least 2
media buses of each type (Ethernet, Token Ring, and FDDI), and access-
Modules corresponding to those media segments. In the remaining slots, the
customer may optionally insert additional accessModules or bridge-
Modules to provide internal internetworking. Because the nodal processor's own
gigabitBus can act as local backbone for all the LAN media that connect to it,
this configuration is equivalent to a collapsed-backbone LAN concentrator
[Zeil92, Skor92]. As such, the gigabitBus is required to be present in this
configuration.

How can we subclass collapsedBackboneHub from nodalProcessor to
specify this new object class? What restrictions do we need to specify for the
component multiplicities inherited by collapsedBackboneHub from
nodalProcessor?

Example: Isochronous Node

In this product, to increase market penetration, we decide to offer in our nodal
processor an interface to a PBX. This enables us to carry voice traffic in addition
to data traffic, using either one of our ISDN PRI, T-1, T-3, OC-1, or OC-3
transportModules. Where can we place the pbxAccessModule in the inheritance hierarchy? How can we specify it in the aggregation hierarchy?

Consider the fact that we need to specify the semantics of the following constraint
in the aggregation hierarchy: "There may or may not be instances of pbx-
AccessModule in the nodalProcessor object. But if there is an instance of
pbxAccessModule, then at least one of the transportModules must be an
ISDN PRI, T-1, T-3, OC-1, or OC-3. This is because we cannot carry voice
through our nodalProcessor if the only transportModules in the enclosure are, say, the x25transportModule, the frameRelayTransport-
Module, or the smdsTransportModule." How can we specify this constraint
in our model? (For the time being, we will ignore the possibility that, because an
SMDS signal is mapped to a DS-1 or DS-3 frame format at the Subscriber-
Network Interface, it is possible to design a transport module which payload-maps

both an SMDS stream and a voice stream into a single outgoing signal. We will revisit this possibility in a later example.)

Example: Video Bandwidth Allocator

In this product, we offer a version of the nodal processor preconfigured as a bandwidth allocator, which makes available bandwidth on demand for use with videoconferencing applications. This configuration will have a new access interface to an MPEG video coder/decoder, or a codec supporting the full H.320 video coding and signaling specifications. Depending on how many sites were involved in the videoconference, it could add or drop incremental amounts of WAN bandwidth in a stepwise manner. The bandwidth allocator can supply this "rubber-bandwidth" by providing ISDN access to services such as $n \times 64$, $n \times 384$, Switched 1536, and other switched digital carrier offerings. We will require this product to have at least one `mpegCodecAccessModule` and at least two `isdnPri-TransportModules`.

On what basis can we subclass `videoBandwidthAllocator` from `nodal-Processor`? How can we specify its component multiplicity with `mpeg-CodecAccessModule` and `isdnPriTransportModule`?

8.7. Architectures for Nodal Processor Products

In this section we will address the changes necessary to our original object hierarchies of the nodal processor to ensure that it can accommodate all the product configurations we proposed in the preceding section. As we make modifications, a general rule will become evident: by first creating appropriate descendant classes for both aggregates and components and then specifying stronger component multiplicities for the component's descendants in the aggregate's descendants, appropriate semantic constraints can be built into the formal specification for all the cases above.

Architecture for Broadband Nodal Processor

The version of the nodal processor was specifically configured for broadband networks and required the presence of either a T-3, OC-1, or OC-3 transport module. In turn, this required the presence of the gigabit bus.

To specify this using our model, we first refine our class hierarchy and create the new intermediate subclass `broadbandTransportModule` from `transportModule`. This allows us to collectively refer to the T-3, OC-1, and OC-3 interfaces via a single superclass. Then, we let `nodalProcessor` **specialize-into** `broadbandNodalProcessor`, using as a basis the component specialization constraint that a `broadbandNodalProcessor` must have at least 1 `broadbandTransportModule` as a component. We further specify a separate aggregation hierarchy for `broadbandNodalProcessor`, so that it contains `gigabitBus` with a multiplicity of exactly [1], which represents a

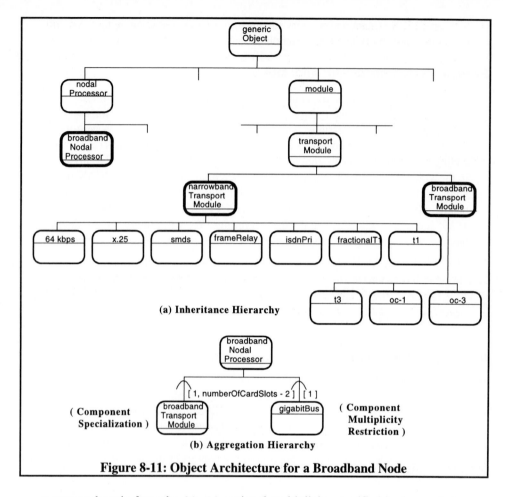

Figure 8-11: Object Architecture for a Broadband Node

narrower domain from the [0,1] optional multiplicity specified in the nodal-Processor superclass. Any configuration created using this aggregation hierarchy will conform to our constraints.

Clearly, the broadbandNodalProcessor will contain other components, such as a systemControllerModule, but we need not specify them again here. These components are available through inheritance because we have already specified them for its superclass nodalProcessor.

Architecture for ATM-Based Node

In this product option, we offered a variation of the Broadband Nodal Processor which used an atmSwitchingFabric for inter-module communication instead of the gigabitBus. To accommodate this variation, we refine our inheritance hierarchy to create a more generalized top-level communicationFabric object class, instead of a top-level bus object class. The communicationFabric object class further **specializes-into** two specific kinds of inter-module communication: the bus object class and the atm-SwitchingFabric object class, as shown in Figure 8-12. The bus object class specializes further, as shown earlier in Figure 8-5. We also create two different kinds of nodalProcessor: we subclass nodalProcessor into either a busBroadbandNode or an atmBroadbandNode. This is also shown in Figure 8-12. Note that Figure 8-12 is a refinement of Figure 8-5, not of Figure 8-11.

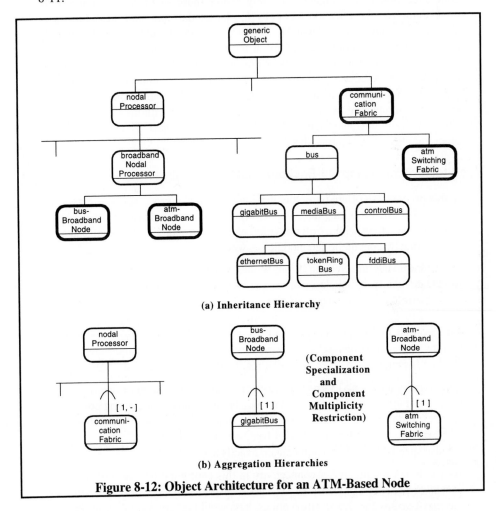

(a) Inheritance Hierarchy

(b) Aggregation Hierarchies

Figure 8-12: Object Architecture for an ATM-Based Node

In the general aggregation hierarchy, we specify that the abstract superclass nodalProcessor must contain at least 1 abstract communicationFabric component object. However, specific subclasses of nodalProcessor may, using component specialization, contain specific subclasses of

communicationFabric. Therefore, we further specify in separate aggregation hierarchies that the busBroadbandNode version of nodalProcessor
must contain exactly 1 gigabitBus object, whereas the atmBroadband-
Node version of the nodalProcessor must contain exactly 1 atm-
SwitchingFabric. This satisfies all the constraints on different versions of
our product.

To be more accurate, there are several other mechanisms which could be used as a
communication fabric: Figure 8-12 only shows those of immediate interest. A
more complete classification hierarchy for intranodal communication fabrics is
shown in Figure 8-13 [Newm92, Zegu93, Turn88, Batc68, Cant71, Giac91,
Lee90, Chip92]. Although we do not at the moment use the hierarchy of Figure
8-13 in our model for the nodal processor, it is shown here for completeness; for
example, our atmSwitchingFabric could be implemented with a non-
blocking space-division architecture such as Batcher-Banyan. (Note that the Clos
switching architecture from this figure has nothing to do with the Clos object-oriented programming language — the Common Lisp Object System. Like many
other interdisciplinary terms, this one is overloaded.)

Architecture for Collapsed-Backbone LAN Concentrator

In this product, we offered a simple version of the nodal processor configured as a
collapsed-backbone wiring hub. The wiring hub contains at least two media buses
of each type, along with accessModules for corresponding LAN interfaces. It
may optionally contain bridge modules as well.

To accommodate this version in our model, we modify our inheritance hierarchy
to create another subclass of nodalProcessor, called collapsed-
BackboneHub. We then specify a separate aggregation hierarchy for
collapsedBackboneHub with multiplicity restrictions tighter than the ones
we specified for the general nodalProcessor superclass. That is, we specify
that the aggregation hierarchy for collapsedBackboneHub must contain two
or more instances each of ethernetBus, tokenRingBus, and fddiBus.

A minimally useful collapsedBackboneHub requires at least one access-
Module. Further, bridgeModules may be optionally added, using component
specialization on the resourceModule object class. Since we said that the
gigabitBus served as a collapsed backbone for all LAN traffic in the campus,
we also specify that this version contain exactly 1 gigabitBus.

As we do not require WAN connectivity in this configuration, we further specify
exactly 0 transportModules. We need to specify this because, if we did not,
the collapsedBackboneHub object class would inherit the [0,numberOf-
CardSlots−2] multiplicity of transportModule from its nodal-
Processor superclass, which would mean that a transportModule could
still possibly be present in the collapsedBackboneHub. By explicitly re-

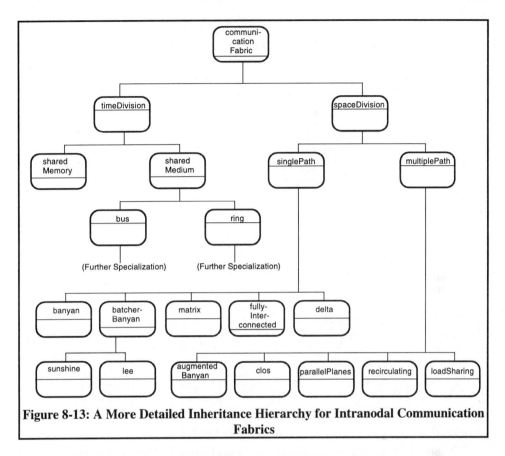

Figure 8-13: A More Detailed Inheritance Hierarchy for Intranodal Communication Fabrics

stricting its component multiplicity to `[0]` in the `collapsedBackboneHub` subclass, we indicate that it is required to be absent. This is shown in Figure 8-14.

Architecture for Isochronous Node

In this product, we offered a version of the `nodalProcessor` which interfaced with a PBX, so that it can transmit voice traffic as well. Clearly, not all versions of `nodalProcessor` are capable of carrying voice traffic; in order to transmit voice, the `nodalProcessor` must contain at least one ISDN PRI, T-1, T-3, OC-1, or OC-3 module as its WAN interface, because other WAN interfaces such as X.25, SMDS, and Frame Relay are incapable of transmitting voice traffic.

We refine our model to accommodate this constraint by making several adjustments to the inheritance and aggregation hierarchies, as shown in Figure 8-15.

To begin, we create a new subclass of `accessModule` called `pbxAccessModule`, which allows our `nodalProcessor` to be connected to a `pbx`. Then, we subclass `nodalProcessor` to create two different kinds of node: a `voiceCapableNode` and a `dataOnlyNode`.

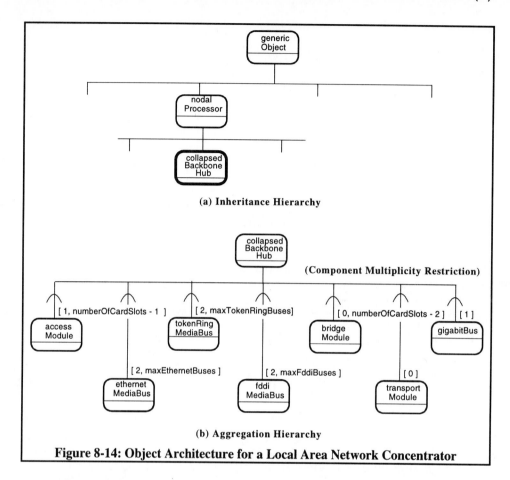

Figure 8-14: Object Architecture for a Local Area Network Concentrator

We further adjust the inheritance hierarchy to also create two intermediate kinds of transportModule classes, called isochronousTransportModule and nonIsochronousTransportModule. This allows a finer granularity of classification of the available transportModules. Under isochronous-TransportModule we group all the modules capable of carrying voice traffic, that is, the ISDN PRI module, T-1, T-3, OC-1, and OC-3 transport modules. All the other transport modules are grouped together under nonIsochronous-TransportModule.

We now specify a tighter aggregation hierarchy for voiceCapableNode. In this aggregation hierarchy, we require voiceCapableNode to contain at least 1 pbxAccessModule, and at least 1 isochronousTransportModule. This uses component specialization. By specifying these constraints in the aggregation hierarchy, we are assured that each version of nodalProcessor configured as a voiceCapableNode is invested with the required capabilities.

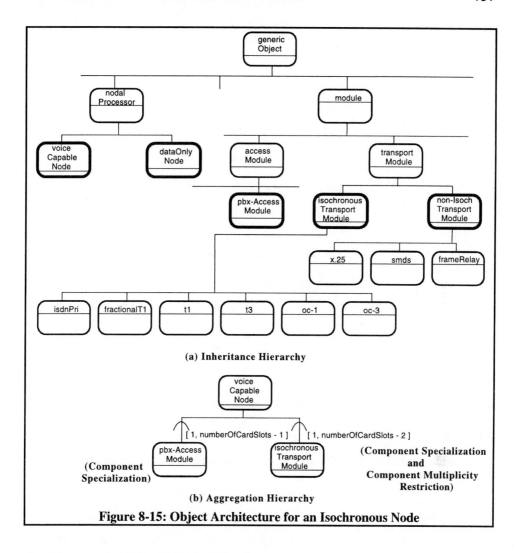

Figure 8-15: Object Architecture for an Isochronous Node

Architecture for Video Bandwidth Allocator

In this product, we offered a version of the nodalProcessor which was configured as a videoBandwidthAllocator. This product accommodated variable demand for videoteleconferencing by dialing up additional bandwidth on its
ISDN PRI interfaces as required. We specified that in this configuration the
nodalProcessor must contain at least one access interface to an MPEG codec
and at least 2 ISDN PRI WAN interfaces.

The inheritance and aggregation hierarchies that specify this configuration are
shown in Figure 8-16.

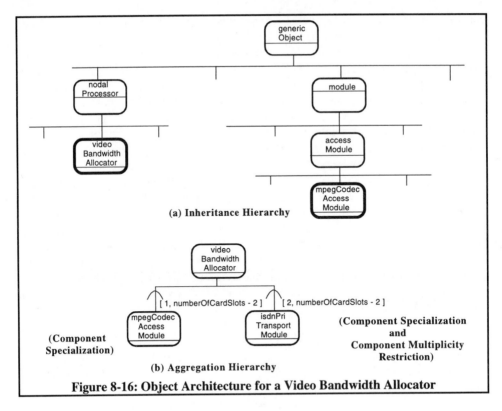

(a) Inheritance Hierarchy

(b) Aggregation Hierarchy

Figure 8-16: Object Architecture for a Video Bandwidth Allocator

In this configuration, we create an additional subclass of nodalProcessor, which we call videoBandwidthAllocator. We also create a new subclass of accessModule, called mpegCodecAccessModule, which allows an external MPEG coder/decoder to interface to the nodalProcessor. (We could in the future use a new access module which executes an onboard codec function, interfacing directly with external camera equipment.) Then, we specify a separate, tighter aggregation hierarchy for the videoBandwidthAllocator. In this aggregation hierarchy, we require that the videoBandwidthAllocator contain at least 1 mpegCodecAccessModule and at least 2 isdnPri-TransportModules. This requirement ensures that any nodalProcessor configured for video applications has the access and transport capabilities it needs to support this service.

8.8. Principles for Architecting Nodal Processor Products

By working through these examples, the reader will have abstracted the general principle of object-oriented architectures for network products: by creating new subclasses where appropriate and specifying stronger component multiplicities and specialized components for the subclasses, the semantics of all of the different product configurations above can be modeled precisely and formally.

A modeling practice that can be inferred by working through these examples is that every time we are required to model a choice among different kinds of objects, we "fork" a class to create subclasses. Every time we are required to model a minimal configuration for a particular assembly, we specify composition relationships with appropriate multiplicities. This is why inheritance is sometimes called an *or* operation (the superclass `module` is either an `accessModule` *or* a `transportModule` *or* a `systemControllerModule` *or* a `resourceModule`) while aggregation is sometimes called an *and* operation (a `nodalProcessor` is a `systemControllerModule` *and* some `accessModules` *and* some `transportModules` *and* some `resourceModules`).

This example also shows why more than one aggregation hierarchy is often necessary to specify the complete model for the system. While a superclass may have its own aggregation hierarchy, a subclass may specify a stronger aggregation hierarchy, either with restricted multiplicities, or containing only specialized components, or both. Thus, the aggregation hierarchies for a given system do not form a single rooted-and-connected directed acyclic graph; they form a forest of such graphs. All of these hierarchies are required together to describe all the composition constraints on the system. By modeling specific aggregations for subclasses of `nodalProcessor`, we can formally instruct our model compiler to impose appropriate constraints for each product option.

We leave it as an exercise for the reader to assimilate the analyses of all the different product configurations above and put back together the new "big picture" of the inheritance hierarchy. This hierarchy should depict all the different subclasses created for the various configurations of `nodalProcessor`. Some of these might appear as subclasses of each other; for example, a `videoBandwidthAllocator` is clearly also an isochronous version of the `nodalProcessor`, and the `broadbandTransportModule` class is a descendant of the `isochronousTransportModule` class.

As an exercise, we propose below a few additional configurations and leave the reader to consider the adjustments necessary to the inheritance and aggregation hierarchies to accommodate these configurations.

Example: Hybrid Access/Resource Modules

After some analysis of manufacturing costs, we find that making a module that bridges FDDI segments to any other segment is rather expensive, because of the speed of the chip sets required to process FDDI. To consolidate costs, we decide to offer a multipurpose module with more than one bridge — that is, a single module that bridges multiple Ethernet segments to an FDDI segment and also bridges the Ethernet segments to each other.

How can we specify this resource module in the inheritance hierarchy? Can we circumvent the use of multiple inheritance by requiring such a module to contain multiple LAN media and bridging protocol entities in the aggregation hierarchy?

Suppose further that we create a variation on such a module — one that provides not just multiple bridging between the backplane media segments but also contains LAN access ports and supports multiple segments on the module itself. Thus, access ports on the module will be grouped according to which segment they belong to; the module will contain onboard bridges which bridge these segments to each other and also to the media buses on the backplane. Clearly, this object class will be a "hybrid" between the `accessModule` and `resourceModule` classes.

How can we normalize the inheritance hierarchy to place such a hybrid module in it? Can we avoid using multiple inheritance? Do we need to use capsules? How can we specify its component object classes in the aggregation hierarchy?

Example: Hybrid Transport/Resource Modules

Suppose we turn the SMDS transport module into an add-on resource module instead. If a customer already owns a configuration with a T-3 transport module, just the SMDS function can now be added as a resource. It is possible to accomplish this because the SMDS physical layer can be payload-mapped to the DS-3 frame format. This variation on the SMDS module now becomes a converter (resource) module which performs the L3_PDU and L2_PDU generation but does not have its own carrier interfaces; instead, it inserts the PLCP payload into the existing DS-3 framer on the T-3 transport module already installed in the box. This allows customers to upgrade an existing unit to SMDS functionality at moderate cost while protecting their investment in the existing transport modules.

How can we place such a new resource module in the inheritance hierarchy? Do we need to normalize the inheritance hierarchy to create intermediate classes? How can we redistribute the placement of protocol entities among the object classes to accommodate this new module?

Applying Object Architecture Principles

Because of the powerful and flexible architecture of the nodal processor, many other modules can be designed for providing specific functions in response to new marketing needs. The family of products generated by our architecture can be further extended by designing a variety of hybrid modules similar to the ones described above. As the density of features on a board increases, modules which hybridize all three functions together — access, resource and transport — can be developed to address specific market niches. We leave it as an exercise to think of the many such possibilities for hybrid modules and to specify the object architecture for each.

By considering actual and hypothetical product variations, we can refine our object hierarchies so that we properly model all aspects of our problem. Once we are satisfied we have the proper model, we can then specify our model and all its constraints formally in our special-purpose language and turn it over to an automated software process. This network synthesis process can use our inheritance and aggregation hierarchies to assemble and configure instances as product orders are received, imposing and applying all our constraints along the way. Part of this program's design must include the ability to compile the formal specification of the model, identify all the aggregation relationships of each object class and all its descendants, and apply the strongest possible aggregation relationship specified for a descendant class as a composition constraint during network synthesis.

In Chapter 27, we will see how a system model so specified can be formally captured as the schema of a *model information base*, a subset of which can be used as an *architecture information base* from which networks can be synthesized.

8.9. High-Order Aggregations

So far our examples have considered aggregation hierarchies for the design of small systems. Small systems, however, do not exist in isolation; they are connected to other systems which together constitute a network. By extending the concept of aggregation to subnetworks and entire networks, we can expand the notion of aggregate-component relationships to obtain the "big picture".

Low-order aggregation hierarchies — those that concentrate on the architecture of small systems and can specify multiplicities accurately — are powerful modeling tools which can actually help us construct systems and create variations on systems, using well-identified component parts. High-order hierarchies have somewhat less utility as system construction tools but are nevertheless useful to convey the larger context.

An example of a high-order aggregation is a wide-area telecommunications network such as an *intelligent network* [ITU-T Q.1200]. The physical configuration of an intelligent network consists of switching systems called *service switching points*, database computers called *service control points*, *adjunct processors* or *services nodes*, voice-processing platforms called *intelligent peripherals*, specialized network management systems called *operations support systems* and *service management systems*, and many other nodes, as depicted in Figure 8-17 [ITU-T Q.1201, ITU-T Q.1205, SR 2247, Robr91, Berm92, Garr93]. We might consider modeling these as the "components" of an "aggregate" `intelligentNetwork` object class. Even if we do so, however, it becomes difficult to specify component multiplicities in a useful and meaningful manner.

Note that Figure 8-17 is a schematic only, representing typical relationships between objects rather than an actual network topology. In the topology of an instantiated intelligent network, many different service switching points will interconnect with each other, signal transfer points will typically be deployed in mated pairs, and multiple operations support systems may be used.

Figure 8-18 shows the high-order aggregation hierarchy for a system modeled in this manner. (Note that the "functions" of this figure are not the same as the functions in our object-oriented model.) Though this figure shows the breakdown of an intelligent network, it is not very instructive: at this level of complexity, decomposition does not convey as much information about the components as it does for smaller systems. For the big picture, *inter-object relationships*, rather than component decompositions, are semantically richer modeling constructs. Clearly, describing the exact nature of the relationship between an SSP and an SCP or adjunct, for example, will convey much more information than knowing how many of each an aggregate network may contain. When we consider inter-object relationships in Chapter 17, we will examine an example of such a relationship in greater detail.

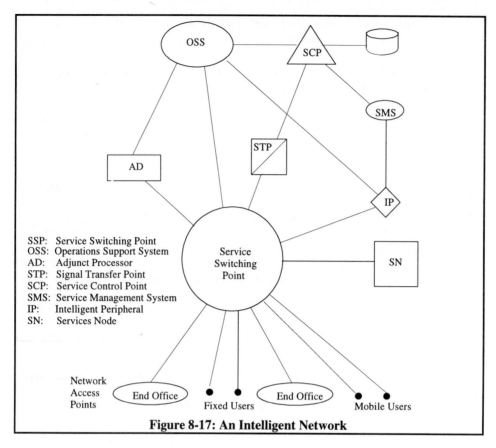

SSP: Service Switching Point
OSS: Operations Support System
AD: Adjunct Processor
STP: Signal Transfer Point
SCP: Service Control Point
SMS: Service Management System
IP: Intelligent Peripheral
SN: Services Node

Figure 8-17: An Intelligent Network

It is intellectually tempting to attempt to model high-order aggregations and low-order aggregations as constituting the same continuous aggregation hierarchy. Thus, an `rj45mediaConnector` object class will, at some level, be considered a component of a `globalTelecomNetwork` object class. Even though this fact is nice to know, it is not terribly useful. Nevertheless, many architects do indeed specify top-to-bottom continuous aggregation hierarchies, because the boundary between high-order and low-order aggregations is extremely fuzzy.

It should be borne in mind though that the way the aggregation hierarchy is used is different at each level of specificity. For smaller systems, it can actually be used in the normative manner we adopted to build our nodal processor, that is, as a construction tool — a set of rules specifying how systems can be put together. The higher we rise in the aggregation hierarchy, the more complex the system gets; the number of options and variations explodes, and so the normative utility of the aggregation hierarchy decreases. It is mostly helpful only in sketching and describing the larger context, rather than in telling us how to build it.

Thus, the notion of aggregation can be used at various levels. When used from a global perspective, aggregation can show us the composition of entire networks, or the

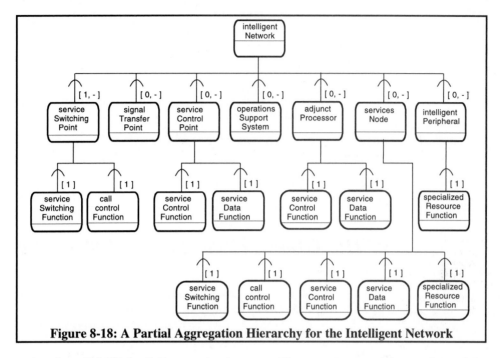

Figure 8-18: A Partial Aggregation Hierarchy for the Intelligent Network

"view from 100,000 feet". By zooming in on specific components and then again on their sub-components, we can examine the "view from 10,000 feet", the "view from 1000 feet", and so on, until we can concentrate on the smallest components of the network that make sense (e.g., individual software modules or hardware chips).

8.10. Summary

To architect products using object-oriented modeling methodologies, the product architecture must be organized using inheritance and aggregation hierarchies. The inheritance hierarchy must enumerate all the versions and different configurations which the product can manifest. A specialized version of the product may be represented as a subclass. This version may be required to contain specialized components. The semantics of such specialization constraints such as these may be formalized by modeling separate aggregation hierarchies for each version. Each such aggregation hierarchy may use Specialization by Component Specialization and/or Specialization by Component Multiplicity Restriction. For individual network devices, aggregation and inheritance hierarchies can be used to specify product architectures in a normative sense and act as construction rules for building devices. For larger networks, object relationships are more useful in describing the overall composition of the network.

9. The Object Registration Hierarchy

> *"The goal of network architecture is to design a network which stays up at least as long as it took to design."*
> — *anonymous network architect.*

9.1. Introduction

This chapter deals with the issue of registering our object modeling constructs so that they can be referenced in communication. The principles of registration are presented, along with a discussion of the different possibilities of structuring registration data. Analogies with existing registration hierarchies are introduced to explain the concept. The structure of the international object registration hierarchy is presented, with a demonstration of how privately registered information can be internationalized.

9.2. Conceptual Background

We have defined many conceptual constructs in our modeling methodology. These include object classes, attributes, functions, capsules, aggregates, and components. If we are to use all these constructs as information to be analyzed at network architecture time, or as information to be exchanged between network objects at run time, we need some way of referring to each construct in an unambiguous manner. That is, every time we need to refer to one of these constructs, we need a unique *label* by which it can be referenced.

To interoperate with other networks, we must be assured that all communicating parties are using the same object model. This means that by some prior arrangement or through preliminary on-line negotiation, they have to agree to use the same model information base; that is, they must all use the same set of conceptual constructs and the same labels to refer to each construct. If we have such an assurance, we can avoid the need to include the complete definition of a modeling construct each time we need to use it in communication; we can save ourselves much effort by simply using their labels.

Therefore, we would like to unambiguously label every object class, every capsule, every attribute, every function, and many other constructs which we will define later.

Labeling a modeling construct is a non-trivial exercise. When a construct is assigned a label, it is officially accepted into the model information base. Automated network synthesis software processes which use the model information base to pick out components of network objects are now free to use the new construct. Other software entities encoding model information for use in run-time protocols may also use the new construct. Before a new construct is accepted into the model information base and assigned a unique label, it must be carefully scrutinized to ensure that it is orthogonal to existing constructs, does not conflict with any existing construct, and indeed accomplishes something useful.

The procedure of accepting a new conceptual construct in the model information base is known as *registration*. Whenever a new object class, a new attribute, or any other construct, is so accepted and labeled, it is said to be *registered*. Since the model information base is published to all processes that require it, registration makes the construct publicly available. It may be further assumed that other entities which understand our model and encounter one of its registered labels during communication will be able to dereference the label and use the actual construct which is its referent.

It should be noted that the labels assigned by the registration procedure refer to modeling constructs and not to any instantiated realizations of the model. The elements of the model information base referred to by the labels are object classes, capsules, functions, and so on, which constitute the *schema* of the network. Many different networks may be realized according the same schema.

For each actual network realized according to the schema, there will be a separate database which identifies the actual *instances* of the constructs in the schema. Such an "instance information base" is different from the model information base. Different networks may use the same model information base but will use different instance information bases. The design of a database for storing actual instance information can be different for each network and is outside the scope of the registration problem. It is possible, and probably sensible, to use the same platform to store both schema and instance information for a given network; however, this choice is properly an implementation concern.

9.3. Design of Registration Name Spaces

The set of all possible labels that can be used to name modeling constructs is called the *name space* of a model. The process of registration essentially assigns to a modeling construct an unused element of the name space. Because of the need to ensure that each such assignment will be unique, registration is usually handled by a central agency known as a *registration authority*. If a team of several people is working together to specify the network model, one person can be elected to act as the registration authority. The role of the registration authority is to act as czar and zealous guardian of the model information base and ensure that it is kept "pure and virtuous" and is not "polluted" by ad hoc definition of non-orthogonal modeling constructs.

Every time a new conceptual construct is defined, it should be generally checked to see that it is indeed useful and does not overlap with existing constructs. If the registration label is a number, the architect creating that construct contacts the registration authority and, literally, "takes a number". The registration authority makes sure that the number handed out is unique, updates the model information base to show that the number is taken, indicates which construct it has been assigned to, and enters the definition of that construct in the model information base.

How then should we design the name space, or labeling scheme, for each of our modeling constructs? One of the requirements is that our labeling scheme should be flexible, so that it can *accommodate growth* as new constructs are defined. We could use alphanumeric strings, but this would involve an alphanumeric search in the model's data dictionary every time a label needed to be dereferenced. While this is not prohibitive, it could have run-time performance penalties. A labeling scheme using only numbers lends itself better to efficient implementations using techniques such as indexing and hashing.

One possibility is a flat name space of integers, say from 0 upward. Each time a new item is registered, the next unused positive integer could be handed out. While this has the advantage of being simple, it has the problem that related objects may not be registered together. Related objects might end up being assigned scattered numbers depending on the sequence in which they were defined. Since items would be assigned numbers from no particular well-defined range, we would be unable to tell by just looking at the number which kind of item it was assigned to. Run-time software entities which dereference scattered labels for related entities would not be able to exploit the efficiency advantages of contiguously "clustering" the registration labels of related information.

Furthermore, this approach would be unsuitable for large networks. For large networks, it is impractical to have a single registration authority that every architect must contact each time she specifies a new modeling construct. It would be much easier if we assign just a subset of the name space to each department and let a *local registration authority* hand out numbers from that *subset* of the name space. The higher-level registration authority can then just ensure that the name space subsets assigned to each department are disjoint. Since each department would use numbers from its assigned range, this approach would have the additional advantage that similar objects would be registered with numbers close together in the name space. More importantly, the central registration authority need no longer be a bottleneck as it need no longer be concerned with minutiae. Thus, our new labeling scheme would have the additional advantage of being *partitionable*, so that each partition could be *delegated*.

This would work fine for a while, but when one department used up all the numbers in its range, it would have to be assigned a new range, which may not be contiguous with its previous range. While we can certainly live with this problem, it may lead to slight inefficiencies in run-time lookup algorithms.

With all these schemes, there is a bigger problem that arises when we connect our network to somebody else's network. Assuming that both networks use the same model, if our network uses numbers starting from 0 up, and theirs does also, it is almost inevitable that somewhere there will be a conflict of the name space. A little later, we will see how this problem can be solved.

9.4. Structuring Registration Hierarchies

One way to accommodate the needs of uniqueness, indefinite growth, and delegative partitioning is to use a hierarchical data structure. This structure can consist of non-negative integers, each of which defines a node in the hierarchy. The integers can be so assigned that at every level all sibling nodes are differently numbered. By assigning to our items registration numbers from different branches of the hierarchy, we can be assured that all registered items can be uniquely labeled. By extending the hierarchy as deep as we need to at the leaves, we can be assured of indefinite growth. By assigning different branches of the hierarchy to each group and giving each group the authority to grow its branch of the tree, we can be assured of delegative partitioning.

Such a hierarchy is called an *object registration hierarchy*. It should be noted that the items registered in the hierarchy are not just object classes as defined in the model but also attributes, functions, capsules, aggregations, and so on. The term *object* is somewhat of a misnomer here. In the context of registration, the term "object" means "anything that is registered", rather than an instance of a class in the object-oriented sense. Often, we will refer to the hierarchy as simply a *registration hierarchy*.

To identify each construct in the registration hierarchy, we must now specify not just one integer but a sequence of integers. It is this *sequence of integers* which constitutes a single label. We start off at an unnumbered root and proceed to follow this sequence of integers, which causes us to traverse the hierarchy downward, with each number in the sequence identifying each successive branch. Upon exhausting all the integers in the sequence, the node at which we find ourselves is the construct of interest. All possible sequences of integers will not necessarily correspond to a well-defined path in the hierarchy, since each branch could have different allocations at each level, and sibling nodes need not be consecutively numbered.

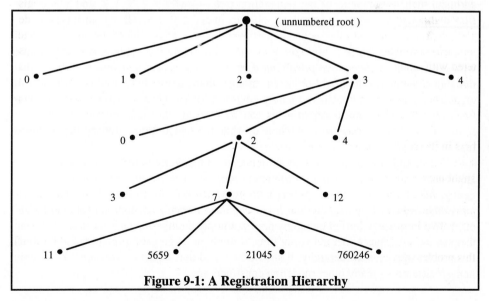

Figure 9-1: A Registration Hierarchy

For example, if we register an object class in the registration hierarchy as shown in Figure 9-1, every time we need to refer to it we can simply specify its label as { 3 2 7 760246 }. Assuming that this hierarchy is publicly advertised and available, anyone who uses the same model can dereference that label and identify the complete specification of the object class — all its attributes, all its functions, all its capsules, and so on. Of course, each of these properties will have its own registration label which itself must be dereferenced.

Since we want to accommodate indefinite growth, we cannot tell in advance how many integers will be required to specify any one particular item. The sequence of integers could be indefinitely long. Therefore, if we are to carry these labels in any sort of protocol, we cannot assign fixed-length fields in the protocol frame to carry these labels. We must have some mechanism in the protocol which identifies a label, tells us how long it is, and then tells us what it is. Fortunately, this can be easily accomplished in most protocols.

How should we structure the registration hierarchy for all our items of interest? The answer is "any way we want". The actual structure of the hierarchy is irrelevant, as long as it can grow, be delegated, and results in unique assignments. Remember we need to register not just object classes but also attributes, capsules, and so on. We can, if we wish, assign the branch { 0 } to mean "all object classes", { 1 } to mean "all attributes", { 2 } to mean "all functions", and so on. Under each of these branches, we might create some additional structure of sub-branches under each branch. Alternatively, we might use a flat naming scheme under each branch, so if we define 1000 object classes, they might all be registered as { 0 0 } to { 0 999 }.

With such a scheme, numbers can also be assigned based on institutional organization. If we have three departments working on the model, we might assign each department their own branch of the registration tree — say { 0 }, { 1 }, and { 2 }. The first department now registers all its objects under { 0 0 }, all its attributes under { 0 1 }, and so on, while the second department registers all its objects under { 1 0 }, all its attributes under { 1 1 }, and so on, as shown in Figure 9-2. This is perfectly in line with our notion of *delegative partitioning* of the name space, and this is indeed what many institutions do. It should be noted, though, that partitioning based on institutional organization should be considered purely advisory. This is because, over time, organizations can change — entire departments can be merged, shuffled, reorganized, bought, sold, split, laid off, or otherwise obliterated, while the registration numbers they assigned to their items will continue to be in use.

It should be emphasized that the registration hierarchy is just a *data structure for labels* and conveys no semantic information whatsoever about the actual model. In particular, *the registration hierarchy has nothing whatsoever to do with either the inheritance hierarchy or any aggregation hierarchy*. Just because an item appears below another item in the registration hierarchy does not imply an inheritance association between them in the inheritance hierarchy, nor does it imply an aggregation relationship between them in the aggregation hierarchy. It should be noted that object classes are not the only items registered — many other modeling constructs are.

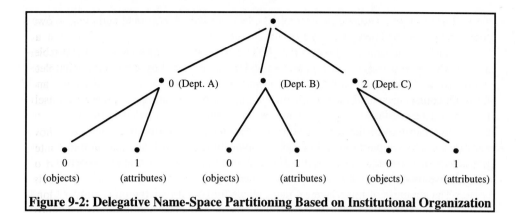

Figure 9-2: Delegative Name-Space Partitioning Based on Institutional Organization

Nevertheless, because each object class must appear exactly once in the registration hierarchy, it may seem tempting to structure the branches of registration hierarchy to parallel the branches of the inheritance hierarchy. Whether or not this is done is actually quite irrelevant. All we really want is a unique label for each registered item. Even if the registration structure is aligned with the inheritance structure to begin with, it can very soon get misaligned if we start defining classes with multiple inheritance. A good guiding principle for designing the labeling structure is its use by run-time algorithms which will dereference the labels. If we can assign related labels to related information, storage for run-time lookups is likely to be more efficiently organized.

Once a label has been assigned, it *absolutely cannot be changed*, because the information is published to all users of the model. In the event that a particular item was either incorrectly registered, or has become obsolete and is no longer used, a question may arise as to whether we should free up its registration number for reuse by a new item. The answer is no. Registration number reuse is not advisable, on the off-chance that there may still be some entities in the network that do not know that a number has changed its meaning. New items should be assigned numbers which have never previously been used; the magnitude of the number is irrelevant. If need be, we can always create new branches in the registration hierarchy. Positive integers are a cheap natural resource and need not be recycled; the probability that their indiscriminate consumption will cause depletion or environmental damage is commonly considered small.

9.5. The International Registration Hierarchy

Assume that we have defined all our modeling constructs and have labeled them using our own registration hierarchy. We can begin to use our model to synthesize and architect networks, to operate them, and to manage them. What happens when we federate our network, and interconnect it to other networks over whose registration labels we have no control? Clearly, there can be a conflict of name spaces. To keep the name spaces disjointly partitioned, we need a mechanism to which *everybody* subscribes.

The solution to this is to have an *international registration authority*. With such a mechanism, everybody can register all their items with the international authority. Thus,

we will never have any name space conflicts, because the international authority will ensure that the assigned name space partitions are disjoint.

Such a mechanism actually exists [ITU-T X.660]. This mechanism has been created for the express purpose of registration and is administered by the international standards organizations ISO and ITU. These organizations define the *universal name space*
for registering objects and partition it for assignment to the national standards organizations of various countries. Each national organization has been delegated responsibility
for its own partition of the name space. The national organization may then create sub-
partitions in its own partition and delegate responsibility for each sub-partition to institutions in its own country, and so forth. The end result is that every number assigned from
the universal name space is guaranteed to be internationally unique.

The structure of this universal name space for object registration is similar to that
described in Figure 9-2. That is, it is hierarchical, and uses non-negative integers to
identify registered items nestled somewhere within the branches of its registration tree.
Starting off at the root of this tree and working our way down through the various
branches and sub-branches delegated to various national standards bodies and sub-bodies,
we can precisely locate a specific registered item. The important concept here is that *there
is only one tree for the whole world.* Every registered item must somehow, somewhere,
link up with this single, global tree, so that it can be universally uniquely identified.

The international registration label, which is a sequence of integers such as
{ 1 3 6 ... }, has a name — it is known as an OBJECT IDENTIFIER. Once again, the
term *object* is a misnomer, because it actually identifies any item registered in the international registration hierarchy. Such items need not just be object classes or instances in
the sense of object-oriented modeling. The label is called an OBJECT IDENTIFIER because, as we shall see, it is a recognized data type in the international syntax specification
language known as ASN.1, or Abstract Syntax Notation One.

The registration tree of international OBJECT IDENTIFIERs starts off at an unnumbered conceptual root. Immediately under this root are three branches, numbered 0, 1,
and 2. Branch 0, labeled "CCITT" for historical reasons, is administered separately by the
ITU; branch 1 separately by ISO; and branch 2 jointly by both ISO and ITU. Each authority then delegates further responsibility to various organizations by assigning numbers
under each branch. Under ISO, for example, there are sub-branches assigned for 0 (for
standards), 1 (any recognized registration authority), 2 (for ISO member bodies), and 3
(for any other identified organizations). Figure 9-3 shows the upper levels of the international registration hierarchy.

In a later section, we will see how object model constructs defined by private organizations can be accommodated within this universal labeling structure. As a prelude,
we present the analogy of this structure to other international registration hierarchies
which may possibly be more familiar.

9.6. Other International Registration Hierarchies

The concept of a hierarchically structured application-specific universal name space is not
new. Neither is the concept of delegative partitioning of the name space to various

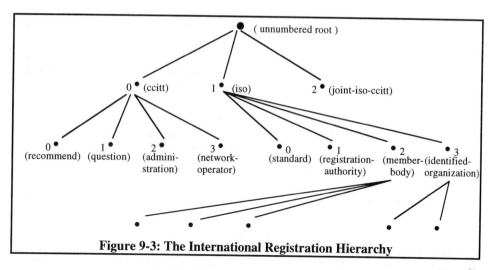

Figure 9-3: The International Registration Hierarchy

authorities which perform the actual assignment. Consider the analogy with the North American Numbering Plan (NANP) which is largely used by telephone networks in the geographic continent of North America. The NANP was privately administered for many years but is now administered by the U.S. Federal Communications Commission. To uniquely identify telephone numbers, the NANP creates at the highest level several branches from its unnumbered conceptual root [TR 93]. These branches are identified by a three-digit integer known as an *area code*.

In an earlier version of the NANP, area codes were restricted to a particular syntax, so only about 150 or so were allowed; this restriction has since been removed due to growth requirements. An area code usually covers a particular geographic area and is usually administered by a regional telephone company providing service to that area. Although there used to be a one-to-one mapping between geographic areas and area codes, the new NANP allows multiple *overlay codes* to provide service to overlapping territories in the same geographic area. Special area codes such as 800 and 900 have no particular geographic mapping and can provide service in a distributed fashion.

Further down the NANP hierarchy, each regional telephone company creates under each area code approximately 700 branches, each branch being identified by a three-digit integer known as a *prefix*. Each prefix is then assigned to a particular switch, providing service to a narrow local area. Multiple prefixes may be assigned to a single switch. Since prefixes are just registration mechanisms, their allocation need not be contiguous. Figure 9-4 illustrates how numbers might be allocated under the NANP hierarchy.

The authority in charge of a prefix can delegate branches under the prefix to subscribers. Up to 10,000 branches can be created underneath each prefix, each identified by a 4-digit integer. With prior arrangement, the subscriber can receive authority to further delegate underneath that 4-digit integer. The subscriber may register branches underneath that 4-digit integer, called *extensions*, to individuals on its campus. Alternatively, instead of registering for a single 4-digit number from the phone company, the subscriber may register for a whole block of 4-digit numbers directly underneath the prefix. If the sub-

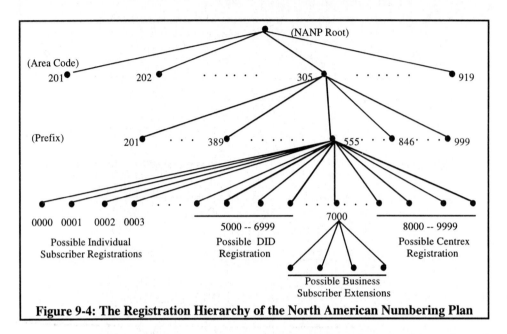

Figure 9-4: The Registration Hierarchy of the North American Numbering Plan

scriber has a PBX on campus, it may use that block of numbers for *Direct Inward Dialing*, which has the effect of registering internal PBX extensions as part of the block assigned to the subscriber. If it does not have a PBX on campus, it may use that block of numbers for *Centrex* service, which has the same effect, as the phone company's central office switch mimics a virtual PBX for that block of numbers.

Thus, the telephone networks in the NANP are in fact a registration authority. An interesting aspect of this registration mechanism is that it allows delegative partitioning of the name space but, for various technical reasons, it cannot accommodate indefinite growth. Another interesting issue is whether this name space, large as it is, is still a private name space, or whether it can be used to interoperate with other networks internationally.

Telephone communication was one of first application areas which addressed the problem of creating federated networks. In order for telephone systems worldwide to interoperate, the appropriate jurisdictional authorities first had to work out a registration mechanism whereby every telephone terminal in the world could be uniquely identified. It was not practical to force everyone into the same numbering format, as every jurisdiction already had an installed base with its own proprietary number registration format; further, this format was not necessarily internally consistent within each jurisdiction either.

The addressing problem was solved by a convention that specified the use of additional integers. All the jurisdictions met under the aegis of the ITU and created a standard known as E.163 to assist in federating their respective networks [ITU-T E.163]. Each jurisdiction could continue to use its own proprietary format for internal communication. This is known as a *National Specific Number*. But if it wanted to interoperate with other telephone systems, it would first have to obtain and publicize an official number, known as a *Country Code*, from the ITU. Country codes themselves are assigned based on geographically defined "World Zones". By agreeing to use official country codes assigned by the ITU prior to dialing proprietary-format numbers, telephone networks could address each other internationally without ambiguity.

By controlling the assignment of country codes and ensuring that all assignments are unique, the ITU acts as a registration authority. It creates a universal name space of telephone numbers, such that if each telephone terminal in the world is addressed by its full universal label, it is guaranteed to be unique. This name space also allows delegative partitioning, because once each jurisdiction obtains an official country code from the ITU, it is free to allocate as it pleases any further number registration underneath that country code. It may further sub-partition its assigned partition of the universal telephone number name space and delegate the authority for each sub-partition to sub-authorities, and so on. Figure 9-5 illustrates some allocations by the ITU, creating a superstructure above the numbering plans of individual countries, including the NANP.

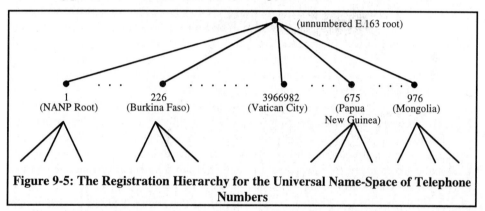

Figure 9-5: The Registration Hierarchy for the Universal Name-Space of Telephone Numbers

The assignment by the ITU of country codes is similar to creating branches of the registration tree based on *institutional organization*, except on a greater scale. Thus, all the caveats of patterning a registration hierarchy based on an institutional hierarchy apply. Just as the departments of an institution can be split and merged, so can countries. In certain cases, some countries which already shared the same numbering plan now share the same "country code": the countries of World Zone 1 (Canada, the United States of America, and many Caribbean nations) share the NANP "country code" 1. Aside from this, political change resulting in the disappearance and creation of nations (through disintegration and unification) means that some old ITU country code registrations are no longer valid. Certain numbers are made obsolete, never to be reused, and other new ones assigned. This is not merely a paper activity, because if a new nation should choose to keep its telephone networks aligned with its political autonomy, it requires database and software upgrades to thousands of telephone switches worldwide.

Network-layer addresses — the level at which data networks identify specific nodes in the network — are another example of a *universal name space of network nodes*, whose assignment is controlled by a central registration authority [Mats89]. All of these also allow delegative partitioning. The numbering plan X.121, administered by the ITU, specifies the address format for X.25 data networks, partitioning it as a Data Network

Identification Code and a Network Terminal Number [ITU-T X.121]. The Internet numbering plan, administered by the Network Information Center, partitions the Internet address name space into a Network ID and a Host ID, whose length differs depending on the class of the address [RFC 1117, RFC 1060]. The numbering plan E.164, administered by the ITU, specifies the format for international ISDN addresses, partitioning it as a Country Code, a National Destination Code, and a Subscriber Number [ITU-T E.164]. The OSI network numbering plan, defined in the standard ISO 8348, specifies the format for OSI network-layer addresses, partitioning it as an Authority and Format Identifier, an Initial Domain Identifier, and a Domain-Specific Part [ISO 8348].

9.7. Linking to the International Hierarchy

If we want our network to interoperate with other networks, we must subscribe to some universal numbering scheme. In our case, we are not trying to register network addresses; we are trying to convey the semantics of our network model. Thus, all we want is the ability to uniquely identify our modeling constructs such that they will not conflict with other constructs. Since the internationally administered registration mechanism for objects guarantees that the labels of all objects registered within it will be unique, we can use this mechanism to register our modeling constructs.

In doing so, we must reconcile our private registration tree with the international hierarchy, because our privately assigned numbers could very easily be in conflict with the allocations already made in the universal name space. And indeed this is often the case, but this problem can be solved very simply. Because the international registration tree can be grown indefinitely, we do not actually have to *relabel* our private tree. We can just *attach* our private tree to one of the leaf nodes of the international hierarchy.

All we need is *one number* assigned to us by some authority which already has an official assignment in the tree. Once we have that number, we can link the root of our private tree at that number. The reason we can do this is because sub-branching authority is also delegated with number assignment. Once we have one number in the tree, we are free to create further branches as we please and expand the tree downward from that number. Of course, we can choose to do this by retaining the same configuration we have in our private tree. Thus, all our assignments will remain the same, except that our labels, instead of starting at our private root, will now start off at the international root. Thus, each of our labels will have a new sequence of integers prefixing its old value, and this new prefixing sequence will be the same for all our labels. Figure 9-6 illustrates how a private tree might be linked to the international hierarchy.

Do we need to wait for an official number before beginning to use our object model? No — the process of obtaining an official number can take time. We can create our own tree from a private root, begin to use it right away, and eventually link up somewhere with the international tree. Therefore, we can start assigning numbers to register items in our object model as we define them. When we are finally attached to the universal name space, all the labels for our registered items will change to add the same new prefixing integer sequence. At this point, all we will need to do is possibly change a directive in a header file and recompile the model.

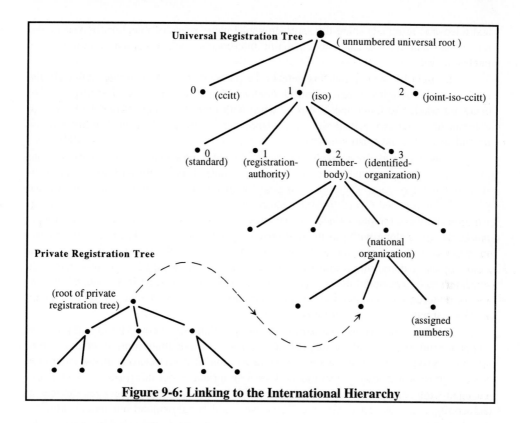

Figure 9-6: Linking to the International Hierarchy

9.8. Achieving Interoperability

A genuine question may be raised with regard to registering our subtree internationally. When we assigned labels from the private tree we originally built, we registered those items which we thought were important in our model. What guarantee do we have that others using the same tree will also be using the same model? If we send them information using a universal label which refers to a construct in our model, how do we know that they can dereference that label correctly with respect to our model? Conversely, if we receive a label from them, we might be able to recognize that label as a valid universal label, but we might not know anything about its referent construct. The registration mechanism, while guaranteeing that each assigned label will be unique, *makes no guarantee that the semantics associated with that label will be understood by everyone who subscribes to the international registration hierarchy.*

As it turns out, this is indeed what happens, and fortunately, it isn't a problem. The reason it isn't a problem is because *there is no requirement that just because we all share the universal name space, we must all use the same object model.* In fact, we can go on quite happily using our *subset* of the name space, as long as we build our applications that understand and dereference that subset. Other organizations can use their subset of the name space, along with their applications. As an analogy, paging devices, fax machines, and telephone terminals share the same universal name space of telephone numbers, but there is no requirement that a fax machine interoperate with a telephone terminal or a paging device.

It might be argued that this defeats the purpose of interoperability. After all, the reason we linked up our registration hierarchy with the international hierarchy was because we wanted to interconnect our network with other networks. If our network is to continue to be our own private semantic island, there really is no reason to publicly register and advertise our registration tree.

This is indeed a reasonable argument. However, now that we have registered our object models internationally, we are at least guaranteed that there will not be any conflicts in the name space. Therefore, it is possible that in future there may be a chance that we could interoperate. To realize this chance, it is not sufficient to merely advertise registration numbers for our objects — we must also publicly advertise the actual *object model* that goes along with our internationally registered numbers. Then, any other institution desiring to interoperate with us merely has to access the formal definition of our object model and compile it into their network. Now, they would be able to dereference our labels and understand the semantics of our model. Conversely, if we wanted our applications to understand and interoperate with another network, we would have to obtain *its* object model and compile it into *our* network.

As an alternative to this extra-systemic negotiation, we could build sufficient intelligence into our network so that it could perform this negotiation on its own as a preliminary activity prior to commencing interoperation. If each network in the federation were cognizant of its own object model, then appropriate model information could be exchanged with other networks on-line at network federation time, or between devices at autoconfiguration handshaking time. Thus, we could autodownload our model information base into an alien intelligent network and accept an autodownload of the alien model information base. We would then have the ability to mutually dereference the semantics associated with each other's universal labels and achieve true interoperation with intra-systemic rather than extra-systemic negotiation.

9.9. Summary

In order to interoperate our network at a high level with other networks, we need to be able to convey the semantics of our object model. Doing so requires that we uniquely identify all our modeling constructs and publicize them. We accomplish this by organizing our constructs in a tree-structured registration hierarchy. For making this hierarchy publicly available, we must link our private tree to the international registration hierarchy. To do this, we must find an authority which already has a number somewhere in the tree and is willing to assign us a branch underneath their number. This usually can be done by approaching a national standards authority or other authorized regulatory body. Once our modeling constructs are registered in the universal name space, we can make available to any party desiring to interoperate with our network the actual model associated with the internationally registered numbers.

10. *Introduction to Network Modeling Syntax*

"Permanent network fixes are temporary.
Temporary network fixes are permanent."

— *anonymous network architect.*

10.1. Introduction

In this chapter, we examine the benefits of a formal approach to modeling communication networks. As a vehicle to couch this formalism, the syntax notation of ASN.1 is introduced. The use of templates created by ASN.1 Information Object Class notation is explained with simple examples. Logical predicates, also couched in ASN.1 notation, are introduced as a tool for use in advanced modeling constructs which will be covered in later chapters.

10.2. Formalism in Network Modeling

Any modeling technique which must be amenable to automatic analysis needs a language in which the semantics of the model can be expressed. Such a model representation language should be designed for both human inspection and for machine interpretation. The language should be precise and formal and should allow us to specify all the constructs we need in order to capture the meaning of our network model. It is not important that the modeling language itself be executable, but it is very important that the syntax of the language be sufficiently rich that we can express all the complexities of a large network. The syntax of the specification language should encourage human understanding of the system in an "accessible" and "natural" manner. In addition, if the syntax is unambiguous so that machine-based interpretation can convert the specifications into actual executable language implementations, we can then translate the formal specification into any desired implementation merely by writing an appropriate "model compiler".

Just as the design of VLSI circuits benefits from the use of formal modeling techniques, so can the architecture of complex networks. The benefits of a formal specification syntax are many, the most important benefit perhaps being that formalism imposes an organization on the architect's thinking. It forces the architect to be precise and resolve potential design conflicts at the specification stage itself, rather than later on in the life cycle at which point they can be expensive to correct.

A number of model representation languages already exist today [Deva91]. Logic programming languages are useful where the problem domain has many actual facts and needs inferential resolution. Production systems are better when the domain is heuristic and is required to produce normative recommendations. Structure-based systems are useful when the domain is hierarchical and displays strong categorization characteristics. Associative systems are applicable when, in addition to hierarchical structure, the domain also displays many cross-structural linkages.

For our use, each of these specification techniques has some elements useful for expressing the semantics of network modeling, but no single technique has all the constructs we need. In addition, we want to ensure that we do not specify our model in a representation language tied to a particular implementation technique. Therefore, we will express our model in a specification syntax which will be independent of any implementation language but can be translated to one or more desired implementation languages with appropriate compilers. By designing our own specification syntax, we ensure that we can express all the elements we need to capture the complete semantics of our model.

Note that a formal syntax is not intended to replace graphical techniques for representing the same information. Graphical techniques are extremely important in human communication: they are relatively concise and can convey a lot of information to the human reader in a single page. While graphical techniques are language-neutral, often many are not tool-neutral, since many are tied to specific modeling methodologies. Formal syntaxes are tool-neutral — once a standard syntax is specified, many different front-end graphical tools could conceivably generate the same syntax. In addition, by ensuring that the formal syntax is designed only to capture modeling semantics and is not itself an implementation language, it can also be made language-neutral.

Historically, many semantic models have been captured in a graphical representation [Chen76, Rumb91a] while others have used formal syntax [Codd90]. These techniques should be seen as being complementary rather than competitive. The ideal modeling tool will support both a graphical technique and a formal syntax. A picture conveys the essence of a high-level model to the human reader. But, by its very nature of being a high-level overview, a picture cannot possible accommodate every detail about properties and attributes. Furthermore, outside of certain selective application domains, *semiotic compilers* — that is, compilers which translate a *pictorial* source representation into an executable software implementation — are not widely available. A formal modeling syntax allows us to both precisely capture details and to write translators which will create implementations given the specification as input. This syntax could either be directly specified by the architect or could be generated by a graphical front-end tool.

Whether the network architect uses a graphical front-end tool to specify the formal model or not, it is important that the specification process be interactive. Network modeling is an iterative process, in which the architect proposes a partial working hypothesis, prototypes and tests it through simulation, then expands and refines it based on the results of the simulation testing.

The specification compiler, therefore, should be capable of digesting partial models and should allow progressive refinement so that more details and richer structure can be added as the model is refined. In particular, any new modeling construct specified should be checked against the model information base. Potential conflicts and ambiguities with existing constructs should be indicated and resolved through an interactive process with the network architect [Sara87]. The model information base acts as a repository of specification information and admits new specification constructs only if they do not conflict with existing constructs.

To maintain a model information base, some sort of supporting system is clearly required. This supporting system will be required to maintain a dictionary of existing modeling constructs, search them for potential conflicts with new constructs, and efficiently store them in a manner suitable for easy retrieval.

In this book. the vehicle we shall use to specify our formal model is the international standard Abstract Syntax Notation One (ASN.1). This notation is one among many which can serve to *demonstrate* how the methodology may be used in a formal specification. It is not an integral part of specialization theory or of any network model constructed using specialization theory. The modeling technique is syntax-independent; any sufficiently precise notation (that is, one capable of being compiled) may be chosen to capture the semantics of the methodology.

10.3. Elements of ASN.1

ASN.1 is a syntax notation designed to express information in a form independent of machine representation. There are two parts to the ASN.1 specification. The first part specifies the syntax notation itself [ITU-T X.680]. The second part specifies how this syntax notation may be encoded for transmission as a sequence of bits using one of many *encoding rules*, such as the Basic Encoding Rules [ITU-T X.690]. In OSI protocol stacks, ASN.1 encoding and decoding is generally done at the presentation layer, although ASN.1 has been used in many places including non-OSI protocol stacks.

For our network model, we are not concerned with the encoding of ASN.1 for transmission; we know this can be accomplished using any appropriate set of encoding rules. We will use just the syntax notation to express the semantics of our model.

It should be noted that, by itself, ASN.1 lacks many semantic features which are built into other formal specification languages (some of which we shall consider in Chapter 13). In some cases, the semantic concepts of specialization theory can be expressed more concisely in a language other than ASN.1. However, ASN.1 provides "building blocks" for creating constructs on which user-defined semantics can be imposed. These constructs can be both human-readable and machine-processable. Nevertheless, it is important that the user-imposed semantics associated with user-defined ASN.1 constructs be documented precisely; otherwise, ambiguity may arise due to differing interpretations.

This chapter is not intended to be a tutorial on the basics of ASN.1, as there are many excellent sources for that information. For a detailed explanation of the ASN.1

syntax, the reader is referred elsewhere [Rose90, Chap89, Whit89, Stee90, Scot90]. We will cover a few elementary constructs by way of introduction.

Types and Values

Two of the more important notations in ASN.1 are *type assignments* and *value assignments*. A type assignment creates new types, based either directly on built-in ASN.1 types, or on existing types defined using built-in ASN.1 types. A type can be either a *simple type* or a *structured type*.

A simple type can be created by a type assignment with three syntactic components: the name of the type, the assignment symbol ": : =", and the appropriate type notation. Thus

```
TypeName ::= TYPE
```

is the general form of a type notation. For example,

```
IpAddress ::= OCTET STRING (SIZE (4))
```

defines `IpAddress` as an ASN.1 type using the built-in `OCTET STRING` type.

Value assignments create values of built-in or user-defined types. A value assignment is similar to a type assignment, but each value also carries with it its type. Thus

```
valueName TypeName ::= VALUE
```

defines a value of that type. For example,

```
myNetAddress IpAddress ::= 'C0210414'H
                       -- 192.33.4.20
```

assigns to the variable `myNetAddress` the specified value of the `OCTET STRING`. The double hyphen delimits an ASN.1 comment-to-end-of-line.

The name `IpAddress`, which is a new type created by the type assignment, is called a *type reference name*. The name `myNetAddress`, which is an instance of the type created by the value assignment, is called a *value reference name*. An important rule in ASN.1 is that a type reference name must always start with an upper-case letter, and a value reference name must always start with a lower-case letter.

A type can also be created as a subtype of an existing type, such that the subtype can only take a subset of values of the existing type. Such a type is created using a *value set type assignment*. A value set type assignment has four syntactic components: the type reference name of the subtype being created, the type reference name of the existing type, ": : =", and a list of permissible values of the existing type. The list of permissible values is typically separated with the symbol "|", an expansion known as an ASN.1 *production*.

Because it has four components, a value set type assignment looks rather like a value assignment, but it really creates a type. For example, the value set type assignment

```
CompanyXAddress IpAddress ::= {
                                'C0210414'H  |
                                'C0210415'H  |
                                'C0210416'H
                              }
```

creates `CompanyXAddress` as a subtype of `IpAddress` whose values can only come from the enumerated list of `IpAddress` values. Subject to this restriction, `CompanyX-Address` can be legally used as any other type reference name, for example, to create values.

Object Identifiers

An example of a built-in ASN.1 type is the `OBJECT IDENTIFIER` type. As we said before, an `OBJECT IDENTIFIER` is a sequence of integers which serves to uniquely identify a modeling construct in a registration hierarchy. It is possible to assign an `OBJECT IDENTIFIER` to any modeling construct so that that construct becomes uniquely registered in some registration hierarchy. This registration hierarchy could be a private tree or could be part of the global registration hierarchy. Even if we start off using a local form of `OBJECT IDENTIFIER`s in a private hierarchy to begin with, we can redefine the prefix when we link up to the global hierarchy, so we will not worry about the distinction between local and global values of `OBJECT IDENTIFIER`s as a modeling concern.

Recall that an `OBJECT IDENTIFIER` is a sequence of integers, each integer identifying an arc in a registration hierarchy. We can therefore say

```
Label ::= OBJECT IDENTIFIER


labelOfMyObject Label ::= {2 5 4 20}
```

These statements create a new type reference name called `Label` which is simply the same type as `OBJECT IDENTIFIER`. The value reference name `labelOfMy-Object`, which has the type `Label`, is then assigned a particular value which is an actual `OBJECT IDENTIFIER`.

Subtypes

ASN.1 has many other built-in types for simple values, including bit strings, Booleans, integers, reals, and various kinds of character strings. Aside from value set type assignments, subtypes in ASN.1 can be created by using the mechanism of *subtype constraints*.

A subtype constraint restricts values of existing types to particular ranges or sets of values. For example, the type assignment

```
PositiveInteger ::= INTEGER (1..MAX)
```

constrains the type `PositiveInteger` to only possess values between the range 1 and the maximum value supported by the compiler. As an example of a constraint defining a set of values, the type assignment

```
TouchToneKey ::= IA5String ("0"|"1"|"2"|"3"|"4"|"5"|
                            "6"|"7"|"8"|"9"|"*"|"#")
```

constrains the type `TouchToneKey` to contain only the indicated single-character string values from the built-in type `IA5String`, which represents the international alphabet. Constraints can also be specified as inclusions or exclusions from the permitted values of another type; for example, the type assignment

```
DialedDigit ::= TouchToneKey (EXCEPT("*"|"#"))
```

permits any value of the type `DialedDigit` to have any value of `TouchToneKey` except the indicated values.

Structured Types

The notation also permits the use of structured types, in which simple types can be combined in various ways to create more complex types. The basic structured types in ASN.1 are the SEQUENCE type, the SEQUENCE OF type, the SET type, the SET OF type, and the CHOICE type. We provide a few elementary examples of these types below.

     A SEQUENCE OF construct is used to indicate a collection of values of the indicated type. All the values in this collection must be of the same type. Its length may be indeterminate, but the ordering is significant. For example, the type

```
DigitString ::= SEQUENCE OF DialedDigit
```

defines `DigitString` as any ordered collection of `DialedDigit` values of indeterminate length. To limit the length of this collection, a constraint may also be specified as a *size constraint*. The type assignment

```
ThreeDigitString ::= SEQUENCE (SIZE(3)) OF DialedDigit
```

limits the type `ThreeDigitString` to the indicated size. A size constraint can be equivalently specified using the alternative form

```
FourDigitString ::= DigitString (SIZE(4))
```

A SEQUENCE type is used to create a record or structure of other types, each named with an identifier. As an example, the type assignment

```
NanpNumber ::= SEQUENCE
{
        areaCode                ThreeDigitString,
        prefix                  ThreeDigitString,
        number                  FourDigitString,
        extension               DigitString OPTIONAL
}
```

creates the type NanpNumber as a structure with four fields; the OPTIONAL keyword for the extension field indicates that that field may be omitted. Any value of this type must contain the field names against each of their values. For example, the value assignment

```
myPhoneNumber NanpNumber ::=
{
        areaCode                {"3","0","5"},
        prefix                  {"5","5","5"},
        number                  {"0","0","0","0"}
}
```

creates myPhoneNumber as a legal value of type NanpNumber.

The SET OF type is similar to the SEQUENCE OF type, with the difference that the ordering is not significant. For example, the type assignment

```
PreferredCallForwardingList ::= SET OF NanpNumber
```

defines PreferredCallForwardingList as a type consisting of a collection of values of the NanpNumber type, in which the ordering of the collection is not significant. A SET type, like a SEQUENCE type, contains field names and their type; it is similar to a SEQUENCE type with no significance for the internal ordering of the fields.

The CHOICE construct is used to create a type which resolves to one of several other types. For example, given the type assignments

```
CountryCode ::= DigitString
```

```
EuropeanNumber ::= SEQUENCE
{
      cityCode              DigitString,
      number                DigitString
}
```

we may then define the type

```
InternationalNumber ::= SEQUENCE
{                             -- number in E.163 format
      countryCode    CountryCode,
      number         CHOICE
                     {    -- national specific number
                       northAmerican [0] NanpNumber,
                       european      [1] EuropeanNumber,
                       other         [2] DigitString
                     }
}
```

In this definition, the number field in any value of the International-Number type can resolve to a value which is either an NanpNumber type, a EuropeanNumber type, or a DigitString type. Any value of a CHOICE type must indicate which field of the CHOICE has been selected by using the field name and a ":" to prefix the value. For example, the value assignment

```
myInternationalNumber InternationalNumber ::=
{
      countryCode    "1",
      number         {northAmerican: myPhoneNumber}
}
```

creates myInternationalNumber as a legal value of the type International-Number. In the definition of a CHOICE type, all the fields must be tagged with an integer tag appearing within brackets; this helps ensure distinctness of the selected value when the chosen field is encoded for transmission in a PDU. The fields of a SET type should also be similarly tagged.

Many excellent texts provide a detailed language tutorial of ASN.1 [Stee90, Scot90]. In the next section, we will examine a more complex form of structuring, called an *information object class*, which we will use frequently in the formal specification of our model.

10.4. Information Object Classes

An *information object class* is a structuring mechanism in ASN.1 to support the packaging of a set of other types together in a single construct [ITU-T X.681]. An information object class is used to create *information objects*. The term "information object class" is an unfortunate overloading of terminology: the words "object" and "class" have nothing whatsoever to do with objects and classes in the sense of object-oriented modeling. An ASN.1 information object class is merely a template which allows the definition of packages of other syntaxes; such a package need not necessarily be an object class in the object-oriented sense. Neither does an information object class support inheritance in the manner of an object class in an object-oriented model.

We will always refer to these templates as "information object classes" and always attempt to have sufficient context to make this usage distinct from object classes in the object-oriented model. In general, the terms "object class", "object", and "instance" will refer to our object-oriented network model, while the terms "information object class" and "information object" will refer to syntactic constructs in ASN.1. As we shall see later, all constructs in our object-oriented network model — including object classes, attributes, functions, and relationships — will be defined as ASN.1 information objects of an appropriate information object class.

An information object class is created by an *information object class assignment*. This describes the elements of each information object class, known as *fields*. Its syntax is

```
CLASSNAME ::= CLASS
{
     &field1,
     &field2,
     ...
}
```

Here, CLASSNAME is the name of the information object class being created and is called an *information object class reference*. The term CLASS is a reserved keyword in ASN.1 syntax. The constructs &field1 and &field2 are *field names*. Field names must all begin with an ampersand. Once an information object class has been defined, we may create information objects of that class. Information objects are structured collections of actual data values. These objects are created using a notation called an *information object assignment*:

```
informationObjectName CLASSNAME ::=
{
     &field1    valueOfField1,
     &field2    valueOfField2,
     ...
}
```

This assignment creates `informationObjectName` as an information object of the `CLASSNAME` information object class. The construct `informationObject-Name` is the name of the created information object and is called an *information object reference*. We may reference the value of an individual field in any information object simply by suffixing the field name to the information object reference. This mechanism is known as a *value from object*. For example, the construct

```
informationObjectName.&field1
```

is equivalent to the value `valueOfField1`. The definition of an ASN.1 information object class permits us to specify the default value which information objects of that class may have for any given field.

An important rule is that an information object class reference must be all upper-case letters, and an information object reference must begin with a lower-case letter. As is obvious, the information object class assignment notation is analogous to the type assignment notation, and the information object assignment notation is analogous to the value assignment notation. However, unlike many object-oriented programming languages, an information object class is *not* a type, and an information object is *not* a value. We shall see later how they are different.

The information object class assignment notation allows the definition of the an *extended syntax* for defining information objects of that information object class. This is known as a *with-syntax* specification; it permits the creation of information objects with a *user-defined* notation. This allows the specification of user constructs in a friendlier, more readable manner, as it allows the specifier to add sufficient syntactic sugar to each construct to make it palatable to the human reader. Information object classes replace the ASN.1 Macro Definition Notation which some readers may be familiar with from the earlier ASN.1 standard.

Each field of an ASN.1 information object class may be one of seven different varieties:

1. A field may contain just a type reference name, without containing any value (*Type Field*).

2. A field may contain a single value of a specified type (*Fixed-Type Value Field*).

3. A field may contain a value whose type varies for different information objects of that class and is determined depending on the contents of a Type Field (*Variable-Type Value Field*).

4. A field may contain a set of values of specified type (*Fixed-Type Value Set Field*).

5. A field may contain a set of values whose type varies for different information objects of that class and is determined depending on the contents of a Type Field (*Variable-Type Value Set Field*).

6. A field may contain an information object of a specified information object class, including the information object class currently being specified (*Object Field*).

7. A field may contain a set of information objects from a specified information object class (*Object Set Field*).

Having defined an information object class, we need some way of distinguishing information objects of that class from each other. To do this, we may select one of the fixed-type value fields as the *identifier field* for that information object class. By specifying this to be UNIQUE, we ensure that each information object in any set of information objects of that information object class has a different value for the identifier field.

The identifier field, if we so choose to assign its value, may also serve to uniquely identify the information object within a context broader than just a set of information objects of the same information object class. For example, the identifier field could be an OBJECT IDENTIFIER. The value of this identifier field could be assigned as a new node in some registration hierarchy. Therefore, it may uniquely identify the information object not only within that information object class but also among information objects created from other information object class templates. If this is desired, it is incumbent on the specifier to organize the registration values properly; the ASN.1 compiler, when it sees the UNIQUE keyword, can only enforce uniqueness among information objects of a set of the same information object class.

To define an information object class, then, we need to specify

1. The name of each field of the information object class;

2. The nature of each field of the information object class, that is, whether it is a type field, a fixed-type value field, a variable-type value field, a fixed-type value set field, a variable-type value set field, an object field, or an object set field;

3. Whether each field is optional and/or possesses any default settings;

4. Which field, if any, is the identifier field.

In our model, we need to specify many constructs, which include object classes, attributes, functions, capsules, relationships, and so on. We will develop modeling constructs for all of these in the next chapter using information object class notation. As an introductory example to the usage of ASN.1 information object classes, we will consider the specification of attributes in this chapter.

10.5. Using Information Object Classes

Information object classes may be used to specify constructs in our object-oriented network model. To illustrate their application, we attempt in this section to create a specification for the ATTRIBUTE construct; in subsequent chapters, we will present full-fledged definitions of other object-oriented constructs.

An Example with Information Object Classes

We know that an attribute is a property of an object which, with appropriate permissions, can be read as a data value and assigned a data value. Since there are many different kinds of attributes, the data type of each attribute will be different. In addition, each attribute must also be uniquely identifiable so it can be referenced in a database or encoded in a protocol frame. Thus, every defined attribute must possess a value field whose type is `OBJECT IDENTIFIER` as its identifier field.

The specification of each attribute as an information object class must also have a type field which specifies the type of the attribute. We specify the information object class for an attribute as follows:

```
ATTRIBUTE ::= CLASS
{
     &AttributeType,
                         -- a type field
     &attributeLabel     OBJECT IDENTIFIER UNIQUE
                         -- a fixed-type value field
}
WITH SYNTAX
{
     ATTRIBUTE-TYPE      &AttributeType
     IDENTIFIED BY       &attributeLabel
}
```

This specification creates a new information object class named `ATTRIBUTE`. The keywords `CLASS`, `UNIQUE`, and `WITH SYNTAX` are reserved keywords in the ASN.1 information object class notation.

This specification not only sets up the structure of the class but also tells the ASN.1 compiler in the `WITH SYNTAX` clause to accept a more user-friendly definition for information objects of that information object class. We may begin to use that syntax to specify many different kinds of attributes. Assume, for example, that we have already set up the following prior type assignment:

```
BandwidthInBps ::= INTEGER (0..MAX)
```

This type definition creates a new type reference name, `BandwidthInBps`, which is constrained to possess non-negative integer values up to the maximum integer value supported by the compiler. We may now begin to use this type definition in the specification, for example, of the attributes of a `multiplexer` object class:

```
compositePortSpeed ATTRIBUTE  ::=
{
        ATTRIBUTE-TYPE          BandwidthInBps
        IDENTIFIED BY           {multiplexerAtts 1}
}

channelPortSpeed ATTRIBUTE  ::=
{
        ATTRIBUTE-TYPE          BandwidthInBps
        IDENTIFIED BY           {multiplexerAtts 2}
}
```

and so on. These definitions assume that `multiplexerAtts` is already an OBJECT IDENTIFIER defined elsewhere earlier and create new OBJECT IDENTIFIERs for `compositePortSpeed` and `channelPortSpeed` by suffixing `multiplexer-Atts` with another unique integer.

Information Object Sets

Just as we can define value sets, we can also defined *information object sets*. For example, we may define the information object set {`MultiplexerAttributes`}, consisting of all the ATTRIBUTE information objects which denote attributes of the `multiplexer` object class. The identifier `MultiplexerAttributes` is called an *object set reference* which must begin with an upper-case character. We may define this using a notation known as an *object set assignment*. This creates a defined object set qualified by its information object class. This is structurally similar to a value set type assignment except that it uses information objects instead of values:

```
MultiplexerAttributes ATTRIBUTE  ::=
                      {
                              compositePortSpeed   |
                              channelPortSpeed     |
                              ...
                      }
```

This permits us to refer to all the attributes of `multiplexer` as a set by simply using the object set reference `MultiplexerAttributes`.

This example has been intentionally simplified in order to illustrate the concept of an ASN.1 information object class. In an actual model, each port speed would not necessarily be modeled as an individual attribute of a `multiplexer` object class. A generic `portSpeed` attribute could be modeled for a generic `port` object class, and a decomposition relationship could be specified for the `port` object class in the `multiplexer` object class, with an appropriate multiplicity for the decomposition. We shall define the syntax for such specifications in the next chapter.

Caveats

The following are important points to remember while using information object classes:

- An information object class is not a *type*. It can only be used in the following circumstances:

  i)   to create a stand-alone information object

  ii) to create a stand-alone information object set

  iii) to create an object field in an information object class definition

  iv) to create an object set field in an information object class definition

  v)   on the right-hand side of another information object class assignment.

  It *cannot* be used, for example, as the type of a field in an ordinary structured type such as a SEQUENCE or CHOICE. This is because the components of a structured type must be other typed values; they cannot be information objects.

- Just as an information object class is not a type, an information object is not a *value*. An information object cannot appear in situations where a value is required; for example, it cannot appear as a field in a CHOICE among other types. An information object is not intended for being encoded for transmission in a PDU as values of other types are, although value fields and value set fields of any information object may be extracted, encoded, and transmitted. For the same reason, information object sets are not value sets.

- The name of an information object class must be all upper-case. The names of information objects created using that class must begin with a lower-case character, *as if* they were values. The names of all information object sets created using that class must begin with an upper-case character, *as if* they were value sets.

- All *type field references* in an information object class definition must begin with an upper-case character after the "&".

- All *set-valued field references* in an information object class definition must begin with an upper-case character after the "&". This applies to fixed-type value set fields, variable-type value set fields, and object set fields. The type name or information object class name which qualifies the field, if any, applies to every element of the set-valued field.

- All *single-valued field references* in an information object class definition must begin with a lower-case character after the "&". This applies to fixed-type value fields, variable-type value fields, and object fields. The lower-case initial indicates to the compiler that this field is single-valued.

- All *variable-type fields* must use a type name which is the name of a type field in that information object class. This applies to variable-type value fields and variable-type value set fields. (Note that although types are similar to information object classes and values are similar to information objects, there is no such thing as a "variable-class object field" or a "variable-class object set field".)

10.6. Attribute Value Predicates

We now introduce an important concept known as an *attribute value predicate*. A "predicate", from mathematical logic, is a formula with at least one "free variable". A predicate can be meaningfully evaluated only when its free variables stand for particular items. An attribute value predicate is similar; it is a set of three elements: an attribute, a value, and some sort of equality, inequality, or membership relation between them. Among other things, an attribute value predicate helps us declare that a particular attribute possesses a particular value. For example, we may need to state that the compositePortSpeed attribute of the t1Multiplexer object class cannot exceed 1.544 Mbps. Doing this requires three elements in an attribute value predicate: the compositePortSpeed attribute, the inequality relation, and the value 1.544 Mbps.

We set up an attribute value predicate as a structured type consisting of three elements, that is, the triad

```
{attribute, is, value}
```

where the field attribute identifies the label of the attribute of interest, the field value indicates the value of interest, and the field is indicates the exact relation that the indicated attribute bears with value. We specify that the is field be of type Comparator and define the type Comparator as

```
Comparator ::= ENUMERATED
{
    equalTo (0),
    greaterThan (1),
    greaterOrEqualTo (2),
    lessThan (3),
    lesserOrEqualTo (4),
    notEqualTo (5)
}
```

Recall that an ASN.1 specification is not itself intended to be executable. This is why the enumeration of the `Comparator` type is not an actual relational symbol which can be executed and enforced in a programming language environment. Rather, it is an integer placeholder for the actual relational symbol. For any given `AttributeValue-Predicate`, it is this indicator which will be stored in the model information base. When the network model is realized, the formal ASN.1 specification must be translated into an appropriate implementation language. It is in this implementation language — the "concrete syntax notation" — that the attribute value predicate can actually be tested and enforced.

It is important for us to specify all manner of attribute value predicates. As we shall see in the next chapter, these will be crucial in formally expressing the basis of specialization for each object class. In subsequent chapters, they will be important in specifying relationships and in reasoning about network operations.

Contexts of Use

An attribute value predicate can convey many different semantics, depending on the context in which it is used. If used against an identified network object in an actual run-time network, the predicate may *ask a question* as to whether the attribute bears the specified comparison to the indicated value in that network object. It may be used to *make a statement* that the attribute does in fact bear the specified comparison to the indicated value. It may be used *as a command* to set the attribute in the specified comparison to the indicated value. Or, it may be used to *qualify for some operation* a set of objects for which the attribute bears the specified comparison to the indicated value.

The context in which the predicate is used cannot be determined by examining just the predicate itself; the scope of the context must be externally identified by some indicator of the way the predicate is intended to be used. For example, if an attribute value predicate is used in database operations executed against a relational implementation of the model information base, the context could be specified by database primitives analogous to `SELECT`, `UPDATE`, and `WHERE` clauses of the SQL language. Alternatively, if an attribute value predicate is used in a protocol data unit, the context of usage could be specified by a field in the protocol data unit external to the attribute value predicate itself.

Aside from using an attribute value predicate against object *instances* in an actual network, it may also be used against object *classes* in the *model* of the network. The organization of the object model in the model information base — the specification of attributes, classes, inheritance, and aggregation hierarchies — is also known as the *schema*. In a network schema, no object instances exist; the schema only contains the specifications of classes. The usage of an attribute value predicate against *classes* in a network schema carries a completely different meaning than when used against *objects* in an actual network.

If an attribute value predicate is used against the network schema, it may be used to *ask a question* as to whether the attribute of the identified class *can bear* the specified comparison with the indicated value. It may be used to *make a statement* that the attribute can indeed bear the specified comparison with the indicated value. It may be used *as a command* to establish a bound to constrain that attribute to bear the specified comparison with the indicated value. Or, it may be used to *create a subset* of a class for some schema operation (e.g., further specialization).

Such querying of the schema of the model information base typically occurs during architecture time when classes and hierarchies are being specified. However, an external network may also query the schema of a given network at run time, if the model information base is available on-line and is amenable to being queried by a run-time protocol. We summarize the contexts in which we may use the elements {`attribute`, `is`, `value`} of an attribute value predicate in operations against the network schema:

1. ***Interrogative***: Usage of an attribute value predicate in this context poses a query: *Can the attribute specified by* `attribute` *bear the comparison specified by* `is` *to the indicated* `value`?

2. ***Declarative***: Usage of the attribute value predicate in this context makes a statement of actual fact, possibly in response to a query. A declarative predicate may be considered to have a BOOLEAN returned value, because it must either be TRUE or FALSE: *The attribute specified by* `attribute` *can (or cannot) bear the comparison specified by* `is` *to the indicated* `value`.

3. ***Imperative***: Usage of an attribute value predicate in this context issues a command: *Establish a bound so that the attribute specified by* `attribute` *is constrained to bear the comparison specified by* `is` *to the indicated* `value`.

4. ***Qualificative***: Usage of an attribute value predicate in this context acts as a subsetting clause for externally specified operations on objects: *Create (or do not create) a subset of the class for an externally specified operation such that the attribute specified by* `attribute` *bears the comparison specified by* `is` *to the indicated* `value`.

Our primary interest is to use an attribute value predicate as a *basis of specialization* for the derivation of subclasses in the model information base. When used as a basis of specialization, the qualificative form of the attribute value predicate is used on the superclass to create a subset for further evolution and refinement. The usage is also *imperative* on the created subclass, because the attribute logical predicate establishes a bound for the value of the attribute which acts as a constraint on all the members of the subclass.

As we shall see later, the notion of logical predicates will be extended to not only statements about attributes and their values but also statements about objects which stand in particular relationships to other objects. This will give us a very powerful modeling construct.

10.7. Constrained Types

To formally specify attribute value predicates, we cannot just create a regular SEQUENCE type consisting of the triad {`attribute`, `is`, `value`} because of a syntactic complication. That complication arises due to the fact that, at the time we create this SEQUENCE type, we do not know what the type of the `value` component will be. Clearly, the type of value will vary with each attribute: for some attributes it may be numeric, for others a character string, and for yet others some complex structured type. When we create a general `AttributeValuePredicate` type applicable to all attributes, we know we can indicate the actual attribute of interest using the `OBJECT IDENTIFIER` which is the registration label of the attribute; we can simply use this as the `attribute` component. However, we cannot specify the `value` component, because we do not know its type. Since its type changes for every attribute, there is no way to specify ahead of time to the ASN.1 compiler what type it should assign to this component, and we would be stuck at the following point:

```
AttributeValuePredicate ::= SEQUENCE
{
      attribute          OBJECT IDENTIFIER,
      is                 Comparator,
      value              ????????????
}
```

Recall, however, that in the `ATTRIBUTE` information object class, we had a *type field* called `&AttributeType` whose purpose was simply to specify the type of the attribute. Clearly, the type of the `value` field in `AttributeValuePredicate` should be the same as the `&AttributeType` field of the current attribute of interest for which we are using the attribute value predicate. Somehow, we need to obtain this information and use it in our specification of `AttributeValuePredicate`.

We must address the problem that the `&AttributeType` field changes for every `ATTRIBUTE` information object. Rather than declaring a different `Attribute-ValuePredicate` type for each `ATTRIBUTE` information object, we describe a mechanism for writing a general `AttributeValuePredicate` type for all attributes, regardless of their type.

ASN.1 provides a notation known as *constraint specification*, which allows us to create, among other things, *constrained types* [ITU-T X.682]. A constrained type limits the possible values which values of that type may possess. There are many types of constraints which are permitted in ASN.1 syntax, but we will most often use the type known as a *table constraint*. A table constraint uses a hypothetical table of values, known as the *associated table*. The associated table is conceptually formed by some defined set of information objects, typically with more than one field. This is known as a *defined object set*. The fields of the information object class act as the "columns" of this table, and their values in the information objects in the defined object set act as the "rows". Columns of this table may be used as lists of permissible values to constrain the values of any other new type reference name we might wish to create.

There are two ways in which we might use the associated table formed by a defined object set to constrain a new type reference name. The first, known as a *simple table constraint*, creates a new type whose values must come from the distinct set of values of some identified *column* of the table. The second, known as a *component relation con-*

straint, requires two fields of the new type to be related such that both their values must come from the same *row* of this table.

Simple Table Constraint

As an example, assume that we create a defined information object set called `{Attributes}`, consisting of all `ATTRIBUTE` information objects:

```
Attributes ATTRIBUTE ::= {
                              attribute1      |
                              attribute2      |
                              ...
                      }
```

where `attribute1`, `attribute2`, and so on, stand for actual defined ASN.1 information objects of the `ATTRIBUTE` information object class, each with its own `&AttributeType` and `&attributeLabel` fields. The object set reference `{Attributes}` now denotes a *defined object set*. We can now use this set to constrain the `AttributeValuePredicate` type, as follows:

```
AttributeValuePredicate ::= SEQUENCE
{
       attribute      ATTRIBUTE.&attributeLabel
                              ({Attributes}),
       is             Comparator,
       value          ATTRIBUTE.&AttributeType
                              ({Attributes}{@attribute})
}
```

This definition for the type reference name `AttributeValuePredicate` is not an information object class definition — it simply uses the ASN.1 structuring primitive `SEQUENCE`. The definition states that the type `AttributeValuePredicate` consists of three elements: the value reference name `attribute`, the value reference name `is`, and the value reference name `value`.

In this specification, the construct `ATTRIBUTE.&attributeLabel` creates a *type*. This construct is known as ASN.1 *object class field type*. The ASN.1 compiler recognizes that if the name of an information object class is suffixed with the name of one of its fields, what is desired is the *type* of that field. (By contrast, if the name of an actual information object were to be suffixed by that field, it evaluates to the *value* of that field in that particular information object.) If the field name used to suffix the information object class name is itself a type field, then it is understood to mean an *open type*, that is, a type that could represent any value. Since the type of `&attributeLabel` field of the

ATTRIBUTE information class is an OBJECT IDENTIFIER, the construct
ATTRIBUTE.&attributeLabel is simply equivalent to OBJECT IDENTIFIER.

By suffixing this construct with the simple table constraint ({Attributes}),
which is the set of all defined ATTRIBUTE information objects, we create a *constrained
type*. This means that values of this type are confined to a limited pool of permissible values. The attribute component of AttributeValuePredicate is constrained
such that it cannot take just any OBJECT IDENTIFIER value but must take a value
from the &attributeLabel field from an element of the set ({Attributes}),
that is, from any *defined* ATTRIBUTE information object.

Component Relation Constraint

The value component is also constrained. This field also has an object class field type,
since its type is ATTRIBUTE.&AttributeType. However, the &AttributeType
component of ATTRIBUTE is itself a type field which varies for every ATTRIBUTE information object. When used as the type of the value component of Attribute-
ValuePredicate, it represents an open type.

This component also has a simple table constraint applied by the defined object
set {Attributes}, so it must represent a type from the &AttributeType field of
one of the information objects in the set {Attributes}. In addition to this, we would
like to ensure that this component takes the &AttributeType from the *same*
ATTRIBUTE information object whose &attributeLabel field was identified in the
attribute component. In effect, in any value of type AttributeValue-
Predicate, both the components attribute and value must come from the *same
row* of the conceptual table associated with the defined object set {Attributes}.

To enforce this, we introduce a *component relation constraint*; we further constrain the value component with the attribute component. The construct
@attribute is called an *at-notation*, and it requires the ASN.1 compiler to enforce that
the &AttributeType field chosen for value must belong to the same ATTRIBUTE
information object whose &attributeLabel is indicated by the attribute component.

We can now state the fact that the compositePortSpeed of the t1-
Multiplexer object class is constrained to an upper bound with the following value of
an AttributeValuePredicate:

```
SEQUENCE
{
    attribute        compositePortSpeed.&attributeLabel,
    is               lesserOrEqualTo,
    value            15440000
}
```

The &attributeLabel field of the ATTRIBUTE information object
compositePortSpeed is identified in the attribute field of the Attribute-

ValuePredicate value above. The &AttributeType field of this information object is BandwidthInBps. Thus, the value field in the specification above must also be of the type BandwidthInBps. Because the value 15440000 specified for this field is compatible with the type BandwidthInBps, this specification is accepted by the compiler. We reiterate that although an attribute value predicate requires a label, a comparator, and a value, it does not imply that the label itself is compared against the value; rather, the current contents of the attribute indicated by the label are tested against the value.

10.8. Parameterized Types

A *parameterized type* allows any parameter in the type specification to be "passed in" [ITU-T X.683]. This acts as a formal parameter which qualifies or *parameterizes* the entire type reference name. A parameterized type reference name provides a shorthand to create a whole family of types in a single specification. All the members of this family of types are structurally identical, except for the variation introduced by the parameter. Parameterized type reference names are analogous to the *template* types available in some object-oriented programming languages.

Types can be both constrained and parameterized. For example, the constraining set can be passed in as a parameter. This eliminates the need to have a *defined* object set to create the associated table which indicates the permissible values of the constrained type. Because the constraining set is passed in as a parameter, we can now have a constrained type whose permissible values are determined with reference to an *undefined* object set, the "rows" of whose associated table will be specified later, possibly on a case-by-case basis.

As an example, the set {Attributes} which constrains the Attribute-ValuePredicate type could be passed in as a *parameter*. This means we need no longer have {Attributes} as a *defined* object set, listing all defined ATTRIBUTE information objects as elements of the set. We can simply let it be a placeholder for *any* object set of ATTRIBUTE information objects which will be passed in later:

```
AttributeValuePredicate {ATTRIBUTE:Attributes} ::=
SEQUENCE
{
    attribute        ATTRIBUTE.&attributeLabel
                                        ({Attributes}),
    is               Comparator,
    value            ATTRIBUTE.&AttributeType
                         ({Attributes}{@attribute})
}
```

In this specification, the construct {ATTRIBUTE:Attributes} acts as the parameter which qualifies the entire AttributeValuePredicate. The construct

`ATTRIBUTE:` is known as the *parameter governor*, and its operand `Attributes` is known as the *formal parameter* (also sometimes called a *dummy reference*). If the formal parameter is a value or a value set, the governor indicates the type of the parameterizing value or value set. If the formal parameter is an information object or an information object set, the governor indicates the information object class of the parameterizing information object or information object set. If the formal parameter is itself the name of a type or an information object class, no governor is required.

With this specification in place, the ASN.1 compiler can generate an entire family of `AttributeValuePredicate` types if we pass in a set of `ATTRIBUTE` information objects. The identifier `Attributes` no longer refers to a specific, defined list of `ATTRIBUTE` information objects but is a symbolic placeholder for *any* list of `ATTRIBUTE` information objects which we may define later.

A defined object set which is passed in to the parameterized type is known as an *actual parameter*. The result of passing in such a set is a type generated by conceptually replacing the formal parameter with the actual parameter and removing the parameterization. By passing in different such lists to the specification of an `AttributeValue-Predicate`, we can create a different set of permissible values for a new member of the `AttributeValuePredicate` family of types.

Because the identifier `{Attributes}` in the parameterized specification is simply a formal parameter and no longer represents a defined object set with a fixed name, we can give it any name we want. For example, we could parameterize the entire `AttributeValuePredicate` with the construct `{ATTRIBUTE:Alist}`, as long as we replaced every occurrence of the identifier `Attributes` in the specification with `Alist`. This would preserve the same semantics of parameterization. On the other hand, if we have created a list of actual `ATTRIBUTE` information objects as a defined object set, we may omit the parameterization if we use the object set with the fixed name instead of the formal parameter. In general, any type specification which is parameterized can also be expressed without parameterization, provided we fix the name of the parameter to some defined value, some defined value set, some defined object, or some defined object set.

Throughout this book, we will have many occasions to use types constrained with respect to some information object set. In many cases, we will assume that the constraining set is a defined object set (i.e., an explicitly created list of actual information objects). This will allow us to constrain each specification without necessarily parameterizing it, since the constraint will use a set with a fixed name.

It should be remembered, however, that without loss of generality, each constrained type can also be parameterized, with the constraining set being passed in rather than being fixed. For readability and easier comprehension, we will express all constrained types without parameterization under the assumption that the name of the constraining object set is fixed. Nevertheless, they can just as well be expressed with parameterization should it be so desired.

10.9. Specifying Collections

From time to time, we will be required to specify types which are lists of permissible values of fields from some defined object set. We know that we can create the set {Attributes} of all ATTRIBUTE information objects by simply enumerating them in an object set reference. Similarly, we can create a set of just *one field* from a defined object set. For example, suppose we wished to create a list of just the &attributeLabel fields of all ATTRIBUTE information objects. This would be similar to defining the associated table of the set {Attributes}, but rather than using the entire table, we can use just one column of that table.

Collections as Constrained Object Class Field Types

Recall that we said earlier that the construct ATTRIBUTE.&attributeLabel generates a *type*, because it is an object class field type. The construct ATTRIBUTE.-&attributeLabel({Attributes}) adds a constraint to this type, thus creating a *constrained object class field type*. We can use this in a simple type assignment, for example,

```
AttributeLabel ::= ATTRIBUTE.&attributeLabel
                                            ({Attributes})
```

In this assignment, the newly created type AttributeLabel has the same type as the &attributeLabel field of the ATTRIBUTE information object class (that is, an OBJECT IDENTIFIER). Moreover, its value is constrained by the set {Attributes} of all defined ATTRIBUTE information objects. This means that the type AttributeLabel is a *subtype* of OBJECT IDENTIFIER; each value of type AttributeLabel cannot be just any OBJECT IDENTIFIER but must be drawn from the limited pool of OBJECT IDENTIFIERs defined by the &attributeLabel fields of the set {Attributes}.

Collections as Value Sets from Objects

ASN.1 permits us to define the same type using an alternative mechanism called a *value set from objects*. With this mechanism, we may extract the values of all &attributeLabel fields of all ATTRIBUTE information objects by simply referencing the entire set {Attributes} *as if* it were a single information object. This acts as a simultaneous reference to every information object of the set, creating a set of all their &attributeLabel fields. For example, we may define the set

```
AttributeLabel ::= {Attributes}.&attributeLabel
```

The construct AttributeLabel is now a *value set from objects*: it is the set of OBJECT IDENTIFIERs taken from all the &attributeLabel fields of the set {Attributes} of all defined ATTRIBUTE information objects. The interesting feature of a value set from objects is that it is also a *type*. We may use it just as we use any other type; for example, we could create values with it. Thus, both the different ways of defining `AttributeLabel` above are type assignments, the first one as a constrained object class field type, and the second as a value set from objects. Both create `Attribute-Label` as a type reference name; moreover, since they both use the same defined object set {`Attributes`}, both specify exactly the same list of permissible `OBJECT IDENTIFIER` values. Either mechanism may be used at the specifier's discretion.

Collections as Object Sets from Objects

Using a similar mechanism, we may create a list of *information objects* which are fields of other information objects. This mechanism is known as an *object set from objects*. For example, we need not list the set {`Attributes`} as an enumerated list of all `ATTRIBUTE` information objects, if we can extract the same list as shorthand from another list of defined information objects. We know that all attributes belong to object classes (that is, classes in our object-oriented network model). If we have a defined set of `OBJECT-CLASS` information objects, we can simply extract from this defined object set the set {`Attributes`} of all fields of the information object class `ATTRIBUTE`.

In Chapter 11, we will present the ASN.1 information object class templates which will be used to formally specify our object classes. Assume for the time being that some object classes have been already defined, using a structure similar to the following:

```
OBJECT-CLASS ::= CLASS
{
      &Attributes            ATTRIBUTE,
      ...,
      &objectClassLabel   OBJECT IDENTIFIER UNIQUE
}
```

where `&Attributes` is an *object set field* specifying a set of `ATTRIBUTE` information objects, indicating all the attributes which belong to this object class. The details of the `OBJECT-CLASS` structure will be filled in in Chapter 11; for the time being, assume that some object classes have already been defined and that we have collected them together in the defined ASN.1 information object set {`ObjectClasses`}, as follows:

```
ObjectClasses OBJECT-CLASS ::= {
                                 objectClass1   |
                                 objectClass2   |
                                 ...
                        }
```

Here, `objectClass1`, `objectClass2`, and so on, are all defined ASN.1 information objects of the `OBJECT-CLASS` information object class. We can now specify

{Attributes} as the set of all attributes belonging to all the object classes in this set, using the shorthand notation

```
Attributes ATTRIBUTE ::= {{ObjectClasses}.&Attributes}
```

This specification defines {Attributes} as an *object set from objects*. It is an information object set which enumerates all the ATTRIBUTE information objects specified in the &Attributes field of all the OBJECT-CLASS information objects in the information object set {ObjectClasses}.

This, however, is not sufficient to enumerate all the attributes in a set of object classes. Recall that our object class may contain capsules, both mandatory and optional, which may bring in their own attributes. A more detailed object class specification would look like

```
OBJECT-CLASS ::= CLASS
{
     &Attributes                   ATTRIBUTE,
     &MandatoryCapsules            CAPSULE,
     &OptionalCapsules             CAPSULE,
     ...,
     &objectClassLabel             OBJECT IDENTIFIER UNIQUE
}
```

where both &MandatoryCapsules and &OptionalCapsules are *object set fields* indicating the CAPSULE information objects which belong to that object class. Each CAPSULE information object would bring in its own attributes, using a definition (to be fully detailed in Chapter 11) such as

```
CAPSULE ::= CLASS
{
     &Attributes                   ATTRIBUTE,
     ...,
     &capsuleLabel                 OBJECT IDENTIFIER UNIQUE
}
```

To fully enumerate the attributes of an object class, we must not only enumerate its direct attributes but also those brought in by the capsules belonging to that object class. We expand the definition of the information object set {Attributes} as follows:

```
Attributes ATTRIBUTE ::=
{
   {{ObjectClasses}.&Attributes}                          |
   {{{ObjectClasses}.&MandatoryCapsules}.&Attributes}     |
   {{{ObjectClasses}.&OptionalCapsules}.&Attributes}
}
```

Parameterized Collections

In the specification above, if {ObjectClasses} were a parameter of the specification instead of a defined object set, it could represent any set of OBJECT-CLASS information objects. It could even represent a single object class, in which case the *parameterized information object set* Attributes created would stand for all the attributes of just that one object class. For example, we may define the parameterized information object set ATTRIBUTES using a *parameterized information object set assignment*:

```
Attributes {OBJECT-CLASS:ObjectClasses} ATTRIBUTE ::=
{
   {{ObjectClasses}.&Attributes}                          |
   {{{ObjectClasses}.&MandatoryCapsules}.&Attributes}     |
   {{{ObjectClasses}.&OptionalCapsules}.&Attributes}
}
```

With this specification in place, if multiplexer is an information object of the OBJECT-CLASS information object class, then the object set assignment

```
MultiplexerAttributes ATTRIBUTE ::=
                              Attributes{multiplexer}
```

creates MultiplexerAttributes as a defined object set consisting of all the ATTRIBUTE information objects which belong to multiplexer.

With the mechanism of object set from objects, we need no longer explicitly enumerate the information object set {Attributes} in terms of every ATTRIBUTE information object. We can extract it when needed from the defined object set {Object-Classes}. In general, we need to maintain just the list {ObjectClasses}; from this defined object set, we can extract lists of all attributes, functions, and capsules used in the model using object sets from objects, extract other lists of values from those lists using value sets from objects, and so on.

Unlike a value set from objects, which can be used as a type, an object set from objects cannot be used as a type. It remains a defined set of individual information objects. This is because an information object class is not a type; it can only be used to create stand-alone individual information objects or information object sets and object fields or object set fields in information object class definitions. For the same reason, an information object *set* is not a value set and hence is not a type either. Thus, an object set from objects is also not a type.

10.10. Specifying Domains

We indicated that each attribute in our model has a domain, which may be a set of discrete values, a continuous range of values, or sets of discontinuous ranges of values. In the formal specification of an attribute, we must indicate what the domain of the attribute is. To accommodate this, we expand the definition of the ATTRIBUTE information object class to include a new field:

```
ATTRIBUTE ::= CLASS
{
      &AttributeType,
      &attributeDomain            Domain {&AttributeType}
                                                 OPTIONAL,
      &attributeLabel             OBJECT IDENTIFIER UNIQUE
}
WITH SYNTAX
{
      ATTRIBUTE-TYPE              &AttributeType
      [ ATTRIBUTE-DOMAIN         &attributeDomain ]
      IDENTIFIED BY              &attributeLabel
}
```

We added the new variable-type value field &attributeDomain. This is a variable-type field because its type, Domain, is parameterized by the type field &AttributeType. The type Domain expands into all the possibilities of allowable values for that attribute. The permissible values defined for that attribute in the expansion of Domain must all have the same type as &AttributeType. This is why the type field &AttributeType parameterizes Domain:

```
Domain {Type} ::= CHOICE
{
      theSet          [0]   SET OF Type,
      theRangeWith    [1]   SEQUENCE
                            {
                              lowerBound [0] Type OPTIONAL,
                              upperBound [1] Type OPTIONAL
                            }
```

```
        and                [2]   SET OF Domain {Type}
}
```

This specification indicates that `Domain` is either indicated as a discrete set of values (`theSet` alternative), or as a range of values (`theRangeWith` alternative). Each range specifies both an `upperBound` and a `lowerBound`. Both bounds are `OPTIONAL`; if either is omitted, it is assumed to be unspecified. The `and` alternative itself expands into a `SET OF` allowable `Domain` types; if the domain is discontinuous, this permits us to specify multiple ranges, or a set and a range, or any combination thereof. All the discrete values in `theSet` alternative and the limits in `theRangeWith` alternative must be of the type `Type`, which is passed in as a parameter.

The entire `&attributeDomain` field is optional in the `ATTRIBUTE` information object class. If omitted, the domain of the attribute is considered to be its *natural domain*. The natural domain of an attribute is the full domain of its specified `&AttributeType`, respecting any subtype constraints which may have been applied. For example, if `&AttributeType` is specified as `INTEGER`, then the natural domain is the set of all integers; if it is specified as `INTEGER(2..10)`, then the natural domain is the set of all integers between 2 and 10 inclusive. If it is specified as `INTEGER(2|4|6|8|10)`, then the natural domain is the set of all even integers between 2 and 10 inclusive.

It is in fact possible to express all the permissible sets or value ranges of the attribute as the natural domain of `&AttributeType`, using the built-in subtyping features of ASN.1. However, the `Domain` type is important in our model because, as we shall see, it is used to indicate the domains of many other constructs, including multiplicity values, function arguments, and function results. We know that multiplicities may be specified as attribute-defined expressions; in Chapter 11, we shall see how the `Type` parameter of the `Domain` construct may be redefined to accommodate such expressions, so that multiplicity values are not restricted to constants.

We know that attribute domains may be restricted as they are inherited down the hierarchy. Thus, we can merely specify the new domain for the inherited attribute, causing our model compiler to conceptually apply the new domain in the subclass without changing the `&AttributeType`.

Attribute Domain Predicates

We have already seen that one way of specifying attribute domain restriction during specialization is to use an `AttributeValuePredicate`. We provide an alternative mechanism using a new predicate called an `AttributeDomainPredicate`, which permits us to vary the value of the domain of any construct. This consists of two elements: a construct label and a new domain specification:

```
AttributeDomainPredicate ::= SEQUENCE
{
        attribute           ATTRIBUTE.&attributeLabel
                                            ({Attributes}),
        is                  Domain {ATTRIBUTE.&AttributeType
                                            ({Attributes}{@attribute})}
}
```

This predicate simply indicates that the attribute indicated by the `attribute` field has a new domain defined by the `is` field. The type of the `is` field is `Domain`, which is parameterized by the `&AttributeType` field of the same `ATTRIBUTE` information object whose `&attributeLabel` is indicated in the `attribute` field.

This predicate can be used to create the same semantics as an `Attribute-ValuePredicate`, because it changes the domain for an inherited attribute in the subclass. In fact, the basis of specialization by attribute domain restriction can be expressed either as an `AttributeValuePredicate` or an `AttributeDomainPredicate`; both are considered equivalent by our compiler. We define the type `Attribute-LogicalPredicate`, which expands to either one of these two predicates:

```
AttributeLogicalPredicate ::= CHOICE
{
        newValueOf          [0]  AttributeValuePredicate,
        newDomainOf         [1]  AttributeDomainPredicate
}
```

For example, if `compositePortSpeed` is an information object of the `ATTRIBUTE` information object class, then the bound `t1CompositePortSpeed-Restriction` may be specified in either form of an `AttributeLogical-Predicate`. With the following supporting definition

```
compositePortSpeedLbl OBJECT IDENTIFIER ::=
                        compositePortSpeed.&attributeLabel
```

we may specify the logical predicate in the `AttributeValuePredicate` form:

```
t1CompositePortSpeedRestriction
                        AttributeLogicalPredicate ::=
{
        newValueOf:
        {
                attribute        compositePortSpeedLbl,
```

```
        is              lesserOrEqualTo,
        value           1544000
    }
}
```

or we may specify it in the `AttributeDomainPredicate` form:

```
t1CompositePortSpeedRestriction
                        AttributeLogicalPredicate ::=
{
    newDomainOf:
    {
        attribute       compositePortSpeedLbl,
        is              { theRangeWith:
                            { upperBound 15440000 }}
    }
}
```

Both of these specifications are semantically equivalent in our model; both create a value of type `AttributeLogicalPredicate`, which may be used as a basis of specialization, which must be a logical predicate. Both establish a new domain for the `compositePortSpeed` attribute when it is inherited in a subclass, and either may be used in our model.

It is important to note that the use of an `AttributeDomainPredicate` or an `AttributeValuePredicate` as a basis of specialization does not change the value of the `&attributeDomain` field in the `ATTRIBUTE` information object in the model information base. Rather, when the attribute is inherited by a subclass, the compiler conceptually replaces the copy of the permissible domain values in the subclass with the newly specified domain. This conceptual substitution occurs only for the `&attribute-Domain` field, and only in that subclass. The `&attributeLabel` for that attribute in the subclass remains the same, so that the attribute is identified using the same `&attributeLabel` in both the superclass and the subclass, even though it has different domains in each. The `ATTRIBUTE` information object remains unchanged in the model information base and may be used with its original domain values by other object classes which wish to specify it for themselves.

10.11. Other Logical Predicates

Aside from attribute value predicates, we will require many other types of logical predicates to make various formal statements and declarations in our object model. We introduce some of these below.

In Chapter 6, we indicated that the basis of specialization for creating subclasses is formally specified as a logical predicate. When the basis of specialization is attribute domain restriction, we can use an `AttributeLogicalPredicate` to indicate this restriction. However, there are other modes of specialization as well; classes may specialize by any of the *addition* modes, such as attribute addition or function addition. In order to formally state an *addition* basis of specialization, we need a new logical predicate.

In order to specify that a property has been added, all that is necessary is to indicate the label of the property being added. For example, if the `&attributeLabel` field of any `ATTRIBUTE` information object class is used as a predicate, we interpret it as a basis of specialization indicating the addition of the attribute. Hence, any value of the type `AttributeLabel`, defined as

```
AttributeLabel  ::= ATTRIBUTE.&attributeLabel
                                        ({Attributes})
```

if used by itself, can act as an addition predicate. Along the same lines, we may indicate that a function or a capsule has been added by simply using the types `FunctionLabel` and `CapsuleLabel` as predicates. These types are defined as

```
FunctionLabel  ::= FUNCTION.&functionLabel({Functions})
CapsuleLabel   ::= CAPSULE.&capsuleLabel({Capsules})
```

where `{Functions}` and `{Capsules}` are both defined object sets of the `FUNCTION` and `CAPSULE` information object class respectively, which will be fully detailed in Chapter 11.

The types `AttributeLabel`, `FunctionLabel`, and `CapsuleLabel`, if interpreted as predicates indicating the presence of a property, may also be used in contexts other than as an addition basis of specialization. For example, they may be used in an interrogative context. From time to time, any external network querying a the schema of a given network may need to know whether or not a particular property is possessed by an object class. By merely referencing the value of the property label in a protocol request against the network schema (with the interrogative context being specified in some other field of the protocol request), the querying network may determine whether or not the property is present in a given object class.

Aside from being used at architecture time, these "label predicates" can also be used at run time if the schema is available on-line. They can be used not only to ask whether a property is present but also to respond to the query. By simply using it in a response (the declarative context and the target class being specified in some external field of the protocol) we can state in a protocol response whether or not the property has been added to a given class. We summarize the contexts of usage below.

1. *Interrogative*: Usage of a label logical predicate in this context poses a query: *Is the indicated attribute, function, or capsule a property of the object class?*

2. *Declarative*: Usage of a label logical predicate in this context makes a statement of actual fact, possibly in response to a query. A declarative

predicate may be considered to have a BOOLEAN returned value, because it must either be TRUE or FALSE: *The indicated attribute, function, or capsule is (or is not) a property of the object class.*

3. ***Imperative***: Usage of a label logical predicate in this context issues a command to extend or modify the network schema: *Add the indicated attribute, function, or capsule to this object class.*

4. ***Qualificative***: Usage of a label logical predicate in this context acts as a subsetting clause for externally specified operations on objects: *Perform (or do not perform) the externally specified operation only on those object classes which possess the indicated attribute, function, or capsule as a property.*

Aside from predicates indicating property addition, labels can also be used as predicates indicating a *variance* in an inherited property. For example, a capsule label could be used in specialization by capsule fixing, indicating that an inherited capsule, optional in the superclass, is now being fixed in the subclass. The formal statement of the basis predicate must clearly indicate whether the capsule label is being used to add a new capsule or fix an optional inherited capsule.

We will have occasion to add more elements to the logical predicates we have defined here, as we develop our object model further. As newer kinds of properties (aside from attributes, functions, and capsules) are defined, their labels may also be used as addition predicates. In addition, other predicates similar to attribute value predicates will be defined as we determine the need for stating other facts about our object model.

10.12. Putting It All Together

The development of the preceding constructs has been explained in an incremental, evolutionary fashion to expound the underlying conceptual basis fully. In this section, we present an overall view of all logical predicates by defining the general type Logical-Predicate, which expands to any of the other logical predicates. We do this because we often need to use multiple logical predicates simultaneously in some logical combination, using and, or, and not connectives. We define the general Logical-Predicate type as follows:

```
LogicalPredicate ::= CHOICE
{
      simplePredicate      [0]   SimpleLogicalPredicate,
      compoundPredicate    [1]   CompoundLogicalPredicate,
      negatedPredicate     [2]   LogicalPredicate
}
```

which allows us to express combinations of logical expressions with full generality. The types in this definition have their own expansions:

```
CompoundLogicalPredicate ::= SEQUENCE
{
        connectBy               LogicalConnective,
        predicates              SET OF LogicalPredicate
}
```

where

```
LogicalConnective ::= ENUMERATED
{
        and (0),
        or  (1)
}
```

The type `CompoundLogicalPredicate` is interpreted as an instruction to conceptually place the `connectBy` (either an `and` or an `or`) between each pair of the set of `LogicalPredicates` indicated by `predicates`. This permits us to evaluate the result of a set of logical predicates "*and*-ed" or "*or*-ed" together at once. If we are required to negate a particular fact, we can express it as a `negatedPredicate` which, as the general `LogicalPredicate` type indicates, expands into another `Logical-Predicate`, permitting us to negate any simple or compound logical predicate.

All the other logical predicates of the preceding section — each of which expresses a single fact — are simple logical predicates, which can be expressed in the type `SimpleLogicalPredicate`:

```
SimpleLogicalPredicate ::= CHOICE
{
        attributeAdded            [0] AttributeLabel,
        functionAdded             [1] FunctionLabel,
        capsuleAdded              [2] CapsuleLabel,
        capsuleFixed              [3] CapsuleLabel,
        attributeDomainRestricted [4]
                                  AttributeLogicalPredicate
}
```

We also expand the type `Comparator` which was used in the type `AttributeValuePredicate`. For attribute values that vary over a continuous domain, our earlier enumeration of comparisons was adequate. However, we could also have attributes whose domain is restricted to a discrete set of values. In this case, we need to be able to express interrogation, declaration, imperation, and qualification with regard to the membership of an individual attribute instance within a specified *set* of values. We extend our notion of Comparator to include set comparisons and redefine Comparator as follows:

```
Comparator ::= ENUMERATED
{
        equalTo (0),
        greaterThan (1),
        greaterOrEqualTo (2),
        lessThan (3),
        lesserOrEqualTo (4),
        notEqualTo (5),
        setEqualToSet (6),
        setNotEqualToSet (7),
        aMemberOf (8),
        notAMemberOf (9),
        aSubsetOf (10),
        aSupersetOf (11),
        setIntersectionNullWith (12),
        setIntersectionNotNullWith (13)
}
```

This allows us to express the relation between an attribute and its value with full generality. Strictly, all these comparators are not necessary, because we have the ability to express any AttributeLogicalPredicate as a negatedPredicate. Thus, greaterThan, lessThan, and notEqualTo can technically be expressed as the negations of the predicates containing lesserOrEqualTo, greaterOrEqualTo, and equalTo respectively. Similarly, the set-oriented enumerations can also be used in negatedPredicates to express semantics such as set inequality, null intersections, and non-subset and non-superset properties. Technically, even the equality relations are not necessary: the numeric equalTo can be expressed as the simultaneous conjunction of greaterOrEqualTo and lesserOrEqualTo, and setEqualToSet can be expressed as the simultaneous conjunction of aSubsetOf and aSupersetOf. Nevertheless, we leave all the possible comparisons in for convenience and economy of expression.

All of the constructs specified so far will be used heavily and expanded upon throughout the development of our formal object model.

10.13. Summary

The network model can be expressed in a formal specification language which is amenable to machine interpretation. Aside from being unambiguous and machine-parsable, the specification language should allow human inspection, that is, the syntax should be sufficiently readable that it is immediately understandable. The constructs for specifying our model are couched in ASN.1, in particular its Information Object Class notation, Constraint Specification notation, and Parameterization notation where necessary.

ASN.1 is also used for specifying logical predicates. Attribute logical predicates ask questions and make declarations about the domains of attribute values. Property labels may be used as logical predicates to indicate any basis of specialization by property addition. All these predicates are used against classes in the schema of the model information base. The same predicates may be used against object instances in an actual network, with completely different meanings.

The use of a formal specification language is not any more complicated or difficult than any programming language and is a natural vehicle in which to express the semantics required in the process of network architecture.

11. Formal Modeling of Network Objects

*"Tech writer who spend too much time on first ten chapters
of manual, make company file Chapter 11."*
— *anonymous Chinese proverb.*

11.1. Introduction

In this chapter we will introduce formal definitions of ASN.1 information object classes
to model all the semantics of a network object class, including bases of specialization,
attributes, functions, and capsules. Examples will demonstrate the usage of these information object classes. Syntax will also be provided for modeling aggregation relationships between object classes.

11.2. Object Classes

The formal model of network object classes is expressed using ASN.1 information object
class constructs. The model must provide adequate syntax for expressing all the semantics of object modeling we have developed in the preceding chapters. In particular, we
must be able to express specialization, attributes, functions, and capsules.

Each object class in the model is an ASN.1 information object, specified using the
`OBJECT-CLASS` information object class template. Thus, each information object of the
`OBJECT-CLASS` information object class template represents a network object class (in
the object-oriented sense). The model information base will only be populated with these
network object classes and related modeling constructs. When the model is realized in
any actual network, instances of these network object classes — that is, all the actual
network objects required in a given instance of the network — can be created and named.

We specify the `OBJECT-CLASS` ASN.1 information object class template for
network object classes as follows:

```
OBJECT-CLASS ::= CLASS
{
        &SpecializesFrom              Specialization,
        &Attributes                   ATTRIBUTE,
        &Functions                    FUNCTION,
        &MandatoryCapsules            CAPSULE,
        &OptionalCapsules             CAPSULE,
        &objectClassLabel             OBJECT IDENTIFIER UNIQUE
}
```

This simplistic-looking definition contains a very rich internal structure. This
definition is only a first cut; we will refine this definition as we go along. We examine
each of the fields in the definition.

&SpecializesFrom: This is a *fixed-type value set field*. This field contains a
   set of values, each of whose type is Specialization. The purpose of this
   field is to indicate the object's genealogy in the inheritance hierarchy. The type
   Specialization is a structured type indicating which immediate superclass
   the specificand object class is derived from. Recall that the basis of specialization
   is a condition that must be satisfied by all members of the class. To allow the
   model compiler to enforce this condition, we formally specify the basis of specialization to the compiler as a logical predicate:

```
Specialization ::= SEQUENCE
{
        superclass                    ObjectClassLabel,
        basisOfSpecialization         LogicalPredicate
}
```

where

```
ObjectClassLabel ::= OBJECT-CLASS.&objectClassLabel
                                    ({ObjectClasses})
```

Since an object class deriving with multiple inheritance could have more than one
superclass, with a different basis of specialization from each superclass, the
&SpecializesFrom field could list more than one specialization for the same
object class. This is why it is a value set field rather than a value field. Note that
although each object class technically **specializes-from** all its ancestral classes,
we only list the immediate superclass in the immediate superclass in the superclass field. When actual objects are created using the specificand template, the

entire genealogy of the class is telescoped into the objectClass attribute, as explained in Chapter 4.

In addition, an object class might not have a superclass. (The only object class for which this is actually true is the genericObject root class, but it must nevertheless be accommodated.) Therefore, the &SpecializesFrom field of the OBJECT-CLASS information object class template must really be an OPTIONAL field. We will specify this in our second cut at the OBJECT-CLASS template.

Furthermore, even if a superclass exists, a formal basis of specialization may not have been specified. For example, the top-level classes which are immediate descendants of genericObject have no basis of specialization. To allow for free specialization, the basisOfSpecialization component of the Specialization type must also be OPTIONAL.

&Attributes: This is an *object set field*. The value of this field is an information object set created using the ATTRIBUTE information object class, which we defined in Chapter 10. All the elements of this set-valued field are the attributes of the network object class being defined.

The &Attributes field should really be OPTIONAL since the OBJECT-CLASS being defined may not add any original attributes of its own to its specification, as it may use only those attributes which it inherits from its ancestors.

&Functions: This is also an *object set field*. The value of this field is an information object set created using the FUNCTION information object class. We shall examine the detailed definition of this template later. All the elements of this set-valued field are functions of the network object class being defined. The &Functions field should be optional for the same reason that the &Attributes field is optional.

&MandatoryCapsules: This is also an *object set field*. The value of this field is an information object set created using the CAPSULE information object class. We shall examine the detailed definition of this template later. All the elements of this set-valued field are mandatory capsules of the network object class being defined. Because the class need not specify any original mandatory capsules and could only possess inherited mandatory capsules, the &MandatoryCapsules field should be OPTIONAL.

&OptionalCapsules: This *object set field* is similar to the &Mandatory-Capsules field, with the difference that its elements are *optional* capsules of the network object class being defined. While &Attributes, &Functions, and &MandatoryCapsules are specifications of core behavior for the object class, &OptionalCapsules are a specification of variant behavior. Again, because the class need not originate any optional capsules, the &OptionalCapsules field should itself be OPTIONAL.

&objectClassLabel: This is a *fixed-type value field*. This is the identifier field for the object class and defines the label which can be used to uniquely reference this object class. The &objectClassLabel field is the only really required field in any specification for an OBJECT-CLASS.

We now take a second cut at defining the OBJECT-CLASS template and also introduce a WITH SYNTAX specification for more user-friendly definition, where brackets correspond to OPTIONAL fields of the information object class specification:

```
OBJECT-CLASS ::= CLASS
{
        &SpecializesFrom              Specialization OPTIONAL,
        &Attributes                   ATTRIBUTE OPTIONAL,
        &Functions                    FUNCTION OPTIONAL,
        &MandatoryCapsules            CAPSULE OPTIONAL,
        &OptionalCapsules             CAPSULE OPTIONAL,
        &objectClassLabel             OBJECT IDENTIFIER UNIQUE
}
WITH SYNTAX
{
        [ SPECIALIZES-FROM            &SpecializesFrom ]
        [ ATTRIBUTES                  &Attributes ]
        [ FUNCTIONS                   &Functions ]
        [ MANDATORY CAPSULES          &MandatoryCapsules ]
        [ OPTIONAL CAPSULES           &OptionalCapsules ]
        IDENTIFIED BY                 &objectClassLabel
}
```

ASN.1 is not an object-oriented specification notation; as such, it does not inherently provide any mechanism to support subclassing or inheritance of information object class specifications. Therefore, we have to explicitly create our own constructs, outside the set of ASN.1 primitives, to support these semantics. This is why we create our own SPECIALIZES-FROM clause in the OBJECT-CLASS information object class specification. This varies from conventional object-oriented programming languages which provide inherent syntactic support for these concepts.

ASN.1 does, however, provide strong support for subtyping — it is possible to easily define a subtype of any type reference name by simply restricting its domain. In specialization theory, subclasses are also subtypes, because of the monotonic inheritance condition and the desirability of maintaining substitutability of subclass instances for instances of ancestral classes. The question may be posed as to why we indicate the basis of specialization using our own clauses, rather than specify an attribute domain restriction using ASN.1's built-in subtyping syntax. This is indeed a reasonable question; if we chose to do this, we would make our definitions more compact, since subtyping in ASN.1 would adequately convey the semantics of domain restriction.

We do not do this because object classes specialize on the basis of many other features and not just attribute domain restriction. If we required a subtype specification (possibly in a type field) for every object class, we would be unable to supply it when a subclass specialized by, say, attribute addition.

We will consider a complete example of an OBJECT-CLASS definition when we have specified all the supporting templates as information object classes. Since we already know the ATTRIBUTE construct introduced in the previous chapter, we will use it in a simple example right now.

11.3. Using Attributes in Classes

Since every object has a name and knows its class, it must possess attributes which hold that information. These are modeled as the attributes objectName and object-Class. Recall from Chapter 5 that these are original attributes of genericObject, the root of the inheritance hierarchy, from which they are available by inheritance in every object class. We now formally specify these attributes using the ATTRIBUTE information object class template.

For the time being, assume that the objectName attribute has the type ObjectName, reflecting some simple object-instance-naming convention for the purposes of illustration. In a real network model, the objectName attribute can be specified so that its ATTRIBUTE-TYPE is a CHOICE among different instance naming schemes — either flat or hierarchical — any of which might be followed in a given network.

Also for the time being, assume that we are registering constructs in our own private registration hierarchy, which begins at an unnumbered root from which arc {1} identifies all classes, arc {2} identifies all attributes, and so on.

```
attributes OBJECT IDENTIFIER  ::= {2}
  -- root of registration subtree for all attributes

objectName ATTRIBUTE ::=
{
      ATTRIBUTE-TYPE        ObjectName
      IDENTIFIED BY         {attributes 1}
}


objectClass ATTRIBUTE ::=
{
      ATTRIBUTE-TYPE        SEQUENCE OF ObjectClassLabel
      IDENTIFIED BY         {attributes 2}
}
```

In this syntax, we created two attributes, `objectName` and `objectClass`, and registered them as {2 1} and {2 2} using their `IDENTIFIED BY` clause. We created the labels merely by suffixing an integer value to another `OBJECT IDENTIFIER` value, namely, `attributes`, which identifies the root of the branch of the registration hierarchy where we choose to store all attributes.

The reason `objectName` and `objectClass` are attributes of every network object is because every object *instance* must know what its name is and what class it **is-an-instance-of**. The constructs above specify that the `ATTRIBUTE-TYPE` of `object-Class` is simply a `SEQUENCE OF OBJECT IDENTIFIER` which, for every object, holds the registration labels of all the classes representing the genealogy of that object. Conceptually, the `&objectClassLabel` with which that class is registered in the model information base, prefixed by its genealogy, is copied into the `objectClass` attribute of every instance of that class in the run-time network. Thus, the `&object-ClassLabel` of every *ancestral* class is also conceptually available in every instance. The sequence is ordered: the label of the actual leaf class which that object **is-a-member-of** is the last element of the sequence, and the label of the root of the hierarchy — `genericObject` — is the first. (Implementations may reverse this ordering for faster comparisons.) This is unlike some object-oriented programming environments, where object instances do not necessarily know their class or their ancestry.

Recall also from Chapter 5 that the `objectClass` attribute is specially implemented in every instance: it compares equal to the `&objectClassLabel` of every class which it **is-a-member-of**; that is, it compares equal to any element of the sequence. This makes it possible to test whether an object **is-a-member-of** a given ancestral class.

The `objectName` attribute simply contains the name of each instance so that it can be identified uniquely among other instances. Any convenient naming scheme may be followed for naming instances. We assume that the structure of all instance names is captured in the `ObjectName` type reference name. If we wish, we could decide to name instances uniquely only within their class, so that the `ObjectName` type would have some mechanism for identifying the class name as well the instance name. If we wish to have globally unique names for instances, all values of type `ObjectName` must be drawn from some global name-space. There are many useful naming schemes. We do not specify any particular scheme in our model, as specialization theory works with all naming schemes; no single scheme is preferable to any other. For the purposes of demonstration, if we wish, we could simply specify

```
ObjectName ::= PrintableString
```

Because `objectName` and `objectClass` are attributes of every object class, we model them as attributes of `genericObject`. By inheritance, these two attributes are available in every object instance:

```
classes OBJECT IDENTIFIER    ::= {1}
  -- root of registration subtree for all object classes
```

```
genericObject OBJECT-CLASS ::=
{
        ATTRIBUTES              {objectName, objectClass}
        IDENTIFIED BY           {classes 1}
}
```

The `genericObject` class is specified without a `SPECIALIZES-FROM` field since it has no superclass. Its `ATTRIBUTES` field, which is an object set field, consists of a defined information object set with the two elements `objectName` and `object-Class`, each of which is an information object of the `ATTRIBUTE` information object class. The whole class is then assigned a registration label in its `IDENTIFIED BY` field.

11.4. Attributes

The information object class specification for an attribute is the same as that defined in the previous chapter, that is

```
ATTRIBUTE ::= CLASS
{
        &AttributeType,
        &attributeDomain              Domain {&AttributeType}
                                                      OPTIONAL,
        &attributeLabel               OBJECT IDENTIFIER UNIQUE
}
WITH SYNTAX
{
        ATTRIBUTE-TYPE                &AttributeType
        [ ATTRIBUTE-DOMAIN           &attributeDomain ]
        IDENTIFIED BY                &attributeLabel
}
```

Here, the `&AttributeType` is a *type field* which specifies the type of the attribute, while the `&attributeLabel` is a *value field* which holds the registration label which identifies the attribute. Examples of information objects of this information object class are `objectName` and `objectClass`, specified in the preceding section.

11.5. Functions

A function is an operational capability possessed by an object. For example, the coding of image frames for transmission is a function of a video codec, and the forwarding and filtering of packets is a function of a MAC-layer bridge. The formal specification of such operational capabilities has two parts to it. In the first part, we treat the function as a black box and are interested only in the external interfaces it presents, that is, its inputs and outputs. In the second part, we attempt to specify the behavior of the function, that is, how it is expected to transform its inputs to its outputs.

Because many different objects can act together to provide a single function, a function can be viewed as a composite. Composite functions are analogous to higher-level subroutines which call lower-level subroutines to provide required services, except that in our model such "calls" can occur across objects. For example, the composite operational capability of an `eightHundredService` object class could potentially be expressed in terms of a `globalTitleTranslation` function of an `ss7sccp` object class, a `tableLookup` function of a `relationalDatabase` object class, and so on. In Chapter 20, we will examine how such "cross-object" functions may be specified.

To specify the external interfaces of a function, we need to specify its inputs, its outputs, and any externally visible exceptions it can possibly raise. We also need to register each function so that we can uniquely identify it and reference it during invocation. We now make our first cut at the definition of a `FUNCTION` information object class.

```
FUNCTION ::= CLASS
{
        &Arguments              ARGUMENT,
        &Results                RESULT,
        &Exceptions             EXCEPTION,
        &functionLabel          OBJECT IDENTIFIER UNIQUE
}
```

We now consider each field in this definition.

&Arguments: This is an *object set field* which lists the arguments which act as input to the function. Each argument is specified using the supporting ARGUMENT information object class definition. Because the function may accept more than one input parameter, this field is an object set field rather than an object field. The supporting information object class ARGUMENT specifies the type of the argument required by the function. It has a definition very similar to that of ATTRIBUTE, but because a function could accept any input — not necessarily an attribute (e.g., a PDU) — this is defined in its own information object class, as follows:

```
ARGUMENT ::= CLASS
{
        &ArgumentType,
        &argumentDomain         Domain {&ArgumentType}
                                               OPTIONAL,
        &argumentLabel          OBJECT IDENTIFIER UNIQUE
}
```

```
WITH SYNTAX
{
       ARGUMENT-TYPE                &ArgumentType
       [ ARGUMENT-DOMAIN            &argumentDomain ]
       IDENTIFIED BY                &argumentLabel
}
```

The nature of the input depends on what the function does. For example, the `loopbackTest` function of a `digitalServiceUnit` object class may accept an argument with the `&ArgumentType` of `INTEGER`, representing the duration of the `loopbackTest` function. The `routePacket` function of a `router` object class may accept an argument with an `&ArgumentType` of `NetworkProtocolPDU`. Input parameters which are ASN.1-defined PDUs can be expressed as structured ASN.1 types; stream inputs and other PDUs can simply be specified as `ABSTRACT-SYNTAX.&Type`, which uses a special built-in information object class in ASN.1 whose `&Type` field represents an open type.

The optional `argumentDomain` field, like an `attributeDomain` field, specifies the domain of the argument if necessary. If the argument to a function happens to be an attribute of the object class, then that `&attributeLabel` field may be used instead of an `&argumentLabel` in the invocation of the function; otherwise, the argument must be registered separately in its own `ARGUMENT` template.

The definition of an argument does not indicate which function that argument belongs to, for the same reason that the definition of a function does not indicate which object class the function belongs to: it is possible for the same argument to be specified for use by different functions and for the same function to be specified for use by different object classes. Since a function may accept no arguments, the `&Arguments` field must be `OPTIONAL`.

&Results: This is an *object set field* which indicates the output parameters of the function. Because a function may have multiple outputs, this is an object set field rather than an object field. Each output is specified using its own supporting information object class definition. The `RESULT` information object class is defined as follows:

```
RESULT ::= CLASS
{
       &ResultType,
       &resultDomain               Domain {&ResultType}
                                                OPTIONAL,
       &resultLabel                OBJECT IDENTIFIER UNIQUE
}
```

```
WITH SYNTAX
{
        RESULT-TYPE                     &ResultType
        [ RESULT-DOMAIN                 &resultDomain ]
        IDENTIFIED BY                   &resultLabel
}
```

The &Results field must also be OPTIONAL as the function may produce no
output.

&Exceptions: This is an *object set field* whose value is a set of externally visible
exceptions which can possibly be raised by the function. This field must also be
OPTIONAL. Any external request which causes the object instance to invoke the
function must be able to identify exactly which exception the function has raised
in the event of invocation failure. Therefore, every exception must also be registered. In addition, since an exception may also produce additional information,
each exception is also allowed to carry an associated parameter.

```
EXCEPTION ::= CLASS
{
        &ExceptionParamType             OPTIONAL,
        &exceptionParamDomain           Domain
                                        {&ExceptionParamType}
                                                        OPTIONAL,
        &exceptionLabel                 OBJECT IDENTIFIER UNIQUE
}
WITH SYNTAX
{
        [ EXCEPTION-PARAMETER-TYPE
                                        &ExceptionParamType ]
        [ EXCEPTION-PARAMETER-DOMAIN
                                        &exceptionParamDomain ]
        IDENTIFIED BY                   &exceptionLabel
}
```

In this definition, the &ExceptionParamType is an optional *type field* which
indicates the type of any parameter associated with that exception.

&functionLabel: This is a *fixed-type value field* of type OBJECT IDENTIFIER
which serves to uniquely identify the function in a registration hierarchy. This label is useful when referencing the function during network synthesis, or during
network operation in a protocol request invoking the function. The protocol re-

quest simply references the function using its &functionLabel and provides its &Arguments parameters.

All the preceding fields specify the external interface of a function. Aside from this, we also need a mechanism to formally specify the behavior of the function, so that we can convey in our model the semantics of what the function does. We do so with the use of one or more *formal description techniques.*

For the time being, assume that the description of the capabilities of a function is specified in the *fixed-type value field* &specification, whose type is SET OF SEQUENCE OF FormalSpecification. In Chapter 14, we will examine the nature of this type in greater detail and consider many different formal description techniques which can be used to specify a function.

We now take a second cut at our template for the FUNCTION information object class:

```
FUNCTION ::= CLASS
{
        &Arguments          ARGUMENT OPTIONAL,
        &Results            RESULT OPTIONAL,
        &Exceptions         EXCEPTION OPTIONAL,
        &specification      SET OF SEQUENCE OF
                                FormalSpecification
                                OPTIONAL, -- new field
        &functionLabel OBJECT IDENTIFIER UNIQUE
}
WITH SYNTAX
{
        [ ARGUMENTS         &Arguments ]
        [ RESULTS           &Results ]
        [ EXCEPTIONS        &Exceptions ]
        [ SPECIFICATION     &specification ]
                                        -- new field
        IDENTIFIED BY       &functionLabel
}
```

This template is sufficient to specify most functions. In Chapter 13, we will provide additional techniques for specifying functions as extensions to existing functions which may have already been defined. At that time, we will extend the above template further to allow for specification reuse of prior function definitions.

11.6. Capsules

Capsules contain collections of properties which are either present all together or not at all. Because a capsule contains attributes, functions, and possibly other capsules, the formal specification of a capsule is similar to that of an object class. The difference is that capsules are never instantiated and are not arranged in any kind of hierarchy, and so carry no reference to any object classes.

The specification of a capsule is

```
CAPSULE ::= CLASS
{
        &Attributes            ATTRIBUTE OPTIONAL,
        &Functions             FUNCTION OPTIONAL,
        &Capsules              CAPSULE OPTIONAL,
        &capsuleLabel          OBJECT IDENTIFIER UNIQUE
}
WITH SYNTAX
{
        [ATTRIBUTES            &Attributes]
        [FUNCTIONS             &Functions]
        [CAPSULES              &Capsules]
        IDENTIFIED BY          &capsuleLabel
}
```

If an object class specifies an original capsule, the capsule must be listed either in its &MandatoryCapsules field if it is mandatory, or in its &OptionalCapsules field if it is optional. If an object class inherits either a mandatory or an optional capsule from its ancestral classes, it need do nothing in its definition.

If a subclass specializes using capsule fixing — that is, it turns an optional capsule inherited from an ancestral class into a mandatory capsule — then the Simple-LogicalPredicate of Chapter 10 must indicate the fixed capsule and must be used (along with other predicates, if any) as the basis of specialization. On determining that an inherited optional capsule has been fixed, our model compiler conceptually "moves" it from the information object set of the &OptionalCapsules field to that of the &MandatoryCapsules field, so that it becomes mandatory for subsequent descendants.

11.7. The Inheritance Hierarchy

We now consider examples of object classes arranged in an inheritance hierarchy to demonstrate how an inheritance hierarchy may be specified formally.

Quantitative Basis of Specialization

We revisit the example of the `multiplexer` object class introduced in Chapter 10. Assume for the purposes of this example that this class is derived from `customer-PremisesEquipment`. We take a first cut at formally specifying this class as follows:

```
multiplexer OBJECT-CLASS ::=
{
  SPECIALIZES-FROM    {{
                        superclass
                         customerPremisesEquipmentLbl,
                        basisOfSpecialization
                        {simplePredicate:
                          {attributeDomainRestricted:
                           {newValueOf:
                            {attribute equipmentTypeLbl,
                             is          equalTo,
                             value       multiplexers
                        }}}}
                       }}
  ATTRIBUTES          {
                        numberOfChannelPorts,
                        numberOfCompositePorts,
                        maxChannelPortSpeed,
                        compositePortSpeed
                      }
  FUNCTIONS           {
                        timeDivisionMultiplex
                      }
  IDENTIFIED BY       multiplexerLbl
}
```

Several assumptions have been made in this specification. We have assumed that `multiplexerLbl` is a defined `OBJECT IDENTIFIER` and so is `customer-PremisesEquipmentLbl`. In particular, we have assumed that

```
customerPremisesEquipmentLbl ::=
        customerPremisesEquipment.&objectClassLabel
```

Generally, we will use the convention that any variable name ending in `-Lbl` is an appropriately chosen `OBJECT IDENTIFIER` from the registration hierarchy. For example, we have assumed that equipmentTypeLbl is the &attributeLabel of an equipmentType information object of the ATTRIBUTE information object class. We also assume that multiplexers is some fixed value reference name which is type-compatible with equipmentType.&AttributeType. Recall that an Attribute-ValuePredicate requires a label and a value, but that does not mean that it tests the *label* against the value; rather, it tests the current contents of the attribute indicated by the label against the value. The predicate used here as the basis of specialization — {equipmentTypeLbl, equalTo, multiplexers} — defines the constraint on the value of the equipmentType attribute which any instance of customer-PremisesEquipment must satisfy before it can qualify to be a member of multi-plexer. In all examples, assumptions similar to these will hold.

Our model requires us to distinguish between different kinds of multiplexers, so we create two subclasses from this class — a broadbandMultiplexer class with compositePortSpeed greater than 44.736 Mbps, and a narrowband-Multiplexer class with compositePortSpeed less than 44.736 Mbps. We therefore get

```
broadbandMultiplexer OBJECT-CLASS ::=
{
    SPECIALIZES-FROM        {{
                            superclass
                             multiplexerLbl,
                            basisOfSpecialization
                            {simplePredicate:
                             {attributeDomainRestricted:
                              {newValueOf:
                               {attribute
                                    compositePortSpeedLbl,
                                is        greaterOrEqualTo,
                                value     44736000
                            }}}}
                            }}
    FUNCTIONS               {
                            determineNetworkTopology
                            }
    IDENTIFIED BY           broadbandMultiplexerLbl
}
```

and

```
narrowbandbandMultiplexer OBJECT-CLASS ::=
{
        SPECIALIZES-FROM       {{
                                superclass
                                 multiplexerLbl,
                                basisOfSpecialization
                                {simplePredicate:
                                 {attributeDomainRestricted:
                                  {newValueOf:
                                  {attribute
                                      compositePortSpeedLbl,
                                   is          lessThan,
                                   value       44736000
                                }}}}
                                }}
        IDENTIFIED BY          narrowbandbandMultiplexerLbl
}
```

The basis of specialization for narrowbandMultiplexer is now the negation of the basis predicate for specializing broadbandMultiplexer, assuring us of disjoint and complete partitioning. Note that the examples above are intended to illustrate the concept and are not intended to be a complete specification of multiplexer objects. More subclasses must be created and additional functions specified before we arrive at instantiable leaf classes. For example, further subclasses of the broadband-Multiplexer class could be refined with additional functions such as ds3Framing, cBitParity, oc1Framing, and so on.

Qualitative Basis of Specialization

The example above demonstrated how subclasses could be defined based on a *quantitative* basis of specialization. As an example of *qualitative* basis of specialization, we will formally specify the customCallingService object class of Chapter 6. For brevity, its genealogy and basis of specialization are not shown here.

```
customCallingService OBJECT-CLASS ::=
{
        ATTRIBUTES       {
                          serviceType,
                          softwareVersionNumber,
                          dateOfDeployment,
                          vendorName,
```

```
                              hostSwitchIdentifier
                          }
          IDENTIFIED BY   customCallingServiceLbl
    }
```

where

```
    serviceType ATTRIBUTE ::=
    {
          ATTRIBUTE-TYPE        CustomCallingServiceTypes
          IDENTIFIED BY         serviceTypeLbl
    }


    CustomCallingServiceTypes ::= ENUMERATED
    {
          callWaiting (0),
          threeWayCalling (1),
          speedCalling (2),
          distinctiveRinging (3),
          ringWhenFree (4),
          callBlocking (5),
          callingNumberDelivery (6),
          callScreening (7),
          callReturn (8),
          anonymousCallReject (9),
          selectiveForwarding (10),
          callTracing (11)
    }
```

We now specify two set-valued supporting value reference names to partition this enumerated type:

```
    callingNumberServiceTypes
          SET OF CustomCallingServiceTypes ::=
    {
          callBlocking,
          callingNumberDelivery,
          callScreening,
          callReturn,
```

```
        anonymousCallReject,
        selectiveForwarding,
        callTracing
    }
```

and

```
nonCallingNumberServiceTypes
        SET OF CustomCallingServiceTypes ::=
    {
        callWaiting,
        threeWayCalling,
        speedCalling,
        distinctiveRinging,
        ringWhenFree
    }
```

We can now use this partitioning as the basis of specialization:

```
callingNumberService OBJECT-CLASS ::=
    {
        SPECIALIZES-FROM {{
                        superclass
                         customCallingServiceLbl,
                        basisOfSpecialization
                         {simplePredicate:
                          {attributeDomainRestricted:
                           {newDomainOf:
                            {attribute serviceTypeLbl,
                             is      {theSet:
                                     callingNumber-
                                     ServiceTypes
                        }}}}}
                        }}
        FUNCTIONS       {
                         retrieveCallingNumber,
                         databaseLookup
                        }
        IDENTIFIED BY   callingNumberServiceLbl
    }
```

and

```
nonCallingNumberService OBJECT-CLASS ::=
{
      SPECIALIZES-FROM {{
                          superclass
                           customCallingServiceLbl,
                          basisOfSpecialization
                           {simplePredicate:
                            {attributeDomainRestricted:
                             {newDomainOf:
                              {attribute serviceTypeLbl,
                                is    {theSet:
                                        nonCallingNumber-
                                          ServiceTypes
                          }}}}}
                         }}
      IDENTIFIED BY    nonCallingNumberServiceLbl
}
```

In this manner, a qualitative basis of specialization can be formally expressed, allowing the compiler to enforce the constraint. Individual services may be derived from these subclasses, for each of which the basis of specialization will further tighten the domain of allowable values for `serviceType`. For example, `callWaitingService` will have its basis of specialization formally expressed as `{serviceTypeLbl, equalTo, callWaitingServiceType}`. Of course, each individual service object class will add many more FUNCTIONs which characterize its operation.

Other Bases of Specialization

In an analogous manner, we can formally state the basis of specialization for each one of the specialization principles we explored in Chapters 6 and 7. We summarize below how different `LogicalPredicates` may be used to specify each basis of specialization:

Specialization by Attribute Addition: Use a `SimpleLogical-Predicate` to indicate the `&attributeLabel` of the new attribute in the `attributeAdded` field.

Specialization by Function Addition: Use a `SimpleLogical-Predicate` to indicate the `&functionLabel` of the new function in the `functionAdded` field.

Specialization by Capsule Addition: Use a `SimpleLogical-Predicate` to indicate the `&capsuleLabel` of the new capsule in the `capsuleAdded` field.

Specialization by Capsule Fixing: Use a `SimpleLogicalPredicate` to indicate the `&capsuleLabel` of the fixed capsule in the `capsuleFixed` field.

Specialization by Attribute Domain Restriction: Use an `Attribute-ValuePredicate` with a `Comparator` indicating the numeric or subset value restriction for the attribute, or use an `AttributeDomainPredicate` for the same purpose. If both upper and lower numeric restrictions on the domain are specified, use a `CompoundLogicalPredicate` which ands together two `AttributeValuePredicates`, or indicate both bounds of the domain in an `AttributeDomain-Predicate`.

All Compound Specializations: Use a compound form which ands multiple `SimpleLogicalPredicates` together.

We will examine the function-based modes of specialization (that is, result covariance and argument contravariance) in Chapter 14 after we have studied the formal modeling of functions. The formal specification of more advanced specialization modes (for example, specialization by component multiplicity restriction and specialization by component specialization) will be covered in subsequent chapters after additional consideration of aggregation and other types of relationships.

11.8. Aggregation Hierarchies

We have developed constructs for formally specifying object classes, attributes, functions, modules, and inheritance hierarchies. To construct complex networks, we also need to specify aggregation hierarchies formally. We will now develop constructs to indicate how object classes may be aggregated together in other object classes, each with its appropriate component multiplicity.

An aggregation relationship is either a composition (`is-a-part-of`) relationship or a decomposition (`has-as-a-part`) relationship. Both these relationships are semantically equivalent, and either could be used depending on one's perspective. In any event, two object classes are involved in an aggregation relationship. We will therefore develop a construct which is an ASN.1 information object class, involving both the aggregate object class and the component object class.

```
AGGREGATION ::= CLASS
{
      &aggregateClass          OBJECT-CLASS,
      &componentClass          OBJECT-CLASS,
      &componentMultiplicity   Multiplicity,
      &aggregationLabel        OBJECT IDENTIFIER UNIQUE
}
```

The construct above represents both the `is-a-part-of` and `has-as-a-part` relationships. The fields in the definition above are explained as follows:

&aggregateClass: This is an *object field* which identifies the OBJECT-CLASS ASN.1 information object that acts as the aggregate class in the specificand aggregation relationship.

&componentClass: This is an *object field* which identifies the OBJECT-CLASS ASN.1 information object that acts as the component class in the specificand aggregation relationship.

&componentMultiplicity: This is a *fixed-type value field* whose type is Multiplicity. This specifies the component multiplicity for the aggregation relationship. Because we said in Chapter 7 that the component multiplicity need not be explicitly specified if it is exactly one, this field should be optional. The compiler understands its absence to mean exactly one component instance must be contained in each aggregate instance.

&aggregationLabel: This is a *fixed-type value field* which serves to identify the specific aggregation relationship. Its type is OBJECT IDENTIFIER. All aggregation relationships are also registered in the registration hierarchy. This allows the network architect constructing an aggregate object to pull in its components merely by referencing each specific aggregation relationship using its label.

Further, because all aggregations are presumed exclusive by default, it is assumed that the component object `is-a-part-of` exactly one aggregate object. However, some aggregations may be inclusive, in which case we must also specify an "aggregate multiplicity" to indicate how many different instances of the aggregate class can `have-as-a-part` the same instance of the component class. We now take a second cut at the AGGREGATION information object class, introducing a WITH SYNTAX specification:

```
AGGREGATION ::= CLASS
{
        &aggregateClass              OBJECT-CLASS,
        &aggregateMultiplicity       Multiplicity OPTIONAL,
        &componentClass              OBJECT-CLASS,
        &componentMultiplicity       Multiplicity OPTIONAL,
        &aggregationLabel            OBJECT IDENTIFIER UNIQUE
}
WITH SYNTAX
{
        AGGREGATE                    &aggregateClass
        [ WITH MULTIPLICITY          &aggregateMultiplicity ]
              HAS-AS-A-PART
        COMPONENT                    &componentClass
        [ WITH MULTIPLICITY          &componentMultiplicity ]
```

```
        IDENTIFIED BY                    &aggregationLabel
}
```

The presence of a WITH MULTIPLICITY clause immediately after the AGGREGATE clause advises the compiler that this is an inclusive aggregation relationship with a sharable component; otherwise, the value of &aggregateMultiplicity also defaults to exactly [1], implying exclusive aggregation. The keyword HAS-AS-A-PART in the WITH SYNTAX specification is unnecessary for compilation purposes but is included as syntactic sugar for readability.

Formal Multiplicity Specifications

We must also specify the type Multiplicity. As we indicated in Chapter 7, the component multiplicity of any aggregation relationship can be expressed in one of several ways. It could be specified as a range with an upper and lower limit, or as a set of enumerated constants, or in terms of attribute-defined expressions. We already know how to specify sets or ranges of permissible values using the parameterized type Domain of Chapter 10. Therefore,

```
    Multiplicity ::= Domain {MultiplicityValue}
```

where

```
    MultiplicityValue ::= CHOICE
    {
        constant [0] INTEGER (0..MAX),
                                    -- non-negative integer
        ade      [1] AttributeDefinedExpression
    }
```

The type AttributeDefinedExpression further expands into a simple grammar allowing mathematical and logical operations on attributes. The terminal symbols of this grammar are the &attributeLabels with which the attributes involved in the expression are registered. An AttributeDefinedExpression may also use the return results of a FUNCTION, and so the grammar permits as terminal symbols &functionLabels with their &argumentLabels and &resultLabels, including an indication of which values are to be assigned to each &argumentLabel to evaluate the function. The expansion of AttributeDefinedExpression into such a grammar is fairly straightforward and is omitted here for brevity.

Each actual aggregation relationship can now be represented as an ASN.1 information object. Using the example from Chapter 7 of a wiringHub object class which has a numberOfCardSlots attribute, we can formally specify its aggregation relationship with its component hubCard object class:

```
numberOfCardSlots ATTRIBUTE ::=
{
      ATTRIBUTE-TYPE            INTEGER (0..MAX)
      IDENTIFIED BY             numberOfCardSlotsLbl
}


wiringHub-hubCard AGGREGATION ::=
{
      AGGREGATE                wiringHub
          HAS-AS-A-PART
      COMPONENT                hubCard
      WITH MULTIPLICITY        {theRangeWith:
                                  { lowerBound { constant:1 },
                                    upperBound { ade:
                                      {numberOfCardSlotsLbl}}
                               } }        -- attribute-defined
                                          -- expression
      IDENTIFIED BY            {...}
}
```

This specification is general enough to hold for all aggregations of a hubCard component in a wiringHub object, irrespective of the capacity of the wiringHub.

11.9. Summary

The formal model of network object classes can be expressed in the syntax of ASN.1 information object classes, with supporting type definitions such as the ones defined in this chapter. The information object class syntax for each network object class specifies its genealogy, its basis of specialization, and its attribute and function properties. Each property is also formally defined using its own ASN.1 information object class definition. Aggregation hierarchies are defined notationally by specifying both the aggregate and component object classes as well the component multiplicity in an ASN.1 information object class template designed for that purpose.

12. Object Modeling Application Examples

*"I checked my horoscope on the 900 number, and it
predicted my service charges would go up next month."*
— *anonymous information service subscriber.*

12.1. Introduction

Some of the object classes typically encountered in a communications network include physical network equipment and devices, protocol stacks, and network services. In this chapter, examples are provided of modeling these object classes in accordance with the model developed so far.

12.2. Device Object Classes

As an example of a device entity, consider the example of a generic modem superclass which **specializes-into** a `leasedLineModem` object class and a `dialModem` object class. Assume the modem object class **specializes-from** the generic `customerPremisesEquipment` object class specified below. The `customerPremisesEquipment` object class is a descendant of the `networkDevice` object class; for brevity, its genealogy and basis of specialization are not shown.

```
customerPremisesEquipment OBJECT-CLASS ::=
{
      ATTRIBUTES       {
                            productName,
                            manufacturerIdentifier,
                            vendorIdentifier,
                            productReleaseNumber,
```

```
                              manufacturerSerialNumber,
                              manufacturerPartNumber,
                              customerAssetNumber,
                              equipmentType,
                              operationalStatus,
                              dateOfPurchase,
                              dateOfDeployment,
                              expectedDateOfSuperannuation,
                              equipmentLocation,
                              depreciationSchedule,
                              maintenanceSchedule,
                              serviceContractNumber,
                              serviceContact,
                              troubleHistory
                         }
        IDENTIFIED BY   customerPremisesEquipmentLbl
    }
```

This specification is a typical (but incomplete) list of all the attributes of interest for any customer premises equipment. Each attribute will have its own supporting ATTRIBUTE definition specifying an appropriate ATTRIBUTE-TYPE; these are not shown here for brevity. The definition above lists many interesting aspects of customer premises equipment; in Chapter 20, we will see that some of these attributes (such as manufacturerIdentifier, vendorIdentifier, serviceContact) are not real attributes of this class but arise as pseudo-attributes by virtue of the fact that this class participates in relationships with other object classes.

We now specialize the modem object class from customerPremises-Equipment:

```
    modem OBJECT-CLASS ::=
    {
      SPECIALIZES-FROM   {{
                          superclass
                           customerPremisesEquipmentLbl,
                          basisOfSpecialization
                           {simplePredicate:
                            {attributeDomainRestricted:
                             {newValueOf:
                              {attribute equipmentTypeLbl,
                               is         equalTo,
```

```
                                   value      modems
                         }}}}
                      }}
ATTRIBUTES            {
                       modemType,
                       normalSpeed,
                       delayToDTR,
                       ctsAlwaysOn,
                       rtsToCtsDelay,
                       acceptRemoteTestCommands,
                       currentTestModeStatus
                       carrierLossDisconnectTimer
                      }
FUNCTIONS             {
                       modulateData,
                       demodulateData,
                       resynchronizeOnCarrierLoss,
                       performSelfTest,
                       performEndToEndErrorTest,
                       performLocalAnalogLoopback,
                       performLocalDigitalLoopback,
                       performRemoteAnalogLoopback,
                       performRemoteDigitalLoopback
                      }
IDENTIFIED BY         modemLbl
}
```

We now create the subclass `leasedLineModem` from the modem object class:

```
leasedLineModem OBJECT-CLASS ::=
{
 SPECIALIZES-FROM    {{
                      superclass  modemLbl,
                      basisOfSpecialization
                        {simplePredicate:
                         {attributeDomainRestricted:
                          {newValueOf:
                           {attribute    modemTypeLbl,
                            is           equalTo,
```

```
                              value          leasedLineModems
                    }}}}
                  }}
ATTRIBUTES        {
                  modulationType,
                              -- AM, PSK, or FSK
                  builtInConstellations,
                  possibleDownspeedValues,
                  rxCarrierStatus,
                  txCarrierStatus,
                  dialBackupStatus,
                  dialBackupOutboundPhoneNumbers,
                  dialBackupLocalPhoneNumbers,
                  orientation,  -- central or remote
                  structure,
                    -- point-to-point or multipoint
                  worstTolerableLineConditioning,
                  txLevel,
                  txLevelProgrammable,
                  streamingTimer,
                  testingEnabled,
                  trainingTime
                  }
FUNCTIONS         {
                  fourWireOperation,
                  twoWireFallback,
                  autoDownspeed,
                  autoUpspeed,
                  initiateDialBackup,
                  acceptRemoteDialBackup,
                  testLineAttenuationDistortion,
                  testLineEnvelopeDelay,
                  testLineSignalToNoise,
                  }
IDENTIFIED BY     leasedLineModemLbl
}
```

The subclass dialModem could be specified as follows:

```
dialModem OBJECT-CLASS ::=
{
 SPECIALIZES-FROM      {{
                        superclass   modemLbl,
                        basisOfSpecialization
                         {simplePredicate:
                          {attributeDomainRestricted:
                           {newValueOf:
                            {attribute     modemTypeLbl,
                             is            equalTo,
                             value         dialModems
                        }}}}
                       }}
 ATTRIBUTES            {
                        localPhoneNumber,
                        jackType,
                        numberOfRingsBeforeInboundAnswer,
                        numberOfRingsBeforeOutboundFail,
                        dialToneWaitTime,
                        intervalBetweenTouchToneDigits,
                        remoteCarrierStartWaitTime,
                        remoteCarrierSustainWaitTime,
                        carrierLossToleranceDelay,
                        escapeCharacter,
                        escapeGuardDelay,
                        carriageReturnCharacter,
                        lineFeedCharacter,
                        backspaceCharacter,
                        commaCharacter,
                        commaPauseDuration,
                        commandEchoOn,
                        responseSendOn,
                        touchToneDialingOn,
                        answerModeOn,
                        longSpaceDisconnectModeOn,
                        speakerOn,
                        numberOfDataBits, -- 7 or 8
                        parity, -- Even, Space, Odd, Mark
```

```
                           transmissionMode, -- sync or async
                           clockSource
                                -- internal, external or slave
                           }
              FUNCTIONS     {
                           dialDataCall,
                           acceptDataCall
                           }
              IDENTIFIED BY  dialModemLbl
         }
```

In all of these object class definitions, each attribute and function would have its supporting ATTRIBUTE and FUNCTION definitions, which would be required for the complete specification of the object class. These are fairly straightforward to define and are not shown here for brevity.

This specification for a modem object is not complete but is intended to illustrate the overall approach. Depending on the exact abilities of the modem we are modeling, the modeling specifications above could be extended as required by further specialization. For example, modems with data compression capabilities (such as V.42bis or MNP-5 modems) could be subclassed further from the preceding classes. Alternatively, if some modems offer these functions as optional capabilities, they could be modeled using capsules.

12.3. Protocol Object Classes

We now consider an example of a protocol entity object class. A *protocol object* is considered to have a physical embodiment, as either a hardware, firmware, or software entity. Each protocol object must be deployed on some host system, such as a computer system in an end-user network or a switching or routing system in a carrier network. The host object is considered to possess the protocol object as a component via an aggregation relationship.

The following example models a hypothetical connection-oriented transport protocol designed to provide reliable, guaranteed service with error detection and correction. This model is typical of many transport protocols but does not reflect any particular standard protocol. Assume that the specificand transportProtocol object class derives from a top-level protocolEntity object class, which in turn is defined as follows:

```
protocolEntity OBJECT-CLASS ::=
{
  ATTRIBUTES        {
                    protocolName,
                    protocolIdentifier,
```

```
                         refModel,
                         operativeLayer,
                         operativePlanes,
                         implementedOptions,
                         hostSystemIdentifier,
                         embodimentType,
                         embodimentProductIdentifier,
                         vendorIdentifier,
                         manufacturerIdentifier,
                         productReleaseNumber,
                         manufacturerPartNumber,
                         manufacturerSerialNumber,
                         productVersionNumber,
                         activityStatus
                         }
   IDENTIFIED BY         protocolEntityLbl
   }
```

The detailed semantics of some of the more significant attributes listed above will
be explained in Chapter 15 where we deal with modeling network protocols. We can now
subclass transportProtocol from protocolEntity as follows:

```
transportProtocol OBJECT-CLASS ::=
{
  SPECIALIZES-FROM    {{
                         superclass    protocolEntityLbl,
                         basisOfSpecialization
                           {simplePredicate:
                             {attributeDomainRestricted:
                               {newValueOf:
                                 {attribute   operativeLayerLbl,
                                  is          equalTo,
                                  value       transport
                           }}}}
                         }}
  ATTRIBUTES          {
                         transportEntityType,
                         localTransportAddress,
                         maxConnectionCapacity,
```

```
                             upTime,
                             numberOfCurrentConnections,
                             currentConnectionTable,
                             transportLayerStatistics,
                             layerMaxPDUsize,
                             minimumRetransmissionTimeout,
                             maximumRetransmissionTimeout,
                             congestionWindowLimit
                             }
    FUNCTIONS                {
                             openConnection,
                             closeConnection,
                             abortConnection,
                             transmitNormalPDU,
                             receiveNormalPDU,
                             retransmitPDU,
                             executeTimerBackoff,
                             executeCongestionControl
                             }
    IDENTIFIED BY            transportProtocolLbl
    }
```

Each attribute and function of this object class can be defined using its own sup-porting definitions. We will, however, provide detailed definitions of two of the more in-teresting attributes. The attribute `transportLayerStatistics` lists the statistical values of various counters within the protocol entity. Such statistics are typically interest-ing to network management functions, and this attribute could be structured as follows:

```
    transportLayerStatistics ATTRIBUTE ::=
    {
         ATTRIBUTE-TYPE         TransportLayerStatistics
         IDENTIFIED BY          transportLayerStatisticsLbl
    }
```

where the supporting type reference name `TransportLayerStatistics` could be defined as follows:

```
TransportLayerStatistics ::= SET
{
        numberOfOutgoingRequests              [0]   INTEGER,
        numberOfFailedOutgoingRequests        [1]   INTEGER,
        numberOfIncomingRequests              [2]   INTEGER,
        numberOfRejectedIncomingRequests      [3]   INTEGER,
        numberOfLocalDisconnectRequests       [4]   INTEGER,
        numberOfRemoteDisconnectRequests      [5]   INTEGER,
        numberOfProviderAborts                [6]   INTEGER,
        numberOfResets                        [7]   INTEGER,
        numberOfPDUsSent                      [8]   INTEGER,
        numberOfPDUsReceived                  [9]   INTEGER,
        numberOfPDUsRetransmitted             [10]  INTEGER,
        numberOfUnassociatedPDUs              [11]  INTEGER,
        numberOfChecksumErrors                [12]  INTEGER,
        numberOfFormatErrors                  [13]  INTEGER,
        numberOfBadUpperPorts                 [14]  INTEGER,
        numberOfOctetsSent                    [15]  INTEGER,
        numberOfOctetsReceived                [16]  INTEGER,
        numberOfOctetsRetransmitted           [17]  INTEGER
}
```

Another interesting attribute of the `transportProtocol` entity is the `currentConnectionTable`, which lists all the currently active connections held by the entity. This attribute could be structured as follows:

```
currentConnectionTable ATTRIBUTE ::=
{
        ATTRIBUTE-TYPE        TransportConnectionTable
        IDENTIFIED BY         currentConnectionTableLbl
}
```

where the supporting type reference name `TransportConnectionTable` can be defined as a SEQUENCE of rows, each row specifying an individual transport connection:

```
TransportConnectionTable ::=
                        SEQUENCE OF TransportConnection
```

```
TransportConnection ::= SEQUENCE
{
  localConnectionIdentifier    INTEGER,
  remoteConnectionIdentifier   INTEGER,
  localEndpoint                Address,
  remoteEndpoint               Address,
  localNetworkAddress          Address,
  remoteNetworkAddress         Address,
  connectionInitiatedBy        Address,
  connectionState              FSMState,
  connectionMaxPDUSize         INTEGER,
  connectionStatistics
                               TransportConnectionStatistics
}
```

Here, the supporting type reference name Address could be defined as an
OCTET STRING, FSMState could be defined as an ENUMERATED number representing the current state from all the possible states of the finite state machine of the
transportProtocol object, and TransportConnectionStatistics could
list all the counters which may be of statistical interest to network management. In this
situation, these counters could collect per-connection statistics (as opposed to per-entity
statistics, which were specified in TransportLayerStatistics):

```
TransportConnectionStatistics ::= SET
{
    numberOfPDUsSent            [0]   INTEGER,
    numberOfPDUsReceived        [1]   INTEGER,
    numberOfPDUsRetransmitted   [2]   INTEGER,
    numberOfChecksumErrors      [3]   INTEGER,
    numberOfFormatErrors        [4]   INTEGER,
    numberOfBadUpperPorts       [5]   INTEGER,
    numberOfOctetsSent          [6]   INTEGER,
    numberOfOctetsReceived      [7]   INTEGER,
    numberOfOctetsRetransmitted [8]   INTEGER
}
```

This is a typical example of how a connection-oriented transport protocol object
can be modeled. Protocol entities possessing additional features may be specified by further specialization. For example, a transport protocol with the additional capability of
transmitting expedited data may subclass from transportProtocol and add the

functions `transmitExpeditedPDU` and `receiveExpeditedPDU`. Many other protocol objects at various layers can be modeled using similar techniques.

12.4. Service Object Classes

We now consider typical examples of service object classes. The term *service* is heavily overloaded in communications and carries different meanings in different contexts. Each layer provides a different kind of service to the layer above. Clearly, a service such as electronic mail provided by an application-layer entity is different from a data transfer service provided by a link layer. In our model, the concept of a service is meaningful only with reference to an appropriate protocol entity or entities which provide that service. Usually, a particular service is meaningful only with respect to one or more layers in a protocol stack; each service will therefore be specified relative to its operative layers.

The relationship between a protocol object and the service it provides is not an inheritance association, nor is it an aggregation relationship. A single protocol entity may furnish more than one service, while a single service may be furnished by the co-operative action of multiple protocol entities. The exact relationship between a `protocolEntity` object class and a `service` object class is called a *service provision* relationship; a `protocolEntity` is said to `provide` one or more `services`, while a `service` `is-provided-by` one or more `protocolEntity` objects. In Chapter 17, we shall see how this special relationship can be brought within the regime of our general relationship model.

Each type of communication application requires different services from its lower-layer protocols, depending on the nature of the application. Applications such as broadcast digital HDTV do not typically care about error detection and correction as they are error-tolerant, but they generate source bits at a constant rate and require delivery at the same constant rate. Applications such as voice communication are also error-tolerant, but are delay-sensitive. On the other hand, applications such as file transfer, electronic mail, and software download are highly error-sensitive, but their source bit generation activity can be blocked, buffered, and flow-controlled if necessary, and transmission delays can be tolerated. Different applications with different requirements may be multiplexed within the same bitstream. For example, a downstream digital-HDTV transmission between a CATV head-end system and a subscribing monitor (which is not error-sensitive) may be mixed with an upstream signal containing home shopping orders (which is error-sensitive), and thus must be processed by a different protocol stack.

For each application, therefore, the services required at each layer are different. The nature of the application determines the services that will be invoked in the stacks supporting that application. To illustrate the notion of services available at each layer, we will study the services offered by two important layers: the data-link layer and the application layer.

Link-Layer Services

Various services are provided by different link layers, depending on the nature of the applications they support. We can distinguish these services based on several criteria:

Isochronicity: An *isochronous* service is one that requires both the source and destination to operate to the same clock. This means that the receiving system consumes bits at the same rate as they are produced by the source system, and the service must assure synchronization between transmitted source bits and received destination bits. If for any reason this synchronization is lost, mechanisms for automatic resynchronization must be provided. This means that timing information must be built into the service. If the source application happens to be asynchronous but transmits data over a synchronous line, an isochronous mode of transmission is still required: even when the application has nothing to send, it is incumbent on the sending host to keep on transmitting synchronously clocked null codes, so that an appropriate density of bit boundary transitions is provided to maintain the timing reference. We include in this category transmissions which are *plesiochronous*, that is, almost synchronous — any two signals which are nominally at the same rate and whose rate variation is between small, specified limits. A *non-isochronous* service does not require a common timing reference between source and destination.

Source Bit Generation Rate: A *continuous bit rate* or *constant bit rate* (CBR) service must be able to carry a bitstream from any source generating bits at a constant rate. This is also sometimes referred to as a *continuous bitstream organization* (CBO) service. By contrast, a *variable bit rate* (VBR) or *variable bitstream organization* (VBO) service is not required to guarantee a constant transmission rate.

Link-Layer Multiplexing: A *multiplexed* service allows multiple applications (or multiple instances of the same application) to share the link simultaneously. By contrast, a *dedicated* service requires that only one application have exclusive use of the link at a given time and that it not relinquish it until it completes. Multiplexed services are more complex to implement since they must carry some identifier field in the link-layer format which will assist in demultiplexing at the destination.

Link-Layer Error Detection: A service *supporting* link-layer error correction contains a mechanism in the link-layer format to detect payload errors. By contrast, a service which *does not support* link-layer error detection leaves it to higher layers to detect and correct errors. Implementing detection at the link layer adds complexity to its protocols, since it requires additional fields to carry error detection mechanisms such as CRC. However, for marketing reasons some network providers offer this service at the link layer itself because of the higher margins on sophisticated services. Some users may choose to perform this function at higher layers in their terminal equipment stacks rather than in the network, thereby expending additional CPU cycles but saving by subscribing to a less expensive service.

Link-Layer Frame Loss: A service *detecting* lost or mis-inserted link-layer frames will carry additional overhead to indicate a sequence number for each frame. A service *not detecting* lost frames will not incur this overhead but must depend on higher layers to detect lost or mis-sequenced data.

Connection Mode: A *connection-oriented* service is required to provide a connection between the source application and the destination application. By contrast, a *connectionless* service need not establish such a connection before communication can occur. Connection establishment is required for isochronous and constant-bit-rate services. It is also generally required when the service is interactive (i.e., bidirectional and real-time), or when the volume of data to be transmitted is sufficiently large as to make connectionless transmission cumbersome. Typically, even though a link layer may be aware of whether its payload is connection-oriented or connectionless, it need not itself perform the actual connection establishment; this can be handled at some layer higher in the stack.

In our object model, we could use each one of these criteria as the *basis of specialization* for link-layer services. We could select further criteria depending on the detail of granularity we want in our classification; usually two or three are sufficient to cover most possibilities, because of dependencies between various categories. If we wish, we can also choose additional criteria such as *content indication* (provided or not-Provided), *frame length* (fixed or variable), *segmentation and reassembly* (supported or notSupported), and so on, as bases of specialization. If we choose n different criteria as bases of specialization, we could in effect create 2^n disjoint subclasses, but many will be empty.

In the case of link-layer services, we could create disjoint subclasses using isochronous and nonIsochronous as one basis of specialization, continuousBitRate and variableBitRate as another, and so on. Many of these subclasses are empty: for example, there is no such thing as a continuousBitRate-nonIsochronous service; all continuousBitRate services are isochronous.

These criteria were considered by the ITU in the definition of the service model for Broadband ISDN standards [ITU-T I.211, ITU-T I.150, Day91]. The B-ISDN "link layer" produces fixed-length cells called *asynchronous transfer mode* (ATM) cells. The cells produced by the "link layer" in B-ISDN are transported by the ATM layer, which is responsible for delivery across the network. Because the "link layer" in any terminal equipment adapts its applications to the ATM layer, it is often called the *ATM adaptation layer* (AAL). Each AAL also has a sublayer to provide a *segmentation and reassembly* function, which divides PDUs arriving from higher layers into fixed-length ATM cells

In the original model to define the services offered by the AAL layer, the ITU considered only isochronicity, source bit generation rate, and connection mode as possible bases of specialization for B-ISDN link-layer services. ATM cells have 5 fixed octets of header information, up to 4 octets of variable control information, and up to 48 octets of payload, with the total being exactly 53 octets. For this model, therefore, frame length need not be considered as a basis of classification. Using the chosen bases, four "service classes" were defined, termed Class A through D respectively. These "service classes" were specialized according to the criteria shown in Figure 12-1.

Based on these service classes, four different protocolEntity classes were defined for the AAL layer. These were termed AAL Type 1, AAL Type 2, AAL Type 3, and AAL Type 4 respectively, matching the definitions of the service classes.

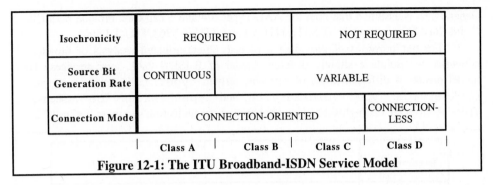

Figure 12-1: The ITU Broadband-ISDN Service Model

However, it soon became clear that the distinction between AAL Types 3 and 4 was artificial. Both AALs were intended to transport data. As we shall see in Chapter 15, typically any terminal equipment producing and consuming data has several layers of protocol entities for performing error correction and detection. These higher layers typically also perform connection establishment and tear-down, if any is required. The intended distinction between AAL Types 3 and 4 was that Type 3 would be used for connection-oriented data and Type 4 for connectionless. However, if the need for connection establishment can be detected at a higher layer and executed there, then the link layer can simply transmit both connection-oriented and connectionless data in an identical manner. Since this is a common situation, AAL Types 3 and 4 were merged into a single entity termed AAL Type 3/4.

In addition, the internetworking industry was evaluating B-ISDN standards for transmission of LAN data over broadband networks. Through years of experience of running data over varied network substrates, this industry already had considerable experience with designing reliable error-correction protocols such as TCP/IP at the middle layer in terminal equipment. This industry needed a simple bare-bones transmission facility from the AAL layer. The proposed AAL types, with their ability to detect cell loss and errors at the link layer, over-provided for functionality which was already present in the middle layers of much existing terminal equipment.

To accommodate the needs of the internetworking industry, an additional AAL type was proposed: a "simple and efficient" type which dispensed with the functionality of detecting cell loss and errors, relegating that to the upper layers. This also resulting in freeing up an additional 4 octets' worth of overhead, which could now be used for payload. This also resulted in the loss of the ability to multiplex different AAL-layer users onto the same physical connection; this was not a problem as such multiplexing between different user applications can also be done higher up in the stack. AAL Type 5 therefore uses all 48 octets of an ATM cell's payload field, with a minimal 5-octet header. A simple segmentation and reassembly function can convert packets or datagrams produced by upper layers to ATM cells [RFC 1483], thus simplifying most of the processing at the AAL layer.

With the merging of AAL Types 3/4 and the creation of AAL Type 5, the original service classes A, B, C, and D no longer corresponded to the AAL types. The ITU then decoupled service classes from AAL types, stating that although they were still "in consonance" with each other, the user was free to select any AAL type for any service class.

Generally, it is assumed that both the AAL Types 3/4 and 5 can each provide both Class C and Class D services [ITU-T I.321, ITU-T I.362, ITU-T I.363, ITU-T I.364].

For our purposes of providing a precise object-oriented analysis of broadband networks, we define a slightly different model of B-ISDN AAL-layer services. This model creates 4 different kinds of services, termed `type1LinkService`, `type2-LinkService`, `type3-4LinkService`, and `type5LinkService` respectively. These services are distinguished using the bases of specialization shown in Figure 12-2.

Isochronicity	REQUIRED		NOT REQUIRED	
Source Bit Generation Rate	CONTINUOUS	VARIABLE		
Connection Mode	CONNECTION-ORIENTED		EITHER	
Link Level Multiplexing	DEDICATED		MULTIPLEXED	DEDICATED
Link Level Error Detection	NOT SUPPORTED	LIMITED SUPPORT	SUPPORTED	NOT SUPPORTED
Link Level Cell Loss	DETECTED			NOT DETECTED
	type1 LinkService	type2 LinkService	type3-4 LinkService	type5 LinkService

Figure 12-2: Bases of Specialization for Link-Layer Services

`type1LinkService`: This supports a continuous source bit generation rate and provides isochronous timing to guarantee that the destination consumes data at the same rate that the source produces it. It is always connection-oriented and does not support error detection in the link layer. Examples of applications which may use this service are telephone conversations and videoteleconferencing.

`type2LinkService`: This supports sources which may generate data at a variable rate but still need timing synchronization between source and destination. It is also connection-oriented and sometimes performs limited forward error correction at the link layer. Applications using this service typically are distributive audio and video services with consumer presentation control, such as interactive video games, audio message retrieval, and many multimedia services. Although video is often thought of as a continuous bitstream application, video compression techniques such as MPEG which use image differencing, motion compensation, predictive/interpolative encoding, or fractal algorithms often tend to produce bursty encodings of constant-rate bitstreams.

`type3-4LinkService`: This is a variable-bit-rate service intended for transmission of data. Both connectionless and connection-oriented data can be transmitted; connection handling, if necessary, may be done higher up in the stack. This service allows multiple applications between the same end-points to share the same the link simultaneously and also performs error detection at this layer. Its typical users may include both volume data transmission applications (the original ITU "Class C" services, such as software distribution) as well as sporadic low-volume data applications (the original ITU "Class D" services, such as credit card validation, electronic funds transfer, travel reservations, and lottery ticket purchasing).

`type5LinkService`: This supports variable bit rate sources, does not require a common timing reference between source and destination, and does not care about the connection characteristics of the application. A `type5LinkService` provides a fairly low level of functionality within the network and is used when higher layers provide sophisticated frame resequencing, connection control, and error detection and correction. It also assumes that only one network layer at a given time will use the same link-layer circuit, thus cutting down on multiplexing overhead at the link layer. Typically, applications using a `type5LinkService` are data only — for example, text and graphics transmission. Such applications could be interactive, such as library catalog browsing, remote login, and text conferencing, or non-interactive, such as bulk file transfer.

In the next section, we will see how each of these service types fits into the inheritance hierarchy, **specializing-from** the `service` object class. The criteria of Figure 12-2 are useful for classifying not just AAL layers but other link-layer protocols as well; for example, protocols such as SDLC or LAPB can also be analyzed and classified with respect to these criteria.

Application Services

Once we begin to consider application services, we need different criteria as the basis of specialization. Some possible criteria are

Delay Sensitivity: A *delay-sensitive* service is required to guarantee a maximum (and usually very small) upper bound on the transmission delay. Interactive real-time services are typically delay-sensitive. A *delay-tolerant* service need not provide any such guarantee and is permitted to possibly delay bits in the network during transmission if necessary.

Error Sensitivity: An *error-sensitive* service is required to guarantee reliable transmission and recovery from network errors. Text and data transmission services are always error-sensitive. An error-sensitive service is typically required to traverse some non-trivial middle or upper-layer protocol responsible for error detection and correction. An *error-tolerant* service — such as broadcast digital-HDTV — is usually unaffected by a non-zero bit error rate in network transmission.

Depending on the speed of the underlying network and the processing power of its end-nodes, it may not always be possible to satisfy both stringent delay-sensitivity bounds and stringent error-sensitivity bounds, due to the inherent delays in processing error-recovery algorithms in error-correcting protocols. With increasing bandwidth and faster processing capacity, this limitation will become less restrictive with time.

The classification of application services according to the bases of specialization above, together with additional parameters such as *throughput,* is often used by many protocols (including B-ISDN AAL Types 1 and 2, and Frame Relay) to negotiate *QOS (Quality-Of-Service) parameters* with the network. Some even distinguish two kinds of delay parameters — propagation delay versus variational delay. Generally, a multi-way negotiation involving all the terminal devices involved in the communication, and the network itself, must occur for each connection. Special protocols are often defined for this purpose: for example, the protocol *Q.93B* [ITU-T Q.93B] handles these negotiation parameters in B-ISDN during connection establishment [Smit93b].

Using delay tolerance and error tolerance in combination as orthogonal bases of specialization, we can create four disjoint subclasses for application services. All of these four subclasses are non-empty, as shown in Figure 12-3. Similar classifications of application services have been proposed elsewhere in the literature [Schi93] under different terminologies (e.g., "reliable real-time", "unreliable real-time", "reliable non-real-time", and "unreliable non-real-time").

	ERROR SENSITIVE	ERROR TOLERANT
DELAY SENSITIVE	Space Vehicle Telemetry Real-Time Data Operate-By-Wire	Voice Conferencing Video Conferencing
DELAY TOLERANT	Text Mail File Transfer Software Distribution	Voice Mail Fax Mail Video Mail

Figure 12-3: Bases of Specialization for Higher-Layer Services

Clearly, there are many dependencies between the services provided by different layers. Each application service will require different services from the layers below; the nature of each application dictates the nature of the underlying protocol stack required to support it. For example, a non-interactive service such as software download is highly delay-tolerant but completely error-intolerant. Being delay-tolerant, it requires few, if any, guarantees on service time or variance limitation on service delay distributions from the lower layers. Being error-intolerant, it does require error detection and correction. However, because the destination can afford to receive all packets, store them, resequence them, and then request retransmission of missing information at leisure, packet mis-sequencing need not be corrected in flux. While the transport layer supporting such an application must be able to retransmit errored or missing information, it need not even calculate the round-trip delay, since it need never estimate how long to wait before re-transmitting an unacknowledged packet; it can simply wait for the destination to request it.

Thus, there is a mapping between application services classified using error and delay tolerances and the link-layer services classified by other criteria in the preceding section. In fact, there is a mapping between different application services and the services provided by *every* layer in the stack. As we shall see in Chapter 15, the knowledge of these dependencies can be formalized as a set of *layering rules* for the construction of protocol stacks. When these dependencies are formally specified, they can be used to advantage by a network synthesis program to correctly construct the protocol stack for a given application service.

12.5. Specifying Service Objects

Using the formal notation of our model, we can now define a top-level generic `service` object class based on the considerations in the preceding section:

```
service OBJECT-CLASS ::=
{
  ATTRIBUTES              {
                          serviceName,
                          serviceType,
                          serviceEntityIdentifier,
                          operativeLayer,
                          }
    IDENTIFIED BY         serviceLbl
}
```

The `operativeLayer` attribute identifies the layer or layers of the protocol entities which provide that service. Using this as the basis of specialization, we can define the services offered by each layer. For each layer, we can create further subclasses for services with different characteristics.

As an example, at the link layer we can create subclasses for `type1Link-Service`, `type2LinkService`, `type3-4LinkService`, and `type5Link-Service`, reflecting the characteristics we chose as the bases of specialization in our model. For example,

```
linkService OBJECT-CLASS ::=
{
  SPECIALIZES-FROM      {{
                        superclass    serviceLbl,
                        basisOfSpecialization
                          {simplePredicate:
                          {attributeDomainRestricted:
```

```
                              {newValueOf:
                               {attribute   operativeLayerLbl,
                                is          equalTo,
                                value       dataLink
                              }}}}
                             }}
ATTRIBUTES                   {
                              timingReference,
                               -- isochronous or non-isochronous
                              sourceBitRate,
                               -- constant or variable
                              connectionMode,
                               -- connOriented or connectionLess
                              multiplexing,
                               -- multiplexed or dedicated
                              errorDetection,
                               -- supported or not
                              frameLoss,
                               -- detected or not
                              }
 IDENTIFIED BY               linkServiceLbl
}


type1LinkService OBJECT-CLASS ::=
{
 SPECIALIZES-FROM            {{
                             superclass   linkServiceLbl,
                             basisOfSpecialization
                              {compoundPredicate:
                               {connectBy   and,
                                predicates
                                {{simplePredicate:
                                  {attributeDomainRestricted:
                                   {newValueOf:
                                    {attribute
                                            timingReferenceLbl,
                                     is       equalTo,
                                     value    isochronous
                                   }}}},
```

```
                                  {simplePredicate:
                                   {attributeDomainRestricted:
                                    {newValueOf:
                                     {attribute sourceBitRateLbl,
                                       is        equalTo,
                                       value     constant
                                   }}}}
                                  }}}
                                 }}
    ATTRIBUTES               {
                              ratedSpeed,    -- bps
                              maxVCIsSupported,
                              managementStatistics,
                              ...
                             }
    FUNCTIONS                {
                              transmitCell,
                              receiveCell,
                              forwardCell,
                              ...
                             }
    IDENTIFIED BY            type1LinkServiceLbl
    }
```

It is important to note that we are modeling `service` classes, which are different from the `protocolEntity` classes we modeled in preceding sections. When the desired service is identified, the service provision relationships between `protocol-Entity` classes and `service` classes will allow us to select the correct protocol entities which provide the desired service. It is interesting to note that `service` classes are generally fully abstract. This implies that a `service` class may not have any "instances" which are hardware, software, or firmware implementations. However, the `protocol-Entity` classes which provide that `service` will have concrete instances. The `service` class remain abstract, serving only as a guideline (through its service provision relationships) to correctly synthesize stacks of concrete `protocolEntity` objects which collectively furnish the desired service.

In a similar manner, different services may be specified for other protocol layers as well. If, for example, we were modeling transport protocols which provided congestion control for transport-layer protocol data units, a `congestionControlService` could be subclassed from `transportService` and invested with the appropriate FUNCTIONs to provide congestion control for transport layer protocols.

For application-layer services, we need to consider delay tolerance and error tolerance as attributes which can be set to various values. These could then be specified as constraints in the basis of specialization, allowing the compiler to automatically enforce them. For example, we can specify the following subclasses:

```
applicationService OBJECT-CLASS ::=
{
  SPECIALIZES-FROM    {{
                        superclass  serviceLbl,
                        basisOfSpecialization
                         {simplePredicate:
                          {attributeDomainRestricted:
                           {newValueOf:
                            {attribute  operativeLayerLbl,
                             is         equalTo,
                             value      application
                        }}}}
                       }}
  ATTRIBUTES          {
                        errorTolerance,
                        delayTolerance
                       }
  IDENTIFIED BY       applicationServiceLbl
}


errorSensitiveApplicationService OBJECT-CLASS ::=
{
  SPECIALIZES-FROM    {{
                        superclass  applicationServiceLbl,
                        basisOfSpecialization
                         {compoundPredicate:
                          {connectBy  and,
                           predicates
                           {{simplePredicate:
                             {attributeDomainRestricted:
                              {newValueOf:
                               {attribute
                                        errorToleranceLbl,
                                is      equalTo,
```

```
                                     value    0
                          }}}},
                          {simplePredicate:
                           {attributeDomainRestricted:
                            {newValueOf:
                             {attribute
                                     delayToleranceLbl,
                              is        equalTo,
                              value     acceptableLimit
                                   -- defined elsewhere
                             }}}}
                           }}}
                          }}
    IDENTIFIED BY         errorSensitiveApplicationServiceLbl
    }
```

We can now begin to define specific application services, for example:

```
bulkFileTransferService OBJECT-CLASS ::=
{
  SPECIALIZES-FROM      {{
                          superclass
                                  errorSensitive-
                                  ApplicationServiceLbl,
                          basisOfSpecialization
                           {simplePredicate:
                            {attributeDomainRestricted:
                             {newValueOf:
                              {attribute     serviceTypeLbl,
                               is            equalTo,
                               value         bulkFileTransfer
                              }}}}
                          }}
  ATTRIBUTES            {
                          currentUserAuthorizations,
                          fileTranferLog
                         }
  FUNCTIONS            {
                          listRemoteDirectory,
                          listLocalDirectory,
```

```
                        changeRemoteDirectory,
                        changeLocalDirectory,
                        transmitFile,
                        receiveFile,
                        convertFileFormat,
                        changeTransmissionMode,
                        reportAccessRestrictions,
                        changeAccessRestrictions
                        deleteRemoteFile,
                        deleteLocalFile
                        }
    IDENTIFIED BY       bulkFileTransferServiceLbl
    }
```

Following taxonomic principles such as the ones used in the examples above, one categorization of `service` object classes could be made as suggested in Figure 12-4.

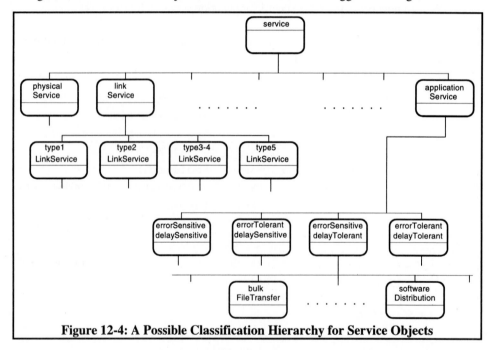

Figure 12-4: A Possible Classification Hierarchy for Service Objects

We can automate the knowledge that each service, depending on its bases of specialization, requires a particular profile for its underlying protocol stack. If the architect indicates that a `bulkFileTransferService` is required by an application in the network, a network synthesis tool can automatically pull in all the protocol modules required to support this service. This is because the network synthesis tool knows that the `bulkFileTransferService` object class derives from the `errorSensitive-ApplicationService` object class and therefore knows what stacks are required in order to support the error and delay tolerance requirements of such services. In Chapter 17, we shall see how the service provision relationships between service classes and protocol classes may be formally specified to the model compiler.

The relationship between `protocolEntity` object classes and `service` object classes allows us to model the semantic linkage between *service definitions* and *protocol specifications*. Generally, a service definition is an implementation-independent description of "what the service does", while the protocol specification describes "how it does it" [ITU-T X.210, ITU-T X.407]. Among other things, the `service` object class can accommodate such service definitions as abstracted and encapsulated classes within an object-oriented model. If the service definition is sufficiently detailed, the protocol specification to implement the service can often be extracted from it almost mechanically. In our model, the `protocolEntity` class reflects implemented protocol instances, while their related `service` class reflects their (explicit or implied) fully abstract service definition.

In some situations, a distinction can be drawn between the *control* aspects of a particular service and its *payload* aspects. For example, the control and signaling bitstream that supports a `videoteleconference` service may not have the same characteristics as the payload bitstream for that service. The control and signaling bitstream (which may contain information such as dialed number and tariff rate) may be highly error-sensitive, while the payload bitstream may be error-tolerant. In Chapter 15, we shall also see how, for a given service, the control bitstream can be specified to use a different underlying protocol stack than its payload bitstream.

12.6. Summary

Object classes such as physical equipment, protocol entities, and network services are frequently encountered in a communications network. All of these can be modeled using the ASN.1 information object class template defined for specifying network object classes. When specifying classes such as these, care must be taken to ensure that the basis of specialization has been correctly specified to allow the model compiler to enforce it as a constraint. Equipment classes are typically subclassed on the basis of their equipment type. Protocol classes may be subclassed on the basis of their operative layer. Protocol classes have service provision relationships with service classes. Service classes may be subclassed using those characteristics which are important at that level in the protocol stack.

13. Object Function Behavior

"The real expert is the network consultant whose cost and time estimates are the highest."
— *advice from anonymous systems integrator.*

13.1. Introduction

In this chapter, we introduce techniques for modeling the behavior of the functions of an object class. After an introduction to graphical techniques, we cover notational techniques in greater detail. Several different techniques are explained for the modeling of protocol objects, software objects, and hardware objects. A mechanism is described for the integration of these function behavior models into our object model. Finally, additional specialization principles are considered based on behavior specialization of functions.

13.2. Formal Description Techniques

In Chapter 11 we created the formal model of an OBJECT-CLASS with a FUNCTIONS field, which is a set-valued field whose type is the FUNCTION information object class. A FUNCTION itself is modeled as having inputs, outputs, and exceptions, along with a SPECIFICATION field. The SPECIFICATION describes "what the function does", and has as its type a FormalSpecification. In this chapter, we focus exclusively on various techniques which can be used to describe the FormalSpecification of a function. These are termed *Formal Description Techniques*.

A formal description technique is a specification mechanism for the behavioral aspects of any dynamic operational capability. Some formal description techniques are mostly diagrammatic and are intended largely to assist in human comprehension of the behavioral aspect of functions. Among the diagrammatic techniques we shall consider are State Transition Diagrams, Data Flow Diagrams, Timing Sequence Diagrams, and Case Diagrams.

To specify the dynamic model of a function formally enough so that it can be interpreted by a model compiler, an analytical description is desirable. Some formal description techniques can be provided as input to machine interpreters, which produce as their output a partial or complete executable implementation of the specification. Since our focus is to provide a complete description of a network object to our model compiler, we will be more interested in notational rather than pictorial techniques.

Some of the formal description techniques we shall consider for specifying the functions of protocol entity objects are Estelle, LOTOS, SDL, and CHILL. Excellent overviews of these techniques may be found in [Boch90a, Boch90b, Brui87, Sidh90, Turn93]. Aside from protocol entities, we shall also consider formal descriptions of dynamic models of functions in both software objects, using specification languages such as Z and VDM, as well as hardware objects, using specification languages such as VHDL. All of these techniques provide a machine-interpretable textual notation for describing the problem domain.

13.3. Graphical Formal Descriptions

The formal description of protocol objects has been the subject of much research, and many advanced techniques have been devised to capture the dynamic properties of a protocol machine. These are often based on State Transition Diagrams, Data Flow Diagrams, Timing Sequence Diagrams, and Case Diagrams. The following is a brief discussion of some of these techniques.

State Transition Diagrams

State Transition Diagrams are a well-understood concept in engineering and software systems design, and many different ways of representing them have been devised in the literature. When it is known that an object will react in a predictable way to a certain *stimulus* and produce a certain *response*, the object is said to be in a known *state*. When the stimulus is actually received, the object produces the expected response and may remain in the same state or move to a different state. The object is then said to have executed a *state transition*, which is said to have been *fired* by the stimulus. By providing other stimuli in its new state, it may be possible to keep the object in the same state, move it back to its original state, or move it to yet another state. By abstracting this pattern of stimuli, responses, states, and state transitions for all objects of a given class, we can represent it as a *state transition diagram* for that class.

A state transition diagram represent states as circles and ovals, with transitions represented by directed arcs. Each arc is typically labeled *I/O*, with *I* representing the input which causes the transition to fire, and *O* representing any possible output produced by the object as a consequence of executing this transition. An implementation of a state transition diagram with a predictable number of states is known as a *finite state machine*.

As an example, Figure 13-1 shows the State Transition Diagram for the protocol machine of the Transmission Control Protocol (TCP, [RFC 793, Come91]).

For large systems, however, simple state transition diagrams tend to become cumbersome, because of the explosion of states. In the worst case, if every state could have a

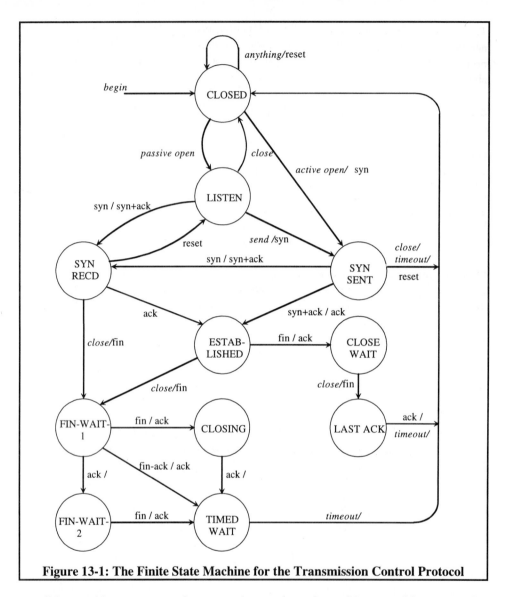

Figure 13-1: The Finite State Machine for the Transmission Control Protocol

possible transition to every other state, the number of transitions would grow as the square of the number of states.

Harel statecharts [Hare87] are a technique for managing this complexity by introducing structure. In a Harel statechart, states can be nested by allowing a *superstate* to contain nested *substates*. The high-level set of transitions can then be represented as a transition diagram of superstates only. Each superstate can then contain a set of nested transitions between substates, with each substate possibly containing further nested substates, and so on. At any given time, an object can be in only *one* superstate of the superstate diagram; within that superstate, it can be in only *one* substate of that superstate.

Therefore, a superstate may be considered a generalization of its nested substates; the nesting model actually defines a *state specialization hierarchy*. By applying structuring principles such as these, a complex State Transition Diagram can be modeled in a reasonable, understandable fashion.

In later sections, we will examine some techniques for representing state transition diagrams in a textual, notational form, such that they can be used for the automatic generation of implementations of state machines.

Data Flow Diagrams

Data Flow Diagrams [Your89, Dema79, Gane78, Ward86] have been used to describe the functional model for many complex systems. Data flow diagrams describe the interactions between *processes* and the *data stores* they use. By tracing the directed arrows between processes (represented by circles or ovals) and data stores (represented by horizontal parallel lines), the various transformations undergone by a unit of data can be accurately described. The directed arcs representing *data flows* carry an indication of the type of data which acts as input and output from each processing element. Data stores are conceptual stores only; in any given implementation, a data store could be a large complex database system with persistent storage, or simply a location in volatile memory.

Unlike State Transition Diagrams, Data Flow Diagrams do not describe the interactions between *events*, that is, they do not indicate the mapping between inputs that fire specific state transitions and the corresponding output of that transition. It should be noted that the circles representing processing elements in a data flow diagram have absolutely no correlation with the circles representing states in a state transition diagrams.

Figure 13-2 represents a data flow diagram for a secure network mail application which includes a user-level encryption mechanism for processing encrypted messages to and from the network. This data flow diagram is incomplete, as it is only intended to illustrate the concept; a complete email application would also include many other details, such as message stores for copies of outgoing messages. Further, some email applications may use encryption features which may be available in the protocol stack itself, rather than at the user level as indicated in this figure.

It should be remembered that if data flow diagrams are used in our methodology, they should be used only as specification tools for mapping the inputs for a function to its outputs. In particular, the data flow diagram should make no attempt to specify a particular computation path inside the function. For example, the specifier may not introduce any processes or data stores which may be internally required by the function, if such processes and data stores are not externally visible outside the function. Specifying such internal details is tantamount to suggesting a particular implementation path [Haye91].

At this time, very few attempts have been made to create a textual notational representation of the semantics of a data flow diagram, so that it can be analyzed and verified mechanically. This is an area ripe for further research, because parts of an implementation could be derived automatically from a formal notational description of a data flow diagram such as the above.

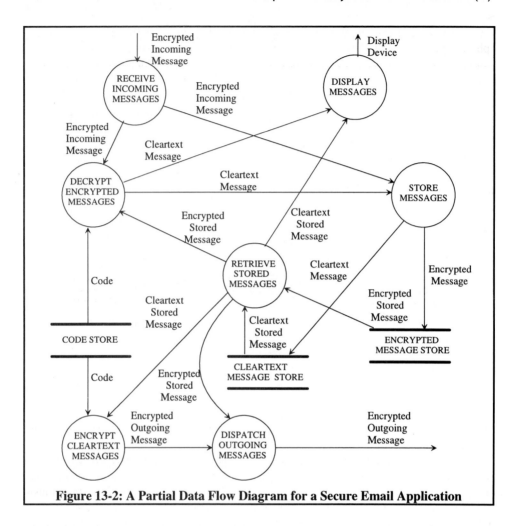

Figure 13-2: A Partial Data Flow Diagram for a Secure Email Application

Timing Sequence Diagrams

Timing Sequence Diagrams describe the sequence of communication between two objects by indicating the timing interactions between bidirectional message exchanges. In a timing sequence diagram, the time axis is assumed to start at the top of the diagram and flow downward. The exchange of messages between objects is indicated by arrows between two vertical parallel lines which correspond to the boundaries of the communicating objects. Because each message takes finite time to traverse the network, the arrows always slope downward in the direction of travel.

A timing sequence diagram is a schematic only, that is, the slope of the arrows or distance between events on the object boundary does not necessarily bear any proportion to actual time durations in a real network.

As an example, Figure 13-3 shows the timing sequence diagram covering all the phases of peer X.25 objects exchanging messages at Layer 3.

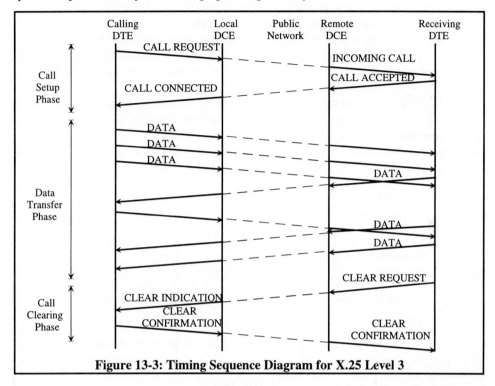

Figure 13-3: Timing Sequence Diagram for X.25 Level 3

To date there has been little work on capturing the semantics of a timing sequence diagram in a formal, textual notation, which can be analyzed by protocol verifiers and simulators. Clearly, if a protocol object class is fully defined in terms of its state transitions, two distinct objects of this class can be instantiated in a simulation and made to communicate. A timing sequence diagram could then be derived as the graph of messages exchanged between these objects during the simulation. However, the reverse situation — where the *a priori* specification of a timing sequence diagram results in the automatic derivation of a (possibly partial) finite state machine for a protocol entity — has been inadequately addressed in the network modeling literature so far.

Case Diagrams

Case Diagrams [Rose93] are an excellent graphical technique for representing the internal behavior of protocol entities. A Case diagram provides a description of the "ultimate fate" of each input received by a protocol layer. It does so by illustrating how each input protocol data unit affects its *counters*, that is, variables which keep running totals of these units. It thus traces the path that a particular PDU may take through a layer, showing the possibilities of discards due to errors or lack of resources.

Case diagrams represent PDUs using upward or downward data flows, indicating inputs transiting through a layer to either a higher or a lower layer in the protocol stack. As the PDU is processed by the layer, various counters are updated. Counters in a Case diagram are either *additive* counters, *subtractive* counters, or *filter* counters. An additive counter meters the PDUs in each horizontal tributary feeding PDUs into the main vertical data flow; a subtractive counter meters the PDUs in each horizontal distributary taking PDUs away from the main vertical data flow; a filter counter merely meters the PDUs in the main vertical data flow itself.

Figure 13-4 depicts the internal behavior of an Internet Protocol entity (IP, [RFC 791]) as it processes datagrams received from a network interface layer before they are passed on to the transport layer.

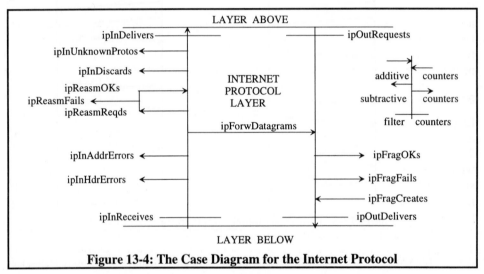

Figure 13-4: The Case Diagram for the Internet Protocol

Case diagrams are an important visual aid to understanding the internal workings of a protocol layer object, but they are an incomplete description of everything that the layer object does. It should also be noted that Case diagrams do not necessarily dictate a particular implementation, that is, the counters are not necessarily updated in the sequence in which they occur in the data flow on the Case diagram.

The formal knowledge arising from a Case diagram is a mathematical equality constraint on the number of PDUs received from the layer below (or delivered to the layer above) as it relates to a linear combination of various counters. In Figure 13-4, for example, it must always be the case that

```
ipOutDelivers = ipOutRequests + ipForwDatagrams -
          ipFragOKs - ipFragFails + ipFragCreates
```

If counters are modeled as attributes of the layer entity object class, a Case diagram describes a mathematical invariant that always holds between these attributes. This invariant implies that the attribute may be computed from other attributes. For this reason, `ipOutDelivers` is not formally modeled by the SNMP Management Information Base. Mathematical relations such as these between the counter attributes of a protocol object class are called *Case Invariants*. In Chapter 20, we shall see how such invariants may be formally modeled.

13.4. Notational Formal Descriptions

Aside from the diagrammatic techniques considered above, many notational techniques also exist for specifying the formal behavior of protocol objects. Both connection-oriented and connectionless protocol entities may be described using these techniques. Connectionless protocols can also be modeled as state machines — even though they do not maintain connection information, features such as error handling, flow control, and fragmentation and reassembly require that they be aware of some concept of state. The following is a brief discussion of the highlights of some of these techniques. For a comprehensive treatment, particularly of Estelle, LOTOS and SDL see [Turn93].

Estelle

Estelle, a name derived from *Extended State Transition Language*, is a standardized formal description technique for the specifying communication protocols and services [ISO 9074]. An Estelle specification for a protocol describes communicating state automata whose internal actions are defined by Pascal-like statements. Because it uses a syntax similar to Pascal, it is not only relatively easy to specify behavior formally in Estelle, but it is also fairly straightforward to automate the generation of implementation code from such a specification as well.

A distributed system in Estelle is a collection of communicating *tasks* [Budk87]. These are sometimes called *module instances*. A task has a number of *interaction points*, which are either *internal* or *external*. At each interaction point the task receives certain inputs and produces certain outputs. A task is generally a finite state machine and is formally described as a nondeterministic communicating state automaton using a Pascal-like syntax. If a task includes at least one transition, it is said to be an *active* task; otherwise it is an *inactive* task.

Tasks in Estelle themselves may be nested in a hierarchy, much like a Harel statechart. The sequence in which tasks in a hierarchy are to be executed is specified by performing a *binding* between their interaction points. If an external interaction point of a nesting (outer) task is bound to an external interaction point of a nested (inner) task, the interaction points are said to be *attached*. If the external interaction point of any task is bound to an external interaction point of a sibling task, the interaction points are said to be *connected*. At any given time, an interaction point is either attached to at most one other interaction point, or connected to at most one other interaction point.

The link that binds two interaction points serves as the conceptual medium of a message exchange, or an *interaction*, between tasks. Each interaction point is associated with a conceptual unbounded FIFO queue to which it appends its interactions. Synchronization semantics between tasks are expressed by partitioning tasks into *subsys-*

tems. Tasks in different subsystems may execute asynchronously in parallel. To enforce synchronization, tasks must belong the same subsystem.

Figure 13-5 shows the model for an Estelle system.

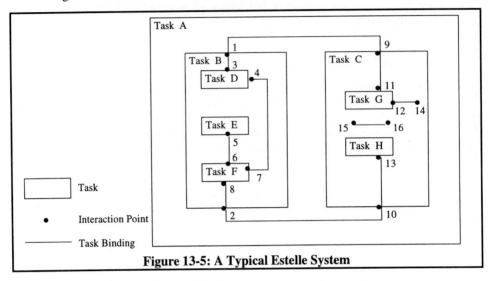

Figure 13-5: A Typical Estelle System

The detailed internal actions of a task are formally specified using *transitions*. A transition may be *simple* or *nested*. Nested transitions are analogous to transitions between the substates of the same superstate in a Harel statechart. A transition moves the task from one state to another and fires only when its formally specified input conditions have been met at some interaction point. If more than one transition is ready to fire based on a given set of input conditions, the transition with the highest priority is the one that fires. On firing, the transition executes a *transition block* which is a sequence of Pascal statements between begin and end keywords. On completion, the transition moves the task from the state specified in the from keyword to the state specified in the to keyword.

The following is an example [Linn88] of the syntax for an Estelle transition, with comments in brackets:

```
state       state_a, state_b;      [declares two states]

trans                              [declares a transition]
priority    integer_constant       [prioritization among
                                     peer transitions]
from        state_a                [current state]
to          state_b                [next state]
provided    predicate              [boolean expression]
```

```
when        ip1_name.event        [input event at named
                                    interaction point]
      begin                       [transition block]
      ...                         [executable statements]
      output    ip2_name.pdu      [possible output action]
      end
```

As an example, consider the TCP state machine of Figure 13-1. Such a machine could be modeled in Estelle with at least two interaction points: one with the application entity above (such as an `ftp` or `telnet` application) and one with the IP layer below. Each transition shown in Figure 13-1 would have a separate Estelle `trans` declaration, one of which is demonstrated as an example below:

```
state established, fin_wait_1;

trans from established to fin_wait_1
when application_layer.close_received
      begin
      ...
      output internet_layer.fin
      end
```

A complete Estelle specification for the TCP protocol machine would model each transition similarly, with the body of the transition filled out with executable statements for the actions to be taken. More interaction points could also be modeled. It is possible to build a "hybrid" Estelle compiler which understands the state machine constructs but which allows the procedural statements in the transition block to be specified in some other programming language such as C++. The entire TCP finite state machine, which Figure 13-1 represents pictorially, can be captured in Estelle notationally and fed to an Estelle compiler. We could then verify the correctness of the transitions and automatically generate a partial implementation of a TCP protocol machine.

If the specificand object in our methodology exhibits state transitions for one of its functions, Estelle could be used as an appropriate formal technique to specify that function. This may be accomplished by binding its &Arguments and &Results parameters to events at the external interaction points of an Estelle task and referencing an Estelle specification for the internal behavior. For more details on Estelle the reader is referred to [ISO 9074, Budk87, Cour88].

LOTOS

LOTOS, a name derived from *Language of Temporal Ordering Specifications*, is a formal description technique which specifies communication systems by defining the temporal relations between its externally visible interfaces [ISO 8807].

The LOTOS view of a communication system is that of a *process*, which may contain within it nested *subprocesses*. A process executes in an *environment* which may consist of other processes. A process has an externally observable impact on its environment and may also be capable of performing internal, unobservable actions. The behavior of each process is conceptually a tree structure whose root represents the initial state of the process, and whose branches represent the possible interactions a process could undertake, ordered in time according to the depth of the nodes in the tree.

Synchronization between processes is specified in terms of *events*. Events are considered to occur instantaneously and have zero duration. An event happens at one of the *gates* of the process. A gate is analogous to an interaction point in Estelle. The LOTOS *process definition* specifies the behavior of a process by defining the sequences of events that are externally observable at all the gates of the process.

The following is an example of LOTOS syntax for a process specification:

```
process    proc-name [ args ]   :=
           subproc1-name [ args ] ||
           subproc2-name [ args]
where
     process subproc1-name [ args ] :=
             . . .
     endproc
     process subproc2-name [ args ] :=
             . . .
     endproc
endproc
```

The process is defined in terms of its *behavior expressions*. Behavior expressions are specified in terms of reserved LOTOS keywords and operators which allow for all possible behaviors for the transitioning process. The complete syntax for behavior expressions allows for process action, process inaction, choices, parallel composition, sequential composition, nested process instantiation, process hiding, disabling, and successful termination. Precedence relations between operators are defined rigorously enough to allow compilers to unambiguously parse LOTOS behavior expressions. The foundation for defining data types and values in LOTOS is ACT ONE, which is based on the theory of abstract data types.

Table 13-1 describes some selected LOTOS operators [Diaz89]. Lower-case identifiers represent event names; upper-case identifiers represent process names, while G represents a set of gate identifiers.

Behavior expressions may be conditionally triggered by prefixing them with *guarded expressions*, which govern behavior expressions by allowing their execution only if their conditional predicate is true. Other LOTOS syntax allows for the specification of multi-process synchronization to satisfy the requirements of interprocess communication and broadcast messaging.

Inaction	`stop`	deadlock
Action	`a;B`	event a precedes process B
Choice	B_1 `[]` B_2	choice between processes B_1 and B_2
Parallel	B_1 `|||` B_2	interleaving
	B_1 `||` B_2	full synchronization
	B_1 `|[G]|` B_2	synchronization on events in G
Sequence	B_1 `>>` B_2	process B_1 precedes process B_2
Disrupt	B_1 `[>` B_2	process B_2 disrupts process B_1
Hiding	`hide G in B`	hide events in G from environment of B

Table 13-1: Some LOTOS Operators

A function in our methodology may be formally specified using LOTOS, if it is suitable to do so, by binding the `&Arguments` and `&Results` fields to events at the gates of a LOTOS process and referencing a LOTOS description for internal behavior. For more details on LOTOS, the reader is referred to [ISO 8807, Bolo87, Brin86], with excellent examples in [Logr90, Faci91, Kouy91].

SDL

SDL — *Specification and Description Language* — is a widely used language for formal specification of real-time, interactive, distributed systems [ITU-T Z.100]. Partial specifications for many telecommunications systems have been described using SDL. The popularity of SDL arises from the fact that it possesses both a graphical and a textual representation. The graphical representation, SDL/GR, expresses concepts such as input, output, processes, delays, and many others by using diagrammatic constructs. The text-only syntax, SDL/PR, conveys all the semantics of the graphical representation using equivalent notational constructs. For expressing certain concepts which cannot be accommodated graphically (for example, the structure of abstract data types of the input and output parameters) the textual notation may be used to complement the graphical representation.

SDL models the system as a number of *processes*, each of which is an extended finite state machine. Each process works autonomously and internally executes in a conceptually serial fashion. A process may cooperate with other processes, with multiple processes executing asynchronously in parallel within the same system. While each process may have its own local data store for storing internal variables, processes are encapsulated in the sense that they do not have direct access to the variables of other processes.

Processes communicate with each other using *signals*, which always carry source and destination process addresses. Processes read signals from an infinite *input queue* and execute state transitions in response to those signals. When a transition is executed in response to a signal, the signal is said to be *consumed*. A transition may involve reading and writing of variables, execution of conditional statements, creation of new processes, and emission of signals to other processes.

SDL provides a rich set of structuring principles for specifying the behavior of a system at various levels of hierarchical decomposition. An important structuring principle in SDL is known as a *block*. A block may contain one or more processes. A block may also contain sub-blocks which in turn contain processes. The scope of definitions made in a nesting block extends to all its nested blocks. Blocks are connected to each other by way of *channels*. Channels themselves may be structured using blocks and other channels, a feature which provides a very powerful abstraction.

Channels may also be used by blocks to communicate with the external environment. A well-defined system boundary encapsulates the SDL system, and information may be exchanged across this boundary using environment signals. The stimulus-response model of an SDL specification, where the response to any external stimulus is described in the formal specification, is fairly intuitive and easy to understand.

An SDL specification must formally define the block structure of an SDL system, the channel descriptions, the signal descriptions, the process descriptions, and data type descriptions. The process description must formally define for each process its name, input and output parameters, variable descriptions, timer descriptions, procedure descriptions, and the process graph for its finite state machine. Figure 13-6 describes some of the graphical constructs in SDL.

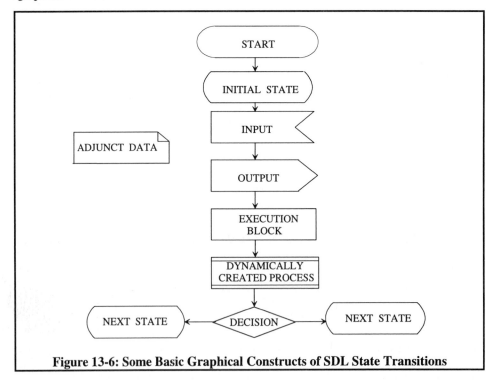

Figure 13-6: Some Basic Graphical Constructs of SDL State Transitions

As an example of SDL representation, consider again the TCP protocol machine of Figure 13-1. Figure 13-7 shows the SDL representations of some of the transitions of that protocol machine.

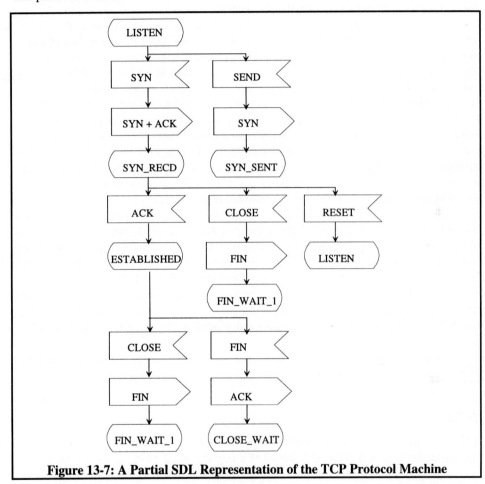

Figure 13-7: A Partial SDL Representation of the TCP Protocol Machine

To model a state-transition-oriented function for a specificand object in our methodology, the &Arguments and &Results fields of a function may be bound to the external signals received at an SDL block boundary. For more details on SDL the reader is referred to [ITU-T Z.100, Sara87, Beli89], with excellent examples in [Hogr88].

CHILL

The *CCITT High-Level Language* — CHILL — is a suitable description technique for highly concurrent, real-time systems [ITU-T Z.200]. It was originally devised for programming switching systems with stored program control and is suitable for applications such as call handling, operations system support, on-line and off-line maintenance and acceptance testing. CHILL is essentially a programming language derived from PL/1, ALGOL 68, and Pascal and provides the normal features of such languages. Aside from these, CHILL has capabilities which make it an efficient specification vehicle for the behavior of both large and small switching elements.

A CHILL program describes the *actions* which must be performed, the *objects* which are the operands to these actions, and the *program structure*. Each data object is either a value or the location of a value and has a *mode* associated with. The mode of a data item in CHILL is analogous to the class of an object in a class-based language: it enforces strong typing, enumerates allowable values, restricts access methods, and specifies valid operations on the data. Data objects may be structured using other data objects.

Actions in CHILL allow the program to invoke built-in or externally supplied procedures. Sequential actions can be specified using normal flow-of-control statements. It is possible to structure the program for concurrency, which is important in highly parallel systems such as switching elements. The unit of concurrency is a *process*: a process may execute concurrently with other processes but is internally sequential. To permit coordination between processes, interprocess communication is necessary.

Like SDL, CHILL provides *signals* as the mechanism for asynchronous interprocess communication. In addition, lightweight processes can be dynamically created and deleted. CHILL allows each process to wait selectively on multiple signals simultaneously. It also enforces critical regions for internal executions of a process when it cannot be interrupted by signals. Arriving messages are processed from a FIFO queue.

CHILL allows information-hiding through modules, which consist of data and procedure definitions. This is accomplished using a *grant/seize* mechanism where selective access can be provided to certain data and procedures by the granting process to the seizing process.

For more details on CHILL, the reader is referred to [ITU-T Z.200, Chap90]. Many attempts have been made to extend CHILL with object-oriented features; examples may be found in [Maru91, Guen93].

TTCN

TTCN — the *Tree and Tabular Combined Notation* — is a mechanism for formally specifying the expected external behavior of a protocol [ISO 9646-3]. TTCN has largely been used in the design of test suites and test cases for protocol validation. As a test suite design tool, it may be considered a formal description of the testable behavior of a function. By itself, TTCN is not a complete specification technique because it has no mechanism for describing the internal state transitions and procedures of its specificand system.

TTCN specifies dynamic system behavior by defining combinations of allowed events. Such combinations can specify the sequence in which events are expected to occur and may also specify a choice of one among several successor events in response to a given predecessor event. Undesired external inputs can be trapped using an `otherwise` clause as an alternative to desired events.

The overall organization of a TTCN test suite is in terms of a collection of tables defining aspects of a test, including service primitives, PDUs, their parameters, value constraints on parameters, and ordering of interactions. The interaction ordering is defined as a conceptual tree where each branch represents a possible order of execution, which is what gives the notation its name. There is also a linear representation of this tree structure which allows the specification of TTCN test cases in machine-readable code. Examples of use of TTCN may be found in [Naik92, Eswa90].

13.5. Formal Description of Software Objects

All the formal specification techniques described so far are applicable to distributed systems which communicate using protocols. Therefore, they are applicable to protocol object classes — typically in the middle layers of a protocol stack — and to aggregate object classes which possess protocol object classes as components. However, in a protocol machine — or in any other communicating system — there will be regions in which the machine will execute a series of procedural actions uninterrupted by external inputs. Even if the protocol machine is specified in terms of some special-purpose finite state notation, the procedural actions within the body of any given state transition are typically specified using a conventional programming language. We need a way of formally specifying the operational capabilities of the software procedures within a finite state machine without recoursing to any particular implementation language.

In addition to uninterruptible procedural regions within the states of a protocol machine, software can exist in a network as pure applications as well. For example, an application-entity user in our network may be a pure software process which communicates with a display device or a storage device. Even though this process may not be a protocol machine, it is still a functionary in our network and should be modeled as an object. A formal specification technique for software specicands will be useful in describing the functions of such application entities in our network.

The purpose of formal description techniques for software entities is to describe a software process independent of its implementation [Neuh91]. The software process could possibly be implemented in C, C++, Smalltalk, Pascal, or any other language and still meet the same specification irrespective of its implementation language. Therefore, such an implementation-independent formal specification is clearly important in our object-oriented modeling methodology, because we are only interested in the behavior specification of the object class; we are not concerned with which of its many possible polymorphic implementations has been actually realized in any given object instance.

Many formal software specification techniques are oriented not just toward describing the internal and external models of software processes but also for analysis by proof-verification automatons. These techniques include the specification languages *Z* [Spiv86, Spiv89, Spiv92], *VDM*, or the Vienna Development Method [Jone90], and *Larch* [Gutt85, Gutt93]. These specification languages incorporate concepts and import notation from set theory and first-order logic. VDM, for example, has several dialects based on denotational semantics [Gunt92, Wins93]. Its specification language — VDM-SL — supports the generation of implementations from abstract models and is undergoing international standardization [Dawe91, Plat92].

Operations in Z, VDM, and Larch are specified in terms of preconditions and postconditions. It is the operation's client objects which are responsible for guaranteeing that the preconditions indeed hold before invoking the operation, while it is the implementer's responsibility to ensure that its postconditions are satisfied on termination. An operation invariant indicates a logical condition which remains unaffected by the operation; in many methods, it is permissible for the invariant to become temporarily false during the execution of the operation. Current efforts are focused on adding object-oriented notions to these techniques to standardize notations such as *Object Z* [ISO WG7/N6089, Duke90, Duke92, Rose92, Kilo93a].

By feeding the specification to a theorem prover, it can be determined whether that specification is internally logically consistent. Thus, correctness can be proven without compiling, executing, or testing any implementation of the specification. This is accomplished by ensuring that the operations of a given state description are compatible with the state invariant. By working through a series of proof obligations for every transaction, the correctness of an entire specificand program can be verified. An example of such a proof mechanism is provided in [Lafo91]. Environments which support these formal software description techniques generally include tools that reason about specifications.

There are many other formal software description techniques, some of which have profoundly influenced the development of formal protocol description techniques. These include CSP (Communicating Sequential Processes [Hoar85]), CCS (The Calculus of Communicating Systems [Miln80]), Temporal Logic [Pneu86], Transition Axioms [Lamp83], and many others [Olde91, Feij92]. In addition, there is an emerging class of type-checkers and other software tools for direct machine-processing of mathematical expressions in formal specification languages.

Examples of formal specifications for models of software entities can be found in [Spiv90, Wing90]. Their use, though not widespread, is increasing, especially for large and complex software systems. These techniques will no doubt gain in popularity with the more extensive development of software specification theory and the greater availability of supporting tools which can cater to industry-scale software projects. Ideally, formal software specification techniques such as Z and VDM should be integrated with CASE tools already in industrial use, all of which should be a subset of larger computer-aided design tool for distributed application development which follows a formal network modeling methodology.

13.6. Formal Description of Hardware Objects

The fact that formal specification languages are not just useful but essential is perhaps best demonstrated in the area of Electronic Design Automation (EDA). In this area, several important mechanisms have been devised for specifying electronic component designs in an implementation-independent manner. Two of the most popular EDA modeling and specification languages are Verilog and VHDL (the *VHSIC Hardware Description Language* [IEEE 1076]).

Many vendors concentrating on the Verilog and VHDL market have developed an extensive body of supporting compilation tools, analysis tools, and simulation tools around these languages. To assure model interworking, various interoperability tools between these two specification languages are being developed. These include translation tools, standard file formats, and heterogeneous environments for simultaneous simulation. Both Verilog and VHDL are important and will continue to evolve further. For the purposes of illustrating the concept of a formal hardware specification language in this book, we will concentrate on VHDL in the rest of this section.

VHDL allows the physical implementation of an electronic system to be specified both structurally and behaviorally. It provides abstraction at many levels — from the high-level architecture level down to the gate level. Because it is possible to focus at different levels of abstraction at different stages of design, it is possible to adopt a true top-down approach to hardware systems design.

VHDL has excellent notational capabilities to describe the structural (*netlist or schematic*) aspects of the design of the hardware system. Aside from structural description, it has exceptional facilities for modeling behavioral descriptions as well. For modeling timing characteristics of components, for example, VHDL supports min/max timing, setup, hold, and spike detection facilities. VHDL can be used to build generic models which can then be back-annotated with timing for specific devices.

This allows the construction of generic libraries of VHDL components — for example, a library model of an and gate can represent any manufacturer's device and can be used as an off-the-shelf component in the system. Most VHDL vendors supply the basic building blocks of a design in a pre-built and pre-compiled format, ready for the simulation environment. Many specialized semiconductor vendors also supply VHDL model libraries for their custom devices, so that designers can simulate systems using those devices.

As an elementary example, the VHDL specification for the structure and behavior of a nand gate, shown in Figure 13-8, could be specified as follows:

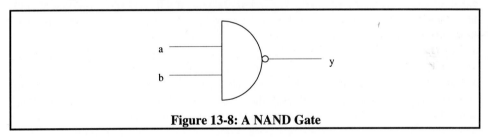

Figure 13-8: A NAND Gate

```
ENTITY nand_gate IS
      PORT       (a,b: IN BIT; y: OUT BIT)
END nand_gate;


ARCHITECTURE behavioral OF nand_gate IS
BEGIN
      y <= a NAND b AFTER 1 ns;
END behavioral;
```

Building up from the gate level, more complex chip-level and board-level designs can be specified. Once a system design has been described in VHDL, it can then be compiled and simulated. The VHDL simulator is supplied the *netlist*, which is the schematic or structural description of the design; the *model library*, which specifies the behavior for each device in the design; and the *test vectors*, which are the stimuli that drive the simulation.

In addition, VHDL has built-in facilities for specifying design management and version control information. The designer may specify which configuration of the circuit is to be used during simulation. This information determines what level of the hierarchy should be simulated, and if more than one version of the circuit is available, determines which version will be selected for simulation.

An alternative to VHDL is the *Verilog Hardware Description Language*, which is also a popular formal description technique and enjoys the support of many design automation and simulation vendors. Either could be used in our model as the formal specification for hardware object classes, such as the component card classes of an aggregate network device object class. Work is proceeding on various aspects of model interoperability between VHDL and Verilog. For more details on VHDL the reader is referred to [IEEE 1076, Coel89, Perr91b].

13.7. Specialization by Function Extension

We now consider additional specialization principles based on behavioral aspects of functions. In Chapter 6, we said that all properties which are common among sibling subclasses should be elevated to the superclass. In general, all common properties should be applied at the highest level possible in the inheritance hierarchy. This applies to function behavior as well.

Consider a situation in which a superclass is an abstract superclass, that is, it has no instances. All members of the superclass are therefore instances of one of its subclasses. Each subclass possesses functions which are similar but not identical. We can then abstract the *common behavior* of all these functions and elevate it to a function of the superclass. The superclass would then possess a function which has a formally described behavior. Even though this behavior specification might possibly be incomplete — that is, no implementation of the function as specified in the superclass may be practically executable — there is no problem as long as the superclass is abstract, and so it will never have instances which may invoke this incompletely specified function.

The subclasses now inherit this incompletely specified function but refine the specification of the function by adding more detail to it. If the subclass adds sufficient detail to the formal specification of the function to complete it, it is permissible for the subclass to have instances which invoke the function. If not, the subclass must remain abstract and depend on its further subclasses to refine and complete the formal specification of the function.

As an example, consider the abstract superclass `transportProtocol` which describes all the possible transport-layer protocols in the protocol stack of some hypothetical family of standards. Each actual transport protocol may have some options which make it different from every other transport protocol. For example, one transport protocol may be designed for a reliable underlying network service and may provide only basic transport-layer functionality, while another transport protocol may be designed for an unreliable network layer service and may provide sophisticated error detection and recovery. Nonetheless, some parts of their finite state machine may be common. We may therefore abstract the *common states* and *common transitions* into the formal description of a function in the superclass `transportProtocol`. The superclass could specify, for example, the state transition diagram of Figure 13-9 in the textual notation of some formal description technique.

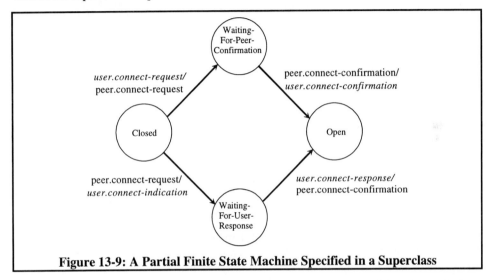

Figure 13-9: A Partial Finite State Machine Specified in a Superclass

Note that this diagram is incomplete — it only shows the states for the initial operation of the protocol machine which transition it from `closed` to `open`. There is, for example, no transition for the finite state machine to return to its `closed` state. This is not a problem because the superclass serves as a specification vehicle for only the transitions which are *common* to all subclasses. The fact that these transitions specify an incomplete finite state machine is irrelevant as long as the superclass is abstract, because this machine will never be instantiated. Due to specialization, each subclass may define different additional states and return to the `closed` state in its own way, thus completing the finite state machine.

Because the subclass inherits the finite state machine from a function in its superclass, it does not have to specify the inherited states and transitions again. It need only *incrementally refine* the function by specifying just the *new* states and transitions it adds to the inherited finite state machine. A subclass could, for example, extend the finite state machine as in Figure 13-10.

The principle of monotonic inheritance is at work here as well. A subclass may only *add new states* and *add new transitions* between states. This implies that no inherited states or state transitions may be deleted. If deletions were permitted, the subclass would no longer behave in accordance with the partial state machine specified in the su-

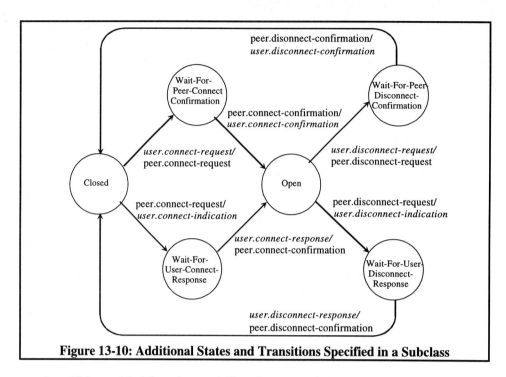

Figure 13-10: Additional States and Transitions Specified in a Subclass

perclass. This would violate the **specializes-from** association, as the subclass would no longer be fully substitutable for the superclass as a subtype. Further, since a state transition is analogous to a function invocation, a subclass may *expand the set of input messages* which cause the transition to fire (similar to argument contravariance), and it may *restrict the set of output messages* arising from the transition (similar to result covariance). Thus, if the message sets associated with a transition are {I}/{O}, then it is permissible to expand the set {I} and restrict the set {O} with increasing specialization.

This principle is known as *Specialization by Function Extension*. Note that this is different from *function addition*, in which an entirely new function is added in the subclass. By contrast, function extension allows the subclass to refine an inherited but partially specified function with more detail: adding more states, adding more transitions, expanding input message sets, or restricting output message sets. In combination with argument contravariance and result covariance, function extension gives us a very powerful mechanism to increase the functional capabilities of the subclass. We continue to follow the precept that specialization "describes it in greater detail, narrows it for specific focus, and expands it for richer function".

Specialization by function extension is not restricted to formal descriptions of protocols alone. If the superclass of a set of hardware objects has abstracted the common properties of their functions in a VHDL description, each subclass may add more VHDL code to the description to refine and extend this specification. In an analogous manner, the formal description of software functions can be extended as well.

Furthermore, function extension can be used as a *basis of specialization* as well. This means that the incremental refinement to the behavior of a function may be used as a reason for creating the subclass in the first place. This leads us to the specialization principle of *function extension*:

Specialization Principle:	*A descendant may extend the behavior of a function inherited from an ancestral class (**Function Extension**).*

Function extension need not necessarily be restricted to adding more constructs in the same formal description technique which was used in the superclass. For any inherited function, the subclass may extend behavior by specifying the extended behavior in a different formal description technique.

Function extension may also proceed by adding *wrappers* to inherited functions. If a superclass has a complete, executable specification for a function, a subclass may extend it by requiring that new code, specified in the subclass, be always executed along with the inherited function. If this new function is to be executed prior to the inherited function, it is called a *before wrapper*; if it is to be executed subsequently, it is an *after wrapper*. Of course, it is possible for a subclass to specify both before and after wrappers, wrappers on inherited wrappers, and so on.

13.8. Reuse of Formal Specifications

Extensional reuse of function specifications is a mechanism which permits a function to be extended with additional specification techniques. In this section, we present some more ways in which extensional reuse may be availed of.

Consider a router device, which has the responsibility of routing PDUs of some connectionless network-layer protocol. This router accepts an incoming packet, performs a lookup in its routing table, and routes the packet out of one of its ports. This may be modeled as the `routePacket` function, whose formal description is specified using some locally defined methodology.

Aside from its normal capability, this router can also respond to some user-defined route administration policy. The user may wish to route packets differently depending on the Administrative Domain the packet will transit through [Estr90, Clar90, RFC 1125]. For example, the user may have determined that, during peak hours of operation, costs are minimized by routing packets through one Administrative Domain, while during off-peak hours the tariff differentials shift in favor a different Administrative Domain.

Our `policyRouter` has the capability of supporting such user-specified routing policy by automatically switching between two different sets of routing criteria. It does this by using different sets of routing tables depending on the time of day. The `routePacket` function may have the state transition diagram of Figure 13-11 as part of its formal description.

The formal description of this State Transition Diagram may be specified in, say, Estelle notation. These state transitions are part of the formal specification of the `routePacket` function. Because the behavior formally specified for this function is

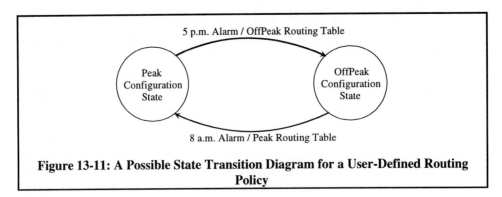

Figure 13-11: A Possible State Transition Diagram for a User-Defined Routing Policy

included along with its registered FUNCTION information object, it is now well known. Thus, it can be reused by any other function in any other object class which desires to extend this behavior.

As an example, we may reuse the specification of the state transitions of the policyRouter object class in an unrelated object class. Consider a different network object — say a pbx object — whose peak and off-peak offered loads vary not just by time of day but also by day of week. Peak load is exhibited between 8 a.m. and 5 p.m. on weekdays; off-peak load is exhibited after 5 p.m., and weekends exhibit a "weekend load" which is even lower than off-peak. We may now consider this, much like a Harel statechart, to be the nested set of transitions of Figure 13-12.

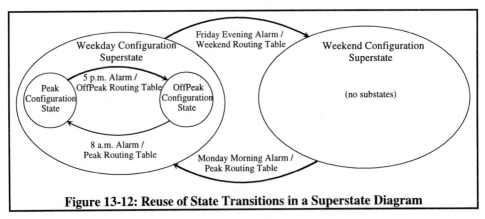

Figure 13-12: Reuse of State Transitions in a Superstate Diagram

When we now specify the "outer" set of transitions formally, we can reference the "inner" set of transitions whose specification we have already specified formally, merely by referencing the formal specification of Figure 13-11. This provides our modeling methodology with a very powerful mechanism for reuse of function specifications.

13.9. Summary

Many formal description techniques exist for modeling the functions of a network object class. Notational techniques include Estelle, LOTOS, and SDL for protocol objects, Z, VDM, and Larch for software objects, and VHDL and Verilog for hardware objects. The functions of an object class may be defined in terms of a combination of these techniques. By incrementally refining the specification of a function, a subclass may extend a function inherited from a superclass for increased capabilities. This is known as Function Extension. Function Extension may also be used as a basis of specialization, which is formally indicated by a logical predicate identifying the extension as present.

Research efforts are in progress to architect an integrated specification environment. Work in new areas such as Architectural Semantics [MacK90] and the SPECS architecture [Brui87] attempts to accommodate different high-level specification languages (e.g., Estelle, Lotos, and SDL), abstract their content, and translate this information down to a common semantic information base. Computer-aided network modeling tools should in the future accommodate formal protocol models, software models and hardware models in an integrated fashion, following a confluence of object-oriented modeling, CASE, and EDA design methodologies.

14. Formal Behavior Models

"May thy packets never collide, and thy tokens always come to pass."

— *blessing from anonymous networking guru.*

14.1. Introduction

In this chapter, we introduce the formal notation which may be used to model the function behavior specifications of Chapter 13. We describe how models of formal function behavior may be identified and located. The notation for specialization by function argument contravariance, result covariance, and function extension is presented.

14.2. Referencing Formal Specifications

The focus of Chapter 13 was to address techniques which could be used to provide a formal description for the &specification field for each FUNCTION information object, whose template was defined in Chapter 11 as

```
FUNCTION ::= CLASS
{
        &Arguments              ARGUMENT OPTIONAL,
        &Results                RESULT OPTIONAL,
        &Exceptions             EXCEPTION OPTIONAL,
        &specification          SET OF SEQUENCE OF
                                        FormalSpecification
                                            OPTIONAL,
```

```
          &functionLabel              OBJECT IDENTIFIER UNIQUE
}
WITH SYNTAX
{
        [ARGUMENTS                &Arguments]
        [RESULTS                  &Results]
        [EXCEPTIONS               &Exceptions]
        [SPECIFICATION            &specification]
        IDENTIFIED BY             &functionLabel

}
```

Any of the formal description techniques described in Chapter 13 may be used to model the &specification of a function of an object class. Aside from the formal description techniques we have discussed, system architects often use their own methodology for dynamic modeling. This local methodology could use a descriptive natural-language text format, some locally defined graphical convention, or a combination thereof. This freedom is accommodated in our model by allowing local specification methodologies in addition to formal description techniques.

The &specification field of a function has the type SET OF SEQUENCE OF FormalSpecification. This is a set-valued field because we allow the same function to be described using more than one technique; each element of the set provides one view of the function using exactly one description technique. The set collects together all the descriptions of the function, each providing a different perspective, in a single construct. The elements of each set are internally ordered in a SEQUENCE; as we shall see in a later section, this ordering allows us to describe the function in progressively greater detail, using function extension, as we proceed down the hierarchy.

Because each instance of a FormalSpecification could be very large, it is impractical to include an entire formal specification for the behavior of each function in an embedded form within any FUNCTION information object itself. These formal descriptions are largely used at architecture time to determine the exact behavior of the function. In future networks, if the model information base is available on-line in a run-time network, external networks could also possibly query this behavior dynamically. We incorporate the formal description into the function by reference. Each Formal-Specification in our methodology refers to a document containing the actual specification:

```
FormalSpecification ::= DocumentLabel
```

The DocumentLabel could be any valid manner of referring to a document, such that it can be looked up by a model compiler, validated, and passed on as an argument to a supporting compiler appropriate for the description technique contained in that document. For example, the DocumentLabel could point to a document object in some directory (such as an X.500 Directory Information Tree [ITU-T X.500]). Alternatively, the document itself could be structured and contain nested documents, with the structure of the document being formally described in terms of ODA (Office Document Architecture [ITU-T T.411]), SGML [ISO 8879], or any other document description standard. In a later section, we will see one method of specifying documents which includes an indication of the formal description technique used in the document.

In addition to the name of the document, its semantic content — that is, each formal description of the function — must also be well known. To permit this, we need a way of identifying which formal description technique has been used in the document. Because the model for a function may use more than one formal description technique, we define the type `FormalSpecificationType` which expands into any allowable formal description technique:

```
FormalSpecificationType ::= CHOICE
{
        protocol [0] ProtocolFormalSpecification,
        software [1] SoftwareFormalSpecification,
        hardware [2] HardwareFormalSpecification,
        local    [3] LocalMethodologyFormalSpecification
}


ProtocolFormalSpecification ::= OBJECT IDENTIFIER
                                ( estelle |
                                  lotos   |
                                  sdl     |
                                  chill   |
                                  local   )


SoftwareFormalSpecification ::= OBJECT IDENTIFIER
                                ( z     |
                                  vdm   |
                                  local )


HardwareFormalSpecification ::= OBJECT IDENTIFIER
                                ( vhdl    |
                                  verilog |
                                  local   )


LocalMethodologyFormalSpecification ::=
                                OBJECT IDENTIFIER
```

Each one of the values estelle, lotos, and so on, are simply registered OBJECT IDENTIFIERs. Each formal description technique is thus uniquely identifiable. The types ProtocolFormalSpecification, SoftwareFormal-Specification, and HardwareFormalSpecification are also OBJECT IDENTIFIERs but are subject to a *subtype constraint*: they can only take the values of the listed OBJECT IDENTIFIERs. Because each formal description technique is registered, the program which analyzes our entire network model knows which specific supporting compiler (or set of supporting compilers) to invoke for analyzing the formal specification of each function.

This provides the ability to uniquely identify which formal description technique has been used. In addition, each FormalSpecification which provides all or part of the description of some actual function in some actual object class must itself be registered. We accomplish this by using an adjunct DOCUMENT information object class with three simple fixed-type value fields: a document name, an indication of the formal description technique used, and its registration label. This allows any document to be registered:

```
DOCUMENT ::= CLASS
{
        &documentName           PrintableString,
        &documentType           FormalSpecificationType,
        &documentLabel          OBJECT IDENTIFIER UNIQUE
}
WITH SYNTAX
{
        DOCUMENT-NAME           &documentName
        DOCUMENT-TYPE           &documentType
        IDENTIFIED BY           &documentLabel
}
```

If {Documents} is the set of all DOCUMENT information objects, we may simply extract DocumentLabel as an OBJECT IDENTIFIER from the &document-Label fields of this set:

```
DocumentLabel ::= DOCUMENT.&documentLabel
                                        ({Documents})
```

Therefore, each FormalSpecification in the &specification field of any FUNCTION information object simply resolves to a list of OBJECT IDENTIFIERs. Given this definition, and provided we have already created a place in the registration hierarchy to label all function specifications, such as

```
functionSpecs OBJECT IDENTIFIER ::= {...}
-- root of registration subtree for all function specs
```

we can begin to register function specifications, for example,

```
dummyProtocolSpec DOCUMENT ::=
{                                 -- a protocol spec in Estelle
      DOCUMENT-NAME         "/dfs/bigtime.com/users/guru/
                                  dummy_protocol.estelle"
      DOCUMENT-TYPE         {protocol:estelle}
      IDENTIFIED BY         {...}
}


extensionToDummy DOCUMENT ::=
{                                 -- a protocol spec in SDL
      DOCUMENT-NAME         "/dfs/bigtime.com/users/guru/
                                  dummy_extn.sdl"
      DOCUMENT-TYPE         {protocol:sdl}
      IDENTIFIED BY         {...}
}


tcpProtocolSpec DOCUMENT ::=
{
      DOCUMENT-NAME         "/dfs/nic.ddn.mil/rfc793.txt"
      DOCUMENT-TYPE         {protocol:local}
      IDENTIFIED BY         {...}
}


tcpBigWindowAndNAKOptions DOCUMENT ::=
{
      DOCUMENT-NAME         "/dfs/nic.ddn.mil/rfc1106.txt"
      DOCUMENT-TYPE         {protocol:local}
      IDENTIFIED BY         {...}
}
```

and so on. These examples are included to illustrate the concept of how protocol behavior may be formally made available on-line for automatic inspection. The on-line availability of formal models of network behavior, and the automated determination of its compatibility with other behavior, will be of great assistance during the process of computer-assisted network design and architecture.

By registering actual function specifications and providing the name of their source documents using an agreed-upon document-naming convention — possibly in some universally accessible wide-area distributed file system — we can make the exact working of each function available to all devices and systems in the federated network. If the function specification uses a standard well-known description technique and the device possesses the intelligence to parse that technique, it can, if it so chooses, determine dynamically at operation time the capabilities of other objects in the network which claim to support that function. Potentially, this allows each object in a federated, multi-vendor network to figure out at operations time how another object may be expected to behave. More practically, a network synthesis tool could interrogate these documents at architecture time to determine the behavior of objects which may be candidates for use in a proposed network configuration.

As a trivial example, a hot-connected resource (such as a networked printer) could interrogate some local database at run time for the specifications of all available device drivers, determine which driver matched its own capabilities most closely, and automatically trigger that device driver to be dynamically loaded in each client workstation. This will save users from having to specify the type of the shared printer to each workstation individually. This is beneficial as it reduces the overhead of separately specifying the same information to each client which uses that resource and also reduces the associated potential for error. It will also be beneficial for remote printing scenarios where the printer may be across a WAN and its type may not be easily accessible to a remote user. Such autoconfiguration ability will significantly increase the plug-and-play capabilities of networked devices and reduce the human administrative overhead. The benefits which will be derived for large and complex pieces of telecommunication network objects will be considerably greater than those described in the everyday example above.

At architecture time, a new function which is a variation of an extension of an existing function could simply source in the existing specification and specify just the variations. This is explored in greater detail in subsequent sections.

14.3. Covariance and Contravariance

In Chapter 6, we indicated that an object class may specialize from its subclass using the modes of *argument contravariance*, in which it expanded the domains on the arguments of an inherited function, and *result covariance*, in which it restricted the domains on the results of those functions. We now define the formal notation for indicating how this specialization occurs.

Argument Predicates

Recall that each function argument is registered in its own ARGUMENT information object template. To indicate the value of a function argument, we use a predicate similar to the predicate we used to indicate the value of an attribute. We call this an Argument-ValuePredicate, which we define as follows:

```
ArgumentValuePredicate ::= SEQUENCE
{
        function                FunctionLabel,
        argument                ARGUMENT.&argumentLabel
                                        ({Arguments}),
        is                      Comparator,
        value                   ARGUMENT.&ArgumentType
                                        ({Arguments}{@argument})}
}
```

where

```
FunctionLabel ::= FUNCTION.&functionLabel({Functions})
```

In this specification, the field `function` indicates the label of the function whose argument is chosen as the basis of specialization. The field `argument` indicates the argument of that function chosen for contravariance; it is constrained to belong to the pool of all OBJECT IDENTIFIERs which are `&argumentLabel` fields of the set {Arguments} of all ARGUMENT information objects. As in Chapter 10, the `is` field indicates stated comparison. The field `value` indicates the value against which that argument is compared; it is constrained to be of the same type as the `&ArgumentType` field of the ARGUMENT information object chosen by the `argument` field from the set {Arguments}.

An `ArgumentValuePredicate`, when used as a basis of specialization for argument contravariance, describes the new expanded domain on the indicated function argument. Just as we specified an alternative mechanism for attributes, we also specify one for function arguments, which may be equivalently described in an `Argument-DomainPredicate`:

```
ArgumentDomainPredicate ::= SEQUENCE
{
        function                FunctionLabel,
        argument                ARGUMENT.&argumentLabel
                                        ({Arguments}),
        is                      Domain{ARGUMENT.&ArgumentType
                                        ({Arguments}{@argument})}
}
```

Since the semantics of both these constructs are equivalent, we may specify argument contravariance using either construct. As with `AttributeLogical-`

`Predicates`, we combine the choice between these two constructs into a single logical
predicate:

```
ArgumentLogicalPredicate ::= CHOICE
{
       newValueOf      [0]   ArgumentValuePredicate,
       newDomainOf     [1]   ArgumentDomainPredicate
}
```

Result Predicates

Using similar constructs, we can make statements about the return result of a function as
well:

```
ResultValuePredicate ::= SEQUENCE
{
       function              FunctionLabel,
       result                RESULT.&resultLabel
                                          ({Results}),
       is                    Comparator,
       value                 RESULT.&ResultType
                                ({Results}{@result})}
}


ResultDomainPredicate ::= SEQUENCE
{
       function              FunctionLabel,
       result                RESULT.&resultLabel
                                          ({Results}),
       is                    Domain{RESULT.&ResultType
                                ({Results}{@result})}}
}


ResultLogicalPredicate ::= CHOICE
{
       newValueOf      [0]   ResultValuePredicate,
       newDomainOf     [1]   ResultDomainPredicate
}
```

The types `Domain` and `Comparator` continue to be the same as those defined in Chapter 10. With an `ArgumentLogicalPredicate` and a `ResultLogical-Predicate`, we can make statements about the domains of function arguments and results. For example, if we wish to indicate the values of the new end-points of the permissible domain of a function argument, we may use two `ArgumentValuePredicates` "*and*-ed" together, one with a `lesserOrEqualTo` comparator to indicate the upper end-point, and one with a `greaterOrEqualTo` comparator to indicate the lower end-point. Or, we may use a single `ArgumentDomainPredicate` indicating both the upper and lower bounds of the range. Both are considered equivalent by our compiler. The compiler checks to ensure that the newly specified domains do not in fact cause any restriction of inherited argument domains or relaxation of inherited result domains; if so, it rejects the specialization.

Contexts of Use

As with other predicates, these predicates can be used against the network schema with the following meanings:

1. *Interrogative*: Usage of a logical predicate in this context poses a query: *Can the specified* `argument` *of the specified* `function` *have the indicated domain? Or, can the specified* `result` *of the specified* `function` *have the indicated domain?*

2. *Declarative*: Usage of the value logical predicate in this context makes a statement of actual fact, possibly in response to a query: *The specified* `argument` *of the specified* `function` *can (or cannot) have the indicated domain. Or, the specified* `result` *of the specified* `function` *can (or cannot) have the indicated domain.*

3. *Imperative*: Usage of the value logical predicate in this context issues a command: *Establish the indicated domain for the specified* `argument` *of the specified* `function`. *Or, establish the indicated domain for the specified* `result` *of the specified* `function`.

4. *Qualificative*: Usage of a value logical predicate in this context acts as a subsetting clause for externally specified operations on objects: *Perform (or do not perform) the externally specified operation only on those classes for which the specified* `argument` *of the specified* `function` *can have the indicated domain. Or, perform (or do not perform) the externally specified operation only on those classes for which the specified* `result` *of the specified* `function` *can have the indicated domain.*

When a subclass specializes using either argument contravariance or result covariance, the argument domain relaxation or result domain restriction occurs only in the subclass. Conceptually, the new domain values are substituted for the old domain values only in the copy of the permissible value information stored in the subclass. The domain values in the superclass are not altered. The specification of the `ARGUMENT` and `RESULT` information objects in the model information base is not altered; they continues to possess their originally specified domain values, if any, and other functions may specify them for use with the original specification intact. The function argument, the function result, and the inherited function itself continue to possess the same identifying labels in the subclass as they do in the superclass, even though the argument and result domains might be different.

Logical Predicates

Because these predicates pose questions or make statements about the values of function arguments and results, they are like any other logical predicate. To accommodate them formally as a permitted `LogicalPredicate` type, we expand the definition of `SimpleLogicalPredicate` (which is one of the `CHOICE`s that the general `LogicalPredicate` type expands to) to include these as well:

```
SimpleLogicalPredicate ::= CHOICE
{
        attributeAdded              [0] AttributeLabel,
        functionAdded               [1] FunctionLabel,
        capsuleAdded                [2] CapsuleLabel,
        capsuleFixed                [3] CapsuleLabel,
        attributeDomainRestricted   [4]
                                    AttributeLogicalPredicate,
        argumentDomainRelaxed       [5]
                                    ArgumentLogicalPredicate,
        resultDomainRestricted      [6]
                                    ResultLogicalPredicate
}
```

We will add more elements to this `CHOICE` construct when we consider other types of logical predicates in subsequent chapters. We can now use the types `ArgumentLogicalPredicate` and `ResultLogicalPredicate` in any place that calls for a `LogicalPredicate`, if they are appropriate. For example, we may use them as a basis of specialization when we wish to specialize using a function-based mode:

Specialization by Argument Contravariance: Use an `Argument-LogicalPredicate` to indicate the expanded domain on the desired argument of the desired function. If a numeric domain is expanded in both directions, use two `Argument-ValuePredicates` compounded together, or indicate both bounds in an `ArgumentDomainPredicate`.

Specialization by Result Covariance: Use a `ResultLogical-Predicate` to indicate the restricted domain on the desired result of the desired function. If a numeric domain is restricted in both directions, use two `ResultValuePredicates` compounded together, or indicate both bounds in a `Result-DomainPredicate`.

14.4. Specialization by Function Extension

In Chapter 13, we stated that subclasses may also specialize by *extending the behavior* of inherited functions. We must also accommodate the addition of extended behavior when stating the formal basis of specialization. Fortunately, this is easy: recall that the type of the `&specification` of the FUNCTION information object class is a SET OF SEQUENCE OF `FormalSpecification`. The subclass can thus add an extended function description to that set using a different formal description technique, or another element to an existing SEQUENCE within the set using the same formal description technique.

If the subclass extends the `FormalSpecification` by adding a different formal description technique (e.g., adding a software specification in Z to a protocol specification in Estelle), another element is added to the `&specification` set. However, if the same formal description is extended (e.g., adding more states in Estelle to a partial protocol machine already specified in Estelle) then another element is added to the SEQUENCE of Estelle descriptions which itself is an element of the set. Thus, our compiler considers each element of the `&specification` set a collection of progressively detailed formal descriptions which all use the same technique, while the set itself consists of such collections which use different techniques. In any given SEQUENCE of the value set, our model compiler requires all the elements of the SEQUENCE to use the same formal description technique and considers that each successive element incrementally refines and extends the description provided by the previous elements of the SEQUENCE.

To formally specify function extension, we define a predicate for that purpose. This predicate specifies a new value for the `&specification` field, which contains the extended specification for the inherited function. Conceptually, this new specification replaces that of the inherited function in the subclass, thereby providing richer detail for the same function in the subclass. This predicate does not indicate any comparison or range; instead, like a label predicate, it indicates merely a list of `Formal-Specification` values:

```
FunctionExtensionPredicate  ::= SEQUENCE
{
      function                    FunctionLabel,
      newSpecification            SET OF SEQUENCE OF
                                        FormalSpecification
}
```

We also accommodate this as a `SimpleLogicalPredicate`:

```
SimpleLogicalPredicate ::= CHOICE
{
        attributeAdded                 [0] AttributeLabel,
        functionAdded                  [1] FunctionLabel,
        capsuleAdded                   [2] CapsuleLabel,
        capsuleFixed                   [3] CapsuleLabel,
        attributeDomainRestricted  [4]
                                   AttributeLogicalPredicate,
        argumentDomainRelaxed        [5]
                                   ArgumentLogicalPredicate,
        resultDomainRestricted       [6]
                                   ResultLogicalPredicate,
        functionExtended             [7]
                                   FunctionExtensionPredicate
}
```

With this in place, we can now use logical predicates to specify specialization by function extension. We summarize this as:

Specialization by Function Extension: Use a `FunctionExtension-Predicate` to indicate the extended specification of the inherited function.

14.5. Summary

The formal behavior of a function may be identified by a document which contains the behavior description. Each such document describes the behavior using some formal or local methodology. We may include a reference to the formal description of each function in the `&specification` field for that `FUNCTION`. The formal statement of the basis of specialization using any of the function-based modes must be specified by logical predicates. For example, the formal bases of specialization using argument contravariance and result covariance are specified using logical predicates defined for the purpose.

15. Modeling Network Protocols

"On the first six layers, God created The Stack. And on the seventh layer He rested, for thereupon He enjoyed huge margins."

— *anonymous chapter and verse.*

15.1. Introduction

In this chapter, we describe modeling techniques for network protocols. We introduce the topic by first providing a model for reference models which give rise to families of protocols. Using this model, we demonstrate a basis for classifying protocol entities. The notion of creating protocol stacks by assembling component protocol entities according to permitted layering rules is introduced. Various types of stacks are evaluated with respect to their suitability for transferring different kinds of traffic. The concept of protocol planes is introduced. Finally, we consider the possible ways of specializing network devices with respect to the protocol stacks they support.

15.2. Conceptual Background

The trend of networks becoming increasingly multifaceted is accelerating. Monolithic proprietary networking architectures are insufficient to interoperate easily with the many different protocols in other networks; the concept of a single suite of network protocols providing universal service has proved unrealistic. Networks of the future will use multiple protocols defined by multiple standards bodies [Mala91, GOSIP 92]. They will interface with multiple operating systems on a variety of hardware architectures supplied by different vendors. A wide diversity of equipment will provide services within the network and perhaps an even wider range of end-user devices — all manner of data, voice, image, video, and consumer electronics equipment — will connect to this network on the customer's premises.

In a multifaceted and multistandard universe, no single family of protocols, whether proprietary or open, will suffice to solve the entire networking problem. Wherever a need is perceived for a particular application, specialized architectures and protocols will create a communication infrastructure for that application — much as data networks, telephone networks, and community access television networks evolved independently over the years. As it evolves, a network which originated as a tightly knit, special-purpose, application-specific network changes to accommodate newly perceived application needs and enhancements to existing services. This is accomplished by adding new operating software, supporting new applications, introducing new equipment, and interworking with other networks through appropriate multiprotocol gateways.

Because such gateways typically convert either protocol frames, transmission formats, or encoding schemes from one standard to another, the gateways are themselves specialized. They often possess little more than the ability to convert between two network formats, allowing binary, pairwise interoperability between just two special-purpose networks. Each such pairwise-interoperability requirement between two special-purpose networks creates a market niche. Hundreds of such niches — and niches between niches — are created for each price-point the market supports. Each such gateway — whether an automatic call distributor attached to a PBX or an interactive multimedia device attached to a CATV receiver — adds value by adding new functionality to an existing limited-purpose infrastructure. Eventually, if this added value is sufficiently large, the gateway is integrated into and subsumed within newer models of networking equipment. The cable-ready desktop workstation represents an evolutionary step similar to the voice-mail-ready PBX.

15.3. Reference Models

To completely model networks, we must know not only what each protocol does; we must also know exactly which protocols are supported in each device in the network. The importance of this knowledge arises from the fact that the set of protocols and interfaces supported in each device dictates how that device can interoperate with other devices. During the network architecture and planning phase, when synthesizing a network out of various candidate devices, the protocols supported in each device act as architectural rules which specify how that device may connect with other devices. Since only like protocol families can communicate, these architectural rules dictate that each device may only directly connect to another device which supports the same protocol families as itself. By undertaking this activity of pairwise-matching protocol suites, a network architecture program can automatically apply and enforce connectivity rules.

All communication protocols are layered, with each layer using and building upon the services provided by the layer below. Layering provides a mechanism for decomposition and reuse such that different upper-layer protocols, providing different application services, may use the same set of primitives supplied by a lower-layer protocol. The reverse situation is also possible — the same upper-layer protocol may use different lower-layer protocols depending on which set of interfaces it wants to use for external communication.

There are various systems for layering network protocols. Each system is called a *reference model*. A reference model identifies the layers of a family of protocol suites and the layering relationships between protocol entities in that family. When any protocol entity is developed, it must implement a particular layer from a particular reference model. Furthermore, the services it provides to other protocol entities in the layer above, as well as the services it expects from the layer below, must be identified.

A reference model sets a *context*. This context serves as an overarching architecture to which all implementations must conform. Individual protocol entities must belong somewhere within the context. Reference models allocate functions to each layer in a protocol stack. It is not permissible for a protocol entity to violate this separation of functional responsibilities and still conform to that reference model. (It could, of course, conform to a different reference model.)

By convention, the layers of a reference model are specified bottom up, the first layer being the one closest to the physical port where data enters or leaves the device. Thus, "lower" layers are the ones closest to the physical port, and the "upper" layers are the ones closes to the application which produces or consumes data. One also speaks of layers being "above" or "below" other layers with respect to this convention.

The OSI Reference Model

There are several reference models used in communication networks, each suitable for a different combination of applications and infrastructure. Perhaps the most famous of these is the Open Systems Interconnection (OSI) Reference Model. This model identifies seven layers in a communication protocol stack: from the bottom up, they are the Physical, Data Link, Network, Transport, Session, Presentation, and Application. Each of these layers is specified in rich detail, with many having intricate substructures, sub-layers, and optional components. We will not describe the OSI Reference Model in detail, as this description is available in many excellent texts and papers.

The OSI Reference Model was specified in the late 1970s [ISO 7498, Hens88] and was designed for data communication only; it was not designed for transporting any isochronous traffic. Furthermore, it was designed assuming that the network substrate for wide-area communication would be the existing copper-wire-based plant then in use for voice communication. Because copper-based data communication tends to be relatively lossy and unreliable in terms of bit error rates, the end-user equipment sending and receiving the data had to have robust error-detecting and correcting mechanisms. Seven layers were specified for the OSI Reference Model, the assumption being that each end-point involved in data communication would be a powerful computer capable of implementing the full protocol stack, thereby assuring reliable transfer of data.

The development of superior substrate materials eroded many of the assumptions underlying the architecture of the OSI Reference Model. With technologies such as optical fiber, the error rates across the network substrate were dramatically reduced. Data transfer across such networks, while not entirely eliminating the need for error detection and correction, became much more reliable. Transfer rates also increased by orders of magnitude. The network substrate was no longer the bottleneck in data communication; the limiting factor now became the rate at which data could be produced and consumed by the end-user computing equipment. The proliferation of inexpensive desktop computers meant that many of the nodes being added to the network were relatively small machines with limited memory and limited CPU resources, incapable of implementing a full OSI stack. As such, the need for each transferred data bit to traverse seven layers of processing at each end became perceived to be not just unnecessary but actually undesirable. To adjust to the new realities of networking, many other reference models have been proposed [Haas91].

For all these reasons (and some others such as protracted standardization cycles) OSI communication protocols today are not the universal data communication architecture they were once envisioned to become. They have, however, achieved some measure of success: many OSI application-layer standards are popular because of their rich functionality, and some OSI lower-layer standards have also been widely deployed. Rather than implementing the entire standard, many vendors have "cherry-picked" the useful and better parts of OSI and deployed them on other efficient communication infrastructures more suitable for today's networks. Such "cross-pollination" among various reference models has contributed to the thriving mix of heterogeneous, multifaceted, and multiprotocol networks we have in use today.

Despite its lack of universal deployment, OSI has been largely successful in the sense that its biggest contribution has been its reference model architecture. The concept of conquering the communication problem by dividing it into layers has shaped and molded the thinking of numerous network architects, programmers, and users. Although few use the complete stack of OSI communication protocols, all networking architectures continue to be compared and evaluated against the OSI reference model. Thus, the most significant contribution of OSI is perhaps the establishment of the layered model as a baseline against which useful and workable protocol entities — mostly non-OSI — can be developed.

Newer Reference Models

Another reference model which has been very successful commercially is the Internet Reference Model [Come91]. This model was also originally designed for non-isochronous data communication. It is less complex than the OSI Reference Model and has behind it the solid robustness of many years of implementation experience. It dispenses with many of the redundancies and some of the niceties of the OSI model, which results in fast, reliable, no-nonsense communication.

For isochronous communication, perhaps the most important model is the B-ISDN (Broadband Integrated Services Digital Network) Reference Model. This has been designed bearing in mind the need for both isochronous and non-isochronous services. Although it can be used for data communication, it does not specify the upper layers of a data communications stack, preferring to leave that to other models.

Figure 15-1 shows some typical reference models. All these models have been specified in various international standards. Commonly used protocol families do not necessarily always fall into any particular standardized reference model. Many proprietary networking architectures (e.g., SNA, DECNET, NetWare) often specify their own reference models depending on the context desired. Of course, between any given pair of reference models, there are always many analogies and rough approximations between the

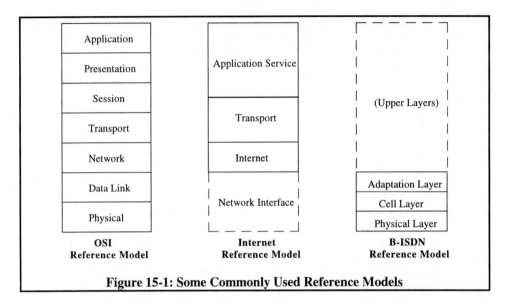

Figure 15-1: Some Commonly Used Reference Models

responsibilities assigned to corresponding layers. For example, Figure 15-2 examines the details of the lower layers of the OSI and B-ISDN reference models and shows some approximate analogies between the functions of the lower layers of OSI and the lower layers of B-ISDN (up to AAL 3/4) [DePr93].

Newer reference models take advantage of the processing power of high-performance microprocessors and collapse multiple complex functions into single layers. For example, the functions allocated to the network and transport layers of the OSI model might be allocated to a single *transfer* layer in a newer reference model. Many high-speed protocols support multiple complex functions — such as rate-based flow control, timer-based connection management, and multicast addressing — in a single layer [Zitt91]. Examples of such protocols include the *Versatile Message Transaction Protocol* (VMTP [RFC 1045, Cher89]) and the *Express Transfer Protocol* (XTP [Ches89]).

Newer lower-level high-speed interfaces possess richer and more detailed sublayer definitions analogous to the data-link and physical layers of OSI. Examples of these include the *High-Performance Parallel Interface* (HIPPI [Tolm92, ANSI X3-183]) and *FiberChannel* (FC [ANSI X3T9, Getc92]). These new protocols working with new reference models will make gigabit networking common. Figure 15-3 illustrates an example of a special-purpose high-speed network whose protocol architecture must be modeled with respect to one of the newer reference models.

This mechanism to describe reference models formally is not restricted to protocol stacks alone — any layered architecture can be so described. If we wish, the layered architecture of Figure 15-4 for a generic file processing application program may also be described formally using our syntax. Although we will largely use examples dealing with protocol stacks, Figure 15-4 illustrates the concept that a layered reference model can be generically applied in many other situations. A vendor of spreadsheet and word processing applications, for example, might choose to adopt Figure 15-4 as the standard context within which all applications must be constructed.

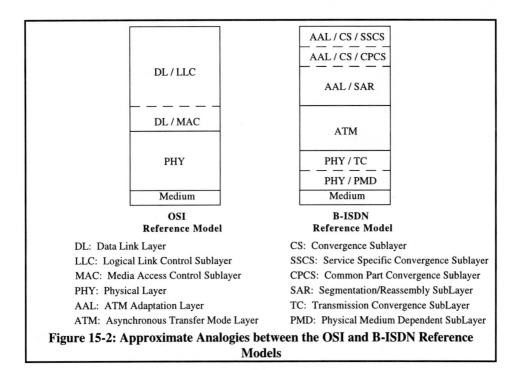

DL: Data Link Layer   CS: Convergence Sublayer
LLC: Logical Link Control Sublayer   SSCS: Service Specific Convergence Sublayer
MAC: Media Access Control Sublayer   CPCS: Common Part Convergence Sublayer
PHY: Physical Layer   SAR: Segmentation/Reassembly SubLayer
AAL: ATM Adaptation Layer   TC: Transmission Convergence SubLayer
ATM: Asynchronous Transfer Mode Layer   PMD: Physical Medium Dependent SubLayer

Figure 15-2: Approximate Analogies between the OSI and B-ISDN Reference Models

Modeling Reference Models

Reference models can themselves be modeled as object classes. The top-level class `referenceModel` serves as the common ancestor of all reference models. Individual reference models, such as `osiReferenceModel`, `internetReferenceModel`, and `bisdnReferenceModel`, may be subclassed from `referenceModel`. The `referenceModel` class is a fully abstract class because there is no such thing as an object which is an instance of a reference model; only protocol entities which conform to particular reference models have instances. Rather, `referenceModel` serves as a baseline class against which instantiable classes (such as `protocolEntity`) may be subclassed, using as a basis their relationship with `referenceModel`. In Chapter 17, we will examine relationship-based modes of specialization which will make this possible. Figure 15-5 illustrates reference models as object classes.

In Chapter 16, we will see how entire reference models may be specified in a formal notation. The complete specification of a reference model will identify the layers of the reference model and the sequence in which they occur.

15.4. Protocol Entities

So far we have only modeled the layers of a reference model and not the protocols which may belong to a layer. Individual protocol entities must belong to a particular reference

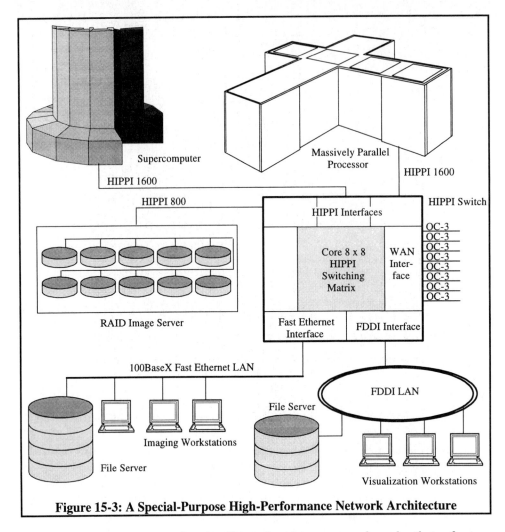

Figure 15-3: A Special-Purpose High-Performance Network Architecture

model and implement some functionality assigned to any one layer by that reference model. In Chapter 12, we saw an example of how the `protocolEntity` object class may be formally specified. This object class had the attributes `refModel` and `operativeLayer`. In any member of this object class, the value of the `refModel` attribute must be one of the recognized reference models, and the value of the `operativeLayer` attribute must be one of the recognized layer names from that reference model. This allows our network model compiler to accurately associate each protocol entity with a particular layer in a particular reference model.

In Chapter 12, when we formally specified a `transportProtocol` object class, we indicated that its basis of specialization was the restriction of its `operative-Layer` attribute to the value `transport`. The implicit assumption at that point was that `transport` indeed was some registered layer name belonging to some registered refer-

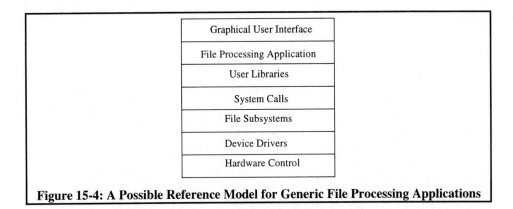

Figure 15-4: A Possible Reference Model for Generic File Processing Applications

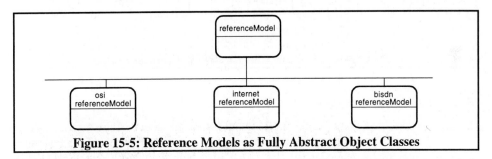

Figure 15-5: Reference Models as Fully Abstract Object Classes

ence model. In general, our formal specification of any protocol entity must carry with it some information indicating which layer of which reference model that protocol entity implements.

Classifying Protocol Entities

Reference models can be used as a basis of specialization for protocol entities. We can choose to perform a high-level classification of the `protocolEntity` object class using the reference model as a basis, if we find such an inheritance hierarchy meaningful. We do this by restricting the domain of the `refModel` attribute to a particular value. As the next level down the hierarchy, the layers of each reference model can be used to further classify its protocols. We can categorize all entities implementing layer-n functions in a generic `layer-N-entity` object class, using as a basis of specialization the fact that the domain of the `operativeLayer` attribute is restricted to a specific layer name.

Figure 15-6 shows one possible classification technique for protocol entities. This is a more accurate classification than that described in Figure 8-6, Figure 8-7, and Figure 8-8; those classifications were not made using the reference model as a basis.

More than one protocol entity may belong to a given layer in a given reference model. Each such entity implements a different set of features assigned to that layer. We can further specialize the `layer-N-entity` superclass into individual subclasses for each protocol entity, using some function-based basis of specialization.

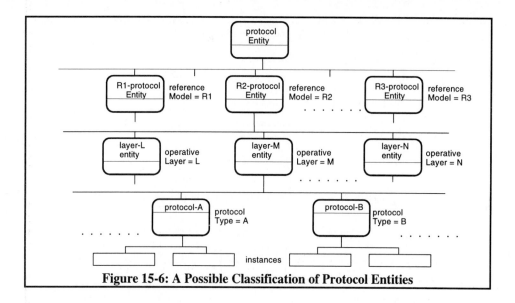

Figure 15-6: A Possible Classification of Protocol Entities

Subclasses and Subtypes

If one protocol object class exhibits a strictly monotonic extension of the functionality of another protocol object class in the same layer, it may be possible to model the extending class as a subclass of the extended class. That is, if both the classes `protocolA` and `protocolB` are descendants of the `protocolEntity` object class, both have the same value of `refModel` and `operativeLayer`, and `protocolB` implements everything `protocolA` does plus additional functionality, then `protocolB` can be a subclass of `protocolA`. The specialization principles of either Function Addition or Function Extension, or both, may be applied here, depending on how the additional functionality is defined.

Bear in mind, however, that a subclass is also a subtype, and hence its instances must be substitutable for instances of all its concrete ancestral classes. If `protocolB` is a subclass of `protocolA`, and if both are concrete, then it must be possible to replace an instance of `protocolA` with one of `protocolB`; in particular, it must be possible for two devices, one with `protocolA` on its stack and one with `protocolB`, to interoperate exactly as if both had `protocolA`. This is represented in Figure 15-7. If such substitution is not possible, it would be incorrect to model `protocolB` as a subclass of `protocolA`. Where two protocol entities share significant functionality but are not strictly substitutable, they should be modeled with common capsules or abstract normalized intermediate superclasses.

Many protocol specifications contain optional features that a protocol entity implementation may or may not choose to implement. Under these situations, it becomes important to indicate which specific features have been implemented for each such protocol in a defined stack. In international standards, this is often accomplished by the use of *functional profiles* which indicate the specific optional features included for each entity.

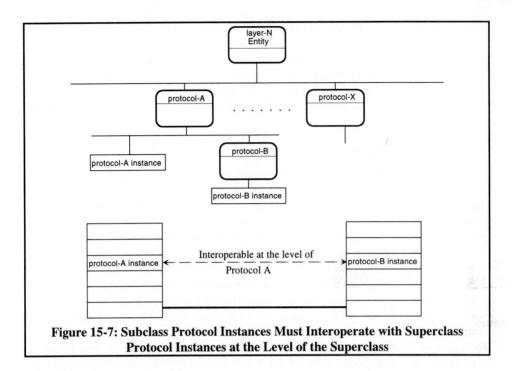

Figure 15-7: Subclass Protocol Instances Must Interoperate with Superclass Protocol Instances at the Level of the Superclass

15.5. Protocol Layering

Protocols exhibit well-formed relationships with each other, called *layering relationships*. Layering relationships specify permissible ways in which protocols can be combined to create a protocol stack, which can then be deployed for use by a particular class of applications. Only certain protocols can be layered on top of other protocols. In our modeling methodology, we formally specify these layering rules to our model compiler.

Any given protocol may have several other protocols on the layer "above" it. Conversely, it may be possible to layer a given protocol on any one of several other protocols which would reside "below" it. Typically, when a data packet is received by a device through an external port, there is only one physical-layer and link-layer entity associated with that port through which that packet can go. At the middle layers, however, there could be several candidate protocol entities which could process it. It is important for each protocol entity to identify the correct protocol entity in the layer above to which the packet must be delivered. In other words, every layer entity performs a *demultiplexing* function with respect to the entities in the layer above it.

To correctly identify the sequence of layers a data packet must traverse up a recipient stack, reference models require that the header for each layer identify the corresponding peer layer entity in the recipient stack to which the packet is addressed. This identification is given various names; in various reference models it is called a *port, well-known port, upper-layer protocol number*, or *service access point*. For the purposes of being sufficiently general, we shall call this the *demultiplex point*. It should be understood that we are not inventing a new term but using a generic name to denote the actual proto-col upper-layer-identifying parameter at each layer in the context of any standardized reference model. We include the demultiplex point in our specification for the layering relationship. For standard reference models, the demultiplex point is defined in the ap-propriate standards documents. Sometimes, when two protocols must be layered together for ad hoc purposes, it is necessary to assign this parameter using some locally agreed-upon convention.

Use of Layering Rules

The set of all such protocol layerings is normally represented as a "layer cake" with sev-eral protocols at each layer. Most specifications of network architectures represent this information diagrammatically. With the formal notation for permitted protocol layerings which we will describe in Chapter 16, we will have in our model a precise notation to formally describe this layer cake in a specification language, so we can automate its analysis and manipulation as a data structure in software.

When our architecture compiler analyzes the specified protocol dependencies and represents the layer cake as a data structure in memory, the protocol layerings form a *di-rected acyclic graph*. In this graph, the protocols are the nodes and the layering rules are the edges [Hege88, Valt91]. For each protocol which is a node of the graph, it is possible to construct a tree structure going downward toward all the protocols below it (following the chain of "layers-above" relationships), and another tree structure going upward to-ward all the protocols above it (following the chain of "layers-below" relationships). By traversing the tree structure downward, we can enumerate the *transitive closure of proto-cols supporting* the given protocol entity. By traversing the tree structure upward, we can enumerate the *transitive closure of protocols supported* by the given protocol entity.

It is not necessary in our model that each layering rule can only associate proto-cols in adjacent layers of a reference model. It is possible to define a layering rule which "skips" layers, that is, allows a layering between protocols implementing non-adjacent la-yers of a reference model. This is rarely done due to the ensuing complications with de-multiplex point identification, but it is sometimes necessary for efficiency in the lower la-yers. In this case, the upper protocol is said to be *direct-mapped* to the lower protocol through a *convergence function*, rather than through the normal intermediate layer entity. By the reverse token, it is also possible for two protocols in the *same* layer of the refer-ence model to be layered one above the other under special circumstances.

It is also not necessary to require that only protocols belonging to the *same refer-ence model* be layered on top of each other. It is possible, and often desirable, to construct "hybrid" protocol stacks by layering together protocol entities belonging to different ref-erence models. Multiprotocol gateways often do this at the highest layer they support. Also, some reference models do not specify some layers of a protocol stack. For example, almost any middle- and upper-layer data communication stack can be layered above the Adaptation Layer (AAL 3/4) of the B-ISDN Reference Model. Similarly, almost any con-venient physical and link layer stack can be layered below the Internet Layer of the Internet Reference Model if the appropriate network interface drivers are available.

We also permit the notion of *inverse-layering*. Inverse-layering allows a protocol which would normally be "above" its supporting protocol to be temporarily layered "below" it. Inverse layering destroys the acyclic nature of the directed graph of protocol layerings; nevertheless, as it is not very common, the graph's cyclomatic complexity remains of low order, and cycle detection remains relatively easy. Inverse layering is only permitted for bridging across stacks; no protocol layering cycle is permitted inside any one stack.

Inverse layering is often required when data frames are presented to a gateway device in some low-level format but need to be encapsulated in a higher-level protocol amenable to routing across a WAN or an internet. Inverse-layering is also called *tunneling*. A common example of tunneling is the capturing of an SDLC frame from an FEP, or an LLC2 frame from a Token-Ring LAN, as the payload of an IP datagram, so that SNA traffic can be routed across an internet. Thus, unroutable traffic intended for a point-to-point or shared-medium-broadcast topology is converted into routable traffic over a mesh topology. Because of its special purpose, such inverse layering generally works without well-known demultiplex points. Its disadvantage is that it requires ad hoc configuration of routing table addresses. We represent such encapsulation in our model as a conceptual inverse layering, that is, the link-layer entity of the SNA Reference Model is layered above the internet-layer entity of the Internet Reference Model, as shown in Figure 15-8.

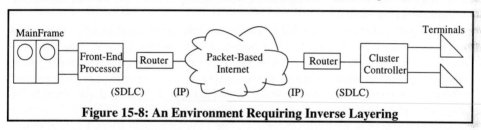

Figure 15-8: An Environment Requiring Inverse Layering

Applying Layering Rules to Network Architecture

With the formal specification of layering rules, it is now possible to automate in software the process of construction of protocol stacks to service specific application requirements. For a given protocol at a given layer, a simple graph traversal algorithm can identify each possible protocol which could layer immediately below it. For each one of those protocols, the protocols immediately below them can be identified. It thus becomes possible to automate in software the answer to questions like:

a) *We wish to set up an enterprise-wide WAN to support a forms-routing workflow application. What kind of network should we set up?* Identify which protocols are called by the application. For each one of those protocols, traverse the allowable layerings downward to enumerate possible stacks which could support that application.

b) *We have a Token-Ring LAN in our department. What applications can we deploy?* Starting from the Token-Ring protocol, traverse the supported protocols upward to enumerate possible applications which can be supported on it (which admittedly will be a very large set).

c) *If we acquire Brand X suite of protocols, what will it do for us and what kind of networks can we run it on?* Traverse the stack both upward and downward from the layers of Brand X to enumerate potential applications and supporting network types.

15.6. Protocol Stacks

We define a *protocol stack* as a *path* which a Protocol Data Unit (PDU) may take through a network device. We model a protocol stack as an object class, which is always deployed on an aggregate *host* object as a component. A host does not necessarily imply a mainframe computer system; the object hosting a protocol stack could be any `network-Device`. A *full protocol stack* is one where a PDU travels between a physical-layer port in the device and an application or layer which produces or consumes it. All other protocol stacks are termed *substacks*. Network devices are not required to implement full protocol stacks; bridges, gateways, and switches, for example, implement only substacks since they neither produce nor consume user PDUs. (Technically, these devices do produce and consume control, routing, and network management PDUs; we will address this question in a later section.)

A protocol stack is modeled as an object of the `protocolStack` class, which has its constituent `protocolEntity` objects as components. Thus, it plays the `has-as-a-part` role with them in an inclusive-aggregation relationship. By layering these component protocol entities together as specified by the layering rules, complete protocol stacks can be erected. These are sometimes called *tower sets*. As an example, consider the stack of Figure 15-9, which represents the mechanism used in a SONET network to download software to network elements via the Data Communications Channel (DCC) [TR 253].

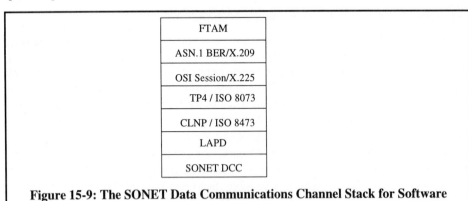

| FTAM |
| ASN.1 BER/X.209 |
| OSI Session/X.225 |
| TP4 / ISO 8073 |
| CLNP / ISO 8473 |
| LAPD |
| SONET DCC |

Figure 15-9: The SONET Data Communications Channel Stack for Software Download

We follow the convention that a stack is always specified bottom-up, with the lowest layer being the first element in the sequence. The lowest layer need not necessarily be the bottommost layer of a reference model; we could specify substacks of just middle layers for use in other stack definitions. We must ensure, however, that the protocols constituting a stack are not layered together in any arbitrary sequence; we must follow the layering rules. In Chapter 16, we will specify the formal notation for the layering rules which permit protocol entities to be sequenced together to create a stack.

Each protocol entity in a stack has a set of mandatory and possibly some optional features implemented. The options actually implemented in any instance can be described in the flag attribute `implementedOptions`. The set of options implemented in any one entity in any one layer often depends on the set of options implemented in some other entity in some other layer. This is because only certain combinations of options in different layers can be meaningfully implemented together. This combination of options for the various layer entities in a stack, taken together, is often called the *functional profile* of the stack. Some reference models have predefined functional profiles which are suitable for specific applications. Each predefined functional profile is given a name, which is shorthand for indicating the combination of subsets, options, and parameters required in the protocol entities. Sometimes functional profiles are themselves standardized; for example, OSI stacks may conform to certain *international standardized profiles* (ISP) [ISO TR 10000].

In our model, we model the profile of a stack as the `functionalProfile` attribute of the `protocolStack` object class. As the model is developed, we will see how assigning a particular value to the `functionalProfile` attribute can algorithmically influence the options implemented in the `protocolEntity` components constituting the `protocolStack`.

15.7. Isochronous Communication

The discussion of protocol stacks in the preceding section was largely oriented toward data communication. For isochronous communication, transmitted information is not generally processed by deeply layered stacks. Rather, it is encoded directly by some hardware in the sending terminal equipment, communicated in some standard transmission format over its medium, and directly reconstructed by hardware in the receiving terminal equipment. Isochronous signals are not processed as discrete PDUs which could be independently fragmented, routed, reassembled, error-detected, and error-corrected by protocol entities. Terminal equipment conventionally used for isochronous communication includes PBXs, key systems, telephone sets, digital cameras, video codecs, CATV receivers, CATV head-end systems, radio receivers, and radio transmitters. All of these have appropriate hardware to directly transmit or receive signals for their medium as defined by the relevant transmission standards. Where the transmission medium is not a broadcast or a dedicated facility, these devices have the ability to set up switched paths through the network prior to data transmission, so that a fixed path is reserved for the duration of the transmission.

A Historical Perspective

The historical difficulties with respect to sending isochronous signals over layered communication stacks were many. In many *packet-switched* networks of the 1970s and 1980s, the network protocol used was connectionless. This implied that each protocol data unit — often called a datagram — contained complete source and destination address information. In theory, different protocol data units from a single application stream addressed to the same destination could each be routed independently and individually. If in fact each packet arrived by a different route, packets in the same stream could arrive out of sequence, and some could even be dropped if problems were encountered along their path. Even if it so happened that they were all directed along the same route and arrived in the proper sequence, the destination address in the header of each packet would still have to be fully resolved by a routing table lookup at every router along the path. This would result in variable routing delays at different routers along the path.

Some packet-switched data networks were connection-oriented but performed positive acknowledgments node-to-node rather than end-to-end. While connections were established during a call setup phase (as in Figure 13-3), packets were still processed and error-checked at the network layer at each node. While this was necessary given the relatively high error rates of the copper plant infrastructure of that time, it made network performance inadequate for isochronous traffic. Because the content of an isochronous message is invalidated if parts of it arrive late or mis-sequenced, all of these considerations made packet-switched networks — whether connection-oriented or connectionless — unsuitable for such traffic.

Traditionally, isochronous communication has been carried over frame formats such as DS-1 or DS-3 which were synchronously clocked. Since their content was error-tolerant, it was not necessary to reconstruct each and every bit correctly at the receiving terminal equipment. Thus, layered protocol entities performing acknowledgment and error detection were unnecessary. The important consideration was transmitting the content promptly, rather than accurately, because variable transmission delays would invalidate the content. Low-bit-rate signal streams were formatted and multiplexed within a high-speed frame format, but they were not packetized. Even though the information contained in each slot (or channel) in the multiplexed frame format did not carry any address, header, or checksum information, it could still be delivered to the correct destination on time. This was accomplished by making the network *circuit-switched*: that is, the correct path had been established and the required bandwidth reserved ahead of time, either on a dedicated basis during network provisioning, or on a switched basis during call setup. Once established, a constant data rate was guaranteed along this path, and information could flow continuously.

If remote multimedia communication consisting of voice, video, image, and data streams were to be conducted using conventional technologies, the stack profile for such an application would appear as in Figure 15-10.

We can easily specify complete stacks such as the data transmission stack of Figure 15-10 in our model using the techniques in the preceding sections. We can treat the hardware entities encoding the transmission formats for isochronous traffic — such as ds1Framer — as single-layer "stacks". Although this is not very useful in the protocol sense, it is helpful in our methodology to model a network device as possessing this "stack" so we have some knowledge of its capabilities in our model information base.

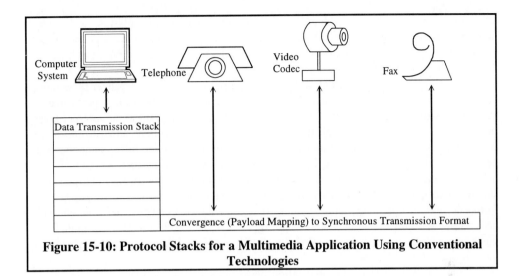

Figure 15-10: Protocol Stacks for a Multimedia Application Using Conventional Technologies

New Technologies

In today's networks, the situation has changed. The bandwidth available from the underlying network infrastructure has increased by orders of magnitude. Cell-oriented substrate technologies such as ATM are optimized to deliver both isochronous and non-isochronous traffic [Bhar91]. Being a hardware-implemented packet technology, ATM provides virtual circuits and virtual paths which can be viewed as "wires" for communication — that is, a physical layer with a rapidly reconfigurable medium and extremely elaborate multiplexing facilities [Aoya93]. Its adaptation layer — especially AAL 3/4 — can be viewed as a link-layer format for data communication [DePr91, DePr93]. Even though information is packetized, the short, fixed cell size ensures that isochronous signals can be delivered on a regular basis without being blocked or flow-controlled [Onvu94]. This becomes possible because, for each isochronous source, the rate of cell generation from the adaptation layer is known. Since the cells are short, isochronous traffic is guaranteed not to be interrupted by non-isochronous data packets of large and variable length. Even when the rate of cell generation from a source is not known (such as data arriving due to bursty LAN activity), a sufficient number of offered cells can still be accepted until the bandwidth is saturated, and the rest can be flow-controlled. If a cell is lost in transit, error-tolerant traffic is not usually affected, while error-sensitive traffic must detect this using some protocol entity higher than ATM in the stack; this is normal for many middle-layer substacks for data.

ATM cells do not require complete routing resolution at each node. The cell headers do not carry the full destination address; they only indicate some variety of link identifier which identifies the link on which the packet originated relative to the node. The sequence of links along which the cell will be routed from node to node is established ahead of time during a call setup phase (for *switched virtual circuits,* or SVCs) or during a network administration phase (for *permanent virtual circuits*, or PVCs). During the data transfer phase, each incoming packet is looked up in a virtual circuit mapping table, the contents of the link identifier field are changed for transmission to the next node, and the outgoing packet is relayed. Because such processing can guarantee an upper bound on the routing delay at each node, this technology is suitable for both isochronous and non-isochronous traffic.

At layers higher than ATM and AAL in the protocol stack, the packet processing performance of protocol entities has also improved significantly due to high-performance microprocessors. Even with full address resolution of each datagram at the internet layer in each router in the path, overall transfer delays have been brought down to the point where it is now feasible to transmit isochronous information over fully connectionless network protocols. Thus, it is no longer technologically necessary to reserve dedicated bandwidth ahead of time during call setup to deliver isochronous traffic, although it is still less expensive to do so. Many isochronous applications now show acceptable performance and quality over connectionless datagram networks. Thus, the conventional networking wisdom of "connectionless protocols for data and connection-oriented for voice and video" has lost currency as the traditional lower-layer distinctions between these services have blurred.

The stack profile for an application performing remote multimedia communication using modern technologies would be similar to that depicted in Figure 15-11. Isochronous traffic could either be layered above some routed, connectionless network-layer protocol, or could be adapted directly to a connection-oriented protocol at the cell layer, depending on the existing infrastructure. This figure is representative only; it is in fact possible to use even more layers in the stacks for isochronous traffic, such as the sequence consisting of the Internet Protocol (IP [RFC 791]), the User Datagram Protocol (UDP [RFC 768]), and the Real-Time Transport Protocol (RTP [Schu92]), or the sequence consisting of the Streams-II Protocol (ST-II [RFC 1190]) and the Real-Time Transport Protocol.

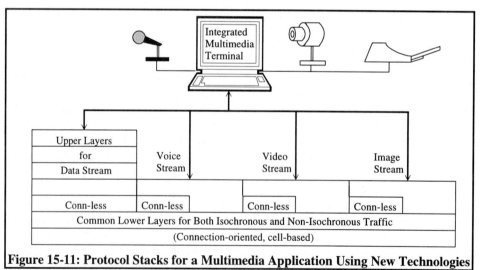

Figure 15-11: Protocol Stacks for a Multimedia Application Using New Technologies

We can now specify the common lower layers used by both isochronous and non-isochronous traffic as a common substack for the different streams. Even though all streams use common lower-layer protocols, data packets will still need additional higher-level protocols due to their error sensitivity. The upper layers of such a protocol stack can be implemented in end-user computing equipment. Throughout the network, features and capabilities of transmission, switching, signaling, and routing equipment can be implemented using common hardware for cell-processing at the lower layers of the stack.

15.8. Protocol Planes

So far, we have only dealt with protocols for transfer of information which is directly produced and consumed by the end-user. Normally, the content of the information generated by the end-user is not normally of interest to the devices involved in networking; they merely treat it as payload and transmit it without analyzing or interpreting it (unless it is a wiretap device). Payload information could be encoded in any manner the user desires: isochronous, non-isochronous, compressed, or encrypted. Only the higher-level substack or appropriate decoding hardware in the receiving terminal equipment must interpret content in this format; other devices in the network need merely relay it.

Aside from information of interest to the end-user, every network carries messages which are of internal interest to the devices involved in networking. These internal messages are not normally visible to the end-user; she need not be aware of their existence, even though some actions she performs may trigger these messages. Messages containing user payload information are called *user messages*; the internal messages generated by network devices are of two kinds: *control messages* and *management messages*. Control messages are those which are required for operating the network in real time to ensure delivery of the user messages. Management messages are those which are of interest to the network service provider (and sometimes to the user) for network management.

User, Control, and Management Planes

The ISDN Reference Model [ITU-T I.320] divides protocol stacks into three *planes*: the *User Plane*, the *Control Plane*, and the *Management Plane*. Without loss of generality, this concept can be extended to all reference models. These are often abbreviated U-Plane, C-Plane, and M-Plane respectively. Planes can be thought of as dividing protocol stacks "vertically" much as layers divide them "horizontally".

A protocol entity usually performs a highly specific service and usually belongs to only one plane. However, it is possible (and common among protocol stacks for data streams) for a protocol entity to belong to more than one plane.

For connection-oriented traffic, C-Plane activity usually involves *signaling messages* to establish and tear down connections between terminal equipment for transferring U-Plane traffic. If a connection cannot be established, the connection-reject is sent back through another C-Plane message. Identifying terminal capabilities, negotiating options, and allocating bandwidth for each party of a multicast session are all activities that occur in the C-Plane prior to U-Plane data transfer. Some newer protocols reduce C-Plane activity by piggybacking it over U-Plane messages, for example by triggering the connection establishment state machine only upon the arrival of the first U-Plane message and timing out to tear down the connection.

For connectionless traffic, signaling for connection establishment is not necessary because each packet carries the full address and can be individually routed as it is received. This requires the presence of routers, which need to maintain a reasonably current representation of their immediate topology in their routing database. Unbeknown to U-Plane traffic, routers periodically exchange *routing messages* to communicate network topology and reachability information. In connectionless networks, these constitute the C-Plane traffic.

M-Plane messages carry information about administrative activities which the providers or managers of the network wish to perform, such as remotely interrogating operating parameters and device configurations, commanding network reconfiguration, provisioning new services, receiving reports of unfavorable operating conditions, monitoring overall network performance, retrieving usage information for trending analysis and accounting, and downloading new operating software.

The distinguishing characteristic of all C-Plane and M-Plane messages is that they are *always all data*. Even when the U-Plane traffic is an error-tolerant isochronous stream, C-Plane and M-Plane messages which assist in transmitting that U-Plane traffic are still error-sensitive data streams. For example, the information indicating the network address in a telephone call (e.g., dialed or translated digits, sometimes called a *global title*) is conveyed through data packets and must be transmitted error-free, even though the actual voice traffic stream is error-tolerant.

Because they are data, C-Plane and M-Plane messages always require some higher-level protocols in a protocol stack to process them correctly. Therefore, even when U-Plane traffic goes through only a trivial single-layer stack as in Figure 15-10, we still need to implement a separate non-trivial data stack for C-Plane and M-Plane messages. Internetworking devices for non-isochronous traffic, such as repeaters, bridges, and routers, implement only substacks for U-Plane traffic since they neither produce nor consume U-Plane PDUs. However, they do produce and consume C-Plane and M-Plane PDUs and so must implement full stacks for these. Consequently, to correctly synthesize a network out of candidate devices, we must match not just one protocol stack but *three*: one for each of the planes.

Control-Plane Stacks

There are many standards for C-Plane message stacks. When the U-Plane traffic is isochronous, *Signaling System Number 7* [ITU-T Q.700] is used between telecommunications switching equipment (called the *Network-Network Interface*, or NNI). The *Q.931 suite* is used over ISDN's D-channel [ITU-T Q.931] for signaling and call control between end-users and the network (called the *User-Network Interface*, or UNI). At the UNI in Broadband ISDN, the protocol *Q.93B* negotiates quality-of-service parameters with the ATM network. For videoconferencing, additional UNI protocols such as H.230 and H.242 specify how call setup, disconnect, and control information is exchanged between video codecs which use H.261 and H.221 for U-Plane traffic. Even the familiar DTMF (Dual-Tone Multi-Frequency, commonly known as "Touch-Tone") is technically an example of C-Plane data, though it is not always processed by a non-trivial data stack.

For connectionless, non-isochronous U-Plane data traffic, commonly used C-Plane stacks include the *Routing Information Protocol* (RIP [RFC 1058]) and the *Open Shortest Path First* protocol (OSPF [RFC 1131]) in conjunction with the Internet Protocol (IP [RFC 791]) for interior gateway communication. The *Intermediate-System-to-Intermediate-System* protocol (IS-IS [ISO 10589]) is also used for the same purpose in conjunction with both the Internet Protocol and the Connectionless Network Protocol (CLNP [ISO 8473]). A class of protocols known as *Inter-Domain Routing Protocols* are used to communicate routing policy information between routers in different administrative domains (IDRP [RFC 1125, Estr93, ANSI X3S3]). Because all these protocols are used only between gateways in hierarchically structured internets (the "Network-Network Interface"), they are the analogues of Signaling System No. 7. C-Plane protocols commonly used for control messages between end-users and gateways (the "User-Network Interface") include the *Address Resolution Protocol* (ARP [RFC 826]) and the *End-System-to-Intermediate-System* Protocol (ES-IS [ISO 9542]); they are the analogues of the Q.931 suite. Further, the *Internet Control Message Protocol* (ICMP, [RFC 792]) is a general C-Plane protocol used in IP networks to relay error and control messages.

For connection-oriented, non-isochronous U-Plane data traffic, C-Plane messages are typically required to establish and tear down connections between the communicating systems over the underlying stacks. Examples of connection-oriented non-isochronous U-Plane protocols include X.25 [ITU-T X.25], the *Transmission Control Protocol* (TCP [RFC 793]), and the *Transport Protocol-4* (TP4 [ISO 8073]). When control activity is required for this U-Plane data, the C-Plane traffic is carried over *the same protocols* as the U-Plane traffic. This is obviously the most convenient solution: since a stack exists to carry the U-Plane data anyway, it can carry C-Plane traffic — which is also data — just as well. Thus, protocols such as X.25 and TCP are *both* C-Plane and U-Plane protocols, because the same protocol handles both connection control and user data transfer. Some experimental protocols such as the *Network Block Transfer Protocol* (NETBLT [RFC 998]) separate user and control-plane activities to allow efficient implementations of both. Figure 15-12 illustrates some commonly used C-Plane protocol stacks [Perl92, Mitr91].

When we categorized protocol entities earlier in Figure 8-7 and Figure 8-8, we made an intuitive distinction between user protocols in one subclass and routing and signaling protocols in another. We see now that this distinction can be made rigorous by formalizing our new knowledge of control and user planes in our model for the `protocolEntity` object class. We accomplish this formalization by modeling an `operativePlanes` attribute for the `protocolEntity` object class. The value of this attribute indicates which of the three planes the protocol entity supports. By performing attribute domain restriction on `operativePlanes`, we can, if we wish, classify user protocols, routing and signaling protocols, and management protocols in different branches of the inheritance hierarchy.

Management-Plane Stacks

M-Plane stacks are also standardized, and generally include additional higher-layer protocols than C-Plane stacks, as they need to interface to user-level network management applications. Standard M-Plane protocols include the *Common Management Information*

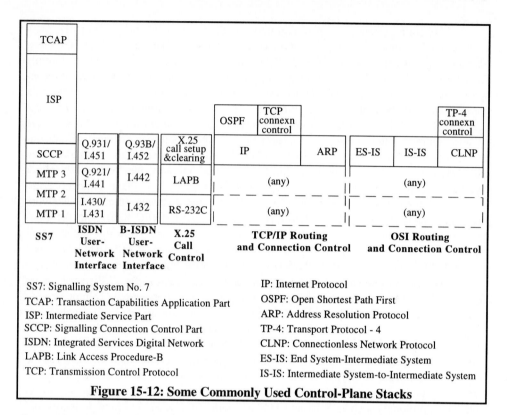

Figure 15-12: Some Commonly Used Control-Plane Stacks

Protocol (CMIP [ITU-T X.710, ITU-T X.711]), used in the *Telecommunications Management Network* (TMN [ITU-T M.3010]) for the management of SONET transmission elements, loop carriers, and telecommunications switching elements; *Transaction Language-1* (TL-1 [TR 62, TR 831, TR 1093, SR 2723]), a standard used for the management of telecommunications transmission devices such as cross-connects; and the *Simple Network Management Protocol* (SNMP [RFC 1441, RFC 1448]), used for the management of customer-premises equipment, internetworking devices, and SMDS networks [TR 1062]. The SONET DCC stack of Figure 15-9 is actually an M-Plane stack; Figure 15-13 illustrates additional commonly used M-Plane stacks.

Just as a protocol entity can be characterized for use in a particular plane, so can an entire protocol stack. The protocolStack object class has a stackPlanes attribute with a definition virtually identical to the operativePlanes attribute of the protocolEntity object class. This attribute indicates the planes for which that entire stack could be deployed for service. The value of the stackPlanes attribute for a protocolStack object is always the intersection of the values of the operative-Planes attribute for each of its component protocolEntity objects. For example, if all protocolEntity objects in a protocolStack support both the C-Plane and the U-Plane, then the entire stack will support both the C-Plane and the U-Plane. If even one component protocolEntity object does not support the C-Plane, then the entire stack cannot support the C-Plane.

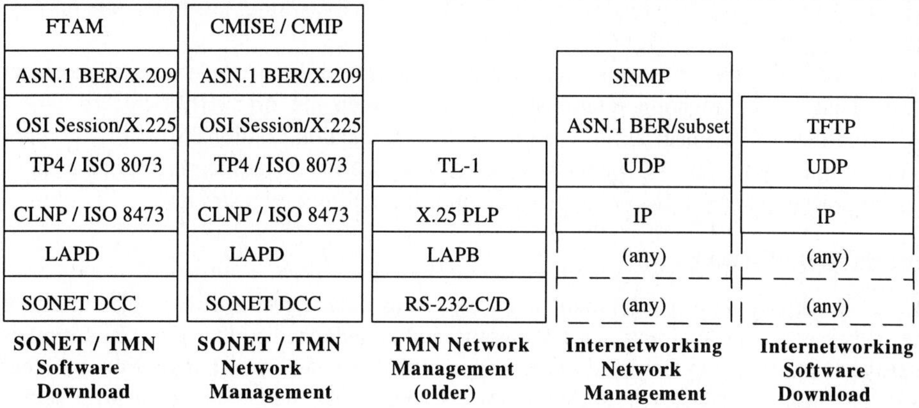

SONET / TMN Software Download	SONET / TMN Network Management	TMN Network Management (older)	Internetworking Network Management	Internetworking Software Download
FTAM	CMISE / CMIP			
ASN.1 BER/X.209	ASN.1 BER/X.209		SNMP	
OSI Session/X.225	OSI Session/X.225		ASN.1 BER/subset	TFTP
TP4 / ISO 8073	TP4 / ISO 8073	TL-1	UDP	UDP
CLNP / ISO 8473	CLNP / ISO 8473	X.25 PLP	IP	IP
LAPD	LAPD	LAPB	(any)	(any)
SONET DCC	SONET DCC	RS-232-C/D	(any)	(any)

FTAM: File Transfer, Access and Manipulation
BER: Basic Encoding Rules
TP4: Transport Protocol 4
CLNP: Connectionless Network Protocol
LAPD: Link Access Procedure - D
SONET: Synchronous Optical Network
DCC: Data Communications Channel
TL-1: Transaction Language 1
TMN: Telecommunications Management Network

CMISE: Common Management Information Service Element
CMIP: Common Management Information Protocol
PLP: Packet Level Protocol
LAPB: Link Access Procedure - B
UDP: User Datagram Protocol
IP: Internet Protocol
SNMP: Simple Network Management Protocol
TFTP: Trivial File Transfer Protocol

Figure 15-13: Some Commonly Used Management-Plane Stacks

Note that the `protocolStack` class does not have a `refModel` attribute; unlike a `protocolEntity` object, it does not have to belong to any particular reference model, as it could be a "hybrid" stack created by layering together protocol entities belonging to different reference models.

15.9. Ports

All devices in the network must communicate with other devices; they execute this communication through well-defined interfaces called *ports*. In our model, we define a port as always having a physical realization. This means that our definition of a port excludes such things as socket connections to software programs, PDU demultiplexing points in protocol objects, or API parameters to call software objects from other software objects. If these objects require external communication, they must go through a physical port.

A port always belongs to a physically realized network device and possesses at least a physical-layer interface to the outside world. If the port is involved in *wireline* networking, it has a *transceiver/connector interface* which can potentially connect to some transmission medium such as a cable. If the port is involved in *wireless* networking, it has a *transceiver/antenna interface* which is statically or dynamically tuned to signals modulated over the appropriate wavelengths in the electromagnetic spectrum. Both wireline and wireless ports can be easily modeled; they possess similar attributes, the distinction between them occurring only in the lower layers.

We model the `port` object class as a component of the `networkDevice` object class. Thus, an aggregation relationship exists between the `networkDevice` object class and the `port` object class. We model this aggregation relationship with a component multiplicity of `[0,-]`. Subclasses of `networkDevice` containing specific numbers of ports can restrict this range using component multiplicity restriction.

Interface Substacks

A port contains at least one protocol stack, known as its *interface substack*. The interface substack has at least one physical-layer entity and is dedicated to that port. This implies that the substack is implemented exclusively for that port and not shared with any other port. In contrast, instances of substack objects containing middle- or upper-layer protocols could be implemented just once for the entire network device and shared by different full stacks. We model this as an exclusive-aggregation relationship between the `port` object class and the `interfaceSubstack` descendant of the `protocolStack` object class. Multiple instances of interface substacks could exist in a network device if it contains multiple ports.

For *wireline* ports, if the stack performs any link control, then the substack up to the link control layer is normally the interface substack. The interface substack for a *wireless* port follows a different reference model, which generally combines multiple functions in a single layer partitioned into sublayers [Buch91]. The sublayer analogous to link-level control may perform additional fragmentation for lengthy data frames. Due to the higher error rates of wireless media, additional fragmentation reduces bandwidth requirements for retransmission of lost or bad data. For lost data, the sublayer performs *selective retransmission*, that is, it retransmits only lost fragments rather than the entire data frame. Synchronization and modulation, based on any appropriate technology (such as CDMA or TDMA for digital cellular or CDPD for packet data over existing analog cellular facilities) is performed by a sublayer analogous to the physical layer.

In the C-Plane, one sublayer is responsible for device registration and antenna selection, which must be performed each time since the device could function in a mobile environment with frequent changes in its physical address. Another sublayer executes spectrum request/grant activity. Because all these functions are implemented in hardware or firmware, the interface substack for a wireless port tends to be more complex than that of a corresponding wireline port; it is often treated as a single layer, and even the partitioning into sublayers is not always clear-cut. Of course, different wireless technologies, just like wireline technologies, could follow different reference models.

Classifying Ports

To classify ports, we can subclass at the highest level on the basis of whether it is wireless or wireline, using attribute domain restriction. At the next level, we can further classify ports on the basis of the type of link-level control it supports; this uses component specialization as it depends on specialization of the component protocol entities of its component interface substack. Finally, we can subclass further with respect to its

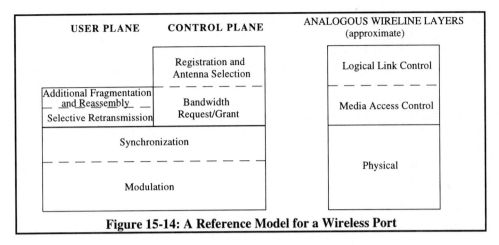

Figure 15-14: A Reference Model for a Wireless Port

physical-layer connectors, using component specialization again. Of course, as with all classifications, all bases of specialization must be selected such that our model becomes meaningful. For example, we could classify ports on the basis of their speed attribute first if we decided that such classification was more meaningful. Figure 15-15 illustrates a possible classification for ports.

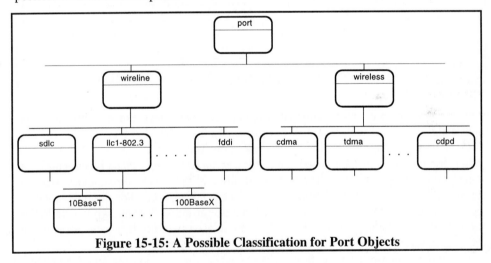

Figure 15-15: A Possible Classification for Port Objects

Ports Shared among Planes

Some devices have only one network port and must conduct all external communication through that port. Consider a desktopWorkstation object class which has a single IEEE 802.3 connection to the other devices. This connection is carried over twisted-pair wiring to a LAN concentrator, through which the workstation can internetwork. The workstation runs the Internet protocol stack so that it can support applications such as file transfer, remote login, and distributed file sharing. The workstation also supports an

SNMP agent so that it can be remotely managed by the network administrator. New software releases and upgrades can be downloaded to the workstation by the network administrator through the TFTP protocol.

We model this aggregate `desktopWorkstation` object as possessing only one `port` object as a component. This port has a dedicated interface substack consisting of the sequence {`tenBaseT, llc1-802dot3`}. Several full `protocolStack` objects use this port. Figure 15-16 illustrates a model of the stacks associated with this device. Since they share the same port, all the full protocol stacks use the layers in the interface substack implemented as hardware for that port.

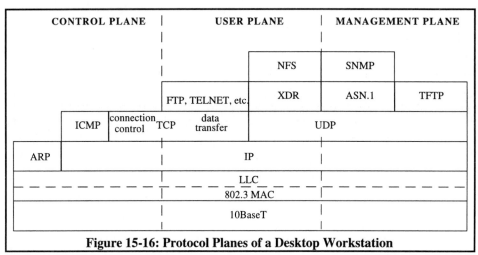

Figure 15-16: Protocol Planes of a Desktop Workstation

Each stack provides functionality from one or more planes. For example, the stack consisting of the protocol sequence {`tenBaseT, llc1-802dot3, arp`} provides C-Plane functionality for routing; the stack {`tenBaseT, llc1-802dot3, ip, tcp`} provides both U-Plane functionality for data transfer and C-Plane functionality for connection control, and so on. The number of different PDU paths through each stack is never less than the number of different planes the stack supports. For example, connection control PDUs from the TCP protocol terminate at the TCP layer, while data PDUs are passed on to the application. Thus, there are at least two different paths through the TCP layer, which is consistent with the fact that it supports two planes.

If the same workstation object were to possess a second port for data communication (for example, if it were configured to act as a gateway), the number of full stacks available in the workstation would increase by a factor of two, since the number of paths a PDU could take would also increase twofold. The second port would have its own interface substack; higher-level protocol entities would interface with either port, depending on the source and destination of their data.

Ports Dedicated to Planes

We now consider an example where the planes are completely separated, each with its individual port. Consider the example of a voice-mail-ready PBX system. Its purpose is to serve as a local exchange for intra-campus traffic among a number of extensions and to allow voice traffic from these extensions to access the switched public network. It contains an interface to multiple DS-1 trunks which connect the campus to its local exchange carrier. It performs call control signaling to the local exchange carrier's switch using the Q.931 protocol suite. In addition, it supports a network management agent which receives its commands through an interface port called the administrative port.

The network management system which supervises this PBX is an integrated system which also manages other devices such as automatic call distributors and some computer-assisted telephony application systems; as such, it communicates to all its managed elements over an Ethernet LAN, over which a combination of TP4/CLNP protocols is run. Because the voice-mail system embedded in the PBX is hosted on a computer which exchanges data with other systems over an Ethernet LAN, this interface can also be used by the network manager to manage the entire PBX. Its network management agent supports call detailing, handling overload and other alarms from the switching element, and monitoring and database administration on the storage database for the embedded voice-mail system. In addition, software upgrades for both the switching element and the voice-mail system can be downloaded through this port. By routing this network management traffic across a wide-area CLNP internet, network management for the PBX can be performed remotely if necessary.

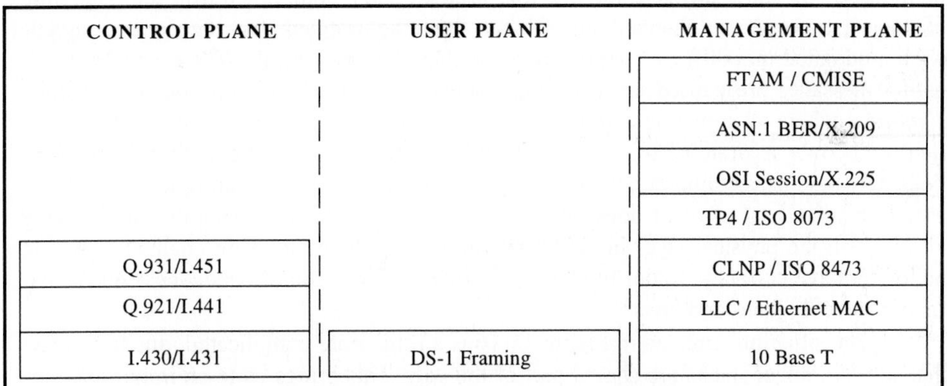

CONTROL PLANE		USER PLANE		MANAGEMENT PLANE
				FTAM / CMISE
				ASN.1 BER/X.209
				OSI Session/X.225
				TP4 / ISO 8073
Q.931/I.451				CLNP / ISO 8473
Q.921/I.441				LLC / Ethernet MAC
I.430/I.431		DS-1 Framing		10 Base T

Figure 15-17: Protocol Planes of a Voice-Mail-Ready PBX

Figure 15-17 represents the stacks for this PBX. The planes in this case are completely separate, that is, no stack implements more than one plane. This is often the case in situations where the device presents separate interface ports for user traffic, control traffic, and management traffic.

In Chapter 21, we will show how the full protocol stacks contained in a `networkDevice` object do not have be directly specified: they can be inferred from the knowledge of the component interface stacks of the component `port` objects, combined

with the knowledge of the middle- and upper-layer substacks which are directly components of the device. By using the permitted protocol layerings to associate applications,
mid-level protocol stacks and interface substacks of component ports together, we can
infer which full protocol stacks are supported in the device, and hence infer with which
other devices it may interoperate.

15.10. Bandedness

We use special terminology to indicate concisely whether the user, control, and management planes share protocol stacks. This is called the *bandedness* of the device.
Bandedness is a Boolean property and is always expressed with reference to the user
plane. Bandedness can have two values: *in-band* and *out-of-band*. The term *band* refers to
the U-Plane. If any particular data stream is carried via the same stack as the U-Plane, it is
considered to be *in-band*; if it is carried via a different stack, it is considered to be *out-of-
band*.

In the example of Figure 15-17, M-Plane traffic is carried in an entirely separate
stack than the U-Plane. The PBX is said to support *out-of-band network management*.
Furthermore, C-Plane traffic is also carried in a separate stack. Thus, the PBX performs
out-of-band signaling to its external carrier switch. (However, individual stations making
intra-campus calls to other stations may signal in-band to the PBX if they use DTMF.)

In the earlier generation of telecommunication networks, the distinction was often
made between *in-channel in-band signaling* and *in-channel out-of-band signaling*. In
both cases, the same physical facility was used to carry both call traffic and signaling
messages; however, in-channel out-of-band signaling implied that the control signals
were modulated in a different frequency range than the voice traffic. The case where signaling messages are carried on a different physical facility is termed *common channel
signaling*, where all signaling activity for different end-user calls is consolidated and carried on its own separate network. Because the new generation of digital telecommunications networks uses common channel signaling, the choice of modulating in-channel signals in-band or out-of-band does not arise. Further, due to the elaborate multiplexing
available in the physical layer in ATM networks, considerations of in-channel signaling
no longer have currency. In our model, we formalize the notion of bandedness on the basis of protocol planes and layers.

The situation depicted in Figure 15-16 is a little more complicated, due to the fact
that some protocol stacks are shared part of the way. This brings us to an important concept: *Bandedness is not an absolute Boolean but is relative only to a layer*. In Figure
15-16, incoming management and control traffic remains in-band with respect to the
physical and link layers but gets separated from the U-Plane further up the stack. At the
IP layer, for example, ARP messages are out-of-band, but TCP connection control message and all SNMP messages are in-band. This means that the IP layer treats all PDUs the
same; it does not know the difference between U-Plane, C-Plane, and M-Plane PDUs.
The SNMP network management for this workstation is in-band relative to UDP, IP and
below, but out-of-band with respect to TCP and its applications. Even if a remote network manager sends a message to retrieve an IP-layer parameter, that message is not interpreted by the IP layer, which treats it simply as in-band data and passes it on the SNMP

entity via UDP. The SNMP entity interprets the data and retrieves the required data from the instrumentation for the IP entity and sends the response back via another message which is also treated by IP as in-band data received from UDP. (Note that TCP supports the concept of an "out-of-band" or "urgent" data which is treated rather like a connection control message, in that it bypasses the buffers reserved for "normal" data. This is analogous but not strictly equivalent to our definition of out-of-band.)

If any network control or management activity is *fully out-of-band*, it uses a completely separate stack and has its own separate physical port. Fully out-of-band network management is sometimes implemented for remote internetworking devices by adding a separate RJ-11 or RJ-45 port which accepts dialed telephone calls for supporting remote network management activity. If the control or management activity is *fully in-band*, it uses the entire U-Plane stack and behaves exactly like any other U-Plane application. If it is neither, then its bandedness changes value somewhere along the way while going up the stack, either from in-band to out-of-band (e.g., if the activity uses the same physical port as the U-Plane but has separate applications) or from out-of-band to in-band (if the activity has a separate physical port but uses upper layers in common with the U-Plane). When indicating the bandedness of any network control and management activity, it is essential to indicate the layer at which this value changes.

It is also possible for planes to service each other. For example, the transfer of M-Plane messages may itself require supporting routing or signaling activity in the C-Plane. By the same token, protocol entities constituting the C-Plane may themselves need to be managed by M-Plane applications.

15.11. Classifying Network Devices

When classifying network devices, clearly one of the most important bases of specialization is the function of that device, which is largely dictated by the protocol stacks it supports. In our model, a network device may directly contain protocol stacks as components; often, upper- and middle-layer substacks can be modeled as immediate components of their containing device, or as indirect components if they happen to be part of, say, an operating system component. A network device may also contain port components which in turn contain protocol stacks as interface substacks. Figure 15-18 shows the overall aggregation hierarchy for network devices, ports, protocol stacks, and entities.

When constructing an inheritance hierarchy for network devices, the principle of component specialization is used in many bases of specialization. This principle permits subclasses of the `networkDevice` superclass to contain specialized subclasses of `port`, `protocolStack`, and so on. In addition, component addition is also important: as devices get more specialized going down the inheritance hierarchy, they could add more protocol entities, more stacks, and more ports for increased functionality. We can use the following rules for classifying network devices:

- *A network device may be subclassed for its use of specialized component protocol stacks* (Component Specialization).

- *A network device may be subclassed for its use of specialized component protocol entities in its component protocol stacks* (Component Specialization).

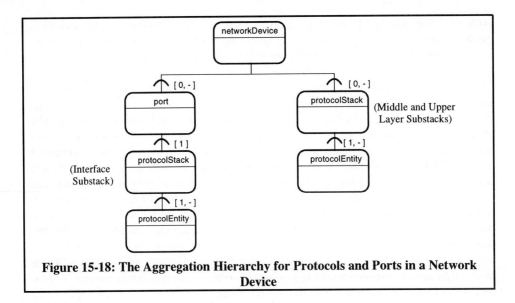

Figure 15-18: The Aggregation Hierarchy for Protocols and Ports in a Network Device

- *A network device may be subclassed for its use of specialized component ports* (Component Specialization).

- *A network device may be subclassed for its use of specialized component protocol stacks as interface substacks in its component ports* (Component Specialization).

- *A network device may be subclassed for its use of specialized component protocol entities in the interface substacks in its component ports* (Component Specialization).

- *A network device may be subclassed for adding component protocol stacks* (Component Addition).

- *A network device may be subclassed for adding component protocol entities in its component protocol stacks* (Component Addition).

- *A network device may be subclassed for adding component ports* (Component Addition).

- *A network device may be subclassed for adding component protocol stacks as interface substacks in its component ports* (Component Addition).

- *A network device may be subclassed for adding component protocol entities in the interface substacks in its component ports* (Component Addition).

These bases of specialization are frequently used for classifying network devices. Of course, they are not the only ones used for this purpose; there could be many others. As always, in accordance with our principles of monotonic inheritance, a network device is not permitted to remove inherited component protocol stacks, inherited component ports, protocol entities in inherited component protocol stacks, interface substacks in inherited component ports, or protocol entities in the interface substacks in inherited component ports.

15.12. Summary

To describe the protocols used in any network device correctly, it is important to indicate the reference model and the layer functions which each protocol entity implements. The relationship of a protocol entity to other protocol entities is formally described by specifying a set of permissible protocol layerings. A sequence of protocol entities, assembled using the permitted layerings, is considered a protocol stack. The protocol stack object class is considered an aggregate class which contains its protocol entities as components. An attribute of the protocol stack object class specifies the order in which its component entities must appear. Isochronous traffic may be carried over single-layer transmission formats or over complex stacks; data traffic always requires non-trivial stacks to be correctly transmitted.

Each protocol entity implements activity from one or more protocol planes. There are three planes: the user plane, the control plane, and the management plane. Entire protocol stacks may service more than one plane. While isochronous traffic may use trivial stacks in the user-plane, its associated control and management planes require non-trivial data stacks.

Ports are physical interfaces for external communication and possess an interface substack. The full stacks associated with a port may service the user, control, or management planes, or some combination thereof. If the three planes share a common substack at the port level, control and management activity is said to be in-band with respect to their common layers; otherwise, it is said to be out-of-band.

16. Formal Protocol Models

"The manual for retrieving files over the network is now available on-line on the remote file server."
— *notice on anonymous corporate bulletin board.*

16.1. Introduction

In this chapter we introduce the formal notation for modeling reference models, protocol stacks, ports, and various attributes of protocol entities described in Chapter 15. This notation is also couched within the formalism of ASN.1 information object class notation.

16.2. Modeling Reference Models

To formally describe communication networks, it is helpful to indicate the reference model which has served as the baseline for the design of each protocol supported in each network device. A device could support more than one protocol stack, with each stack possibly belonging to a different reference model. Many multiprotocol gateways and protocol translators — such as FTAM-FTP gateways — fall into this category.

We specify a reference model as a fully abstract top-level object class, using the OBJECT-CLASS template. We also need to identify what the layers of that reference model are; this is accomplished in the layers attribute:

```
referenceModel OBJECT-CLASS ::=
{
     ATTRIBUTES          {
                              referenceModelName,
                              layers
                         }
}
```

318

```
        IDENTIFIED BY          referenceModelLbl
}
```

The attribute `layers` is defined as

```
layers ATTRIBUTE ::=
{
        ATTRIBUTE-TYPE         Layers
        IDENTIFIED BY          layersLbl
}
```

where the type reference name `Layers` is defined as

```
Layers ::= SEQUENCE OF Layer

Layer ::= SEQUENCE
{
        layer                     LayerLabel,
        subLayerStructure         Layers  OPTIONAL
                                      -- specified bottom-up
}


LayerLabel ::=       OBJECT IDENTIFIER
```

This allows us to label each reference model with an OBJECT IDENTIFIER. Its constituent layers are also assigned individual OBJECT IDENTIFIER labels. By concatenating these layer labels bottom-up in a SEQUENCE, we can formally describe the reference model to a network synthesis compiler. Because a layer recurses into an optional sublayer structure, we can specify as many levels of sublayering as are necessary.

Individual reference models may now be specified as subclasses of the `referenceModel` object class. For example, we may specify the OSI Reference Model as

```
osiReferenceModel OBJECT-CLASS ::=
{
  SPECIALIZES-FROM    {{
                        superclass  referenceModelLbl,
                        basisOfSpecialization
                         {compoundPredicate:
```

```
                    {connectBy   and,
                     predicates
                     {{simplePredicate:
                       {attributeDomainRestricted:
                        {newValueOf:
                         {attribute
                                   referenceModelName,
                          is       equalTo,
                          value    "OSI"
                     }}}},
                     {simplePredicate:
                       {attributeDomainRestricted:
                        {newValueOf:
                         {attribute  layers,
                          is         equalTo,
                          value      osiLayers
                     }}}}
                     }}}
                    }}
          IDENTIFIED BY   osiReferenceModelLbl
   }
```

where the new value of the `layers` attribute, `osiLayers`, is specified as

```
   osiLayers Layers ::=
   {
        { layer    osiPhysical},
        { layer    osiDataLink},
        { layer    osiNetwork},
        { layer    osiTransport},
        { layer    osiSession},
        { layer    osiPresentation},
        { layer    osiApplication}
   }
```

where each of the identifiers `osiPhysical`, `osiDataLink`, and so on, are values of type LayerLabel, that is, OBJECT IDENTIFIERs. The value `osiReference-ModelLbl` is assumed to be an appropriately chosen OBJECT IDENTIFIER.

By registering entire reference models within our model information base, we facilitate the ability of our network architecture and planning programs to synthesize a network from a description of the objects in the information base. By working with multiple reference models and by deriving connectability information through matching protocol stacks implementing a common reference model, programs that assist in network architecture, planning, and design can correctly construct heterogeneous, multiprotocol networks.

We assume that the information object set {ReferenceModels} is the set of all OBJECT-CLASS information objects which denote reference models. We now specify the constrained type ReferenceModelLabel as

```
ReferenceModelLabel ::=
        OBJECT-CLASS.&objectClassLabel({ReferenceModels})
```

which constrains it to be an OBJECT IDENTIFIER only from that set.

16.3. Protocol Entities

As specified in Chapter 12, protocol entities in our model are members of the protocolEntity object class. We examine some of its more important attributes in detail below. Recall from Chapter 12 that we modeled a refModel attribute for the protocolEntity object class. This attribute identifies which reference model the protocol entity conforms to. We may formally specify this attribute thus:

```
refModel ATTRIBUTE ::=
{
        ATTRIBUTE-TYPE              ReferenceModelLabel
        IDENTIFIED BY              refModelLbl
}
```

In this definition, the type of the refModel attribute is simply an OBJECT IDENTIFIER, constrained to come from the set ReferenceModelLabel. (Note that the identifier refModelLbl is the attribute label of the refModel attribute and is not the label of any reference model.)

When a protocol entity conforms to a particular reference model, it must implement one of the layers of that reference model. The protocolEntity class also has an operativeLayer attribute. Its value indicates which layer within its reference model is implemented by the protocol entity:

```
operativeLayer ATTRIBUTE ::=
{
        ATTRIBUTE-TYPE              LayerLabel
        IDENTIFIED BY              operativeLayerLbl
}
```

The type of the `operativeLayer` attribute is `LayerLabel`, which is simply an `OBJECT IDENTIFIER`. Although we have not defined this as a constrained type, this must be a `LayerLabel` from one of the layers of the protocol entity's reference model, identified in its `refModel` attribute.

Besides `refModel` and `operativeLayer`, the `protocolEntity` object class also has an `operativePlanes` attribute indicating the planes — user, control, and management — which that protocol entity supports. This is specified as follows:

```
operativePlanes ATTRIBUTE ::=
{
        ATTRIBUTE-TYPE              SET OF Plane
        IDENTIFIED BY              operativePlanesLbl
}


Plane ::= ENUMERATED
{
        user (0),
        control (1),
        management (2)
}
```

Our compiler now knows the plane or planes for which each `protocolEntity` may be used. Using this knowledge, it can construct `protocolStack` objects which are targeted for providing service for a specific plane. It is possible, and common for non-isochronous error-sensitive traffic, to use the same protocol stack for both the user plane and the control plane. This does not imply the existence of two different copies of the same stack with identical layer entities; rather, it means that both C-Plane PDUs and U-Plane PDUs are processed along the same path as they traverse the stack.

The core functions of any protocol entity can be specified either in the `&Functions` field of the information object defining that entity, or in a capsule listed in the `&MandatoryCapsules` field. The optional features can be specified in capsules listed in the `&OptionalCapsules` field.

For any instance of a protocol entity, it is sometimes necessary to ascertain dynamically which optional features have been implemented in that instance. For this we use the attribute `implementedOptions` of the `protocolEntity` object class. This is a flag attribute, evaluating to a set of `OBJECT IDENTIFIER`s. More precisely, it evaluates to some subset of `{&OptionalCapsules}.&capsuleLabel`; the field `&OptionalCapsules` lists all the `CAPSULE` information objects which may optionally occur in that information object class. The attribute `implementedOptions` lists all the `OBJECT IDENTIFIER`s of the optional capsules which actually occur in that protocol entity instance. We may formally model this attribute as

```
implementedOptions ATTRIBUTE ::=
{
        ATTRIBUTE-TYPE              SET OF CapsuleLabel
        IDENTIFIED BY              implementedOptionsLbl
}
```

The attribute `implementedOptions` lists the original or inherited optional capsules actually occurring in that protocol entity. Knowing the value of the `implementedOptions` attribute in each `protocolEntity` object, the network synthesis compiler is now able to automatically determine not only which pairs of protocol stacks in different network devices may interoperate with each other but also the level of service at which they may interoperate, depending on the optional features implemented in the protocol entities of each stack.

16.4. Protocol Layering

As indicated in Chapter 15, protocol entities can be layered only according to certain rules. The rules which define the permitted combinations of protocol entities above or below other protocol entities are known as protocol layerings. We assume that the information object set {Protocols} enumerates all the OBJECT-CLASS information objects which denote concrete, instantiable descendant classes of the general `protocolEntity` object class. Using this set, we define the constrained type `ProtocolLabel` as

```
ProtocolLabel ::= OBJECT-CLASS.&objectClassLabel
                                        ({Protocols})
```

We may now use this definition in the formal notation for protocol layerings, which we formally specify using the PROTOCOL-LAYERING information object class:

```
PROTOCOL-LAYERING ::= CLASS
{
        &upperProtocol              ProtocolLabel,
        &lowerProtocol              ProtocolLabel,
        &demultiplexPoint           INTEGER OPTIONAL,
        &layeringLabel              OBJECT IDENTIFIER UNIQUE
}
WITH SYNTAX
{
        PROTOCOL                    &upperProtocol
            LAYERS-ABOVE
```

```
        PROTOCOL                        &lowerProtocol
        [DEMULTIPLEX POINT              &demultiplexPoint]
        IDENTIFIED BY                   &layeringLabel
}
```

This information object class defines a permitted layering between two protocols which are identified by their `ProtocolLabel`. We specify one such `PROTOCOL-LAYERING` information object in our model information base for each permissible layering between a pair of protocols. This allows our network synthesis programs to correctly construct a protocol stack by combining protocol entities using appropriate layering rules. An example [RFC 1060] of one such rule is

```
udp-ip PROTOCOL-LAYERING  ::=
{
        PROTOCOL                        udp
            LAYERS-ABOVE
        PROTOCOL                        ip
        DEMULTIPLEX POINT               17
        IDENTIFIED BY                   udp-ip-layeringLbl
}
```

The `demultiplexPoint` field of the `PROTOCOL-LAYERING` information object class is optional because, under special circumstances such as inverse layering and other ad hoc layerings, no well-defined demultiplexing parameter is used. As an example of an inverse layering or tunneling, consider the capturing of SDLC frames within IP datagrams for routing across a packet-based internetwork, as shown in Figure 15-8:

```
sdlc-ip-tunnel PROTOCOL-LAYERING  ::=
{
        PROTOCOL                        sdlc
            LAYERS-ABOVE
        PROTOCOL                        ip
        IDENTIFIED BY                   sdlc-ip-tunnelingLbl
}
```

We know that each descendant of the `protocolEntity` object class possesses both a `refModel` and an `operativeLayer` attribute. Given the knowledge of these attributes, it is a reasonable question to pose as to why the compiler cannot *infer* a permitted layering between protocol entities if they happen to implement adjacent layers of the same reference model. The reason is that each layer-*n* entity of a given reference model cannot necessarily be layered above *every* layer-*(n-1)* entity of the same reference model;

some upper layer entities only work with a subset of the possible entities that could layer below it in the same reference model. In addition, it is sometimes possible to layer together entities which do not necessarily belong to the same reference model. For this reason, we only construct stacks using explicitly defined permitted layerings.

With the set of all permitted layerings formally defined, we now have a software representation of the "layer cake" of protocols. By representing this in our architecture as data structures in the model information base (rather than the conventional representation as a diagram on paper), we can now manipulate and reason with this information. Network synthesis programs can use the permitted layerings as *synthesis rules* which drive the construction of protocol stacks during the process of automated network architecture.

16.5. Protocol Stacks

We specify a protocol stack in our model as an object class:

```
protocolStack OBJECT-CLASS ::=
{
     ATTRIBUTES      {
                          numberOfLayers,
                          protocolSequence,
                          functionalProfile,
                          stackPlanes,
                          ...
                      }
     IDENTIFIED BY        protocolStackLbl
}
```

Here, `protocolStack` is an object class with no specialization (it is a top-level class), no functions (since its functions are executed by its component `protocolEntity` object classes), and a number of attributes. The attribute `numberOfLayers` indicates the number of protocol entities in the stack. The attribute `stackPlanes` indicates the planes (user, control, or management) for which that stack may be used. The attribute `protocolSequence` lists the protocols actually contained in the stack. The attribute `functionalProfile` indicates the profile assigned to the stack; as we mentioned in Chapter 15, only certain combinations of options in different layers can be meaningfully implemented together. Generally, each such meaningful combination of options is given a name so that it can be referred to concisely.

We do not provide a formal specification for these attributes, because many of them need not actually be specified for any instance of a protocol stack; their values can be *inferred* from the component protocol entity objects in that instance of that stack. The attribute `numberOfLayers` can be inferred by counting the number of `protocolEntity` components. The attribute `protocolSequence` can be inferred by enumerating in a bottom-up sequence the `&objectClassLabel` fields of the `protocol-Entity` components. The attribute `stackPlanes` can be inferred as the intersection of the values of the `operativePlanes` attribute for each of its component `protocolEntity` objects. In Chapter 20, we will see how all of these may be computed as *virtual attributes* of the `protocolStack` object class merely by following its decomposition relationship with its component `protocolEntity` objects.

The attribute `functionalProfile`, depending on the value assigned to it, constrains the values of the `implementedOptions` attribute of the `protocolEntity` components. In Chapter 22, we will see how a constraint between related object classes can be formally specified.

Unlike a `protocolEntity`, a `protocolStack` object does not have a `refModel` attribute. As we stated in Chapter 15, a protocol stack does not belong to a particular reference model. A protocol stack can be a "hybrid" stack created by layering together protocol entities belonging to different reference models.

It should be noted that the `protocolSequence` attribute cannot list any arbitrary sequence of `protocolEntity` objects; the protocols layered together must follow the layering rules specified as `PROTOCOL-LAYERING` information objects. If a particular pair of protocols does not occur in any permitted protocol layering, then those two protocols cannot be layered as adjacent entities in any instance of a `protocolStack`.

Since a `protocolStack` object itself may be contained as a component of a `networkDevice` object (which is typically the case for many middle-layer and application substacks), we specify an aggregation relationship between the `networkDevice` object class and the `protocolStack` object class as follows:

```
device-stack AGGREGATION ::=
{
        OBJECT-CLASS                    networkDevice
            HAS-AS-A-PART
        OBJECT-CLASS                    protocolStack
        WITH MULTIPLICITY               zeroOrMore
        IDENTIFIED BY                   deviceStackAggLbl
}
```

A protocol stack is itself an aggregate object and contains several protocol entities. One complication arises when modeling this aggregation relationship: when we described the general aggregation relationship in Chapter 7 and its formal specification in Chapter 11, we did not consider the *order* in which component objects appear in the aggregate. For aggregation relationships in general, the order of appearance of component objects in the aggregate is irrelevant. For protocol stack objects, however, the order is significant: the sequence of component protocol entity objects determines the function of the stack. Furthermore, this sequence must be constrained by the set of protocols available and the permitted layerings between them.

The ordering cannot be imperatively imposed by specifying a value for the `protocolSequence` attribute because, as we said earlier, this is an inferred attribute whose value is implicitly determined by enumerating the components. In Chapter 20, we will provide a modeling technique which will solve this dilemma, through the notion of an *ordered relationship*. For the time being, we assume it is somehow possible to order all the `protocolEntity` components of a `protocolStack` object in a bottom-up fashion, and that the `protocolSequence` attribute does reflects the proper order.

We specify two aggregation relationships for the `protocolStack` object class, one permitting a stack to contain protocol entities as components, and another permitting it to contain substacks:

```
stack-entity AGGREGATION ::=
{
        OBJECT-CLASS              protocolStack
             HAS-AS-A-PART
        OBJECT-CLASS              protocolEntity
        WITH MULTIPLICITY         zeroOrMore
        IDENTIFIED BY             stackEntityAggLbl
}


stack-subStack AGGREGATION ::=
{
        OBJECT-CLASS              protocolStack
             HAS-AS-A-PART
        OBJECT-CLASS              protocolStack
        WITH MULTIPLICITY         zeroOrMore
        IDENTIFIED BY             stackSubStackAggLbl
}
```

These aggregation relationships permit a protocol stack object to contain not just protocol entity components but also other protocol stacks, such as partially defined sub-stacks. By assembling component substacks together, many different protocol stacks can be created with a relatively small number of building blocks. The `protocolStack` object class is implemented such that its `numberOfLayers` attribute always reflects not just the number of `protocolEntity` components it directly contains but also the re-cursive total of the `numberOfLayers` attributes of its substack `protocolStack` components. Further, its `protocolSequence` attribute specifies the order in which its contained `protocolEntity` objects, including the `protocolEntity` objects in its component substacks, must appear. In Chapter 20, we will see how inferred attributes such as these can be made to reflect recursively determined values as well.

Useful protocol stacks may now be subclassed from the `protocolStack` object class. For example, the SONET DCC stack for software download shown in Figure 15-9 is an instance of the `sonetDccStack` object class, which can be modeled as a descendant of the `protocolStack` object class. To specialize from the general `protocol-Stack` superclass, specific stacks use specialization by component specialization. As explained in Chapter 7, this means that while the general `protocolStack` superclass contains the general `protocolEntity` superclass as a component, specialized subclasses of `protocolStack` (such as the `sonetDccStack`) are permitted to contain specialized subclasses of `protocolEntity` (such as `ftamEntity`) as components.

In all cases, the `protocolSequence` attribute of each specialized concrete stack will reflect the sequence of the concrete descendants of `protocolEntity` contained within it. For example, the `protocolSequence` attribute of an instance of SONET DCC stack would have the following embedded value of type SEQUENCE OF `ProtocolLabel`:

```
{
        sonetDCC-Lbl,
        lapb-Lbl,
        dccCLNP-Lbl,
        dccTP4-Lbl,
        dccSession-Lbl,
        dccASN1BER-Lbl,
        dccFTAM-Lbl
}
```

where all sequence elements are values of type `ObjectClassLabel` denoting descendants of `protocolEntity`. Each such descendant class describes a possible protocol implementation, that is, it carries in its `implementedOptions` field an indication of the options which are necessary for correctly implementing this stack.

Recall that in Chapter 7 we permitted two modes of aggregation: *exclusive* aggregation, with non-sharable components, and *inclusive* aggregation, permitting component sharing. Generally, the `protocolEntity` components of a `protocolStack` are modeled with inclusive aggregation. We have defined a stack as a path taken by a PDU. In many network devices, many different protocol stacks — that is, many different paths a PDU might take — often use the same `protocolEntity` object. This is typical for middle-layer entities, which are generally implemented only once per network device.

For example, if we were to define a `sonet-OS-NE-Stack`, we would specify different component protocol entities for the upper layers (such as `cmise`) and lower layers (such as `rs232c`, `lapb`, and `x25plp`), but many middle layers (`dccCLNP`, `dccTP4`, `dccSession`, and `dccASN1BER`) might stay the same. SONET devices implementing both these stacks will reuse the same middle-layer entities, which will demultiplex PDUs for delivery to the appropriate upper layers. Thus, different `protocol-Stack` objects may `have-as-a-part` the same `protocolEntity` object. This is modeled as an inclusive aggregation because many devices have just one instance of a middle-layer entity, whereas it may have multiple upper-layer entities (and multiple lower-layer entities, if it has more than one port). Usually, only the aggregation of the interface substack within a `port` object is considered exclusive, since that substack is not shared with any other `port`.

In Chapter 21, we will provide an alternative mechanism for modeling full protocol stacks. This mechanism will demonstrate how full protocol stacks need not be specified as actual objects but can be *inferred* from the knowledge of the interface substacks, middle-layer substacks, and applications deployed on the network device, combined according to the permitted layering rules. Such inferred objects are known as *virtual objects*. If multiple stacks exist in the device, not all of them need be actual instantiated objects; some full stacks can be inferred as virtual objects from other specified actual `protocolStack` and `protocolEntity` objects.

16.6. Ports

We model the `port` object class as a component of the `networkDevice` object class. Thus, an aggregation relationship exists between `networkDevice` and the `port`. We model this aggregation relationship with a component multiplicity of $[0,-]$; of course, subclasses of `networkDevice` containing specific numbers of ports can restrict this range using component multiplicity restriction.

```
port OBJECT-CLASS ::=
{
        ATTRIBUTES              {
                                    wireline,
                                        -- wireline or wireless
                                    speed,
                                    ...
                                }
        IDENTIFIED BY           portLbl
}


networkDevice-port   AGGREGATION ::=
{
        OBJECT-CLASS                    networkDevice
            HAS-AS-A-PART
        OBJECT-CLASS                    port
        WITH MULTIPLICITY               zeroOrMore
        IDENTIFIED BY                   devicePortAggLbl
}
```

The interface substack of a port is a protocol stack with at least one physical-layer entity and is a component of that port. The interface substack is dedicated to that port, as opposed to middle- or upper-layer substacks which could be implemented just once for the entire network device. We model the interface substack as a `protocolStack` component of a `port` object. We omit all multiplicity specifications for this aggregation to allow them to default to exactly `[1]`.

```
port-interfaceSubstack          AGGREGATION ::=
{
     OBJECT-CLASS               port
          HAS-AS-A-PART
     OBJECT-CLASS               protocolStack
     IDENTIFIED BY              portInterfaceStackAggLbl
}
```

16.7. Summary

The formal specification of reference models is performed using subclasses of the `referenceModel` object class defined for that purpose. This notation lists all the layers which belong to that reference model. The `refModel` attribute of a `protocolEntity` object class must indicate a defined reference model, and its `operativeLayer` attribute must indicate one of its defined layers. A `protocolEntity` object also has an `operativePlanes` attribute indicating the planes it supports, as well as an `implementedOptions` attributes listing the optional features it implements. Protocol entities may be layered according to the permitted layering rules defined in the `PROTOCOL-LAYERING` information object class template.

A protocol stack is modeled as an aggregate `protocolStack` object class whose components are concrete descendants of the `protocolEntity` object class. Most attributes of the `protocolStack` class, such as `numberOfLayers`, `stackPlanes`, and `protocolSequence`, can be inferred from its component `protocolEntity` objects. A `port` object is modeled as a component of a `networkDevice` object; in turn, it contains a `protocolStack` component, which is its interface substack.

17. Object Class Relationships

"I got engaged to this LAN guru, and all he gave me was a token ring."
> — *fiancee of anonymous network architect.*

17.1. Introduction

In addition to classifying the objects constituting a network in taxonomical hierarchies, the methodology of specialization theory (like many others) abstracts the relationships among them as a fundamental underpinning of the model. In this chapter, we present an approach to relationship modeling, providing many examples of relationships among network objects. We introduce the notions of relationship roles and multiplicities and consider various specialization modes arising from the consideration of the relationships an object class participates in.

17.2. Conceptual Background

A *relationship* is said to exist between object classes when the operation of one object class affects another object class. The specification of the relationship describes the nature of this influence. The knowledge of such relationships is especially important in any information model describing the network. Many types of relationships exist in a network, for example:

- A SONET cross-connect *terminates* OC-1 circuits.

- A file transfer service is *deployed* on a computer system.

- A LAN administrator *supervises* a file server.

- A PBX may be *connected* to an automatic call distributor.

- A subscriber may *subscribe* to a network service.

331

- A switched circuit may *back up* a dedicated circuit.

In the methodology developed so far, we can model individual object classes such as cross-connects, circuits, services, and computer systems, but we cannot yet model the interaction that occurs between them during network operation. We *can* model some special cases of couplings: the aggregation relationship of Chapter 7 and the protocol layering relationship of Chapter 15 are both examples of relationships which operationally couple together pairs of object classes. For the time being, we will continue to treat these as special cases; later in this chapter we will show how these may also be subsumed within the general relationship model.

In specialization theory, a *relationship* is defined to be an *operational coupling* between two objects. Like a property, we abstract it as an operational coupling between their *object classes*, and so we sometimes call it an *inter-class relationship*. Just as the characteristics of a set of similar objects are modeled as the *properties* of their object class using *property assignment*, so a set of similar operational couplings between similar object-pairs is modeled as a relationship between their object classes using *relationship assignment*. Each such relationship is specified as a first-class conceptual construct. This means that the semantics of this coupling cannot be captured using any other construct and so must be defined independently. Depending on how a relationship between two classes is defined, all instances of those classes may or may not participate in that relationship

To model relationships in the abstract, we need to define not just the pair of object classes which participate in the relationship but also the exact nature of the coupling between them. Any pair of object classes could participate in more than one relationship with each other. Each relationship, therefore, must be distinguished from other relationships. The two object classes which participate in a relationship need not be genealogically related; they could be located anywhere in the inheritance hierarchy.

A *relationship instance* is an instance of the abstract relationship construct. A relationship instance couples a pair of *object instances* which participate in that relationship. The two object instances must exist before the relationship instance can exist. When a pair of object instances is so linked, the relationship is said to be *instantiated*. An instantiated relationship *operationally couples* a pair of object instances; it is not *equivalent* to a pair of object instances. A relationship instance exists separately from its participant object instances.

The traditional representation of relationships uses a pictorial representation called an *Entity-Relationship Diagram*. This is a well-known modeling methodology which has been extensively used for many years and has many variations [Chen76]. In our model, we will use an analogous pictorial representation called a *Class Relationship Diagram*. There is a one-to-one correspondence between the object classes of a class relationship diagram and the entities of an entity-relationship diagram. Like the entities of an Entity-Relationship (ER) model, our object classes are encapsulated closures of attributes, functions, capsules, and so on. However, object classes in our model are not exactly equivalent to the entities of an ER model. This is because we have defined an object class as an extensible type having a well-defined place in the inheritance hierarchy. The entities of an ER model do not typically participate in any hierarchical taxonomy.

Some modeling methodologies attempt to show both inheritance hierarchies and relationships in the same connected graph. We will not do so in our model. Such graphs often create more confusion than clarity, because they attempt to mix two orthogonal modeling concepts. Even though we might draw them together, we will always draw class relationship diagrams as separate graphs from class inheritance hierarchies. We will use class relationship diagrams as pictorial aids which will only be informal adjuncts to our model; the precise specification of relationships will be performed using constructs in the formal notation.

17.3. Subjects, Relatants, and Roles

We will occasionally focus on a particular object class and model all its relationships. In specialization theory, we use the term *subject* for the object class on which we are currently focused. Each object class participating in a relationship with the subject is said to be its *relatant*. The set of all relatants of any given subject is the set of all object classes which participate in any relationship with that object class. Together, the subject and relatant classes of any relationship are called the *participant classes* or simply the *participants* of that relationship. In any relationship instance, the term *subject instance* will be used to denote the instance or member of the class we consider the subject. The term *relatant instance* will denote the instance or member of the class we consider the relatant; the term *participant instance* will denote either.

Roles and Role-Pairs

Since a relationship couples two object classes, it could be traversed from either participant to the other. A relationship is bidirectional. Each of these two directions is given a name: we call each relationship direction a *role*. For each role, the object class originating that direction is the subject for that role; the object class which terminates that direction is the relatant for that role. For succinctness, we often say the subject *plays* that role with the relatant. A role indicates the precise semantics of the interaction between the participants. Roles are useful both for human comprehension and for formal specification of relationships [Elma88].

In any relationship, roles always appear as *reciprocal pairs*. In the context of any one subject, the role played by the subject with its relatant is said to be the *forward role;* the role played by the relatant with the subject is called the *reciprocal* role. In a class relationship diagram, the forward role is represented by an arrow going away from the subject toward its relatant, while the reciprocal role is represented by an arrow coming from the relatant toward the subject. In general, the semantics of the forward and reciprocal roles are different. Each role is uniquely paired with its reciprocal; it is not possible for any one role to be paired with two different reciprocal roles. Together, the mutually reciprocal roles are called a *role-pair*.

An approximate analogy is that a relationship may be considered a "sentence" in which one object class ("the subject") plays a role ("the verb") with another object class ("the object"). If the forward role is considered analogous to casting the sentence in the active voice, the reciprocal role is analogous to recasting it in the passive voice.

When specifying a relationship formally, it is irrelevant which particular class we choose to be the subject in any relationship; we can just as easily specify the same semantics if we reverse our perspective and make the other class the subject. Identical semantics are stored in the model information base in either case. Figure 17-1 illustrates a class relationship diagram with the participant classes and the roles they play. In any class relationship diagram, the choice of subject and relatant classes can be interchanged as long as the choice of forward and reciprocal roles is also simultaneously interchanged; this is equivalent to conceptually "flipping the diagram around horizontally".

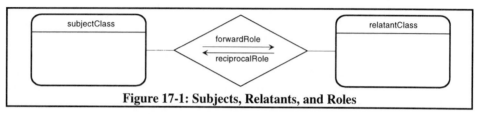

Figure 17-1: Subjects, Relatants, and Roles

Referring to a defined relationship construct uniquely identifies the participant classes and the roles they play with each other. However, referring just to a pair of mutually reciprocal roles does not uniquely identify a relationship, nor does it identify the classes playing those roles. This is because several pairs of object classes could play the same roles with each other in several different relationships. A given subject class could play the same role with different relatants in different relationships. A given subject class could play a forward role with one relatant in one relationship and play the reciprocal of the same forward role with another relatant in another relationship. Two relationships in which the same role-pair occurs are considered *isomorphic* to each other.

Because every relationship uniquely defines a pair of object classes and a pair of roles, it is not correct in specialization theory to say "Object class A has the same relationship with object classes B and C". It is correct to say "Object class A plays the same role in its relationship with object class C as it does in its relationship with object class B." The relationship between object classes A and C is a separate construct from the relationship between A and B. If both these constructs are specified with the same pair of roles, the two relationships are isomorphic. Thus, it is equally correct to say "Object class A has *isomorphic* relationships with object classes B and C."

Figure 17-2 provides examples of class relationship diagrams, along with their relationship instances. In this figure, the `sonetCrossConnect` object class plays the `terminates` role with respect to the `ocl-circuit` object class; in the reciprocal direction, the `ocl-circuit` object class plays the `is-terminated-at` role with respect to the `sonetCrossConnect` object class [Eame91]. Similarly, in the relationship between the `switchedCircuit` and `dedicatedCircuit` object classes, the roles `backs-up` and `is-backed-up-by` are reciprocals of each other.

Relationship Associations

Since a relationship in specialization theory is independently specified as a first-class modeling construct, it has connotational associations with other first-class modeling

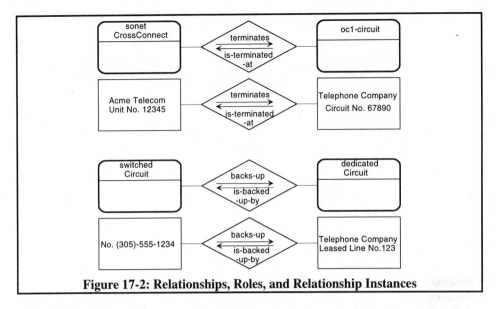

Figure 17-2: Relationships, Roles, and Relationship Instances

constructs. The association between an object class and a relationship in which it is involved is **participates-in**; the complementary association between the relationship and the object class is **involves**. Similarly, the association between an object class and the role it exhibits in the relationship is **plays**; the complementary association is called **is-played-by**. Each role has the association **is-a-role-of** with the relationship construct itself, for which the complementary association is **has-as-a-role**. Figure 17-3 illustrates some of the connotational associations involved in general relationship modeling.

In specialization theory we permit the specification of *involute* relationships [Hugh91]. An involute relationship is one in which both the subject and relatant classes are the same class. An instance of an involute relationship operationally couples two fellow members of the same class. Many examples of involute relationships exist in network modeling, one of the most commonly encountered being connectivity relationships between network devices. Note that such a relationship involutes on the class, not on the object. This means that a member of the class bears the relationship with a fellow member, not that an object bears the relationship with itself. Since a relationship in specialization theory is defined as an operational coupling between two objects, an object cannot bear any relationship with itself. If the two coupled objects happen to be members of the same class, then we say that the class bears a relationship with itself, which by definition is an involute relationship.

A relationship instance cannot be created in the model information base unless the two participant instances already exist. A relationship instance may be destroyed without destroying the participant instances, since it merely decouples them from each other operationally, possibly freeing them to be coupled with other participant instances. If a participant instance itself is destroyed, however, all its relationship instances are also automatically destroyed, since it is impossible to have "free-hanging" relationship instances with a participant object only at one end [Ditt91, Klem91, Bapa93a]. This must appear to

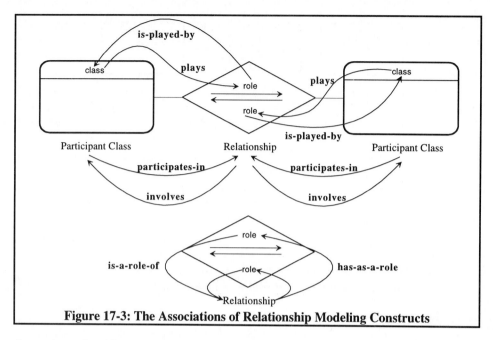

Figure 17-3: The Associations of Relationship Modeling Constructs

be performed as if a cascaded-delete mechanism were being used (even if it is actually performed subsequently by garbage collection).

17.4. Subject and Relatant Multiplicity

Each relationship role possesses a *multiplicity*, which specifies a quantification for that role. This multiplicity is similar to the component multiplicity we specified for the aggregation relationship in Chapter 7. Each role in the relationship has its own multiplicity specification. The multiplicity value for one direction of the relationship is in general different from the multiplicity value in the other direction. The multiplicity with which a subject participates in the relationship is called *subject multiplicity*; it quantifies the number of instances of the subject which could play the forward role with each instance of the relatant. The multiplicity with which a relatant participates in the relationship is called *relatant multiplicity*; it quantifies the number of instances of the relatant which could play the reciprocal role with each instance of the subject. Together, subject and relatant multiplicities are called *relationship multiplicities*.

These multiplicities are specific to each relationship: the same subject may have one set of relationship multiplicities with one relatant in one relationship and a different set of relationship multiplicities with another relatant in another relationship.

Relationship multiplicities combine the notions of *optionality*, which indicates whether or not an instance of the relatant is obligated to participate in that relationship with each instance of the subject, and *cardinality*, which indicates how many instances of the relatant may participate in the relationship with each instance of the subject. In entity-relationship models, relationship cardinality has traditionally been specified as either *one-to-one*, *one-to-many*, or *many-to-many*.

Multiplicity Intervals

We use the same multiplicity specifications for relationships as we did for aggregations in Chapter 7. As the general form of a multiplicity specification, we will specify at each end both a *lower limit*, N, and an *upper limit*, M, for the number of instances which can participate in that relationship. As before, both N and M must be non-negative integers with M greater than or equal to N. If for a given role both the limits N and M are specified, we interpret it to mean that an instance of the role's subject must participate in the relationship with *at least* N and *at most* M instances of the role's relatant. This is called the *multiplicity interval* of the role. In a class relationship diagram, we specify the multiplicity interval of each role using the bracketed notation [N,M] at the *relatant* end of the role direction.

As with aggregation, there are a number of special cases to be considered with respect to the specification of the multiplicity interval:

[N,M] :   N and M both specified. A subject instance must play its role with *at least* N and *at most* M relatant instances.

[N] :   Only N specified; assume N = M. A subject instance must play its role with *exactly* N relatant instances.

[N,-] :   N specified, M open-ended. A subject instance must play its role with *at least* N relatant instances.

[-,M] :   N unspecified, M specified. A subject instance must play its role with *at most* M relatant instances.

[0,1] :   Special case of [N,M]. Participation in the relationship is *optional*.

[0,-] :   Special case of [N,-]. A subject instance must play its role with *zero or more* relatant instances.

[1,-] :   Special case of [N,-]. A subject instance must play its role with *one or more* relatant instances.

[0] :   The object class *does not participate* in the relationship.

none: None specified. The default is considered to be the case [1]. A subject instance must play its role with *exactly* 1 relatant instance.

Quantifying each end of the relationship with a multiplicity becomes especially important with many-to-many relationships. An example of a many-to-many relationship is the `subscription` relationship between a `subscriber` object class and a `networkService` object class. A single `subscriber` may subscribe to one or more `networkServices`, while each offered `networkService` may be subscribed to by zero or more `subscribers`.

Optional and Mandatory Relationships

For any role, if the lower bound of the relatant multiplicity is zero, the relatant is said to be an *optional* relatant for the subject; if non-zero, it is said to be *mandatory*. When we specify the syntax for relationships, we will see how all these different cases of multiplicity may be formally specified in our object model. Figure 17-4 demonstrates examples which use the multiplicity interval notation above.

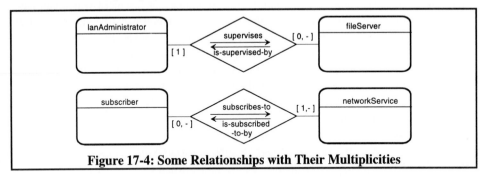

Figure 17-4: Some Relationships with Their Multiplicities

The formalized relationship knowledge represented by Figure 17-4 indicates the participant classes, the roles they play, and the multiplicity of each role. The relationships represented in this figure may be cast in "sentence" form by simply reading across them forward and backward:

- *"A LAN administrator supervises zero or more file servers."*

- *"A file server is supervised by one LAN administrator."*

- *"A subscriber subscribes to one or more network services."*

- *"A network service is subscribed to by zero or more subscribers."*

In the first relationship, if `lanAdministrator` is chosen as the subject, then its relatant is `fileServer`, the forward role is `supervises`, the reciprocal role is `is-supervised-by`, the relatant multiplicity is `[0,-]`, and the subject multiplicity is `[1]`. If `fileServer` is chosen as the subject, then everything "flips around".

If the destruction of an object instance in the model information base violates the minimum multiplicity required in any of its relationships with its relatants, then the destruction of the model instance is flagged as erroneous. For example, if an attempt is made to delete an instance of `lanAdministrator` from the model information base, and if that instance has been coupled in a `supervises` role with existing instances of `fileServer`, then the deletion attempt is flagged. If allowed to proceed, this deletion will leave the `fileServer` instances playing the `is-supervised-by` role with no instance of `lanAdministrator`, thus violating the minimum multiplicity requirement of `[1]`. In general, operations on object instances can be constrained by the multiplicities with which they participate in their relationships.

17.5. Attribute-Defined Multiplicity

Even though the multiplicity specifications above are adequate to cover a majority of the situations, they are still not semantically powerful enough to cover all cases. As with aggregation hierarchies, specialization theory permits subject and relantant multiplicities to be defined in terms of *attribute-defined expressions*. The ability to do this considerably enhances the generality of the model. Consider a sonetCrossConnect object class, which possesses numberOf-OC1-Ports as an attribute. For some instance of sonetCrossConnect this attribute may have a fixed value — say, 64. This object class participates in a termination relationship with the oc1-circuit object class, with which it plays the terminates role. Clearly, this is a one-to-many relationship: a single sonetCrossConnect object may terminate many oc1-circuit objects, while an oc1-circuit object terminates at only one sonetCrossConnect. To specify the relantant multiplicity of the terminates role, we may decide to use the interval [0,64].

However, this is not sufficient, because each instance of sonetCrossConnect may play the terminates role with oc1-circuit with a *different* multiplicity. Depending on the number of OC-1 ports available, a high-end instance of this class may have a relantant multiplicity of [0,2048] for its terminates role, a mid-range instance may have a multiplicity of [0,512], while a low-end instance may have [0,64]. Therefore, modeling the multiplicity of this relationship as [0,64] for the entire sonetCrossConnect class would be wrong.

To solve this problem, we reason that even though each instance of sonet-CrossConnect may have a different upper bound for the relantant multiplicity for its terminates role, we nevertheless know that this upper bound is available in its numberOf-OC1-Ports attribute. Therefore, we do not specify the relantant multiplicity of the oc1-circuit object class in terms of an integer *constant*; rather, we specify it in terms of an *attribute* of sonetCrossConnect. We know that, no matter what value each instance of sonetCrossConnect possesses for that attribute, the upper bound for the number of oc1-circuit objects terminated there is defined by that attribute.

As we did with component multiplicities of aggregation relationships, we allow relantant multiplicities to be specified not merely in terms of integer constants but also in terms of *attribute-defined expressions* involving attributes of the subject. Usually, these attribute-defined expressions involve some *capacity-related* attribute of the subject class. The correct relantant multiplicity for the terminates role which sonetCross-Connect plays with oc1-circuit is [0, numberOf-OC1-Ports]. In a class relationship diagram, the attributes in such an expression are indicated in the multiplicity specification. For any role, the attributes in an expression for *relantant multiplicity* must belong to the *subject*; the attributes in an expression for *subject multiplicity* must belong to the *relantant*.

Figure 17-5 is an example of an attribute-defined multiplicity expression. Like component multiplicities, subject and relantant multiplicities could in general be specified as integer constants, ranges of integer constants, or ranges in which either the lower bound, or the upper bound, or possibly both, could be specified in terms of attribute-defined expressions. In addition, because subject and relantant multiplicities need not always

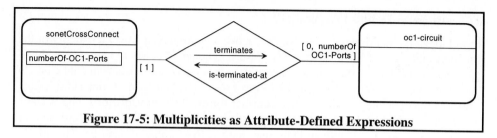

Figure 17-5: Multiplicities as Attribute-Defined Expressions

conform to a continuous domain, we permit them to be specified in terms of a discrete set
of enumerated values as well.

In general, in any situation where we find that the multiplicity of a relatant must
be expressed in terms of a non-trivial integer, it is advisable to examine the attributes of
the subject to see if they can be used as operands to some appropriate algorithm yielding
an expression for relatant multiplicity. Typically, capacity-related attributes of the subject
are used to set the bounds for relatant multiplicity.

17.6. Relationship Attributes

Further consideration of the nature of relationships between object classes leads us to
several semantically useful concepts. One of these is the concept of qualifying relationship constructs with their own attributes. We shall call these *relationship attributes*. A
relationship attribute is an attribute which characterizes the entire relationship instance; it
does not belong to either of the participant classes.

As an example, consider the subscription relationship between a subscriber object class and a networkService object class. This is a *many-to-many*
relationship, that is, each subscriber could subscribe to many different network-
Services, while each networkService may be subscribed to by many different
subscribers. The subscription relationship could have its own attributes. A
subscriber could conceivably subscribe to different networkServices on different dates and could conceivably have a different account balance for each one. Therefore,
each instance of a subscription relationship could be characterized by attributes
such as serviceOrderDate, accountBalance, creditLimit, and so on.

It is not correct to model these as attributes of a subscriber object, because
their values could be different for each networkService the subscriber subscribes to. Neither is it correct to model these as attributes of a networkService object, because their values could be different for each subscriber subscribing to that
networkService. Placing these attributes inside either participant would make it difficult to link their values with the correct instance of the other participant. Therefore,
these attributes are most properly modeled as *relationship attributes* which characterize
the *entire relationship* between the two classes, rather than characterizing either class by
itself.

Consider another example in the administration of a wide-area distributed file
system, of which many exist [Spec85, Kaza88]. In this network, we have a file system
constructed on file servers in different geographic locations. The distribution is transpar-

ent; to its users, the system appears as a single, homogeneous file system. To administer this file system, we divide it into *cells*. Naturally, with our penchant for using overloaded terminology, these cells have nothing to do with ATM packets. A cell in our distributed file system is a logical grouping of file servers and client workstations constituting one subtree of the file system. The grouping is logical, but for convenience, cells could be defined based on geographic location. Our policy for administering this file system requires that each cell be supervised by at least two, and possibly more, local system administrators. These system administrators are responsible for monitoring and configuring the cell as required. Of course, a system administrator could supervise more than one cell.

We might further decide, also as a matter of system administration policy, that each system administrator would be entitled to one of three levels of access with respect to each cell. We define these as follows:

- *No Access*: The system administrator is allowed no access to the cell.

- *Monitor Access*: The system administrator is allowed to monitor the cell non-interruptively, for example, to check percentage disk utilization and process activity.

- *Reboot Access*: The system administrator is allowed unlimited access to the cell, including all "root privileges" which permit her to reboot constituents of the cell.

These access levels permit us to give limited access to the cell to "external" system administrators if we wish, without compromising the security of the cell. The access levels can be defined as enumerated values for an `accessPermission` attribute. Because each system administrator could have different access permissions with respect to different cells and because each cell could give different access permissions to different system administrators, the `accessPermission` attribute is best modeled as a *relationship attribute* of the `supervision` relationship between the `sysAdmin` object class and the `dfsCell` object class. In a class relationship diagram, we depict the attribute or capsule in the diamond which represents the relationship, as illustrated in Figure 17-6.

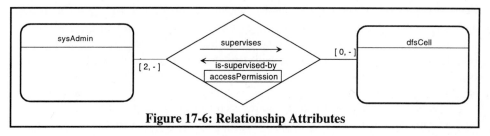

Figure 17-6: Relationship Attributes

We have now extended the notion of relationships to include attributes which qualify each relationship instance. These relationship attributes may be collected together in a capsule. These capsules are similar to the capsules which belong to object classes but are slightly restricted: they cannot contain FUNCTIONs. This is because a relationship does not execute any functions; it is just an operational coupling between two object classes (which may individually execute functions).

17.7. Relationship Inheritance

Aside from participating in relationships, object classes **specialize-into** subclasses based on various considerations. Subclasses are representations of their superclasses which have undergone more evolution and refinement. The principle of *Relationship Inheritance* states that *all relationships defined for an object class are inherited by its descendants*. In accordance with monotonic inheritance, a descendant class may not choose to drop or cancel any relationships defined for its ancestors. This is necessary because a subclass is also a subtype, and hence an instance of a descendant class must be substitutable for an instance of any of its concrete ancestral classes. If a descendant class were to cancel any relationships specified for its ancestors, it would destroy this substitutability.

A relationship couples two object classes operationally, either or both of which could undergo specialization. Descendant classes of either participant will inherit the entire relationship with the other participant, that is, all descendants of the subject will inherit their ancestor's relationship with its relatant, and all descendants of the relatant will inherit their ancestor's relationship with the subject.

A Relationship Inheritance Example

Consider the earlier example of a `subscription` relationship between a `subscriber` object class and a `networkService` object class. This relationship is defined on the general superclasses `subscriber` and `networkService`, each of which could undergo further specialization. For the purposes of this example, assume that we further categorize `subscriber` into three subclasses, possibly using its `usageVolume` attribute as a basis: `smallBusinessSubscriber`, `midGrowthSubscriber`, and `largeAccountSubscriber`. We might make this classification because we might have different marketing strategies for each market segment. The object class `networkService` also undergoes specialization: assume we create the subclasses `basic-800-Service` (also called `freephoneService` in many international markets), `virtualPrivateNetworkService`, and `originBasedRoutingService`. The principle of relationship inheritance states that each subclass of `subscriber` inherits its relationship with `networkService`, and each subclass of `networkService` inherits its relationship with `subscriber`. Figure 17-7 illustrates this concept.

While relationship inheritance requires each descendant to play the same role with the same relatant, it does not require each descendant to play the same role with the *subclasses* of the relatant. In this example, where each participant superclass specializes into 3 subclasses, the number of implicit relationships generated by relationship inheritance is 6, not 9. Relationship inheritance only requires the subclasses `smallBusinessSubscriber`, `midGrowthSubscriber`, and `largeAccountSubscriber` to relate to `networkService` and not to subclasses of `networkService`. Conversely,

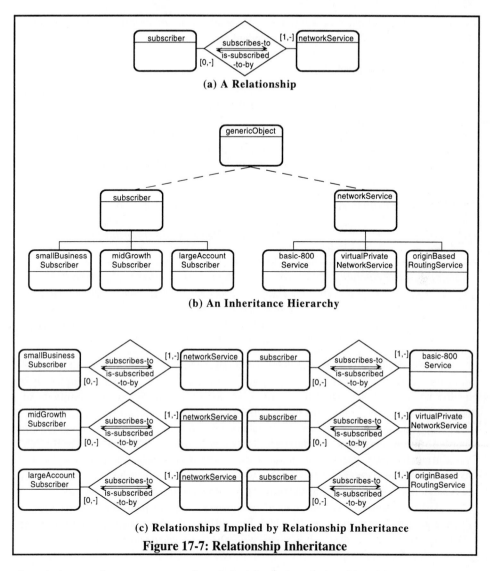

(a) A Relationship

(b) An Inheritance Hierarchy

(c) Relationships Implied by Relationship Inheritance

Figure 17-7: Relationship Inheritance

the subclasses of `networkService` only inherit the relationship with `subscriber`, not with the subclasses of `subscriber`.

Along with ancestral relationships, a descendant class by default also inherits the relatant multiplicity for each relationship. As we shall see later, there are some permissible ways in which the descendant can modify this inherited multiplicity. Thus, each subclass of `subscriber` by default has the same relatant multiplicity for the `subscribes-to` role with `networkService` that the superclass `subscriber` had; conversely, each subclass of `networkService` by default has the same relatant multiplicity for the `is-subscribed-to-by` role with `subscriber` that the superclass `networkService` had. In addition, if the relationship had any attributes (such as `serviceOrderDate`), they continue to be available as relationship attributes in the implicit relationship inherited by the descendant class.

Relationship Principles

We formalize these notions below as the *relationship principles* of specialization theory. These are called *relationship inheritance, monotonic relationship inheritance*, and *relatant multiplicity inheritance*:

Relationship Principle:	*A descendant class inherits the relationships of an ancestral class* (***Relationship Inheritance***).

Relationship Principle:	*A descendant class may not cancel any relationship defined for an ancestral class* (***Monotonic Relationship Inheritance***).

Relationship Principle:	*A descendant class inherits by default the relatant multiplicity for each relationship inherited from an ancestral class, which it may modify in permissible ways* (***Relatant Multiplicity Inheritance***).

These principles govern the behavior of descendant classes with respect to the relationships defined for their ancestors. Each class must respect these principles. It is equally important to note what these principles do *not* require. Relatant multiplicity inheritance, for example, only says that a subclass inherits the *relatant* multiplicity by default; it does not require each subclass to inherit the *subject* multiplicity of a relationship inherited from its ancestors. In a later section, we will examine what happens to the subject multiplicity under specialization and state an appropriate principle governing its behavior. We will also detail the permissible ways in which a descendant class may modify the relatant multiplicity it inherits according to relatant multiplicity inheritance.

We now consider various specialization modes arising from the relationships in which an object class participates [Boch91, Benz93]. All the mechanisms discussed in the following sections are collectively termed *relationship-based specialization modes*.

17.8. Relationship Addition

A subclass inherits all its superclass relationships and, in accordance with monotonic inheritance, is not permitted to cancel or drop them. It is permitted to *add* new relationships which did not exist in the superclass. This is in keeping with the precept that subclasses represent more evolved definitions of superclasses. The addition of a new relationship may be used as a basis of specialization, in which case it is called *Specialization by Relationship Addition*.

There is, however, one caveat with respect to relationship addition: the specializing subclass is not permitted to add a relationship with an existing relatant in the same role, or with any *ancestor* of an existing relatant in the same role. If this were allowed, a subclass would be effectively permitted to redefine an existing relationship, possibly changing its multiplicities in illegal ways. The newly added relationship must be with a "brand-new" relatant class (that is, not an ancestor of any existing relatant class). A subclass is permitted to add a new relationship with a *descendant* of an existing relatant in the same role, but, as we shall see, this becomes equivalent to another specialization mode which we shall examine in a subsequent section.

Aside from adding brand-new relatant classes, specialization by relationship addition also allows the specification of a new relationship having different roles with an existing relatant class. If a subject participates in a relationship with a relatant, its subclass is permitted to play a new role with the same relatant. This is because in specialization theory a relationship is defined in terms of a specific role and a specific pair of relatant classes; thus, a subject which adds a new role with an existing relatant class in fact adds a new relationship.

17.9. Relatant Multiplicity Restriction

There is another important consideration in the inheritance of relationships. Normally, a subclass inherits the relationships of a superclass and their relatant multiplicities. While a subclass may not cancel any inherited relationships, it may in fact *restrict the multiplicity of the relatant*. This is similar to a subclass restricting the domain of an attribute value when it specializes using attribute domain restriction. A superclass may have indicated, for example, that the relatant multiplicity for a particular relatant in a particular relationship is [0, -], even if its specialized subclasses do not all use the same multiplicity in that relationship. A superclass represents a generalization and must necessarily indicate the most general form of the multiplicity domain used in all its subclasses. This means that the domain for the relatant multiplicity in the superclass must be a *superset* of all the domains for that relatant multiplicity in its subclasses. (It can be a minimal superset, that is, a union.) Since a subclass represents a more specialized form of the superclass, it is permitted to use a *subset* of this domain to make it more meaningful for its own use.

An Example with Relatant Multiplicity Restriction

Consider the example of a switching system in an *intelligent network*, modeled as a serviceSwitchingPoint object class [ITU-T Q.1200]. This system is equipped with the capability of identifying calls that need intelligent network services and determine any special handling required for those calls from a *service logic execution environment* (SLEE). The service logic execution environment normally exists in a serviceControlPoint object, which is a computer system (typically hosting a database) that supplies the rules for special handling of calls. These rules may apply to services such as 800 database lookup [Bowe91], called-party locator service (in mobile and wireline environments), forwarding through digit translation, transferring to an in-network voice mailbox, transferring to an in-network call distributor, and many others [SR 1623, Berm92].

Normally, a serviceSwitchingPoint accesses a serviceControl-Point through the signaling (SS7) network. For high-capacity switching systems, however, faster access is often required. In these cases, the SLEE may be hosted on an adjunctProcessor object, which is a computer system directly connected to the serviceSwitchingPoint by means of a high-speed interface and usually dedicated to it. This provides faster access to the service logic than going through the SS7 network to a serviceControlPoint [TR 29, TA 1123, TA 1126, TR 1127, TA 1129, TA 1280].

We might model this as the serviceLogic relationship between the serviceSwitchingPoint and the adjunctProcessor object class, in which serviceSwitchingPoint plays the requests-service-logic-from role with adjunctProcessor, and adjunctProcessor reciprocates with the role supplies-service-logic-to. Since not all serviceSwitchingPoints have an adjunctProcessor, we model the requests-service-logic-from role with the relatant multiplicity of [0,-]. This fact may be restated as "A service-SwitchingPoint requests-service-logic-from [0,-] (zero or more) adjunctProcessors". Figure 17-8 illustrates this relationship.

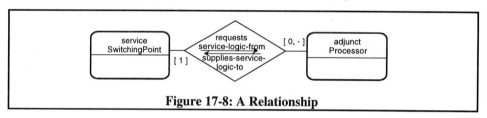

Figure 17-8: A Relationship

When architecting our network, suppose we have a rule which states that for high-capacity switches, an adjunctProcessor is always required. Low- and moderate-capacity switches may or may not have an adjunctProcessor; if they do not, they must request their service logic from a serviceControlPoint (or possibly a servicesNode). Assume for the sake of this example that a high-capacity switch is defined as one serving more than 50,000 lines. We create a subclass of service-SwitchingPoint, called highCapacitySwitch, using as its basis of specialization the attribute domain restriction {numberOfLines >= 50000}.

The subclass highCapacitySwitch inherits the serviceLogic relationship with adjunctProcessor from its superclass. Normally, the highCapacity-Switch would also inherit the default relatant multiplicity of [0,-] for the requests-service-logic-from role, in accordance with the principle of relatant multiplicity inheritance. If it accepted this default, it would be possible to have a high-CapacitySwitch which requests-service-logic-from zero adjunct-Processors. This would make our network model incorrect, since our architecture rule requires a highCapacitySwitch to have at least one adjunctProcessor. We therefore permit highCapacitySwitch to *restrict* the inherited relatant multiplicity with adjunctProcessor to [1,-]. This represents a narrowing of the domain from

[0,-]. This phenomenon is known as *relatant multiplicity restriction*. Figure 17-9 illustrates this principle.

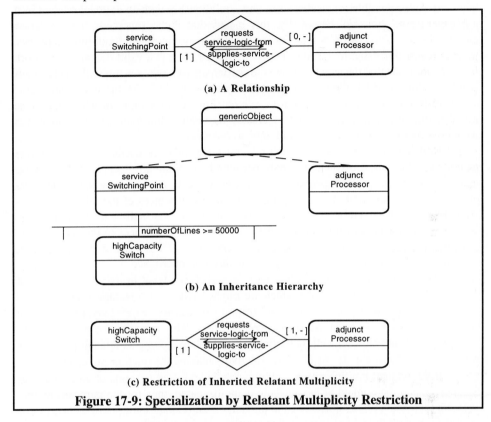

Figure 17-9: Specialization by Relatant Multiplicity Restriction

In general, a descendant class is permitted to restrict the relatant multiplicity of an inherited relationship by narrowing its domain, just like an attribute. If it uses this restriction as a basis of specialization, it exhibits *Specialization by Relatant Multiplicity Restriction*.

Degenerate Relationships

As we see from the example above, this principle can also be used by descendant classes to turn *optional* relatants into *mandatory* ones. If a superclass specifies a relatant multiplicity as [0,n], indicating optional participation in the relationship with up to n instances, a descendant class may restrict this to [m,n] with a non-zero m, meaning that each instance of that descendant is required to participate in that relationship with at least m instance of the relatant.

It is not possible to turn *mandatory* relatants into *optional* ones through inheritance. Any attempt to do so will cause a non-zero lower bound for the relatant multiplicity in the superclass to be changed to a zero lower bound in the subclass. Because this represents an expansion rather than a restriction of the relatant multiplicity domain, the specialization will be rejected by our model compiler.

It is also possible for a subclass to turn a relationship with an optional relatant into a *degenerate relationship*. Essentially, this means that if the superclass has a relatant multiplicity of [0,n] with its relatant, the subclass may use relatant multiplicity restriction to change this value to [0,0]. This is permitted, as it is a valid domain restriction. In effect, it means that the subclass ceases to participate in a relationship with the relatant. A relationship in which the relatant multiplicity turns into [0,0] through legal multiplicity restriction is called a *degenerate relationship*. Any relationship which has non-trivial multiplicity domains — whether created by relationship assignment, or inherited without becoming degenerate — is said to be *well-founded*.

Relationship degeneracy through relatant multiplicity restriction does not violate monotonic inheritance, because it is only permitted for optional relatants. If the relatant multiplicity domain in the superclass includes the value 0, it means that some members of the superclass are permitted to play their role with 0 instances of the relatant class. If we collect all such members in a subset, we can define that subset to be a subclass. Because every member of this subclass plays its role with 0 instances of the relatant, this subclass has effectively made the relationship degenerate. It is not possible to make a relationship with a *mandatory* relatant degenerate through inheritance.

As an example, we might have a subclass lowCapacitySwitch of serviceSwitchingPoint for which we might have an architectural rule which requires it to always obtain its service logic from a serviceControlPoint, in which case it will never have an adjunctProcessor. The subclass lowCapacity-Switch might now use relatant multiplicity restriction to narrow its relatant multiplicity with adjunctProcessor to [0,0], effectively making the relationship degenerate.

If the relatant multiplicity in a relationship is specified in terms of an attribute of the subject, and the domain of the attribute is multi-valued, then for the purposes of specializing that subject into subclasses, the domain of the relatant multiplicity is interpreted to be the one with the widest latitude. For example, if object class A participates in a relationship with object class B, the relatant multiplicity of B with A may be specified as [minB, maxB] where minB and maxB are both attributes of A. The attribute minB may have the discrete domain "2 or 4 or 8" because different instances of A have a different minimum demand for the number of instances of B they require. The attribute maxB may have a continuous domain between 32 and 64 because different instances of A have a different maximum capacity for the number of instances of B they can accommodate. If A is now to be specialized into subclasses using relatant multiplicity restriction, then the restrictable domain of the relatant multiplicity which subclasses of A can work with is [2,64]. By restricting the domains of attributes minB and maxB appropriately, subclasses of A can in effect restrict their relatant multiplicity with B.

This example illustrates the close ties between the principles of relatant multiplicity restriction and attribute domain restriction. The relatant multiplicities for any relationship in which a subject participates are often specified in terms of attributes of the subject. When such an attribute — typically representing an upper or lower bound of the relatant multiplicity — is restricted by a subclass of the subject to a new value out of all possible values in its domain, it could restrict the relatant multiplicity as well.

In our earlier example of the `sonetCrossConnect` object class, the relatant multiplicity of its `terminates` role with `oc1-circuit` was expressed in terms of its `numberOf-OC1-Ports` attribute as `[0,numberOf-OC1-Ports]`. This attribute had the domain of values `{64, 512, 2048}`, because each instance of `sonetCross-Connect` had a different number of OC-1 ports. This meant that the maximum multiplicity for the `terminates` role in all possible instances of `sonetCrossConnect` — that is, the maximum multiplicity of the entire object class — was `[0,2048]`. If this class now undergoes specialization, one of its subclasses might choose to use attribute domain restriction and limit the value of `numberOf-OC1-Ports` to just `{64,512}`, representing a restriction of its original domain of values. In effect, this would also restrict the maximum relatant multiplicity of its terminates role to `[0,512]`. Generally, if the relatant multiplicity is specified as an attribute-defined expression, and this attribute undergoes domain restriction during specialization, our compiler treats relatant multiplicity restriction as equivalent to attribute domain restriction.

17.10. Subject Multiplicity Regression

It is important to get a clear understanding of how relationship multiplicities are affected by specialization and generalization over the inheritance hierarchy. We have seen an example of how a class may specialize by restricting its *relatant multiplicity*. We will now study what happens to *subject multiplicity* when a class specializes.

An Example with Subject Multiplicity Regression

Consider the `access` relationship between a `workstation` object class and a `server` object class. The `workstation` class plays the `accesses` role with the `server` class, which reciprocates with the role `is-accessed-by`. This is a many-to-many relationship, as each `server` could be accessed by multiple `workstations`, and each `workstation` may access multiple `servers`. In the following discussion, the role `accesses` should be broadly interpreted as "has-access-permission-to", and the role `is-accessed-by` as "gives-access-permission-to"; that is, these roles should be viewed in terms of *potential accessibility* rather than as an active set of current connections.

Assume that we have the following rules as part of our administration policy:

- To ensure an equitable distribution of load, each `server` is accessed by at least 6 and no more than `20 workstations`.

- To ensure reasonable network performance, no `workstation` shall access more that 5 `servers`.

This is easily modeled by specifying a multiplicity of `[6,20]` for the `is-accessed-by` role, and `[0,5]` for the `accesses` role. This is shown in Figure 17-10. (In an actual model, these will not be specified as hard-coded constants but in terms of the attributes `minWorkstations` and `maxWorkstations` of the `server` class. Also, the upper limit of the multiplicity of the `server` class would be specified as the interval between 0 and the attribute `maxServers` of `workstation`. If our policy changes, we can simply update these attributes, which will automatically change the multiplicity.)

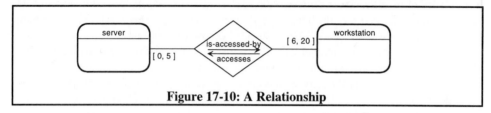

Figure 17-10: A Relationship

Assume now that the `server` object class **specializes-into** two subclasses — an `enterpriseServer` class and a `departmentalServer` class, as shown in Figure 17-11.

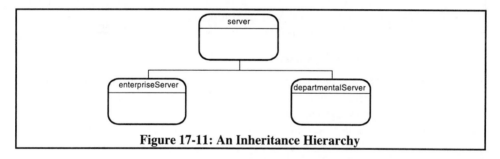

Figure 17-11: An Inheritance Hierarchy

To economize, we may have a policy that we will not purchase a new `enterpriseServer` until there are at least 10 new `workstations` for it to serve. Thus, we have the policy:

• Each `enterpriseServer` must serve at least 10 `workstations`.

Further, we notice that the performance of a `departmentalServer` suffers under heavy loads, so we further rule that

• No `departmentalServer` shall be accessed by more than 12 `workstations`.

None of these additional guidelines conflict with our original policies. This situation is easily modeled: for the `enterpriseServer` subclass, we restrict the domain of the multiplicity of its inherited `is-accessed-by` role with `workstation` from [6,20] to [10,20]. This is permitted by the specialization principle of relatant multiplicity restriction. (In an actual model, we would not have to do this explicitly. We would simply restrict the attribute `minWorkstations` in `enterpriseServer` to one value of all possible values in its domain. Then the relatant multiplicity of `workstation` with `enterpriseServer`, specified in terms of this attribute, would change automatically.) The `departmentalServer` subclass would also change its relatant multiplicity with `workstation` from [6,20] to [6,12] — also permitted by relatant multiplicity restriction — reflecting its new upper limit. This overall situation, a normal one for relatant multiplicity restriction, is modeled in Figure 17-12.

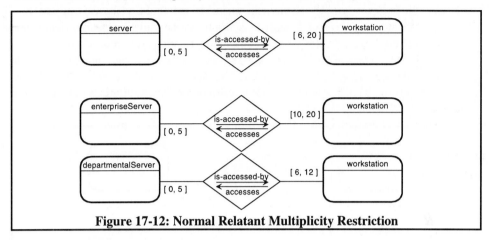

Figure 17-12: Normal Relatant Multiplicity Restriction

Zero-Regression

In this situation, the *subject multiplicity* of [0,5] for the is-accessed-by role stayed the same — it was inherited without change by both enterpriseServer and departmentalServer. This is proper, because the guideline that no workstation shall access more than 5 servers implies both that no workstation shall access more than 5 enterpriseServers and that no workstation shall access more than 5 departmentalServers. Suppose now we wish to ensure redundancy, that is, when a server is down, we still desire each workstation to have access to at least one other server. We further specify the additional policy:

• Each workstation shall access at least 2 servers.

This is easily modeled: we change the subject multiplicity for the is-accessed-by role from [0,5] to [2,5]. However, it is instructive to examine the behavior of this multiplicity under specialization.

If we permit enterpriseServer to inherit from server this subject multiplicity for the is-accessed-by role without change, it would inherit the value [2,5]. This would imply "each workstation accesses at least 2 enterpriseServers", that is, that the *minimum* number of enterpriseServers which a workstation is required to access is 2. If we also permit departmentalServer to inherit the same value, it would additionally imply that the *minimum* number of departmentalServers which a workstation is required to access is also 2. In effect, we would be making the statement that "Each workstation accesses at least 2 enterpriseServers *and* at least 2 departmentalServers" for a total minimum of 4 servers. This is clearly not in conformance with our stated policy.

How many enterpriseServers must a workstation access? We know that a workstation must access at least 2 servers. However, both (or all, if more than 2) could be departmentalServers. Hence, the *minimum* number of enterpriseServers a workstation *must* access is 0. The same argument applies to departmental-Servers. The servers accessed by a workstation could all be enterprise-Servers; as long as it accesses at least 2, it would not be violating policy. Hence, the *minimum* number of departmentalServers a workstation *must* access *is also* 0.

Thus, the *subject multiplicity* of the is-accessed-by role inherited by both enterpriseServer and departmentalServer from their server superclass is not [2,5] but [0,5]. Clearly, this is *not* a restriction of the multiplicity domain. This is represented in Figure 17-13.

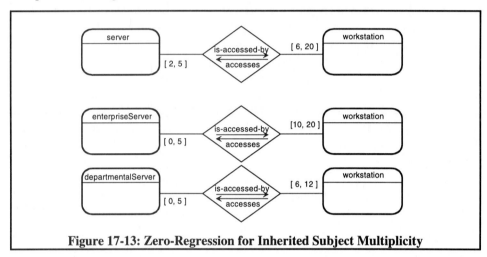

Figure 17-13: Zero-Regression for Inherited Subject Multiplicity

The reason subject multiplicity drops to include a zero minimum becomes apparent on a little reflection. Each time a superclass specializes, all of its subclasses are substitutable for the superclass. The number of choices which could be substituted for the superclass has multiplied: any of its subclasses could fulfill the role. Thus, if some minimum number of members of the superclass are required to participate in one of its relationships, that minimum number can now be made up of members of only one of its subclasses, or members of only another of its subclasses, or some combination of members of all its subclasses. Thus, the minimum number of members required to participate in the relationship *from any one subclass* is zero. This phenomenon occurs because, with each specialization, we now have a wider range of instances which could be used to make up the required minimum number of superclass instances. As we said earlier, specialization is an "or" relationship: if specialization is disjoint and complete, then any member of the superclass is *either* a member of its first subclass *or* a member of its second subclass *or*... and so on.

This creates a new specialization rule: even if a superclass exhibits a non-zero minimum for the domain of its subject multiplicity in any relationship, *all its subclasses must drop that minimum down to zero.* This phenomenon is termed *Zero-Regression*, since the lower bound of the subject multiplicity "regresses" to zero.

We do not have to specify zero-regression explicitly: it is automatically applied by our compiler. Every time the compiler sees a superclass specialize, it examines all relationships in which that superclass is a participant. If the subject multiplicity for that superclass in any relationship has a non-zero lower bound, that relationship is bequeathed to all the subclasses (though relationship inheritance) with its lower bound changed to zero.

Overriding Multiplicity Regression Defaults

It is possible to override the zero-regression of any subject multiplicity with an explicitly specified non-zero value for the lower bound. For example, we could specify the policy guideline that

- Of all the `servers` accessed by any `workstation`, at least one must be its local `departmentalServer`.

In this case the subject multiplicity of the `is-accessed-by` role which `departmentalServer` plays with `workstation` changes from [0,5] to [1,5], since each `workstation` now accesses at least one `departmentalServer`.

The upper bound of the multiplicity domain is not affected by specialization. If a finite upper bound is specified for the subject multiplicity of a superclass, then that maximum can now be made up of instances from some combination of all its subclasses. Hence, the upper bound limiting the participation *of any one subclass* is still the same upper bound which limited the participation of the superclass.

Each subclass, by default, inherits the subject multiplicity domain from its superclass with its upper bound unchanged. However, if any of its sibling subclasses has explicitly overridden the zero-regressed lower bound for its own subject multiplicity, then that value is subtracted from the upper bound for all other subclasses. Thus, if a workstation can access no more than 5 servers of which at least 1 must be a `departmentalServer`, then a `workstation` can access no more than 4 `enterpriseServers`. The override of the zero-regressed lower bound in `departmentalServer` to [1,5] changes the subject multiplicity of `enterprise-Server` to [0,4]. This does not have to be explicitly specified, as the calculation is automatically applied by our compiler.

It is, of course, possible to explicitly lower this upper bound in the subject multiplicity as well, just as it was possible in relatant multiplicity. For example, if we wish to enforce certain security policies for corporate data stored on `enterpriseServers` and provide access only on a need-to-know basis, we could specify the additional guideline

- No `workstation` shall access more than one `enterprise-Server`.

This changes the multiplicity of the `accesses` role which `workstation` plays with `enterpriseServer` from [0,5] to [0,1]. This situation is depicted in Figure 17-14.

In Figure 17-14, the subject multiplicity of `enterpriseServer` is [0,1], which bears no apparent relation to the subject multiplicity of that relationship in its superclass, which was [2,5]. The constraints on the superclass still hold: it is still the case that a `workstation` shall access at least 2 and no more than 5 servers. The addi-

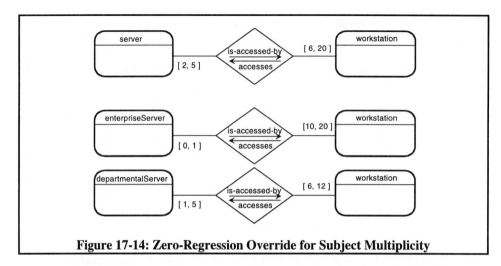

Figure 17-14: Zero-Regression Override for Subject Multiplicity

tional constraints on the same relationships in the subclasses, namely that at least 1 of these `servers` shall be a `departmentalServer` and no more than 1 shall be an `enterpriseServer`, do not conflict with the constraint on the superclass relationship.

In particular, it should be noted that from the inherited relationship in the subclasses, there is no way to recover the original subject multiplicity for the same relationship in the superclass. The value `[2,5]` for the subject multiplicity of `server` cannot be reconstructed from the values `[0,1]` and `[1,5]` for the subject multiplicities of `enterpriseServer` and `departmentalServer` in the same relationship. It is important to note that once relationships are inherited by all subclasses of a subject, we cannot forget about the subject multiplicity in the superclass. We still need to maintain and work with the subject multiplicity bounds in the superclass, applying them as superordinate participation constraints governing the conjunction of all the relationship instances of the subclasses.

How Subject Multiplicity Regression Works

We know that *relatant* multiplicities behave differently: in any relationship, the relatant multiplicity of the superclass must be the union of all the relatant multiplicities for the subclasses. Subclasses can only restrict the domain of the relatant multiplicity to a subset of their original domain. However, no such statement can be made about *subject* multiplicity. If the lower bound for the subject multiplicity in the superclass is not already zero, subclasses "expand" the domain at the lower end because of zero-regression. Because it is also permissible to explicitly lower the upper bound of the subject multiplicity, subclasses could "restrict" the domain at the upper end. The behavior of subject multiplicities does not show *domain restriction*. Rather, it exhibits *regression* on both the upper and lower bounds on the multiplicity interval.

Some observations can be made about the nature of this regression. It must be the case that the lower bound of the subject multiplicity in the subclass (if explicitly specified to override zero-regression) cannot exceed the corresponding lower bound in the superclass. For example, since we have already said that a `workstation` must access at least 2 `servers`, then we cannot also say that a `workstation` must access at least 3 `departmentalServers`. Since each `departmentalServer` also **is-a** `server`, such a statement would imply that a `workstation` must access at least 3 `servers`, which is not the case. By the same token, it also must be the case that the upper bound of the subject multiplicity in the subclass cannot exceed the corresponding upper bound in the superclass. Since we have said that a `workstation` can access no more than 5 `servers`, then we cannot also say that a `workstation` can access no more than 6 `departmentalServers`. If we permitted this, an instance of `workstation` which accessed 6 `departmentalServers` would satisfy the subclass constraint but in doing so would violate the superclass constraint. Furthermore, it must also be the case that the sum of the lower bounds in all the subclasses cannot exceed the upper bound in the superclass. Since we have said that a `workstation` can access no more than 5 `servers`, then we cannot also say that a workstation must access at least 3 `departmental-Servers` and at least 3 `enterpriseServers`.

The only permissible way that a subclass can affect subject multiplicity is to "regress" it at both ends of the domain. The lower bound of the subject multiplicity, if not already zero in the superclass, regresses to zero by default in the subclass. If we wish to override zero-regression by explicitly specifying a non-zero lower bound, this must still be lower or equal to the lower bound in the superclass. The upper bound of the subject multiplicity in the superclass stays the same by default in the subclass. It can also be explicitly regressed in the subclass to any lower non-zero value (but obviously, not lower than the new lower bound).

The subclass is permitted to use this subject multiplicity regression as a basis of specialization. If, for example, instead of using any other basis of specialization, we had chosen to *define* the class `enterpriseServer` as "that subclass of `server` of which a `workstation` can access no more than 1", then we would be using the change in its subject multiplicity in its relationship with `workstation` as the basis of specialization. This specialization mode is called *Specialization by Subject Multiplicity Regression*.

One caveat must be applied with respect to subject multiplicity regression: the mechanism only applies when any specialization proceeding from the superclass creates *at least two* subclasses. If the superclass specializes into only one subclass, then there are no other sibling classes with which participation in the relationship can be "*or*-ed", and thus the lone subclass inherits subject multiplicity without any regression. However, if at any level of the hierarchy we create only one subclass as the result of a specialization, it is perhaps better to redesign the hierarchy to eliminate this specialization entirely. In practice, such a situation is so rare that, while we recognize this possibility, we will ignore it in the formal statement of subject multiplicity regression. We will assume that every specialization creates more than one subclass.

While it was legal for a subclass to use relatant multiplicity restriction for optional relationships to make an inherited relationship degenerate, it is not legal to use subject multiplicity regression for this purpose. When a subclass regresses the lower bound of its inherited subject multiplicity automatically to zero and wishes to explicitly regress the upper bound also, the upper bound can only be regressed to a non-zero value. If subject multiplicity for the subclass were [0,0], the subclass would effectively cease participation in the relationship, thereby violating monotonic inheritance.

If a situation arises where a subject subclass "must" regress its subject multiplicity to [0,0] because the semantics of the subclass "simply cannot" permit it to participate in the inherited relationship, it suggests that the relationship specification has been applied too high in the inheritance hierarchy. Rather than assigning the relationship to the superclass, it is better to respecify the relationship as a set of isomorphic relationships assigned to some of its subclasses one level down. With this change, the non-participating sibling subclass will not inherit the relationship at all, while its participating siblings will continue to enjoy well-founded relationships with the relatant. Thus, monotonic inheritance will not be violated.

When our compiler sees subject multiplicity regression in any specialization, it checks that the explicitly specified lower and upper bounds, if any, for the subject multiplicity in the subclass do not exceed the corresponding lower and upper bounds for the superclass. Further, it ensures that the sum of the lower bounds of the subject multiplicities for the same relationship of all its known sibling subclasses, when augmented by the lower bound in the specificand subclass, does not exceed the upper bound in the superclass. If it does, the compiler rejects the subclass definition.

17.11. Relatant Specialization

There is yet another mode in which a subclass may modify its participation in an inherited relationship. Through relationship inheritance, a subclass of a subject normally inherits the relatant with which its superclass participates in a relationship. We now consider what happens if the *relatant* also undergoes specialization. If this happens, the subclasses of the relatant inherit its relationship with the subject. If the subject has *n* subclasses and the relatant has *m* subclasses, the number of implicit relationships generated by normal relationship inheritance is *n+m*: *n* relationships from the subclasses of the subject with the relatant, and *m* from the subclasses of the relatant with the subject.

Relationship inheritance does *not* require all the subclasses of the subject to relate to *all* the subclasses of the relatant. If the relatant is optional, some subclass of the subject might turn the inherited relationship into a degenerate relationship. However, if the relatant is mandatory, relationship inheritance requires each instance of a subject subclass to relate to *an* instance or instances of the relatant. If any specialization proceeding from the relatant class is complete, then every member of the relatant class is also a member of at least one of its subclasses. Thus, each subclass of the subject must relate to at least one subclass of the relatant. As long as a subject subclass participates in the relationship with *at least one* relatant subclass, it satisfies relationship inheritance. Of course, it may participate in a relationship with multiple relatant subclasses if it so chooses.

An Example of Relatant Specialization

To illustrate this concept, we revisit our example of the subscription service between the subscriber and networkService object classes. In Figure 17-7, we created subclasses of networkService such as basic-800-Service, virtual-

PrivateNetworkService, and so on, and subclasses of subscriber such as smallBusinessSubscriber, midGrowthSubscriber, and so on. Assume that, instead of these immediate subclasses, we had first created the intermediate subclasses corporateSubscriber and residentialSubscriber, and the intermediate subclasses corporateService and residentialService. The descendant classes basic-800-Service, virtualPrivateNetworkService, and so on, would now be subclasses of corporateService, while residentialService may have its own subclasses such as callReturn, callingNumber-Identification, callWaiting, and callForwarding.

For the purposes of this example, assume that all specializations are complete, that is, there is no other kind of subscriber and no other kind of networkService aside from ones we defined. Since each subclass of subscriber must subscribe-to at least one networkService, and since every networkService also belongs to at least one subclass of networkService, each subclass of subscriber must relate to at least one subclass of networkService. In effect, we "permit" a descendant class to participate in the relationship with only selected descendants of its relatant. It is possible for the residentialSubscriber to play the subscribes-to role with only residentialService, and corporateSubscriber to play the sub-scribes-to role with only corporateService.

If we indicate to the model information base which selected descendants of the relatant are chosen by each descendant of the subject, the run-time environment will permit only those relationships to be instantiated. If we formally restrict the sub-scribes-to role played by the residentialSubscriber subclass of sub-scriber to only the residentialService subclass of networkService, the model information base will consider the relationship residentialSubscriber subscribes-to corporateService illegal and will reject any attempt to instantiate this relationship.

Restricting the participation of a subclass in an inherited relationship to only selected descendants of the relatant may be used as a basis of specialization. This is known as *Specialization by Relatant Specialization*. Figure 17-15 illustrates this principle.

17.12. Relationship Attribute Restriction

When a subclass inherits a relationship, it inherits any attributes the relationship may have as well. We permit a mode of specialization in which subclasses may restrict the domain of this relationship attribute. This is similar to specialization by attribute domain restriction, except that the attribute undergoing domain restriction belongs not to the specializing class but to one of its *relationships*.

To illustrate this concept, consider the testing relationship between the cir-cuit object class and the lineTest object class (which may be a component of a lineTestEquipment object class). In this relationship, the circuit object class plays the is-tested-by role with lineTest, the reciprocal role being tests. This is a many-to-many relationship, since each circuit may be tested using different lineTests. Each test is executed according to the maintenance schedule for that circuit:

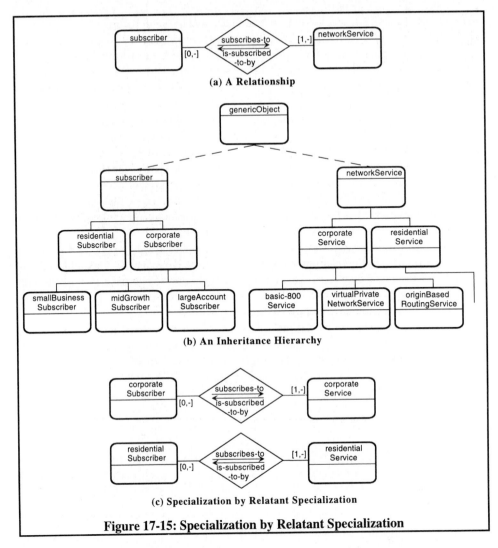

(a) A Relationship

(b) An Inheritance Hierarchy

(c) Specialization by Relatant Specialization

Figure 17-15: Specialization by Relatant Specialization

line integrity tests may be run at least once daily, line quality and bit error rate tests may be run at least once weekly, and so on. Thus, each test that can be run on each circuit has its own test frequency, which is properly modeled as the *relationship attribute* test-Frequency of the testing relationship.

Assume that some circuits are provisioned as dedicated lines for use by a large corporate subscriber in its private network. Because these circuits are mission-critical to the client, we designate them priority circuits. We also require that, while ordinary circuits have bit error rate tests done at least once weekly, priority circuits must have a bit error rate test done at least three times weekly. Thus, the domain of the test-Frequency attribute of the tests relationship, whose value is normally "one or more per week" for an ordinary circuit, changes to "three or more per week" for priority circuits. Since the value "three or more" is a subset of the domain "one or more", the relationship attribute has undergone a restriction. In effect, the `priorityCircuit` subclass of `circuit` has restricted the domain of the `testFrequency` attribute of its `tests` relationship with the `bitErrorRateTest` subclass of `lineTest`. If such a restriction is used as a basis of specialization, it is called *Specialization by Relationship Attribute Restriction*. Figure 17-16 illustrates this concept.

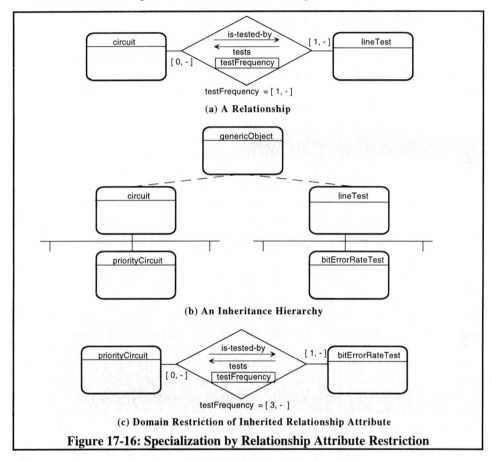

(a) A Relationship

(b) An Inheritance Hierarchy

(c) Domain Restriction of Inherited Relationship Attribute

Figure 17-16: Specialization by Relationship Attribute Restriction

As another example of this specialization mode, consider the situation of file servers which allow anonymous remote users to retrieve data files from them. We could model this as the `retrieval` relationship between a `user` object class and an `ftpServer` object class, the roles being `retrieves-from` and `supplies-to`. Clearly, each instance of `ftpServer` would offer different access privileges to different users; we might model this as the `accessPermission` attribute of the relationship. For the `anonymousUser` subclass of `user`, the value of the `accessPermission` attribute in its inherited `retrieval` relationship with `ftpServer` might be `readOnly`; for the `localDeveloper` subclass it might be `readWrite`, and for the `sysAdmin` subclass it might be `readWriteReboot`. Thus, each subclass of `user` participating in the `re-trieval` relationship is defined by the restricted domain of the `accessPermission` attribute, which belongs not to the `user` class (since a `user` could be a `local-Developer` on one `ftpServer` and an `anonymousUser` on another) but to the `re-trieval` relationship it participates in with `ftpServer`.

17.13. Relatant Attribute Restriction

The specialization modes of relationship addition, relatant multiplicity restriction, subject multiplicity regression, relatant specialization, and relationship attribute restriction are important, as they commonly occur in network models. In addition, there are other relationship-based specialization modes which are not as commonly encountered, but which we mention for completeness of the modeling methodology.

The specialization mode called *Specialization by Relatant Attribute Restriction* is closely tied to specialization by relatant specialization. To illustrate this mode, consider the example of the `leasing` relationship between `dedicatedCircuit` and `sub-scriber`. In this relationship, `subscriber` plays the `leases` role with `dedicatedCircuit`, the reciprocal role being `is-leased-by`. The `subscriber` object class may possess the attribute `priority`, which could take values in the domain `{high, low}`, possibly based on the total volume of business generated by the account. For the dedicated circuits leased by a high-priority subscriber, we create a special subclass of `dedicatedCircuit` called `priorityCircuit`. We might want to create an explicit subclass for these circuits because we might wish to treat them differently (for example, we might want to test them more often).

We could also create a subclass of `subscriber` called `priority-Subscriber` based on restricting the domain of its `priority` attribute to `{high}`. If we did this, the basis of specialization for creating `priorityCircuit` would be relatant specialization by restricting its inherited `is-leased-by` role only with `prioritySubscriber`. However, for several reasons we may not wish to explicitly create the subclass `prioritySubscriber` (for example, there may be no new properties added in such a subclass). We might be content to simply keep `subscriber` as a leaf class in our model.

Under these circumstances, to specify the basis of specialization for the creation of `priorityCircuit`, we must indicate that it plays its inherited `is-leased-by` role *only with* those instances of `subscriber` whose `priority` is `high`. This mode of specialization is called *Specialization by Relatant Attribute Restriction*. This is similar to specialization by attribute domain restriction, with the difference that the attribute undergoing domain restriction does not belong to the specializing class but to another class coupled with it through a relationship. Figure 17-17 illustrates this specialization mode.

In general, the new domain to which the relatant attributes have been restricted may be specified in terms of constants, or in terms of other variables. For example, it is permitted to restrict the domain of a relatant attribute to a value defined by an attribute of the subject. This applies in the other direction as well: when a subject specializes by ordi-

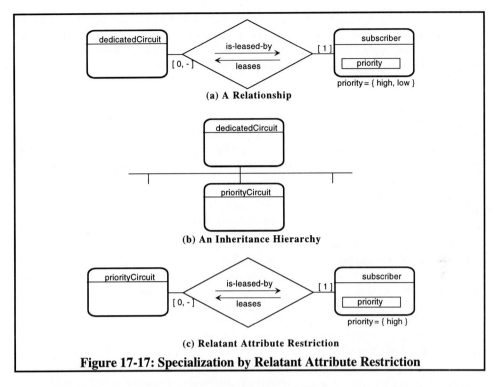

(a) A Relationship

(b) An Inheritance Hierarchy

(c) Relatant Attribute Restriction

Figure 17-17: Specialization by Relatant Attribute Restriction

nary attribute domain restriction, it is permitted to specify the restricted domain to a value defined by an attribute of the relatant.

Specialization by relatant attribute restriction is also closely tied to specialization by subject multiplicity regression. As we have emphasized, all non-trivial values for the end-points of any multiplicity domain should be expressed in terms of attributes. Both the lower and upper bounds of the subject multiplicity could be expressed using some attributes of the relatant class. If, during specialization, we choose to appropriately restrict those particular relatant attributes, we could effectively regress the subject multiplicity. If a subclass is created using such subject multiplicity regression, it can often also be created by applying relatant attribute restriction on those attributes of the relatant which define subject multiplicity. In many cases, both these modes turn out to be equivalent, and either could be used.

Additionally, there are other specialization modes which enable object classes to specialize by restricting or expanding domain values in their relatants. These are analogous to the specialization modes which object classes use to restrict or expand domain values in themselves. The new modes are called *Specialization by Relatant Argument Contravariance*, *Specialization by Relatant Result Covariance*, and *Specialization by Relatant Capsule Fixing*. Although these are permitted by the methodology, they are rarely encountered in practice.

There are no relatant specialization modes analogous to the *addition* modes which classes use for themselves; that is, there are no modes called Specialization by Relatant

Attribute Addition, Specialization by Relatant Function Addition, or Specialization by Relatant Capsule Addition. This is because it is impossible to add anything to the relatant without first creating a subclass for it. If a subclass is indeed created, then these situations become equivalent to Specialization by Relatant Specialization.

17.14. Specialization Principles

We summarize all our relationship-based specialization modes as additional principles of specialization theory. These are called *relationship addition, relatant multiplicity restriction, subject multiplicity regression, relatant specialization, relationship attribute restriction,* and *relatant attribute restriction*:

Specialization Principle:	*A descendant class may add a new relationship* ***(Relationship Addition).***

Specialization Principle:	*A descendant class may restrict the domain of the relatant multiplicity in a relationship inherited from an ancestral class* ***(Relatant Multiplicity Restriction).***

Specialization Principle:	*A descendant class may regress the domain of the subject multiplicity in a relationship inherited from an ancestral class* ***(Subject Multiplicity Regression).***

Specialization Principle:	*A descendant class may restrict its participation in a relationship inherited from an ancestral class to selected descendants of the relatant class* ***(Relatant Specialization).***

Specialization Principle:	*A descendant class may restrict the domain of a relationship attribute in a relationship inherited from an ancestral class* ***(Relationship Attribute Restriction).***

Specialization Principle:	*A descendant class may restrict the domain of an attribute of a relatant class in a relationship inherited from an ancestral class* ***(Relatant Attribute Restriction).***

Based on our knowledge of the effect of specialization on relationship multiplicities, we restate a more specific version of the relationship principle of relatant multiplicity inheritance along with a formal statement about *subject multiplicity inheritance*:

> **Relationship Principle:**   *A descendant class inherits by default the relatant multiplicity for each inherited relationship, which it may restrict (**Relatant Multiplicity Inheritance**).*
>
> *A descendant class inherits the subject multiplicity for each inherited relationship with its lower bound regressed to zero by default, which it may override, and its upper bound unchanged by default, which it may regress to a non-zero value (**Subject Multiplicity Inheritance**).*

We know from the principle of relatant specialization that the subclasses of a subject may restrict their participation in a relationship only to selected subclasses of the relatant. The principle does not, however, specify a lower bound on how many descendants of the relatant each descendant of the subclasses could select. Taken to its logical extreme, this principle would permit us to specialize the relatant without having the subject's subclasses participate in the relationship with *any* subclass of the relatant. This is not permitted in specialization theory if the relatant is mandatory and has specialized completely with respect to a given basis; if it were permitted, it would be equivalent to the subclasses of the subject degenerating an inherited relationship with a mandatory relatant. To prevent this from happening, we formally state the relationship principle of *specialized relatant inheritance*:

> **Relationship Principle:**   *A descendant class participates in a relationship inherited from an ancestral class with at least one descendant of a mandatory relatant class, if any specialization of the relatant class is complete (**Specialized Relatant Inheritance**).*

If a mandatory relatant has *not* specialized completely, there may not be an appropriate subclass of the relatant with which each subclass of the subject can play its role. In this case, each descendant of the subject must play its role with at least the relatant class itself. We need not formally state another relationship principle to this effect, as this requirement is already covered in the principle of relationship inheritance. Further, if the relatant is optional, then a subclass of the subject may turn its inherited relationship into a degenerate relationship. Specialized relatant inheritance does not apply, as we have covered this situation in the principle of relatant multiplicity restriction.

Specialized relatant inheritance places a lower bound on the number of selected subclasses of a completely specialized mandatory relatant to which an inherited relationship may be restricted through relatant specialization — at least one relatant subclass must be selected. This principle is valid for all specializations at multiple levels descending from the relatant. This can be proved recursively, since each time a mandatory relatant specializes completely, at least one of the subclasses so created also becomes a mandatory relatant. This principle is important as it preserves monotonic inheritance. Without this principle, the substitutability of every descendant for its ancestors in their defined relationships would be destroyed.

Relationship-based specialization modes are the mechanisms whereby *fully abstract classes* interact with other classes in the object model. As per our definition, fully abstract classes can have neither instances nor members, and so it might appear quite pointless to specify them. However, their utility lies in the fact that other classes participate in relationships with them. Even though such a relationship can never have relationship instances, other classes can use this relationship to further specialize themselves using any of the relationship-based modes of specialization. Thus, a fully abstract class provides a formalization of any abstract notion in the model (such as `service` or `referenceModel`) which, though non-instantiable, creates a baseline against which other instantiable classes (such as `protocolEntity`) can specialize themselves via their relationship with it.

Another View of Relatant Specialization

To emphasize the internal logical consistency between the various relationship-based specialization modes, we offer a perspective of how relatant specialization may also be equivalently expressed in terms of subject multiplicity regression and relatant multiplicity restriction. Relatant specialization can be viewed as a two-step process: first, the subject class specializes, and bequeaths to all its subclasses the subject multiplicity with the lower bound regressed to zero and the relatant multiplicity without change. If n subclasses are created in this specialization, there are now n different implicit relationships: one between each subject subclass and the relatant class.

We now change our perspective and focus on the relatant class, making that our subject class, and allow that to specialize. Each one of *its* subclasses now inherits n relationships, with the lower bound of their *relatant* multiplicity already being zero. This means that those relatants are optional. A subclass might now use relatant multiplicity restriction for *some* of these optional inherited relatants — those with which it cannot have a "meaningful relationship", as it were — to restrict the relatant multiplicity domain such that the upper bound equals the lower bound. Both bounds are now set to zero for some inherited relatant multiplicities, making the relationships degenerate. We now have an inherited relationship between subclasses in which one of the relationship multiplicities is $[0,0]$, implying that no relationship exists between those classes. All other classes for which multiplicities remain non-trivial are the specialized subclasses of the relatant with which the specialized subclasses of the subject participate in their inherited relationship; the remaining well-founded relationships thus demonstrate relatant specialization. Figure 17-18 illustrates this perspective.

We will not formally state the principles of Specialization by Relatant Attribute Restriction, Relatant Argument Contravariance, Relatant Result Covariance, and Relatant Capsule Fixing. They are very similar to the corresponding modes for object classes themselves mentioned in Chapter 6. These modes can be applied in the modeling methodology when appropriate.

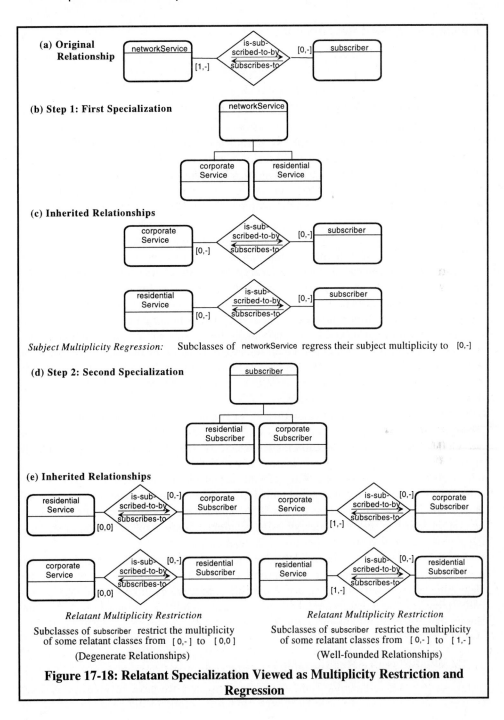

Figure 17-18: Relatant Specialization Viewed as Multiplicity Restriction and Regression

Implicit and Defined Relationships

It is also important to understand the difference between *defined* relationships and *implicit* relationships. We specify the difference between these as follows:

- All relationships between object classes explicitly created by relationship assignment are *defined* relationships;

- All relationships available to an object class through inheritance are *implicit* relationships, *unless* during specialization the object class explicitly uses relatant multiplicity restriction, subject multiplicity regression, relatant specialization, or relationship attribute restriction to modify the default characteristics of the inherited relationship. If it does, then that inherited relationship is also a *defined* relationship.

The importance of this distinction becomes apparent on closer examination of the relationship principle of Monotonic Relationship Inheritance, which forbids an object class from canceling any inherited relationship *defined* for its ancestors. This implies that an object class must be substitutable for its ancestors in all relationships *defined* for them. However, it does not require an object class to be substitutable for its ancestors in any of their *implicit* relationships. For example, the subclass `residentialSubscriber` must be substitutable for its superclass `subscriber` in the original defined relationship of Figure 17-18(a), but need not be substitutable for `subscriber` in the implicit relationships of Figure 17-18(c). In particular, because of relatant specialization, it is legal for `residentialSubscriber` not to be substitutable for `subscriber` in its implicit relationship with `corporateService`; this is because, as we see in Figure 17-18(e), this becomes a degenerate relationship.

As a special note, we mention that for a class participating in any defined *involute* relationship (in which a class participates in a relationship with itself), we forbid any of the relationship-based specialization modes which use that relationship. For example, if object class A participates in a relationship R with itself, it is illegal for A to specialize into a subclass A' on the basis of, say, relatant specialization with itself through R. In our experience, this creates too many problems for our model compiler, and the semantics of this situation are not always clear. Of course, A can continue to specialize using any of the several other specialization modes, or using relationship-based specialization modes using any of its non-involute relationships with other classes.

To explain the various specialization modes, the figures of this chapter have depicted both defined and implicit relationships in our class relationship diagrams. In the diagrammatic representation of an actual network model we would not draw implicit relationships. Through relationship inheritance, their availability is automatic in descendant classes that accept all multiplicity defaults.

17.15. What Else Is a Relationship?

In this section, we re-examine some modeling constructs we have covered in previous chapters and show how they can be brought under the rubric of the general relationship model defined in this chapter.

Aggregation

It should be apparent that the treatment of relationships in this chapter is a generalization of the treatment of aggregation in Chapter 7. In fact, aggregation relationships can be treated exactly like all other relationships. The roles of all aggregation relationships are always `is-a-part-of` and `has-as-a-part`. Because all aggregation relationships have the same role-pair, they are isomorphic with each other. In fact, the use of this role-pair is the defining characteristic of all aggregation relationships.

Component and aggregate multiplicity specifications are simply a special case of relatant multiplicity specifications. If an aggregation relationship is exclusive, it is one-to-many; that is, while the component multiplicity may be a range of values, the aggregate multiplicity is always one. If the relationship is inclusive, the aggregate multiplicity may also be a range of values, since it is possible that the same component object `is-a-part-of` more than one aggregate object. Furthermore, the roles `is-a-part-of` and `has-as-a-part` are transitive. For a transitive role, the relatant of a relatant is also a relatant; this is true of aggregation relationships, as the component of a component is also a component. Finally, they are relationships with no relationship attributes. Because the `has-as-a-part` role is transitive and, in an exclusive-aggregation relationship, also one-to-many, such relationships belong to a special category of relationships which are *hierarchically structurable*. This combination of special properties is what allows us to concatenate pairs of aggregation relationships together to construct a rooted aggregation hierarchy.

The aggregation principles of Composition Inheritance and Decomposition Inheritance are simply special cases of Relationship Inheritance. The aggregation principle of Monotonic Aggregation Inheritance, which forbids descendants from canceling inherited components or aggregates, is simply a restatement of the corresponding relationship principle of Monotonic Relationship Inheritance. The aggregation principle of Component Multiplicity Inheritance is also simply a restatement of the relationship principle of Relatant Multiplicity Inheritance. Diagrammatically, our convention of the little parabola we draw on the lines representing aggregation relationships may just as well be replaced by a relationship diamond containing the `is-a-part-of` and `has-as-a-part` role arrows.

Figure 17-19 illustrates how aggregation may be treated as a relationship. (In this figure, `<aggregateClass>` and `<componentClass>` are not actual object classes, but are metavariables which stand for the names of aggregate and component classes of each actual aggregation relationship.) One such relationship must be defined for each aggregation, with the actual aggregate and component class names being appropriately substituted.

In Chapter 7, we indicated in an aggregation principle that if an aggregate class specialized, its subclasses inherited the component multiplicity with the component class. They were, of course, permitted to restrict this inherited multiplicity. We left undefined the situation of what happened to the component multiplicity if the *component* class specialized. Based on our knowledge of relationships, we know now that if the component class is the class undergoing specialization, the component multiplicity in the aggregation relationship corresponds to the subject multiplicity. Thus, its lower bound undergoes

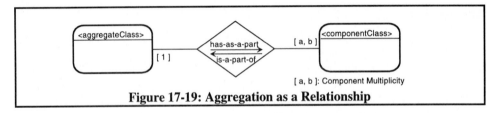

Figure 17-19: Aggregation as a Relationship

zero-regression in the subclass. We can now conclude that an inherited aggregation relationship between an aggregate and any *subclass* of its component must have a component multiplicity in which the lower bound has regressed to zero by default, and the upper bound is unchanged by default. At the discretion of the subclass, the zero lower bound can be overridden, and the upper bound can be regressed. As an example, the component multiplicity for all the aggregation relationships Figure 7-7(b) must be [0,numberOf-CardSlots].

It should also be apparent that component classes can use the principle of relatant multiplicity restriction to turn an inherited inclusive-aggregation relationship into an exclusive-aggregation relationship. Assume it is possible that the same instance of a sharable component class is-a-part-of one or more aggregate objects. However, subclasses of the component may choose to be non-sharable: it is legal for them to turn the inherited relatant multiplicity with the aggregate class from [1,-] to exactly [1], thus making the aggregation relationship exclusive. We can also now permit a situation which we did not consider in Chapter 7: the concept of an *optional aggregate*. This arises when it is possible for a component object to exist on its own, without necessarily being a part of an aggregate object. If component instances can occur as "free-standing" objects, the aggregate class is considered *optional*. In this case, the multiplicity of the aggregateClass in Figure 17-19 must include 0 in its domain, for example, [0,1] for an optional exclusive-aggregation relationship or [0,-] for an optional inclusive-aggregation relationship.

We might be tempted to define all aggregation relationships the easy way: that is, to specify just one aggregation relationship as an *involute* relationship for the highest possible class in the inheritance hierarchy (genericObject). This would permit any object to contain any other object as a component. If this is defined at the highest possible level, all object classes will inherit that single aggregation relationship through relationship inheritance. As useful classes derive from genericObject, they could use relatant multiplicity restriction and relatant specialization to restrict their components to the set of those useful classes they choose to contain.

Specifying aggregation relationships in this way is not, however, advisable, first because it overloads the run-time mechanism in our model to resolve inherited relationships, but more importantly, because it does not convey the semantics of specific aggregations we wish to model. It would require too many descendant classes to turn too many inherited aggregations into degenerate relationships. It is best to continue to define individual aggregation relationships between pairs of object classes with specific multiplicities as required by their semantics.

Henceforth, it should generally be borne in mind that aggregation is not semantically different from any other relationship. When we consider general relationships in subsequent chapters, we also include aggregation. In particular, the roles `is-a-part-of` and `has-as-a-part` are also registered in our model information base as a role-pair, just like all other relationship role-pairs. In subsequent chapters, when we define operations on relationship roles, those operations will be just as applicable to these roles as any other relationship roles.

One important consequence of treating aggregation like any other relationship is that all aggregation-based modes of specialization become special cases of relationship-based modes of specialization and can be specified using the same formal mechanisms. For example, specialization by component or aggregate addition is formally specified using the mode of relationship addition; specialization by component multiplicity restriction is formally specified using the mode of relatant multiplicity restriction; and specialization by component and aggregate specialization are formally specified using the mode of relatant specialization. In addition, new specialization modes are available, such as specialization by "component attribute restriction", arising from relatant attribute restriction. The relationship used in all these specializations should be any of the aggregation relationships in which the specializing subclass participates in the appropriate role.

Protocol Layerings

The operational coupling between protocol entities defined in Chapter 15 is also a relationship. The `protocolLayering` relationship is an *involute* relationship on the `protocolEntity` object class. The roles of the relationship are `layers-above` and `layers-below`, and the `demultiplexPoint` parameter is a relationship attribute. This is a *many-to-many* relationship, since a given protocol entity could layer above or below more than one protocol entity. The relatant multiplicity for both the upper and lower protocol entities is `[0,-]`; the lower bound must be zero because, in a protocol stack, no entities layer above the highest entity or below the lowest entity. This is illustrated in Figure 17-20.

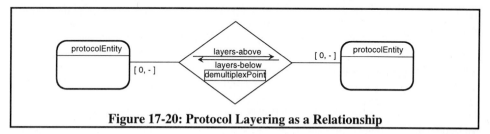

Figure 17-20: Protocol Layering as a Relationship

Protocol-Service Provision

The operational coupling between protocol entities and the services they provide, defined in Chapter 12, can also be modeled as the `serviceProvision` relationship. In this relationship, `protocolEntity` plays the role `provides` with `service`, and `service` plays the role `is-provided-by` with `protocolEntity`. This is a *many-to-*

many relationship, since it is possible that a single `protocolEntity` provides
more than one `service` and also that a single `service` is-provided-by the co-
operative action of more than one `protocolEntity`. As noted before, `service` is a
fully abstract class whose descendants are useful only to participate in relationships with
`protocolEntity` classes, so that descendants of `protocolEntity` can be created,
if necessary, using a mode of specialization involving this relationship.

Figure 17-21 illustrates this relationship, along with a more specialized form of
the same relationship which may become available to descendants of its participant
classes through relationship inheritance, relatant multiplicity restriction, and relatant specialization.

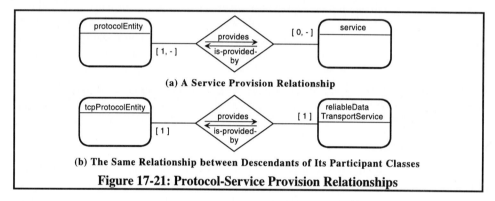

(a) A Service Provision Relationship

(b) The Same Relationship between Descendants of Its Participant Classes

Figure 17-21: Protocol-Service Provision Relationships

The relationship between the `protocolEntity` object class and the
`referenceModel` object class may be specified in a similar manner. While
`referenceModel` is also a fully abstract class (having descendants but no members), it
participates in a relationship with `protocolEntity`; the utility of this is that
`protocolEntity` may use this relationship to specialize further. For example, the
`clnpProtocolEntity` descendant of `protocolEntity` may restrict this inherited
relationship to the `osiReferenceModel` subclass of `referenceModel`, using relatant specialization.

17.16. Associations versus Relationships

We introduce here the exact distinction between relationships and associations. All along,
we have called linkages such as inheritance and instantiation "associations", while the
couplings of this chapter have been called "relationships". Some modeling methodologies
recognize no difference between the two and treat *inheritance* as a relationship, as it is
also a coupling between a pair of classes. It is sometimes argued that **specializes-from** (or
is-a) and **specializes-into** are really the "roles" of an "inheritance relationship". This may
have some meaning in environments where inheritance is a mechanism for implementation reuse rather than specification reuse, or in delegation environments where properties
are referred by objects to prototype objects (though in this case, the roles are perhaps
better named **refers-to** and **is-referred-to-by**).

Connotational versus Operational Semantics

In specialization theory, however, inheritance is a mechanism for specification reuse, as well as for taxonomy definition. As such, inheritance couples object classes *connotationally* rather than *operationally*. To illustrate this distinction, an operational coupling between two classes can always be instantiated as a *relationship instance* between two objects. By contrast, it is difficult to create a relationship instance for an "inheritance relationship". If we attempted to do so, we might pick two objects of some class, but then both objects would be members of both their class and its superclass. If we considered this object-pair an instance of an "inheritance relationship", then each object, being a member of the superclass, would play the `specializes-into` role with the other; further, being a member of the subclass, each object would also play the `specializes-from` with the other. This would imply that the roles were symmetric, which they clearly are not. Rather than wrap ourselves in such semantic paradoxes, we will not model inheritance as a "relationship" in the sense of an instantiable, operational coupling between classes.

Some modeling methodologies also consider *instantiation* a relationship. It is sometimes argued that the **is-an-instance-of** and **has-as-an-instance** associations defined in Chapter 5 are actually the "roles" of an "instantiation relationship" between a `class` object class and an `instance` object class. This also leads to many semantic difficulties, because this too cannot be instantiated; what do we mean by an instance of the `class` object class or an instance of the `instance` object class? For this reason, we will not treat instantiation as a "relationship" in the operational sense of the term.

Throughout this book, we have called connotational couplings between modeling constructs (such as **specializes-from**, **specializes-into**, **is-an-instance-of**, and **has-as-an-instance**) *associations* rather than relationships. In specialization theory, an association is defined as a *connotational coupling* between *modeling constructs*, rather than an *operational coupling* between *object classes*. Associations are connotational in the sense that they serve only to assist our understanding of the system model, without affecting the operation of the actual system.

A real object in the network — such as a `multiplexer` — does not really "care" what class we assign it to, nor how many levels of generalization we construct above its class, nor how we change the inheritance structure above its class if we so wish (subject, of course, to the rules of Chapter 6), because all these activities do not affect how it operates in the network. By contrast, if we create a `connectivity` relationship between a `multiplexer` and a `pbx`, then that does affect how it operates in the network.

Besides specialization and instantiation, associations include generalization, membership, property assignment, and so on. (A slightly better term would be *meta-associations*, since they reflect couplings between modeling constructs.) Both the terms *association* and *relationship* are defined in specialization theory in a very narrow, precise, and technical sense. (Other methodologies use the same terms in other narrow, technical senses.) An association expresses *connotational semantics* (i.e., couplings between *modeling constructs within the methodology*) such as generalization, specialization, property assignment, inheritance, instantiation, membership, subtyping, or supertyping. A relationship expresses *operational semantics* (i.e., couplings between *object classes in the modeled system*) for any actual interaction that objects might have, such as backup, connectivity, termination, subscription, or supervision.

We will continue to treat associations as being *orthogonal* to relationships as defined in this chapter. If the participant classes of a relationship happen to have an association between them (e.g., ancestor and descendant), that fact is incidental to the establishment of the relationship. The majority of this chapter has been devoted to explaining how the semantics of the specialization association influence the semantics of relationships. Such interplay is possible only because of their orthogonality; if specialization were treated just like any other relationship as in some other methodologies, it would be impossible to derive important principles such as relatant specialization, relatant multiplicity restriction, subject multiplicity regression, and so on.

Metamodels

Treating inheritance and instantiation as relationships is useful when we are building a *metamodel* for our object model. A metamodel is a model of the modeling methodology itself. If we were to build one, and if we were to use the modeling methodology itself to build its own metamodel, examples of object classes would be `object`, `object-Class`, `attribute`, `function`, `capsule`, `relationship`, and so forth; examples of relationships would be {`attribute is-a-property-of objectClass`}, {`objectClass specializes-from objectClass`}, {`objectClass participates-in relationship`}, {`object is-an-instance-of object-Class`}, and so on.

Building metamodels can be a very entertaining exercise but is not very useful unless one is building the modeling tool itself or related CASE tools. Metamodels are used in such tools to create *data dictionaries* (such as the IRDS standard) and define the *conceptual schema* which indicate the nature of the data stored in the model information base [ANSI X3-138, ISO 10027, ISO 9007, Hazz89, Gadr87, Gadr93]. For readers interested in tools which support modeling methodologies, the metamodel of specialization theory is presented in Chapter 25. (Readers interested only in applying specialization theory to create models of actual networks may skip that chapter entirely.)

Table 17-1 summarizes some of the major differences between associations and relationships in our methodology.

To summarize, the definition of *relationships* in specialization theory is a circumscribed definition which applies only to operational interactions between any two object classes, without consideration of any connotational taxonomical or genealogical dependencies between them. This definition includes aggregation as a relationship, but precludes us from considering inheritance and instantiation as relationships. We will continue to treat inheritance and relationships as orthogonal notions; diagrammatically, we will largely draw relationships as "horizontal" and inheritance hierarchies as "vertical" to emphasize this conceptual orthogonality. It is the interplay between these two orthogonal concepts that gives rise to the relationship-based specialization modes discussed in this chapter.

	Associations	Relationships
What they are	Connotational couplings between modeling constructs	Operational couplings between object classes
Examples	• Specialization (**specializes-from, specializes-into**) • Instantiation (**has-as-an-instance, is-an-instance-of**) • Property Assignment (**has-as-a-property, is-a-property-of**) • Membership (**has-as-a-member, is-a-member-of**) etc.	• Connectivity (`connects-to, is-connected-to`) • Subscription (`subscribes-to, is-subscribed-to-by`) • Aggregation (`has-as-a-part, is-a-part-of`) • Protocol Layerings (`layers-above, layers-below`) etc.
What they do	Assist our understanding of the system model	Describe interactions between concrete objects
When they are created	Always exist as part of the modeling methodology	Created by architect when applying the methodology to a modeled system
How many of them exist	A fixed, limited number; modeling constructs can be connotationally coupled in only a few ways	Indefinite number; as many as are created by the architect to express different operational couplings
When they are available	Predefined; are always available to connotationally associate modeling constructs created by architect	Not predefined; must be explicitly created by architect before object classes can be operationally coupled
If they are modified	Only affect our understanding of the system model; have no effect on actual system	Have observable effect on actual modeled system
Can they be instantiated	Instantiation not meaningful (except in metamodel)	Instantiation meaningful and possible
How they are used	Help to build modeling tools for the methodology (e.g., design, synthesis, and simulation tools)	Help to build an actual system model

Table 17-1: Associations and Relationships

17.17. Normalization of Relationships

The issue of normalizing relationships deals with selecting which class in the inheritance hierarchy is the best one to which the relationship specification may be applied so that it can be inherited by its subclasses. It may be tempting to specify all relationships as involute relationships at the root of the inheritance hierarchy and leave it to each individual class to decide which of the relationships bequeathed to it by `genericObject` it will participate in, use relatant specialization to throw out all the relatants it does not want, and restrict or regress multiplicities as it sees fit. This actually turns out to be more work, because by default each object class would inherit all relationships, and with each specialization we would have to indicate all the relationships and relatants which do *not* apply. It is conceptually simpler, and less burdensome at processing time, to apply each relationship specification only as high up in the inheritance hierarchy as is absolutely necessary.

Isomorphic Relationships of Siblings

We therefore need to determine for each relationship an appropriate superclass to which that relationship specification can be best applied, such that the relationship is available through inheritance to all the subclasses that need it. We approach this is in a bottom-up fashion. If we find all sibling subclasses playing the same role with the same relatant class, that role can be "promoted" to their superclass. This means that instead of specifying several different isomorphic relationship assignments — one for each sibling subclass — we specify *one* relationship assignment for their *superclass*. The relationship is now available to all the subclasses through inheritance. The ground rule for normalization is

> If all sibling subclasses of a common superclass have isomorphic relationships with the same relatant, then those relationships can be replaced by a single relationship between the superclass and that relatant.

We must, of course, also consider what happens to multiplicities when relationships are promoted. It is easy to deal with relatant multiplicities: since each subject subclass specifies a lower and upper bound for the number of relatant instances with which it will play its role, the lower bound for the superclass must be the lowest of all subclass lower bounds, and the upper bound for the superclass must be the highest of all subclass upper bounds. In other words, the relatant multiplicity for the subject superclass must be the union of the intervals of the relatant multiplicities of the subject subclasses.

For subject multiplicities the situation is more complex. If the relatant requires a minimum number of subject instances from any one subject subclass, clearly the lower bound for the subject multiplicity in the superclass must be at least this minimum number. If the relatant also requires a minimum number of instances from more than one subclass, the lower bound for the subject multiplicity in the superclass must be the sum of all the minima, since each instance of the subclasses also **is-a** superclass instance.

The upper bound for the subject multiplicity in the superclass must also be at least as great as the upper bound of any of its subclasses. However, it cannot be less than its own lower bound, so if the lower bound in the superclass, calculated as above, exceeds the maximum of the upper bounds of all the subclasses, the upper bound in the superclass is reset to the lower bound in the superclass. We thus get the following normalization rules:

If all sibling subclasses of a common superclass have isomorphic relationships with the same relatant, then those relationships can be replaced by a single relationship between the superclass and that relatant, with the following multiplicity bounds:

- *The lower bound of the relatant multiplicity in the superclass is the lowest of the lower bounds of the relatant multiplicities in the subclasses.*

- *The upper bound of the relatant multiplicity in the superclass is the highest of the upper bounds of the relatant multiplicities in the subclasses.*

- *The lower bound of the subject multiplicity in the superclass is the sum of the lower bounds of the subject multiplicities in the subclasses.*

- *The upper bound of the subject multiplicity in the superclass is either the highest of the upper bounds of the subject multiplicities in the subclasses, or its own lower bound, whichever is greater.*

- *An unspecified lower bound is considered equal to zero.*

- *An unspecified upper bound is considered to be greater than all specified upper bounds.*

Figure 17-22 illustrates these guidelines.

By applying these rules at multiple levels, isomorphic relationships in which all subjects are cognate can be promoted all the way up their cognation ancestor. Promotion of relationships up the hierarchy must stop when we reach a level where some sibling class does not have the same isomorphic relationship with the relatant that the other siblings do. If we promoted a relationship any higher, the sibling class would not inherit the relationship from its superclass, requiring it to become degenerate for that class. This would suggest that the relationship is being promoted too high. If we reach a level where, say, three sibling classes have isomorphic relationships with the same relatant but three do not, it may indicate that the hierarchy should be redesigned. Two intermediate subclasses could be introduced, with the three classes having the isomorphic relationship placed under one intermediate subclass, specializing by relationship addition, and the three non-participating ones under the other.

Isomorphic Relationships between Sets of Siblings

It is also possible to normalize relationships where sibling subclasses have isomorphic relationships not with the same relatant but with *subclasses* of a common relatant superclass. If the relatants of the subject sibling subclasses are themselves all sibling subclasses of a common superclass, and if that common superclass has no other subclasses, then that relationship can be promoted to both the superclasses.

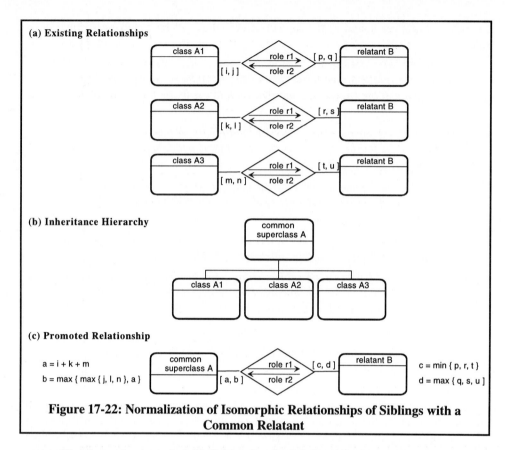

(a) Existing Relationships

(b) Inheritance Hierarchy

(c) Promoted Relationship

$a = i + k + m$

$b = \max \{ \max \{ j, l, n \}, a \}$

$c = \min \{ p, r, t \}$

$d = \max \{ q, s, u \}$

Figure 17-22: Normalization of Isomorphic Relationships of Siblings with a Common Relatant

The determination of multiplicities for the relationships between the two super-classes is somewhat simpler, because the rules for calculating all multiplicities must be symmetric in this situation. We simply take the union of both subject and relatant multi-plicities. We therefore get the following rules of normalization, which are illustrated in Figure 17-23.

If all sibling subclasses of a common superclass have isomorphic relationships with a set of relatants which are also all sibling subclasses of another common superclass, then those relationships can be replaced by a single relationship be-tween the two superclasses, with the following multiplicity bounds:

- *The lower bound of the relatant multiplicity in either superclass is the lowest of the lower bounds of the relatant multiplicities in its sub-classes.*

- *The upper bound of the relatant multiplicity in either superclass is the highest of the upper bounds of the relatant multiplicities in its sub-classes.*

- *The lower bound of the subject multiplicity in either superclass is the lowest of the lower bounds of the subject multiplicities in its sub-classes.*

- *The upper bound of the subject multiplicity in either superclass is the highest of the upper bounds of the subject multiplicities in its sub-classes.*

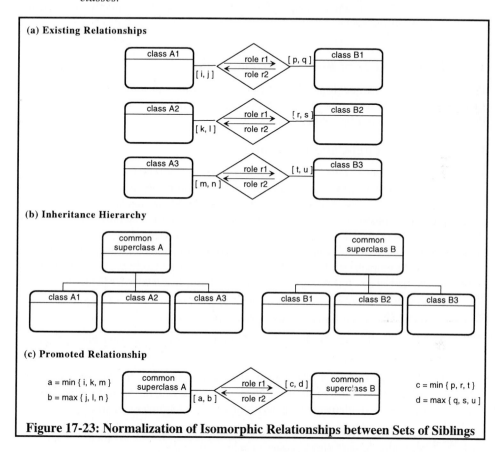

Figure 17-23: Normalization of Isomorphic Relationships between Sets of Siblings

Normalization of isomorphic relationships between two sets of siblings can be treated as a multi-stage process of normalization of isomorphic relationships of siblings with a common relatant. For example, in Figure 17-23 we could first normalize the relationships of all subclasses of A with respect to class B1 using the rules for normalization from Figure 17-22, assuming that the multiplicities for the relationships of A2 with B1 as well as A3 with B1 are all degenerate with multiplicities of [0,0]. Similarly we could then normalize the relationships of all subclasses of A with respect to B2, and then respect to B3; finally, we could now normalize the relationships of all subclasses of B with A. Or we could do this the other way around — first normalizing all subclasses of B with A1, and so on.

These procedures will tend to produce multiplicities which, while still correct, are somewhat looser and less restrictive than the direct union rules specified in Figure 17-23. The reason is that there is less information available for use in Figure 17-22 than in Figure 17-23, because we lose information about minimum multiplicity requirements in the superclass due to zero-regression of subject multiplicity in the subclasses. Hence, if the normalization rules of Figure 17-22 are applied to Figure 17-23, the multiplicities produced by the normalization, though correct, will be looser than directly normalizing Figure 17-23 by its own rules.

17.18. Other Methods of Modeling Relationships

Different modeling methodologies have treated relationships in different ways, some as first-class constructs and some not. Each one of them has some advantages and some drawbacks. We discuss a few of them below.

Relationships as First-Class Constructs

In specialization theory, relationships are modeled as *first-class constructs*, and the specification of relationships is not tied to the specification of object classes or to that of attributes of object classes. A first-class construct is one whose semantics cannot be inferred from other constructs. As a consequence, the construct must be directly specified to the information model. There are many typical software consequences of implementing first-class modeling constructs in a model information base, some of which are listed below. It should be emphasized that the following features are merely the consequences of implementing first-class constructs, and not their defining characteristics [Mody92]:

- First-class constructs can be declared as primitive or defined language constructs in a programming environment;
- First-class constructs can be passed into routines as arguments, and out of routines as results;
- First-class constructs have their storage management handled internally by the model information base, without having the specifier write routines to implement this in terms of storage of simpler constructs;
- First-class constructs can be created and deleted from the model information base as single, cohesive units;
- First-class constructs can be read, modified, and written back into the model information base as single, cohesive units.

We discuss below other methods of modeling relationships, many with similarities and some with differences from specialization theory.

Conjugate Pointer Attributes

In certain areas of research, the concept of object classes and attributes as first-class constructs predated the concept of relationships. When it became apparent that object models, to be semantically complete, required the modeling of abstract inter-class relationships, attempts were made to incorporate relationships into the model in terms of existing first-class constructs. One such attempt was to "attribeautify" relationships, that is, represent relationships in terms of attributes of existing object classes. Thus, if an object class A were to participate in a relationship with object class B, A would have an attribute, say bPointer, which pointed to the particular instance of B with which it participated in the relationship, while B would have a reciprocal attribute aPointer pointing to the corresponding instance of A. This is called the *conjugate pointer* approach; it defines relationships "in" object classes rather than "on" or "between" them.

There are several drawbacks to the conjugate pointer approach, not the least being its inability to specify relationship attributes for many-to-many relationships. If the relationship were many-to-many, A would need several bPointers and B would need several aPointers. This would require making both aPointer and bPointer array-valued attributes. If the relationship had its own attributes, they could not be easily stored in either A or B. The other problem arises with the modification of relationship instances. When the nature of a relationship changes (for example, if we wish to make the bPointer of some A point to a different B, or if we wish to delete the coupling between particular instances of A and B), we would be required to simultaneously update reciprocal attributes in two different object instances atomically through external imperative operations. This may not always be possible, depending on the distribution of the participant instances across platforms and on access and authorization restrictions. If for any reason one update succeeds and the other fails, the system will be left in an inconsistent state. If we wanted such simultaneous modification to be handled internally, we would have to install additional functions in both A and B to send a message to its relatant and wait for a response before it updated its own pointer. These functions would be required to operate multiple-phase commit protocols between the objects to ensure atomicity and concurrency of information modification. These functions would be pure housekeeping functions for updating attributes properly and would have nothing to do with modeling the intrinsic functions of the referent class from the system model which they represent; we would thus tend to clutter up the object class with such housekeeping functions.

Relationship Objects

Other modeling methods "objectify" relationships instead of "attribeautifying" them. This approach arises from the argument that, if relationships themselves are first-class constructs which could have their own attributes, then they could be conceptually accommodated within existing first-class constructs which already possess attributes, namely object classes [Rumb87]. Thus, relationships are cast as an independent object class, two attributes of which are the names of the two participant instances. One instance of this object class is created for each relationship instance. Although such construction of a relationship easily accommodates the notion of relationship attributes, in some ways it is an overkill. Object classes are designed to abstract and encapsulate relevant functionaries in the network model which can be evolved and refined through specialization. Further, the notion of relatant multiplicities, for example, cannot be satisfactorily implemented for many-to-one relationships. If one instance of A participates with many instances of B in such a relationship, many instances of the "relationship object" must be created, all pointing to the same instance of A and each to a different instance of B. If the A instance undergoes modification, (e.g., it changes its name) then all these "relationship objects" must be atomically and simultaneously modified.

Further, the casting of relationships as independent object classes is somewhat unnecessary, because such classes do not participate in any type of taxonomical hierarchy; they do not **specialize-from** any "relationship superclasses", nor are there "relationship subclasses" which they **specialize-into**. Object classes are best used as abstractions to define taxonomies of resources whose commonalities can be captured through the notions of inheritance and specialization. Relationships are best used to define operational interactions between object classes. Though there have been attempts at constructing relationship specialization hierarchies in the literature, most can be modeled more simply in a flat, unstructured space of relationships which are bequeathed down structured *class* specialization hierarchies.

Implementation-Independent Specification

The problem with many relationship-modeling approaches is the confusion of specification with implementation. Specialization theory, like some others [Kilo90, Rumb91a], is a pure specification approach, which does not concern itself with any details of how relationships might be implemented. Each relationship could be implemented in any manner that best suited it. One-to-one relationships could be implemented as conjugate pointers in object classes; many-to-one relationships could be implemented as a one-way pointer in the instances on the "many" side pointing to the same instance on the "one" side, or as an array-valued pointer in the instance on the "one" side, or both; many-to-many relationships could be implemented as "relationship objects", or as tables resident in some data structure external to the participant instances. Each implementation mechanism will undoubtedly have its disadvantages, many similar to those we discussed above. However, instead of using an implementation-dependent specification mechanism and thrusting the same disadvantages on all relationships, we use a pure specification approach so that each relationship can pick an implementation mechanism which minimizes the disadvantages for itself.

In general, the implementation mechanism for a relationship must take into account the ease with which relationship information can be queried; the importance of being able to traverse the relationship from either end; the appropriate location for relationship attributes if any; the frequency with which relationship instances might be created, updated, or deleted; the frequency with which its participant instances might be created, updated, or deleted; the tolerance of the model information base to temporary inconsistencies; and the ease with which relationship-based queries might be processed. Different relationships in the same model could have different implementation mechanisms based on their consideration of these factors. Even different instances of the same relationship could be implemented differently if desired, as long as they preserved the semantics of our specification. We are not concerned with these issues here; we strive for abstraction in our specification of relationships. We accomplish this by casting them as independent first-class constructs, leaving open the possibility of multiple implementation mechanisms as appropriate.

The Entity-Relationship (ER) model and its various derivatives generally have a very strong treatment of relationships and have served as the foundation for many enterprise modeling activities leading to the design of several corporate and technical information system databases. The pure ER model, however, does not deal with subtyping, generalization, and specialization of entities and does not attempt to classify its entities in any taxonomical hierarchy. Recently, many attempts have been made to integrate Entity-Relationship modeling and object-oriented modeling [Kilo91a, Kilo91b, Rumb91a] to arrive at a uniform, multiparadigmatic modeling methodology, much as this book does. However, each of these places a different emphasis on the importance of inheritance, composition, and inter-class relationships. In particular, many of these treat inheritance also as a relationship [Rumb91a, Booc94], a practice which we have not followed in this book due to the narrow, technical definition of relationships in specialization theory stated earlier in this chapter.

Extensions to the Entity-Relationship model have been proposed which model *ternary* relationships, that is, relationships in which three entities participate. In general, examples of *n*-ary relationships where *n* exceeds 2 are relatively uncommon. Some *n*-ary relationships can be reduced to a set of binary relationships, which can be easily modeled. Other examples of ternary relationships are really three-body interactions of finite duration and could be better modeled as *events* rather than persistent steady-state relationships.

17.19. New Relationship Modeling Approaches

NIAM

One methodology that bears special mention is NIAM, the *Nijssen Information Analysis Methodology* [Nijs89, Gadr87, Gadr93]. NIAM breaks the entire universe of discourse into a set of extremely elementary binary associations between participating "objects". NIAM "objects" are not the same as objects in an object-oriented model; they are very low-level descriptions of the functionaries in the universe of discourse. As a binary semantic model, it exposes the lowest level of coupling and functional dependency between its objects. If we were to further decompose the universe, we would begin to lose semantic information. The NIAM model is analogous to the relational model normalized down to the fifth normal form.

After defining binary associations, NIAM defines constraints on them. These constraints could be subtyping constraints, role constraints, uniqueness constraints, exclusion constraints, and equality constraints. We can choose which type of constraints are applicable to which binary association. The interesting facet of NIAM is that all the other modeling methodologies (entity-relationship, object-oriented, relational, etc.) drop out as special cases depending on which constraints are applied to the binary semantic model. Since specialization theory combines elements of all three, it can also be derived as a special case of NIAM.

Kilov Diagrams

Another powerful approach with many conceptual similarities to specialization theory is the one developed by Bellcore in "The Materials" [SR 2010, Kilo94a]. This approach yields an excellent harmonization of object-oriented modeling with entity-relationship modeling. Like specialization theory, it makes a distinction between associations and relationships. (As such, it can also be used to describe its own metamodel.) Associations are connotational couplings between entities, while relationships are operational couplings. Like specialization theory, this approach recognizes only a limited number of predefined associations and an infinite number of user-definable relationships [Kilo94b].

The Bellcore approach is pictorially described using a graphical technique known as a *Kilov diagram*. Kilov diagrams can describe both an application model and a metamodel. In a Kilov diagram, entities are represented by rectangles and the association between them is represented in a triangle. Because there are only a limited number of predefined associations, only a few standard labels can go inside the triangle. Examples of associations recognized in a Kilov diagram are `"D"` (a dependency association between an independent or "strong" entity and a dependent or "weak" entity), `"Ref"` (a reference association between a "maintained" entity and a "reference" entity), and `"S"` (a subtyping association between a supertype entity and a subtype entity, similar to our **specializes-into**). The S-association is by default assumed to be disjoint and incomplete; it can be further qualified as `"SE"` (disjoint and "exhaustive", or complete), `"S+"` (overlapping and incomplete), or `"SE+"` (overlapping and complete). Figure 17-24 is an example of a Kilov diagram for specialization.

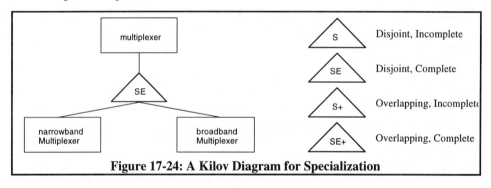

Figure 17-24: A Kilov Diagram for Specialization

Kilov diagrams can also indicate relationships. The relationship itself, like its participant entities, is represented as a rectangle containing the name of the relationship. The participant entities always have the association `"Rel"` with the relationship itself; this is similar to the associations **participates-in** and **involves** of specialization theory, shown in Figure 17-3. Because of this arrangement, it is possible to have more than two entities participating in the same relationship and thus model general *n*-ary relationships. Multiplicity specifications (called "cardinality" in a Kilov diagram) with lower and upper bounds can also be specified, with the usual convention that a lower bound of 0 signifies optional participation. Figure 17-25 shows a Kilov diagram for a relationship.

Kilov diagrams do not specifically indicate relationship roles. In specialization theory, roles introduce directionality semantics which, as we shall see later, are essential to performing relationship-based navigation and inferring extended semantic knowledge. The Bellcore approach focuses heavily on CRUD operations (Create, Read, Update,

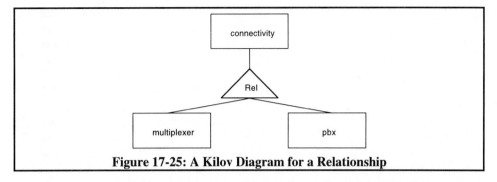

Figure 17-25: A Kilov Diagram for a Relationship

Delete) on the information model and defines the preconditions and postconditions that a protocol request and an entity implementation must meet to guarantee integrity.

The Bellcore approach recognizes two kinds of aggregation: a "composition" aggregation which permits optional as well as "free-standing" components and a "containment" aggregation which permits neither. One difference between the Bellcore approach and specialization theory is that in specialization theory, aggregation is considered an *operational relationship*, whereas in the Bellcore approach it is considered a *connotational association*. As such, the Bellcore approach also represents composition in an association triangle of a Kilov diagram, with either a "C" (general composition) or a "CC" (containment). In specialization theory, the benefits of treating aggregation like any other operational relationship is that connotational associations such as inheritance can then "orthogonally operate over" it, leading to important specialization principles such as component multiplicity restriction and component specialization. Figure 17-26 illustrates a Kilov diagram for composition, along with another diagram indicating how aggregation in specialization theory would be represented if it were cast into a Kilov diagram.

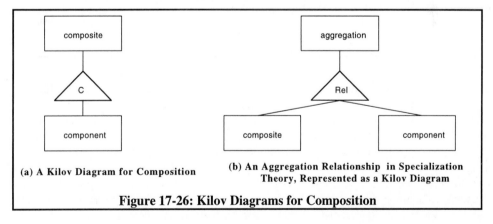

(a) A Kilov Diagram for Composition

(b) An Aggregation Relationship in Specialization Theory, Represented as a Kilov Diagram

Figure 17-26: Kilov Diagrams for Composition

17.20. Summary

The modeling of relationships as operational couplings between object classes is a powerful modeling tool. Relationships are modeled with both subject and relatant multiplicities, which quantify the participation of each class. Relatant multiplicities may be defined in terms of attributes of the subject. A relationship can also have its own attributes which have different semantics than the attributes of either participant.

The interaction between relationships and inheritance gives rise to several specialization modes for object classes. Collectively, they are known as relationship-based specialization modes. An object class may specialize by adding new relationships, by restricting the multiplicity of inherited relatants, by regressing its own subject multiplicity in an inherited relationship, by participating in the relationship with only selected descendants of inherited relatants, by restricting the domain of relationship attributes, or by restricting the domain of attributes in its relatant. These mechanisms are formalized in several specialization principles and relationship principles.

Relationships can be normalized by promoting them higher in the inheritance hierarchy if all sibling subclasses at any one level play the same role with the same relatant or different subclasses of the same relatant. Aggregations are also considered relationships whose roles are `has-as-a-part` and `is-a-part-of`. Protocol layerings can also be subsumed within the general relationship model. We do not, however, consider inheritance a relationship and continue to treat it as an association which is orthogonal to abstract binary inter-class relationships.

18. Virtual Relationships

"I got married to this WAN guru, and all I got was a narrow band."

— *bride of anonymous network architect.*

18.1. Introduction

In this chapter we introduce new concepts in the modeling of object relationships by exploiting special properties of relationship roles. By defining operations on roles, we can enhance our general relationship model to include several semantically useful concepts. These concepts allow us to express extended relationships within our model precisely and succinctly.

18.2. Conceptual Background

A *virtual relationship* is a relationship whose existence can be inferred from other relationships. A virtual relationship is not created by relationship assignment; it is dynamically computed and resolved by the run-time environment from specified relationships [Bapa93c]. The supporting relationships which generate a virtual relationship are termed *base relationships*. The virtual relationship is said to **arise-from** its base relationships, which in turn are said to **give-rise-to** the virtual relationship. A virtual relationship is implicitly generated when the roles of its base relationships have certain special *properties*.

In specialization theory, an *actual relationship* is a relationship which cannot be inferred from the properties of roles of other relationships, and therefore must be explicitly created by the architect using relationship assignment. The base relationships which give rise to a virtual relationship may be actual relationships, or may themselves be virtual. Figure 18-1 illustrates the associations of a virtual relationship with other modeling constructs.

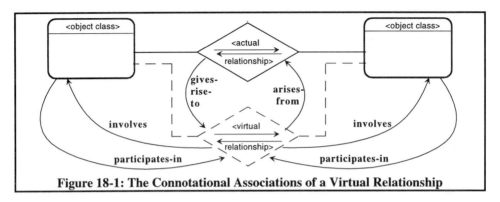

Figure 18-1: The Connotational Associations of a Virtual Relationship

A *virtual relationship instance* is formed by a pair of object instances which participate in the virtual relationship. A virtual relationship does not make existing objects participants in a new relationship. Rather, objects which are already participants in *actual relationship instances* become automatic participants in virtual relationship instances, because of the special properties of the roles in their actual relationships. Thus, although a virtual relationship may have instances, it can never be imperatively *instantiated*; only actual relationships can. Consequently, a virtual relationship can never be modified or deleted. Any change made to its supporting actual base relationships will be automatically reflected in the virtual relationship, since the virtual relationship instances are, in effect, dynamically resolved from actual base relationship instances every time they are queried.

A virtual relationship instance may be queried exactly like an actual relationship instance. If we query any participating object class for its relatant via one of its virtual relationships, the form of our interrogative query predicates and of the ensuing declarative response predicates is the same as it is for actual relationship. Each object "knows" what virtual relationships it participates in, since it "knows" the roles it plays in its actual relationships and the properties of those roles. Because all the actual base relationships which give rise to a virtual relationship must be well-founded (i.e., not degenerate), a virtual relationship is also considered well-founded.

Properties of Roles

A virtual relationship arises as a consequence of special *properties* possessed by the roles of its supporting base relationships. A property of a role is not analogous to a property of an object class, which, as we indicated in Chapter 4, is either an attribute or a function. Rather, a property of a role is a shorthand mechanism for specification reuse, which allows us to define many extended relationships from a single construct. By indicating the properties a role possesses, we create a mechanism which captures within a single relationship specification *more* semantics than just the usual binary association between participant object classes, their multiplicities, and their roles. By specifying our knowledge of the special properties of roles in our formal notation, we can compile into our run-time environment the ability to interpret extended relationship semantics.

There are five important properties which a relationship role-pair may possess:

- The *Commutativity* property;

- The *Transitivity* property;

- The *Distribution* property;

- The *Convolution* property; and

- The *Implication* property.

It is important to emphasize that these properties belong to role-pairs, not relationships. Thus, if a role-pair possesses these properties, they will be operative in all relationships in which that role-pair is used. In Chapter 19, we will examine how these properties can be formally specified along with the specification of a role-pair. The following sections define these properties and consider them in turn.

18.3. Commutative Virtual Relationships

A *commutative virtual relationship* is a relationship which arises from the *commutativity* property of the role-pair in its base relationship. We define a commutative role-pair as follows:

A role-pair {r1,r2} is said to be *commutative* if, given two participant object classes A and B such that A plays role r1 with B and B plays role r2 with A, it can be inferred that B plays role r1 with A and A plays role r2 with B.

This definition implies that any base relationship with a commutative role-pair automatically implies the existence of a virtual isomorphic relationship in which the subject and relatant classes of each role are "flipped around".

An Example of a Commutative Virtual Relationship

Many examples of commutative virtual relationships exist in network modeling. The most common examples of these are *connectivity* and *interconnectivity* relationships between instances of network devices. Consider the connectivity relationship between a pbx object class and an ocl-multiplexer object class. In this relationship, pbx might play the role connects-to with ocl-multiplexer, which would reciprocate with the role is-connected-to. (As we will clarify in Chapter 27, our precise definition of connectivity implies a direct connection between adjacent network-Devices, whereas our precise definition of interconnectivity — which has the roles interconnects-to and is-interconnected-to — includes indirect connections as well.)

In the formal specification of the role-pair connects-to and is-connected-to, we can specify that it possesses the commutativity property. Given this definition, our compiler can additionally infer that the ocl-multiplexer class also plays the role connects-to with pbx, which in turn reciprocates with is-connected-to.

Figure 18-2 illustrates a commutative relationship. In this class relationship diagram, we have indicated the virtual relationship in a dashed diamond. We have a more

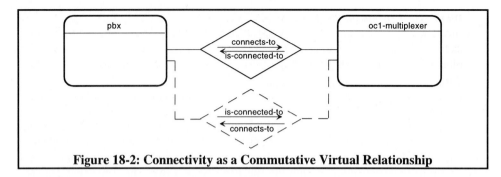

Figure 18-2: Connectivity as a Commutative Virtual Relationship

concise diagrammatic convention for this: we may indicate in the diagram for the base relationship the keyword COMMUTATIVE, so that the implied virtual relationship does not have to be explicitly drawn. Figure 18-3 illustrates this convention.

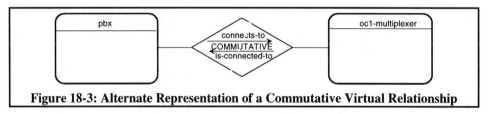

Figure 18-3: Alternate Representation of a Commutative Virtual Relationship

More Commutative Virtual Relationships

Another common example of commutative relationships are *mutual backup relationships*. It is important to understand that *all* backup relationships are not commutative. Suppose we define a backup relationship with the role-pair backs-up and is-backed-up-by without investing it with the commutativity property. Being non-commutative, this relationship is not mutual; it is only a one-way relationship. When we use this relationship to inform our compiler that object class A plays the role backs-up with object class B, the only information the compiler can infer is that B is-backed-up-by A. It *cannot* infer that B backs-up A (or its reciprocal, A is-backed-up-by B).

We might not wish to invest the role-pair backs-up and is-backed-up-by with the commutativity property, because in some contexts it may be used as a non-commutative (one-way) backup relationship. Where we require it to be commutative, we need to specify a new relationship — say, the mutualBackup relationship. This relationship has a different role-pair — say, mbacks-up and is-mbacked-up-by, standing for "mutually backs up" and "is mutually backed up by". We invest *this* role-pair with the commutativity property. Thus, this role-pair carries more semantics than the one-way role-pair backs-up and is-backed-up-by. In a later section, we will see how the semantics of a single mutualBackup relationship can be made to imply the semantics of the one-way backup relationship in both directions.

Consider an example of a signalTransferPoint object class, instances of which are generally deployed in "mated pairs" with each other. By cross-linking pairs of `signalTransferPoint` objects, we provide redundancy in the signaling network. This may be specified as a relationship with `mutualBackup` roles. If so, it implies that for each relationship instance between pairs of `signalTransferPoint` objects, the compiler can also infer a commutatively derived virtual relationship instance, as illustrated in Figure 18-4.

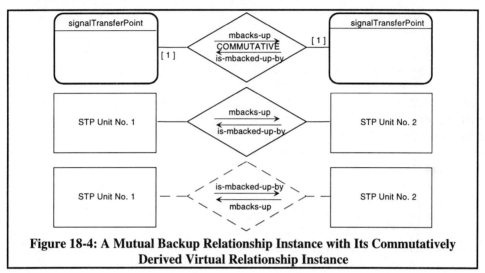

Figure 18-4: A Mutual Backup Relationship Instance with Its Commutatively Derived Virtual Relationship Instance

Note that if a commutative relationship is also *involute*, our compiler requires that the subject and relantant multiplicities have identical domains. An involute relationship is a relationship in which both the participant classes are the same class; if two instances of the same class commutatively play the same roles with each other, then they must do so with identical multiplicity domains. As an example, the backup relationship between two `signalTransferPoint` objects described above is both commutative and involute.

In Chapter 17, we indicated that isomorphic relationships may be normalized by "promoting" them up the hierarchy if all sibling subclasses of a common superclass played the same role with a set of relantants which themselves were also all sibling subclasses of another common superclass. If the subject classes and relantant classes are cognates of each other, executing this normalization may in fact turn this relationship into an involute relationship on their cognation ancestor.

We can, of course, also execute this normalization procedure on isomorphic relationships in which the role-pair is commutative. If promoting different isomorphic commutative relationships through normalization turns them into a single involute relationship on their cognation ancestor, we call the cognation ancestor the *Abelian ancestor* of that relationship. An Abelian ancestor of a commutative relationship is an object class whose every descendant participates in that relationship with another descendant. (This terminology arises from considering a relationship role as a function which maps every member of a group to another.)

18.4. Transitive Virtual Relationships

A *transitive virtual relationship* is a relationship which arises from the *transitivity* property of the role-pair in its base relationships. We define a transitive role-pair as follows:

A role-pair {r1,r2} is said to be *transitive* if, given three participant object classes A, B, and C such that A plays role r1 with B and B plays role r2 with A, *and* B plays role r1 with C and C plays role r2 with B, then it can be inferred that A plays role r1 with C and C plays role r2 with A.

This definition implies that relationship roles are transitive if, given a common "linking" participant, they can be "chained together". Well-known examples of transitive relationships are all *aggregation* relationships, of which we have modeled many examples in previous chapters. The role-pair in all aggregation relationships is {has-as-a-part, is-a-part-of}. This role-pair is transitive because a component of a component is also a component, and an aggregate of an aggregate is also an aggregate.

An Example of a Transitive Virtual Relationship

There are other examples of transitive relationships in network modeling. Consider a network of electronic mail application processes, which exchange electronic mail messages among themselves over local and wide-area computer networks. These application processes may all have different implementations and protocols: some could be Message Transfer Agents, some could be mail handling demon processes, and so on. All these mail handlers may use different standards [ITU-T X.400, RFC 821]. However, through the use of programs like sendmail or other electronic mail gateways with address translation mechanisms, they may all have the ability to forward mail to each other.

We might model them all as subclasses of a common mailHandler superclass. Their mailForwarding relationship with each other might be modeled with the roles {forwards-mail-to, receives-mail-from}. Clearly, this relationship is commutative. We could further provide additional information about this relationship to our compiler by specifying this relationship as being *transitive*. This implies that once we create any two different mailForwarding relationships between any three different mailHandler objects, we also automatically create a transitively derived virtual relationship instance between the third pair. Figure 18-5 illustrates this principle.

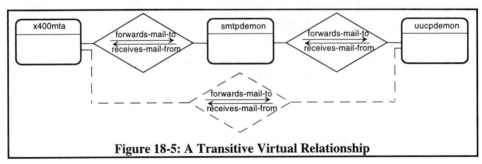

Figure 18-5: A Transitive Virtual Relationship

As a diagrammatic convention, we indicate in the class relationship diagram of the base relationship the keyword TRANSITIVE, as shown in Figure 18-6.

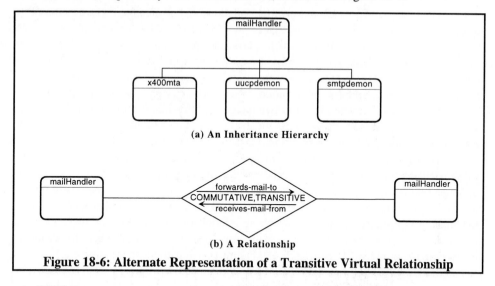

(a) An Inheritance Hierarchy

(b) A Relationship

Figure 18-6: Alternate Representation of a Transitive Virtual Relationship

18.5. Distributive Virtual Relationships

A *distributive virtual relationship* is a relationship which arises from the *distribution* property of the role-pairs in its base relationships. We define distributive roles as follows:

A role-pair {r1,r2} is said to *distribute over* another role-pair {r3,r4} if, given three participant object classes A, B, and C such that A plays role r1 with B and B plays role r2 with A, *and* B plays role r3 with C and C plays role r4 with B, it can be inferred that A plays role r1 with C and C plays role r2 with A. The role r1 is said to distribute *ahead of* role r3, and the role r2 is said to distribute *behind* role r4.

This definition states that, given a common "linking" relatant, the *distributing* role-pair {r1,r2} *distributes over* the *distributand* role-pair {r3,r4}. That is, the role-pair {r1,r2} can be "superimposed" on the role-pair {r3,r4} if the subject of role r3 is replaced by the subject of role r1.

An Example of a Distributive Virtual Relationship

As an example, suppose we wish to model geographic information about network-Device objects. We model this as a housing relationship between a site object class and the networkDevice object class, in which site plays the role houses with networkDevice, which reciprocates by playing is-housed-at with site. The class site is modeled as a separate class because it could have its own attributes, such as streetAddress, telephoneNumber, and so on. It could also be subclassed into, say, centralSite and remoteSite if necessary. Further, multiple network-Device objects could be-housed-at a single site.

There may also be a termination relationship between the networkDevice object class and the circuit object class, in which networkDevice plays the role terminates with circuit, which plays the role is-terminated-at with networkDevice. Occasionally, rather than knowing which networkDevice terminates a given circuit, it may be useful for certain outside-plant engineers to know the physical address or location where the circuit is-terminated-at. Ordinarily, we would have to perform two queries for this information: one to determine which instance of networkDevice the circuit is-terminated-at, and another to determine which instance of site that networkDevice is-housed-at.

To make this more concise, we may simply say that the termination relationship *distributes over* the housing relationship. More specifically, this means that the is-terminated-at role distributes *ahead of* the is-housed-at role. This creates a *distributive virtual relationship* between circuit and site. The distributive virtual relationship is isomorphic to the distributing relationship: the circuit objects play a virtual is-terminated-at role with the same instance of site where its terminating networkDevice is-housed-at. Figure 18-7 illustrates this example.

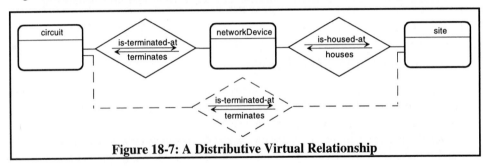

Figure 18-7: A Distributive Virtual Relationship

Equivalently, we could say that the terminates role *distributes behind* the houses role. This means that if a networkDevice terminates a circuit, and a site houses the same networkDevice, then the site also terminates the circuit.

It is important to understand the distinction between distribution *ahead of* a role and distribution *behind* a role. In this example, is-terminated-at distributes *ahead of* is-housed-at, and terminates distributes *behind* houses. A role distributing ahead of another role extends "forward" beyond its relatant. A role distributing behind another role extends "backward" beyond its subject.

Generally, care must be exercised when we simply say that one role-pair distributes over another: the semantics are different depending on which role in each role-pair has been specified as the forward role. If the role-pair for termination is specified as {is-terminated-at, terminates} and for housing as {is-housed-at, houses}, it is correct to say that the termination role-pair distributes over the housing role-pair. If the role-pair for termination is specified as {terminates, is-terminated-at} and for housing as {houses, is-housed-at}, then we must say that the *inverted* termination role-pair distributes over the *inverted* housing role-pair. In either case, is-terminated-at distributes ahead of is-housed-at and terminates behind houses.

In Figure 18-7, there is no interaction defined between the roles is-terminated-at and houses, nor is there any between terminates and is-housed-at. Interactions between these, even if they existed, would not be available from our definition of distribution. Although the semantics of this distinction are precise in our notational formal specification, sometimes they are not immediately obvious upon inspection; in such circumstances, the presence of a class relationship diagram as an adjunct to the formal specification often helps.

More Distributive Virtual Relationships

Often, aggregation relationships are commonly encountered as distributand relationships. Many role-pairs distribute over the has-as-a-part and is-a-part-of roles. For example, the houses role which the site object class plays with networkDevice in Figure 18-7 distributes ahead of the has-as-a-part role. If a site houses a networkDevice and a networkDevice has-as-a-part some component, then it is true that the site also houses that component.

The houses role of Figure 18-7 may also act as a distributand role with respect to other distributing roles. Suppose we have a situation in which we decide to ease our burden of administering central and remote sites in our private wide-area data network. To conserve our resources, we turn over the administration of our site objects to outsourcing vendors. We may have different outsourcing vendors at different sites, but each site is assigned to only one outsourcing vendor. To keep track of this knowledge in our model information base, we may model an administration relationship between an outsourcingVendor object class and a site object class. In this relationship, the class outsourcingVendor plays the role administers with respect to site, which in turn plays the role is-administered-by.

When we create a relationship instance in which an outsourcingVendor administers a site, it is in fact our intent that the outsourcingVendor administers every networkDevice which that site houses. To convey this intent, we may simply say that administration distributes over housing; this implies that the administers role distributes ahead of the houses role. In effect, this creates a distributive virtual relationship between the outsourcingVendor object class and the networkDevice object class. This automatically implies that outsourcingVendor plays the role administers with respect to networkDevice, which reciprocates with is-administered-by. Figure 18-8 illustrates this example.

As a diagrammatic convention, we indicate in the class relationship diagram of the distributing base relationship the keywords DISTRIBUTES AHEAD OF <role>, which is taken to mean that the role just above these keywords in the diagrammed relationship distributes ahead of the indicated <role> in any relationship in which the dia-

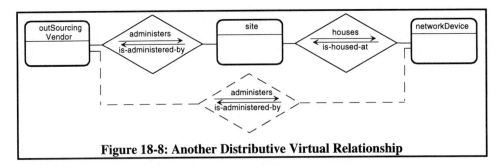

Figure 18-8: Another Distributive Virtual Relationship

grammed relatant of the distributing role plays the indicated <role> as a subject. Alternatively, this could also be diagrammed with the keywords DISTRIBUTES BEHIND <role> using the reciprocal of the distributand role. This is shown in Figure 18-9.

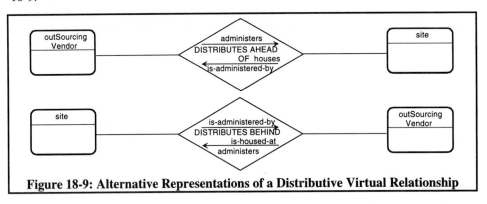

Figure 18-9: Alternative Representations of a Distributive Virtual Relationship

Relationships may distribute over base relationships regardless of whether the base relationships are actual or virtual. In the example of Figure 18-8, the base distributand role houses is an actual role between site and networkDevice. However, the houses role may also be virtually played by site with components of networkDevice, since houses distributes ahead of has-as-a-part. Further, since administers distributes ahead of houses, it follows then that there is yet another distributive virtual relationship in which outsourcingVendor administers all *components* of all networkDevice objects at the site. Figure 18-10 illustrates this concept.

Since a virtual relationship instance may be queried exactly like an actual relationship instance, this implies that if we asked an instance of a component of network-Device for the object responsible for administering it (that is, we queried it for the relatant of its is-administered-by role) we would directly get the correct instance of outsourcingVendor, without having to compose any relational joins in our query. Under conventional modeling, some form of a join condition between entities would be required in the query in order to elicit the desired response — even if the implementation platform for the model information base is not relational.

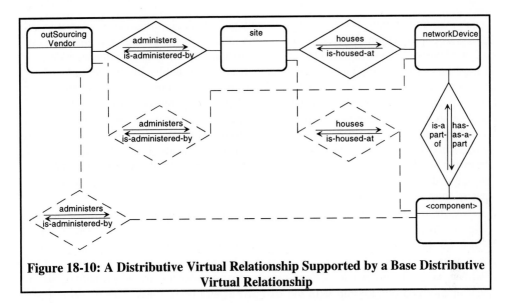

Figure 18-10: A Distributive Virtual Relationship Supported by a Base Distributive Virtual Relationship

A little reflection indicates that a transitive virtual relationship is a special case of a distributive virtual relationship in which both the distributing and distributand role-pairs are the same role-pair.

18.6. Convolute Virtual Relationships

A *convolute virtual relationship* is a relationship which arises from the *convolution* property of the role-pairs in its base relationships. We define convolute roles as follows:

A role-pair {r1,r2} is said to *convolute from* the role-pairs {r3,r4} and {r5,r6} if, given three participant object classes A, B, and C such that A plays role r3 with B and B plays role r4 with A, *and* B plays role r5 with C and C plays role r6 with B, it can be inferred that A plays role r1 with C and C plays role r2 with A. The role r1 is said to *convolute above* the roles r3 and r5, and the role r2 is said to *convolute below* the roles r4 and r6.

This definition states that, under certain circumstances, two base relationships with different role-pairs may give rise to a virtual relationship with an entirely different role-pair. The virtual relationship is said to *convolute from* the base relationships; its forward role *convolutes above* the two base forward roles and its reciprocal role *convolutes below* the two base reciprocal roles. As with distribution, the order in which the roles of the base relationships occur in the specification is important; if this order is reversed, the convolution property of the base roles will in general vanish.

An Example of a Convolute Virtual Relationship

Consider an example in which an information service provider operates a data network which supplies multiple information services to multiple clients. Corporate clients subscribe to one or more information services. The terms of a typical subscription contract require the information service to automatically provide the information of interest to the client. The information service downloads this information to the desktop computers of all employees of the corporate client. Typical examples of this application include brokerage houses subscribing to a stock quotation service, or publishing houses subscribing to a news wire service. The subscription contract is negotiated for an unlimited number of desktop licenses, because all employees of the client wish to receive information from the service provider. Because the information of interest is dynamic and useful only within a small life span, and also because individual desktop computers may be located at geographically different sites, each desktop computer downloads this information directly from the service provider, rather than from any internal central redistribution database owned and operated by the client company itself. If the client adds more desktop computers, they too will receive information directly from the service provider.

Since we have modeled `subscription` relationships before, we know that the roles of these relationships are `subscribes-to` and `is-subscribed-to-by`. Thus, we might model a `subscription` relationship in which an `information-Service` object class `is-subscribed-to-by` a `corporateClient` object class. Further, we might also model a `desktopComputer` object class which participates in an `ownership` relationship with the `corporateClient` class. The `corporate-Client` class plays the role `owns` with the `desktopComputer` class, which reciprocates with the role `is-owned-by`. We also know that the `informationService` class must play a `downloads-to` role with respect to the `desktopComputer` class. This would be a `download` relationship, in which the `desktopComputer` reciprocates with the role `downloads-from`. This situation is illustrated in Figure 18-11.

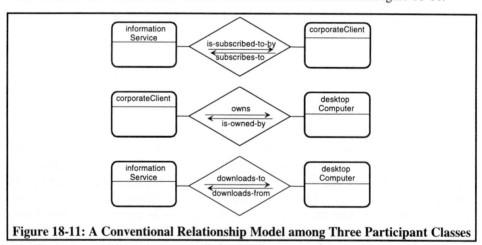

Figure 18-11: A Conventional Relationship Model among Three Participant Classes

In this situation, each time the `corporateClient` adds a new `desktop-Computer`, we must create a new instance of the `ownership` relationship between these two classes. Ordinarily, we must also create a separate instance of the `download` relationship between the `informationService` object class and the same instance of `desktopComputer`. We will always have to check to ensure that all such parallel relationships are consistently maintained. This means that, every time the `corporate-Client` class decommissions or scraps a `desktopComputer`, we must delete the `ownership` relationship instance with that `desktopComputer`. We must then ensure that we also delete the corresponding instance of the `download` relationship between the `informationService` object and the same `desktopComputer`. We would have to maintain this consistency using some mechanism external to the relationships, since we have no mechanism *within* the relationships to automatically shadow the changes of one set of relationship instances in another.

We can eliminate this problem entirely by defining the `download` relationship to be a *convolute virtual relationship* which *convolutes from* the `subscription` and `ownership` relationships. The forward role `downloads-to` *convolutes above* the first forward role `is-subscribed-to-by` played by `informationService` with `corporateClient`, *and* the second forward role `owns` played by `corporate-Client` with `desktopComputer`. The reciprocal role `downloads-from` *convolutes below* the two roles `subscribes-to` and `is-owned-by`. With this specification, a virtual relationship instance of the `download` relationship is automatically created or destroyed every time an actual relationship instance of the `ownership` relationship is created or destroyed. (Or, several instances of the `download` relationship are automatically created or destroyed each time a `subscription` relationship is created or destroyed.) Figure 18-12 illustrates this mechanism.

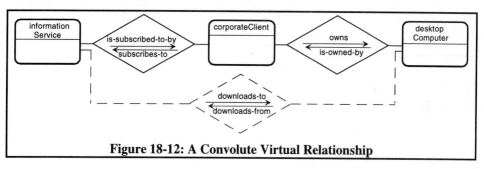

Figure 18-12: A Convolute Virtual Relationship

As with distribution, care must be exercised when we talk about convolution, with due consideration for the order in which the roles are specified. If the role-pair for `download` is specified as `{downloads-to, downloads-from}`, for `subscription` as `{is-subscribed-to-by, subscribes-to}`, and for `ownership` as `{owns, is-owned-by}`, then it is correct to say that the `download` role-pair convolutes from the `subscription` and `ownership` role-pairs. If the role-pair for `subscription` is specified as `{subscribes, is-subscribed-to-by}`, then we must say that the `download` role-pair convolutes from the *inverted* `subscription` role-pair and the (non-inverted) `ownership` role-pair. In either case, `downloads-to` convolutes above `is-subscribed-to-by` and `owns`, in that order, and `downloads-from` convolutes below `subscribes-to` and `is-owned-by`, in that order.

The definition of this convolution does not specify any interaction between the roles `subscribes-to` and `owns`, or between the roles `is-subscribed-to-by` and `is-owned-by`. Moreover, if the order of the base role-pairs is reversed — for example, if we mistakenly specify that the `download` role-pair convolutes from the ownership and `subscription` role-pairs — the compiler will generate the corresponding role convolutions, but the semantics will be incorrect.

More Convolute Virtual Relationships

The base relationships of a convolute virtual relationship may themselves be virtual. As an example, suppose we define a new `consulting` relationship in which the `corporateClient` object class plays the `engages` role with a `consultingGroup` object class. Because the `corporateClient` desires that the information from the subscribed service be also made available to the `consultingGroup`, it may wish to stipulate that certain `desktopComputer` objects owned by the `consultingGroup` be additional recipients of the `informationService`. Thus, the `stipulates` role between `corporateClient` and `desktopComputer` convolutes above the `engages` role between `corporateClient` and `consultingGroup` and the `owns` role between `consultingGroup` and `desktopComputer`. This convolute virtual relationship may act as a base relationship to another virtual relationship; for example, the `downloads-to` role between `informationService` and `desktopComputer` can convolute above the `is-subscribed-to-by` role between `informationService` and `corporateClient` and the virtual `stipulates` role between `corporateClient` and `desktopComputer`. Figure 18-13 shows how this might happen.

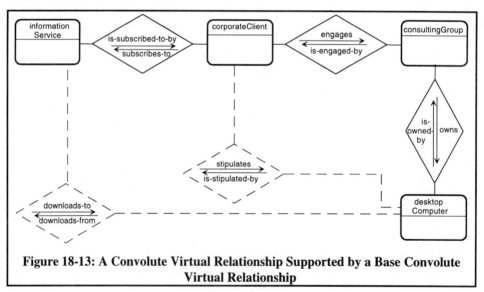

Figure 18-13: A Convolute Virtual Relationship Supported by a Base Convolute Virtual Relationship

A little reflection indicates that a distributive virtual relationship is a special case of a convolute virtual relationship in which the convolute virtual role-pair is the same as the base distributing role-pair.

18.7. Implicate Virtual Relationships

An *implicate virtual relationship* is a relationship which arises from the *implication* property of the role-pair in its base relationship. We define an implicate role-pair as follows:

> A role-pair {r1,r2} is said to *implicate* another role-pair {r3,r4} if, given two participant object classes A and B such that A plays role r1 with B and B plays role r2 with A, it can be inferred that A plays r3 with B and B plays role r4 with A.

This definition states that a relationship with the base role-pair automatically *implicates* (implies) the existence of a virtual relationship between the same participants with different roles.

Implication is actually one of the most general forms of virtual relationships. It is important to note the details of its definition: the definition does not require that the implicate role-pair have the same *properties* as the base role-pair. It is possible that the base role-pair may have properties such as commutativity, transitivity, and so on, which do not necessarily carry over to the implicate role-pair. It is also possible that the implicate role-pair possesses properties which the base role-pair does not. Generally, the implicate virtual relationship conveys different semantics than its base relationship. A few examples will clarify this point.

Implication for Synonymous Virtual Relationships

In its most simple form, implication can be used in situations where all that is necessary is to create a synonym for an existing relationship. A *synonymous virtual relationship* is simply a special case of an implicate virtual relationship in which the semantics, properties, and multiplicities of the virtual relationship are the same as those of the base relationship. A synonymous role permits different external objects to query an object for its relatants in different ways.

For example, we modeled the relationship between outsourcingVendor and site in Figure 18-8 with the roles administers and is-administered-by. We might also have in our model information base the role-pair manages and is-managed-by, registered under separate role labels, which we might normally use for other pairs of participant classes in other relationships. To determine the outsourcingVendor responsible for a particular site object, some objects might query that site object for its relatant via its is-administered-by role, while other objects — possibly from external networks — might query it for its relatant via its is-managed-by role. If we inform our compiler that the role-pair {manages, is-managed-by} is *implicated* by (is a synonym for) the role-pair {adminsters, is-administered-by}, the run-time environment resolves both queries identically.

The base and implicate role-pairs are registered with separate role-labels, so each can be used to create actual relationships in its own independent context when necessary. Implication is a one-way dependency. If we specify that the role-pair {manages, is-managed-by} is a synonym for {administers, is-administered-by}, then an actual relationship instance created with roles {administers, is-administered-by} implies that its participants also play the roles {manages, is-man-aged-by}. However, if we create an actual relationship instance whose participants play the roles {manages, is-managed-by}, it does not mean that they play the roles {administers, is-administered-by}. This would only be possible if we specified a second implication in the reverse direction as well. Generally, synonyms for role-pairs are created to harmonize terminological differences between the internal models of two different networks. Figure 18-14 illustrates this use of implicate virtual relationships.

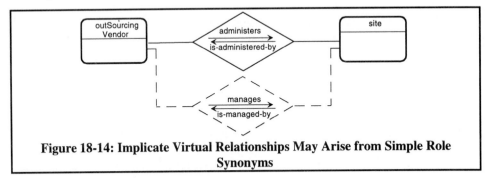

Figure 18-14: Implicate Virtual Relationships May Arise from Simple Role Synonyms

Implication with Different Semantics

A more interesting form of implicate relationships arises when a base relationship gives rise to virtual implicate relationships with different semantics, different properties, and possibly different multiplicities. This generally happens when the base relationship acts as a "stronger" expression or shorthand for a collection of several "looser" relationships. Consider the relationship between object classes workstation and server which we modeled in Figure 17-10, in which workstation plays the role accesses with server, and server plays the role is-accessed-by with workstation. Generally, the fact that workstation accesses server tells us that they also participate in several other relationships. For example, it tells us that workstation interconnects-to server, workstation stores-files-on server, workstation forwards-mail-to server, and so on. Clearly, these roles have different semantics and are often independently used by themselves between other participant object classes. Nevertheless, all of them automatically hold between workstation and server the moment we assert that workstation accesses server. Thus, the access relationship gives rise to several implicate virtual relationships between the same two participant classes; this is illustrated in Figure 18-15.

In general, implicate virtual relationships arise because they indicate consequential roles which exist because the base roles exist. If used as shorthand for a collection of relationships, they may also indicate preconditional roles which must exist for the base roles to exist. As a general guideline, if a consequential role-pair arises from a single base relationship, it is specified as an implicate virtual relationship. If a consequential role-pair

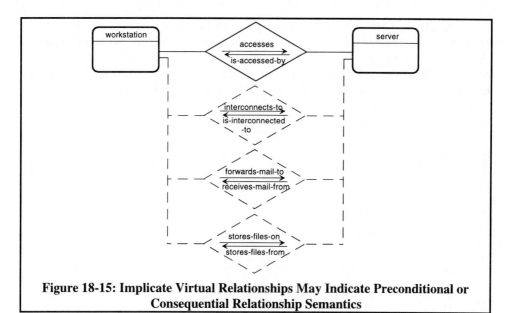

Figure 18-15: Implicate Virtual Relationships May Indicate Preconditional or Consequential Relationship Semantics

arises from two base relationships with a common "linking" relatant, it is specified as a transitive, distributive, or convolute virtual relationship.

Implicate virtual relationships may have properties which their base relationships do not. For example, the implicate role-pair {`interconnects-to, is-interconnected-to`} between `workstation` and `server` is commutative, whereas the base role-pair {`accesses, is-accessed-by`} — which gives rise to the implicate role-pair — is not.

As a more complex example, consider the `backup` relationship in which the roles are `backs-up` and `is-backed-up-by`. If object class A `backs-up` object class B and object class B `backs-up` object class C, it is not true that object class A `backs-up` object class C. This is because if an instance of C fails, it is not true that an instance of A will take over. Thus, the role-pair {`backs-up, is-backed-up-by`} is not *transitive*.

However, this role-pair gives rise to the implicate `pointOfFailure` role-pair {`is-a-point-of-failure-for, has-point-of-failure`}. This conveys different semantics than the `backup` relationship and also has different properties: it *is* transitive. While it is not the case that A `backs-up` C, due to the transitivity of B `is-a-point-of-failure-for` C and A `is-a-point-of-failure for` B, it is true that A `is-a-point-of-failure-for` C. Further, this implicate role-pair also has a *distribution* property which its base role-pair does not have: the role `has-point-of-failure` distributes ahead of the `has-as-a-part` role. If C `has-point-of-failure` A and A `has-as-a-part` D, then it is true that C `has-point-of-failure` D. Thus, it is possible to have implicate virtual relationships with completely different properties than their supporting base relationships.

Implicate virtual relationships are a powerful mechanism to capture extended semantics in a concise manner. In the example above, we create only the actual relationships A backs-up B, A has-as-a-part D, and B backs-up C. Because the
backup relationship gives rise to implicate virtual relationships which have a distribution property, the three actual relationships generate four virtual relationships, as Figure
18-16 shows.

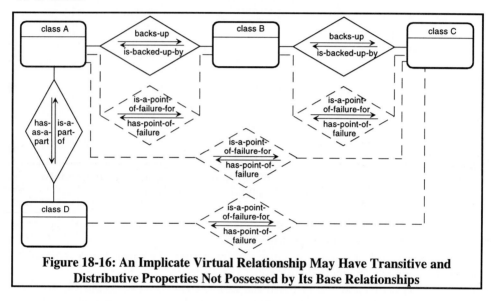

**Figure 18-16: An Implicate Virtual Relationship May Have Transitive and
Distributive Properties Not Possessed by Its Base Relationships**

In Figure 18-16, if we query an instance of C for all its points of failure (that is, all
its relatants via the has-point-of-failure role) the response will include the instances of B, A, and D. In fact, due to the transitivity of aggregation, the transitivity of
pointOfFailure, and the distribution of pointOfFailure over aggregation, the
response will include *all* component objects of A, *all* component objects of B, the transitive closure of A's has-point-of-failure role (that is, all objects which may
back-up A, their back-ups, and so on) and all *their* components as well. By simply
specifying the correct properties for relationship role-pairs, we can equip our run-time
environment with the power to navigate through an extensive semantic network in our
model information base.

Implication for Commutative Breakdown

Implicate virtual relationships are also sometimes used to "break down" commutative relationships into two one-way relationships where necessary. For example, the mutual-
Backup relationship can be broken down into two one-way backup relationships. This
can be accomplished by specifying that the role-pair {mbacks-up, is-mbacked-
up-by} of Figure 18-4 implicates *both* the one-way role-pairs {backs-up, is-
backed-up-by} and {is-backed-up-by, backs-up}, as illustrated in Figure
18-17.

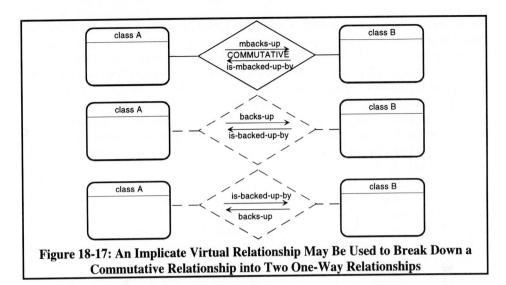

Figure 18-17: An Implicate Virtual Relationship May Be Used to Break Down a Commutative Relationship into Two One-Way Relationships

This is useful in situations where both the commutative and one-way roles are used. Assume that we have specified to our compiler that the `mutualBackup` relationship implicates both directions of the one-way `backup` relationship. Object classes A and B have a `mutualBackup` relationship with each other, in which they play the roles `mbacks-up` and `is-mbacked-up-by`. Also, class C has a *one-way* `backup` relationship with A, such that C `backs-up` A but A does not `back-up` C.

In this situation, when we query an instance of A for all its backups (that is, all its relatants via the `is-backed-up-by` role), the response will include the instances of both B and C. If we had not informed the compiler that the `mutualBackup` relationship implicates both directions of the one-way `backup` relationship, the response would have included only the instance of C. We would have had to make a separate query to the instance of A for its relatants via the `is-mbacked-up-by` role to get a response of B.

The synonymity does not affect the base relationship: if we wish to determine all the *mutual backups* of A, we can continue to query A for its relatants via its `is-mbacked-up-by` role, which continues to hold, and obtain a response of just B.

18.8. Applying Virtual Relationships

It is important to remember that virtual relationships arise as properties of role-pairs, not of relationships. The properties of commutativity, transitivity, and implication are unary operations on role-pairs; distribution and convolution are binary operations on role-pairs. When a relationship is specified with a particular role-pair, all the properties of the role-pair continue to hold in that relationship. A relationship desiring to use a role-pair cannot choose to "drop" certain properties of that role-pair, nor can it invest that role-pair with new properties which hold only between its two participant classes. If a role-pair carrying the same semantics needs to have certain properties in one relationship and different properties in another, we must define two different role-pairs for this purpose. To equate the semantics, we can then synonymize the two role-pairs through implicate virtualization. This was done in the example above where the `mutualBackup` and `backup` relationships were created with different role-pairs because one was commutative and the other was not. Later, the commutative role-pair was synonymized with the one-way role-pair in both directions to equate the semantics.

A relationship instance between two participant objects indicates a particular role-pair behavior between them. If this is an actual relationship instance, the role-pair behavior is imperatively imposed by the specifier. If this is a virtual relationship instance, the role-pair behavior arises as a result of the special properties of other role-pair behaviors which have been imperatively imposed.

Only relationships are virtual; role-pairs are not. When a role-pair is specified, it may be used in any relationships between any pair of participant classes at the discretion of the network architect. The role-pair "does not know" whether it is going to be used imperatively in an actual relationship, or arise virtually from one. Once a role-pair is defined, we may use it directly in an actual relationship, or define a second role-pair with some property that gives rise to the first role-pair in a virtual relationship, or both. The definition of a role-pair does not restrict how or where it may be used: we cannot constrain a role-pair to occur only in virtual relationships or only in actual relationships.

As an example, we indicated in Figure 18-12 that the `downloads-to` role arises as a convolution above the `is-subscribed-to-by` and `owns` roles. When we formally specify the `download` role-pair {`downloads-to, downloads-from`}, we indicate in its definition that it may arise as a convolution from the role-pairs {`is-subscribed-to-by, subscribes-to`} and {`owns, is-owned-by`}. This does not restrict it to *only* occur as a convolution of its base role-pairs. It is possible to directly specify an actual relationship which uses the role-pair {`downloads-to, downloads-from`}. We are permitted to specify this role-pair in any relationship between any two participant classes at our discretion. We can even use it to create an actual relationship between the `informationService` object class and the `desktopComputer` object class. If we do so, we will have the ability to imperatively specify relationship instances in which individual `informationService` objects can directly `download-to` individual `desktopComputer` objects regardless of whether any `corporateClient` objects exist.

Of course, the convolution property continues to hold. This means that any time the compiler sees an object class B which both `subscribes-to` an object class A and `owns` an object class C, it *automatically establishes* a virtual `downloads-to` role between A and C. *Because properties belong to role-pairs, not relationships, this virtual convolution will be established regardless of what the classes* A, B, *and* C *are.* For this reason, it is good modeling practice to make the semantics of relationship roles as limited as possible and apply them to the lowest and most specific descendants of the participant classes as possible.

For the more mathematically inclined, we present below a concise summary of the types of virtual relationship we have defined using informal logical expressions [Benz93]. These expressions help in analyzing which role-pairs of actual relationships can give rise to other role-pairs of virtual relationships. In these expressions, A, B, and C are object classes, and r, s, and t are roles of relationships. The construct $r(A,B)$ is read "r is the role played by A in its relationship with B". If "∧" is read as *and* and "→" is read as *gives-rise-to*, then

- *Commutative Virtual Relationship*:

$$r(A,B) \quad \rightarrow \quad r(B,A)$$

- *Transitive Virtual Relationship*:

$$r(A,B) \quad \wedge \quad r(B,C) \quad \rightarrow \quad r(A,C)$$

- *Distributive Virtual Relationship*:

$$r(A,B) \quad \wedge \quad s(B,C) \quad \rightarrow \quad r(A,C)$$

Note that a distributive virtual relationship of the form

$$r(A,B) \quad \wedge \quad s(B,C) \quad \rightarrow \quad s(A,C)$$

can be written as the first form using reciprocal roles. If r' and s' are the reciprocal roles of r and s respectively, then the second form is semantically equivalent to

$$s'(C,B) \quad \wedge \quad r'(B,A) \quad \rightarrow \quad s'(C,A)$$

which is syntactically equivalent to the first form.

- *Convolute Virtual Relationship*:

$$r(A,B) \quad \wedge \quad s(B,C) \quad \rightarrow \quad t(A,C)$$

- *Implicate Virtual Relationship*:

$$r(A,B) \quad \rightarrow \quad s(A,B)$$

Virtual relationships provide an effective mechanism for extending relationship semantics. Because of their ability to automatically shadow the changes of one set of relationship instances in another, they reduce the potential for inconsistency. Even if an object has a relatant via a virtual relationship arising from a chain of supporting actual relationships, we can query the object for this relatant exactly as we query it for any other relatant. The run-time environment of the object internally and transparently resolves the virtual relationship in terms of its chain of supporting actual relationships. This eliminates the need for us to compose any relational joins in our query, which otherwise can be quite complex. Consequently, virtual relationships considerably enhance the semantic richness of our model.

18.9. Multiplicities of Virtual Relationships

We must also consider the behavior of relationship multiplicities in virtual relationships. Fortunately, it is easy to compute the multiplicity values of virtual relationships from the base relationships. The value of the multiplicity of the virtual relationship depends on the type of the virtual relationship.

Commutative and Implicate Virtual Relationships: There is no change in the relationship multiplicities. For example, in Figure 18-2, the pbx object class will play the virtual is-connected-to role with ocl-multiplexer with exactly the same multiplicity as it plays the actual connects-to role. Similarly, the ocl-multiplexer object class plays its role in both its actual and virtual relationships with the same multiplicity. This is true of implicate virtual relationships as well. Of course, if the implicate virtual relationship also has the transitivity, distribution and convolution properties, then it must be treated accordingly.

Transitive, Distributive, and Convolute Virtual Relationships: Upper bounds of relationship multiplicities *multiply* in the direction of the forward roles. We will demonstrate this phenomenon in the multiplicities of convolute virtual relationships; transitive and distributive relationships also behave in the same manner, since they are simply special cases of convolute relationships.

In Figure 18-12, the upper bound for the relatant multiplicity of the downloads-to role is the product of the upper bounds for the relatant multiplicities of the is-subscribed-to-by role and the owns role. For example, if each informationService is-subscribed-to-by up to 50 corporate-Clients, and each client owns up to 1000 desktopComputers, then each informationService must download-to up to 50000 desktop-Computers. If either base multiplicity has an upper bound which is unlimited, the upper bound of the multiplicity of the virtual relationship is also unlimited.

The lower bound for the relatant multiplicity of a virtual relationship role remains equal to the lower bound of the relatant multiplicity of the "second" or "distant" base relationship role. If each corporateClient subscribes-to at least 3 informationServices, and each desktopComputer is owned by exactly 1 corporateClient, then each desktopComputer downloads-from at least 3 informationServices. Even if it were somehow possible for a desktopComputer to be-owned-by more than one corporateClient, each of which could subscribe-to at least 3 informationServices, then each desktopComputer would still be able to download-from at least

3 informationServices, because all its owners may subscribe-to the same informationServices.

Subject multiplicities may be computed using the same considerations as relatant multiplicities going in the opposite direction. The general algorithm for computing relationship multiplicities for virtual relationships is illustrated in Figure 18-18.

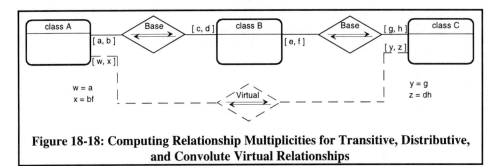

Figure 18-18: Computing Relationship Multiplicities for Transitive, Distributive, and Convolute Virtual Relationships

18.10. Virtual Relationships for Specialization

Virtual relationships may be used in relationship-based modes of specialization. In the example of Figure 18-12, a corporateClient could instruct certain desktop-Computers to download-from only selected informationServices, possibly on a departmental or need-to-know basis. If the corporateClient subscribes-to multiple informationServices, it may use relatant specialization or relatant multiplicity restriction on different subclasses of desktopComputer based on their *virtual relationship* with subclasses of informationService.

For example, the corporateClient might characterize different desktop-Computers for different purposes (that is, create subclasses of desktopComputer). To economize on subscription charges, it may restrict a stockTradingComputer to download-from only a stockQuotationService, and a bondTrading-Computer to download-from only a bondQuotationService. It thus uses relatant specialization to restrict the subclasses of desktopComputer to download-from only selected subclasses of informationService. This is possible because, even though the download relationship is a virtual relationship, we permit relationship-based modes of specialization based on virtual relationships as well. Figure 18-19 illustrates this example.

We are permitted to use virtual relationships in a relationship-based mode of specialization because, during specialization, a relationship predicate is used in its *declarative* context. A virtual relationship behaves like an actual relationship in all contexts of interrogation, declaration, and qualification. Thus, a virtual relationship may be used in place of an actual relationship in any of these contexts. However, because it can never be instantiated, it cannot be used in place of an actual relationship in the *imperative* context.

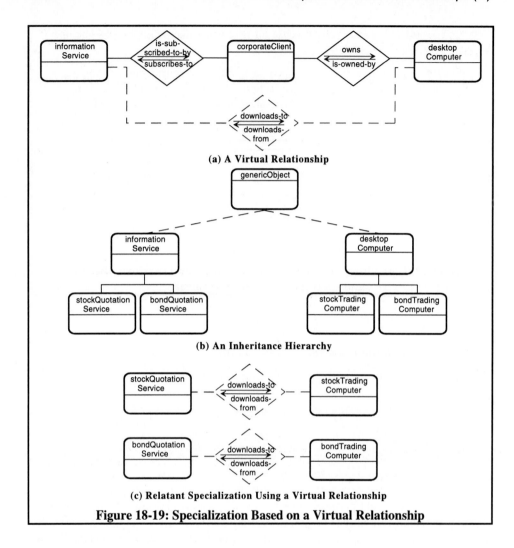

(a) A Virtual Relationship

(b) An Inheritance Hierarchy

(c) Relatant Specialization Using a Virtual Relationship

Figure 18-19: Specialization Based on a Virtual Relationship

18.11. Use of Virtual Relationships

Virtual relationships provide us with a robust mechanism to enforce consistency between a chain of links in a semantic network of objects. The presence of virtual relationships enables us to drop certain constraints which would otherwise be imposed across the semantic network.

For example, a requirement which traverses many links in the semantic network, such as: "*The operator responsible for addressing an alarm generated by a network device must be an employee of the vendor who administers the site which houses that network device*" is normally specified in most systems of knowledge as a sequence of multiple *constraints*. These constraints are explicit: the user must specify how to enforce them by equating values of identifier attributes of *pairs of objects* across binary links in the semantic network [Sowa91].

In specialization theory, we regard a relationship instance to be a *predicate*, in the logic programming sense, between "atom" objects. Thus, asserting a relationship instance is a statement of a fact, just as asserting an attribute value is a statement of a fact. By a logical conjunction of such facts, we can *infer* the identity of attribute values across *multiple* links in the semantic network. By specifying virtual relationships between objects such as `operator`, `alarm`, `networkDevice`, `vendor`, and `site` extending over actual roles such as `is-responsible-for`, `is-generated-by`, `is-employed-by`, `administers`, and `houses`, the semantic constraint falls out automatically and does not have to be explicitly specified. Virtual relationships provide us with the ability to extend the "reach" of nodes in the semantic network to nodes other than their immediate neighbors.

Virtual relationships are part of the general relationship model of specialization theory. As we shall see later, this relationship model is the cornerstone of many other advanced features of the methodology, including inter-object information transfer through virtual attributes, inter-object constraint enforcement, and inter-object rule processing.

18.12. Summary

The concept of virtual relationships is a powerful abstraction which permits us to capture multiple associations between object classes in a single specification. Virtual relationships arise from special properties possessed by the roles of its supporting base relationships. Virtual relationships can never be instantiated; changes in a virtual relationship occur automatically as a consequence of changes in its supporting actual relationships.

Because they automatically reflect the changes in one set of relationship instances in another, virtual relationships reduce the potential for inconsistency in our model. An object may be queried for its relatants via a virtual relationship exactly as it may be queried for its relatants via an actual relationship. This eliminates the need to compose any relational joins in our query.

The properties of the roles of its supporting base relationships are commutativity, transitivity, distribution, convolution, and implication. The virtual relationships which arise as a consequence of these properties may be used exactly like actual relationships in all contexts of interrogation, declaration, and qualification. In particular, virtual relationships may also be used in relationship-based modes of specialization. Virtual relationships provide an elegant shorthand to capture the notion of extended relationships in a concise manner.

19. Formal Modeling of Relationships

"He always needs a hundred words to tell me 'I love you'
— 32 header, 3 data, and the rest all CRC."
— girlfriend of anonymous protocol designer.

19.1. Introduction

Having defined our general relationship model, its interaction with the various modes of specialization, and its extension to virtual relationships, we introduce in this chapter the notation for the formal specification of these modeling constructs. The constructs for relationship templates are introduced along with some examples. We also present constructs for querying and setting relationship multiplicities, as well as logical predicates to operate on relationship instances.

19.2. Formal Specification of Roles

In Chapter 17, we indicated that each relationship between a pair of object classes must be modeled with its role labels and relationship multiplicities. The roles of a relationship must be uniquely paired. Before we specify the formal notation for relationships, we introduce a construct for associating roles in pairs. Each role is assigned an OBJECT IDENTIFIER label so we can formally register all roles in our model information base. This is accomplished using the ROLE information object class template:

```
ROLE ::= CLASS
{
      &roleName                 PrintableString,
      &roleLabel                OBJECT IDENTIFIER UNIQUE
}
```

```
WITH SYNTAX
{
     ROLE NAME                    &roleName
     IDENTIFIED BY                &roleLabel
}
```

This construct registers each role in our model information base. For the time being, we assume that the &roleName of each ROLE is a PrintableString; if we later move to some other structured scheme for role names, we must change the type in this definition.

We can now define the information object set Roles as the set of all ROLE information objects registered in our model information base:

```
Roles ROLE ::= {
                    role1      |
                    role2      |
                    ...
               }
```

where role1, role2, and so on, denote actual ROLE information objects. This set can now be used to constrain the type reference name RoleLabel, which is the same type as an OBJECT IDENTIFIER, except that values of type RoleLabel are constrained to come from the limited pool of OBJECT IDENTIFIERs constituting the &roleLabel fields of all the ROLE information objects in the set {Roles}:

```
RoleLabel ::= ROLE.&roleLabel({Roles})
```

While each role is registered with its own label, roles are never used singly. A role is always used together with its reciprocal role. The information object class ROLE-PAIR pairs two roles together so that they are registered as a mutually reciprocal pair:

```
ROLE-PAIR ::= CLASS
{
     &forwardRole                 ROLE,
     &reciprocalRole              ROLE,
     &rolePairLabel               OBJECT IDENTIFIER UNIQUE
}
WITH SYNTAX
{
     ROLE                         &forwardRole
           RECIPROCATES
```

```
        ROLE                        &reciprocalRole
        IDENTIFIED BY               &rolePairLabel
    }
```

This construct associates two roles together as a pair and uses a label to register the entire role-pair construct. Of course, it is irrelevant which element of the role-pair we specify to be the `&forwardRole` and which the `&reciprocalRole`. The roles of any `ROLE-PAIR` must be uniquely paired, that is, a role cannot occur in more than one `ROLE-PAIR` construct. Also, it is forbidden for a role to be its own reciprocal. We will extend this definition further when we consider the properties of role-pairs which give rise to virtual relationships.

We can now enumerate the set `RolePairs` of all defined `ROLE-PAIR` information objects:

```
RolePairs ROLE-PAIR ::=  {
                            rolePair1 |
                            rolePair2 |
                            . . .
                         }
```

where `rolePair1`, `rolePair2`, and so on, denote actual `ROLE-PAIR` information objects. We may now use this set to define the type reference name `RolePairLabel`, which is an `OBJECT IDENTIFIER` constrained to come from the pool of all `&role-PairLabel` fields of the set `RolePairs` of all defined `ROLE-PAIR` information objects:

```
RolePairLabel ::= ROLE-PAIR.&rolePairLabel({RolePairs})
```

19.3. Formal Relationship Notation

We now define the formal templates for specifying relationships as first-class conceptual constructs using the following information object class:

```
RELATIONSHIP ::= CLASS
{
    &subject              OBJECT-CLASS,
    &forwardRole          ROLE,
    &subjectMultiplicity  Multiplicity OPTIONAL,
    &relatant             OBJECT-CLASS,
    &reciprocalRole       ROLE OPTIONAL,
```

```
            &relatantMultiplicity       Multiplicity OPTIONAL,
            &relationshipLabel          OBJECT IDENTIFIER UNIQUE
    }
    WITH SYNTAX
    {
            OBJECT-CLASS                &subject
            IN ROLE                     &forwardRole
            [ WITH MULTIPLICITY         &subjectMultiplicity ]
                RELATES TO
            OBJECT-CLASS                &relatant
            [ IN ROLE                   &reciprocalRole ]
            [ WITH MULTIPLICITY         &relatantMultiplicity ]
            IDENTIFIED BY               &relationshipLabel
    }
```

This template is a first cut, which we shall use as a working base. As we expand the semantics of relationships, we will extend this template to include additional fields as we need them.

As we stated in Chapter 17, it is irrelevant which particular class we choose to be the subject in any relationship; we can just as easily specify the same semantics if we reverse our perspective and make the other class the subject. The choice of subject and relatant may be reversed, as long as the corresponding roles and multiplicities are also reversed. Although this template may not appear to be symmetric, identical semantics are stored in the model information base irrespective of the direction chosen for specifying the relationship.

In this template, &subject and &relatant are *object fields* of type OBJECT-CLASS which denote the participant classes of the specificand relationship. The clause RELATES TO is unnecessary but is included for readability. The fields &forwardRole and &reciprocalRole are also *object fields* of type ROLE which indicate the role played by each object class.

The fields &forwardRole and &reciprocalRole of any RELATIONSHIP information object must come from the same ROLE-PAIR. Strictly, our template for the RELATIONSHIP construct includes redundant information: it is not necessary to include the field &reciprocalRole in the template. If the compiler knows that the &subject class plays the &forwardRole, it can infer that the &relatant class must reciprocate with the role registered as the reciprocal of the &forwardRole in its ROLE-PAIR construct. This is why the &reciprocalRole field is OPTIONAL; if omitted, it is inferred by the compiler. We often include it in the specification for readability and symmetry.

Multiplicity Specification

The value fields &subjectMultiplicity and &relatantMultiplicity indi-
cate the multiplicity with which the subject and relatant classes participate in the relationship. They are of the type Multiplicity which is the same as that used in the formal
specification of the aggregation relationship, specified in Chapter 11:

```
Multiplicity ::= Domain {MultiplicityValue}
```

where the types Domain and MultiplicityValue are defined as

```
Domain {Type} ::= CHOICE
{
      theSet          [0]   SET OF Type,
      theRangeWith    [1]   SEQUENCE
                            {
                              lowerBound [0] Type OPTIONAL,
                              upperBound [1] Type OPTIONAL
                            }
      and             [2]   SET OF Domain {Type}
}


MultiplicityValue ::= CHOICE
{
      constant [0] INTEGER (0..MAX),
                              -- non-negative integer
      ade      [1] AttributeDefinedExpression
}
```

Any Multiplicity value may involve an AttributeDefined-
Expression, which, as indicated in Chapter 11, further expands into a simple grammar
allowing common mathematical and logical operations on attributes. The attributes in any
expression for &subjectMultiplicity must belong to the &relatant, and the
attributes in any expression for &relatantMultiplicity must belong to the
&subject. Each Multiplicity value is OPTIONAL because, if omitted, it defaults
to exactly 1. If the lower end of the multiplicity domain is not 0, it implies that the relationship is mandatory for that participant, that is, at least one instance of that object class
must participate in the relationship.

Each relationship construct itself is registered in the model information base using
a &relationshipLabel. This label is useful during the creation of individual relationship instances; it is used to identify which relationship is being instantiated. Since a
relationship is bidirectional, creating a single relationship instance in effect creates two

pieces of information: first, that the `&subject` instance plays `&forwardRole` with the `&relatant` instance, and second, that the `&relatant` instance plays `&reciprocalRole` with the `&subject` instance. Once we instantiate a relationship, we may query either the instance of the `&subject` for the instance or instances of `&relatant` with which it plays `&forwardRole`, or we may query the instance of the `&relatant` for the instance or instances of `&subject` with which it plays `&reciprocalRole`. No particular direction is preferred; each role implies its reciprocal, and the semantic importance of both roles is equal.

A relationship label uniquely identifies the participant classes, the roles they play with each other, and their multiplicities. However, a role-pair does not uniquely identify a relationship, or the classes playing those roles. For example, isomorphic relationships would have the same role-pair but different pairs of participant classes.

Querying Relationships

From the context of a given subject class, its relatant in a given relationship can be identified merely by providing the relationship label. Assume there are two classes A and B which participate in relationship R1, in which A plays role r1 with B and B plays role r2 with A. Then, the expression "relatant of A in R1" indicates B, while the expression "relatant of B in R1" indicates A. The expression "the class playing role r1 in R1" indicates A, while the expression "the class playing role r2 in R1" indicates B. If there is a third object class C which plays the same role with A that B does — that is, A plays r1 also with C and C reciprocates with r2 — then the relationship between A and C must be registered separately as R2 (unless C is a descendant of B, in which case it is available through inheritance). The expressions "the class playing role r2 with A" and "the class with which A plays r1" now evaluate to both B and C.

Queries such as those described above are often made at architecture time against the classes of a network schema in the model information base. Analogous queries may be made at operation time against object *instances* in an actual network. From the context of a given instance a of A, the expression "relatant of a in R1" stands for that instance of B (if the relatant multiplicity is 1) or set of instances of B (if the relatant multiplicity exceeds 1) which participate in R1 with instance a of A. The expressions "relatants with which a plays r1" or "relatants which play r2 with a" stand for those instances of both B and C for which relationship instances of R1 and R2 have been created with instance a of A.

An Example of a Relationship Specification

As an example, consider the `subscription` relationship between a `subscriber` object class and a `networkService` object class, which we modeled in Figure 17-4. Each participant class of this relationship will be specified in its own `OBJECT-CLASS` template and will have its own attributes; these are not shown here for brevity. In the traditional entity-relationship approach, this relationship would be modeled as *many-to-many*, that is, a subscriber may subscribe to many network services, and a network service may have many subscribers. With the more precise multiplicity notation of specialization theory, we can specify this relationship formally as indicated below. Throughout this

chapter, we will make the assumption that any identifier ending in the suffix -Lbl is the
value of an appropriately chosen OBJECT IDENTIFIER from the registration hierarchy.

```
subscribes-to ROLE::=
{
      ROLE NAME                  "subscribes-to"
      IDENTIFIED BY              subscribesToLbl
}


is-subscribed-to-by ROLE::=
{
      ROLE NAME                  "is-subscribed-to-by"
      IDENTIFIED BY              isSubscribedToByLbl
}


subscriptionRoles ROLE-PAIR ::=
{
      ROLE                       subscribes-to
          RECIPROCATES
      ROLE                       is-subscribed-to-by
      IDENTIFIED BY              subscriptionRolesLbl
}


subscription RELATIONSHIP ::=
{
      OBJECT-CLASS               subscriber
      IN ROLE                    subscribes-to
      WITH MULTIPLICITY          zeroOrMore
          RELATES TO
      OBJECT-CLASS               networkService
      IN ROLE                    is-subscribed-to-by
      WITH MULTIPLICITY          oneOrMore
      IDENTIFIED BY              subscriptionLbl
}


zeroOrMore Multiplicity ::=
      {theRangeWith: { lowerBound { constant:0 }}}
                                 -- upperBound unspecified
```

```
oneOrMore Multiplicity ::=
      {theRangeWith: { lowerBound { constant:1 }}}
                                    -- upperBound unspecified
```

The "sentence" form of this relationship, which was available by simply reading across its class relationship diagram (Figure 17-4) forward and backward, is also available by reading the fields of this template in the appropriate order. This relationship construct may be read:

- *"A subscriber subscribes to one or more network services."*

- *"A network service is subscribed to by zero or more subscribers."*

19.4. Relationship Attributes

In the preceding section, we modeled an example of a relationship without considering its relationship attributes. As we know, a relationship may be specified with its own attributes. To formally specify these, we extend our specification of the RELATIONSHIP information object class as follows:

```
RELATIONSHIP ::= CLASS
{
      &subject                  OBJECT-CLASS,
      &forwardRole              ROLE,
      &subjectMultiplicity      Multiplicity OPTIONAL,
      &relatant                 OBJECT-CLASS,
      &reciprocalRole           ROLE OPTIONAL,
      &relatantMultiplicity     Multiplicity OPTIONAL,
      &Attributes               ATTRIBUTE OPTIONAL,
      &Capsules                 CAPSULE OPTIONAL,
      &relationshipLabel        OBJECT IDENTIFIER UNIQUE
}
WITH SYNTAX
{
      OBJECT-CLASS              &subject
      IN ROLE                   &forwardRole
      [ WITH MULTIPLICITY       &subjectMultiplicity ]
           RELATES TO
      OBJECT-CLASS              &relatant
      [ IN ROLE                 &reciprocalRole ]
      [ WITH MULTIPLICITY       &relatantMultiplicity ]
      [ ATTRIBUTES              &Attributes ]
```

```
[ CAPSULES                   &Capsules ]
IDENTIFIED BY                &relationshipLabel
}
```

In this extended specification, both `&Attributes` and `&Capsules` are object set fields representing the attributes which qualify the entire relationship. These attributes are syntactically identical to attributes of object classes (that is, they use the same `ATTRIBUTE` information object class template). However, an attribute of a relationship belongs to the entire relationship and not to either participant class.

An Example of Relationship Attributes

As an example, our formal definition of the relationship between the `sysAdmin` object class and the `dfsCell` object class of Figure 17-6 can now be specified as follows, assuming that its role-pair has already been separately defined:

```
dfsCellSupervision RELATIONSHIP ::=
{
        OBJECT-CLASS                 sysAdmin
        IN ROLE                      supervises
        WITH MULTIPLICITY            twoOrMore
                RELATES TO
        OBJECT-CLASS                 dfsCell
        IN ROLE                      is-supervised-by
        WITH MULTIPLICITY            zeroOrMore
        ATTRIBUTES                   {accessPermission}
        IDENTIFIED BY                dfsCellSupervisionLbl
}
```

where the attribute `accessPermission` could be specified as follows:

```
accessPermission ATTRIBUTE ::=
{
        ATTRIBUTE-TYPE               AccessPermission
        IDENTIFIED BY                accessPermissionLbl
}
```

```
AccessPermission ::=        ENUMERATED
{
      noAccess (0),
      monitorAccess (1),
      rebootAccess (2)
}


twoOrMore Multiplicity ::=
      {theRangeWith: { lowerBound { constant:2 }}}
                                    -- upperBound unspecified
```

19.5. Virtual Relationships

In Chapter 18, we modeled virtual relationships as operations on roles. If we indicate the special properties possessed by a role-pair, the compiler has sufficient information to generate all the virtual relationships which arise when that role-pair is used in the specification of actual relationships.

A role-pair may possess the special properties of commutativity, transitivity, distribution, convolution, or implication. We expand our specification of the ROLE-PAIR information object class to allow the specification of these properties as follows:

```
ROLE-PAIR ::= CLASS
{
      &forwardRole             ROLE,
      &reciprocalRole          ROLE,
      &commutative             BOOLEAN DEFAULT FALSE
                                            OPTIONAL,
      &transitive              BOOLEAN DEFAULT FALSE
                                            OPTIONAL,
      &distributesOver         DistributandRolePairs
                                            OPTIONAL,
      &convolutesFrom          ConvolutandRolePairPairs
                                            OPTIONAL,
      &implicates              ImplicandRolePairs
                                            OPTIONAL,
      &rolePairLabel           OBJECT IDENTIFIER UNIQUE
}
```

```
WITH SYNTAX
{
        ROLE                          &forwardRole
            RECIPROCATES
        ROLE                          &reciprocalRole
        [ COMMUTATIVE                 &commutative ]
        [ TRANSITIVE                  &transitive ]
        [ DISTRIBUTES OVER            &distributesOver ]
        [ CONVOLUTES FROM             &convolutesFrom ]
        [ IMPLICATES                  &implicates ]
        IDENTIFIED BY                 &rolePairLabel
}


DistributandRolePairs ::=     SET OF DirectedRolePair


ConvolutandRolePairPairs ::=  SET OF
                                  ConvolutandRolePairPair


ConvolutandRolePairPair ::=   SEQUENCE
{
        firstPair                 DirectedRolePair,
        secondPair                DirectedRolePair
}


ImplicandRolePairs ::=        SET OF DirectedRolePair


DirectedRolePair ::= SEQUENCE
{
        rolePair                  RolePairLabel,
        inverted                  BOOLEAN DEFAULT FALSE
                                              OPTIONAL
}
```

These constructs provide a flexible way to specify a role-pair along with its properties. The properties indicate all the role-pairs which the specificand role-pair distributes over, convolutes from, or implicates. We present a few examples below of some relationships we have already modeled in Chapters 17 and 18.

An Example of a Virtual Relationship

We indicated in Chapter 17 that aggregation could be treated just as any other relationship. We also saw in Chapter 18 that this relationship was transitive. In a subsequent section, we will see how the special-purpose AGGREGATION template we defined in Chapter 11 can be restated in terms of the RELATIONSHIP template of this chapter. For the time being, we define the role-pair aggregationRoles for the aggregation relationship as follows:

```
aggregationRoles ROLE-PAIR ::=
{
        ROLE                        has-as-a-part
            RECIPROCATES
        ROLE                        is-a-part-of
        TRANSITIVE                  TRUE
        IDENTIFIED BY               aggregationRolesLbl
}
```

Here, we assume that the roles has-as-a-part and is-a-part-of have already been independently specified in their own ROLE templates. (We make similar assumptions about all roles in the following examples.) We know from Figure 18-16 that the roles of a pointOfFailure relationship are transitive and distribute over the aggregation roles:

```
pointOfFailureRoles ROLE-PAIR ::=
{
        ROLE                        is-a-point-of-failure-for
            RECIPROCATES
        ROLE                        has-point-of-failure
        TRANSITIVE                  TRUE
        DISTRIBUTES OVER            {{rolePair
                                        aggregationRolesLbl}}
        IDENTIFIED BY               pointOfFailureRolesLbl
}
```

We also know from Figure 18-16 that the roles of a one-way backup relationship implicate the roles of a pointOfFailure relationship:

```
backupRoles ROLE-PAIR ::=
{
        ROLE                      backs-up
               RECIPROCATES
        ROLE                      is-backed-up-by
        IMPLICATES                {{rolePair
                                    pointOfFailureRolesLbl}}

        IDENTIFIED BY             backupRolesLbl
}
```

We know from Figure 18-17 that the role-pair for a `mutualBackup` relation-ship, which is commutative, also implicates both directions of the one-way backup re-lationship:

```
mutualBackupRoles ROLE-PAIR ::=
{
        ROLE                      mbacks-up
                RECIPROCATES
        ROLE                      is-mbacked-up-by
        COMMUTATIVE               TRUE
        IMPLICATES                {
                                     {rolePair
                                         backupRolesLbl},
                                     {rolePair
                                         backupRolesLbl,
                                      inverted      TRUE}
                                  }
        IDENTIFIED BY             mutualBackupRolesLbl
}
```

As explained in Chapter 18, virtual relationships arise entirely as a consequence of properties of role-pairs. Thus, we never use a RELATIONSHIP template to specify a virtual relationship; the template is only used to specify actual relationships. In fact, the ROLE-PAIR specifications above are sufficient for the compiler to automatically gener-ate all the virtual relationships that arise (such as those in Figure 18-16) when the actual base relationships are created.

As a prelude to the example of the convolute virtual relationship of Figure 18-12, we specify the roles of ownership relationships:

```
ownershipRoles ROLE-PAIR ::=
{
        ROLE                          owns
                RECIPROCATES
        ROLE                          is-owned-by
        IDENTIFIED BY                 ownershipRolesLbl
}
```

We have already specified the roles of subscription relationships earlier. We now specify the roles of the download relationship of Figure 18-12:

```
downloadRoles ROLE-PAIR ::=
{
        ROLE                          downloads-to
                RECIPROCATES
        ROLE                          downloads-from
        CONVOLUTES FROM               {{firstPair
                                          {rolePair
                                            subscriptionRolesLbl,
                                            inverted        TRUE},
                                        secondPair
                                          {rolePair
                                            ownershipRolesLbl}
                                      }}
        IDENTIFIED BY                 downloadRolesLbl
}
```

Note that in this specification, the role-pair subscriptionRoles must be inverted. This is because our definition of this role-pair earlier in the chapter was the sequence {subscribes-to, is-subscribed-to-by}, while we know the download relationship convolutes from the role-pairs {is-subscribed-to-by, subscribes-to} and {owns, is-owned-by}. The inverted flag allows us to "flip" the roles of the role-pairs where this is significant.

19.6. Aggregation as a Relationship

In Chapter 17, we examined how aggregation could be modeled as a relationship. Instead of using its own template specified in Chapter 11, we can in fact specify aggregations using the general RELATIONSHIP template. The following example of the aggregation between a wiringHub object class and a hubCard object class illustrates this notation.

```
numberOfCardSlots ATTRIBUTE ::=
{
        ATTRIBUTE-TYPE          INTEGER (0..MAX)
        IDENTIFIED BY           {...}
}


wiringHub-hubCard-aggregation RELATIONSHIP ::=
{
        OBJECT-CLASS            wiringHub
        IN ROLE                 has-as-a-part
            RELATES TO
        OBJECT-CLASS            hubCard
        IN ROLE                 is-a-part-of
        WITH MULTIPLICITY       {theRangeWith:
                                  {lowerBound
                                    {constant:1},
                                   upperBound
                                    {ade:{numberOfCardSlotsLbl}
                                  }} }      -- attribute-defined
                                            -- expression
        IDENTIFIED BY           {...}
}
```

The differences between our specification of the AGGREGATION information object class in Chapter 11 and the template above are purely syntactic. In Chapter 11, aggregation relationships between two object classes were information objects of the AGGREGATION information object class, whereas here, aggregation relationships between two object classes will be information objects of the RELATIONSHIP information object class. The roles of any aggregation relationship specified using the RELATIONSHIP information object class template will always be has-as-a-part and is-a-part-of.

To specify aggregation relationships, either the RELATIONSHIP template or the AGGREGATION template of Chapter 11 may be used. Our compiler accepts either construct and considers both equivalent, as one is simply special-purpose notation for limited cases of the other. Identical semantics are stored in the model information base in either case.

Any aggregate object may be decomposed into its aggregation hierarchy simply by querying it for its relatants via the has-as-a-part role. Because this role is transitive, all component objects with which the queried object has actual or virtual decomposition relationships will be returned as a response. Thus, each object "knows" how to enumerate the transitive closure of its components.

19.7. Protocol Layerings as Relationships

We indicated in Chapter 17 that protocol layerings could also be modeled as relationships. We can specify a `protocolLayering` relationship between two `protocolEntity` object classes using our formal RELATIONSHIP template instead of the PROTOCOL-LAYERING template of Chapter 15, as follows:

```
protocolLayering RELATIONSHIP ::=
{
        OBJECT-CLASS              protocolEntity
                                            -- upper entity
        IN ROLE                   layers-above
        WITH MULTIPLICITY         zeroOrMore
              RELATES TO
        OBJECT-CLASS              protocolEntity
                                            -- lower entity
        IN ROLE                   layers-below
        WITH MULTIPLICITY         zeroOrMore
        ATTRIBUTES                {demultiplexPoint}
        IDENTIFIED BY             protocolLayeringLbl
}
```

This definition is semantically equivalent to our PROTOCOL-LAYERING information object class of Chapter 15; as with the AGGREGATION template, the differences again are purely syntactic. In this specification `protocolLayering` is an information object of the RELATIONSHIP information object class, not a separate information object class. Individual layerings between two actual protocols will also be information objects of the RELATIONSHIP information object class, rather than of the PROTOCOL-LAYERING information object class. In addition, `demultiplexPoint` is now an attribute of the relationship (and will have its own supporting ATTRIBUTE information object definition) rather than simply being a value field of the PROTOCOL-LAYERING information object class. The `protocolLayering` relationship is inherited by descendants of `protocolEntity` through relationship inheritance, with each descendant using relatant specialization to appropriately curtail the set of other protocols it will layer above or below.

The compiler accepts protocol layering specifications either as the special-purpose PROTOCOL-LAYERING template or as relationships inherited by descendants of `protocolEntity` from the construct above. As long as the roles `layers-above` and `layers-below` are specified in an instance of the RELATIONSHIP information object class above, the compiler considers that instance equivalent to a PROTOCOL-LAYERING information object.

19.8. Multiplicity-Based Specialization

In this section, we specify a formal mechanism which object classes may use to specialize by relatant multiplicity restriction and subject multiplicity regression. To do so, we must be able to formally describe relationship multiplicity domains. As a prelude to doing this, we define the types `ObjectClassLabel` and `RelationshipLabel` which resolve to labels for the modeling constructs we will use. These are similar to the `RoleLabel` and `RolePairLabel` types we defined earlier in the chapter:

```
ObjectClassLabel ::= OBJECT-CLASS.&objectClassLabel
                                    ({ObjectClasses})


RelationshipLabel ::= RELATIONSHIP.&relationshipLabel
                                    ({Relationships})
```

In these type assignments, we assume that `ObjectClasses` and `Relationships` are defined sets of information objects of the corresponding information object class. The definitions above simply resolve to lists of `OBJECT IDENTIFIER`s. The type `ObjectClassLabel` is the same type we defined in Chapter 11; the type `RelationshipLabel` is constrained to be drawn from the limited pool of `OBJECT IDENTIFIER`s from the name space of the `&relationshipLabel` fields of all `RELATIONSHIP` information objects of the set `Relationships`.

We need additional type reference names to formally state that the multiplicity of a particular role in a particular relationship possesses a particular value of type `Multiplicity`. We define the following type reference names for this purpose:

```
RelatantMultiplicity ::= SEQUENCE
{
    relationship     RELATIONSHIP.&relationshipLabel
                        ({Relationships}),
    role             ROLE.&roleLabel
                        ({{Relationships}.&forwardRole}
                                {@relationship}),
    relatantMultiplicity
                     RELATIONSHIP.&relatantMultiplicity
                        ({Relationships}{@relationship})
}
```

This constrained type is shorthand to quickly extract just the items of interest from a particular relationship. The type of the `relationship` field is `OBJECT IDENTIFIER`. The type of the `role` field is also `OBJECT IDENTIFIER`, constrained to the indicated set; the set `{{Relationships}.&forwardRole}` is an object set from objects, as explained in Chapter 10. The table constraint {Relationships} ensures that the values of all fields come only from defined RELATIONSHIP information objects. The component relation constraint (@relationship) between the fields ensures that all field values come from the same RELATIONSHIP information object. We can define a similar type reference name to extract the subject multiplicity as well:

```
SubjectMultiplicity ::= SEQUENCE
{
        relationship      RELATIONSHIP.&relationshipLabel
                              ({Relationships}),
        role              ROLE.&roleLabel
                              ({{Relationships}.&reciprocalRole}
                                              {@relationship}),
        subjectMultiplicity
                          RELATIONSHIP.&subjectMultiplicity
                              ({Relationships}{@relationship})
}
```

With the class undergoing specialization assumed to be the subject, these constructs are sufficient to indicate which role of which relationship has been chosen for multiplicity restriction or regression. To combine both sets of roles into a single type, we define the type RelationshipMultiplicity as

```
RelationshipMultiplicity ::= CHOICE
{
        subjectMultiplicity      [0]   SubjectMultiplicity,
        relatantMultiplicity     [1]   RelatantMultiplicity
}
```

To use relationship multiplicities as a basis of specialization, we must be able to make statements about their values which can be evaluated as logical predicates. This is necessary because any basis of specialization must have the type LogicalPredicate. To state that a relationship multiplicity has a particular Multiplicity value, we define a logical predicate called a MultiplicityLogicalPredicate:

```
MultiplicityLogicalPredicate ::= SEQUENCE
{
   relationshipMultiplicity   RelationshipMultiplicity,
   domain                     Multiplicity
}
```

This type reference name formally associates a particular relationship multiplicity (either the subject multiplicity or the relatant multiplicity) with a particular value of type `Multiplicity`.

Contexts of Use

As with `AttributeLogicalPredicates`, the `MultiplicityLogical-Predicate` can also be used in four contexts against the classes of the network schema in the model information base:

1. ***Interrogative***: Usage of a multiplicity logical predicate in this context poses a query: *Is the specified* `relationshipMultiplicity` *permitted to possess the values indicated by* domain?

2. ***Declarative***: Usage of a multiplicity logical predicate in this context makes a statement of actual fact, possibly in response to a query. It returns a BOOLEAN: *The specified* `relationshipMultiplicity` *is (or is not) permitted to possess the values indicated by* domain.

3. ***Imperative***: Usage of a multiplicity logical predicate in this context issues a command: *Establish the values indicated by* domain *as permitted values for the specified* `relationshipMultiplicity`.

4. ***Qualificative***: Usage of a multiplicity logical predicate in this context acts as a subsetting clause for externally specified operations: *Perform (or do not perform) the externally specified operation only on those classes for which the specified* `relationshipMultiplicity` *is permitted to possess the values indicated by* domain.

Within such an externally specified context, we can query the multiplicity values of various relationships and change them as appropriate during the specialization of their participant classes. A class undergoing specialization may formally state the multiplicity changes it makes as follows:

> ***Specialization by Relatant Multiplicity Restriction***: Use a `MultiplicityLogicalPredicate` to indicate the new values of the domain for the relatantMultiplicity.

> ***Specialization by Subject Multiplicity Regression***: Use a `MultiplicityLogicalPredicate` to indicate the new values of the domain for the subjectMultiplicity.

In a later section, we will see how the general `SimpleLogicalPredicate` type may be expanded to include the specialization modes of relatant multiplicity restriction and subject multiplicity regression.

19.9. Relationship Addition and Relatant Specialization

To formally specify the modes of relationship addition and relatant specialization, we need constructs which can identify the relatant classes of interest. This is easy: just as we indicate the addition of properties by simply using the property labels, we indicate the addition of relationships by simply using the relationship label.

We may define the type `RelationshipPredicate` simply as the type `RelationshipLabel`:

```
RelationshipPredicate ::= RelationshipLabel
```

This predicate is interpreted to mean that the specializing subclass adds the indicated relationship. The specializing subclass (or some ancestor thereof) must participate in the relationship indicated by the relationship label. It is not necessary to identify the relatant class and the role, because simply indicating a relationship label determines both.

Contexts of Use

As with other "label predicates", a `RelationshipLabel` may also be used in four contexts against the classes in the schema of the model information base to check whether the queried class is a participant in the indicated relationship:

1. *Interrogative*: *Does the queried class participate in the relationship indicated by the* `RelationshipLabel`?

2. *Declarative*: *The queried class does (or does not) participate in the relationship indicated by the* `RelationshipLabel`.

3. *Imperative*: *Establish the relationship indicated by the* `RelationshipLabel` *for the queried class.*

4. *Qualificative*: *Perform (or do not perform) the externally specified operation only on those classes which participate in the relationship indicated by the* `RelationshipLabel`.

For formally expressing the mechanism of relatant specialization, we need a construct which accommodates a list of selected subclasses of the relatant object class to which the inherited relationship is restricted. We may define a `Relatant-SpecializationPredicate` as follows:

```
RelatantSpecializationPredicate ::= SEQUENCE
{
    relationship             RelationshipLabel,
    relatantSubclasses       SET OF ObjectClassLabel
}
```

This predicate is interpreted to mean that the specializing subclass restricts its participation in the inherited relationship with only those subclasses of the relatant indicated by the `relatantSubclasses` field. The `relationship` field must indicate a relationship in which the specializing subclass participates, and the elements of the `SET OF ObjectClassLabel` listed in the `relatantSubclasses` field must be defined subclasses of the relatant class of the relationship identified by the `relationship` field, assuming that the specializing subclass is the subject.

We summarize the use of the `RelationshipPredicate` and `Relatant-SpecializationPredicate` types as below:

Specialization by Relationship Addition: Use a `Relationship-Predicate` to indicate the addition of the new relationship in the subclass.

Specialization by Relatant Specialization: Use a `Relatant-SpecializationPredicate` to indicate the selected subclass of the relatant in the `relatantSubclasses` field.

We expand the type `SimpleLogicalPredicate` in order to accommodate all the modes for relationship-based specialization:

```
SimpleLogicalPredicate ::= CHOICE
{
        attributeAdded       [0]        AttributeLabel,
        functionAdded        [1]        FunctionLabel,
        capsuleAdded         [2]        CapsuleLabel,
        capsuleFixed         [3]        CapsuleLabel,
        attributeDomainRestricted        [4]
                        AttributeLogicalPredicate,
        argumentDomainRelaxed            [5]
                        ArgumentLogicalPredicate,
        resultDomainRestricted           [6]
                        ResultLogicalPredicate,
        functionExtended                 [7]
                        FunctionExtensionPredicate,
        subjectMultiplicityRegressed     [8]
                        MultiplicityLogicalPredicate,
        relatantMultiplicityRestricted   [9]
                        MultiplicityLogicalPredicate,
        relationshipAdded                [10]
                        RelationshipPredicate,
        relatantSpecialized              [11]
                        RelatantSpecializationPredicate
}
```

19.10. **Relatant-Property-Based Specialization**

To specify formally the specialization modes which use properties of relatant classes, such as relatant attribute restriction, relatant argument contravariance, relatant result co-variance, and relatant capsule fixing, we need a mechanism to track down the relatant of the given subject class. This mechanism is simple: the additional prefix of a single relationship label, which is simply an OBJECT IDENTIFIER, will serve our purpose. A relationship label uniquely identifies both the subject and relatant classes. The subject class is assumed to be the class undergoing specialization. If it uses a property of a relatant class as the basis for its own specialization, the relationship label (which must belong to a relationship in which the specializing subclass participates) will identify the relatant class whose property has been chosen as a basis of specialization.

Once the environment of a relatant class is identified, then any of the ordinary specialization modes (such as attribute domain restriction, function result domain restriction, etc.) which we have already identified in the type SimpleLogicalPredicate may be used. Thus, in order to express specialization using any relatant property, all we need to do is to prefix a SimpleLogicalPredicate with some indication of a *context* which declares that the property identified in the SimpleLogicalPredicate belongs not to the specializing subclass but to its relatant.

We accomplish this by expanding the general type LogicalPredicate to accommodate the new type ContextLogicalPredicate:

```
LogicalPredicate ::= CHOICE
{
        simplePredicate      [0]   SimpleLogicalPredicate,
        compoundPredicate    [1]   CompoundLogicalPredicate,
        negatedPredicate     [2]   LogicalPredicate,
        contextPredicate     [3]   ContextLogicalPredicate
}
```

where

```
ContextLogicalPredicate ::= SEQUENCE
{
        context                    Context,
        simplePredicate            SimpleLogicalPredicate
}
```

The context field of a ContextLogicalPredicate indicates the context to which the SimpleLogicalPredicate identified by the simplePredicate field is applied. Most often, the context field identifies an object class which is a relatant of the class undergoing specialization. However, in some cases, classes specialize using *relationship attribute restriction* rather than relatant attribute restriction. In this situation, the context field identifies the label of the relationship to which attribute domain restriction applies, rather than the label of an object class. Therefore,

```
Context ::= CHOICE
{
  relationship   [0]   RelationshipLabel,
  relatant       [1]   RelationshipLabel
}
```

Prefixing a context to an ordinary mode of specialization is interpreted to mean that the property used in the specialization belongs to the indicated relatant, or to a relationship in which the specializing subclass participates. There are, however, a few restrictions on the ways in which a `ContextLogicalPredicate` may be used:

- If the `context` field of a `ContextLogicalPredicate` indicates a `relatant`, then none of the *addition* modes are permitted for the `simplePredicate` field. This is because an object class cannot specialize by adding any property to a relatant class.

- If the `context` field of a `ContextLogicalPredicate` indicates a `relationship`, then the only permitted mode of specialization for the `simplePredicate` field is `AttributeLogicalPredicate`, which is used to indicate the restricted domain of the relationship attribute.

With these specifications in place, we now have a general mechanism for using any relationship attribute or any property of any relatant class as a basis of specialization. We summarize two of the more important modes below:

Specialization by Relationship Attribute Restriction: Use a `ContextLogicalPredicate` to indicate the relationship in the `context` field, and use an `AttributeLogicalPredicate` to specify the relationship attribute and its new domain in the `simplePredicate` field.

Specialization by Relatant Attribute Restriction: Use a `ContextLogicalPredicate` to indicate the relatant in the `context` field, and use an `AttributeLogicalPredicate` to specify the relatant attribute and its new domain in the `simplePredicate` field.

This mechanism may be used for other relatant-property-based specialization modes as well, although they are less commonly used. For example, if an object class wishes to specialize using relatant function argument contravariance, it formally specifies its basis of specialization in a `ContextLogicalPredicate` in which it identifies the relatant class in the `context` field and then uses an appropriate `ArgumentLogicalPredicate` for the `simplePredicate` field.

19.11. Relationship Instance Predicates

Just as we use a `RelationshipPredicate` to query object classes in the schema of a network model information base, we use a `RelationshipInstancePredicate` to query object *instances* in an actual network for their relatant instances. This is akin to querying object instances for values of their attributes but uses a different predicate. Like an `AttributeLogicalPredicate`, a `RelationshipInstancePredicate` consists of three elements: a field denoting the subject instance, a role label, and a field denoting the relatant instance. The predicate states whether that particular role is being played by the subject instance with the relatant instance. Since we are dealing with object instances, not classes, we must use the `objectName ATTRIBUTE` defined in Chapter 11 to indicate the names of the two instances. The predicate may be defined as follows:

```
RelationshipInstancePredicate ::= SEQUENCE
{
        subject         ObjectName,
        role            RoleLabel,
        relatant        ObjectName
}
```

The fields `subject` and `relatant` both have the type `ObjectName`, which, as defined in Chapter 11, is the `&AttributeType` of the attribute `objectName` of `genericObject`, which identifies the name of every object in the system. The type `ObjectName` is structured to conform to whatever naming scheme we have chosen for object instances.

As with the `AttributeLogicalPredicate` type of Chapter 10, a relationship instance predicate can be used in four distinct contexts:

1. ***Interrogative***: Usage of a relationship instance predicate in this context poses a query: *Does the specified* `subject` *instance play the specified* `role` *with the specified* `relatant` *instance?*

2. ***Declarative***: Usage of the relationship instance predicate in this context makes a statement of actual fact (possibly in response to a query) and returns a BOOLEAN: *The specified* `subject` *instance does (or does not) play the specified* `role` *with the specified* `relatant` *instance.*

3. ***Imperative***: Usage of a relationship instance predicate in this context issues a command: *Establish a relationship instance such that the specified* `subject` *instance plays the specified* `role` *with the specified* `relatant` *instance.* (This has no effect if the `subject` already plays that `role` with the `relatant` in an actual relationship.)

4. ***Qualificative***: Usage of a relationship instance predicate in this context acts as a subsetting clause for externally specified operations on objects: *Perform (or do not perform) the externally specified operation*

on the specified `subject` *instance only if it plays the specified* `role` *with the specified* `relatant` *instance.*

As we said before, the {`subject role relatant`} triad is semantically equivalent to its symmetric triad, that is, {`relatant reciprocalRole subject`}; no particular direction is preferred. In any relationship, we can choose to make either participant instance the subject; this does not affect the semantics of a `Relationship-InstancePredicate`.

In Chapter 24 we will consider another qualificative or selection predicate which applies to entire relatant classes rather than relatant instances. Given a subject instance, a role label, and a relatant *class*, the predicate will be able to select the set of *all* instances of the relatant class with which the subject instance plays the indicated role. If the relatant class name is omitted, the predicate will select all instances of *any* class with which the subject instance plays that role.

19.12. Summary

The formal specification of relationships is accomplished using ASN.1 information object class templates. Roles are defined using `ROLE` information object class templates and paired as mutual reciprocals using `ROLE-PAIR` information object class templates. The `ROLE-PAIR` template also indicates the properties of each role-pair, if any, which may give rise to virtual relationships. Each relationship between participant classes is specified as a `RELATIONSHIP` information object. This template contains fields for the participant classes, their roles, multiplicities, and relationship attributes if any. Only actual relationships are specified using this template. Virtual relationships are never specified, as they are completely determined by the properties of role-pairs used in actual relationships.

The specification of multiplicity values can be performed in a logical predicate defined for that purpose. When an object class specializes using either relatant multiplicity restriction or subject multiplicity regression, it must use a multiplicity logical predicate. The specialization modes of relationship addition and relatant specialization also have predicates defined for their formal expression. Finally, any specialization modes which use either a relationship attribute or any property of a relatant are specified using a context logical predicate, which first identifies the context of the selected relationship or the selected relatant class before applying a simple logical predicate.

20. Virtual Attributes

"It'll take 4 months to fully upgrade our network, but only 3 months before it becomes obsolete again, so if we do nothing, we'll come out ahead."
— *recommendation of anonymous MIS director.*

20.1. Introduction

Very often, the information desired about a particular object is not simply the value of one of its attributes or the result of one of its functions but is some computation based on them. Since we model only orthogonal properties, we do not yet have a mechanism for modeling information which is not directly available but is derivable from the values of these orthogonal properties. In this chapter, we describe such a mechanism and show how the general relationship model can be used as a foundation for deriving information from relatant objects as well. An additional benefit of derived information is that it helps in network privacy, as it permits us to expose only derived information to external networks without necessarily divulging confidential basic information. Thus, security mechanisms arise from the network model itself, rather than from any protocol used to query and manipulate the network model. With the ability to model derived information, we considerably enhance our modeling semantics to provide a rich set of features.

20.2. Conceptual Background

In Chapter 4, we adopted the modeling guideline that an object class is only modeled with attributes which are orthogonal to each other. Features of object classes which can be algorithmically inferred from other features are not modeled. If we model non-orthogonal attributes, we will have attributes within the object class with mutual dependency. In the absence of some monitor process which perpetually inspects and enforces this dependency, we run the risk of these dependent attributes becoming mutually inconsistent.

435

For those values of interest which can be algorithmically inferred from values of existing attributes, it is a simple matter to specify the computation which produces the desired result. However, if an external network which interoperates with our network requests these values, we must expose to the external network both the computation algorithm itself and all the attributes required as input to that algorithm. For various security reasons, we may not wish to expose all this information.

The mechanism of *virtual attributes* acts as a solution to this problem [Bapa93a]. A virtual attribute is an attribute which is specified in terms of other attributes. The attributes supporting the definition of a virtual attribute are called its *base attributes*. The specification of the virtual attribute includes the computation which must be executed on the values of the base attributes in order to generate the value of the virtual attribute.

Because the computation is specified as part of the attribute definition, it is assumed that the algorithm implementing this computation is implicitly encapsulated within the object itself. In particular, it is assumed to be encapsulated as the value-reporting mechanism for the virtual attribute. This means that every time the current value of the virtual attribute is required, *the algorithm for computing its value is in effect implicitly re-executed*. This ensures that the virtual attribute is always computed from the current values of its supporting base attributes.

With this mechanism, we eliminate the problem of modeling dependencies between attributes. Rather than imposing the mutual dependency as a *constraint* to be applied to values of non-orthogonal attributes, we turn the mutual dependency into a *function* which calculates the value of the virtual attribute from orthogonal attributes. With such a specification, any useful value which is algorithmically derivable from existing attributes can now be modeled as a virtual attribute.

We define an *actual attribute* as an attribute of an object class whose value cannot be inferred from any other attributes and so must be explicitly specified by the architect using explicit property assignment. All actual attributes, as we indicated before, must be orthogonal, that is, mutually independent. In any computation for the value of a virtual attribute, the base attributes need not necessarily be actual; they themselves could be virtual. If virtual attribute A has a base attribute B which is also virtual, then the base attributes of B are also base attributes of A. The base attributes at the leaf nodes of this dependency tree must all be actual.

Functional Dependency Associations

A virtual attribute arises as a consequence of a *functional dependency* between two values. This implies that, given one value, there exists some mathematical function which can map that value to the second value. Thus, the dependent value need never be directly specified, as it can be inferred from the independent value merely by application of the mathematical function. Functional dependency theory has been extensively developed in the field of relational database design [Codd70, Arms74, Bern76, Maie83, Ullm88]. It should be noted that a change in a base attribute value does not necessarily change the virtual attribute value, because the functional dependency could map different base attribute values to the same virtual attribute value.

Like other attributes, a virtual attribute is a property of an object class. It is, however, a functionally dependent property rather than an independent property. Like other properties, it has the property assignment associations **is-a-property-of** and **has-as-a-property** with its object class. In addition, a virtual attribute is said to have the association **is-functionally-dependent-on** with its base attributes. The complementary association between the base attribute and the virtual attribute is **functionally-determines**. Together, these are known as the *functional dependency associations*. Figure 20-1 illustrates the associations of the general model of a virtual attribute.

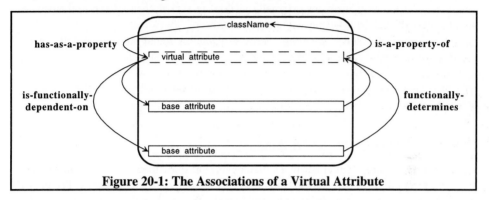

Figure 20-1: The Associations of a Virtual Attribute

The computation algorithm for determining the value of a virtual attribute from its base attributes is generally an *attribute-defined expression*. This attribute-defined expression is part of the specification of the virtual attribute. Syntactically, this is the same as the attribute-defined expressions we used in Chapter 17 to specify relationship multiplicities: it expands to a simple grammar whose expressions allow common mathematical operations on its operands. The terminal symbols of this grammar are other attributes and results of functions.

Using Virtual Attributes

The advantage of modeling algorithmically derivable information as virtual attributes lies in the fact that the external manifestation of virtual attributes is the same as that of actual attributes. A virtual attribute can be interrogated using the same query primitives as any other attribute, and its value is returned using the same response mechanism. The external object or network issuing this query need not be aware of the fact that the interrogated attribute is virtual and that its value is being internally computed using an algorithm involving values of other attributes.

For most purposes, virtual attributes behave exactly like actual attributes. Virtual attributes defined for any object class are bequeathed down the inheritance hierarchy to all descendant classes. There is, however, one important difference between virtual and actual attributes: *virtual attributes can never be updated*. The value of a virtual attribute changes only if there is a change to the value of one of its actual base attributes. If we use a logical predicate of Chapter 10 with a virtual attribute, it can only be used in the *interrogative*, *declarative*, and *qualificative* contexts; it cannot be used in the *imperative* context. Any attempt to imperatively set the value of a virtual attribute will result in the object generating an error.

By specifying appropriate external visibility for both actual and virtual attributes, we can enjoy fine granularity in the control of our security policies. By making only the values of virtual attributes available to external objects, we can implement a privacy policy which protects the values of those attributes we do not wish to expose, while at the same time making necessary data available to external objects. We also automatically protect any of our attributes from being updated by external objects, either accidentally or maliciously. If the only attributes externally visible are virtual, then all exposed attributes are always read-only because they can never be updated.

A virtual attribute is sometimes used to *spoof* an actual attribute simply for the purposes of making it read-only. We can define a virtual attribute whose value is *equal* to that of a read-write actual attribute. By making only the virtual attribute visible to external objects, we ensure that external objects can never inadvertently modify the supporting actual attribute.

20.3. An Example of Virtual Attributes

As an example of how virtual attributes may be used to implement security policies, consider the example of a hypothetical middle-layer protocol X. In this example, Protocol X is a high-speed *transfer* protocol which combines the functions traditionally present in the network and transport layers of many conventional reference models. By piggybacking C-Plane requests on U-Plane PDUs and using flow control, rate control, and timer-based connection management, Protocol X can work with high-speed links when embodied as an efficient parallel implementation in VLSI. For data-link layers with limited frame sizes, Protocol X provides the functionality of assembling PDUs received from the link layer, detecting errors by computing checksums, reassembling fragments of X-layer PDUs, and delivering them to an appropriate upper-layer protocol. An X-router may also forward PDUs not intended for local consumption. For outbound PDUs, Protocol X provides fragmentation capabilities depending on the frame size of the underlying link layer. Each instance of Protocol X — that is, each protocol entity object — is instrumented with certain counters which keep track of how many PDUs are processed by that entity, and what the ultimate resolution of each PDU is. These counters could be used for management and trending purposes by a network management object, or any other object requiring their values. The counters affected as the PDUs are processed are depicted in the Case diagram of Figure 20-2.

The Case diagram for Protocol X represents the counters which indicate the ultimate fate of each PDU processed by the protocol entity X. As explained in Chapter 13, some counters are additive, some are subtractive, and some are filter counters. Each counter meters the number of PDUs undergoing a particular feature of the processing performed by the protocol X entity. As with all Case diagrams, the counters do not suggest the sequence in which this processing is performed. These counters could be modeled as attributes of the `xProtocolEntity` object class. All attributes of this object class need not necessarily be represented on the Case diagram; it may also have non-PDU-counting attributes such as `xMaxConnections`, `xActiveConnections`, `xConnectionsInitiated`, `xConnectionsResponded`, `xConnectWait-`

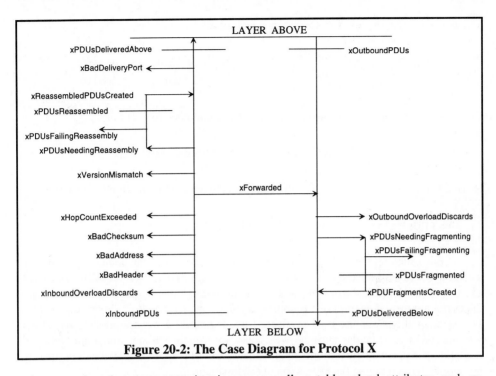

Figure 20-2: The Case Diagram for Protocol X

Timer, and xDisconnectWaitTimer, as well as table-valued attributes such as xCurrentConnectionsTable.

All the PDU counters are not, however, independent. Certain mathematical relationships exist among them; in Figure 20-2, at least four can be derived as linear combinations of the others. From the specialization theory perspective, only orthogonal counters are modeled as actual attributes, with the rest being modeled as virtual attributes. For example, we could choose to make the counter xPDUsDeliveredAbove virtual and express its value in terms of the values of other counters, as follows:

```
xPDUsDeliveredAbove =    xInboundPDUs
                       - xInboundOverloadDiscards
                       - xBadHeader
                       - xBadAddress
                       - xBadChecksum
                       - xHopCountExceeded
                       - xForwarded
                       - xVersionMismatch
                       - xPDUsNeedingReassembly
                       + xReassembledPDUsCreated
                       - xBadDeliveryPort
```

and, we could also express xPDUsReassembled as

```
xPDUsReassembled =        xPDUsNeedingReassembly
                        - xPDUsFailingReassembly
```

Certain inequality constraints also hold among these counters, for example,

```
xReassembledPDUsCreated <= xPDUsReassembled
```

Since all counters are non-negative integers, from the three relations above we can infer

```
xPDUsDeliveredAbove <= xInboundPDUs
```

Each such relation which expresses a constraint between the counter attributes of a protocol entity is called a *Case Invariant*. If a Case Invariant is an equality constraint expressing the dependency of one counter as a linear combination of other counters, it reduces the number of degrees of freedom available in the modeling of the protocol entity. For each equality Case Invariant available from Figure 20-2, we can model *one* virtual attribute. Which particular attribute we choose to virtualize is not important from the modeling perspective; any attribute in an equality Case Invariant may be made virtual by appropriately rearranging the expression of the invariant.

An equality Case Invariant can be modeled as an attribute-defined expression in a straightforward manner. Each time the value of the virtual attribute is interrogated, the attribute-defined expression arising from the Case Invariant is implicitly re-computed using the current values of its base attributes.

For the outbound stream, assume that we make the attribute xPDUs-DeliveredBelow a virtual attribute. Then, the Case Invariant for its computation is

```
xPDUsDeliveredBelow =    xOutboundPDUs
                       + xForwarded
                       - xOutboundOverloadDiscards
                       - xPDUsNeedingFragmenting
                       + xPDUFragmentsCreated
```

Suppose that it is necessary for us to make the attribute xPDUsDelivered-Below available to an external network. For example, the layer below the X entity to which we deliver outbound PDUs might be the link layer of some WAN service provider. Our billing arrangement with the service provider requires that we pay for each PDU which we submit as offered load to their carrier network. Thus, we may have to make the counter xPDUsDeliveredBelow in our xProtocolEntity object available to an accounting management system belonging to the service provider.

If we had not had the mechanism of virtual attributes, we could have modeled only orthogonal base attributes. We would then have had to expose to the external service provider two pieces of information: first, the values of all of the base attributes involved in the computation of the offered load, and second, the algorithm whereby this value may be computed. For privacy reasons, we may not wish to expose all this information to the external service provider. By making the attribute virtual and by providing external access to only the virtual attribute, we protect our internal privacy. In the example above, when the external service provider queries xPDUsDeliveredBelow, it "knows" how to compute itself from its base attributes without exposing them to the external service provider. We can also define virtual attributes to expose only some aggregate or summary values of the "health" of the network (e.g., average utilization) rather than its input parameters [Gold93]. Because the virtual attribute can never be updated, we also automatically eliminate the possibility that it may be inadvertently modified by an external network.

20.4. Conditional Virtual Attributes

There are other virtual attributes whose values are determined by logical rather than arithmetic combinations of their base attributes. These attributes are called *conditional virtual attributes*, because their attribute-defined expressions include conditions which govern the computation of their values.

As an example, consider a circuit object class, which possesses percentageUtilization as an attribute. The type of this attribute may be REAL, as we need to assess the percentage utilization of each circuit object to, say, two decimal places. We may also have a saturationWatermark attribute for the circuit object as a coarse categorization of its utilization. The value of the saturation-Watermark attribute may act as a trigger for different precautionary or restorative actions to be performed on each circuit object. The type of the saturation-Watermark attribute is one of the set of three discrete values {green, yellow, red}. The saturationWatermark attribute may be specified as

```
saturationWatermark =
    green
        if percentageUtilization < 70.00%;
    yellow
        if 70.00% <= percentageUtilization < 90.00%;
    red
        if percentageUtilization >= 90.00%;
```

Clearly, the saturationWatermark attribute is virtual, as its value is completely determined by the percentageUtilization attribute. However, its value is determined differently depending on the conditions governing the computation. It is thus a *conditional virtual attribute*.

There is an important aspect of conditional virtual attributes which must be considered. Although the value of the conditional virtual attribute is completely determined from its supporting base attributes, sometimes its *type* cannot be inferred from the types of the supporting base attributes. Often, the types of conditional virtual attributes must be explicitly specified; if so, they are known as virtual attributes with *explicit syntax.*

For example, the fact that `saturationWatermark` has an enumerated type from the discrete set `{green, yellow, red}` cannot be implicitly inferred from the known type of the `percentageUtilization` attribute, which is simply `REAL`. This is because the expression defining the virtual attribute is logical rather than arithmetic. Although our grammar for attribute-defined expressions allows such logical expressions, the compiler cannot automatically infer its type. Hence, the type of this attribute must be explicitly specified along with its definition. Thus, it is an *explicit-syntax* virtual attribute.

In the example of Figure 20-2, we specified virtual attributes of the X protocol entity without specifying their syntax. It was possible to do this because the virtual attributes were expressed as linear combinations of other attributes. All the base attributes had the same syntax: they were all of type `INTEGER`. Elementary dimensional analysis indicates that the resulting virtual attribute must also have the type `INTEGER`. Usually, if the computation of the virtual attribute is specified as an arithmetic expression, then the compiler can infer the type of the virtual attribute from the types of its supporting base attributes. This type of virtual attribute is termed an *implicit-syntax* virtual attribute.

20.5. Tracked Virtual Attributes

In Chapter 17, we specified relationships as abstract binary associations between object classes. We also considered various alternative methods of implementing relationships, including the specification of relationships as "pointer" attributes in object classes. We argued that although a relationship could be *implemented* as pointers in its participant objects if convenient, it ought not to be *specified* in that manner, due to the various problems of maintaining mutual consistency between different pointers in different object instances indicative of the same relationship instance.

To query the existence of an association between two object instances, we defined in Chapter 19 a *relationship logical predicate.* This essentially took the form `{subjectInstance roleLabel relatantInstance}`, which, if used in an interrogative context, issued a query to determine whether the indicated subject played the indicated role with the indicated relatant. Thus, it determined the existence of a particular relationship instance. We left undefined the mechanism whereby information about relationship instances is stored and accessed, leaving that as an implementation issue, which it rightly is.

There are occasions when it is convenient to query an object instance to determine not just its intrinsic attributes but also the attributes of its *relatants.* For example, information about some attribute of a relatant instance might frequently be required for computations inside a subject instance. It would be convenient to have a mechanism to make this information available without compromising the encapsulation of either the subject or relatant object, and without compromising the implementation-independent nature of our relationship specification mechanism.

We extend the concept of virtual attributes to include the representation of information about an object's *relatants*. A virtual attribute could thus be used to refer to information *outside* a particular object. We accomplish this by permitting a virtual attribute to be defined in terms of base attributes which need not necessarily belong to the same object but could also belong to a *relatant* object, reachable though a relationship instance.

In our model information base, relationship instances are stored as explicit first-class constructs. A relationship instance identifies its participant object instances, which are also first-class constructs. Starting from a participant subject instance, it is an easy matter in our model information base to determine its relationship instances, and thereby enumerate all its relatant instances. Once its relatant instances are identified, it is easy to determine the values of attributes they possess. Thus, using the subject instance as a starting point, it is *algorithmically possible* to track and monitor attribute values in its *relatant* instances.

Virtual attributes can be used as a mechanism to make attribute values of relatant objects automatically available *inside* a subject. In doing so, we do not compromise the encapsulation of either object, because the base attribute remains an intrinsic property only of the relatant; only the relatant can modify that attribute. We also completely eliminate the problem of assuring update consistency to maintain the integrity of the relationship instance, because a virtual attribute can never be updated. *Every time the subject is queried for this virtual attribute, its value is in effect read from the relatant object by tracking it through the relationship automatically and transparently.* Thus, if the relatant instance changes the value of the base attribute, the virtual attribute in the subject instance *automatically reflects this change.*

When a queried object executes the tracking necessary to resolve a virtual attribute from a relatant object, it does so internally and transparently within the run-time model information base. The external object requesting the value of the virtual attribute need not necessarily know that such tracking is being done; the queried object "knows" how to execute the tracking internally. The external object queries the value of the virtual attribute as if it were a property of the queried object, without necessarily knowing whether it really is.

A virtual attribute whose supporting actual base attributes are all properties of the same object class is called a *native virtual attribute*. If even *one* of its supporting actual base attributes belongs to a relatant class, it is called an *imported virtual attribute* or a *tracked virtual attribute*.

Tracked virtual attributes represent a powerful abstraction to capture information about an object's relatants within the object itself. Because they behave exactly like actual attributes in interrogative (query) predicates and declarative (response) predicates, they require no change in the query or response protocols used on the object. Because they can never be updated, they eliminate the problem of ensuring update consistency of redundant information. Because whenever they are queried they are always automatically tracked to their base attributes into relatant instances, they always guarantee correct and consistent information. Because the tracking is performed transparently by the object, we can query the object for multiple attributes, some native and some tracked, without having to compose any relational joins in our query. Finally, they preserve the spirit of encapsulation because, being virtual, they reflect the object's external links within the object without affecting or changing any of the object's intrinsic actual attributes.

An Example of Tracked Virtual Attributes

Consider a situation where each `networkDevice` in our model is located at some known `site`. We model this as a relationship between the `networkDevice` object class and the `site` object class. The `networkDevice` class plays the role `is-housed-at` with respect to the `site` class, which reciprocates with the role `houses`. Clearly, the multiplicity of the `is-housed-at` role is exactly [1], since a `network-Device` can only be located at one `site`; the multiplicity of the reciprocal `houses` role is [0,-] as a `site` could house multiple `networkDevice` objects. Figure 20-3 illustrates this relationship.

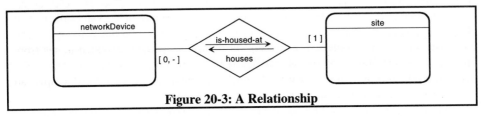

Figure 20-3: A Relationship

Suppose now that we wish to query `networkDevice` objects to determine their current location. Ordinarily, we can accomplish this by specifying that the `network-Device` class has an actual `currentSite` attribute, whose value for each instance is imperatively set to some identifier representing the instance of `site` where it is-housed-at. Many co-located instances of `networkDevice` may have the same value for the `currentSite` attribute. If some of these `networkDevice` objects are moved to another `site`, all of those instances must be individually updated to change their `currentSite` attribute. Alternatively, if any administrative information about the relatant `site` instance changes (for example, a change in the `site`'s name or identifier) then each one of those `networkDevice` instances must be individually updated to reflect that change. If there is no mechanism for automating this update, this leaves open the potential for inconsistency.

We can eliminate this problem entirely by turning the `currentSite` attribute of the `networkDevice` object class into a *tracked virtual attribute*. We know that there is an `is-housed-at` relationship between the `networkDevice` object class and the `site` object class. We further know that the `site` object class has identifier attributes which name it uniquely. It may also have various other useful attributes, such as `streetAddress`, `telephoneNumber`, and `nearestFireStation`. Suppose we decide that the `currentSite` virtual attribute of each `networkDevice` object is most usefully represented as the `streetAddress` attribute of the `site` object with which it plays the `is-housed-at` role. We can then inform our compiler that the `currentSite` attribute of any `networkDevice` instance is a tracked virtual attribute which must be *dynamically computed* by following its `is-housed-at` role link to its relatant `site` object and reading its `streetAddress` value. This is illustrated in Figure 20-4.

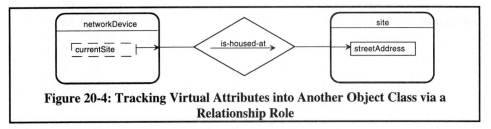

Figure 20-4: Tracking Virtual Attributes into Another Object Class via a Relationship Role

Much of the specification machinery we need to formalize this knowledge is already in place: in specialization theory, a virtual attribute is already computed as an attribute-defined expression. This expands into a grammar permitting simple mathematical and logical operations on the supporting base attributes. The only change we must make is to permit the terminal symbols of this grammar to be supporting base attributes from *relatant* classes as well; they are no longer restricted to being native attributes of the same object class. Thus, a terminal symbol of this grammar, besides being simply an `attributeLabel`, is also permitted to be the sequence `{roleLabel, attributeLabel}`, indicating an attribute in a relatant tracked through a role link.

In general, a virtual attribute could be specified as *any* attribute-defined expression, some of whose base attributes may be native to the same object class, and some could be tracked into relatant classes. Base attributes from *more than one relatant class* may support the same tracked virtual attribute.

20.6. Multiply-Tracked Virtual Attributes

It is permissible for the base attribute supporting a tracked virtual attribute to itself be virtual. If so, the virtual attribute may be tracked through a *chain* of relationship links. We present an example below to illustrate this concept.

Multi-Stage Tracking

We revisit the example of Figure 18-8 in which we turned over the administration of some remote sites to outsourcing vendors. To maintain this knowledge in our model information base, we modeled an `administration` relationship between an `outsourcingVendor` object class and a `site` object class. In this relationship, the class `outsourcingVendor` plays the role `administers` with respect to `site`, which in turn plays the role `is-administered-by`. To make it more convenient to determine which `outsourcingVendor` is responsible for a given `site`, we can create a `siteAdministrator` virtual attribute for the `site` object class. This allows us to query the `site` object directly for its `siteAdministrator` and let the `site` object internally and transparently track its `is-administered-by` role link to the `vendorName` attribute of its relatant `outsourcingVendor` object.

Whenever we create a relationship instance in which an `outsourcingVendor` administers a `site`, we in fact intend that the `outsourcingVendor` administers every `networkDevice` which that `site` houses. We may also find it convenient to directly query each instance of `networkDevice` for the identity of the administrator responsible for administering that device. We therefore model an `administrator` virtual attribute for the `networkDevice` class. Since we know that its value must always be the same as the attribute `siteAdministrator` of the `site` where the `networkDevice` is-housed-at, we track this virtual attribute to the `siteAdministrator` attribute of its relatant `site` object. In effect, the `administrator` attribute of `networkDevice` is tracked through a *chain* of relationship links all the way into the `vendorName` attribute of an `outsourcingVendor` object. Figure 20-5 illustrates this mechanism.

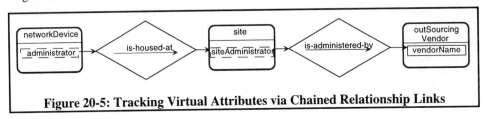

Figure 20-5: Tracking Virtual Attributes via Chained Relationship Links

In general, the resolution of a virtual attribute might result in automatic tracking anywhere through the transitive closure of its relatants. Such consequential tracking is transparent and immaterial to the definition of the specificand virtual attribute. The specification of the `administrator` virtual attribute of `networkDevice` indicates the value of the base `siteAdministrator` attribute of `site` in the same manner regardless of whether `siteAdministrator` is actual or virtual. In Chapter 24, we will see how this knowledge may be formally specified to the compiler.

Role Chaining

A slightly more powerful and abstract variation of this mechanism allows us to track virtual attributes into other objects without necessarily defining intermediate virtual attributes in every object along the relationship chain. For example, in Figure 20-5, it is not incumbent upon us to model the `siteAdministrator` virtual attribute of the `site` object class, if we do not wish to do so. We can directly track `administrator` of `networkDevice` into `vendorName` of `outsourcingVendor` merely by following the chain of role links. Specialization theory permits us to specify for each virtual attribute a role-chain — for example, the role sequence {`is-housed-at`, `is-administered-by`} — rather than a single role link, so we can arrive directly at a supporting base attribute without having to resolve intermediate virtual attributes. In a later section, we will demonstrate how a chain of multiply-tracked role links from actual relationships may be replaced by a single role link from a virtual relationship, if such a virtual relationship is available.

Care must be taken to ensure that, when a virtual attribute is tracked through supporting base attributes which are themselves virtual, it does not end up being indirectly supported by itself. If this happens, the resolution of the virtual attribute may cause infinite loops cycling endlessly through the model schema since there is no actual supporting base attribute. During the compilation of the model, our compiler creates a dependency tree for every virtual attribute, native or tracked, and ensures that all the leaf-nodes of that tree are actual attributes. If definitional cycles are detected, the specification of the virtual attribute is rejected.

20.7. Syntax of Tracked Virtual Attributes

Like native virtual attributes, tracked virtual attributes can also have *implicit* or *explicit* syntax. If they have implicit syntax, the type of the virtual attribute is determined from the type of the supporting base attributes from its relatant classes. Our compiler does this by automatically applying the transformations the base types are subjected to, when they are operated on by the attribute-defined expression. For example, in Figure 20-4, the compiler knows that the syntax of the virtual attribute currentSite of networkDevice is the same as the syntax of the actual attribute streetAddress of site. There is, however, an interesting aspect which we must consider: *the type of an implicit-syntax tracked virtual attribute is affected by the multiplicity of the tracking relationship.*

Consider the reverse situation in the example of Figure 20-5, where we wish to query a site object for a report of all networkDevices housed at the site. To make this easier, we might choose to model a devicesHoused virtual attribute for the site object class, which could be automatically tracked to the objectName attribute of all the members of networkDevice with which the site object plays the houses role. Naturally, since the relationship is inherited by all subclasses of networkDevice, all instances of all subclasses of networkDevice located at that site would be included in this report as well.

Normally, if the attribute type of the base attribute objectName is the type ObjectName and the relatant multiplicity of the houses role is [1], the type syntax of the virtual attribute devicesHoused would simply be ObjectName. However, because each site object can house multiple relatant instances of networkDevice, the multiplicity of the houses role is not [1]; it is [0,-]. Hence, the implicit syntax of the devicesHoused tracked virtual attribute cannot be ObjectName; rather, it must be of the type SET OF ObjectName. This is illustrated in Figure 20-6.

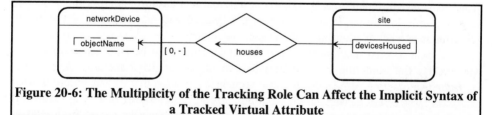

Figure 20-6: The Multiplicity of the Tracking Role Can Affect the Implicit Syntax of a Tracked Virtual Attribute

To accommodate this phenomenon, we do not have to make the tracked virtual attribute devicesHoused an explicit-syntax virtual attribute; the multiplicity knowledge is automatically applied by our compiler. Every time the compiler sees a virtual attribute tracked through a role whose relatant multiplicity does not have an upper limit of 1, the type fed into the type transformation algorithm generated by the attribute-defined expression is a SET OF the type of the supporting base attribute. Thus, it automatically assigns to devicesHoused the type syntax SET OF ObjectName.

If the virtual attribute is tracked through a chain of multiple role links, then if *any* role along the chain of links has a relatant multiplicity with an upper bound greater than 1, the type is transformed to a SET OF the base type. If the base type is already set-valued, no change is made to its type. Thus, the correct implicit syntax is automatically generated for the tracked virtual attribute.

20.8. Relatant Ordering

When the virtual attribute of an object is tracked to multiple relatant instances, the type of the tracked virtual attribute becomes a SET OF the type of the supporting base attribute in the relatant. There is no guarantee of the *order* in which the relatant attributes are enumerated as they are tracked. Therefore, there is no particular *sequence* in which the values of the base attributes from each relatant occur in the tracked virtual attribute.

In some situations, it is necessary to impose an order in which the relatant objects are enumerated. If we can do so, we will be able to predict the sequence in which the relatants are tracked, and thus the sequence in which the supporting base attributes appear in the tracked virtual attribute.

We introduce the concept of an *ordered relationship*. An ordered relationship is a relationship in which the subject class requests that all the relatant instances associated with each subject instance be presented as *ordered* according to some criterion. Since either participant class of a relationship can be viewed as a subject depending on which role we are considering, it is possible that both participating classes request the other to be ordered. Obviously, a subject can only request its relatant to be ordered if the relatant has a multiplicity greater than 1. We call each such request an *ordering criterion*.

Ordering Criteria

Ordering criteria are properties of relationships, just as relationship attributes are properties of relationships. An ordering criterion is not a property of either participant class; a class may have different ordering criteria in different relationships. A class may have one ordering criterion in one relationship with one relatant and may not have any ordering criterion in another relationship with the same relatant.

In an ordered relationship, the ordering criterion must be an *attribute* of the ordered class. Each ordering is specified with both an attribute label and an *ordering comparator*. An ordering comparator is some sequencing relation that creates an order, such as greater-than, greater-or-equal, less-than, or lesser-or-equal. If the relatant class is ordered, then when a subject instance requests values from relatant instances, the values are presented enumerated according to the ordering criterion. It is not necessary that the values requested be those of the attribute used in the ordering criterion, but the values that *are* requested must be arranged as if the instances were enumerated according to the ordering criterion.

The ordering criterion is only effective in the context of the relationship in which it is specified. If the same class participates in another relationship in which it is not ordered, then when its relatant instances are requested, they can be enumerated in an unspecified order in the context of that relationship. More generally, a class can be ordered in any relationship with *more than one* ordering criterion: the first criterion is termed a *primary ordering criterion*, the next a *secondary ordering criterion*, and so on. A secondary ordering criterion is only used as a tie-breaker when values compare equal by the primary ordering criterion. Each such ordering criterion must use a different ordering attribute and may use a different comparator.

Rank

Ordered relationships give us a powerful mechanism to track values into a single *specific* relatant instance out of a set of relatant instances. The order in which a relatant instance is tracked is called its *rank*. In an ordered relationship, a subject instance may request that a particular attribute be tracked into a particular relatant instance merely by indicating its rank. For example, a subject instance may request that a particular attribute be read from the relatant object having rank 1, with the confidence that it will be read from the instance that compares first according to the ordering criterion. More generally, a subject can request multiple values to be read using a range of ranks instead of a single rank. A subject can only specify a rank if an ordering criterion has been specified for the relatant in that relationship; ranking requests are ignored if no ordering criterion has been specified.

As an example, consider the `protocolStack` object class of Chapter 15 which contains the `protocolEntity` object class as a component, with a multiplicity of `[0,-]`. Because each instance of `protocolStack` has-as-a-part multiple instances of `protocolEntity`, it can request that `protocolEntity` be presented as ordered. It may choose the attribute `operativeLayer` of `protocolEntity` and the comparator `less-than` as the ordering criterion. Then, when the `protocolStack` requests any value tracked from its `protocolEntity` components, the value will always be presented in ascending order of `operativeLayer`. Each `protocolStack` can now determine for itself whether it is a substack or a full stack merely by examining the `operativeLayer` attributes of its `protocolEntity` components in the proper order. It can determine the entity at the lowest layer by requesting that particular `protocolEntity` relatant via its has-as-a-part role having rank 1, the next higher entity by requesting the relatant with rank 2, and so forth.

If a virtual attribute is implicit-syntax, if it is supported by base attributes tracked into a relatant class, if the relatant multiplicity of the tracking role exceeds 1, and if the relatant class is ordered with respect to the subject, then the type of the virtual attribute is a SEQUENCE OF the type of the supporting base attribute. This contrasts with the same situation in an unordered relationship, where the type is simply a SET OF the type of the supporting base attribute. For ordered relationships, the type of the tracked virtual attribute is a SEQUENCE OF type regardless of whether the supporting base attribute is the attribute chosen as ordering comparator. (Naturally, if the virtual attribute is computed using an algorithm which is a single-valued reduction of the set of supporting base attributes in the relatant instances — such as their sum or average — then the type is determined by the transformation it undergoes in the algorithm and is not automatically considered to be a SEQUENCE OF type.) If the virtual attribute is supported by different base attributes in multiple relatant classes, then the type of the virtual attribute is still a SET OF type, even if each one of those multiple relatant classes is individually ordered with respect to the subject.

In subsequent chapters, we will consider other relationship examples in which relatant ordering is significant.

20.9. Relatant Information Functions

To facilitate the process of tracking virtual attributes into relatant classes, we equip every object class with a set of functions designed for this purpose. When supplied the name of a relationship role played by a given subject instance, these functions provide information about a *set of relatant instances* by tracking them down through the appropriate relationship instances. The first of these functions is known as the *relatant-tracking* function. There are two important forms of relatant-tracking functions: one which generates a *closed-class relatant set* and one which generates an *open-class relatant set*.

Closed- and Open-Class Relatant Sets

An example of a *closed-class relatant set* is a set of all relatants *of a named object class* with which a given subject plays a given role. By naming both the relatant object class and the role which the subject plays with it, we are in effect restricting the relatant set to exactly *one relationship* in which the subject participates. This is because, in the context of a given subject class, identifying both a relatant class and a role label uniquely identifies a relationship in which the subject is a participant.

An *open-class relatant set* is the set of all relatants *of any object class* with which a given subject plays a given role. This could potentially include relatant instances from more than one relationship, since the subject could play the same role with different relatant classes in different (but isomorphic) relationships. This set is generated by the open-class relatant-tracking function, which takes as its argument only a role label without a named relatant class.

A closed-class relatant set is not necessarily a *closed set*. If more instances of the identified relatant class are created and brought into the relationship with the given subject, more members could be added to the same closed-class relatant set. Further, the set formed by the union of more than one closed-class relatant set is also a closed-class relatant set. For example, when the subject instance identifies two different relatant classes with which it plays the same role in two different relationships, the generated set is also closed. In general, the argument to the closed-class relatant tracking function could be a *set* of identified relatant class names, not just a single class name.

In the example of Figure 20-4, if we supply as arguments to the relatant-tracking function of a site object both the relatant class label networkDevice and the role label `houses`, the function generates a list of all instances of all descendants of `networkDevice` with which that `site` object plays the `houses` role. This would be a closed-class relatant set. On the other hand, if we supply just the role name `houses`, the function generates a list of *all* objects, regardless of class, with which that `site` object plays the `houses` role. Aside from all members of `networkDevice`, this set might include members of other classes as well, such as `backupBatteryPacks`, `cable-Spools` and so on, which may also be relatants of `site` in its `houses` role. This would be an open-class relatant set.

For the purposes of the current discussion, we shall call this function the `track-Relatants()` function. Aside from `trackRelatants()`, every object class is also invested with a *relatant-counting* function, which we shall call `countRelatants()`. This is similar to the relatant-tracking function, in that it also tracks down the relatant objects of a given subject. However, rather than returning a list of the relatant objects, it returns instead an `INTEGER` indicating their count. As with `trackRelatants()`, there are two forms of `countRelatants()`: a *closed-class relatant-counting* function, which takes as arguments a set of identified relatant classes and a role label, and an *open-class relatant-counting* function, which takes as its argument only a role label.

Closed- and Open-Role Relatant Sets

Analogous to the open-class and closed-class forms, these functions also have *closed-role* and *open-role* forms. In the preceding discussion, it was assumed that at least a role label is always specified as an argument to `trackRelatants()` and `count-Relatants()`. We thus described their *closed-role* forms. If we make the role label optional as well, the functions interpret this to mean *"any role"* and generate an *open-role relatant set*. If both the relatant class and role label are unspecified, all relatants of all classes are tracked. If a relatant class is specified but a role label is not, all relatants of the indicated class are tracked irrespective of the roles the subject plays with them: these could come from potentially many relationships. The open-role closed-class and open-role open-class forms of these functions are rarely used but are mentioned here for completeness.

Recall from Chapter 5 that the `objectClass` attribute of every object is specially implemented so that it compares equal not only to the class which that object **is-an-instance-of** but to every one of its *ancestral* classes as well. It thus becomes possible to specify an ancestral class as an argument to these functions and track every relatant which may be an instance of any of its *descendant* classes. This is especially useful when tracking relationships inherited by descendants of the relatant class.

Arguments to Relatant Information Functions

Care must be exercised when using these functions in *transitive* virtual relationships. If a role is transitive, the relatant of a relatant by that role is also a relatant of the subject by the same role. Therefore, a closed-role invocation of `trackRelatants()` with the subject as the root in effect enumerates the entire transitive closure of that role. To control the depth of the search in the transitive closure, these functions take an optional `depth` argument which limits the transitive relatants which are tracked. If the `depth` argument is specified to be 1, only the "first-tier" relatants via the transitive role are returned; "second-tier" relatants which arise as virtual extensions from the "first-tier" relatants are not returned. (A "first-tier" relatant is not necessarily a relatant by an actual relationship; if the transitive role arises by convolution or implication from other roles, a "first-tier" relatant by a transitive role could still be a relatant by a virtual relationship.) The depth argument may be specified to be a range of integers, in which case all the indicated "tiers" are returned. If the depth argument is unspecified, the entire transitive closure is returned. The application to network architecture is obvious: the transitive connectivity relationships between network devices can be used to derive reachability information. We will explore this issue more in Chapter 27.

Another useful capability these functions possess is the ability to accept an implicit rather than an identified class-name as argument. An identified class-name in effect stands for the set of all objects which are members of that class. Specifying a closed-class argument limits the tracking to that set. Both these functions have the ability to accept as their argument an *implicitly* defined set rather than an explicitly defined class-name. The implicitly defined set is the output of a nested call to trackRelatants() itself. Thus, instead of an identified class as an argument, both trackRelatants() and countRelatants() accept instead a set generated by trackRelatants(). Therefore, it thus becomes possible to track or count *relatants of relatants* as well; this mechanism considerably enhances the power of an object to extract information from other objects.

Yet another useful feature these functions possess is their ability to accept a matching argument, which acts as a subsetting mechanism on the returned set of relatant instances. The matching argument is a logical predicate which is conceptually applied to every relatant instance tracked by the class and role arguments. Only instances meeting the matching condition are returned. For example, a matching condition may specify that returned relatant instances have the value of a specified attribute within a specified domain. This feature permits arbitrary subsets of relatant classes to be tracked even if such subsets have not been explicitly created as subclasses. In general, any logical predicate, including those that may be used as a basis of specialization, can be used as a matching condition. If the matching argument is omitted, every member of the tracked relatant class is returned.

In an ordered relationship, trackRelatants() always returns relatant instances sequenced in accordance with the criterion used for ordering the relatant. If the subject wishes to track a specific relatant instance rather than the whole set, it is permitted to invoke trackRelatants() with an optional rank argument. The rank argument must be between 1 and countRelatants(). Alternatively, the rank argument may specify a range of ranks with both end-points being between 1 and countRelatants(). If the rank argument is not used, the entire set of relatants is returned sequenced according to the ordering criterion. If no ordering criterion has been specified for the relatant class, any use of the rank argument is ignored.

From a specification perspective, we do not need to specify trackRelatants() and countRelatants() as FUNCTIONs of an object class. These are environmental functions rather than properties, in that they are automatically provided by the run-time environment to every object class. We reserve the FUNCTION construct to model only those features of its referent object's behavior which are of interest in our network model.

From an implementation standpoint, if our object-oriented network model is implemented in an object-oriented programming environment which does not intrinsically support analogues of `trackRelatants()` and `countRelatants()`, then these functions can be implemented as methods of `genericObject`. If implemented for the root of the inheritance hierarchy, they will be available by inheritance to all object classes.

20.10. Virtual Attributes of Aggregate Classes

Tracked virtual attributes are especially important when the tracking relationship is the aggregation relationship. In Chapter 17, we showed that aggregation could be treated like any other relationship, in which the aggregate class plays the `has-as-a-part` role with its component classes, the reciprocal role being `is-a-part-of`. By defining a virtual attribute for an aggregate class which is tracked into base attributes of its component classes, we can capture within the aggregate class some property representing the totality (or convergence of properties) of its components. For example, we can define the sum or the average of a particular attribute of all components as a virtual attribute of the aggregate.

To illustrate this, we revisit Figure 4-1 in which we argued that the `average-ChannelSpeed` attribute of a `multiplexer` object class should not be modeled as an attribute because, being derivable from individual `speed` values, it was not an orthogonal attribute. Using the modeling techniques developed in Chapter 15, we know that the `speed` attribute really belongs to the `port` objects which are components of the aggregate `multiplexer` object. We can now define `averageChannelSpeed` as a *virtual attribute* of the aggregate `multiplexer` object, whose definition requires that it be dynamically computed by tracking the `has-as-a-part` role which the `multiplexer` object plays with its component `port` objects, reading the values of their `speed` attributes and computing their average. This knowledge can be formally expressed to the compiler as an attribute-defined expression. Informally, we may express this as

```
multiplexer.<averageChannelSpeed> ←
    Sum {{trackRelatants(class:port,
                          role:has-as-a-part)}.speed} ÷
    countRelatants(class:port,role:has-as-a-part)
```

This expression is an informal description of an algorithm whereby such a virtual attribute may be dynamically computed. In this notation, the construct `objectClass.-attribute` represents an actual attribute of an object class, while the construct `objectClass.<attribute>` represents a virtual attribute. The construct

```
{trackRelatants(class:port,role:has-as-a-part)}.speed
```

is a mechanism which iterates over the set of all indicated tracked relatants to generate a set of all their speed attribute values. The operator Sum{ } outside this set performs a plus-reduction, that is, it totals up all its elements. This notation is informal only; the specification to our compiler must be an attribute-defined expression in our formal speci-fication language.

Similarly, we can express many other useful concepts as virtual attributes of ag-gregates which are tracked into their components. In our example of Chapter 7, we mod-eled a wiringHub object class which contained as a component the card object class, with a multiplicity of [1,numberOfCardSlots]. If we wanted to postulate a numberOfInstalledCards virtual attribute for wiringHub, we would simply count the number of card components we could track through its has-as-a-part role, such as

```
wiringHub.<numberOfInstalledCards> ←
        countRelatants(class:card,role:has-as-a-part)
```

and compute the number of ports supported in the wiringHub as its virtual attribute numberOfPorts, expressed in terms of the virtual attribute numberOfPorts of its card components, as

```
card.<numberOfPorts> ←
        countRelatants(class:port,role:has-as-a-part)

wiringHub.<numberOfPorts> ←
        Sum{{trackRelatants(class:card,
                        role:has-as-a-part)}.<numberOfPorts>}
```

and compute the price of each wiringHub object as its price virtual attribute, deter-mined by the cost attributes of all its components, as

```
wiringHub.<price> ←
        {
            Sum{{trackRelatants(role:has-as-a-part)}.cost}
                            -- open-class component set
          + wiringHub.baseCostOfChassis
        }
        × wiringHub.profitMargin
```

and compute its per-port price as the virtual attribute pricePerPort in terms of two supporting base attributes which are both themselves virtual, as

```
wiringHub.<pricePerPort> ←
    wiringHub.<price> ÷ wiringHub.<numberOfPorts>
```

and compute its mean time to failure as

```
wiringHub.<meanTimeToFailure> ←
    Min{{trackRelatants(role:has-as-a-part)}
                                .meanTimeToFailure}
                        -- open-class component set
```

and so on. Clearly, many useful concepts such as these can be postulated as virtual attributes of any aggregate object, which are tracked into base attributes in its components.

20.11. Other Examples of Virtual Attributes

We introduce a slightly more involved example of a *conditional* tracked virtual attribute. Consider an example of a circuit being terminated at some switching equipment, modeled as a `switch` object class which plays the `terminates` role with a `circuit` object class. The `circuit` class has a `status` attribute, whose value is taken from the enumerated domain {busy, idle, dead}. The `switch` class has a `loadingStatus` attribute whose value is taken from the enumerated domain {light, moderate, heavy}. The `switch` has 16384 lines; that is, its `terminates` role with `circuit` has a multiplicity upper bound of 16384. The `loadingStatus` attribute of `switch` is defined to be `light` if the number of busy circuits is less than or equal to 8192, `moderate` if the number is between 8193 and 12288, and `heavy` otherwise.

Clearly, `loadingStatus` is a conditional virtual attribute. However, the conditions governing its computation are not imposed on native base attributes; rather, they apply to the base attributes of a relatant class. In particular, they apply to the totality of the base attributes of multiple relatant objects. We may define it as

```
switch.<loadingStatus> ←
  light IF
    (countRelatants({{trackRelatants{class:circuit,
        role:terminates)}}.status = busy}) <= 8192;
  moderate IF  8192 <
    (countRelatants({{trackRelatants{class:circuit,
        role:terminates)}}.status = busy}) <= 12288;
  heavy IF
    (countRelatants({{trackRelatants{class:circuit,
        role:terminates)}}.status = busy}) > 12288;
```

This construct is permitted since we said earlier that relatant-information functions may take as an argument a set generated by `trackRelatants()` instead of a defined class name. This example shows how the tracked virtual attribute of one object class can be governed by conditions applied to the values of base attributes in a relatant class. Of course, in an actual model the hard constants in this definition should be replaced by appropriate attribute-defined expressions involving attribute values marking the transition boundaries.

Notice that `loadingStatus` is also an explicit-syntax virtual attribute; the fact that its type comes from the enumerated set {`light, moderate, heavy`} cannot be automatically inferred by the compiler from the type of `countRelatants()`, which is simply `INTEGER`.

In general, many of the logical predicates governing the computations of conditional virtual attributes are analogous to the logical predicates indicating bases of specialization. Earlier in this chapter, the conditional virtual attribute `saturation-Watermark` was defined using a condition analogous to *attribute domain restriction* of the supporting `percentageUtilization` base attribute. Here, `loadingStatus` is defined using conditions analogous to a combination of *relatant attribute restriction* and *relatant multiplicity restriction*.

At this point, we indulge in a bit of revisionism. Many of the object classes we have modeled in prior chapters have been specified with attributes which really ought to be virtual attributes. For example, the `maxAge`, `helloTime`, and `forwardDelay` attributes of a transparent LAN bridge in a spanning tree topology can be specified to be virtual attributes tracked into the `rootBridge` object to which it is connected, since they are dictated by the `rootBridge` for all other bridges. For the sake of accuracy, we present some examples below of how other such attributes, earlier modeled as actual, could with our new modeling techniques be specified to be virtual.

In Chapter 12, we modeled the `customerPremisesEquipment` object class with a `manufacturerName` attribute. This is best modeled as a virtual attribute tracked into the `manufacturer` object class through its `is-manufactured-by` relationship role:

```
customerPremisesEquipment.<manufacturerName> ←
    {trackRelatants(class:manufacturer,
                    role:is-manufactured-by)}.objectName
```

Correspondingly, a reciprocal `productLine` virtual attribute could be defined for the `manufacturer` object class by tracking it into the `objectClass` attribute of all the classes with which it plays the role `manufactures`. Since the multiplicity of the `manufactures` role exceeds 1, the implicit syntax of `productLine` would be `SET OF` the type of `objectClass`:

```
manufacturer.<productLine> ←
        {{trackRelatants(role:manufactures)}.objectClass}
                -- open-class relatant set
```

In Chapter 15, we modeled a `protocolStack` object class as an aggregate class which could contain either `protocolEntity` components or other `protocolStack` components as substacks. We can now define `numberOfLayers` as a virtual attribute of the `protocolStack` object class as follows:

```
protocolStack.<numberOfLayers> ←
        countRelatants(class:protocolEntity,
                role:has-as-a-part)
    + Sum{{trackRelatants(class:protocolStack,
                role:has-as-a-part)}.<numberOfLayers>}
```

where the virtual attribute `numberOfLayers` is used recursively in its own definition. In the same chapter, we indicated that a `protocolStack` can be used for serving a particular *plane* (user, control, or management) only if all its component `protocolEntity` objects also serve that plane. If its component `protocolEntity` objects did not all serve a particular plane in common, then the entire `protocolStack` could not serve that plane. We thus define the `operativePlanes` attribute of `protocolStack` in terms of the `operativePlanes` attribute of its component objects:

```
protocolStack.<operativePlanes> ←
        {Intersection{{trackRelatants(class:protocolEntity,
                role:has-as-a-part)}.operativePlanes}}
    Intersection
        {Intersection{{trackRelatants(class:protocolStack,
                role:has-as-a-part)}.<operativePlanes>}}
```

where again we use the virtual attribute recursively in its own definition
    In Chapter 7, we said that we "often informally speak" of some properties as being properties of an aggregate class when in fact they are properties of one of its component classes. For example, the term "speed of a modem" really indicates the `speed` attribute of a `port` component of a `modem` object class. With our new modeling techniques, we can officialize our informal speech by formally specifying a `speed` attribute for the `modem` object class as a virtual attribute tracked into its component `port` object.

20.12. Contingent Base Attributes

There is another mechanism which is occasionally used for virtual attributes tracked into relatants from an open-class relatant set. To recapitulate, an open-class relatant set is a set of all relatants with which the subject class plays a given role, regardless of their class. Because only a role label is specified without a class label, the relatants from an open-class relatant set could potentially come from many different classes. In all of these classes, the supporting base attributes could have slightly different names and slightly different (but compatible) syntaxes but might all convey equivalent semantics. In this case, the virtual attribute might be defined to have one supporting base attribute if the relatant comes from one class, or a different supporting base attribute if the relatant comes from another class [Bert89, Bert91]. Because its base attributes depend on which class they come from, the virtual attribute is said to be defined using *contingent base attributes*.

For example, if our `wiringHub` object class contains components which are manufactured either by ourselves or by a third-party supplier, the attributes used in the computation of its virtual `price` attribute are different depending on a logical predicate which qualifies each tracked relatant:

```
wiringHub.<price> ←
{
    Sum{{trackRelatants(role:has-as-a-part)}.cost
        IF {trackRelatants(role:has-as-a-part)}
                                    .<manufacturerName>
            = wiringHub.<manufacturerName>}
  + Sum{{trackRelatants(role:has-as-a-part)}.oemPrice
        IF {trackRelatants(role:has-as-a-part)}
                                    .<manufacturerName>
            ≠ wiringHub.<manufacturerName>}
  + wiringHub.baseCostOfChassis
}
× wiringHub.profitMargin
```

In this example, the *contingency predicate*

```
{trackRelatants(role:has-as-a-part)}.<manufacturerName>
            = wiringHub .<manufacturerName>)
```

causes a different base attribute from each tracked relatant to be selected into the set depending on whether its `<manufacturerName>` attribute equals the `<manufacturerName>` attribute of the subject `wiringHub` instance. If true, the selected relatant's `cost` attribute is used in the sum; if not, its `oemPrice` attribute is used. The informal notation above permits the expression of such contingency predicates, which can be expressed simply as logical predicates.

Note that this conditional predicate itself equates two tracked virtual attributes: the `<manufacturerName>` attribute of both the `wiringHub` object and the component objects is a virtual attribute tracked through their `is-manufactured-by` role to a `manufacturer` object class. Although contingency definitions for tracked virtual attributes are not commonly encountered, they are occasionally useful and have a place in our modeling arsenal.

20.13. Tracked Virtual Functions

We have said before that reading the value of an attribute is not conceptually different from obtaining the return result of a function. Very similar to the concept of tracked virtual attributes is the concept of *tracked virtual functions*. Tracked virtual functions can be made to "appear" as if they belonged one object class, when in fact they execute in a relatant. An object requested to execute a tracked virtual function will return its result as if that function had been executed internally within that object with the indicated arguments. In actuality, the function is executed by dynamically tracking it through a specified relationship role to a relatant class.

This notion may appear somewhat similar to the concept of *delegation* in some object-based programming environments, but, like virtual attributes, really has its roots in our general relationship model. Unlike delegation environments, for example, the type of the return result of the function is modified by the multiplicity of the tracking role, just as the type of tracked virtual attributes is also modified by the multiplicity of the tracking role. Further, if the multiplicity of the role exceeds 1, then all tracked relatants execute the function.

For example, we may issue a call to a `shutdown()` function of an aggregate object class, whose return value is either 0 for a successful shutdown or 1 for an unsuccessful shutdown. The aggregate actually executes `shutdown()` virtually, by tracking it through its `has-as-a-part` role to the `shutdown()` function of each of its components. Each component might execute `shutdown()` in a manner specific to itself and return either 0 or 1 with the same semantics. We could thus specify `shutdown()` for the aggregate as a tracked virtual function:

```
aggregate.<shutdown()> ←
    Max{{trackRelatants(role:has-as-a-part)}.shutdown()}
```

where the virtual function `shutdown()` for the aggregate class returns 1 if even one of its components could not execute `shutdown()` successfully.

A virtual attribute may be specified as the return result of a function. This function may be a native function or a tracked virtual function; if it is tracked, we still consider the virtual attribute a tracked virtual attribute. By the reverse token, an actual function may use as its argument a tracked virtual attribute. In general, the computation of a tracked virtual attribute might involve any *combination* of supporting base features, including native attributes (actual or virtual), tracked attributes (actual or virtual in the relatant class), native functions (actual or virtual), and tracked functions (actual or virtual in the relatant class).

Consider a `protocolEntity` object implementing a window-based acknowledgement-oriented protocol for transfer of data PDUs. This object may possess an actual averageRoundtripDelay() function, which calculates the average round-trip delay parameter. Another protocolEntity object, layering *above* this protocolEntity object, might possess a maxThroughputLimit virtual attribute. This might be expressed in terms of native base attributes windowSize and maxPacketSize and the return result of the averageRoundtripDelay() function of the *next lower layer*, that is, of the protocolEntity relatant tracked through its layers-below role:

$$\text{protocolEntity.<maxThroughputLimit>} \leftarrow$$
$$(\text{protocolEntity.windowSize} \times$$
$$\text{protocolEntity.maxPacketSize}) \div$$
$$\{\text{trackRelatant(class:protocolEntity,}$$
$$\text{role:layers-below)}\}.\text{averageRoundTripDelay()}$$

Note that our definition of a "virtual function" is very different from the same terminology used in some object-oriented programming environments, where it acts as a placeholder in an ancestral class for a function whose detailed definition will be subsequently provided by a descendant class.

20.14. Tracking through Virtual Relationships

Our definition of tracked virtual attributes creates a mechanism for dynamically resolving the values of an attribute of an object class by querying its relatant instance in an interrogative context. Because virtual relationships behave exactly as actual relationships in the interrogative context, they can also be used as tracking mechanisms for virtual attributes.

Consider the example of Figure 20-5. In this example, we tracked the administrator virtual attribute of networkDevice through a chain of relationship links into the vendorName attribute of outsourcingVendor. However, we also know from Figure 18-8 that the class networkDevice plays the is-administered-by role with the class outsourcingVendor in a distributive virtual relationship. This arises as a consequence of the fact that the is-administered-by role which site plays with outsourcingVendor distributes behind the is-housed-at role which networkDevice plays with site.

To specify the administrator virtual attribute of networkDevice, it is no longer necessary to track a chain of *actual* relationships. We can, in fact, track the virtual attribute through a single *virtual* relationship directly to its base attribute. This is possible because the definition of the role-pair in the virtual relationship internally captures within itself the chain of base role-pairs which support it. Therefore, we no longer have to specify the entire of chain of roles of the actual relationships required to track the virtual attribute. We may use the roles of virtual relationships to reduce the length of the tracking chain in our specification. Figure 20-7 illustrates this mechanism

From an implementation perspective, tracking a virtual attribute through a virtual relationship is generally equivalent to tracking it through a chain of actual relationships.

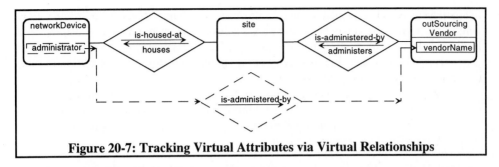

Figure 20-7: Tracking Virtual Attributes via Virtual Relationships

From a specification perspective, it provides us with a slightly more succinct modeling mechanism to convey our semantics correctly.

20.15. Virtual Attributes in Specialization

We have said that virtual attributes behave exactly like actual attributes in the interrogative, declarative, and qualificative contexts. When an attribute is used in a basis of specialization such as attribute domain restriction, it is used in its declarative context. It is possible to use domain restriction on the *virtual* attributes of an object class as a basis of specialization. In effect, this creates subclasses based on partitioning the domain of values the virtual attribute may take. This is called specialization by *virtual attribute domain restriction*.

Tracked virtual attributes bring inside an object the values of base attributes from its relatant objects. If a tracked virtual attribute is used as the basis of specialization, in effect we create subclasses based on domain restriction of an attribute of a relatant. Therefore, specialization by attribute domain restriction (described in Chapter 6), when applied to a tracked virtual attribute, is very closely related to specialization by relatant attribute restriction (described in Chapter 17).

Semantically, virtual attribute domain restriction and relatant attribute restriction are equivalent if the virtual attribute directly tracks a single base attribute of a relatant without subjecting it to any mathematical manipulation. However, the specification of the specialization is different: in virtual attribute domain restriction, the tracking is done in the definition of the virtual attribute itself. The specializing subclass specifies domain restriction on the tracked virtual attribute just as it does for an actual attribute. By contrast, in specialization by relatant attribute restriction, the specializing subclass must indicate both the relatant class and its attribute which it uses in the specialization. In effect, the tracking is not done from within the superclass but in the predicate indicating the basis of specialization for the subclass.

An interesting mode of specialization arises when a single tracked virtual attribute is supported by multiple base attributes in *more than one* relatant class. If so, a tracked virtual attribute may bring into an object a result obtained by applying mathematical operations on attribute values tracked from multiple relatant classes. We are permitted to use domain restriction on such an attribute as a basis of specialization. Unlike specialization by Relatant Attribute Restriction, which permits the subclass to restrict the domain of an attribute in only one relatant, this mechanism effectively permits us to restrict the domain on the result of some mathematical transform of different attributes in different relatants. This transform could be a complex mathematical manipulation of values or a Boolean resulting from comparing attributes of different relatants to constant values or to each other. Thus, we can simultaneously apply multiple conditions on attributes in multiple relatants as a basis of specialization.

Although this mechanism does not commonly occur as a basis of specialization, it is in fact a powerful method of creating highly specialized subclasses based on some complex interaction between multiple relatants of an object class. We express the general form of *virtual attribute domain restriction* as:

Specialization Principle:	*A descendant class may restrict the domain of a virtual attribute inherited from an ancestral class (**Virtual Attribute Domain Restriction**).*

There are specialization modes analogous to Function Argument Contravariance and Function Result Covariance where the function used in the specialization is not a native function of the object class but a tracked virtual function. These are mentioned for completeness, but as they are rarely encountered, we omit a formal statement of the specialization principle. Note that there are no specialization modes corresponding to Virtual Attribute Addition of Virtual Function Addition. If a descendant class adds only a virtual attribute, it in fact adds nothing. A virtual attribute merely represents a new way of looking at values already available in an object class or its relatants; merely adding a new virtual attribute does not extend any of the intrinsic features, properties, or functionality of the object class.

20.16. Summary

A virtual attribute represents an abstraction which reflects the values of one or more supporting base attributes. A virtual attribute is specified using an attribute-defined expression, which may apply a mathematical or logical transform on the values of its supporting base attributes. The value of a virtual attribute is in effect dynamically resolved from the current values of its supporting base attributes every time it is queried.

A virtual attribute is always read-only; it can never be updated. It may be used as a mechanism in our security model when our network is to interoperate with other networks. By making only virtual attributes visible to external networks, we protect the privacy of the supporting base attribute values used in computing the value of the virtual attribute, and the computation algorithm itself. We also ensure that an external network cannot inadvertently modify exposed data.

The base attributes supporting a virtual attribute may be native to the object class or may come from a relatant class. If they come from a relatant class, the virtual attribute is called a tracked virtual attribute and is used to capture within the object information about its relatants. Generally, it may be used to capture within the object some property representing the totality or convergence of properties of its individual relatants. The multiplicity of the tracking relationship affects the syntax of the tracked virtual attribute. The functions of an object class may also be tracked virtual functions which execute in another object class. Virtual attributes and functions may be tracked through actual or virtual relationships.

An object may be queried for its virtual attributes with the same query protocols used for actual attributes. The external object issuing the query need not know that a tracked virtual attribute is resolved from a value in a relatant class. Because the queried object "knows" how to compute its virtual attributes, it executes the tracking internally and transparently. The external object need compose no relational joins in the query.

Domain restriction on virtual attributes may be used as a basis of specialization. Overall, virtual attributes represent a robust, implementation-independent specification mechanism to capture within an object information about its external relationships, without compromising the encapsulation of either the object or its relatants.

21. Virtual Object Classes

*"We've got fax, teleconferencing and email! Now we can
misunderstand each other faster."*

— *anonymous telecom manager.*

21.1. Introduction

The notion of virtual object classes creates additional infrastructure to enhance the security features of a network. By specifying virtual object classes within its model, a network
may fine-tune the granularity with which information about itself is exposed to external
networks. In addition, the mechanism of virtual object classes also provides us with
automatic classification capabilities which are of assistance in executing network operations. In this chapter, we demonstrate how virtual object classes enhance our modeling
semantics, and we present a set of mechanisms with which they may be specified.

21.2. Conceptual Background

A *virtual object class* is a class whose members are completely determined by certain
criteria satisfied by the members of another object class. A virtual object class does not
add structural or functional extensions to any existing object class. In Chapter 5, we said
that a subclass extends the semantics of its superclass by adding more structural detail
(new attributes), adding richer capability (new functions), and narrowing the focus of
applicability (employing any of the specialization principles). A subclass uses a basis of
specialization as a set-partitioning mechanism to isolate some members of its superclass
which it will focus on and evolve further. By contrast, a virtual object class performs no
evolution, extension, or incremental refinement.

The mechanism which creates a virtual object class is called *virtualization*.
Virtualization and specialization are orthogonal concepts. Because a virtual object class
does not refine a superclass to evolve it further, it cannot **specialize-from** ancestral

classes, nor can there be any descendant classes which it **specializes-into**. As such, it does not have a place in the inheritance hierarchy. Any object class which adds, expands, or restricts its superclass properties and has a place in the inheritance hierarchy is called an *actual object class*.

A virtual object class provides a new *perspective* on an existing object class. The existing object class which gives rise to the virtual object class is called its *base object class*, or simply its *base class*. The base class may be an actual object class, or may itself be virtual. If the base class is itself virtual, then *its* base class is also a base class of the specificand virtual class. A virtual object class has only one actual base class, but any base class may give rise to more than one virtual object class.

The properties of the supporting base class which are available in the virtual class are called *aspects* of the virtual class. Aspects are the same as properties (that is, attributes and functions) but belong to virtual object classes. A virtual class is said to *acquire* its aspects from its base class; the base class is said to *grant* them to the virtual class. The terms *inherit* and *bequeath* are not used in the context of virtual and base classes; they are reserved for use only between ancestral and descendant classes. A virtual object class cannot add any new aspects to the properties it acquires from its supporting base classes.

The virtual class is said to **virtualize-from** its supporting base class; the base class is said to **virtualize-into** all the virtual object classes it supports. These are called the *virtualization associations*; they are parallel to (but have different meanings than) the specialization associations **specializes-from** and **specializes-into** between descendant and ancestral classes. Similarly, the associations between the properties of the base class and the aspects of a virtual class are termed **grants-to** and **acquires-from**, also called the *aspect acquisition associations*; these are parallel to (but have different meanings than) the inheritance associations **bequeaths-to** and **inherits-from** between the properties of ancestral and descendant classes.

Virtual Object Instances

An object instance which is a member of an actual object class is called an *actual object* or *actual instance*. An object instance belonging to a virtual object class is called a *virtual object* or *virtual instance*. A virtual object reflects an actual object belonging to an actual class. The virtual object merely happens to be a member of the virtual class because of the manner in which the virtual class has been defined. All instances of a virtual class must be instances of its supporting base class. In particular, they must be concrete instances of some supporting actual base class.

Although a virtual object class may have instances, it can never be *instantiated*. That is, it is not possible to create a new object using the virtual object class as a template. An object can only be created as an instance of an actual object class. Once it is created, it may happen to *automatically* become a member of one or more virtual object classes supported by that actual class, depending on its characteristics and on the definitions of the virtual object classes. Further, it is not possible to destroy an instance of a virtual object class. If the object is destroyed as an instance of an actual object class, it is automatically destroyed as an instance of all virtual object classes supported by that base class.

In addition, a virtual object can never be modified: it is not possible to change the value of an attribute of a virtual object. If a change must be made, it must be made to the supporting actual instance. All virtual objects supported by that actual object will now automatically reflect this change. It is possible that merely changing the value of an attribute of an actual instance destroys the object as a virtual instance, even though it continues to exist as an actual instance.

These limitations imply that the *membership* of a virtual object class (that is, the set of all objects which are its members) can never be explicitly assigned. Once the virtual class definition is in place, actual objects may automatically become or destroy themselves as members of that virtual class depending on their characteristics and on the manner in which the class has been defined. This is because *the membership of a virtual object class is in effect re-enumerated each time that virtual object class is queried.*

Aside from these differences, virtual objects behave externally exactly like actual objects. An external object may query a virtual object exactly as it queries any other object. The external object may request that the virtual object return the value of any of its externally visible attributes, or it may request that the virtual object execute any of its externally visible functions. The external object issues these requests in the same protocol that it uses on any other object; it does not necessarily "know" whether the queried object is actual or virtual. Further, a virtual object class participates in all the relationships defined for its supporting actual base class.

To summarize, a virtual class can only be populated by objects which already exist in its supporting base class. Other than this, virtual objects have no reality internally within the model information base [Abit91, Bars91, Abit93]. Note also that our usage of the term "base class" is different from that of some object-oriented programming languages, where it is used to denote a superclass or an ancestral class.

21.3. Creating Virtual Object Classes

There are three important mechanisms which give rise to a virtual object class:

- *Selection* from its base class
- *Projection* from its base class
- *Conjunction* of its base class with a relatant class.

Each type of virtual object class is used for a different purpose. A virtual object class created by *selection* from its base class is useful for *automatic classification*, in that it helps us easily make the choices we might wish to make while operating the network. Such a class is called a *selected virtual class*. A virtual object class created by *projection* from its base class is useful for *security*, in that it helps us to expose only limited perspectives of our network to external networks. Such a class is called a *projected virtual class*. A virtual object class created by *conjunction* of its base class with a relatant class is useful for *report generation*, in that it helps us to view relationship instances as sets of participant object instances. Such a class is called a *conjunct virtual class*.

The mechanism which creates a virtual object class is called its *basis of virtualization*. It is possible to define a virtual object class which uses multiple selections, projections, or conjunctions as its basis of virtualization. It is also possible to define a virtual object class which simultaneously uses a combination of selection, projection, and conjunction as its basis of virtualization. Further, since the base class of a virtual object class may itself be virtual, it is possible to define a virtual class which uses selection, projection, or conjunction on another virtual class.

In Chapter 5, we said that the semantics of the **specializes-from** association (also called **generalizes-into** or **is-a**) between a descendant class and its ancestors conveyed the notions of specialization, extension, restriction, subtyping, and substitutability, while the semantics of the **specializes-into** association (or **generalizes-from**) between an ancestral class and its descendants implied the notions of generalization and supertyping. By contrast, the semantics of the **virtualizes-from** association between a virtual class and its base classes imply only the notions of selection, projection, conjunction, and non-updatability; the semantics of the **virtualizes-into** association between a base class and its virtual classes imply only the notion of support. Figure 21-1 illustrates this distinction.

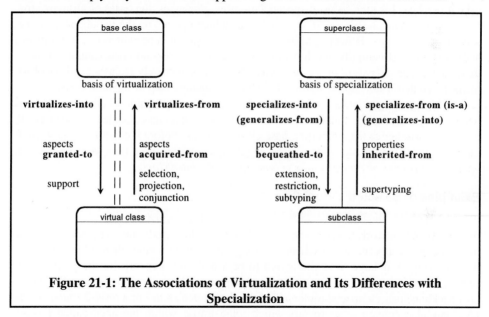

Figure 21-1: The Associations of Virtualization and Its Differences with Specialization

The attributes and functions which a base class grants its virtual classes may be actual or virtual, native or tracked. It is possible to define a virtual object class whose aspects are virtual attributes tracked through virtual relationships.

21.4. Selected Virtual Classes

A selected virtual class is a class defined using a *selection criterion* as its basis of virtualization. Creating virtual classes by selection is a mechanism which permits objects to *autoclassify* themselves. The autoclassification of objects is an important tool in the operation of communication networks. When performing an operation or issuing a request on objects in a network, we may indicate that the operation is to be performed on all members of a selected virtual class. Consequently, it will be performed on all members of the supporting base class which meet the criteria for being selected into the virtual class. Because we have already specified the criteria in the definition of the selected virtual class, *we do not have to supply the selection criteria in the protocol along with our request*. All the objects on which we wish to execute the operation are already preselected, because the objects have *autoclassified themselves*.

The criteria for defining a selected virtual class are essentially set-partitioning operators. They create selected virtual classes by partitioning the members of the supporting base class into *subsets*. A selected virtual class segregates those members of the supporting base class which are likely to be useful as preselected groups during the operation of the network.

The conditions for preselecting objects into the set defined by a selected virtual class look rather like the bases of specialization used by subclasses to **specialize-from** their superclass. Like the bases of specialization for subclasses, the bases of virtualization for selected virtual classes are logical predicates which operate on the membership of the supporting base class. However, unlike a subclass — which is permitted to extend its inherited features structurally and functionally — a selected virtual class cannot add anything new to the definition of the supporting base class. It merely isolates a subset of its members so that it can capture a limited view of the membership of the base class.

The logical predicate used to define the selected virtual class is called the *selector basis of virtualization* or simply the *selector* for that virtual class. A selector specifies all the tests a member of the supporting base class must pass before it can autoclassify itself as a member of the selected virtual class. A selector specifies these tests as *conditions on values of attributes or return results of functions of the base class.*

Examples of Selected Virtual Classes

As an example, a consider a router-based internetwork designed for interconnecting various local-area networks over several geographically dispersed sites. The routers use a link-state-based algorithm to exchange routing information among themselves. Because the internetwork is large, it is configured to be a multi-tier network for the purposes of routing. The network is partitioned into separate *areas*. Each area connects to the wide-area backbone using a special router called the *designated router* or a *level-2 router*. Each area may also contain other routers which route traffic within the area, called *level-1 routers*. Each designated router converses with designated routers in other areas to convey information about the network nodes reachable in its own area [RFC 1247, ISO 10589, Perl91, Perl92].

The designated router for each area is chosen either by assignment, or by election among routers. That is, there may be no special built-in differentiation between level-1 routers and designated routers; it is possible that all router devices may be exactly alike. Although a designated router may choose to invoke some built-in FUNCTIONs which level-1 routers may not invoke, it need not intrinsically possess any additional functionality that level-1 routers do not already have. Thus, all routers may be instances of the same object class. It is also possible that a designated router may automatically become a level-1 router if a new election is held among the routers following a topology reconfiguration.

For these reasons, it is not ideal modeling practice to define `designated-Router` and `level-1-router` as a *subclasses* of `router`. If we created these classes and populated them with instances, it is possible that we may have to explicitly delete instances of `designatedRouter` and add new instances to `level-1-router`, each time a new election is held. We would much prefer that the routers have the ability to *autoclassify* themselves.

We can therefore define both `designatedRouter` and `level-1-router` as *selected virtual classes* supported by the base `router` class. The selector basis of virtualization can use the value of the `level` attribute of the `router` class. The selector for `designatedRouter` constrains this attribute to the value 2; the selector for `level-1-router` constrains it to the value 1. Each time a new election is held, the routers reclassify themselves if necessary, merely by changing the value of their `level` attribute. Thus, when we query the membership of the `designatedRouter` class, we only get those `router` objects whose `level` attribute happens to have the value 2 *at that time*. In effect, the entire membership of `designatedRouter` is re-evaluated by applying the selector basis of virtualization to every member of its base `router` class. Of course, all explicitly assigned designated routers will always be members of the `designatedRouter` class.

There are many situations in network modeling in which it is useful to provide objects with the ability to autoclassify themselves. For example, in a bridge-based LAN internetwork, we could define the selected virtual classes `forwardingPort` and `blockedPort` to classify the `ports` of `transparentBridge` objects using the spanning tree algorithm. Due to topology changes, it is possible for a `forwarding-Port` to become a `blockedPort` (and vice versa) automatically. If we wished to enumerate the set of all `forwardingPorts` in a current configuration, we could simply specify that it is a selected virtual class supported by a `port` base class, using as a selector the value of its `forwarding` attribute.

We also revisit the example of the `circuit` object class of Chapter 20, in which we created a `saturationWatermark` conditional virtual attribute whose value was completely defined by a `percentageUtilization` actual attribute. Instead of modeling a conditional virtual attribute with a three-valued domain for the `circuit` object class, we can create an alternative model by defining three object classes virtualizing from it. We could define, for example, the selected virtual classes `greenCircuit`, `yellowCircuit`, and `redCircuit`, using as a selector the value of its `percentageUtilization` attribute. We can, if we wish, now issue operations which are to be performed on `redCircuit` objects alone; this operation will execute on all `circuit` objects which may happen to belong the `redCircuit` selected virtual class at that time. Figure 21-2 illustrates these examples.

In Figure 21-2, if the `percentageUtilization` of a `redCircuit` object changes, it could automatically destroy itself as a member of the `redCircuit` selected virtual class and instantiate itself as a member of either `yellowCircuit` or `green-Circuit`. In reality, the `circuit` does not destroy and recreate itself in the model information base; all it does is change the value of its `percentageUtilization` attribute. We say that an object "destroys" itself as a member of one selected virtual class

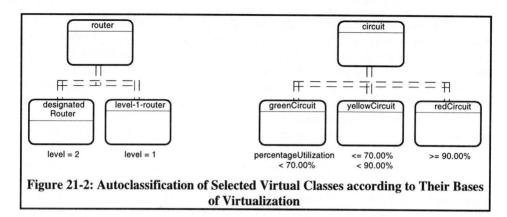

Figure 21-2: Autoclassification of Selected Virtual Classes according to Their Bases of Virtualization

and "recreates" itself as a member of another because, when the membership of the virtual classes is re-enumerated before and after the change in the object's attribute value, it appears that the object has "moved".

This ability objects possess of moving between selected virtual classes (or more generally, to move in and out of a selected virtual class) is called their *autoclassification* ability. It arises as a consequence of the fact that, each time the selected virtual class is queried, its membership is re-enumerated by applying the selector to all members of the supporting base class.

21.5. Modes of Virtualization by Selection

As with specialization, any virtualization by selection may be characterized as *disjoint* or *complete*. This has the same meaning as it did in Chapter 6. If the virtualization is disjoint, then there is no overlap in the partitioning of the domain of the selector attribute chosen as the basis of virtualization. This implies that an actual object can support *no more than one* virtual object in any selected virtual class using that attribute as a selector. If the virtualization is complete, then each value in the domain of the selector attribute is "covered" in some selected virtual class definition supported by the base class. This implies that an actual object supports *at least one* virtual object in some selected virtual class using that attribute as a selector. In the `circuit` example of Figure 21-2, the virtualization is both disjoint and complete. In the `router` example, the virtualization is disjoint, and, if the number of routing tiers supported in the internetwork is no more than 2, is also complete.

Of course, more than one set of virtualizations may proceed from the same base class, each using a different attribute as a selector. In addition, it is also possible to define a virtualization in which simultaneous domain partitioning of more than one attribute is used as the selector. In this case, it is called a *compound virtualization*. The concepts of disjointness and completeness also apply but must be considered in multiple dimensions. In all cases, if the virtualization is not disjoint, it is possible for an actual object to support more than one virtual object in the selected virtual classes using that attribute (or those attributes) as the selector.

The analogies between specialization and virtualization are by now easily apparent. As it turns out, because a selector basis of virtualization is a logical predicate, its formal specification is syntactically identical to the logical predicates used as bases of specialization. In fact, many of the principles which can be used as bases of specialization for creating new subclasses, also have analogues as selector bases of virtualization for creating new selected virtual classes. Notable exceptions are the *addition* modes of specialization: specialization by attribute addition, function addition, capsule addition, and relationship addition do not have analogues as bases of virtualization. This is because, as we stated earlier, a virtual object class cannot extend its base class in any manner.

We define below the bases of virtualization which can be used to create selected virtual classes as analogues of some of the specialization principles. These should be viewed as general guidelines and by no means constitute an exhaustive list of all the ways in which virtual classes can be defined.

- *A virtual object class may select those members of its base class for which an attribute, actual or virtual, native or tracked, has a value restricted to a specified domain (**Attribute Domain Restriction**).*

- *A virtual object class may select those members of its base class for which a result returned from a function, actual or virtual, native or tracked, has a value restricted to a specified domain (**Result Covariance**).*

- *A virtual object class may select those members of its base class for which an optional capsule is present (**Capsule Fixing**).*

- *A virtual object class may select those members of its base class for which relatant multiplicity in a relationship has a value restricted to a specified domain (**Relatant Multiplicity Restriction**).*

- *A virtual object class may select those members of its base class which participate in a relationship with only certain descendants of the relatant (**Relatant Specialization**).*

- *A virtual object class may select those members of its base class which participate in a relationship with only certain selected virtual classes based on the relatant (**Relatant Virtualization**).*

- *A virtual object class may select those members of its base class for which an attribute of a relatant of its base class has a value restricted to a specified domain (**Relatant Attribute Restriction**).*

- *A virtual object class may select those members of its base class for which a relationship attribute of a relationship in which its base class participates, has a value restricted to a specified domain (**Relationship Attribute Restriction**).*

- *A virtual object class may select those members of its base class which use more than one of the above modes simultaneously as a basis of virtualization (**Compound Virtualization**).*

It should be easily apparent how most of these virtualization modes work. We offer below an example illustrating the new mode of *virtualization by relatant virtualization*.

Relatant Virtualization

Consider again the `switch` object class of Chapter 20 which plays the `terminates` role with the `circuit` object class. The `circuit` object class has a `status` attribute which takes its value from the enumerated set {`busy, idle, dead`}. To facilitate our ability to operate on all `circuits` meeting certain criteria as an entire class, we define the selected virtual classes `deadCircuit` and `liveCircuit` which **virtualize-from** the base class `circuit`. The basis of virtualization is that any `circuit` whose `status` is dead belongs to `deadCircuit`; if its `status` is busy or idle, it is a `liveCircuit`. This uses *virtualization by attribute domain restriction*. Individual `circuit` objects may "move" between these selected virtual classes as the value of their `status` attribute changes.

The `switch` class has a `maxCircuits` attribute which indicates the maximum number of circuits it terminates [Yell92]. The `switch` class also **virtualizes-into** the selected virtual classes `operationalSwitch`, `partiallyOperational-Switch`, and `deadSwitch`. The basis of virtualization is the number of dead-Circuits the `switch` terminates. If none of the `circuits` which the `switch` terminates are dead, it is an `operationalSwitch`; if it terminates at least one `deadCircuit`, it is a `partiallyOperationalSwitch`; if every `circuit` it terminates is dead, it is a `deadSwitch`.

In other words, each selected virtual class of `switch` participates in its termination relationship with selected virtual classes of `circuit` with different multiplicities. Further, each selected virtual class of `switch` plays its `terminates` role with only some, not all, selected virtual classes of `circuit`. We may say that each selected virtual class of `switch` "chooses" those selected virtual classes of `circuit` with which it will play the `terminates` role. This situation is known as *virtualization by relatant virtualization* and is illustrated in Figure 21-3.

In this example, the `switch` object autoclassifies itself based not on the values of its own attributes, but based on the values of attributes in its *relatant* objects. Thus a `switch` object may appear to "move" from one selected virtual class to another even though none of its *own* attributes has changed. It moves because a relatant object has "moved" from one of *its* selected virtual classes to another.

Note that the relationships in which the virtual object classes of Figure 21-3 participate are not *virtual relationships*, as defined in Chapter 18. They are actual relationships whose participants happen to be virtual object classes. As permitted by the modes of virtualization, these virtual classes have restricted the multiplicity domains in the relationships they inherited from their base classes. Of course, virtual object classes may participate in virtual relationships as well.

A little reflection will indicate the close ties between the mechanism of *tracked virtual attributes* of Chapter 20 and *virtualization by relatant virtualization*. If we had specified the virtual attribute `numberOfDeadCircuits` for the `switch` object class,

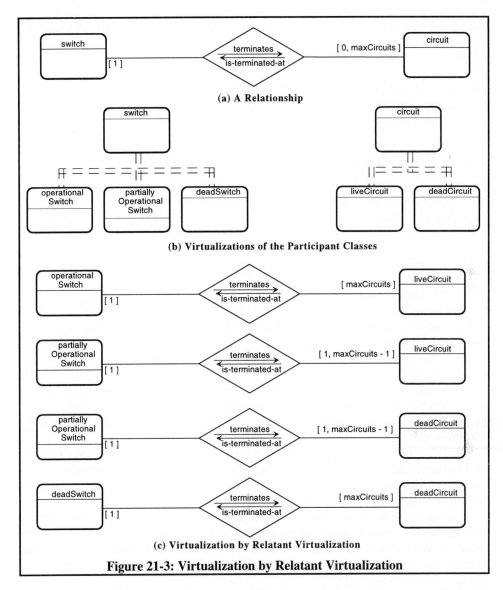

Figure 21-3: Virtualization by Relatant Virtualization

its value would have been defined by counting the number of circuit relatants the switch terminates which are dead, using the countRelatants() function. If such an attribute had indeed been defined, the selected virtual classes operational-Switch, partiallyOperationalSwitch, and deadSwitch could have been virtualized by merely using attribute domain restriction on this attribute.

Virtualization by relatant virtualization can be explained by the same arguments that support specialization by relatant specialization. The only difference here is that in specialization by relatant specialization, the classification takes place by way of defined subclasses of the subject and relatant. Thus, the participant objects of the relationship instance are fixed within their subclasses. In virtualization by relatant virtualization, the participant objects can "move" between their virtual classes as and when values in their relatant objects change. Further, as we said in Chapter 17, relatant specialization can often be equivalently expressed as relatant attribute restriction. This applies here as well: virtualization by relatant specialization and virtualization by relatant virtualization can also be often expressed in terms of relatant attribute restriction.

21.6. Projected Virtual Classes

A projected virtual class is a class which is defined using a *projection criterion* as its basis of virtualization. Creating virtual classes by projection is a mechanism which permits us to focus only on certain selected aspects of the base class. We may wish to capture in a virtual class only certain aspects of the base class which we wish to treat differently; for example, we may wish to expose only those aspects to external networks. We could do this by keeping the entire base class hidden and defining a projected virtual class which includes only those aspects which we wish to expose.

The criterion used for defining a projected virtual class is known as a *projector basis of virtualization*, or simply a *projector*. A projector is a list of the aspects which will be visible in the projected virtual class; essentially, it is a list of attributes and functions granted by the base class. The attributes and functions in a projector list may be actual or virtual, native or tracked. The order in which the aspects appear in the projector list is irrelevant.

All members of the base class are also members of the projected virtual class. If a new member is added to the base class, it is automatically instantiated as a member of all projected virtual classes supported by that base class. Of course, only certain aspects of that object will be available in its virtual instances.

The differences between selected and projected virtual classes are many. A selector basis of virtualization is a logical predicate; a projector basis of virtualization is simply a list. If an object is instantiated in the base class, it may or may not be a member of the supported selected virtual classes, depending on the values of its attributes. However, it is always a member of all supported projected virtual classes. An object may "move" between selected virtual classes as its attribute values change. By contrast, an object never "moves" between projected virtual classes. It remains a member of all projected virtual classes supported by its actual base class until it is explicitly destroyed as an instance of the actual base class.

There is, however, one rare circumstance under which an object instantiated in a base class does not appear as a member of a supported projected virtual class. This is when a projected virtual class is defined using a projector list which contains only properties originating in *optional* capsules of the base class. If an instance of the base class contains no optional capsules, it will not appear as a member of the projected virtual class. This is very uncommon as most projector lists usually contain at least the objectName attribute, so we can correctly link the values of the aspects we see through the projector with the proper object instance. Figure 21-4 illustrates a projected virtual class.

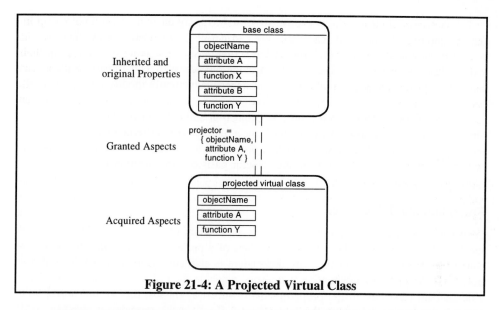

Figure 21-4: A Projected Virtual Class

Like a set of selector bases of virtualization, a set of projector bases of virtualization may also be characterized as disjoint and complete. For a set of projected virtual classes supported by the same base class, the virtualization is disjoint if any property of the base class appears as an aspect in no more than one projected virtual class. The virtualization is complete if every property of the base class appears as an aspect in at least one projected virtual class. In practice, it is very uncommon to encounter a disjoint projected virtualization because, as we indicated before, at least the objectName attribute (or some other unique-valued identifier attribute) usually appears in all projector lists.

In the uncommon situation where a unique-valued identifier attribute is not projected into a virtual class, it is possible that multiple virtual objects in that class appear completely identical. Many instances of the base class may have equal values for those attributes which are granted in the projector list. In the absence of a distinguishing identifier attribute, some of the members of the virtual class may have equal values for all acquired aspects. This is permitted in specialization theory; it is not regarded as an inconsistency to have identical virtual object instances.

21.7. Using Projection

By carefully defining projector lists for projected virtual classes and appropriate external visibility for these classes, we can closely control our security policies. By making projected virtual classes available to external objects, we can implement a privacy policy which protects the values of those aspects we do not wish to expose, while at the same time making necessary data available to external objects. We also automatically protect our objects from being updated by external objects, either accidentally or maliciously. If the only objects externally visible are virtual, then all exposed aspects are always read-only because they can never be updated.

A projected virtual class is sometimes used to *spoof* an actual object class simply for the purpose of making it read-only. We can define a projected virtual class with a projector list containing *all* properties of the actual class. By making only the projected virtual class visible to external objects, we provide full access to its members, while at the same time ensuring that external objects can never inadvertently modify any of their aspects.

It is possible to use selection and projection simultaneously. This will create a virtual object class whose members *both* meet the selector criteria *and* are projected through the projector list. If selection and projection are used simultaneously, it is not necessary that any attributes used in the selector basis of virtualization be granted as an aspect to the virtual class in the projector list.

Projection and Inheritance

We said in Chapter 5 that an instance of any descendant of an ancestral class is also a member of the ancestral class. If the base class of a projected virtual class has descendants, then each new instance of any descendant is also automatically a member of the base class. As such, it will show up as a virtual object in the projected virtual class. Since a descendant class has all the properties of its ancestral classes, this virtual object will have all the aspects defined in the projector list. Recall that a descendant also may add *new* properties. Regardless of how many new properties are added by the descendant, they do *not* appear in the projected virtual class. Only those properties defined in the projector list from the base class appear as aspects in the projected virtual class.

For this reason, it is not permitted to define a projector list which contains properties its base class does not have, in the hope that, after the base class specializes, its descendants will add those properties. This is because while some descendants might add those properties, others might not. Each time a projector list is defined, our compiler checks that it is a subset of the properties currently available in the base class. If not, it rejects the virtualization.

Although it is possible in each actual base class to keep track of which properties of the class are inherited and which are originated in the class, this knowledge is lost in the virtual class. If in its projector list the virtual class is granted both original and inherited properties as aspects, the virtual class does not "know" whence its aspects originated.

Projection and Instantiation

Recall in Chapter 10 we indicated that every object "knows" its class. This knowledge was captured in the attribute `objectClass` which we modeled for `genericObject`, the root of the inheritance hierarchy. For every object, the value of this attribute is set to the class it belongs to; by interrogating this attribute, we can determine what class that object **is-an-instance-of**.

We clarify now that the value of the `objectClass` attribute of every object is always set to its *actual* class. We have said before that an object **is-an-instance-of** only one actual class, although it may be an instance of multiple virtual classes. No matter how many virtual classes the object belongs to, the value of its `objectClass` attribute always reflects its actual class. Because this value is fixed for the lifetime of the object, an object always "knows" what actual class it belongs to. By contrast, it *never* knows which virtual classes it belongs to. An object may belong to more than one virtual class depending on how the virtual classes are defined and "move" back and forth between different virtual classes as its attribute values change, but still "have no idea" that it is doing so. This is because the membership of virtual classes is re-enumerated every time the classes are queried.

If the base class grants `objectClass` as an aspect in a projector list to a virtual class, it is in theory possible for an external object to determine whether or not objects of that virtual class are actual or virtual. It can do this by simply interrogating the value of the `objectClass` attribute of any object in the virtual class. If this is the same as the name of the class it queried, it is an actual object; if not, it is a virtual object. If we do not wish to give external objects the ability to determine this, we can do one of two things. We can choose not to expose the `objectClass` attribute of the virtual class to other objects, using some external security mechanism. Alternatively, we can define the virtual class such that the base class does not grant `objectClass` to the virtual class in its projector list. If need be, we can define two virtual classes, one with `objectClass` as an acquired aspect and another without, and expose the first to trusted external objects and the second to all others.

An Example of a Projected Virtual Class

As an example of a projected virtual class, we may define the virtual object class `directory`. This projected virtual class can be defined on `genericObject` — that is, the root of the inheritance hierarchy — as its base. The projector list can simply be the two attributes `objectName` and `objectClass`. Since every object is a member of `genericObject`, every object will be a member of `directory`. Since every object possesses the attributes `objectName` and `objectClass`, those values will appear for every object in `directory`. No other properties of any object will appear. Figure 21-5 illustrates this example.

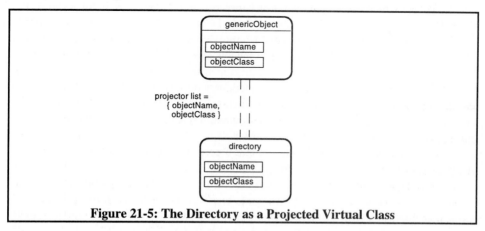

Figure 21-5: The Directory as a Projected Virtual Class

If there are certain objects we do not wish to list in the `directory`, we can simultaneously use a selector to prevent them from appearing. Since the `objectClass` attribute is specially implemented so that it compares equal to `objectClass` values of ancestral classes as well, we can prevent an entire branch of the inheritance hierarchy from being listed by simply specifying a selector using the `objectClass` attribute to exclude the root class of that branch.

21.8. Conjunct Virtual Classes

A conjunct virtual class is a virtual class which is defined using a *conjunction criterion* as its basis of virtualization. Creating a virtual object class by conjunction is a mechanism which permits us to focus on the *relationships* in which its base class participates. Typically, we use conjunction so that we may simultaneously inspect the properties of both an object and its relatants. While each virtual object in a selected or projected virtual class is supported by base *object* instances, a virtual object in a conjunct virtual class is supported by *relationship* instances in which its base objects participate. Thus, each instance of a conjunct virtual class may reflect properties from the base object *and* its relatant. Nonetheless, the conjunct virtual class itself has only one base class. The conjunct virtual class is said to be *defined on* this base class.

The criterion for specifying a conjunct virtual class is known as a *conjunctor basis of virtualization*, or simply a *conjunctor*. A conjunctor identifies one or more relatant classes of the base class whose properties are also to be included in the virtual class. Since a conjunct virtual class reflects the properties of relationship instances, its aspects will include the properties of *both* the base class and of the relatant class. This is especially useful if we desire to use the conjunct virtual classes for *report generation*: for example, to list all the pairs of participant objects of some relationship.

A conjunctor is specified essentially in terms of the `trackRelatants()` function which we introduced in Chapter 20. When used in a conjunctor, the `trackRelatants()` function is applied to every member of the base class. In this context, the `trackRelatants()` function requires a role label and exactly one class label; open-class, multi-class, or open-role flavors of this function are not allowed. Since the `objectClass` attribute of every class compares equal to all its ancestral classes, comparing the `class:` argument in the conjunctor with the `objectClass` attribute of other objects will permit us to create conjunctions with instances of descendants of relatant classes as well. If the objects of the base class have relatants which belong to different but cognate classes, we may create a conjunction with all of them by merely specifying a conjunction with their cognation ancestor.

When executed, the conjunctor creates a conjunct virtual class whose aspects are the properties of its base class, and the properties of the relatant class tracked through the conjunctor. Thus, the values of the aspects of each virtual instance reflect the values of properties of some instance of the base class *and* its relatant instance from the relatant class, tracked as indicated by the conjunctor. Only the properties of correctly related pairs of participant instances will appear as the aspects of a virtual instance. The values are correctly related because, when used in a conjunctor, the `trackRelatants()` function iterates over every member of the base class and tracks the correct relatant instance of each member, object by object. Figure 21-6 illustrates the aspects of a conjunct virtual class.

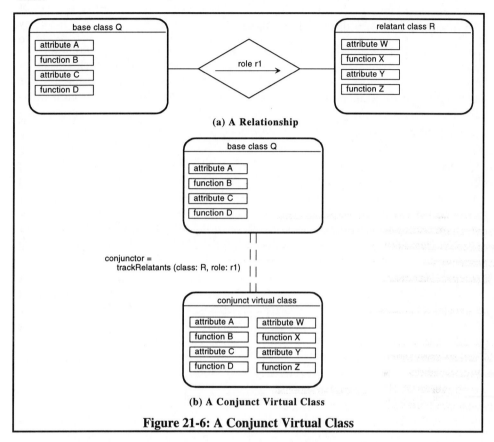

(a) A Relationship

(b) A Conjunct Virtual Class

Figure 21-6: A Conjunct Virtual Class

Aside from requiring a single mandatory class label and at least one role label as arguments, all the features of the `trackRelatants()` function we described in Chapter 20 may be used in a conjunctor. For example, it is possible to specify multiple role labels to track the relatant class by a chain of role links, rather than a single role. Each role link of the chain could indicate an actual or virtual relationship. Since `track-Relatants()` accepts a set generated by its own result instead of a `class:` argument, it is also possible to specify a conjunctor with a nested call to `trackRelatants()`.

It is fairly common to encounter a projector used along with a conjunctor. This is useful when we do not wish to acquire *all* the properties of the base class and its tracked relatant class as aspects of the conjunct virtual class. When used together with a conjunctor, a projector lists the properties of both the base and the relatant class which are to appear as aspects of the virtual class. By using such a projector, we can screen out those properties of either class which we do not wish to see in the conjunct virtual class. If the relationship through which the relatant is tracked also has its own attributes, the projector may also bring in attributes of the relationship.

An Example of a Conjunct Virtual Class

As an example of a conjunct virtual class whose aspects are relationship attributes, consider again the `subscription` relationship of the `subscriber` object class with the `networkService` object class. This relationship may have the relationship attribute `accountBalance`. Suppose we wish to generate a report which lists for each subscriber their `accountBalance` for each `networkService` they subscribe-to. We can define an `accountsReceivable` conjunct virtual class based on subscriber, using the conjunctor `trackRelatants (class: networkService, role: subscribes-to)`. To screen out the aspects we do not wish to see in the report, we also apply a projector which lists simply `{subscriber.objectName, networkService.objectName, subscription.accountBalance}`.

The conjunct virtual class thus created has many virtual objects. For each object, the three aspects we specified in the projector are listed. By enumerating the membership of the conjunct virtual class, we can inspect our report. Figure 21-7 illustrates this class.

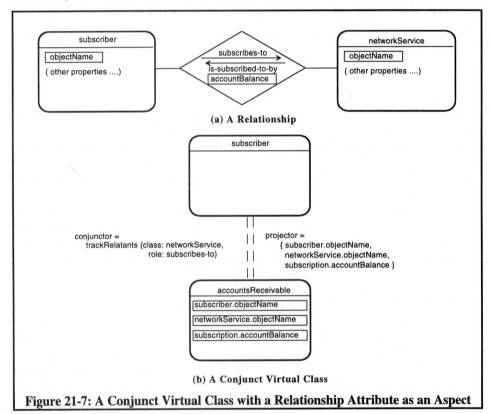

(a) A Relationship

(b) A Conjunct Virtual Class

Figure 21-7: A Conjunct Virtual Class with a Relationship Attribute as an Aspect

We can make the set of virtual objects in the conjunct virtual class as specific as we wish. For example, we may wish to inspect the account balances for only the `fax-DistributionService` subclass of `networkService`. We know that `fax-DistributionService` inherits the `is-subscribed-to-by` role which `networkService` plays with `subscriber`. Thus, we could specify a new conjunct virtual class based on `subscriber`, using the conjunctor `trackRelatants` (`class: faxDistributionService, role: subscribes-to`). Only those `subscriber` objects which have relationship instances with `faxDistribution-Service` objects will appear as members of the conjunct virtual class.

It is also possible to use selectors along with a conjunctor. If a selector is used along with a conjunctor, it may define a selection criterion which uses an attribute of the base class, an attribute of the relatant, an attribute of the relationship, or any combination. The selector is applied to the base instances, relatant instances, and relationship instances, and the conjunction is carried out only between those participant instances which meet the selector criteria. For example, in Figure 21-7, we may apply a selector which selects only those relationship instances which satisfy the predicate {`accountBalance` > `10000`}. A selector may also use variables instead of constants in its predicate: for example, a selector may specify a condition on an attribute of the base class in terms of an attribute of the relatant. If a selector, projector and conjunctor are used together, it is not necessary that the selector attributes be granted as aspects to the base class in the projector list.

It is possible to use a projector list which projects aspects from only the base class, or only the relatant class, or only the relationship. For example, if in Figure 21-7 we defined a projector which listed only the `networkService.objectName` attribute, the members of the conjunct virtual class would reflect all the `networkService` objects which at least one `subscriber subscribes-to`. The `subscriber` class is still the base class of this conjunct virtual class, even though none of its properties appear as aspects. This mechanism can be used to generate a report of all active `network-Service` objects, screening out those which no `subscriber subscribes-to`. If we wished to generate the inverse report — that is, the list of `networkServices` with no `subscribers` — we can define another conjunct virtual class based on the `networkService` object class, using as its selector basis of virtualization the predicate that the number of `subscriber` objects with which it plays the `is-subscribed-to-by` is exactly zero. This uses virtualization by relatant multiplicity restriction.

21.9. Conjunction and Multiplicity

We must also consider the effect of relatant multiplicity on the instances of the conjunct virtual class. It is possible that the relatant multiplicity of the tracking role specified in the conjunctor has a lower bound of 0. This implies that some instances of the base class may not have any relatant instances by that role. If this happens, then those instances of the base class do not appear in the conjunct virtual class. This is because a conjunct virtual class reflects the properties of a pair of relationship participants. If a base object has no relatant, it does not participate in any relationship instance and so cannot support any object in the conjunct virtual class.

It also important to consider what happens when the relatant multiplicity of the tracking role specified in the conjunctor has an upper bound which exceeds 1. In this situation, each instance of the base may participate in a relationship with more than one instance of the relatant. In this case, each instance of the base may support *multiple* virtual instances in the conjunct virtual class. Different instances of the conjunct virtual class may reflect different pairings between the *same* instance of the base class with different instances of the relatant class. Again, this is because the conjunct virtual class reflects relationship instances rather than just object instances.

For example, if there are n members of the base class which play their role with the tracked relatant with a relatant multiplicity of exactly k, with k>1, then each instance of the base class is related to exactly k instances of the relatant class. In this situation, the number of virtual objects in the conjunct virtual class will be n×k. Depending on the subject multiplicity, it is not necessary that each base instance be related to uniquely different relatant instances. In the extreme case, it is possible that there are only k relatant instances altogether, and that every member of the base class is related to all k members of the relatant class. Even then, the number of virtual instances in the conjunct virtual class is still n×k, all of which are considered different virtual objects.

Figure 21-8 illustrates the behavior of conjunct virtual classes when the upper bound of the relatant multiplicity of the tracking role in the conjunctor exceeds 1. In this figure, the base class B plays role q1 with R with a subject multiplicity of [0,j] and a relatant multiplicity [0,k]. When the specified conjunctor and projector are applied, only those objects of B which participate in relationship instances with R appear in the conjunct virtual class. If the same instance of B participates in different relationship instances with different instances of R, then all those relationship instances appear in the conjunct virtual class.

We may compute an upper bound on the number of instances in the conjunct virtual class as follows. Assume that in Figure 21-8, the base class B has n members, its relatant class R has m members, the upper bound for the subject multiplicity is j, and the upper bound for the relatant multiplicity is k. If k≤m, the number of possible R-instances all B-instances can play q1 with is n×k; otherwise, it is n×m. If j≤n, the number of possible B-instances all R-instances can play q2 with is m×j; otherwise, it is m×n. Thus, the upper bound on the number of possible objects in a conjunct virtual class is

```
max((m × min(j,n)),(n × min(k,m)))
```

This upper bound represents the possible number of relationship instances which can exist. Naturally, it is symmetric: the same upper bound applies regardless of whether the conjunct virtual class is defined on B tracking R through q1, or whether it is defined on R tracking B through q2. The actual number of virtual objects in the conjunct virtual class depends on how many of these relationships are actually instantiated. Of course, if a selector is used along with the conjunctor, it will restrict this number even further, as only

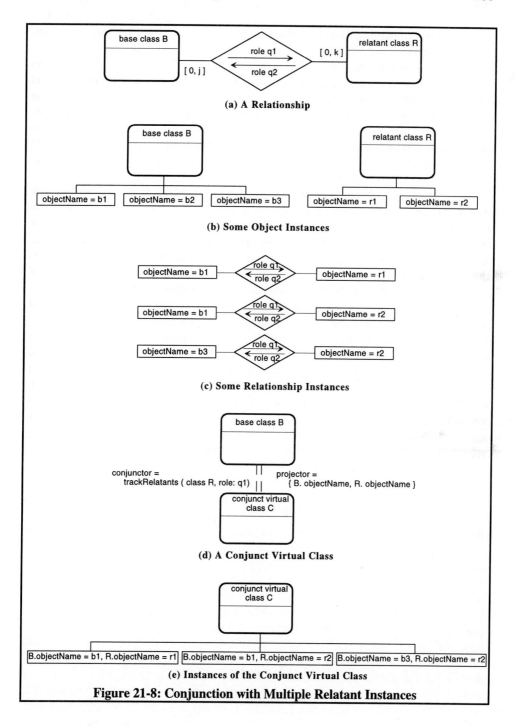

(a) A Relationship

(b) Some Object Instances

(c) Some Relationship Instances

(d) A Conjunct Virtual Class

(e) Instances of the Conjunct Virtual Class

Figure 21-8: Conjunction with Multiple Relatant Instances

those members of the base class meeting the selector criteria will be tracked. If two conjunctors are used simultaneously, this upper bound calculation can be applied recursively by considering the conjunctions as if they occurred one after the other.

This upper bound must be adjusted by a factor of 2 if the relationship is both commutative and involute. As an example, consider the `mutualBackup` relationship of Figure 18-4, in which the `signalTransferPoint` class plays the `mbacks-up` and `is-mbacked-up-by` roles commutatively with itself. Suppose we wish to generate a report which lists the backup object for each `signalTransferPoint` in the network. We can create a conjunct virtual class based on `signalTransferPoint`, using as a conjunctor the function `trackRelatants (class: signalTransferPoint, role: is-mbacked-up-by)`. When applied to the example of Figure 18-4, this conjunct virtual class has *two* virtual objects in it: the first reflecting pair {stpUnit-No1, stpUnitNo2} and the second reflecting the pair {stpUnitNo2, stpUnit-No1}. Even though there is only one relationship instance, when `trackRelatants()` iterates over every object in the class to determine its relatant, the involute and commutative nature of this relationship causes that relationship instance to be listed twice. This is not considered an error, as it correctly generates the information desired in the report.

Generally, because the conjunct virtual class reflects relationship instances rather than object instances, it does not matter which participant class of the relationship we pick as its base. The virtual instances appearing in the conjunct virtual class will be the same whether we pick the first class as the base and track the forward role to the second, or whether we pick the second class as the base and track the reciprocal role to the first. The choice of the base could depend on which participant grants more of its properties as aspects to the conjunct virtual class. If a selector is used along with the conjunctor, then the class whose attributes are used in the selector is generally chosen as the base. If the conjunct virtual class we are creating is to support yet another conjunct virtual class, then the base must be the class whose roles are to be tracked in both the first and the second conjunctions. If two conjunctors are used simultaneously to create one virtual object class, the class which originates both roles must be the base.

An Advanced Conjunction Example

We may also use conjunct virtual classes to "assemble" objects together. For example, we can assemble a number of `fullProtocolStack` virtual objects in a `networkDevice` by using relationships to create conjunctions between the *substacks* contained in the `networkDevice`. In Chapter 15, we mentioned that if a `protocolStack` object represents a middle-layer stack, it can be modeled as a component of a `networkDevice` object. If a `protocolStack` object represents an interface substack, it can be modeled as a component of a `port` object. We can let `protocolStack` **specialize-into** the subclasses `applicationSubstack`, `middleLayerSubstack`, and `interfaceSubstack`, as shown in Figure 21-9(a). Using them in an aggregation hierarchy, we can model `applicationSubstack` and `middleLayerSubstack` as components of `networkDevice`, and `interfaceSubstack` as a component of a `port` component of `networkDevice`. This is shown in Figure 21-9(b). By the transitivity of aggregation, `interfaceSubstack` is also a component of `network-Device`.

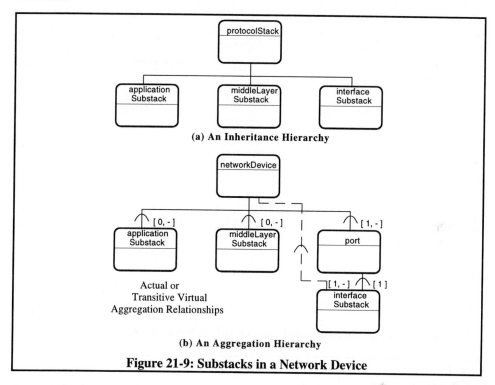

(a) An Inheritance Hierarchy

(b) An Aggregation Hierarchy

Figure 21-9: Substacks in a Network Device

One way of listing all the `fullProtocolStack` objects available in the device is to define them explicitly. These objects can be created so that they `have-as-a-part` the `protocolEntity` objects available in that device. Naturally, these stacks cannot have arbitrary `protocolEntity` components: the permitted layering rules must be followed while constructing the stacks. Furthermore, the `protocolEntity` components must be sharable, so that different `fullProtocolStack` objects can reuse the same instance of `protocolEntity` if necessary. However, the disadvantage of creating `fullProtocolStack` objects in this manner is that their generation is not automatic: every time we add a new application-layer entity, for example, we must remember to explicitly create another new `fullProtocolStack` object.

To automate the generation of new instances of `fullProtocolStack`, we can define it to be a *conjunct virtual class*. To automatically populate this class with instances, we may say that *every* `middleLayerSubstack` creates conjunctions with *every* `interfaceSubstack` and *every* `applicationSubstack` in the `network-Device`. From the permitted-layering relationships, we know that the `network-LayerProtocolEntity` which `is-a-part-of` the `middleLayerSubstack` `layers-above` the `linkLayerProtocolEntity` which `is-a-part-of` the `interfaceSubstack`. We can define a distributive virtual relationship in which the layers-above role distributes ahead of is-a-part-of. This will allow the entire middleLayerSubstack to layer-above the linkLayerProtocolEntity in the interfaceSubstack. By also defining the role layers-below to distribute ahead of is-a-part-of, the entire interfaceSubstack can layer-below the middleLayerSubstack as well. This derivation is shown in Figure 21-10.

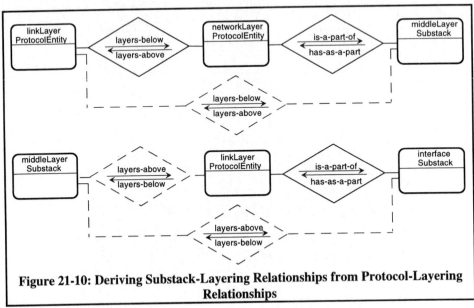

Figure 21-10: Deriving Substack-Layering Relationships from Protocol-Layering Relationships

Using a similar mechanism, we can create virtual layering relationships between middleLayerSubstack and applicationSubstack. We may now define the conjunct virtual class fullProtocolStack based on the middleLayerSubstack class, by conjuncting it simultaneously with the interfaceSubstack class via its layers-above role and with the applicationSubstack class via its layers-below role. We can thus derive fullProtocolStack objects *inferentially*, from the knowledge of the substacks contained in the networkDevice. Figure 21-11 illustrates how this can be done.

Figure 21-11 is an example of using two conjunctors simultaneously. The selectors, which use relatant attribute restriction with respect to the networkDevice relatant, apply to all three classes; they ensure that only those protocolStack objects contained in the device of interest are selected for conjunction.

This conjunction generates all possible combinations in which the protocolStack objects in the given networkDevice can be assembled using the permitted layerings. If after the selector has been applied the number of applicationSubstack objects is j, the number of middleLayerSubstack objects is k, and the number of interfaceSubstacks is n, the number of virtual fullProtocolStack objects created will be j×k×n. This value is governed only by the number of

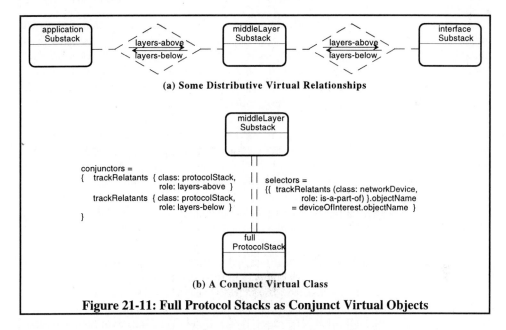

(a) Some Distributive Virtual Relationships

(b) A Conjunct Virtual Class

Figure 21-11: Full Protocol Stacks as Conjunct Virtual Objects

members of each class which satisfy the selector (that is, are all components of the same `networkDevice` object which we are interested in); the upper bounds of the relatant multiplicities are not restrictive in this case. In effect, these virtual `fullProtocol-Stack` objects reflect all the possible paths a PDU may take through the `network-Device`.

We need no longer specify `fullProtocolStack` objects as actual objects, as they can be derived as virtual objects from the knowledge of the substacks supported in the device. For complex network devices supporting many different interfaces, middle-layer entities, and applications, deriving knowledge about the full protocol stacks they support from knowledge about their components can be quite useful in the process of automated network architecture.

21.10. Virtualization, Specialization, and Relationships

The actual base class supporting a virtual class belongs to some inheritance hierarchy. However, a virtual object class has no place in the inheritance hierarchy. A virtual object class is not considered to have the any ancestors; the aspects of a virtual class behave as if they were all original properties. Nor is a virtual object class considered to have descendants, even though its supporting actual class may specialize further. Although a virtual class may **virtualize-from** a base class which is also virtual, we do not formally model virtualization hierarchies, as most often they are very shallow. Virtualization and specialization are orthogonal concepts.

If an actual class adds new members as instances of its descendants, they are automatically reflected as members of the virtual classes it supports (or candidates to be reflected as members of the selected virtual classes it supports). Nevertheless, since the virtual classes it supports cannot reflect the structural and functional refinements added by the descendants, they appear as "flat" members of the virtual class, as if they had been directly created as instances of the base class. Once a virtual object class is defined, it "loses" the memory of its ancestors and "loses" its ability to specialize further. It is illegal to attempt to define a new class which **specializes-from** a virtual object class. It is, of course, possible to specialize its supporting actual base class further and define new virtual object classes based on subsequent descendants of the actual base class.

It is technically legal, though not recommended, in specialization theory to define actual subclasses in the inheritance hierarchy which do not necessarily extend their inherited structure or functions in any way. This happens when the subclasses use their basis of specialization merely as a subsetting mechanism instead of an evolutionary mechanism. In this case, the subclass is semantically equivalent to a selected virtual class. Such subclasses are created on rare occasions as pure, unextended subsets of their superclasses simply in order to isolate those members which will be evolved further by subsequent descendant classes.

On the other hand, if a subclass does not extend its superclass in any way *and* there are no further descendants of that subclass, then that subclass might be better defined as a selected virtual class instead. This selected virtual class would use as its selector basis of virtualization the same logical predicate which would have otherwise been used as its basis of specialization. The superclass will now be a leaf-level concrete class and objects can be created as instances of this superclass itself. Because this class supports virtual object classes, objects will be able to autoclassify themselves among the virtual classes.

If the subclass had been explicitly specified and if objects had been created as instances of the subclass, the objects would be restricted to being members of only that subclass, as instances of actual classes cannot autoclassify themselves. If an attribute value changes, an object may have to be explicitly destroyed as an instance of one actual class and explicitly recreated as an instance of another. On the other hand, if we had created selected virtual classes rather than subclasses, the object would have retained its ability to autoclassify itself by "moving" itself among these selected virtual classes.

A virtual object class is considered to participate in all the relationships defined for its supporting actual class. This applies whether the relationship is actual or virtual. We are permitted to query a virtual object for its relationships, track its relatants, count its relatants, and so on. This gives us the ability to create conjunct virtual classes based on other virtual classes if necessary. For example, all the virtual object classes of Figure 21-3 participate in the same relationships as their base class.

21.11. Comparison with the Relational Model

Readers familiar with the relational model for database management [Codd90] will have no doubt noticed many similarities between the virtual classes of specialization theory and the mechanism of *views* available in that model. If we assume that there is an approximate analogy between the object classes of an object-oriented model and the *table definitions* of the relational model [Bapa91] — an assumption which is not universally accepted — then mechanisms of selection and projection match the corresponding mechanisms available in the relational model. Our mechanism of conjunction is similar to *table joins* in the relational model.

Just as the relational model often treats the *tuples* of a table as a set, so also we treat the members of an object class as a set. However, the ability to model class inheritance hierarchies in specialization theory, together with the ability to model general interclass relationships, creates many advantages (and some limitations) when compared to the relational model. For readers familiar with that model, we present below a summary of some of the key comparisons.

- *Object functions are available* as aspects of a virtual object class. In the relational model, functions are not modeled as fields of a tuple.

- *Union operations are implicit.* We do not need to define a virtual object class as the union of two other object classes because the mechanism of generalization already acts as a supersetting mechanism. The union of the members of cognate classes can be defined as a virtual object class based on their cognation ancestor, along with a projector that projects only the properties of that ancestor (i.e., leaving out the properties added by the descendant classes).

- *Intersection operations are implicit.* Each subclass is a subset of its superclass. If all specializations are disjoint, intersection operations are unnecessary. If some specializations are overlapping, the intersection operation between any two classes can be defined as a selected virtual class on their cognation ancestor, using as a selector merely the overlapping domain regions of the attributes the two classes use as their bases of specialization.

- *Difference operations are implicit.* The difference between two classes can be defined as a selected virtual class on their cognation ancestor, using as a selector the non-overlapping domain regions of the attributes the two classes use as their bases of specialization.

- *Relationships are required for joining.* A conjunct virtual class in specialization theory requires its base class to be a participant in a well-founded relationship with the conjuncted relatant; it is not possible to create a conjunction with a class which is not a relatant of the base class via either an actual or virtual relationship. The relational model does not inherently support the notion of relationships and roles. In the relational model, it is possible to join *any* two tables regardless of any "relationship" semantics between the tuples.

- *Multiple classes may be simultaneously joined.* A conjunct virtual class can be created by using more than one conjunctor simultaneously. This is analogous to the relational model, which permits joining more than one table simultaneously.

- *Theta-joins are not permitted.* A conjunct virtual instance can only be created by correctly relating two participating object instances playing a well-defined role. In the relational model, this would be a join using the primary key of one table with a foreign key of another table. This would be a natural join in which the join keys are compared for equality. The mechanism of a general theta-join — in which the join keys may be compared for inequalities — is permitted in the relational model but not in specialization theory.

- *Inner equi-joins are permitted.* In specialization theory, every base object having a relatant will support a virtual instance in a conjunct virtual class. If it has multiple relatants, it will support multiple virtual instances, just as in the relational model.

- *Outer joins are not permitted.* In specialization theory, any base object which does not have a relatant will not support a virtual instance in a conjunct virtual class. The relational model permits such joins by padding in the fields of the "missing" relatant with null values.

- *Cartesian products are not permitted.* In specialization theory, only object instances participating in a defined relationship can support conjunct virtual objects. It is not possible to create a conjunct virtual class in which every object in the base class appears to play its role with every object in the relatant class, if those relationships have not been actually instantiated. The relational model permits such table joins as Cartesian products.

- *Division operations are not permitted.* We do not need to go "backward" from a conjunct virtual object class to a real object class such that, given a conjunct virtual class and the set of objects in its supporting base class, we must deduce the members of the relatant class. A conjunct virtual class is always defined "forward" from the base class and its relatant.

21.12. Summary

A virtual object class is an object class whose membership is completely defined by the membership of its supporting base class. A virtual object class adds no structural or functional refinements to its supporting base class; it merely provides a new perspective from which to view objects of the base class. The instances of a virtual object class are called virtual objects, which are always supported by actual objects. The properties of the supporting base class which are visible in the virtual object class are called aspects. A virtual object class is said to acquire its aspects from its supporting base class, which is said to grant them to the virtual class.

   A virtual object class is specified using a basis of virtualization. The basis of virtualization may be a selector, projector, or conjunctor. A virtual object class created using a selector is called a selected virtual class. A selected virtual class uses the selector as a logical predicate to define a subset of the members of the base class. The bases of virtualization for creating a selected virtual class are analogous to many bases of specialization for creating a subclass. Selected virtual classes provide a mechanism for virtual objects to autoclassify themselves by moving from one virtual class to another as values of their attributes change.

A virtual object class using a projector is called a projected virtual class. It provides the ability to focus only on selected aspects of the base class. It may be used as a security mechanism to expose only limited information about objects of the base class.

A virtual object class created using a conjunctor is called a conjunct virtual class. Conjunct virtual classes acquire their aspects not just from the base class but also from its relatants. If a base object has many relatants, it will support multiple virtual objects in the conjunct virtual class. It is possible to use selectors, projectors, and conjunctors together.

A virtual object class is not considered to have any descendants, as it cannot project as aspects any new properties which may be added by descendants of its supporting actual base class. However, if a new instance of a descendant of an actual class is created, it may appear as a virtual instance of the virtual classes that actual class supports. A virtual object class is considered to participate in all the relationships defined for its supporting base class.

22. Object Class Constraints

"The most reliable network device, quite obviously beyond
any need of checking, will be the one that has failed."
— *anonymous network manager.*

22.1. Introduction

In order to completely specify network objects, we must be able to describe the constraints that operate on them. Constraints operate both within an object and across objects. Part of the challenge of specifying constraints across multiple objects is to determine the object in which they can be best specified. In this chapter, we explore the issue of modeling object constraints and present new mechanisms which permit us to incorporate them within our model correctly and concisely.

22.2. Conceptual Background

In the preceding chapters, we have introduced many concepts which place limits on what objects can do. Although in specialization theory we do not call them constraints, we already have the ability to specify many structural and behavioral limitations in our model. For example, concepts such as

- *"Attribute A must have values within the indicated bounds"*
- *"Attribute A must have values from the indicated set"*

are already available in specialization theory because attribute domains are built into the definitions of attributes. Further, concepts such as

- *"Object B must relate to at least so many of object C"*
- *"Object B can relate to at most so many of object C"*

are also available because they are built into the definitions of relationship multiplicities. In addition, dependencies such as

- *"Attribute D of object B is determined by attributes E and F"*

- *"Attribute G of object B is determined by attribute H of object C"*

are automatically available from our definitions of native and tracked virtual attributes.

In this chapter, we present a more general form of limitations on the structure and behavior of objects. The modeling concepts we will introduce will permit us to describe the limitations on the structure and behavior of *combinations* of objects, including entire systems.

In specialization theory, a *constraint* is a mechanism which places limits on an object's structure and behavior. A constraint compels an object to confine itself within the bounds it specifies. If an object confines its behavior within the indicated bounds, it is said to *satisfy* the constraint; otherwise, it is said to *violate* it.

A constraint in and of itself is not an object; it does not have any ancestral or descendant classes or belong to any inheritance hierarchy. Rather, a constraint is a *property* of an object class, just as an attribute or a function also **is-a-property-of** an object class. Since a subclass inherits all properties of its superclass, it inherits its constraints as well: once a constraint has been defined in an object class, it is bequeathed to all descendant classes of that object class. Like other properties, a constraint may also be collected with other properties in a capsule.

A constraint is said to *govern* the properties of the objects it affects. A native constraint governs the properties of a single object, while a spanning constraint simultaneously governs the properties of multiple objects. More generally, a constraint is also sometimes said to govern the *objects* whose properties it affects. When a constraint is specified, it is often said to be *imposed* on the objects it governs.

Constraints can be specified both within an object and across objects. If the constraint operates within a single object, it is called an *native constraint*. If the constraint operates across multiple objects, it is called a *spanning* constraint [Wu90, Mazu89]. The *arity* of a constraint indicates the number of objects it affects. A native constraint is always unary; spanning constraints may be binary, ternary, or generally, *n*-ary with some defined value for *n*.

Hard and Soft Constraints

We segregate constraints into two broad categories: *hard* constraints and *soft* constraints. (Categorizations with finer granularity have been proposed [Kers89] but two are sufficient for our purposes of network modeling.) A hard constraint represents an *absolute truth*; it is imposed in order to reflect in our model some immutable physical reality. A hard constraint can never be violated because doing so would invalidate some fundamental law or axiom of nature. Any attempt to violate a hard constraint is immediately rejected by the run-time environment. A hard constraint is sometimes called a *physical constraint* or an *invariant* [Meye88]. When implemented in an object-oriented programming environment, it must be checked for satisfaction before and after an object is modified; therefore, it is sometimes called a *contract* [Meye92, Helm90].

By contrast, a soft constraint represents a *policy* rather than an absolute truth. A soft constraint is imposed in order to operate the communication network in some state which is preferable but not necessarily immutable. We may apply a soft constraint because it represents a desirable condition which we learn from experience, rather than from some natural law. A soft constraint can be violated without invalidating any fundamental law or axiom. From time to time we may operate the network in a state in which a soft constraint has been temporarily relaxed. Occasionally a soft constraint may be permanently violated. A soft constraint is also sometimes called a *policy constraint*, a *heuristic*, or a *business rule* [Kers89].

The formal specification of both hard and soft constraints is performed in exactly the same manner; the constructs which specify them are syntactically identical. However, each constraint carries a flag whose value indicates whether it is hard or soft, thus permitting the run-time environment to determine whether it can be temporarily violated. By default, all constraints are considered hard. All the limitations we can already accommodate in specialization theory — such as attribute domains and relationship multiplicity bounds — are considered the equivalent of hard constraints.

Specifying a Constraint

The properties of an object governed by a constraint may be attributes or functions. These attributes and functions could be actual or virtual, native or tracked. A constraint places a *comparator* — which is some binary mathematical comparison operator — between these properties. The properties appearing on either side of the comparator are called the *operands* or the *comparands* of the constraint. Occasionally, we will speak of the *left comparand* and the *right comparand* of the constraint when such a distinction is significant.

In its most elementary form, a constraint simply places a comparator between two properties, or between one property and a constant. More generally, a constraint may involve mathematical expressions in which multiple properties appear on either side of the comparator. The properties appearing in these expressions can be attributes or functions, actual or virtual, native or tracked.

Because a constraint involves a comparison between expressions of properties, its formal specification requires a comparator between two *attribute-defined expressions*. These are the same expressions involving attributes or functions which we have used throughout our application of specialization theory. As we know from Chapter 20, attribute-defined expressions can combine properties from different object classes. From the context of a given object class, a single attribute label in an attribute-defined expression refers to a native attribute, whereas an attribute label preceded by a role or relationship label refers to a tracked attribute referenced from the indicated relatants. Therefore, using the sequence

```
{AttributeDefinedExpression
 Comparator
 AttributeDefinedExpression}
```

we can express all constraints generally, whether native or spanning. As we shall see later, it is possible to express a spanning constraint as if it were a native constraint involving tracked virtual properties.

The *type* of the constraint depends on the comparator used between the two attribute-defined expressions. The following comparators are permitted between the comparands of a constraint:

- *Equal to*
- *Not equal to*
- *Lesser than or Equal to*
- *Greater than or Equal to*
- *Less than*
- *Greater than*

A constraint with the `equal-to` comparator is called an *equality constraint*; all the rest are called *inequality constraints*, with the last two being *strict inequality constraints*. These comparators can be applied to comparands which are single-valued expressions involving attributes or functions, as well as to single-valued reductions of set-valued attributes and functions using set-reduction operators such as `Sum`, `Product`, `Min`, `Max`, and `Count`. When both comparands are set-valued, the following comparators may be used:

- *Set equal*
- *Set not equal*
- *Set intersection non-null*

Because a constraint is a comparator between two attribute-defined expressions, the entire constraint expression is in essence a *logical predicate*. For hard constraints, this logical predicate is permanently asserted: it must always evaluate to `true`. For soft constraints, it is possible that this logical predicate sometimes evaluates to `false`. The protocols which an object uses to communicate with the external world are equipped with the ability to flag any operation which causes constraint violations. Operations (such as changes in attribute values) which could cause violations of hard constraints are always rejected as they are impossible to perform. Operations which could cause violations of soft constraints are rejected by default but can be overridden. This overriding can be done on a case-by-case basis, or by "squelching" the soft constraint on an instance-by-instance basis, or by permanently "squelching" it system-wide.

When to Use Constraints

In Chapter 20 we said that an equality constraint between attribute values — whether between single-valued or set-valued comparands — can be turned into an expression for computing a virtual attribute. If all the properties governed by a constraint belong to the same object class, this is a native virtual attribute; if not, this is a tracked virtual attribute. This reduces one degree of modeling freedom.

We now clarify that an equality constraint can be respecified as a virtual attribute only if it applies to *all* members of the classes possessing the governed attributes. If so, we redefine any one of the governed actual attributes to be a virtual attribute such that it can be computed from other governed attributes. However, if the equality constraint applies only to *some* members of the classes possessing the governed attributes, it cannot be turned into a definition for a virtual attribute. Since the constraint does not apply to all members, the virtual attribute cannot be inferentially computed from other attributes in those objects in which the constraint does not hold, and therefore that attribute cannot be virtual. In these situations, we continue to model all the governed actual attributes as actual but leave the constraint in as a constraint. We specify the conditions which objects of that class must meet so that the constraint applies within them (for example, they could all belong the same subclass of the object class).

We often encounter inequality constraints during the modeling of communication networks. Inequality constraints do not reduce a degree of modeling freedom because they cannot be turned into a computational expression for one of the governed attributes. Therefore, inequality constraints are always modeled as constraints.

As a general rule, if the constraint involves placing a comparator between just one property and a constant, and if the constraint is a hard constraint, then it should not be modeled as a constraint at all. Rather, it should be recast as a specification for the domain of that property. For example, a hard constraint which limits the value of an attribute to less than some known constant should be absorbed into the attribute's type syntax, rather than modeled as a constraint governing the object in which the attribute appears.

22.3. Modeling Constraints

Native constraints are relatively straightforward to model, as they require simply the statement of a logical predicate which compares two attribute-defined expressions. The formal statement of this constraint is performed along with the specification of the object it governs. In Chapter 24, we will enhance our formal specification syntax for object classes such that it accommodates constructs for constraints.

Anchoring a Spanning Constraint

While a spanning constraint operates over two objects, it cannot operate over any random object pair. *The objects governed by a spanning constraint must participate in well-founded relationships.* In other words, a spanning constraint can only govern objects which are relatants of each other, either by actual or virtual relationships. If two objects are not relatants of each other, it is not possible in specialization theory to define a constraint governing both of them.

If a spanning constraint is *n*-ary with *n*>2, then all *n* objects it governs must be participants in well-founded relationships with *at least one common relatant*. It is not necessary that all governed objects must play the same role with the common relatant. The objects could all play different roles with the common relatant (and possibly with each other), but it is necessary that there be a sequence of well-founded role links that can be tracked from each governed object to every other governed object through the common relatant. If the constraint originates in an optional capsule, then any object possessing that capsule must have as relatants all the objects required by the spanning constraint.

While a common relatant is necessary in a spanning constraint, it is not necessary that the constraint involve some property of the common relatant. It is possible that the spanning constraint only involves properties of objects which have no relationship with each other; however, these objects are all required to have at least one relatant in common. Usually, the constraint is formally specified as a property of that common relatant. If the constraint is binary, then the constraint is specified as a property of either class participating in the relationship but not both.

The common relatant possessing the constraint as a property is said to *anchor* the constraint. All objects governed by the constraint must therefore be relatants of the *anchoring object*, even though they need not be relatants of each other. Figure 22-1 depicts this situation.

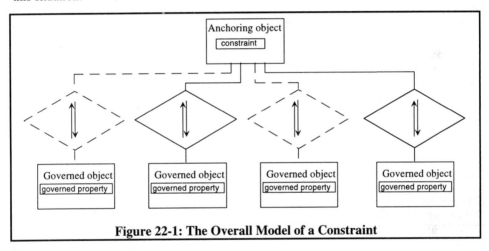

Figure 22-1: The Overall Model of a Constraint

Constraint Associations

The associations of constraint modeling are **governs** and **is-governed-by**: a constraint **governs** the properties involved in it, and each such property **is-governed-by** the constraint. These associations may involve properties of multiple objects if the constraint is a spanning constraint. Of course, since a constraint is a property of its anchoring class, it has the associations **is-a-property-of** and **has-as-a-property** with its anchoring class. Figure 22-2 shows the associations of a constraint model.

Hard Constraints

Consider a `multiplexer` object class. This class has an aggregation relationship with the `port` object class, since each `multiplexer` object has many `ports`. Some of the `ports` which a `multiplexer` contains are `channelPorts`, representing the low-speed feeders which supply signal streams to the `multiplexer`. It also contains a

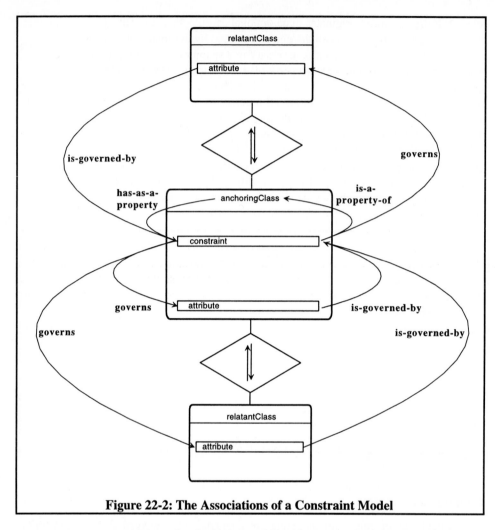

Figure 22-2: The Associations of a Constraint Model

compositePort which carries the high-speed signal stream containing the multiplexed feeder signals. The speed of the compositePort must exceed the sum of the speeds of all the individual channelPorts, otherwise portions of the channel signals will be lost. More generally, a multiplexer may sometimes contain more than one composite-Port (for example, it could be a *dual-composite* or a *dual-aggregate* device). In this case, the sum of the speeds of all the compositePorts must exceed the sum of the speeds of all the channelPorts. Figure 22-3 illustrates such a device.

So far, none of the modeling constructs we have developed are powerful enough to express this requirement. We can model a speed attribute for port objects, we can model port components of multiplexer objects, and we can even model the multiplicities with which different subclasses of port (that is, channelPort and compositePort) are components of multiplexer. Nevertheless, although the se-

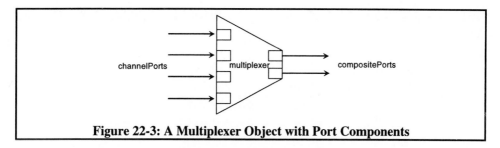

Figure 22-3: A Multiplexer Object with Port Components

mantics behind the speed constraint between the various `port` components can be easily understood and expressed as a logical predicate on various attributes, we have not yet developed any constructs which can formally capture this requirement.

In specialization theory, this requirement can be stated as a *constraint* anchored at the `multiplexer` object class. The `multiplexer` object class anchors the constraint even though none of its own attributes are governed by the constraint. We can still define it as a constraint on `multiplexer` because all the attributes which the constraint governs belong to *relatants* of `multiplexer`; in particular, they are the `speed` attributes of its `port` components. Since `multiplexer` is the common relatant of all governed objects, it is the best class to anchor the constraint.

Using the same informal notation we used in Chapter 20, we may express this constraint as

```
Sum {{multiplexer.<trackRelatants (class:compositePort,
                        role:has-as-a-part)>}.speed}
≥
Sum {{multiplexer.<trackRelatants (class:channelPort,
                        role:has-as-a-part)>}.speed}
```

The notation of this constraint is similar to that of tracked virtual attributes, with the difference that no tracked virtual attributes are actually defined in this expression. The constraint computes its comparands by tracking them into the relatants of `multiplexer` *as if* they were explicitly defined virtual attributes of `multiplexer`, and then applies the indicated comparator between them. We may consider the comparands to be *implicitly defined virtual attributes* of the `multiplexer` class — say `totalChannelBandwidth` and `totalCompositeBandwidth`. This means that `multiplexer` objects cannot be explicitly queried for their values, since they are not explicitly defined. Nevertheless, each time the constraint is applied, they "come into existence" for a limited duration while the constraint is being evaluated.

Since a constraint is a property of an object class, each constraint is given a *name*, which acts as an identifier label with which it is referenced in our model. The formal definition of a constraint assigns this name to the logical predicate which defines the constraint. The constraint can be evaluated as `true` or `false` simply by evaluating this named logical predicate. If we name the constraint above `bandwidthConstraint`, its definition would become

```
multiplexer.bandwidthConstraint ←
    Sum {{multiplexer.<trackRelatants
               (class:compositePort,
                role:has-as-a-part)>}.speed}
    ≥
    Sum {{multiplexer.<trackRelatants
               (class:channelPort,
                role:has-as-a-part)>}.speed}
```

Because this constraint governs attributes from multiple relatants of `multiplexer`, it is a *spanning* constraint anchored at `multiplexer`. By the simple mechanism of specifying the governed relatant attributes in this constraint as explicitly defined virtual attributes `totalChannelBandwidth` and `totalCompositeBandwidth` as properties of `multiplexer`, we can express the spanning constraint as if it were a *native* constraint. Although the constraint remains a spanning constraint because it governs tracked virtual attributes, expressing it in this form makes it simpler for human readability and comprehension. For example, if we define the following virtual attributes of `multiplexer`:

```
multiplexer.<totalCompositeBandwidth> ←
    Sum {{trackRelatants (class:compositePort,
                          role:has-as-a-part)}.speed}
```

```
multiplexer.<totalChannelBandwidth> ←
    Sum {{trackRelatants (class:channelPort,
                          role:has-as-a-part)}.speed}
```

then, we can express the constraint simply as though it were a native constraint:

```
multiplexer.bandwidthConstraint ←
    multiplexer.<totalCompositeBandwidth>
    ≥
    multiplexer.<totalChannelBandwidth>
```

Figure 22-4 illustrates this situation.

Another example of a constraint is the assignment of an "options profile" value to an object which is required to reflect certain options implemented in its relatants. For ex-

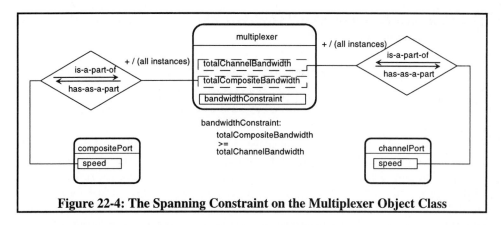

Figure 22-4: The Spanning Constraint on the Multiplexer Object Class

ample, the `functionalProfile` attribute of the `protocolStack` object, when assigned a particular value, requires that certain optional features be present in its component `protocolEntity` objects. Thus, the `implementedOptions` attributes of the component `protocolEntity` objects (reflecting the presence of optional capsules) are constrained by the value of `functionalProfile` in the aggregate `protocolStack` object. This is easily specified as a constraint: the Boolean expression equating `functionalProfile` to a certain value (evaluating to `true` or `false`) must match the Boolean expression requiring a `CapsuleLabel` to be `aMemberOf` the set-valued attribute `implementedOptions` of an appropriate component `protocolEntity`; such a Boolean expression can be compounded if necessary for multiple component `protocolEntity` objects.

Soft Constraints

As an example of a *soft* constraint, consider the example of a router-based internetwork in which multiple routers route packets to each other over some wide-area backbone. This internetwork has a multi-tier topology for the purposes of routing, such that each area has a *designated router* through which nodes within the area communicate with other areas in the internetwork. Other routers called *level-1 routers* route traffic within each area. The designated router may be determined by election among the routers, or may be explicitly assigned. Suppose that some areas in the internetwork are equipped with high-end router devices which, because of their superior packet processing performance, the local administrators wish to manually assign to be the designated router for that area. To assist in deciding when a router device should be manually assigned to be a designated router and when to permit routers to pick one by election, the administrators might have the heuristic that the packet processing capacity of the assigned designated router must be significantly higher than that of other `level-1-routers`. Thus, we might have the spanning constraint

```
assignedDR.speedHeuristic ←
  assignedDR.ppsRate
  ≥
  1.5 × Max {{assignedDR.<trackRelatants
                  (class:level-1-router,
                   role:interconnects-to)>}.ppsRate}
```

This speed heuristic suggests that the ppsRate (that it, the packet-per-second rate, a measure of packet processing capacity) of any assigned designated router be at least 1.5 times greater than that of other level-1-routers it interconnects-to. (Strictly, we need a more complex constraint to ensure that all the tracked level-1-router relatants are also part of the same area as the assignedDR object. This can be done using a variety of mechanisms: by defining an <area> virtual attribute for the router class which tracks its is-a-part-of role to the area class and equating it for all routers in a constraint, or by defining a subclass area-level-1-routers by relatant specialization, and so on. This is omitted here so that we can focus on the relevant constraints.)

Naturally, this speed heuristic is soft and can be violated occasionally if necessary. While some soft constraints may seem obvious, formalizing them is of great assistance during the process of automated network synthesis in software.

Participation Constraints

Constraints can also be specified as *participation* or *counting constraints* in which some minimum or maximum numbers of objects are required to participate in a particular relationship. Normally, if an object class A requires either a minimum or maximum number of instances of a relatant class B in a relationship, we can specify this in the appropriate relatant multiplicity. Suppose object class A is related to two object classes B and C. Both B and C play their roles with A with a subject multiplicity of [0,-], that is, any instance of A requires 0 or more instances of B and 0 or more instances of C.

Suppose now that each A requires at least 1 of *either* B *or* C. This would not normally be a problem for us if B and C are both subclasses of the same common superclass, say D. If the specialization of D into B and C is both disjoint and complete, then we can assert the relationship to hold between D and A with a subject multiplicity of [1,-] for D, and let B and C inherit from D the relationship with A while at the same time regressing the lower bound to 0. This means that each instance of A requires 0 or more instances of B and of C, but requires at least 1 member of D. As explained in Chapter 17, the ancestor multiplicity continues to hold as a constraint; since each D is either a B or a C, it implies that each A requires either a B or a C, and our specification is sufficient to be enforced by the compiler.

However, we have a problem if B and C are *not* sibling or cognate. If B and C are not cognate, we cannot specify a minimum subject multiplicity on a cognation ancestor since there *is* no cognation ancestor. We must therefore specify this as an explicit *participation constraint*.

As an example, we revisit the model for a `protocolStack` object class we specified in Chapter 15. We indicated that a `protocolStack` object could contain as components both `protocolEntity` objects and `protocolStack` objects as substacks. The component multiplicity of both `protocolEntity` and `protocolStack` in the aggregate `protocolStack` was specified to be `[0,-]`; it was not necessary for the aggregate `protocolStack` to contain at least one of each, since it could always contain either. However, this specification is not sufficient, as in the extreme case it permits the aggregate `protocolStack` to contain *neither*. We must require that the aggregate `protocolStack` contain at least *either* a component `protocolEntity` *or* a component `protocolStack`. Since `protocolStack` and `protocolEntity` are not cognate, we cannot define a minimum component multiplicity for their cognation ancestor. Hence, we define the *minimum participation constraint*:

```
protocolStack.minimumComponents ←
    protocolStack.<countRelatants(class:protocolEntity,
                                  role:has-as-a-part)>
    +
    protocolStack.<countRelatants(class:protocolStack,
                                  role:has-as-a-part)>
    ≥ 1
```

Alternatively, if we specify a virtual `<numberOfProtocolEntities>` attribute for the `protocolStack` object class as the sum of the number of `protocolEntity` components and of the recursive `<numberOfProtocolEntities>` attributes of its `protocolStack` components, we can define the `minimumComponents` constraint to simply govern this virtual attribute, thereby expressing the spanning constraint as a native constraint:

```
protocolStack.<numberOfProtocolEntities> ←
    countRelatants(class:protocolEntity,
      role:has-as-a-part)
    +
    Sum{{trackRelatants(class:protocolStack,
      role:has-as-a-part)}.<numberOfProtocolEntities>}

protocolStack.minimumComponents ←
    protocolStack.<numberOfProtocolEntities> ≥ 1
```

22.4. Constraint Addition

We know that a descendant class can add new attributes, new functions, and new relatants to those that it inherits from its ancestors. Since a constraint is also a property, a descendant class is permitted to add a *new constraint* when it specializes from its superclass. This is consistent with our precept that the functionality of a class becomes more detailed as we proceed down the inheritance hierarchy. This phenomenon is known as *Specialization by Constraint Addition*. For example, when the `multiplexer` class of Figure 22-4 specializes from its superclass — say `networkDevice` — it could add the `bandwidthConstraint` as a new property, since this constraint is not specified for its superclass.

Usually, constraints governing properties of an object class are applicable in all members of that object class. Therefore, when proceeding down the inheritance hierarchy, these constraints can be added as new constraints at the same time that the governed properties are added as new properties. This means that the constraint is effective in all members of that object class, even if the object class **specializes-into** multiple descendant classes. Constraints, like other properties, are bequeathed down the inheritance hierarchy.

On some occasions, however, constraints are not added at the same time as their governed properties are added but are added *later*. This means that a superclass may possess these properties as unconstrained properties, but when that superclass specializes, the properties *become* constrained in the subclass. In other words, a subclass need not necessarily constrain only new properties which it adds as original properties; it could also constrain inherited properties which already exist unconstrained in its superclass. We view this as a *property addition* mechanism in which a constraint is added to refine and specialize superclass behavior for narrower focus, rather than as a phenomenon which "cancels" or "drops" superclass properties [Wink92, Abra91]. Conceptually, imposing a logical predicate which only governs a subset of superclass members as a *subclass constraint* is no different from imposing a logical predicate which only applies to a subset of superclass members as a *basis of specialization* for subclass creation.

An Example of Constraint Addition

Consider the example of a `lanBridge` object class, which is the class of all network devices which bridge local area networks. This class has `port` objects as components. Each `port` object contained in the `lanBridge` object class has a `portType` attribute, indicating the type of the `port`. (This could possibly be a virtual attribute defined by the nature of its component `interfaceSubstack` object.)

We might create the subclass `twoPortBridge` of `lanBridge`, as the distinction between `twoPortBridge` and `multiPortBridge` is sometimes useful during the process of automated network synthesis. The `twoPortBridge` class is created using attribute domain restriction, based on restricting its (virtual) `numberOfPorts` attribute to 2. We also create two new tracked virtual attributes for `twoPortBridge`, say `port1Type` and `port2Type`, being tracked from the `portType` attributes of its two `port` components.

Suppose that we further specialize `twoPortBridge` into the subclasses `homogeneousBridge` and `heterogeneousBridge`. We might wish to do this because we find that it helps to hold down costs during automated network synthesis: we might wish to instruct the network synthesis program, when faced with a choice between interconnections, to give preference to the cheaper homogeneousBridge objects to connect similar LANs rather than the more expensive heterogeneousBridge objects to connect dissimilar LANs. The homogeneousBridge object class is specified such that both the port components it contains must have the same portType.

The attributes port1Type and port2Type already exist in the twoPort-Bridge superclass. The general twoPortBridge superclass does *not* require that these two attributes have the same value. However, the homogeneousBridge subclass *does* require them to be constrained to the same value, while the heterogeneous-Bridge requires them to be constrained to necessarily unequal values. This is possible because specialization theory permits constraints to govern virtual attributes as well.

In this situation, the homogeneousBridge subclass uses a specialization mode similar to attribute domain restriction but in a slightly different way: instead of restricting the attribute to a subdomain of its original domain, it restricts it to the value of *another attribute*. In effect, it requires one attribute-defined expression to be equal to another. We know such a construct better as a *constraint*; the subclass effectively adds a new constraint which did not exist in the superclass.

In adding this constraint, the homogeneousBridge subclass does not particularly care what the exact values of these two attributes are, as long as they are equal to each other. It subjects *existing, inherited* properties to a *new* constraint, rather than adding new properties which are constrained at the time of addition. Because the presence of this constraint is the distinguishing characteristic of the homogeneousBridge subclass, such constraint addition may be used as a basis of specialization. This mode of specialization is termed *Specialization by Constraint Imposition*. Figure 22-5 illustrates this situation.

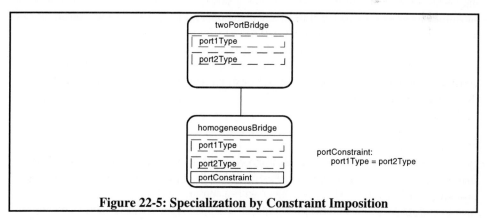

Figure 22-5: Specialization by Constraint Imposition

If the port1Type and port2Type attributes had been constrained to the same value in *every* member of twoPortBridge, then that constraint could have been defined at the level of the twoPortBridge class itself. (In fact, one of the virtual attributes could have been defined in terms of the other.) However, since not every member of `twoPortBridge` is subjected to this constraint, these attributes must be unconstrained in the superclass. It is not possible in the `homogeneousBridge` subclass to *redefine* the `port2Type` virtual attribute to equal the `port1Type` virtual attribute, for this would mean that the subclass overrides the virtual attribute definition specified in the superclass, thereby altering the definition of an inherited property. This is not permitted in specialization theory.

Even if the `port1Type` and `port2Type` attributes had both been *actual* in the superclass, it would not have been possible to make one of them virtual and defined in terms of the other in the subclass. In general, once an attribute has been defined to be actual in its originating class, no descendant class can make it virtual; once an attribute has been defined to be virtual in its originating class, no descendant class can change the virtualizing definition.

Specialization by Constraint Addition

We thus get the specialization principle of *constraint addition* or *constraint imposition*:

> **Specialization Principle:**   *A descendant class may add a constraint as a new property (Constraint Addition or Constraint Imposition).*

Constraint imposition is similar to constraint addition; in fact, our compiler treats them both the same way. Nevertheless, we use the two terms in slightly different ways: we typically use the term "constraint addition" in conjunction with attribute addition when *newly added* properties are constrained and "constraint imposition" when *inherited* properties, unconstrained in the ancestral classes, are constrained in the descendants.

A subclass specializing by constraint imposition is consistent with our precept that the scope of applicability gets narrower going down the hierarchy. It continues to be a substitutable subtype of its superclass, since any object that satisfies some constraint can always be used in situations where it is not necessarily required to satisfy that constraint.

In general, care must be exercised when adding new constraints to ensure that they do not conflict with existing constraints. If our compiler detects a conflict between a new constraint and inherited constraints, or between two new constraints, then the specialization is rejected.

22.5. Constraint Restriction

Besides adding new constraints, a subclass is permitted to specialize by *tightening inherited constraints*. This is permitted because any object with a tighter constraint can always be used in any situation where an object with a looser constraint will do. The subclass thus continues to be substitutable subtype of its superclass. A tighter constraint further narrows the scope of applicability of the subclass, thus increasing its specialization. This mode of specialization is known as *Specialization by Constraint Restriction*.

Constraint Restriction is similar to attribute domain restriction, in that it works essentially by tightening the domains of existing constraints. This domain tightening could either restrict the governed attributes to a subdomain of their original domain, or it could restrict them to a specific value. For example, if a superclass imposes a constraint on attributes x and y such that 2 < x+y < 10, then a subclass can tighten this constraint such that 2 < x+y < 5. Another sibling subclass can tighten it such that x+y = 5, while a third sibling subclass may tighten it to 5 < x+y < 10. In fact, if we were to define the virtual attribute z to be equal to x+y, different subclasses could specialize by using ordinary domain restriction on the virtual attribute z. We could even check this specialization for disjointness and completeness. In all cases, the instances of the subclasses with the tighter constraint will always satisfy the looser constraint in the superclass [Meye92], and thus continue to be members of the superclass.

An Example of Constraint Restriction

As an example, we revisit the `multiplexer` object class which constrains the total bandwidth available on the composite side to be greater than or equal to the total feeder bandwidth on the channel side. We now model a new subclass of `multiplexer`, called `bandwidthOnDemandMultiplexer`. On the composite side, this device does not connect to dedicated lines with fixed bandwidth. Instead, it *dials up* an appropriate amount of bandwidth on the composite side as and when demand increases on the channel side and disconnects some of these dialed connections when demand decreases on the channel side. Assume for the purposes of this example that the feeder channels all carry isochronous traffic; for example, they could originate from PBX devices or videoconferencing systems. The bandwidth demanded by the channels is always presented in increments of 64 kbps. The users of the `bandwidthOnDemandMultiplexer` object subscribe to some $n\times64$ network service; this permits the `bandwidthOnDemand-Multiplexer` to add appropriate amounts of bandwidth in increments of 64 kbps on the composite side as and when required.

Since the `bandwidthOnDemandMultiplexer` adjusts the composite bandwidth up or down in response to the changes in the channel bandwidth, it satisfies a *tighter* constraint than its `multiplexer` superclass. At all times, the total composite bandwidth for this device is *equal* to the total channel bandwidth, rather than being greater-or-equal. In other words, the `bandwidthOnDemandMultiplexer` has specialized by *restricting* to strict equality the constraint it inherited with a greater-or-equal inequality.

```
bandwidthOnDemandMultiplexer.bandwidthConstraint  ←
     multiplexer.<totalCompositeBandwidth>
     =
     multiplexer.<totalChannelBandwidth>
```

Figure 22-6 illustrates this example.
We may generalize this to the specialization principle of *constraint restriction*:

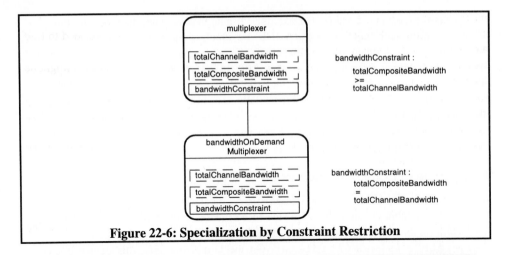

Figure 22-6: Specialization by Constraint Restriction

Specialization Principle:	*A descendant class may restrict a constraint inherited from an ancestral class (Constraint Restriction).*

The compiler ensures that the new restrictions on the constraint do not create any conflict with other constraints. If they do, it rejects the specialization.

Constraint Hardening

In addition to constraint restriction, subclasses are also permitted to specialize using the mode of *Constraint Hardening*. In this mode, a subclass is permitted to turn a *soft* constraint inherited from a superclass into a *hard* constraint in the subclass. Since the constraining predicate remains unchanged, this implies that all instances of the subclass must respect the constraint as mandatory, whereas all that the superclass requires is that its members respect it as advisory. In effect, instances of the subclass remain substitutable in any situation which requires an instance of the superclass, as they apply the constraint on a stricter basis. Once the constraint is hardened in a subclass, it remains hard for all descendants of that subclass.

Some modeling methodologies use a finer granularity for constraint "hardness": instead of just two levels, multiple degrees of hardness can be assigned to constraints. Specialization by Constraint Hardening can still apply in this situation: it implies that a subclass raises the degree of hardness of an inherited constraint to a higher (i.e., stricter) level. We omit a formal statement of the principle of Specialization by Constraint Hardening as it is rarely encountered, but this does belong in our modeling arsenal as a tool which can be used when required.

22.6. System-Spanning Constraints

System-spanning constraints are constraints which are effective across the entire network, or large portions of the network [Ozsu91, Gupt93]. Generally, they simultaneously affect many objects throughout the network, even through those objects may not be related to each other. To find an anchoring object for a system-spanning constraint, we need to find a common relatant which all governed objects collectively relate to. This is easily done: we could choose the highest possible aggregate class in the whole network. This might be the class `network`, which is related to every other object in the network: because of the transitivity of the `has-as-a-part` role, every object is a component of `network` by either an actual or a virtual decomposition relationship. If the constraint does not govern the entire `network`, then we must find an aggregate object lower in the aggregation hierarchy than `network`, but still sufficiently high up so that every object governed by the spanning constraint is its component. After we find this lowest common aggregate, we can then anchor the constraint at this object.

For example, constraints governing attributes such as `cost` are often system-spanning constraints. During network synthesis, we might be required to constrain the total `cost` of an entire network within certain limits. To accomplish this, we can define the virtual attribute `<cost>` of the `network` object class as the recursive sum of the `cost` attributes of all its relatants by the `has-as-a-part` role. Thus, this attribute will represent the total of the `cost` attribute of every object in the transitive closure of that role.

By applying a constraint on the `cost` attribute of `network` at the very start of the automated network synthesis process, we ensure that it will always be enforced and satisfied throughout the process of assembling the network out of its components. This enforcement will be performed automatically and internally within the model information base at all times, without our having to explicitly run any external function to compute the cost of each proposed configuration. Thus, our model permits us to enforce system-spanning constraints pro-actively while doing top-down design, rather than enforcing them reactively. By specifying this constraint to be soft, we will be permitted to temporarily violate and override it if we wish to experiment with hypothetical configurations.

22.7. Summary

A constraint is a property of an object class which limits its behavior. A constraint may govern attributes and functions, actual or virtual, native or tracked. A spanning constraint simultaneously governs properties of more than one object class and is modeled as a property of any object that is a common relatant of all governed objects; this object is then said to anchor the constraint. System-spanning constraints can be anchored at the highest aggregate class in the system, since the highest aggregate is always a common relatant of every other object in the system.

Like other properties, a constraint is bequeathed down the inheritance hierarchy. Under Constraint Addition, a descendant class may add new constraints to new attributes at the same time it adds those attributes. Under Constraint Imposition, a descendant class may impose new constraints on existing, inherited attributes. Under Constraint Restriction, a descendant class may restrict the effectiveness domains of inherited constraints.

23. Object Class Rules

> *"Sure, we believe in computer-assisted network architecture. We've given all our field technicians a BERT tester."*
>
> — *anonymous network manager.*

23.1. Introduction

In this chapter, we present a model for specifying the conditions under which objects exhibit certain behavior. The mechanism of rules allows us to model the semantic link between an object's structural properties and its behavioral properties. By indicating which behavioral properties are exhibited as and when structural properties change, we considerably enhance the completeness of the specification of objects.

23.2. Inference Rules and Triggers

In many methodologies, *rule-based modeling* permits the inferencing of certain facts about the universe of discourse based on other facts. The construct which drives this ability is called an *inference rule*. An inference rule can be either a *deduction rule* if in its specification the consequent precedes its antecedents, or a *production rule* if the antecedents precede their consequent. In some situations, rather than simply inferring a fact based on other facts, a rule can instead invoke a function. If such a rule has been specified, then once certain conditions are established, specific functions can be automatically executed. Such rules are called *trigger rules* or *triggers*. Trigger rules are similar in form to inference rules, but their "consequent" is an invocation of a function rather than an assertion of a fact.

In this chapter, we will focus on modeling trigger rules as properties of object classes. So far, we have modeled many structural properties of object classes (attributes, relationships, constraints) and many behavioral properties (functions), but we have not

510

completely modeled the *link* between structural and behavioral properties. It is easy to model a situation where function execution causes changes in attribute values; we will now explore the reverse situation, that is, changes in attribute values which cause function execution.

So far, we have assumed that functions are executed and attributes are read or modified in response to messages received using some external protocol which operates on objects. The focus of our methodology is not to describe any protocol which operates on objects but rather to evolve constructs to model their static and dynamic characteristics as a specification technique. Without considering protocol issues, we will now model the links between structural and behavioral properties as *rules* [Goya88, Kers89, Rabi89]. In the following discussion, we will refer to rules that infer facts from other facts as *inference rules*, and rules that cause functions to execute as *trigger rules*.

Built-in "Inference Rules"

Certain "inference rules" are implicit in specialization theory: we already have the ability to infer certain facts from other facts. Our entire methodology has been organized such that unstated facts become obvious from stated facts using the constructs and mechanisms we have presented. We can very easily express many of these concepts in the syntax of inference-rule-based languages [Brow84, Ster86, Bhar89]. As examples, we present some of these constructs below. These are only intended to show the equivalences between the "facts" (both connotational and operational) of an object-oriented model and the facts of a knowledge-based model [Zani84, Kahn86, Malp87]. These examples are not intended as a suggestion that our object-oriented methodology be implemented in this manner; among other things, such an implementation would be unable to construct an inheritance hierarchy or to distinguish between associations and relationships.

```
/* Facts */
objectClass(classA).
objectClass(classX).
attribute(a).
function(f).
constraint(c).

/* Property assignment */
has-as-a-property(classA,a).
has-as-a-property(classA,f).
has-as-a-property(classA,c).

/* Instantiation */
object(x).
is-an-instance-of(x,classX).
```

```
/* Specialization */
specializes-into(classA,classX).
specializes-from(Descendant,Ancestor) :-
     specializes-into(Ancestor,Descendant).


/* Inheritance */
has-as-a-property(Descendant,AnyProperty) :-
     has-as-a-property(Ancestor,AnyProperty),
     specializes-from(Descendant,Ancestor).


/* Relationships */
/* for all Subject, Relatant in {ObjectClasses},
   each relationship role becomes a predicate... */


 /* Forward and reciprocal Roles */
anyForwardRole(Subject,Relatant).
correspondingReciprocalRole(Relatant,Subject) :-
     anyForwardRole(Subject,Relatant).


/* Commutative Virtual Relationship */
connects-to(pbx,multiplexer) :-
                            connects-to(multiplexer,pbx).


/* Distributive Virtual Relationship */
administers(vendor,device) :-
     administers(vendor,site),
     houses(site,device).


/* Transitive Virtual Relationship */
is-a-part-of(port,wiringHub) :-
     is-a-part-of(port,card),
     is-a-part-of(card,wiringHub).


/* Convolute Virtual Relationship */
downloads-to(informationService,desktopComputer) :-
     is-subscribed-to-by(informationService,
                           corporateClient),
     owns(corporateClient,desktopComputer).
```

```
/* Implicate Virtual Relationship */
stores-files-on(workstation,server) :-
      accesses(workstation,server).
```

Many other modeling constructs in our methodology have equivalences as inference rules. Inference rules involve the computation of facts from other facts. In specialization theory, facts are represented as attribute values, object instances, and relationship instances. We can already deduce many facts from other facts simply because of the ability to bequeath properties down class inheritance hierarchies, bequeath relationships down class inheritance hierarchies, and derive virtual relationships. For example, if classX is an object class with the attribute a, and object x is an instance of classX, then syllogisms of the form

```
has-as-a-property(x,a) :-
      has-as-a-property(classX,a),
      is-an-instance-of(x,classX).
```

are readily available from our definition of properties and instantiation. Further, syllogisms with induction on ancestral classes are available simply by traversing up the inheritance hierarchy.

Non-Horn Logic and the Closed-World Assumption

As the preceding examples show, many inferences which can be expressed in *Horn-clause logic* are automatically available in specialization theory [Kowa79, Fagi82, Lloy87, Robi92]. A Horn clause is a logical statement with one or more conditions (precedents) which together imply exactly one conclusion (consequent). If the conclusion is of the form (A or B), the statement is not a Horn clause. In specialization theory, some *non-Horn* inferences can also be drawn because of our definition of subclasses as subsets. For example, our statement of Specialized Relatant Inheritance from Chapter 17 may be stated as

```
is-related-to(classA1, classB1) OR
is-related-to(classA1, classB2) :-
      is-related-to(classA, classB),
      specializes-from(classA1, classA),
      specializes-from(classB1, classB),
      specializes-from(classB2, classB).
```

An inference such as the above is not a Horn clause (and thus cannot be expressed in the syntax of many inferencing environments) since the conclusion involves a disjunction (i.e., an or condition) of *two* atomic formulas. It arises as a result of using the *closed-world assumption*, which acts as a meta-rule permitting us to infer the negation of a fact if we cannot infer the fact [Reit78, Mink82].

Using the closed-world assumption, if class A has class B as a mandatory relatant, class A **specializes-into** subclass A1, and class B completely **specializes-into** subclasses B1 and B2, then A1 must be related to either B1 or B2 (it may choose either one due to relatant specialization), or possibly to both B1 and B2. Since we are not told (nor can we infer from other facts) that B has subclasses other than B1 and B2, the closed-world assumption lets us infer that B in fact has no subclasses other than B1 and B2. Similarly, we may infer that A has no subclasses other than A1. Thus, specialized relatant inheritance requires that A1 must play the same role with either B1 or B2 that A played with B.

Equivalences of Inference Rules

If the simplest facts are represented as statements about values of attributes, then at the lowest level, the implication of one fact by another corresponds to the specialization theory mechanism of virtual attributes. All definitions of *virtual attributes*, where certain attribute values (facts) are derived by applying arithmetic and logical computations on base attributes (other facts, whether in the same or another object), can easily be recast as inference rules.

The preceding discussion is intended to illustrate the equivalences between logical inference rules and many aspects of modeling with specialization theory and to emphasize that many logical inferences are *already* implicitly available in specialization theory simply because of the way it has been constructed. However, specialization theory is much more than a system of such logical inferences. Because of abstraction, encapsulation, and inheritance, it can build a rich taxonomical hierarchy of real-world objects and model the relationships between them, something that most logic programming environments do not support.

Because many inference rules are already available in specialization theory, we shall not consider the inference rules of any Horn or non-Horn logic as part of our general rule modeling. If some complex inferencing is required for the derivation of a fact — for example, the updating of an attribute in an object — it can generally be expressed as a sufficiently complex attribute-defined expression which computes that virtual attribute. New virtual attributes can be defined if needed to represent intermediate steps in the reasoning process.

In many knowledge-based systems, inference rules are used in environments where multiple potentially conflicting rules can exist simultaneously in the rule information base. The inference engine then selects the most appropriate rule for use in any given situation, based on some conflict-resolution strategy. This represents a powerful reasoning capability. Incorporating such capability in an abstract object-oriented model is a complex exercise; besides, many objects do not need this power. Therefore, we do not consider conflict resolution as part of our general rule model. Our goal is to maintain, as far as possible, a deterministic object model in which the model information base does not admit potentially conflicting rules, if it can detect them. If such rules are admitted, it would require the model information base to use a conflict-resolution strategy; this is not currently part of our model. Henceforth, our use of the term "rule" will be limited to *de-*

terministic trigger rules which model the semantic link between attribute values, relationship instances, and function execution [Benn89, Eric89, Unla89, Chor90].

23.3. Conceptual Background

In specialization theory, a *rule* is a *property* of an object class, in the same sense that attributes and functions are properties of an object class [Diaz91, Anwa93]. Like other properties, rules are bequeathed down the inheritance hierarchy: descendant classes inherit all the rules of their ancestors. As usual, because of monotonic inheritance, descendant classes are forbidden from dropping or canceling any inherited rules. Like other properties, a rule may also be collected with other properties in a capsule.

A rule establishes a linkage between a *structural change* experienced by an object and the execution of one or more *functions*. This linkage is specified as a set of circumstances defined in terms of structural properties. These circumstances are known as the *preconditions* of a rule. If the defined circumstances are met, the preconditions are said to be *satisfied*. When this occurs, the rule is said to be *activated*, and the functions indicated in the rule are *triggered*. (We do not use the term *fired* which is common in some rule-based reasoning models, because that usually implies the selection of one among a set of potentially conflicting rules after the application of some conflict-resolution strategy.)

Driving Preconditions and Triggered Functions

The structural properties on which the preconditions of a rule are specified are said to *drive* the rule. The functions executed when the rule is activated are said to be *triggered* by the rule. To specify a rule completely, it is sufficient to indicate the preconditions on its driving properties and to identify its triggered functions and the arguments thereof. The functions triggered by a rule must already be properties of the object class, or must be added as new properties at the same time as the rule is added. There is nothing "special" about the triggered functions of a rule — like other functions, they can be invoked directly if needed, without necessarily being triggered by the rule. Usually, when a triggered function is invoked by a rule, it is supplied with arguments which are either constants, or are derivable from one of the driving properties or from some other external property.

Anchoring a Spanning Rule

A rule can operate within a single object, or across objects. Although a rule can affect many objects, a rule is always a property of only one object. The object which possesses the rule as a property is said to *anchor* the rule. However, the conceptual area over which the rule operates can include objects other than the anchoring object. A rule can be driven by preconditions involving properties in other objects. A rule can trigger functions of other objects. In fact, the anchoring object need not be affected by the activation of the rule at all: it is possible that all driving properties and triggered functions of a rule belong to other objects.

If the driving properties and triggered functions of a rule all belong to the object anchoring the rule, the rule is said to be a *native rule*; if they come from multiple objects, it is said to be *spanning rule*. The *arity* of a rule indicates the number of objects spanned by the rule. A unary rule is a native rule; a binary rule spans two objects; a general *n*-ary rule can span multiple objects.

Even though the driving preconditions and triggered functions of a spanning rule need not belong to the anchoring object, they cannot come from any random object. *The objects spanned by a spanning rule must participate in well-founded relationships with the anchoring object.* In other words, a rule can only span objects which are *relatants* of the anchoring object, either by actual or virtual relationships. If any object is not a relatant of the anchoring object, it is not possible in specialization theory to define a rule spanning that object.

This implies that if a spanning rule is *n*-ary with *n*>2, then all *n* objects it spans must have the anchoring object as their common relatant. As with constraints, all spanned objects could play different roles with the anchoring object (and possibly with each other), but it is necessary that there be a sequence of defined role links that can be tracked from each spanned object to every other spanned object through the anchoring object. If the rule originates in an optional capsule, then any object possessing that capsule must have as relatants all the objects required by the spanning rule.

For example, a `dualCompositeMultiplexer` object could have a spanning rule which triggers the `autoUpspeed` function of one of its component `composite-Port` objects, if the `status` attribute of its other `compositePort` object changes to dead. Even though neither the driving attribute nor the triggered function are properties of `dualCompositeMultiplexer`, the rule itself can still be a property of `dual-CompositeMultiplexer`. This is because the `dualCompositeMultiplexer` object has well-defined relationships (aggregation) with the `compositePort` objects, though which it can conceptually monitor the status and invoke functions in those relatants. Being the common relatant of both the `compositePort` object involved in the rule, `dualCompositeMultiplexer` is the best place to anchor the rule. Generally, a spanning rule permits a structural change in one object (e.g., an attribute value update) to trigger desired behavior in any of its relatants, such as a component, an aggregate, or a connected object.

Figure 23-1 illustrates the general model of a rule.

The overall associations for rule modeling are **is-driven-by** and **drives** between a rule and its driving properties, and **triggers** and **is-triggered-by** between a rule and its triggered functions. These associations may operate across object classes for spanning rules. Of course, since a rule is a property of its anchoring class, it has the associations **is-a-property-of** and **has-as-a-property** with that class. These associations are described in Figure 23-2.

Establishing Driving Preconditions

The driving preconditions of any rule can be any one of the structural changes which an object can experience. Typical driving preconditions under which a rule may be activated are

- The value of an attribute changes into (or out of) some indicated sub-domain.

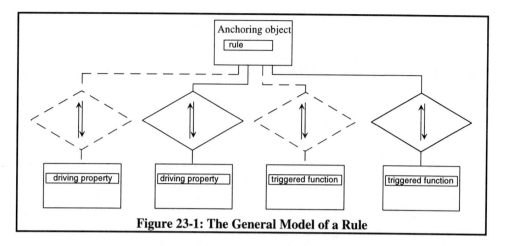

Figure 23-1: The General Model of a Rule

- The value of an attribute changes into (or out of) any one of a set of defined values.

- Some indicated relationship instance is established (or destroyed).

- Some indicated relationship instance is established (or destroyed) in which an indicated participant object has certain indicated properties (e.g., attribute values within some indicated subdomain, out of some indicated subdomain, etc.).

- Some indicated relationship instance is established (or destroyed) in which *either* participant has certain indicated properties.

- Some indicated role is established (or destroyed) for an indicated subject in *any* relationship instance with *any* relatant.

- Some indicated role is established (or destroyed) for an indicated subject with any relatant such that the *subject* has certain indicated properties.

- Some indicated role is established (or destroyed) for an indicated subject with any relatant such that the *relatant* has certain indicated properties.

The list above is by no means an exhaustive list of possible driving preconditions but is suggestive of typical situations in which a rule may be activated. In all cases, the driving preconditions may be expressed as a *logical predicate*. As we know from Chapter 10, it is fairly easy to indicate specific values for attributes as *attribute logical predicates*: they essentially take the form {attribute, is, value} where attribute is an AttributeLabel, is is a Comparator, and value is of AttributeType. A simple attribute logical predicate is assumed to apply to the attribute in the driving precondition. If, as specified in Chapter 19, the attribute label is preceded by a role or relationship label, it implies that the predicate applies to an attribute tracked from the anchoring object to a relatant object.

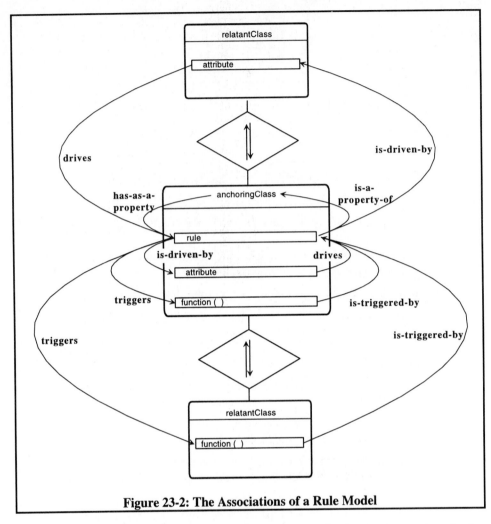

Figure 23-2: The Associations of a Rule Model

To define driving preconditions based on the establishment or destruction of relationship instances, we may use *relationship predicates*. As we know from Chapter 19, a
relationship predicate asserts a relationship instance between a pair of participant object
instances. The context is always assumed to be that of the class anchoring the specificand
rule. From this context, if the driving precondition is expressed simply as a value of type
`RelationshipLabel`, it is interpreted as requiring the rule to be activated every time
an instance of that relationship is established for any instance of the anchoring class. If
the driving precondition is specified simply as a value of type `RoleLabel`, it is interpreted as requiring the rule to be activated every time that role is established for an instance of the anchoring class as the subject, with a relatant instance of any class with
which such a role is valid. Of course, any logical predicate can also be a logical combination of multiple attribute logical predicates and relationship predicates.

We can fine-tune the driving preconditions to be as specific as necessary. For example, we can cause the rules to be activated only after a certain threshold number of relatants has been established with the anchoring class. From Chapter 20, we know that the `trackRelatants()` and `countRelatants()` functions can be used either in open-class or closed-class forms. When used from the context of the anchoring class of the specificand rule, the driving precondition

```
{countRelatants (class:definedClass,
                 role:definedRole) >= 5}
```

holds as soon as the fifth relationship instance is established between any instance of the anchoring class and the defined relatant class. If this predicate drives the rule, it does not activate the rule the first four times such a relationship instance is established but activates it on the fifth. If the predicate is specified as

```
{countRelatants (class:definedClass,
                 role:definedRole) = 0}
```

then the rule is activated only after the last relationship instance is destroyed. In general, driving preconditions which involve non-trivial threshold values should be specified in terms of attribute-defined expressions for threshold attributes rather than hard constants.

Specifying a Rule

A rule is conceptually specified as an `if-then-else` construct. In our informal notation, a rule may be expressed as

```
if (precondition)
then function()
else function()
```

where the `else` part is optional, and executed only if the negation of the precondition is true. The `precondition` is always a logical predicate. Each `function()` specified in the rule must have its own corresponding formal definition as a FUNCTION and must be a property of the anchoring object or a spanned relatant. A single rule may trigger the execution of multiple functions in different objects.

Rules should only be used for specifying object behavior which can be considered to be automatically activated by some hypothetical process which conceptually monitors the driving preconditions perpetually for structural changes. Rules should not be used for specifying behavior which is otherwise part of the normal functionality of the object. For example, the normal execution of a function on the receipt of a protocol message should not be modeled as a rule, as it does not involve the conceptual monitoring for structural changes. (Of course, the execution of a function on the receipt of a protocol message may cause a consequential structural change, which might then activate a rule that triggers yet another function, but the precondition of the rule is modeled as the structural change, not the receipt of the original protocol message.)

Rules are used within network objects in many situations. They include optimum path determination on topology reconfiguration [Benn89], exception overload handling [Cron88], autodiagnosis and autorepair capabilities in network objects [Dupu91, Goya91, Raha91], and bandwidth and capacity allocation [Erfa89]. Work has also been done in automatic learning and induction of rules from existing knowledge in topology information bases [Good91]. We present some examples below as we consider how rules interact with object inheritance hierarchies.

23.4. Rule Addition

Because a rule is a property of an object class, a subclass inherits all rules specified for its superclass. Since a subclass is permitted to add new properties, it may also add new rules to the properties inherited from its superclass. The new rules stay in effect for all subsequent descendants of that subclass.

An Example of Rule Addition

As an example, consider a `switch` object class which plays the `terminates` role with the `circuit` object class. The `circuit` object class may have a `status` attribute enumerated as {`busy`, `idle`, `dead`}. The `switch` may have a `numberOfLiveCircuits` virtual attribute which reflects the number of `circuit` objects it terminates whose `status` is not dead. The `switch` may also have a `numberOfBusyCircuits` virtual attribute which reflects the number of `circuit` objects which are busy at any given time.

While an ordinary `switch` may not have sophisticated overflow diversion features, assume that there is a subclass of `switch` which does. This subclass — say `dSwitch` — adds a new `divert_overflow()` function [Moor89]. In addition, this subclass also possesses a *rule* which can automatically trigger this function. This rule causes each `dSwitch` object to automatically invoke `divert_overflow()` when the `numberOfBusyCircuits` reaches a certain threshold. The `divert_overflow()` function then internally determines whether there is any other `switch` among the possible reroute paths which could handle the overflow, and if so, hands off excess traffic to the other `switch`. We may express this rule as

```
if ((numberOfBusyCircuits ÷
        numberOfLiveCircuits) ≥ 0.9)
then divert_overflow()
```

Although the expression of this rule looks as if it were a native rule, it is actually a spanning rule since its preconditions involve virtual attributes tracked from a relatant object class. If we had not defined the `numberOfBusyCircuits` and `numberOf-`

LiveCircuits as virtual attributes of switch, we could have defined the same rule
with explicit calls to countRelatants(), with the same effect.

Since each rule is a property, we give it a name which can be used for referencing
it. Hence, a more complete definition for the rule becomes

```
dSwitch.overflowRule ←
        if ((numberOfBusyCircuits ÷
            numberOfLiveCircuits) ≥ 0.9)
        then divert_overflow()
```

When the dSwitch object class specializes from the switch superclass, it may
use the addition of this rule as a basis of specialization. This is known as *specialization
by rule addition*, which we may express formally as a specialization principle:

> ***Specialization Principle****:*   *A descendant class may add a rule as a new
> property (**Rule Addition**).*

Figure 23-3 illustrates this specialization mode. Adding rules makes our model
richer and more expressive, as it enforces the semantic link between changes in attribute
values and the execution of various functions.

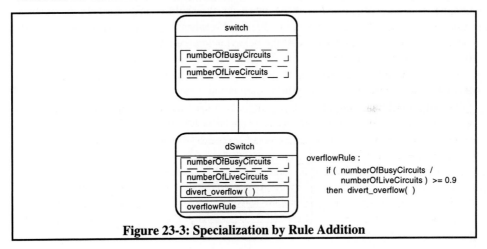

Figure 23-3: Specialization by Rule Addition

23.5. Rule Precondition Contravariance

A subclass inherits rules from its ancestors class and may use them without change.
However, as the functionality of a subclass increases going down the hierarchy, it may invoke the same rule in a variety of circumstances. In particular, it may invoke the rule
when the preconditions are *weaker*. Doing so maintains the subclass as a substitutable
subtype of its superclass, since it is always possible to use an object which activates a rule

at a lower threshold when the superclass only stipulates that the rule must at least be invoked at the higher threshold [Fest93].

An Example of Precondition Contravariance

Assume that there is a subclass of dSwitch which acts more conservatively than its superclass. In other words, it executes the call to divert_overflow() at a lower threshold than it superclass. Suppose that the subclass conservativeDSwitch redefines overflowRule as

```
conservativeDSwitch.overflowRule ←
    if ((numberOfBusyCircuits ÷
        numberOfLiveCircuits) ≥ 0.8)
    then divert_overflow()
```

In this rule, the class conservativeDSwitch computes the same ratio in terms of the same attributes numberOfBusyCircuits and numberOfLive-Circuits but changes the threshold at which it triggers the function divert_overflow(). It is permitted to do this because it meets *more* than the minimum precondition specified by the superclass. The superclass dSwitch requires that every member call divert_overflow() when the threshold reaches 0.9. In the subclass conservativeDSwitch, when the threshold reaches 0.9, the overflow is already diverted; thus the subclass exhibits all the behavior required by the superclass, augmented by *additional* behavior.

Descendant classes are permitted to *weaken* the preconditions under which rules are activated. Because rule preconditions are unlike other properties which are restricted to increase the focus of applicability going down the hierarchy, they are said to exhibit *contravariance*. Figure 23-4 illustrates this specialization mode.

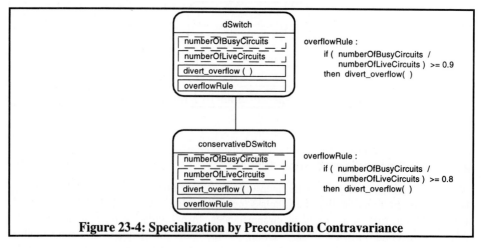

Figure 23-4: Specialization by Precondition Contravariance

An Alternate View of Precondition Contravariance

Precondition contravariance may be viewed in terms of rule addition. For example, the class `conservativeDSwitch` may be considered to inherit the `overflowRule` from its superclass `dSwitch` without change, as follows:

```
conservativeDSwitch.overflowRule ←
    if ((numberOfBusyCircuits ÷
        numberOfLiveCircuits) ≥ 0.9)
    then divert_overflow()
```

Besides inheriting this rule without change, the class `conservativeDSwitch` may also be considered to add the *new* hypothetical rule `overflowRule2`, defined as follows:

```
conservativeDSwitch.overflowRule2 ←
    if (0.8 ≤(numberOfBusyCircuits ÷
        numberOfLiveCircuits) < 0.9)
    then     divert_overflow()
```

Adding the hypothetical rule `overflowRule2` is legal by rule addition, since it does not conflict with any existing rule. By merging these two rules together, we in effect get the rule with the expanded domain.

Descendant classes are not permitted to *strengthen* rule preconditions, because that implies that they cancel inherited behavior. For example, if another hypothetical subclass of `dSwitch`, say `optimisticDSwitch`, changes the threshold to `0.95`, it will not exhibit the behavior of `dSwitch` objects when the ratio is, say, `0.92`. In order to be a member of `dSwitch`, every object must call `divert_overflow()` when the ratio reaches `0.9`. However, members of `optimisticDSwitch` will not exhibit the behavior required of all `dSwitch` objects between ratios of `0.9` and `0.95`, effectively canceling inherited properties. This is not permitted in specialization theory because of monotonic inheritance.

Precondition contravariance may also arise naturally from attribute domain restriction. The threshold for invoking `divert_overflow()` may be specified as the value of an attribute, say `diversionThreshold`. The superclass `dSwitch` may define this attribute value to come from the domain `[0.0, 0.9]`, while the subclass `conservativeDSwitch` may restrict this domain to `[0.0, 0.8]`. When processing this specification, our compiler notes that this attribute domain restriction in effect weakens the rule precondition and accepts the specification. As with relatant multiplicity restriction for attribute-defined multiplicities, it is possible to define attribute domain restriction such that the subclass effectively strengthens the preconditions of any existing rule. If our compiler detects this, it rejects the specialization.

Of course, all other specialization principles continue to be effective simultaneously. For example, if the triggered function is a native function of the specializing subclass, it may simultaneously exhibit function extension, argument contravariance or result covariance as well.

Precondition Contravariance in Logical Domains

Precondition contravariance is not restricted to adjusting values of numeric domains only; it can also be exhibited in logical domains. Weakening a precondition expressed as a logical predicate is essentially equivalent to *adding a logical disjunction* (that is, an or condition). A descendant class may exhibit precondition contravariance by combining its inherited precondition predicate with a *new* predicate, such that the two are combined with an or. This ensures that the subclass will exhibit the superclass behavior under at least the same circumstances as the superclass, but it may also exhibit the same behavior under other circumstances.

For example, the subclass selfMonitoringDSwitch of dSwitch may have the additional capability of monitoring its own internal switching elements. It may have the ability to count the number of switchingElement objects it has-as-a-part, and compute the two counting virtual attributes numberOfSwitchingElements and numberOfFailedSwitchingElements. The virtual attribute numberOf-FailedSwitchingElements counts the number of switchingElement components whose status field indicates failed. Because of this feature, it has the capability to invoke divert_overflow() when the numberOfFailedSwitch-ingElements reaches some threshold. For example, it may change the precondition of overflowRule to

```
selfMonitoringDSwitch.overflowRule ←
      if (((numberOfBusyCircuits ÷
          numberOfLiveCircuits) ≥ 0.9))
        or
        ((numberOfFailedSwitchingElements ÷
          numberOfSwitchingElements) ≥ 0.2))
      then divert_overflow()
```

The subclass selfMonitoringDSwitch displays all the characteristics of its superclass dSwitch with regard to calling divert_overflow(), and it displays additional characteristics as well. This is consistent with the specialization theory precept that a subclass may extend superclass functionality while remaining a substitutable subtype. It is a trivial exercise to express any weakening of a rule precondition by the addition of an *or*-predicate as a *rule addition* mechanism in the subclass.

Descendant classes are not permitted to add another predicate to an inherited precondition with an and conjunction. This would constitute strengthening the predicate, which is not permitted in specialization theory.

Rules with Else-Clauses

Care must be taken when using precondition contravariance, however, as there are some rules for which precondition weakening is *not* permitted. In particular, *it is illegal to weaken the driving preconditions of a rule which has an* `else`*-clause*. To see why this is so, consider a superclass rule of the form {if P then f() else g()}, where P is a logical predicate. This rule may be considered equivalent to the set of two rules, {if P then f()} and {if not P then g()}. If a subclass inherits this rule by weakening the precondition predicate P, it in effect *strengthens* the precondition predicate not P which drives the triggering of g(). This is illegal in specialization theory, because it implies that there may be some situations in which the superclass requires g() to execute, but the subclass does not do so as it requires a *stronger* precondition before g() is triggered. The subclass executes f() instead, which is not what the superclass specified. In effect, the subclass modifies inherited behavior in a manner that renders itself non-substitutable for the superclass.

By the same reasoning, it is also illegal to strengthen the precondition for a rule with an `else`-clause, because while this would weaken the predicate driving the `else`-clause, it would strengthen it for the `then`-clause. This is not permissible if the `then`-clause is non-null. If the `then`-clause *is* null, a subclass may *strengthen* the rule precondition, but this is equivalent to weakening the precondition for the restated rule with the predicate negated and a non-null `then`-clause. Assuming that all rules are stated positively (that is, no rule has a null `then`-clause), the following circumstances describe the applicability of precondition weakening:

- *Rule with no* `else`-*clause*: A subclass is permitted to weaken the rule precondition but not strengthen it.

- *Rule with both* `then`- *and* `else`-*clauses*: A subclass is not permitted to make any change to the rule precondition.

Our compiler has some ability to determine whether precondition weakening on any one rule conflicts with other rules. Because of this, it is difficult to "get away with" precondition weakening on a rule containing an `else`-clause by a straightforward restatement of the rule as two different rules with only `then`-clauses, such as {if P then f()} and {if not P then g()}. If obvious conflicts with other rule preconditions are detected while analyzing any particular precondition weakening, the entire specialization is rejected. Although the compiler's ability to catch rule conflicts is limited, it can generally trap those conflicts which are apparent on superficial inspection.

The phenomenon of precondition weakening, when used in a specialization, is called *Specialization by Rule Precondition Contravariance*, or simply *Precondition Contravariance*. We may state this formally as the specialization principle of *precondition contravariance*:

Specialization Principle:	*A descendant class may weaken a driving precondition of a rule inherited from an ancestral class, if the rule has no else-clause (**Precondition Contravariance**).*

23.6. Rule Function Addition

In addition to weakening the driving preconditions of a rule, a subclass may *add new functions to an inherited rule*. This means that when the rule is activated in the subclass, it exhibits all the behavior which is specified by the superclass, plus additional behavior. This is permitted in specialization theory as subclasses may evolve and extend inherited behavior.

As an example, consider the example of another subclass of dSwitch, called activeDSwitch. Assume that this subclass has the ability to report status information to its operations support system on an unsolicited basis, as opposed to other kinds of dSwitch objects which may have to be polled for their status. This subclass inherits the overflowRule from dSwitch. It modifies the rule such that in the then-clause, in addition to triggering the function divert_overflow(), it also triggers a new function report_diversion_alert(). The intent of this invocation is to cause a diversion report to be generated to its operations support system. In effect, it restates the rule as

```
activeDSwitch.overflowRule ←
        if ((numberOfBusyCircuits ÷
            numberOfLiveCircuits) ≥ 0.9)
        then {
                divert_overflow();
                report_diversion_alert();
            }
```

Thus, this subclass exhibits all the functionality of its ancestors but also adds additional functionality when it invokes the inherited rule. This is permitted in specialization theory. If a subclass exhibits this behavior as a basis of specialization, it is known as *Specialization by Rule Function Addition*. Figure 23-5 illustrates this principle.

If the rule has an else-clause, a subclass may perform rule function addition on either the then-clause, or the else-clause, or both. To see why this is permitted, recall that if the rule has an else-clause, the subclass cannot change the rule precondition. We may therefore equivalently state the rule with the precondition logically negated and the then-clause and the else-clause interchanged. Adding a new function to the then-clause of the negatively stated rule is equivalent to adding a new function to the else-clause of the positively stated rule. Regardless of whether the then-clause or the else-clause is executed in any particular activation of the rule, the subclass exhibits all the functionality of the superclass, plus additional functionality. In general, for spanning rules, the added rule functions may be functions of relatant classes of the anchoring class.

Under no circumstances is the subclass permitted to *drop* rule functions from either the then-part or the else-part. This would mean that it cancels inherited behavior in some situations, which is illegal under monotonic inheritance. Other function-based specialization modes continue to be simultaneously active: for example, a subclass may

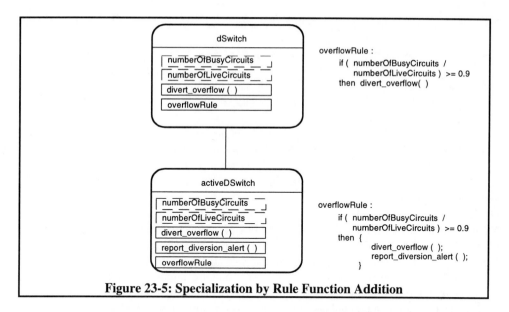

Figure 23-5: Specialization by Rule Function Addition

add a rule function at the same time that it performs argument contravariance or result covariance on that function, or on any other existing rule function, if these functions happen to be native properties of the anchoring class.

We may state this formally as the specialization principle of *rule function addition*:

Specialization Principle:	*A descendant class may add a new triggered function to a rule inherited from an ancestral class (**Rule Function Addition**).*

23.7. Using Rules

As practitioners, our focus is to model the system using a methodology which captures as much structural and behavioral detail as possible. In specialization theory, rules provide only *adjunct* information about objects: they tell us how objects respond to structural changes. Rules are subservient to objects in that they are encapsulated as properties within objects. Of course, this does not limit rules to operate only on a single object; in the examples we have seen of spanning rules, the general relationship model provides a foundation which permits a single rule to affect multiple related objects. For example, if a rule is required to span multiple components of the same aggregate, the rule can be anchored as a property of the aggregate.

Some modeling methodologies use rules as the primary modeling construct, with "objects" being the operands of the rules with no internal structure of their own. While certain applications benefit from this approach, in specialization theory (as in many other methodologies [Bobr83, Fuku86, Kosc88, Wu91]) objects combine taxonomical, structural, behavioral, and rule semantics simultaneously. We thus use an object's encapsulation to specify the rules which span that object and its relatants. This encapsulation makes rules the structural properties of their anchoring object [Stef86, Cone88, Ibra90], rather than making "objects" the unstructured operands of rules.

The rule processing involved in most object model compilers, if at all available, is fairly elementary. For this reason, it is good modeling practice to keep rules simple and easily tractable. If many complex, interdependent rules are specified within an object class, the compiler is often unable to determine rule conflicts. This is because, when a rule is activated, the execution of the triggered function could cause a change in an attribute value, thus activating another rule. In general, it is impossible to analyze a given rule set lexically to ascertain whether any such set of cascaded rule activations is internally self-consistent, or whether a sequence of such activations shall have any deterministic termination [Gode30, Turi37].

A very elementary algorithm is used in our compiler to check for superficial inconsistencies between the driving preconditions of various rules. It is possible that under certain circumstances a complex rule-set with internal inconsistencies will go undetected. If this happens, selecting the most appropriate rule among conflicting candidate rules will require the presence of a full-fledged forward-chaining inference engine which uses a conflict-resolution strategy, conceptually embedded inside each object; this is not part of our object modeling methodology at this time. In Chapter 26, we will examine the potential for implementing objects with internally encapsulated rules in various environments.

In specialization theory, rules are used as the mechanism which cause objects to exhibit desired behavior in response to some structural change. Since rules are properties of object classes, they need to be specified "up front" at schema definition time. In some cases this can be a disadvantage, because the network model cannot "learn" rules on its own. If rules are conceptualized during network operation, the schema must be redefined to explicitly add the formally stated rule as a new property of some class. We mention other rule-processing paradigms which can learn and apply rules adaptively.

Case-based reasoning [Barl91, Kolo93, Lewi93a] stores historical patterns of responses to structural changes and examines each new structural change for similarity with some known historical event. This serves as a starting point for a human operator to recommend a response, which is itself added to the known history. *Artificial neural networks* [Simp90] are proficient in learning by example once sufficient training has been performed to adjust neuron weights. *Fuzzy logic* applies interpolative reasoning techniques to generate responses to events in the network [Lewi93b]. It is most useful when the response must be delivered in real time, without the luxury of waiting for complex rule processing in a rule base. Although these are all excellent techniques, they are not currently tied to specialization theory.

23.8. System-Spanning Rules

System-spanning rules have system-wide scope, in that the structural changes which happen in one part of the network trigger functions in another part. It is not necessary that the object experiencing the changes and the object executing the triggered function be related, but it is necessary that they have at least one relatant in common. For rules that span the entire network, as with constraints, the common relatant which is often chosen to anchor the rule is the highest possible aggregate class in the system.

For example, a system-spanning rule could be anchored at the class `network`, which has every other object in the network as a component. This arises due to the transitivity of the `has-as-a-part` role, making every object in the network a component of `network` by either an actual or a virtual decomposition relationship. By specifying the system-spanning rule as a property of `network`, we enable it to be driven by preconditions of objects anywhere in the network and to trigger functions of objects anywhere else in the network. However, the most useful "rule spans", and the ones most commonly modeled, are generally local to some smaller aggregate class (for example, between the component classes of a `switch` aggregate class).

23.9. Summary

Rules are a general mechanism which permit us to specify the semantic linkage between the structural change experienced by an object and the behavior that it may exhibit as a response. In specialization theory we only model trigger rules which cause the functions of an object class to execute when certain structural changes occur. We do not model inferences in which potentially conflicting rules may simultaneously exist.

A rule is always the property of a single class, called its anchoring class. A rule may affect a single object, in which case it is called a native rule, or multiple objects, in which case it is called a spanning rule. All objects spanned by a rule must be relatants of the anchoring object via either actual or virtual relationships.

A rule has driving preconditions which must be satisfied for it to be activated. The functions executed by the rule are called triggered functions. The driving preconditions and triggered functions of a rule may belong to objects other than the anchoring object. The structural changes which act as driving preconditions of any rule may involve changes in attribute values or the establishment and destruction of relationship instances.

Like all properties, a rule is bequeathed down the inheritance hierarchy. A descendant class inherits all the rules specified for its ancestors. Under Rule Addition, a descendant class may add a new rule. Under Precondition Contravariance, a descendant class may weaken the driving preconditions of any inherited rule.

24. *Formal Models for Inferred Semantics*

> *"Why do we pay so much for our 800 numbers when the constitution guarantees free speech?"*
> — *anonymous corporate general counsel at budget meeting.*

24.1. Introduction

Having defined the concepts of native and tracked virtual attributes, virtual object classes, object constraints and object rules, we introduce in this chapter the notation for the formal specification of these modeling constructs. Many existing constructs, such as those of attributes, object classes, and relationships, are enhanced to permit the specification of new semantics. The formal model of constraints and rules as properties of object classes is also introduced, as well as the notation for specialization modes which use constraints and rules.

24.2. Virtual Attributes and Functions

We specify virtual attributes using the `VIRTUAL-ATTRIBUTE` template. This construct is an information object class whose information objects, like `ATTRIBUTE` information objects, are independently registered. We know that the `ATTRIBUTE` information object class possesses the *type field* `&AttributeType`, which indicates the type syntax of the attribute. The `VIRTUAL-ATTRIBUTE` information object class also contains the type field `&AttributeType`, but it is optional. If omitted, the virtual attribute is assumed to be an *implicit-syntax virtual attribute*. As indicated in Chapter 20, this lets the compiler automatically determine the type of the virtual attribute from the types of its supporting base attributes. If the base attributes are tracked from a relatant object class, the relatant multiplicity of the tracking role affects the type syntax of the virtual attribute. If we wish to specify an *explicit-syntax virtual attribute*, we may include the optional

&AttributeType field in the VIRTUAL-ATTRIBUTE information object specification; this is typically used when the virtual attribute definition uses logical rather than mathematical combinations of its base attributes.

In Chapter 20, we stated that the computation algorithm for a virtual attribute is an attribute-defined expression. The type AttributeDefinedExpression expands into a grammar allowing mathematical and logical combinations of the base attributes. The complete specification of this grammar is conceptually elementary; we do not provide it here because of its length. The terminal symbols of this grammar are either other native or tracked properties. In a later section, we will see how tracked virtual attributes may be specified.

Like actual attributes, each virtual attribute is assigned an OBJECT IDENTIFIER label so we can formally register it in our model information base.

```
VIRTUAL-ATTRIBUTE ::= CLASS
{
     &algorithm              AttributeDefinedExpression,
     &AttributeType          OPTIONAL,
     &virtualAttributeLabel
                             OBJECT IDENTIFIER UNIQUE
}
WITH SYNTAX
{
     COMPUTED-FROM           &algorithm
     [ ATTRIBUTE-TYPE        &AttributeType ]
     IDENTIFIED BY           &virtualAttributeLabel
}
```

We now introduce the formal syntax for virtual functions. It is worth reiterating that the specialization theory definition of a virtual function is not the same as that used in some object-oriented programming environments, where it acts as a placeholder in an ancestral class for a function whose definition will be provided subsequently in a descendant class. In specialization theory, a virtual function is the analogue of a virtual attribute. That is, it is a function which appears to execute as a native function in one object, when in fact it is specified in terms of other functions, which could execute in a tracked relatant object. A virtual function is defined as

```
VIRTUAL-FUNCTION ::= CLASS
{
     &algorithm              AttributeDefinedExpression,
     &Arguments              ARGUMENT OPTIONAL,
     &Results                RESULT OPTIONAL,
```

```
        &Exceptions              EXCEPTION OPTIONAL,
        &virtualFunctionLabel
                                 OBJECT IDENTIFIER UNIQUE
}
WITH SYNTAX
{
        COMPUTED-FROM            &algorithm,
        [ ARGUMENTS              &Arguments ]
        [ RESULTS                &Results ]
        [ EXCEPTIONS             &Exceptions ]
        IDENTIFIED BY            &virtualFunctionLabel

}
```

It should be noted that the &algorithm field does not represent the algorithm for any internal mechanism of the virtual function, as a virtual function has no internal mechanism. Rather, it represents the computations which must be performed on the *results* of the supporting base functions, in order to generate the result of the specificand virtual function. As such, it is an `AttributeDefinedExpression`. As we mentioned in Chapter 7, the term `AttributeDefinedExpression` is a slight misnomer, because its terminal symbols need not just be attributes; they can be the return results of functions as well. This is because using a return result of a function is conceptually no different from using the retrieved value of an attribute. In the specification of a virtual function, the type `AttributeDefinedExpression` can also serve to indicate which supporting base functions must be invoked, and what transformations must be performed on their results in order to generate the result of the specificand virtual function.

In the specification above, as in that of the FUNCTION information object class in Chapter 11, &Arguments, &Results, and &Exceptions are *object set fields* of the ARGUMENT, RESULT, and EXCEPTION information object classes respectively. The &Arguments field is useful because it supplies to the virtual function those arguments, if any, which it in turn needs to supply to its supporting base functions. The &Results field is useful because the type of the result of a virtual function need not be the type of the result of a supporting base function, especially if it undergoes a logical transformation by &algorithm. The &Exceptions field lists any exceptions which the virtual function might generate on its own, other than those generated by its supporting base functions (e.g., to signal an inter-object communication failure while calling a tracked base function).

In Chapter 10, we have used the set {Attributes} as the set of all defined ATTRIBUTE information objects. The type `AttributeLabel` is defined as an object class field type constrained by this set:

```
AttributeLabel ::= ATTRIBUTE.&attributeLabel
                                       ({Attributes})
```

Similarly, the type `FunctionLabel` is constrained by the information object set `{Functions}`:

```
FunctionLabel ::= FUNCTION.&functionLabel({Functions})
```

These definitions only capture label values from actual attributes and functions. To accommodate virtual attributes and functions, we define the types `Virtual-AttributeLabel` and `VirtualFunctionLabel` along similar lines:

```
VirtualAttributeLabel ::=
                VIRTUAL-ATTRIBUTE.&virtualAttributeLabel
                              ({VirtualAttributes})

VirtualFunctionLabel ::=
                VIRTUAL-FUNCTION.&virtualFunctionLabel
                              ({VirtualFunctions})
```

where `{VirtualAttributes}` is the set of all defined `VIRTUAL-ATTRIBUTE` information objects, and `{VirtualFunctions}` is the set of all defined `VIRTUAL-FUNCTION` information objects.

In the future, we will be required to refer to the labels of all attributes and all functions regardless of whether they are actual or virtual. We therefore define new types as the combination of the sets of actual and virtual property labels:

```
AnyAttributeLabel ::=     CHOICE
{
      actual            [0]      AttributeLabel,
      virtual           [1]      VirtualAttributeLabel
}


AnyFunctionLabel ::=     CHOICE
{
      actual            [0]      FunctionLabel,
      virtual           [1]      VirtualFunctionLabel
}
```

```
AnyPropertyLabel  ::=        CHOICE
{
        attribute        [0]          AnyAttributeLabel,
        function         [1]          AnyFunctionLabel
}
```

24.3. Attribute-Defined Expressions

Both virtual attributes and virtual functions are computed from an algorithm specified by
an `AttributeDefinedExpression`. The grammar for the type `Attribute-`
`DefinedExpression` has as its terminal symbols other attributes and functions.
These properties may be native or tracked. If the terminal symbols are defined as the type
`Property`, we may define the type as

```
Property ::= CHOICE
{
        native        [0]          AttributeOrFunction,
        track         [1]          TrackedProperty,
        count         [2]          TrackedRelatants
}
```

where, if native, `Property` is resolved by the compiler within the context of the same
object class as the specificand virtual property; otherwise, it is directly tracked to another
object class. Of course, a "native" base property could be another virtual attribute, already
specified as a property of the same object class, whose specification indirectly tracks it
into another object class; even if this is so, it is not of concern to the specificand virtual
property, for whom such internal tracking is transparent.

We will examine the types `TrackedProperty` and `TrackedRelatants` in
greater detail in the next section. The type `AttributeOrFunction` is either an attribute or the return result of a function:

```
AttributeOrFunction ::= CHOICE
{
        attribute        [0]          AnyAttributeLabel,
        function         [1]          AnyFunctionWithArguments
}
```

If the base property is an attribute, then its value is directly used in the computation of the attribute-defined expression, and its type is directly fed into the type transformation for generating the type of implicit-syntax virtual attributes. If the base property is
a function, it is not sufficient to merely indicate the label of the function. If the function

takes arguments, we must specify what the arguments are which generate the value of the desired virtual property. In the normal course of operation, the &Arguments for a function are typically supplied in the protocol request which invokes this function. When the function is used as a base property in the computation of a virtual property, there is no external protocol request from which the function arguments may be extracted. Thus, the arguments of the base function must be derived from constants, or from the attributes used in the enclosing attribute-defined expression, or from other attributes of the object class. The type AnyFunctionWithArguments is simply a shorthand mechanism to extract just the fields of interest from FUNCTION or VIRTUAL-FUNCTION information object classes. This information is sufficient to cause the execution of the function. This may be specified as

```
AnyFunctionWithArguments ::=   CHOICE
{
      actual    [0]        ActualFunctionWithArguments,
      virtual   [1]        VirtualFunctionWithArguments
}


ActualFunctionWithArguments ::= SEQUENCE
{
   function      FUNCTION.&functionLabel({Functions}),
   arguments     SET OF SEQUENCE
                 {
                    argument   ARGUMENT.&argumentLabel
                               ({{Functions}.&Arguments}
                                {@function}),
                    value      ARGUMENT.&ArgumentType
                               ({{Functions}.&Arguments}
                                {@function,@.argument})
                 }
}


VirtualFunctionWithArguments ::= SEQUENCE
{
   function      VIRTUAL-FUNCTION.&virtualFunctionLabel
                               ({VirtualFunctions}),
   arguments     SET OF SEQUENCE
                 {
                    argument   ARGUMENT.&argumentLabel
                               ({{VirtualFunctions}.&Arguments}
                                {@function}),
```

```
          value      ARGUMENT.&ArgumentType
                     ({{VirtualFunctions}.&Arguments}
                        {@function,@.argument})
        }
    }
```

The type `ActualFunctionWithArguments` identifies a function in the `function` field and supplies values for each argument in the `arguments` field. The `arguments` field itself is a `SET OF` all the arguments whose values must be supplied. Each element within the set is a `SEQUENCE` of two fields: an `argument` field, which is simply an `OBJECT IDENTIFIER` referring to one argument of the function, and a `value` field, which indicates the value which must be assigned to that argument for the execution of the function, so that its result may be used in the algorithm for the virtual property being computed.

The `argument` field is constrained to be an `OBJECT IDENTIFIER` from the `&argumentLabel` fields of the `ARGUMENT` information objects of the information object set `&Arguments`, which must belong to the same `FUNCTION` information object chosen from the set `{Functions}` by the `function` field. The type of the `value` field is constrained to be the `&ArgumentType` of the same argument; the component relation constraint `@.argument` indicates that the constraining component (the `argument` field) is a field of the innermost textually enclosing construct (in this case, the `SEQUENCE` construct). The type `VirtualFunctionWithArguments` is similarly defined.

24.4. Tracked Properties

The types `TrackedProperty` and `TrackedRelatants` were used in the previous section as alternatives in the expansion of the type `Property`. In effect, these types represent the arguments of the conceptual functions `trackRelatants()` and `count-Relatants()`. If the specificand virtual property is implicit-syntax, we need not specify its type at all, because the compiler can automatically infer the type from its knowledge of the types of the supporting base properties and the relatant multiplicity of the tracking role.

If the tracked property is implicit-syntax and determined through `track-Relatants()`, and it does not execute any mathematical transformation on its supporting base attributes, then its type is the same as the type of the base property (if the relatant multiplicity of the tracking role does not exceed 1), or a `SET OF` the type of the supporting base property (if the relatant multiplicity of the tracking role exceeds 1), or a `SEQUENCE OF` the type of the supporting base property (if the relatant multiplicity of the tracking role exceeds 1 and the relatant class is ordered with respect to the subject class). If the tracked property is determined through `countRelatants()`, then its type is always `INTEGER(0..MAX)`, that is, a non-negative integer.

If the tracked property is determined through `trackRelatants()`, we must specify both the base property and the tracking arguments for the call to `track-`

Relatants(). If it is determined through countRelatants(), we need merely specify the tracking arguments. We take a first cut at specifying the type Tracked-Property as follows:

```
TrackedProperty ::= SEQUENCE
{
        instance                TrackedRelatant,
        baseProperty            AttributeOrFunction
}
```

where AttributeOrFunction is the same as specified in the previous section, that is, any attribute or function, actual or virtual, native or tracked. If the base property in the tracked relatant is itself virtual, it may have its own definition which performs additional tracking internally to yet another object class; the specificand virtual property in the subject is oblivious to any such occurrence. It is illegal to define a tracked virtual property of the subject in terms of another tracked virtual property of the relatant, which in turn is supported, directly or indirectly, by the same specificand tracked virtual property of the subject; this would lead to infinite resolution loops for the tracked virtual property.

The definition of TrackedProperty above is not sufficient, however. Recall that in Chapter 20 we said that base properties can be *contingent*, that is, if multiple base properties are tracked into different relatant classes, a different base property may be used depending on some condition imposed on its enclosing class. This is typically used with open-class forms of trackRelatants(), in which the subject class may play the same role with multiple relatant classes, each of which may have a different name for compatible tracked properties. To accommodate this, we make a second cut at defining the TrackedProperty type to include contingent base properties as well:

```
TrackedProperty ::=   CHOICE
{
        normal          [0]   NormalTrackedProperty,
        contingent      [1]   ContingentTrackedProperty
}

NormalTrackedProperty ::= SEQUENCE
{
        instance                TrackedRelatant,
        baseProperty            AttributeOrFunction
}
```

```
ContingentTrackedProperty ::= SEQUENCE
{
        instance                TrackedRelatant,
        contingencies           SET OF SEQUENCE
                                {
                                  baseProperty
                                          AttributeOrFunction,
                                  contingency
                                          LogicalPredicate
                                }

}
```

If the base property is contingent, the tracked relatant objects generally belong to different classes, as the `trackRelatants()` function is used in an open-class form. The field `contingencies` lists all the possible properties which could be used as the base depending on the governing condition. This type is a `SET OF` type; this is interpreted to mean that, if the object tracked by the `instance` field satisfies the `Logical-Predicate` specified by the `contingency` field from any element of the set, then the corresponding property of that object indicated by the `baseProperty` field must be used as the base in the computation of the specificand virtual property. Every one of these `LogicalPredicate` elements of the set of `contingencies` is conceptually applied to each tracked relatant object. The `LogicalPredicate` may simply require that the tracked object's `objectClass` attribute have a particular value (for example, be a descendant of some named superclass), or it may be a more complex condition. The types of all the underlying actual properties from each tracked object must be compatible. That is, they must all either be the same type or be subtypes of each other.

The function `countRelatants()`, which can simultaneously count multiple relatant objects from multiple classes in the same invocation, takes as its argument the type `TrackedRelatants`, which is specified as

```
TrackedRelatants ::= SET OF TrackedRelatant
```

Recall that `trackRelatants()` and `countRelatants()` can be used in both open-class and open-role forms. If the tracking role is transitive, they may also take a `depth` argument which controls the depth of the search within the transitive closure. If the tracking leads to a relatant class which is sequenced in an ordered relationship, they may also take a `rank` argument to indicate one or more specific relatant objects which are to be tracked. Thus, we may define the type `TrackedRelatant` as

```
TrackedRelatant ::= SEQUENCE
{
    role                  SEQUENCE OF RoleLabel
                                              OPTIONAL,
    relatantClass         SET OF AnyObjectClassLabel
                                              OPTIONAL,
    depth                 INTEGER(0..MAX)     OPTIONAL,
    rank                  INTEGER(0..MAX)     OPTIONAL,
    matching              LogicalPredicate    OPTIONAL
}
```

In this specification, the type `RoleLabel` is the same as that specified in Chapter 19: it is constrained to come from the pool of OBJECT IDENTIFIERs of the `&role-Label` fields of the elements of the set `{Roles}` of all defined ROLE information objects. We will formally specify the type `AnyObjectClassLabel` in the next section; at this point, it is sufficient for us to know that it refers to either an actual or virtual object class.

The `role` field is a SEQUENCE OF type because a chain of role links rather than a single role may be directly tracked from the subject, as we did in Figure 20-5. If the `role` field is unspecified, the call to `trackRelatants()` is assumed to be open-role. The `relatantClass` field is a SET OF type because relatant objects from more than one object class may be simultaneously tracked from the subject. For example, if the `relatantClass` field specifies two relatant classes, then all members of both these classes with which the subject plays the role sequence indicated by the `role` field are tracked. If the `relatantClass` field is unspecified, the call to `trackRelatants()` or `countRelatants()` is assumed to be open-class, that is, all objects with which the subject plays the indicated role are tracked regardless of their class. The `matching` field specifies any optional matching condition to be imposed on the tracked relatants, in case only certain members of the tracked relatant class are desired.

The most typical usage of `trackRelatants()` and `countRelatants()` is either in the closed-role closed-class form or in the closed-role open-class form. This means that the optional `role` field of the `TrackedRelatant` type specified above is generally present. It is possible, though not always meaningful, to omit this field, which means that the functions are being used in an open-role form.

24.5. Classes with Virtual Properties

To accommodate virtual properties in our object class specification, we need to enhance our OBJECT-CLASS information object class template. We do this as follows:

```
OBJECT-CLASS ::= CLASS
{
        &SpecializesFrom              Specialization OPTIONAL,
        &Attributes                   ATTRIBUTE OPTIONAL,
        &Functions                    FUNCTION OPTIONAL,
        &MandatoryCapsules            CAPSULE OPTIONAL,
        &OptionalCapsules             CAPSULE OPTIONAL,
        &VirtualAttributes            VIRTUAL-ATTRIBUTE
                                         OPTIONAL,  -- new field
        &VirtualFunctions             VIRTUAL-FUNCTION
                                         OPTIONAL,  -- new field
        &objectClassLabel             OBJECT IDENTIFIER UNIQUE
}
WITH SYNTAX
{
        [SPECIALIZES-FROM             &SpecializesFrom]
        [ATTRIBUTES                   &Attributes]
        [FUNCTIONS                    &Functions]
        [MANDATORY CAPSULES           &MandatoryCapsules]
        [OPTIONAL CAPSULES            &OptionalCapsules]
        [VIRTUAL ATTRIBUTES           &VirtualAttributes]
                                                -- new field
        [VIRTUAL FUNCTIONS            &VirtualFunctions]
                                                -- new field
        IDENTIFIED BY                 &objectClassLabel
}
```

This construct enables us to specify object classes with both actual and virtual properties. As an example, consider the relationship of Figure 20-4. In this relationship, the class `networkDevice` possesses a `currentSite` virtual attribute, which is tracked to the `streetAddress` attribute of its relatant class `site`, with which it plays the `is-housed-at` role. We specify this at the same time that we specify the other attributes of the `networkDevice` object class, as follows:

```
networkDevice OBJECT-CLASS ::=
{
        ...,                                          -- other fields
        VIRTUAL-ATTRIBUTES            {currentSite}
```

```
        ...,
        IDENTIFIED BY                networkDeviceLbl
}
```

The currentSite attribute has its own VIRTUAL-ATTRIBUTE information object definition. The &algorithm field for computing this virtual attribute is simply the value of the streetAddress attribute of the relatant site object. Assume that this tracking is specified in the AttributeDefinedExpression siteStreet-Address:

```
currentSite VIRTUAL-ATTRIBUTE ::=
{
        COMPUTED-FROM                siteStreetAddress
        IDENTIFIED BY                currentSiteLbl
}
```

The value siteStreetAddress is of the type AttributeDefined-Expression. We expand this as shown below; this definition assumes that is-HousedAtLbl is the &roleLabel field of a defined is-housed-at ROLE information object, siteLbl is the &objectClassLabel of a defined site OBJECT-CLASS information object, and that streetAddressLbl is the &attributeLabel of a defined streetAddress ATTRIBUTE information object:

```
siteStreetAddress AttributeDefinedExpression ::=
{ track:
      { normal:
            { instance
                  {
                     role                       isHousedAtLbl,
                     relatantClass              siteLbl
                  }
               baseProperty
                  {
                     attribute: {actual:  streetAddressLbl}
}     }     }     }
```

This attribute-defined expression represents a single base attribute whose value is used directly, without being subjected to any algorithmic computation or type transformation. The entire right-hand side in the above assignment represents a single terminal symbol of the AttributeDefinedExpression. This symbol tracks the street-

Address native attribute of the `site` relatant object with which the `networkDevice` object plays the `is-housed-at` role.

24.6. Ordered Relationships

We are permitted to model certain relationships as *ordered*, that is, a subject class playing a role with a relatant multiplicity greater than 1 may request that all its relatant instances be presented as sequenced according to some criterion. The ordering criterion can be any attribute of the relatant, to which a specified comparator is applied. Multiple ordering criteria may be used, with the first being the primary ordering criterion, the next being the secondary criterion, and so on.

To specify ordered relationships, we need an enhancement to our `RELATIONSHIP` information object class template. This template now takes an optional field indicating the ordering. For each participant class, this field indicates the ordering, if any, requested for that class by its relatant:

```
RELATIONSHIP ::= CLASS
{
        &subject                OBJECT-CLASS,
        &forwardRole            ROLE,
        &subjectMultiplicity    Multiplicity OPTIONAL,
        &subjectOrdering        OrderingCriterion
                                    OPTIONAL, -- new field

        &relatant               OBJECT-CLASS,
        &reciprocalRole         ROLE OPTIONAL,
        &relatantMultiplicity   Multiplicity OPTIONAL,
        &relatantOrdering       OrderingCriterion
                                    OPTIONAL, -- new field

        &Attributes             ATTRIBUTE OPTIONAL,
        &Capsules               CAPSULE OPTIONAL,
        &relationshipLabel      OBJECT IDENTIFIER UNIQUE
}
WITH SYNTAX
{
        OBJECT-CLASS            &subject
        IN ROLE                 &forwardRole
        [ WITH MULTIPLICITY     &subjectMultiplicity ]
        [ ORDERED BY            &subjectOrdering ]
                                        -- new field

            RELATES TO
        OBJECT-CLASS            &relatant
```

```
            [ IN ROLE                    &reciprocalRole ]
            [ WITH MULTIPLICITY          &relatantMultiplicity ]
            [ ORDERED BY                 &relatantOrdering ]
                                              -- new field
            [ ATTRIBUTES                 &Attributes ]
            [ CAPSULES                   &Capsules ]
            IDENTIFIED BY                &relationshipLabel
     }
```

The type OrderingCriterion, used in this template for the &subject-Ordering and &relatantOrdering fields, is defined as

```
OrderingCriterion ::= SEQUENCE OF SEQUENCE
{
        orderingAttribute       AnyAttributeLabel,
        comparator              OrderingComparator
}
```

Here, the orderingAttribute field is AnyAttributeLabel, which must refer to one of the attributes of the participant object class being ordered. The type OrderingCriterion is a SEQUENCE OF type because the first element in the outer enclosing sequence is interpreted as the primary ordering criterion, the next the secondary criterion, and so on. The type OrderingComparator is a subtype of the general Comparator type defined in Chapter 10 and must be one of the following:

```
OrderingComparator ::= Comparator
                      (
                              lessThan            |
                              lesserOrEqualTo     |
                              greaterThan         |
                              greaterOrEqualTo
                      )
```

As an example, consider the aggregation relationship we modeled between a protocolStack and its component protocolEntity object class. A protocol-Stack object may request that its component protocolEntity objects be presented as ordered according to their operativeLayer attribute:

```
stackEntityAggregation RELATIONSHIP ::=
{
        OBJECT-CLASS             protocolStack
        IN ROLE                  has-as-a-part
            RELATES TO
        OBJECT-CLASS             protocolEntity
        IN ROLE                  is-a-part-of
        WITH MULTIPLICITY        zeroOrMore
        ORDERED BY               {{ orderingAttribute
                                      operativeLayerLbl,
                                    comparator   lessThan
                                 }}
        IDENTIFIED BY            stackEntityAggregationLbl
}
```

24.7. Virtual Object Classes

A virtual object class is defined using selection, projection, and conjunction on its base class. These virtualizing mechanisms may be used in isolation, or in combination with each other. We define the information object class VIRTUAL-OBJECT-CLASS in terms of its supporting base class and its bases of virtualization, as follows:

```
VIRTUAL-OBJECT-CLASS ::= CLASS
{
        &baseClassLabel          AnyObjectClassLabel,
        &selector                Selector OPTIONAL,
        &projector               Projector OPTIONAL,
        &conjunctor              Conjunctor OPTIONAL,
        &virtualObjectClassLabel
                                 OBJECT IDENTIFIER UNIQUE
}
WITH SYNTAX
{
        BASE-CLASS               &baseClassLabel
        [ SELECT                 &selector ]
        [ PROJECT                &projector ]
        [ CONJUNCT               &conjunctor ]
        IDENTIFIED BY            &virtualObjectClassLabel
}
```

In this specification, the fields &selector, &projector, and &conjunctor are all OPTIONAL because each virtual object class definition may use any combination of them.

Just as the set {ObjectClasses} represents the set of all defined OBJECT-CLASS information objects for actual object classes, the set {VirtualObject-Classes} represents all defined VIRTUAL-OBJECT-CLASS information objects for virtual object classes. We had also defined the type ObjectClassLabel as a constrained type:

```
ObjectClassLabel ::= OBJECT-CLASS.&objectClassLabel
                                      ({ObjectClasses})
```

Along the same lines, we define the type VirtualObjectClassLabel. This is defined as an OBJECT IDENTIFIER constrained to come from the &virtual-ObjectClassLabel fields of the VIRTUAL-OBJECT-CLASS information objects in the set {VirtualObjectClasses}:

```
VirtualObjectClassLabel ::= VIRTUAL-OBJECT-CLASS.
                                &virtualObjectClassLabel
                                ({VirtualObjectClasses})
```

We can now define the type AnyObjectClassLabel as either of these two types, as follows:

```
AnyObjectClassLabel ::= CHOICE
{
    actual          [0]         ObjectClassLabel,
    virtual         [1]         VirtualObjectClassLabel
}
```

The &baseClassLabel field of the VIRTUAL-OBJECT-CLASS information object class template has type AnyObjectClassLabel. With the definition above, the base class supporting a virtual object class can itself be either an actual or virtual object class.

We now define the types Selector, Projector, and Conjunctor. As we indicated in Chapter 21, the selector basis of virtualization in a virtual object class definition is simply a logical predicate. If multiple selectors are used, multiple logical predicates can be and-ed together in a single logical predicate. As indicated in the various logical predicates defined throughout our model for bases of specialization, a logical predicate can also represent concepts such as relatant attribute restriction, relatant specialization, and so on. Without repeating any of these concepts, we assume that all of them can be expressed when necessary in the `LogicalPredicate` type defining a selector basis of virtualization:

```
Selector ::= LogicalPredicate
```

The type `Projector` is easily defined, as it is simply an unordered list of all attributes and functions acquired as aspects by the virtual object class:

```
Projector ::= SET OF SEQUENCE
{
        grantedAspect           AnyPropertyLabel,
        grantingClass           AnyObjectClassLabel   OPTIONAL
}
```

Here, each granted aspect may be associated with its granting class, because in conjunct virtual classes granted aspects could come from either the base class or any one of the relatants with which it is conjuncted. The `grantingClass` field helps us to properly associate each aspect acquired by the conjunct class with the granting class. The `grantingClass` field is optional; if omitted, it defaults to the base class. The field `grantedAspect` has type `AnyPropertyLabel`. As defined earlier, this represents any attribute or function, actual or virtual, native or tracked. Because the `Projector` type is a list, it must be a SET OF such associated aspects.

As indicated in Chapter 21, conjunctors are conceptually specified in terms of the `trackRelatants()` function to indicate the relatant classes which must be conjuncted with the base class to create the conjunct virtual class. Thus, we may specify the type `Conjunctor` as

```
Conjunctor ::= SET OF TrackedRelatant
```

Because more than one conjunctor may be used at the same time, it must be a SET OF type. When used together with a projector, the specificand conjunct virtual class acquires the indicated aspects from its base and relatant classes. The compiler knows the multiplicity of each tracking role in each value of type `TrackedRelatant` specified in the conjunctor. Thus, the number of members in the conjunct virtual class is governed either by the multiplicity of each tracking role, or the membership of the tracked relatant class, as explained in Chapter 21.

24.8. Object Constraints and Rules

Constraints and rules are properties of object classes. To specify them as such, we need to enhance our definition of the `OBJECT-CLASS` information object class template. If the specified constraint or rule is a spanning constraint or spanning rule, then the OBJECT-

CLASS for which it is specified as a property is assumed to be the anchoring class for that property.

```
OBJECT-CLASS ::= CLASS
{
        &SpecializesFrom            Specialization OPTIONAL,
        &Attributes                 ATTRIBUTE OPTIONAL,
        &Functions                  FUNCTION OPTIONAL,
        &MandatoryCapsules          CAPSULE OPTIONAL,
        &OptionalCapsules           CAPSULE OPTIONAL,
        &VirtualAttributes          VIRTUAL-ATTRIBUTE
                                                  OPTIONAL,
        &VirtualFunctions           VIRTUAL-FUNCTION
                                                  OPTIONAL,
        &Constraints                CONSTRAINT OPTIONAL,
                                           -- new field
        &Rules                      RULE OPTIONAL,
                                           -- new field
        &objectClassLabel           OBJECT IDENTIFIER UNIQUE
}
WITH SYNTAX
{
        [SPECIALIZES-FROM           &SpecializesFrom]
        [ATTRIBUTES                 &Attributes]
        [FUNCTIONS                  &Functions]
        [MANDATORY CAPSULES         &MandatoryCapsules]
        [OPTIONAL CAPSULES          &OptionalCapsules]
        [VIRTUAL ATTRIBUTES         &VirtualAttributes]
        [VIRTUAL FUNCTIONS          &VirtualFunctions]
        [CONSTRAINTS                &Constraints]-- new field
        [RULES                      &Rules]     -- new field
        IDENTIFIED BY               &objectClassLabel
}
```

This information object class definition contains the two new fields &Constraints and &Rules. These fields are *object set fields* defining a set of CONSTRAINT and RULE information objects respectively. Their supporting information object class templates may be specified as follows:

```
CONSTRAINT ::= CLASS
{
        &constraintCondition       ComparedADEs,
        &soft                      BOOLEAN DEFAULT FALSE
                                                   OPTIONAL,
        &constraintLabel           OBJECT IDENTIFIER UNIQUE
}
WITH SYNTAX
{
        CONDITION                  &constraintCondition
        [SOFT                      &soft]
        IDENTIFIED BY              &constraintLabel
}
```

In this specification, the &soft field, if present, indicates whether or not the specificand constraint is soft. If absent, the constraint is assumed hard. The type ComparedADEs is, as explained in Chapter 22, simply a pair of attribute-defined expressions with a comparator between them, which acts as the constraint condition. This may be specified as

```
ComparedADEs ::= SEQUENCE
{
        leftComparand       AttributeDefinedExpression,
        is                  Comparator,
        rightComparand      AttributeDefinedExpression
}
```

Since the type AttributeDefinedExpression has as its terminal symbols properties which are either native or tracked, this definition is sufficient to specify both native and spanning constraints. The type Comparator is the same as that defined in Chapter 10.

Similarly, the information object class RULE may be defined as

```
RULE ::= CLASS
{
        &precondition             ComparedADEs,
        &thenTriggeredFunctions   SET OF Property,
        &elseTriggeredFunctions   SET OF Property OPTIONAL,
        &ruleLabel                OBJECT IDENTIFIER UNIQUE
}
```

```
WITH SYNTAX
{
    IF                          &precondition
    THEN                        &thenTriggeredFunctions
    [ELSE                       &elseTriggeredFunctions]
    IDENTIFIED BY               &ruleLabel
}
```

The type `Property` is the same type defined earlier in the chapter. Since it can accommodate both native and tracked functions, this definition is sufficient to specify both native and spanning rules. When used in the definition of a RULE, the type `Property` must ultimately resolve to the type `AnyFunctionWithArguments`; it is not permitted to resolve to an attribute. The `arguments` field of the type `AnyFunctionWithArguments` defining a triggered rule function typically uses the values of attributes, constants, and return results of functions which occur in the `Attribute-DefinedExpressions` of the `&precondition` field, although it is not mandatory for a triggered rule function to use only these values.

24.9. Specialization Using Constraints and Rules

Subclasses may specialize from superclasses using constraints and rules as bases of specialization. We need mechanisms to formally describe the modes of specialization by constraint addition, constraint restriction, rule addition, rule precondition contravariance, and rule function addition. If a subclass adds a spanning constraint or rule, the constraint or rule is considered to be anchored at that class.

Like other addition mechanisms, constraint addition is simply described using a "label predicate", that is, merely indicating the label of a new constraint as a `SimpleLogicalPredicate` is interpreted to mean that the indicated constraint has been added by the subclass as a property. To assist in this specification, we define the type `ConstraintLabel` as an object class field type:

```
ConstraintLabel  ::= CONSTRAINT.&constraintLabel
                                ({Constraints})
```

where `Constraints` is the set of all defined CONSTRAINT information objects. With this specification, simply specifying a value of the type `ConstraintLabel` in a `SimpleLogicalPredicate` is interpreted to mean that the subclass adds the constraint referred to by that value as a property.

Specialization by constraint restriction requires us not only to specify the constraint label but also to indicate the new condition which acts as the tighter constraint. To accommodate this, we define the new type

```
ConstraintPredicate ::= SEQUENCE
{
        constraint              ConstraintLabel,
        condition               ComparedADEs
}
```

When a `ConstraintPredicate` is used as a basis of specialization, the tighter constraint condition denoted by the `condition` field conceptually replaces the old condition in the `&constraintCondition` field of the inherited constraint. As with other such substitutions, this conceptual replacement occurs only in the copy of the constraint condition in the subclass; the condition in the superclass remains unaffected, as is the definition of the `CONSTRAINT` information object itself stored in the schema of the model information base. The compiler ensures — if it is lexically possible to do so — that the new condition does not cause a relaxation of the inherited constraint condition, and that the new condition does not conflict with the conditions of other constraints. If it does, the specialization is rejected.

As with all predicates, these predicates can also be used in interrogative, declarative, imperative, and qualificative contexts against the schema of a network model. A constraint "label predicate" can be used to query, declare, establish, or qualify a particular constraint in a particular object class. The `ConstraintPredicate` type can be used to query, declare, establish, or qualify a particular condition for a particular constraint of a particular object class.

The mode of specialization by rule addition is similar. A new rule added by a subclass is specified simply as a rule label, which is a value of the type `RuleLabel`. This type is defined as follows, assuming that `Rules` is the set of all `RULE` information objects:

```
RuleLabel ::= RULE.&ruleLabel({Rules})
```

The mechanism of rule precondition contravariance requires a predicate which indicates both the rule label and the new precondition:

```
RulePreconditionPredicate ::= SEQUENCE
{
        rule                    RuleLabel,
        precondition            ComparedADEs
}
```

In addition, the specialization mode of rule function addition requires us to specify not only the label of the rule to which the new functions are added but also the added function and the arguments, if any, which the added function requires. We therefore define the type `RuleFunctionPredicate` as follows:

```
RuleFunctionPredicate ::= SEQUENCE
{
      rule                      RuleLabel,
      thenFunction              Property        OPTIONAL,
      elseFunction              Property        OPTIONAL
}
```

Because the type `Property` can be native or tracked, the predicate above is adequate to express the addition of either a native or tracked function to a rule. When used in a `RuleFunctionPredicate`, the type `Property` must ultimately resolve to the type `AnyFunctionWithArguments`; it cannot resolve to an attribute. In this predicate, the function indicated by the `thenFunction` field is considered to be conceptually added to the `&thenTriggeredFunction` field of the rule inherited by the subclass, and the function indicated by the `elseFunction` field is considered to be conceptually added to the `&elseTriggeredFunction` field. Both fields are optional, because either a `thenFunction` or an `elseFunction` could be added without the other. As with all rule functions, the newly added function must already be an inherited or added property of the specializing subclass, or a property of one of its inherited or added relatant classes.

As usual, these predicates can be used in either the interrogative, declarative, imperative, or qualificative contexts. A rule label "predicate" can be used to query, declare, establish, or qualify a particular rule as a property of a particular class; a rule precondition predicate can be used to query, declare, establish or qualify its precondition; and a rule function predicate can be used to query, declare, establish, or qualify its then- and else- functions.

As with all specializations, the new rule precondition specified by a `RulePreconditionPredicate` and the new rule functions specified by a `RuleFunctionPredicate` are considered to conceptually replace only the copy of the fields of the inherited rule in the subclass; the rule itself remains unchanged in the superclass and in the schema of the model information base.

We summarize the specialization modes using rules and constraints as below:

Specialization by Constraint Addition: Use the constraint label to indicate the addition of the constraint in a `SimpleLogicalPredicate`.

Specialization by Constraint Restriction: Use a `ConstraintPredicate` to indicate the new value of the constraint condition in a `SimpleLogicalPredicate`.

Specialization by Rule Addition: Use the rule label to indicate the addition of the rule in a `SimpleLogicalPredicate`.

Specialization by Rule Precondition Contravariance: Use a `RulePreconditionPredicate` to indicate the new precondition of the rule in a `SimpleLogicalPredicate`.

Specialization by Rule Function Addition: Use a `RuleFunction-Predicate` to indicate the newly added `then` and `else` functions of the rule in a `SimpleLogicalPredicate`.

Finally, we add all these new predicates as permitted modes of specialization in the type `SimpleLogicalPredicate`:

```
SimpleLogicalPredicate ::= CHOICE
{
        attributeAdded          [0]        AttributeLabel,
        functionAdded           [1]        FunctionLabel,
        capsuleAdded            [2]        CapsuleLabel,
        capsuleFixed            [3]        CapsuleLabel,
        attributeDomainRestricted          [4]
                        AttributeLogicalPredicate,
        argumentDomainRelaxed              [5]
                        ArgumentLogicalPredicate,
        resultDomainRestricted             [6]
                        ResultLogicalPredicate,
        functionExtended                   [7]
                        FunctionExtensionPredicate,
        subjectMultiplicityRegressed       [8]
                        MultiplicityLogicalPredicate,
        relatantMultiplicityRestricted     [9]
                        MultiplicityLogicalPredicate,
        relationshipAdded                  [10]
                        RelationshipPredicate,
        relatantSpecialized                [11]
                        RelatantSpecializationPredicate,
        constraintAdded                    [12]
                        ConstraintLabel,
        constraintRestricted               [13]
                        ConstraintRestrictionPredicate,
        ruleAdded                          [14]
                        RuleLabel,
        rulePreconditionRelaxed            [15]
                        RulePreconditionPredicate,
        ruleFunctionAdded                  [16]
                        RuleFunctionPredicate

}
```

24.10. Summary

The algorithm for computing a virtual attribute or function is formally specified in terms of an attribute-defined expression. This expands into a grammar allowing base attributes and functions to combine in various mathematical and logical expressions. The terminal symbols of this grammar can be either native properties of the same object class as the specificand virtual attribute, or tracked properties from relatant object classes. Virtual properties are specified in their own independent information object class templates, which are independently registered.

Tracked properties are conceptually specified in terms of the `track-Relatants()` and `countRelatants()` functions. The definition of a tracked virtual property with a base property in a relatant class must specify both the base property and the relatant class from which it must be tracked. A tracked virtual property representing a count of the relatant instances must specify all the relatant instances which must be counted. These functions are generally used in closed-role closed-class and closed-role open-class forms.

Virtual object classes must be formally specified with selectors, projectors, and conjunctors. A selector is a logical predicate, a projector is a list of properties, and a conjunctor is a list of tracked relatant classes. A virtual object class may be defined with selection, projection, and conjunction simultaneously.

Rules and constraints are defined as properties of an object class, each with its own supporting information object class definition which is independently registered. The definition of a constraint and the precondition of a rule is performed in terms of two attribute-defined expressions with a comparator conceptually placed between them. Because the terminal symbols of these attribute-defined expressions can include native or tracked properties, the formal specifications can be used for both native and spanning constraints and rules. Specialization principles which use rules and constraints are expressed using predicates defined for that purpose.

The complete specification of an object class template includes all the virtual attributes, virtual functions, constraints, and rules which that object class possesses as properties.

25. The Metamodel

"I never metamodel I didn't like."

— *anonymous fashion photographer.*

25.1. Introduction

We present here the metamodel of specialization theory. A metamodel is a model of the modeling methodology itself. This chapter is of use to persons designing and creating software tools which implement modeling methodologies. These include architecture tools for network synthesis and simulation software, CASE tools for network operations software, and model compilers for network management software. Readers desiring only to apply the modeling methodology to actually design networks, rather than build modeling tools, may skip this chapter entirely.

25.2. The Metamodel

In this chapter, we define a model of the methodology of specialization theory itself. We use the modeling methodology itself to define its own metamodel. In specialization theory, the "free variables" (that is, the open "slots" into which user-defined "formulas" can be substituted [Gode30, Gode31]) are object classes and relationships. In the metamodel, therefore, *modeling constructs* are substituted for object classes, and *associations* are substituted for relationships.

Thus, objects, object classes, attributes, functions, relationships, constraints and rules all correspond to the *object classes* of the metamodel, while the connotational couplings between them become operational couplings in the metamodel. These include property assignment (**has-as-a-property**, **is-a-property-of**), instantiation (**has-as-an-instance**, **is-an-instance-of**), inheritance (**inherits-from**, **bequeaths-to**), specialization (**specializes-from**, **specializes-into**), and so forth; all of these correspond to *relationship*

554

roles in the metamodel. Table 25-1 describes the correspondence between the modeling methodology and its metamodel.

Model	→	Metamodel
Modeling construct	→	Object class
Connotational semantics	→	Operational semantics
Association	→	Relationship
Reflexive association	→	Involute relationship
Symmetric association	→	Commutative relationship
Transitive association	→	Transitive relationship
Complementary association	→	Reciprocal role

Table 25-1: Mapping Models to Metamodels

Because the methodology can be described using its own metamodel, it is possible to supply the metamodel as input to a compiler which supports the methodology. Some tools feed both the description of the modeled application system and the methodology metamodel simultaneously as input to their compilers. This enables the run-time environment to dynamically control and operate both the application system and the control environment itself. For our application (the architecture, operations, and management of communication networks), this is not very useful. For our purposes, a limited form of such "self-comprehension" by the methodology is generally only required when the schemas of different networks are negotiated on-line at interconnection time, prior to beginning interoperation. Nevertheless, it is of some benefit that the methodology is *closed under self-description* and so can be *reflective* (i.e., "self-understanding" and "introspective") when necessary.

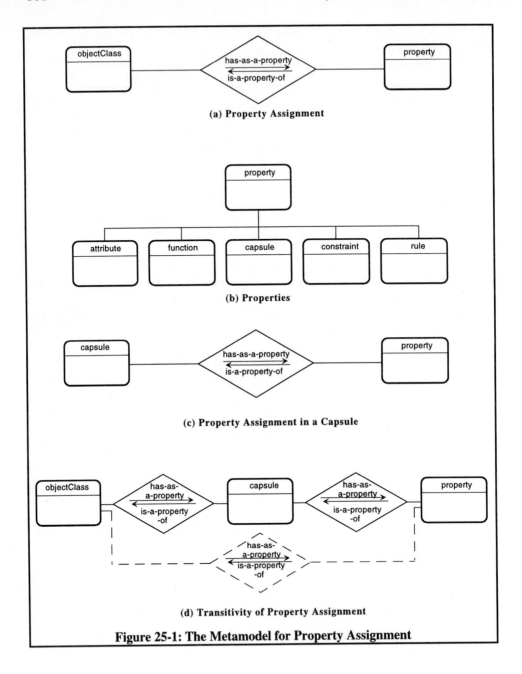

(a) **Property Assignment**

(b) **Properties**

(c) **Property Assignment in a Capsule**

(d) **Transitivity of Property Assignment**

Figure 25-1: The Metamodel for Property Assignment

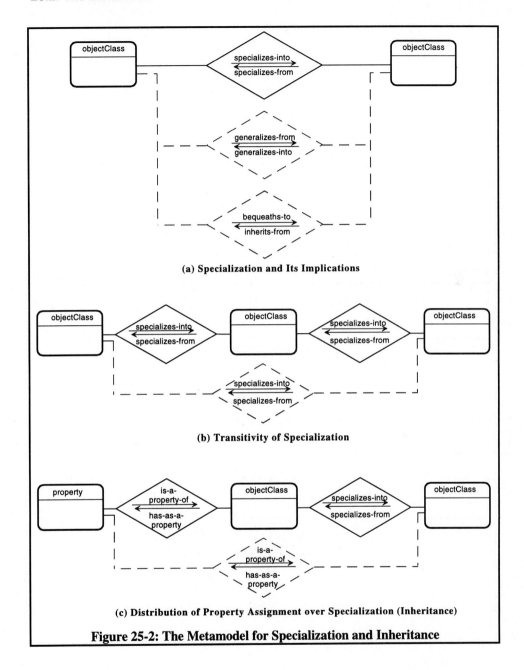

(a) Specialization and Its Implications

(b) Transitivity of Specialization

(c) Distribution of Property Assignment over Specialization (Inheritance)

Figure 25-2: The Metamodel for Specialization and Inheritance

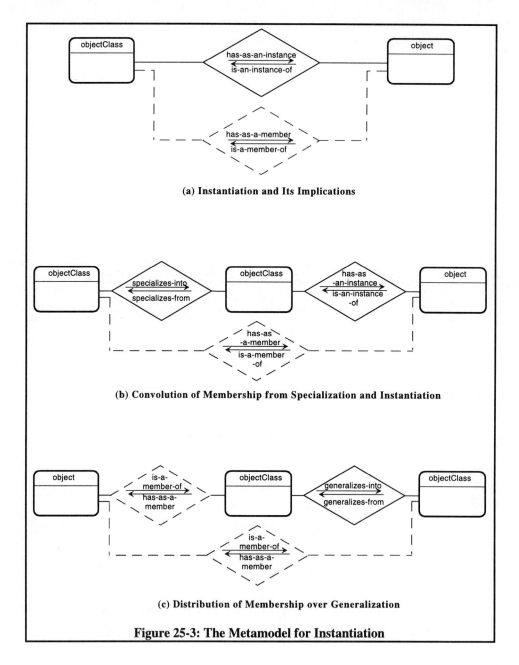

(a) Instantiation and Its Implications

(b) Convolution of Membership from Specialization and Instantiation

(c) Distribution of Membership over Generalization

Figure 25-3: The Metamodel for Instantiation

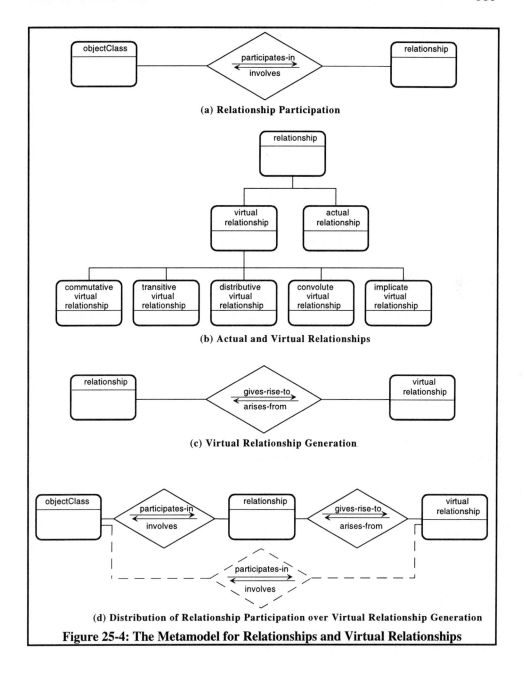

(a) Relationship Participation

(b) Actual and Virtual Relationships

(c) Virtual Relationship Generation

(d) Distribution of Relationship Participation over Virtual Relationship Generation

Figure 25-4: The Metamodel for Relationships and Virtual Relationships

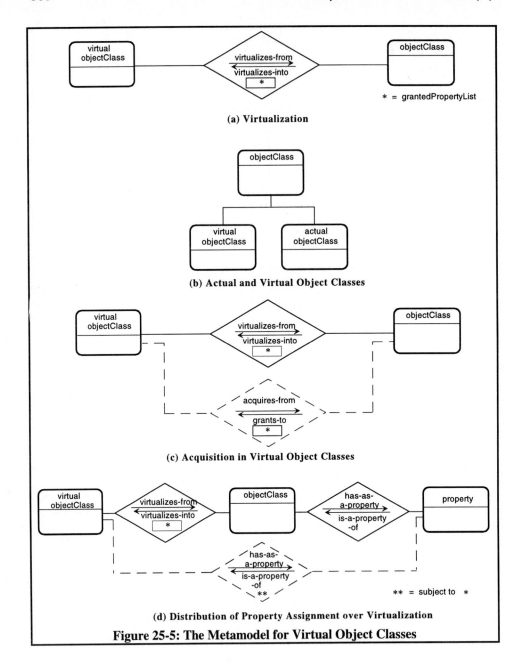

(a) Virtualization

(b) Actual and Virtual Object Classes

(c) Acquisition in Virtual Object Classes

(d) Distribution of Property Assignment over Virtualization

Figure 25-5: The Metamodel for Virtual Object Classes

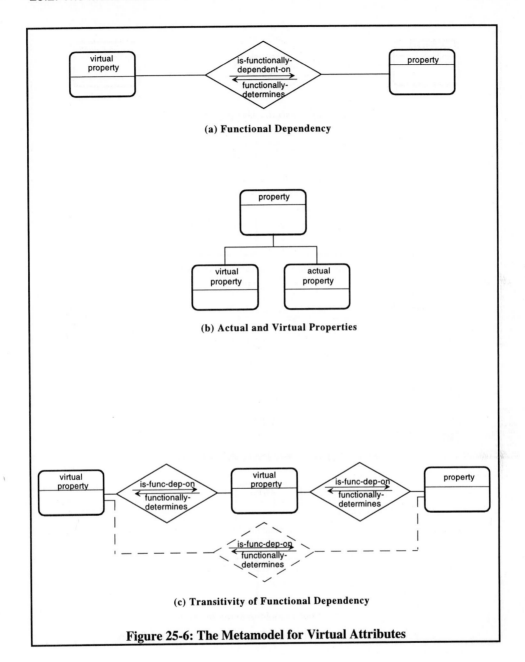

(a) **Functional Dependency**

(b) **Actual and Virtual Properties**

(c) **Transitivity of Functional Dependency**

Figure 25-6: The Metamodel for Virtual Attributes

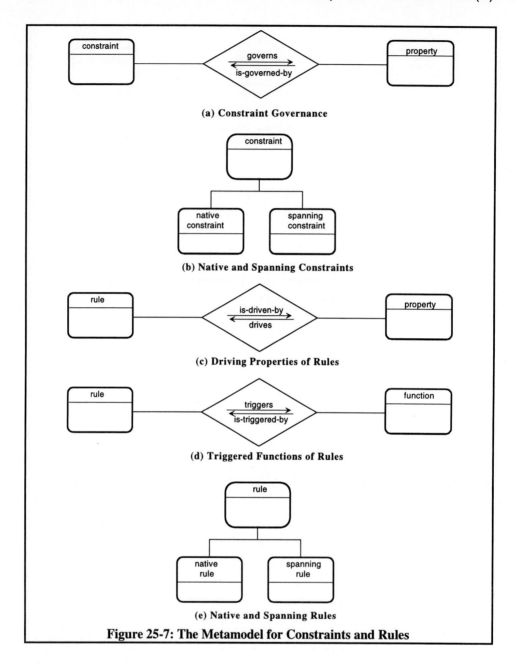

(a) Constraint Governance

(b) Native and Spanning Constraints

(c) Driving Properties of Rules

(d) Triggered Functions of Rules

(e) Native and Spanning Rules

Figure 25-7: The Metamodel for Constraints and Rules

26. The Theory and its Implementation

"The boss sent out email asking for comments on network reliability, but since no one responded he figured everything must be okay."

— *anonymous executive secretary.*

26.1. Introduction

In this chapter, we consider aspects of the mathematical foundations supporting specialization theory. We introduce applications of the methodology which can benefit from the use of an integrated network model. We describe how each such application can use an information base which embodies a subset of a comprehensive network model, and we consider possible implementation environments for the methodology.

26.2. The Modeling Methodology

The entire thrust of our methodology has been to apply the formal principles of specialization theory to network modeling and thereby arrive at a semantically rich set of specifications in an implementation-independent manner. Our methodology attempts to create a symbolic model of a communication network by describing its structural and behavioral properties in a way that minimizes the number of facts a network architect has to specify. It puts the burden on the model information base to infer internally as many extended semantics as it can from the basic primitives provided by the network architect.

As we have seen from our consideration of encapsulation, inheritance, relationships, virtual attributes, virtual relationships, spanning constraints, and spanning rules, we can weave a rich semantic network from a few basic modeling constructs. Much of this semantic network is internally inferred within the model information base; only a few basic facts must be specified by the architect. The network architect need merely specify objects, relationships, and their properties *declaratively*; she need not indicate to the system how to reason with them *procedurally*. The power to use declaratively specified facts to derive extended semantics internally within the model is an important feature of specialization theory. This power arises from its ability to capture many semantics of the application domain precisely and express them formally [Gunt92, Wins93].

Because communication networks themselves are increasingly complex, it is important to provide models for them so that they can be simulated before being constructed. Creating a comprehensive formal model for a network is an extraordinarily complex task. By bringing the formal principles of specialization theory to bear on this problem, we make a start toward formulating it as a series of solvable subproblems by imposing some order and structure using object-oriented techniques.

In the entire development of the methodology, we have endeavored to ensure that the specification technique remains as abstract as possible and completely implementation-independent. Although we have used a formal syntax as our specification notation, this notation has been deliberately chosen to be a non-executable language. Appropriate model compilers can compile the formal specification of any network system into actual implementations in a manner that best suits the target system.

The modeling methodology uses abstractions which are suited to multiple applications. The same abstractions and modeling constructs may be used for a number of different purposes. Multiple activities which require reasoning with a symbolic model of the network — such as network architecture and planning, network operations and network management — can all use the same underlying abstractions provided by our methodology. The creation of a unified application-independent symbolic model of a communication network is an important goal for the network architectures of tomorrow; the methodology of this book attempts to make a modest start in that direction.

26.3. Confluence of Multiple Paradigms

Our application of specialization theory uses features from multiple modeling techniques, and as such represents an *integrated* modeling methodology. Some of the paradigms which contribute features to the methodology are listed below.

- *The Object-Oriented Paradigm* contributes the concepts of abstraction, encapsulation, generalization, specialization, and inheritance, which we use for building up taxonomical and evolutionary hierarchies.

- *The Entity-Relationship Paradigm* is used in our consideration of relationships between object classes. This contributes the notions of roles and cardinalities, which we make more precise with our consideration of bidirectional roles and attribute-defined multiplicity bounds.

- *The Procedural Programming Paradigm* is used to model the internal mechanisms of the functions of an object class where necessary. We use formal techniques for the internal mechanisms of functions to make procedural function specifications as implementation-independent as possible.

- *The Relational Modeling Paradigm* contributes the correspondence between the members of an object class and the tuple sets of a relation, permitting many relational operations on object classes. Other notions contributed by this model include attribute-defined expressions, logical predicates for subsetting, and virtual object classes arising from selection, projection, and conjunction.

- *The Knowledge Representation Paradigm*, a rich subfield of artificial intelligence, contributes the precise specification of bases of specialization as logical predicates. Other uses of logical predicates, such as native and spanning constraints which govern the interaction between objects, also come from this paradigm [Brac92].

- *The Logic Programming Paradigm* contributes the rules which permit objects to execute functions based on the changes in the structural properties of themselves and their relatants. Since inheritance can also be viewed as a logical inference about a consequent subclass property from an antecedent superclass property, the consideration of various bases of specialization (e.g., restriction and contravariance) are driven by the notion that strengthening an antecedent or weakening the consequent preserves the integrity of an inference rule.

- *The Set Theory Paradigm* permits the treatment of the members of an object class as the elements of a set, thus permitting specialization and generalization to be viewed as conceptual subset and superset operations. The process of tracking values from a given object of one class through a relationship role to relatant objects of another class may also be viewed as a mapping function between sets. The concept of virtual object classes also arises as a consequence of the set-theoretic notion of relations [Ullm88].

- *Denotational semantics* provides much of the theoretical foundation for viewing monotonic inheritance as structural induction on object classes. As we will see in the next section, the notion of specialization as a complete partial order and relationships as mapping functions between subject sets and relatant sets are important concepts of the methodology.

Specialization theory is representative of a general trend which uses different paradigms from programming theory, mathematics, and logic to arrive at a unified, comprehensive *multiparadigmatic* methodology [Gogu87, Mese92]. In these methodologies, knowledge is stated declaratively as far as possible, with the housekeeping required to track, record and maintain this knowledge being provided as built-in primitives by the system. This reduces the programming effort on the network architect.

This trend is reflected in many new programming languages [Case91], the new generation of database architectures [Silb91], and in new engineering modeling methodologies similar to ours [Rumb91a]. Figure 26-1 illustrates this trend.

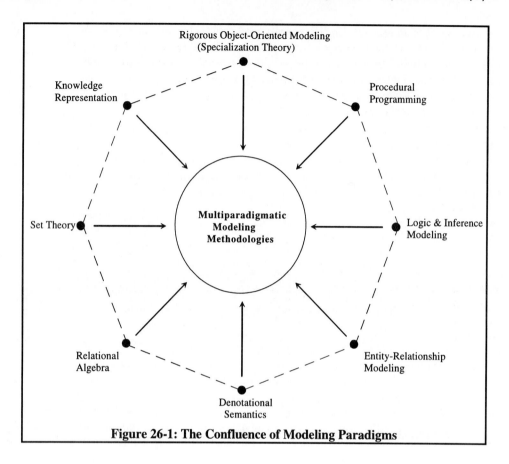

Figure 26-1: The Confluence of Modeling Paradigms

26.4. Toward an Object Calculus

In many modeling methodologies, *mathematical calculi* are used as a notation which can express modeling concepts succinctly. Though expressions in such calculi are mathematical in nature and are generally not machine-processable, they are useful in the initial development of object models and in communicating modeling concepts to network architects and programmers. Experience has shown that much iteration is likely during the early stages of design, and proposed object modeling concepts are best expressed using a mathematical notation. Once sufficient stability has been achieved, expressions or formulas in this notation can then be used as the basis for formal coding in a compilable language. Thus, a calculus can serve as a form of "pseudocode" for software implementations of modeling concepts.

An *object calculus* could be used to express the object modeling concepts of specialization theory as mathematical formulas. Such a mathematical notation could succinctly indicate data types of properties and could express property assignment semantics for object classes. It could define the membership of each object class by writing logical formulas which an object must satisfy in order to be a member of that class. It could be particularly useful in the definition of formulas for creating new object classes by expressing extension and incremental refinement in *assignment statements* which include a formal basis of specialization. It could also be very useful in defining formulas for virtual attribute assignment. Both actual and virtual relationships, as well as closures, could be concisely expressed in such a calculus.

Because specialization theory has underpinnings in set theory and relational modeling, all set-theoretic notation, as well as all notation from the relational algebra and the relational calculus, could be used in an object calculus. Some concepts (e.g., virtual object classes and attribute domain restriction) can already be expressed in standard relational algebra. In addition, both tuple and domain relational calculus [Codd70, Codd72, Codd90, Ullm88] can also express some specialization theory semantics if object class names are used as relation names, property names as field names of the relation, and object instance names as tuple identifiers.

A complete object calculus could become the notation for the mathematical formulas of specialization theory, much as the λ-calculus is the notation for the mathematical formulas of computability theory and semantics, and the relational calculus is the notation for the mathematical formulas of relational modeling theory [Tars41]. These other calculi can be used as the foundation of an object modeling calculus, just as they are used to support the theory of object-oriented programming languages. In such an object calculus, a rich set of theorems expressing the mathematical correctness of various modeling principles can be created. Although we have made intuitive appeals, largely by example, for the correctness of the modeling principles of specialization theory, we have not proved their correctness with mathematical rigor. An object calculus can be used as a vehicle for such rigorous proofs, using as adjuncts a basic set of axioms about objects, properties, and monotonic inheritance, including concepts which are well known in type theory [Pfen92].

Model-Theoretic and Proof-Theoretic Semantics

All along, our approach to methodology has been to provide *model-theoretic semantics*, implying that the "meaning" of any statement in the model (e.g., a property assignment or a relationship assignment) is a fact which can be proved to be either true or false with respect to some actual referent model system. An object calculus will permit us to reinterpret specialization theory in terms of *proof-theoretic semantics*, implying that the "meaning" of any statement in the model is an equation which, through symbolic manipulation using given mathematical rules, can be logically proved or disproved as a "theorem".

One proof-theoretic interpretation of specialization theory (there are many others) can be made as follows:

- A statement of a *relationship* between any two object classes is a well-formed "sentence" or a "theorem" which can be proved or disproved;

- A *specialization principle* is a rule which defines the permitted substitutions in the symbolic manipulation of any "sentence" or "theorem";

- A *virtual relationship* is a rule which defines the permitted conjunctions and disjunctions in the symbolic manipulation of any "sentence" or "theorem".

As with all formal systems, it is possible to start from a premise ("axiom") and "prove" a conclusion ("theorem") using pure token-shunting rules [Russ13, Witt22]. These are also sometimes referred to as *rewriting* rules [Abit93, Mese93]. Thus, all the connotational semantics of specialization theory (specialization, generalization, property assignment, etc.) simply becomes the rules for symbolic manipulation in a formal system. Using such symbolic manipulation rules in an object calculus, it is possible, for example, to prove the existence of one or more inherited relationships between descendant classes (and any consequent virtual relationships arising therefrom) given the actual relationships between ancestral classes, which must exist to axiomatize this particular proof. Indeed, some form of such resolution actually takes place in the model information base at specification time.

There are many other possible proof-theoretic interpretations of the connotational semantics of specialization theory: for example, given a specification for a virtual attribute and the existence of its tracking relationship, it is possible to "prove" a property assignment for that attribute; or, given a spanning constraint or a spanning rule for some ancestral classes, it is possible to "prove" that it is satisfied by their descendant classes using the permitted specialization principles. The specialization principles of specialization theory have sound support in programming language theory as *typing rules*. For example, in denotational semantics, a typing rule called the *subsumption rule* makes possible certain typing judgments about terms; this is equivalent to the specialization principle of attribute domain restriction [Gunt92].

Denotational Semantics

The symbology of *denotational semantics* can also serve as a foundation of an object calculus to provide abstract reasoning about the "meaning" of associations and relationships [Gunt92, Wins93]. In denotational semantics, inheritance (extension and restriction) can be defined in terms of pure structural induction on ordered object classes. We may view inheritance as a *complete partial order* among object classes. Suppose we define the binary *substitutability* association **can-be-replaced-by** between object classes as being the same as **specializes-into**, with the addition that (unlike **specializes-into**) a class can also bear this relation with *itself*. Thus, in any true "sentence" or "theorem" about object classes (that is, a relationship), an object class **can-be-replaced-by** any of its descendants, or by itself, and still yield a true "theorem". This simply asserts relationship inheritance.

The relation **can-be-replaced-by** is *reflexive* (classA **can-be-replaced-by** classA), *transitive* (if classA **can-be-replaced-by** classB and classB **can-be-replaced-by** classC, then classA **can-be-replaced-by** classC), and *antisymmetric* (if classA **can-be-replaced-by** classB, then it cannot be that classB **can-be-replaced-by** classA, unless classB is the same as classA). Thus, **can-be-replaced-by** defines a *partial order* between object classes. (If it were *symmetric*, it would define an *equivalence relation* rather than a partial order.) Further, this partial order is *complete* because every branch in the inheritance hierarchy has a leaf node; in addition, it is also *pointed* as it has a least element (the root of the hierarchy). Indeed, the construction of a monotonic inheritance hierarchy can be viewed as a structural induction in which the structure of every class is inductively defined in terms of its superclass.

Relationships can also be viewed in denotational semantics as *monotonic functions* which map a set of subject classes onto a set of relatant classes. They are monotonic because it is true that if `classA` participates in a relationship with `classX`, then every descendant of `classA` participates in the same (well-founded or degenerate) relationship with some descendant of `classX` (or `classX` itself). This simply asserts specialized relatant inheritance.

Many similar concepts of denotational semantics apply to object modeling [Gunt94], and have been used in various other calculi as the theoretical support of object-oriented programming [Nier93, Lisk93]. Other formal notations such as *Object Z* [ISO WG7/N6089, Carr89, Duke90, Duke91, Rose92, Kilo93a] can also serve as an object calculus to express some basic concepts described herein, although specialization theory provides a stronger treatment of relationships, roles, and virtual semantics. It should be noted that recent work in modeling object-oriented concepts in terms of the bounded second-order lambda calculus $F_\le$, has shown that type-checking $F_\le$ is undecidable [Pier92]. In some cases, though, type-checking for restricted variants of languages based on $F_\le$ is decidable, although the problem remains NP-hard [Bruc93].

In denotational semantics, the specialization principles of our model can axiomatize the proof system from which the relationship principles can be proven as theorems. (Care should be exercised while using inter-disciplinary approaches because of terminology differences. For example, the term *full abstraction* has a different meaning in denotational semantics, and the term *isomorphic* is defined slightly differently in *category theory*, an abstract branch of mathematics which can be applied to sets and partial orders [Aspe91].)

26.5. Some Implementation Issues

The specification of our modeling methodology is implementation-independent. Nevertheless, it is instructive to examine possible implementation vehicles for this methodology. It should be borne in mind that any network system is not restricted to a single choice of implementation; different parts of the network model may be implemented in different ways, each in a manner most appropriate for the part.

Because our methodology formalizes the concepts of specialization theory in a compilable notation, it can be parsed by various translators to generate different implementations in different languages. For each part of the model, the implementation mechanism should be chosen in a manner which best suits that part. For example, if performance is a consideration during run-time operation, then resolution of inheritance structures and tracking relationships by following pointers may be time-expensive; various optimizations can be performed to increase performance. Each implementation is permitted to perform its own optimizations as long as the semantics are preserved.

Fragmented and Replicated Objects

Object classes can be fairly complex if they possess many attributes, functions, virtual attributes, virtual functions, constraints, and rules. When implemented, it is possible that the instances of an object class are not represented as single, cohesive units. Rather, an object instance may be implemented as *fragments*. Some properties of an object may be represented in core memory, others may have a database representation, while yet others may be registers in hardware devices which are directly interrogated to resolve attribute values. All such fragmentary representations of objects are permitted, as long as they can be conceptually pieced back together when required [Kler91].

It is also possible that object fragments, or entire objects, may be *replicated*. This means that the same property of an object instance may be stored in multiple locations. This is sometimes necessary to optimize performance: if the retrieval of a particular object property takes an unacceptably long time, a copy of the property may be stored elsewhere for faster retrieval. Of course, this engenders other problems, such as the resynchronization of all copies of the replicated information when its value changes. This area has been the subject of much research and has many solutions [Bern87]. The trade-offs that must be made when fragmenting and replicating object information must consider such factors as frequency of retrieval, frequency of updates, and so on [Bapa92, Bapa93b].

Eager Evaluation of Intensional Information

Our methodology uses both *actual* and *virtual* facts in reasoning about networks. In an implementation platform, this is often called *extensional* information (facts which must be explicitly specified) and *intensional* information (facts which can be inferred by the platform from other facts) [Ullm88]. Intensional information is also called *derived data*, that is, information which arises from the interdependency between various items [Smit93a]. Many candidate implementation vehicles support the definition of extensional information; only a few support intensional information. For those that do not support derived data, we must write application software ourselves to infer all our virtual features.

If an implementation platform does support virtual or intensional facts, it is possible that for optimal performance much of the intensional information in our model could be evaluated ahead of time, before it is required. This is known as *eager evaluation*. For example, if an object instance has a virtual attribute tracked from a relatant object, the virtual attribute may be implemented as a copy of the actual attribute, the value of the two copies being always maintained in synchronization using some monitoring or change-propagation mechanism. This will ensure that the value is always correctly available when the virtual attribute is queried, without incurring the expense of tracking and resolving it at run time. By contrast, if the retrieval frequency and the cost of run-time resolution is low, the evaluation of the virtual attribute may be *lazy*, that is, it may be actually resolved by tracking to its base attribute every time it is queried. Lazy evaluation eliminates the need to keep multiple copies of the same information synchronized.

Using the same analogy, instances of virtual relationships and instances of virtual object classes may also be determined using either eager or lazy evaluation as their query patterns warrant, as long as they conceptually reflect their underlying base constructs at the time of each query.

Hierarchy Telescoping

A special case of optimization is the technique of *hierarchy telescoping*, which in effect performs eager evaluation over the **specializes-from** and **specializes-into** associations of an inheritance hierarchy [Kim90b]. In this technique, each implemented concrete object possesses not only the attributes and functions which its class originates but also contains *copies* of fixed attributes and functions which it inherits from its ancestral classes. Because the hierarchy is essentially "flattened", this eliminates the need to resolve inherited properties by conducting a dynamic search up the inheritance hierarchy, thus optimizing the performance of the system. It is possible to have an implementation with a *partially telescoped hierarchy* in which some properties are copied into concrete objects and some properties are resolved by searching upwards into ancestral classes. If necessary, telescoping may be selectively performed on a class-by-class basis, or even an object-by-object basis.

Computing Transitive Closures

Many aspects of our model require the evaluation of *transitive closures*. These include the enumeration of descendant classes, the enumeration of the component breakdown of an aggregate, and the enumeration of relatants by transitive virtual relationships (and by virtual relationships which distribute over, convolute from, or are implied by transitive virtual relationships). While evaluation of transitive closures is a complex problem, there are many algorithms for this purpose which are adequate in most situations. The most general treatment of a transitive closure arises as a consequence of operating on it as a *closed semi-ring*, which is a group-algebraic structure [Aho74, Ullm88]. Kleene's algorithm [Klee56] can be applied to all closed semi-rings and so is generally useful for transitive closures. Although not all closed semi-rings can be evaluated in polynomial time, for all our transitive closure evaluations we can obtain $O(n^3)$ time-complexity performance from this algorithm. Many other algorithms which perform more efficiently in special cases are also available [Ioan86, Ioan88, Aho86, Tarj81, Agra87, Jaga87, Vald88].

26.6. Implementation Platforms

If we express our modeling concepts in mathematical notation such as *Object Z* or a similar calculus, we can turn the interpretation of our methodology from being *model-theoretic* (where the "meaning" of any statement in the model is a description of some actual system) to being *proof-theoretic* (where the "meaning" of any statement in the model is a fact which can be mathematically proved). When implemented on some platform, the methodology becomes *operationalized*, implying that the "meaning" of any statement in the model is whatever it means in the model information base on which it happens to be implemented.

It is therefore important that the operational definition of "meaning" have correspondence with the proof-theoretic and model-theoretic definitions of "meaning". The problem of *semantic equivalence* deals with demonstrating the correspondence between *denotational semantics* and *operational semantics* in a rigorous and mathematical manner [Mulm87]. While we shall not go into such a demonstration for our model here, it is important to note that the choice of an implementation platform should minimize the "impedance mismatch" between the built-in primitives whose semantics it supports and the modeling constructs of our methodology.

Many factors govern the choice of implementation platforms [Bapa91a]. Objects or object fragments could be implemented as values retrieved from hardware devices, firmware, volatile memory, or from persistent storage. The persistent storage platforms could be flat-file databases, network databases, hierarchical databases, relational databases, or other proprietary-format databases. For objects or object fragments which are required in the run-time operation of the network, a database implementation may be too slow to meet the performance constraints of real-time network activity. In these situations, the object is best implemented either directly in hardware, firmware, or in volatile memory initialized or downloaded at boot time.

For non-real-time applications such as network synthesis, network simulation, and certain network management activities such as report generation, implementing network objects in some structured database platform is perhaps the most convenient. Many database platforms have built-in integrity checks which reduce the likelihood of errors in network data; these integrity checks can be availed of when implementing our model in the framework of that platform.

Relational Platforms

Relational databases are a stable, mature, and well-understood technology [Date85, Codd90]. Relational platforms have many advantages as implementation vehicles for our model. They have strong support for set-theoretic operations. Relationships between object classes can be easily implemented, as the mapping between the entity-relationship model and the relational model can be performed in an almost algorithmic manner. They may be optimized with well-developed principles of normalization. Relational databases also provide strong support for views, which are analogous to virtual object classes.

Nevertheless, relational databases suffer from some disadvantages. The traditional relational model cannot accommodate functions, constraints, and rules as properties of object classes. Perhaps the biggest disadvantage of the pure relational model is the lack of direct support for taxonomy and inheritance. In many circumstances, the mapping between monotonic-inheritance object-oriented models and the relational model can be performed in a quasi-algorithmic manner [Blah88, Bapa91b, Booc94, Fink92].

One method of implementing an object-oriented model on a relational platform is to perform *normalization across inheritance associations*. This implies that different relations are created for a superclass and a subclass, each with fields that reflect only the original properties for that class. When an instance of the subclass is created, its inherited properties are stored in a record in the superclass relation, while its original properties are stored in the subclass relation. Both relations have an extra field which indicates the record identifier of the corresponding record in the other relation, which serves as the "join key" which pieces the entire object instance together.

An alternative method for imposing an object-oriented model on a relational platform is to perform *denormalization across inheritance associations*, which is similar to *hierarchy telescoping* [Bapa91b, Naka91]. As explained in Chapter 2, this implies that inherited properties of an object class are treated as if they were original properties. When applied to a relational platform, denormalization requires all properties of an object class to be mapped to the fields of a single relation, that is, as the columns of a table corresponding to each instantiable object class. Thus, performance is improved since no joins need be performed across inheritance links, since all the properties of each object are available in a single record. This works well when there are no non-leaf concrete classes. In the presence of object classes which have both instances and subclasses, only partial hierarchy telescoping can be performed and must be combined with normalization across some inheritance links.

The evolution of the relational model to absorb other paradigms such as object-orientation has lead to many newer platforms capable of supporting taxonomy and subtyping semantics [ERL90, Ston89, Silb91, Ston91, Kemn91, Lohm91]. The newer, assimilative models of database systems typically support strong typing, rigorous domain analysis and checking, objects that encapsulate functions and procedures, and implicit property assignment through inheritance.

Non-Normal Databases

Worth special mention is the *nested relational model*. In this model, a single field of a relation (that is, a column of a relational table) is permitted to have a complex internal structure. For example, a single field of a relation may internally have a set-oriented or record-oriented structure. This works well with our methodology since attributes and functions in our model may have structured types such as SET OF and SEQUENCE constructs [Fink93]. A field may also have an internal structure defined by a record in another relation. In fact, since ASN.1 is a strongly typed notation with extensive support for sets and structured records, it is particularly suitable as a data definition language for nested relational and other non-normal databases.

Although the nested relational model is sometimes criticized as being in violation of the first normal form of database design, it actually leads to stricter domain integrity checking. Nested and non-normal relational platforms are promising implementation platforms for our model once issues with respect to querying nested field data in a standardized query language and incorporation of behavioral fields have been worked out.

Object-Oriented Database Platforms

Object-oriented databases are also good candidates as implementation platforms for models based on specialization theory [Kim89, Kim90a, Gupt91]. They support the persistent storage of both attributes and functions, and they naturally support inheritance semantics. Some object-oriented database implementations, however, do not provide constraints and rules; very few provide truly integrated inter-class relationships with support for multiplicities and relationship inheritance. Nevertheless, they represent an evolving technology which, like other database technologies, will undoubtedly be enhanced to capture extended semantics [Atki89, Banc90, Atwo91, Ozsu93].

A reference model for object-oriented database management has been defined by ANSI [ANSI X3-ODM, Kilo92]. This is a comprehensive enumeration of all the properties that a system must have in order to qualify as an *ODM (Object Data Management) system*. This reference model combines the properties of a classical object-oriented software environment (objects, operations, requests, messages, methods, state, binding, polymorphism, encapsulation, identity, classes, types, inheritance/delegation, extensibility, etc.) with the properties of a traditional database-management system (persistence, object lifetimes, transactions, concurrency control, serializability, distribution, data locking, multiple-phase commits, query languages, data dictionaries, namespace management, change management, version and configuration control, schema evolution, security, reliability, fault tolerance, error handling and recovery, etc.). While this standard is not very detailed about the level of information modeling and inter-object relationships which an ODM system must support, it serves as a foundation for the future evolution of sophisticated object-oriented database systems. A similar standard has been defined by the *Object Database Management Group* consortium [ODMG 93].

Intelligent Databases

The emerging database technology of *intelligent databases*, which includes *deductive databases*, *active databases*, and *expert databases*, is a very promising development [Mink88, Kers89, Ullm88, Ullm90]. Like our model, these database systems also integrate multiple modeling paradigms. Many of these systems are evolutions of the object-oriented model and provide rich inheritance and encapsulation semantics [Zani89, Piat89, Piat91, Higa92]. Many also provide advanced reasoning capabilities internally within the database system [Wido90, Gran92]. This is accomplished by the integration of logic programming within the database model, leading to *deductive* or *expert* capabilities [Phip91]. The ability to monitor each object for certain events and automatically trigger other activities based upon those events gives rise to their *active* capabilities [Agra89, McCa89, Geha92, Wido94]. Many support virtual object classes, relationships, and constraints [Geha91, Jaga92]. Virtual relationships can be supported indirectly as Horn-clause inferences on role predicates, in a manner similar to the equivalences we demonstrated in Chapter 23.

At present, few deductive databases support features such as virtual attributes or the formal specialization principles used in our model. Nevertheless, as deductive databases also derive from the confluence of multiple modeling paradigms [Pars90], they are perhaps the implementation platforms which come closest to minimizing the "impedance mismatch" between their built-in primitives and the feature requirements of specialization theory.

Figure 26-2 illustrates some possible implementation choices for our modeling methodology.

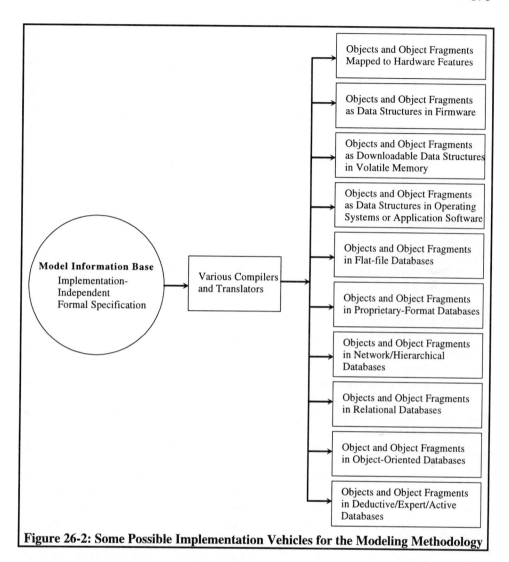

Figure 26-2: Some Possible Implementation Vehicles for the Modeling Methodology

26.7. Application Information Bases

The unified, multiparadigmatic modeling methodology we have developed can be used for various applications, albeit no single application is likely to require all the modeling concepts of the methodology. Subsets of the methodology, each choosing certain features, can be deployed for different applications. We mention a few of the more significant applications for which the network model in our model information base can be utilized.

The activity of *network architecture* is concerned with the design of a network at the planning stage. At this stage, the services which are to be supported in the network are identified. Various candidate software and hardware objects are assembled, and different topologies considered and tested to see that the network delivers the required services correctly and efficiently. Typically, this process is supported by a network modeling tool, which is a software program intended for computer-assisted network architecture. Its front-end usually has a graphical user interface. Such a program usually comprises two subtools: a *synthesis* tool, which selects different devices, circuits, and software applications from a "parts catalog" and assembles them in a proposed configuration; and a *simulation* tool, which tests each proposed configuration against various usage patterns to determine whether the configuration is adequate.

Computer-assisted network architecture is supported by a database which contains the "parts catalog", listing the various items available for network synthesis, and the "assembly blueprint", listing the rules which describe how these parts correctly fit together. We know the parts catalog better as the inheritance hierarchy, and the rules better as relationships. The architecture database can use a subset of our model information base to maintain a rich semantic representation of all the information it needs. We term this an *Architecture Information Base*.

The activity of *network operations* also requires an information base. Once a network configuration is realized, the objects within the network must make run-time decisions as to how best to interoperate with other objects about whom they may have partial or zero knowledge. This makes it necessary for them to maintain, or have access to, a database which contains all the knowledge necessary to operate a run-time environment. This database may also use a subset of our model information base to represent the data it needs. We term this an *Operations Information Base*.

Finally, the activity of *network management* also requires the use of an information base. This database maintains all the knowledge necessary for controlling, diagnosing, monitoring, and configuring the network. As such, it must maintain a representation of the network topology, the various objects in the network, and all their characteristics. Such a database may also use a subset of our model information base. We term this a *Management Information Base*.

Figure 26-3 illustrates how subsets of our methodology may be selected for use in various operations.

26.8. Summary

The modeling methodology can be used to formally specify a comprehensive network model in an implementation-independent manner. Various compilers can translate the model into any implementation vehicle that is appropriate.

The methodology integrates various paradigms, including the rigorous object-oriented paradigm of specialization theory, the entity-relationship paradigm, the knowledge representation paradigm, the logic programming paradigm, the relational paradigm, the procedural programming paradigm, the set-theoretic paradigm, and denotational semantics. Any platform which offers as many of our modeling features as possible as built-in primitives may be selected to host an implementation of our methodology.

In an implementation, objects may be fragmented so that each fragment is implemented differently and retrieved from different locations. Different objects and different

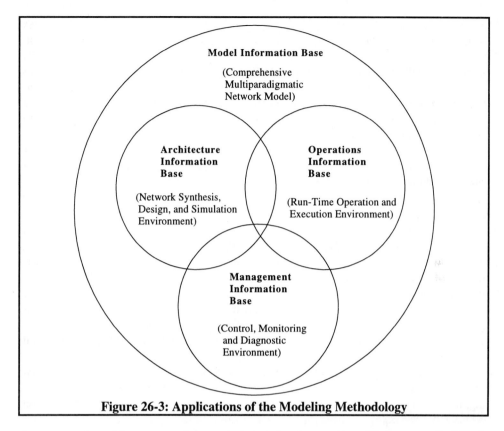

Figure 26-3: Applications of the Modeling Methodology

fragments of an object may each have their own implementation. Since our methodology is a pure specification methodology, different implementation mechanisms are permissible as long as they do not violate the semantics.

For non-real-time applications, the methodology may be implemented on a relational database platform, an object-oriented database platform, or a deductive or expert database platform. Each choice will cause different trade-offs as to which of our modeling features will be directly available from the platform and which must be implemented outside the platform.

The applications of our methodology include network architecture, network operations, and network management. Each may use an appropriate subset of our model information base, termed an Architecture Information Base, an Operations Information Base, and a Management Information Base respectively.

27. Modeling for Network Architecture

> *"Two roads diverged in a wood, and I —*
> *I took the one less traveled by,*
> *And that has made all the difference."*
>   — *algorithm for bandwidth optimization by dynamic*
>   *traffic load allocation, devised by anonymous*
>   *network manager.*

27.1. Introduction

In this chapter, we discuss the application of object-oriented network models to the process of network architecture and planning. The modeling methodology is applied to the phases of network synthesis and network simulation. The derivation of connectivity and interconnectivity relationships is presented, along with algorithms for automated network synthesis. Topology optimization problems in network synthesis are discussed. The benefits of network simulation are presented, along with a discussion of simulation environments and how simulation results can be used to refine the network architecture.

27.2. Network Architecture and Planning

Architecture is the process of mapping *service requirements* to a *system model*. In communication networks, the architecture phase involves designing the network such that it can deliver the services required of it, both current and future. Networks today continue to become faster, more complex, and more enterprise-critical; there is every indication that this trend will continue. The services demanded of communication networks and the performance required from them will doubtless continue to increase.

It is therefore important to apply rigorous design and analysis in the network architecture and planning process. Architecting a network correctly prior to its implementation helps in optimizing deployment costs, minimizing operating costs, predicting response times, meeting performance objectives, planning capacity changes, and accommodating future growth [Norm92a, Norm92b]. A comprehensive object-oriented model can provide the basis for an integrated top-down approach to network architecture. Software programs such as network architecture tools can use object-oriented models to facilitate a high-level approach to this task.

A systematic approach to architecture can also result in a more reliable network. Network architects can analyze failure risks, plan recovery strategies, and prepare for scheduled outages (e.g., for confidence testing). Alternatives can be explored for adding redundancy to improve network survivability. In an optimized network configuration, the costs of excessive redundancy can be eliminated while still providing adequate protection against failure risks.

Synthesis and Simulation

The process of network architecture consists of two phases: the *network synthesis* phase and the *network simulation* phase. During the network synthesis phase, a software model is created for the network: a network topology is proposed and the objects constituting the network (devices, links, protocols, applications) are selected and configured. During the network simulation phase, the software model of the proposed configuration is dynamically exercised using various analytical or experimental operational scenarios. Based on the results of the simulation, the proposed configuration is refined until some objective or combination of objectives (e.g., load handling, adequate performance, operating cost, and future evolvability) is optimized. Clearly, network architecture is an iterative process, in which multiple candidate configurations must be tested against various scenarios, refined, and re-tested until requirements are satisfied.

Each candidate network configuration is tested against both ordinary and exceptional operational scenarios. By simulating both normal and intensive execution of network applications, average as well as excessive traffic loads can be tested. In addition, "what-if" scenarios such as the failure of various network devices or links and the addition of future applications can also be simulated. Simulation assists in pinpointing possible bottlenecks and ensures that adequate capacity exists for the network to handle normal workloads, extraordinary situations, and future growth.

The benefit of an integrated, high-level approach to network synthesis and simulation is that it permits network architects to *recognize, evaluate and select trade-offs* before the network is built. By using an object-oriented model, network architects raise the level of abstraction, as it is easier to conceptualize and understand complex systems at a high level before proceeding with detailed design. A top-down design methodology for complex systems increases the chances of deploying a correctly functioning and properly dimensioned network within a relatively short design cycle. A formal approach to high-level network architecture, involving both synthesis and simulation, is a mechanism for *rapid prototyping* of the network design. It provides a means of verifying the specifications as early as possible in the planning stage.

While network architecture is essential during the planning stage, it can also occur as an ongoing activity throughout the life of the network. Existing networks can be simulated in software to check how well they will handle future growth and evolution. One advantage of simulating an existing network is that the simulation can then be fed actual traffic data captured from the live network, rather than hypothetical traffic distributions generated by some simulation algorithm.

Object-oriented network models can be used in both the network synthesis and network simulation phases, as they incorporate structural as well as behavioral characteristics. As we have emphasized throughout, the inheritance hierarchy serves as a "parts catalog" which maintains a sorted and categorized list of the parts that are available to build the network. By selecting the proper parts and configuring them correctly in the software model, we can perform network synthesis. By providing appropriate input in the software model to the functions representing the behavioral characteristics of these objects, we can also perform network simulation.

The processes of network synthesis and network simulation are carried out with respect to an *architecture information base*. An architecture information base is a subset of the model information base containing all the elements necessary for the activity network architecture. Many network simulation tools use a "model library" or a "reference database". While these serve a similar purpose, an architecture information base is actually more general, in that it not only contains the object models of each device, link, protocol, or application but also the relationships which tell us how they may be correctly synthesized with respect to each other. Figure 27-1 illustrates the overall process of network architecture.

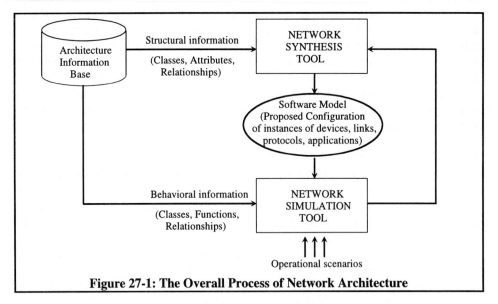

Figure 27-1: The Overall Process of Network Architecture

27.3. Automated Network Synthesis

The activity of *network synthesis* is concerned with creating a proposed network configuration for delivering a given set of services. Network synthesis can be used for topological design at various levels of scale, from small LANs with few nodes [Erso92] to large

WANs serving hundreds of thousands of terminals [Kers93]. The synthesis process usually follows well-defined rules; these are called *recipes* in newer information networking architectures such as ANSA [Ansa92, Herb94]. *Automated network synthesis* is a process which, given the service requirements a network must support, creates an appropriate network configuration in an algorithmic manner. Because the rules for this synthesis activity can be codified, it can be programmed; it is therefore also referred to as *Network Design Automation*.

Creating Object and Relationship Instances

The result of network synthesis is a software model of the proposed configuration. This software model can then be validated through simulation and refined as necessary. The software model is a configuration of *object instances* of the various classes in the architecture information base, and *relationship instances* of the relationships between them in the architecture information base. The architecture information base can store both the schema, that is, a description of classes and relationships, and instances engendered by that schema. It should be remembered, though, that from a given schema, many different instantiated networks can be created — one for each proposed configuration, each containing a different arrangement of instances of the same classes and relationships. Each such configuration can be used to create a software model for simulation.

Relationships are crucial to performing network synthesis correctly. Rather than using relationships as *descriptive statements* that *instruct* us about object interaction in an actual network, we use them as *prescriptive statements* that *construct* for us a proposed network. If a relationship has been defined between two object classes in the architecture information base, we are permitted to establish a relationship instance between their instances in the software model so that they are operationally coupled. Conversely, if there is no relationship defined between two classes in the architecture information base, we cannot couple their instances together in the software model.

Aggregation and Termination Relationships

We have already had a taste of the normative use of relationships in Chapter 8 where we architected a nodal processor. We used aggregation relationships as assembly rules which pieced together different modules to create different configurations of nodal processors. By using both aggregation and other relationships, we can create entire networks by coupling together objects as prescribed.

Aggregation relationships can be used to assemble configurations at higher levels as well. The high-level aggregation for the `network` object class states that it `has-as-a-part` the `networkDevice` object class and the `link` object class. Because networks may contain subnetworks connected to other subnetworks, we also permit the `network` object class to `have-as-a-part` the `network` object class. This is possible because specialization theory permits recursive aggregation; its benefit is that we can synthesize subnetworks first and interconnect them later by making them components of larger networks.

Another fundamental relationship for network synthesis is the `termination` relationship between the `networkDevice` object class and the `link` object class. This is similar to the `termination` relationship described in Figure 18-7, where `circuit` was a descendant of `link`, implying end-to-end terminations. The ancestral class `link` **generalizes-from** `circuit` to accommodate broadcast and shared-media topologies as well. Figure 27-2 illustrates these relationships. As subsequent sections will show, we can derive `connectivity` and `interconnectivity` relationships from instances of the `termination` relationship.

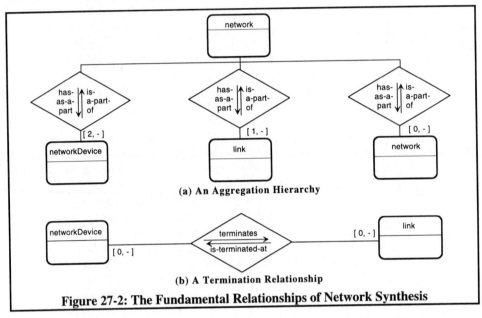

Figure 27-2: The Fundamental Relationships of Network Synthesis

The `networkDevice` object class further **specializes-into** many different types of network devices. Depending on the kind of network we are designing, we can create the appropriate classes in the architecture information base. For carrier-owned networks, these classes will be the ones typically found in a telecommunications WAN; for customer-owned networks, the classes of interest will be those typically found in data internetworks and campus-based voice systems. One possible classification of `network-Device` objects was already provided in Figure 2-3. Of course, each `networkDevice` object will `have-as-a-part` various `protocolEntity` and `protocolStack` objects, as was described in Figure 21-9.

The `link` object class also **specializes-into** various link types. Like `network-Device` objects, these may be subclassed into carrier-owned links and customer-owned links, if such a classification makes sense to the network being synthesized. If the network contains both wireless and wireline links, the `link` object class may also be subclassed at some level into `wirelessLink` and `wirelineLink`, possibly using the medium attribute as the basis of specialization. Various classes of `circuit` (representing end-to-end WAN `links`) can be derived as descendants of `wireline-Link`.

27.4. Connectivity and Interconnectivity

Connectivity relationships are important in the process of automated network synthesis, as they indicate which `networkDevices` are connected together. In our model, we define a `connectivity` relationship as occurring between any two `networkDevices` whose interfaces are directly connected to each other. It has the role-pair {`connects-to, is-connected-to`}. An *interconnectivity* relationship has the role-pair {`interconnects-to, is-interconnected-to`} and occurs between any two `networkDevice` objects which have a chain of `connectivity` relationships between them. As per this definition, if `networkDevice` objects A and B are adjacent neighbors in the network topology, they are both connected and interconnected. If `networkDevice` C is an adjacent neighbor of B but not of A, then C `is-connected-to` B but not to A; however, C still `is-interconnected-to` A because it remains reachable from A. Thus, from a graph theory perspective, `connectivity` defines topological adjacency, whereas `interconnectivity` defines reachability.

Connectivity can be defined as a virtual relationship: the automated synthesis tool can infer connectivity as a convolution from the `termination` relationships between two instances of `networkDevice` and one instance of `link`. That is, if a `networkDevice` terminates a `link` and the same `link` `is-terminated-at` another `networkDevice`, then the automated synthesis tool infers that the two `networkDevice` objects are `connected-to` each other. Clearly, `connectivity` is also a *commutative* relationship and is also *involute* on the `networkDevice` object class. However, it is not *transitive*, since by the definition above only `interconnectivity` is transitive.

Interconnectivity is also a virtual relationship and arises from `connectivity` relationships between `networkDevices`. It arises in three ways: first, in the trivial case, as an *implicate virtual relationship* by implication from `connectivity` (A `connects-to` B implies A `interconnects-to` B); second, as a *distributive virtual relationship* by distribution over `connectivity` (A `interconnects-to` B and B `connects-to` C implies A `interconnects-to` C); and third, as a *transitive virtual relationship* by its own transitivity (A `interconnects-to` B and B `interconnects-to` C implies A `interconnects-to` C). Strictly, the third form is unnecessary since it can be inferred from many steps of the second form, but we specify it anyway to speed up the resolution of `interconnectivity` relationships in the architecture information base. Like `connectivity`, `interconnectivity` is also commutative and involute on the `networkDevice` class.

Thus, `connectivity` and `interconnectivity` relationships are inferred by the automated synthesis tool from base actual `termination` relationships between `networkDevice` and `link` objects specified in the architecture information base. In this manner, `connectivity` and `interconnectivity` act as *topology-building mechanisms* which provide the automated synthesis tool the ability to automatically determine reachability graphs for the entire network. Figure 27-3 illustrates these relationships.

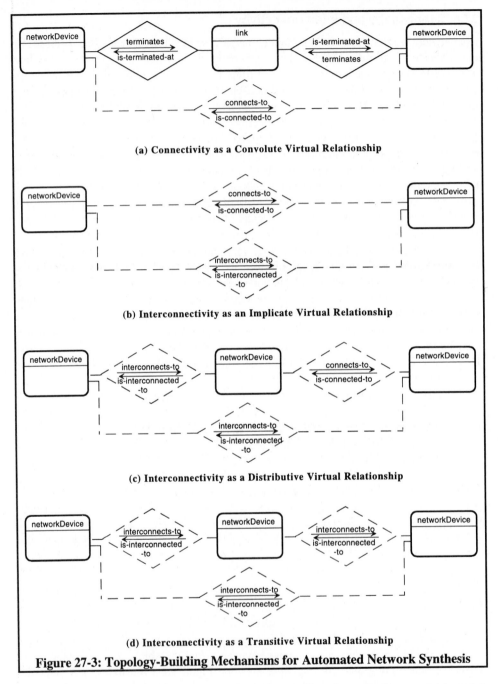

(a) Connectivity as a Convolute Virtual Relationship

(b) Interconnectivity as an Implicate Virtual Relationship

(c) Interconnectivity as a Distributive Virtual Relationship

(d) Interconnectivity as a Transitive Virtual Relationship

Figure 27-3: Topology-Building Mechanisms for Automated Network Synthesis

Note that connectivity need not necessarily arise only from point-to-point termination relationships between networkDevice and link objects. Multidrop, multi-cast, and broadcast topologies can also give rise to `connectivity` relationships. For example, multiple workstations sharing the same LAN segment are also connected to each other, even though each does not arguably "terminate" the segment. (In structured-wiring topologies where workstations on the same LAN segment have point-to-point connections with a `wiringHub`, it is arguably easier to model this as a "`termination`" relationship for some `link`.) We can easily work around this with a few definitions: if we define a `shares-medium` relationship between `networkDevice` and some descendant of `link` (e.g., a `lanSegment` class), then `connectivity` can also arise as a convolution of two instances of the `shares-medium` relationship. Thus, if `networkDevice` objects A and B are on the same `lanSegment`, then they are `connected-to` each other. If B happens to be a `bridge` object, then all the `networkDevice` objects (from any `lanSegment`) which are `connected-to` B are, by the definition of `interconnectivity`, `interconnected-to` A.

In network synthesis, we are permitted to specify a single abstract `link` object in place of a sequence of physical connections: a `link` need not necessarily rigorously track a chain of wire terminations between ports of successive `networkDevice` objects. For example, while synthesizing a private enterprise network consisting of customer-premises equipment, we may create an instance of `t1Circuit` as directly connecting two instances of `t1Multiplexer`. Thus, the two instances of `t1Multiplexer`, possibly very distant geographically, will be considered to be directly `connected-to` each other in the synthesis model. This is, of course, an abstraction; in actuality, the `t1Circuit` originating at one `t1Multiplexer` is likely terminated at some `crossConnect` object in the carrier's network, where the signal is possibly groomed into some higher-speed inter-office trunk, carried through many central offices, and finally degroomed into another `t1Circuit` terminating at the remote `t1Multiplexer`. All these intermediate links are not important to us because our view of the network is simply that of the CPE-based private enterprise network. (Of course, if our view were that of a telecommunications carrier provisioning this network, all these intermediate links would be important.)

It should be noted that so far we have only modeled `connectivity` and `interconnectivity` relationships between network devices. This is not sufficient, because the mere fact that a sequence of wireline or wireless links exists between some pair of `networkDevices` does not mean that they can interoperate. We must also be able to ensure meaningful communication between `networkDevices` by examining their ability to exchange data. Thus, we must have ways of discovering *interoperability relationships* during the process of automated network synthesis. In Chapter 28, we will examine in detail how these relationships may be determined from the knowledge of the `protocolStack` components of each `networkDevice` in the model information base. For the time being, assume that the network synthesis tool has the ability to discover, from the object-oriented model, whether or not the `networkDevices` with `interconnectivity` relationships between them also have an `interoperability` relationship, and that it can use this knowledge in the process of automated network synthesis.

27.5. Network Synthesis Constraints

During automated network synthesis, we may have policies and guidelines for redundancy and reliability. We can apply all these guidelines automatically during the synthesis process as constraints. There are various ways in which constraints can be applied in specialization theory: as attribute domain specifications (requiring an attribute to possess only certain values), as multiplicity domain specifications (requiring a minimum or maximum number of participant objects in a relationship), as functional dependency specifications (requiring a virtual attribute to be consistent with its base attributes), or as the general constraint properties of object classes defined in Chapter 22.

As a typical example, consider the process of synthesizing an enterprise data network, in which we must design a WAN backbone to facilitate data communication between mainframes, front-end processors, terminal clusters, file servers, and multiple LAN internetworks at a number of geographically separate sites. Suppose that the superclass site **specializes-into** the two subclasses backboneSite and remoteSite, representing main offices and branch offices. Also, the superclass circuit **specializes-into** backboneCircuit and remoteCircuit, representing critical high-capacity trunks and feeder links respectively. For this network, we might have the following design guidelines [Ghos92]:

- Each backboneSite must be on at least two different backboneCircuits.

- Each backboneSite must have a backboneCircuit connection to at least two other backboneSites.

- Each remoteSite must have a direct connection to at least one backboneSite.

- No two backboneCircuits should be attached to the same networkDevice.

- There should be a maximum of two hops between any pair of backboneSites.

- There should be a maximum of four hops between any pair of sites.

Using specialization theory, it is an easy matter to formally specify constraints such as these in the architecture information base, so that they are always available to the automated synthesis tool for perpetual enforcement throughout the network synthesis process. Constraints similar to the above can be easily specified using minimum or maximum values for multiplicity domains in the termination relationships of appropriate descendants of site and networkDevice with appropriate descendants of link. Others can be specified as object class constraints, virtual attribute domain specifications, or even as the domain specifications of relationship attributes.

27.6. Algorithms for Synthesis Automation

With all the tools necessary for automating the synthesis phase established, the automated synthesis tool can now proceed to create a network configuration. We present below one possible algorithm which may be used by such an automated synthesis tool. Assume that we are synthesizing a geographically distributed private enterprise network which is required to support many different services. Certain information must be input to this algorithm, such as the services the network must support, the sites which must be included, and the types of facilities or links available from telecommunication carriers to interconnect them.

The initial information for network synthesis is usually provided via a graphical user interface using a point-and-click mechanism to indicate sites and possible links. Many synthesis and simulation tools have graphical front-ends which permit the network architect to define the sites and sketch the desired network topology. These environments support *Network Design Automation*, an activity which is the network design analogue of CASE, CAD/CAM, and EDA tools [Cons93, Doss93, Witt93].

Based on the initial information provided, the synthesis tool attempts to create a network configuration to support the services required which is optimal with respect to some specified criterion (e.g., `cost`). One possible algorithm for this is as follows:

1. Identify the `service` classes which must be supported at each `site`.

2. Follow the `is-provided-by` roles of service provision relationships to determine the possible `protocolEntity` objects which can provide the required services.

3. Follow the `layers-above` roles of protocol layering relationships to identify all the `protocolStack` objects which can support the identified `protocolEntity` objects.

4. Follow the `is-a-part-of` roles of aggregation relationships to identify which `networkDevice` objects contain the required `protocolStacks` (e.g., workstations, mainframes, PBXs, data terminals, telephone terminals, HDTV terminals).

5. Follow the `capacity` attributes of the selected `networkDevices` to determine their processing workload and replicate the number of instances of the selected `networkDevices` at each `site` to support the service workload at that `site`.

6. Follow the `terminates` role of `termination` relationships to identify the types of `link` objects which can be terminated at the selected `networkDevices`.

7. Follow the `interconnectivity` and `interoperability` relationships to insert the appropriate intermediate `networkDevice` objects which can provide local interconnection to the terminal `networkDevice` objects at each `site` (e.g., wiring hubs, LAN bridges, terminal servers).

8. Follow the `interconnectivity` and `interoperability` relationships to insert the appropriate intermediate `networkDevice` objects for LAN-to-WAN interconnection, based on the `links` pro-

vided by the telecommunications carrier (e.g., multiplexers, routers, modems, DSUs, CSUs, video codecs).

9. Follow the `bandwidth` attributes of the available WAN `link` objects and replicate the number of `link` instances to support the anticipated traffic volume between each pair of `sites`.

10. Follow the `is-backed-up-by` roles of `backup` relationships for the critical `networkDevice` and `link` objects and add additional `networkDevices` and `links` to accommodate all redundancy and reliability constraints for the network.

11. Follow the `is-managed-by` roles of management relationships to add the required `networkManagementSystem` objects in the network.

12. Of all the possible network configurations which the preceding steps generate, select the ones which are most optimal with respect to the specified optimizing criterion (e.g., `price` or `operatingCost`).

Using the descendants of `networkDevice` and `link` classes available in the architecture information base, the automated synthesis tool can apply algorithms such as these to create network configurations which support the required services. The process of network architecture does not end here: each configuration proposed by the synthesis algorithm must then be validated by the phase of network simulation. The simulation phase exercises these proposed configurations against actual or hypothetical operations scenarios, helping to refine the overall network architecture.

As we will discuss in the next section, for a variety of reasons it may not always be possible to execute such network synthesis algorithms in a completely automated fashion for very large networks. Nevertheless, the ability to capture much network knowledge in the architecture information base gives us the ability to automate large parts of many network synthesis algorithms, thus considerably easing the process of creating optimal network configurations. Figure 27-4 illustrates an algorithm; recent research has presented similar algorithmic procedures for other types of networks as well [Feri91, Kers93].

27.7. Network Topology Optimization

For complex networks, it may not be possible to execute network synthesis algorithms in a fully automated fashion, as the number of candidate configurations generated may be very large. Thus, searching for the optimum configuration involves the use of operations research techniques such as linear and non-linear programming with a very large number of independent variables [Baza77, Baza79]. Although many well-known techniques have been developed for such optimization, they are generally computationally expensive; the choice of an efficient optimization algorithm [Fan66, Heyd79] is usually tied closely to the characteristics of the matrix of dependent variables of the equation system.

The overall network optimization problem can often be broken down into sub-problems which can be optimized independently [Zolf91]. Some examples are

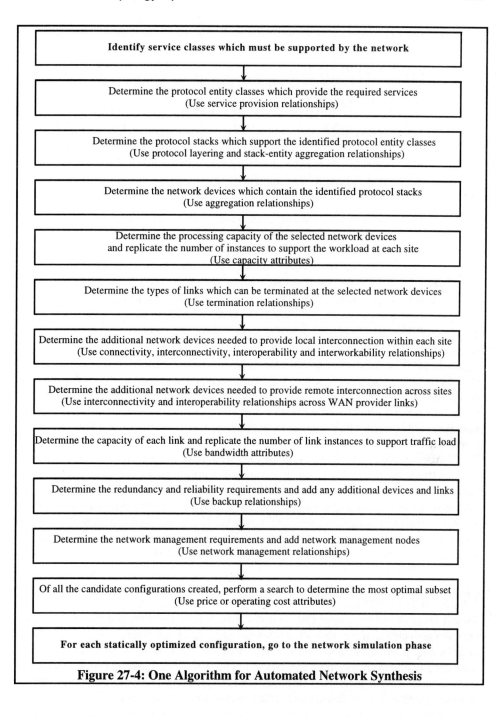

Identify service classes which must be supported by the network

Determine the protocol entity classes which provide the required services
(Use service provision relationships)

Determine the protocol stacks which support the identified protocol entity classes
(Use protocol layering and stack-entity aggregation relationships)

Determine the network devices which contain the identified protocol stacks
(Use aggregation relationships)

Determine the processing capacity of the selected network devices
and replicate the number of instances to support the workload at each site
(Use capacity attributes)

Determine the types of links which can be terminated at the selected network devices
(Use termination relationships)

Determine the additional network devices needed to provide local interconnection within each site
(Use connectivity, interconnectivity, interoperability and interworkability relationships)

Determine the additional network devices needed to provide remote interconnection across sites
(Use interconnectivity and interoperability relationships across WAN provider links)

Determine the capacity of each link and replicate the number of link instances to support traffic load
(Use bandwidth attributes)

Determine the redundancy and reliability requirements and add any additional devices and links
(Use backup relationships)

Determine the network management requirements and add network management nodes
(Use network management relationships)

Of all the candidate configurations created, perform a search to determine the most optimal subset
(Use price or operating cost attributes)

For each statically optimized configuration, go to the network simulation phase

Figure 27-4: One Algorithm for Automated Network Synthesis

- *The Multicommodity Flow Problem*: In this problem, the total traffic volume must be divided over multiple links, with each link possibly having a different cost, in such a manner that the overall flow pattern minimizes the total operating cost [Liu92]. Its solution requires the presence of tariff information for each link type available from the service provider; this is often available in standard tariff databases.

- *The Location Spanning Problem*: This problem involves the coverage of multiple locations with multiple links. Constraints such as "Each `backboneSite` must be on at least two `backboneCircuits`" result in graph-theoretic formulations where a pattern of multiple edges is required to span the vertices at minimal cost.

- *The Shortest Path Problem*: Once a least-cost location-spanning graph has been obtained, it is incumbent on each location to determine the best route through that graph to any other given location. The best route is not necessarily the shortest, that is, the one with the minimum number of hops; the "weights" along each path (varying link tariffs) may suggest a different least-cost route. The solution to the optimum-path problem is not static; cyclical tariff schedules (e.g., off-peak and peak) and extraordinary events (e.g., link failure and return to service) often require that this problem be periodically re-solved.

In general, the computational complexity of many problems such as these is NP-hard. Fortunately, much academic and industrial research has been performed in the area of topological network design over the last several decades. This has resulted in an abundance of algorithms which either generate reasonably good (and sometimes near-optimal) solutions within a limited time, or find an incremental optimization of a known starting solution.

Network synthesis algorithms may be enhanced with heuristics which limit the dimensionality of the search space. For example, we may know that a design based on dedicated data links between routers has a higher operating cost than one based on T-1 links between multiplexers which can also carry PBX traffic; specifying such a heuristic to the automated synthesis tool will help prune the tree of the search possibilities. In addition, manual intervention might be periodically required to perform local optimizations for subnetworks, before proceeding with the global optimization.

27.8. Virtual Classes for Network Views

Once a network has been synthesized from network devices, links, and subnetworks, we can take projections of the network to examine only those components which we wish to view in any given simulation. Assume that we have synthesized an enterprise network consisting of mainframes, front-end processors, cluster controllers, terminals, workstations, Ethernet LANs, token-ring LANs, FDDI LANs, bridges, routers, file servers, PBXs, voice-mail systems, fax stations and telephone terminals. The automated synthesis tool has created a proposed configuration for this network using the permitted relationships between these objects and their components defined in the architecture information base.

Suppose that, in a given simulation, we wish to test for potential congestion of connectionless datagrams. For this simulation, we only wish to view the topology of the various `router` objects in the network; other objects are temporarily irrelevant. We can take a projection of the network which exposes only the `router` devices. This can be accomplished using virtual object classes: we can define a virtual object class, say `routerNetwork`, whose base class is the aggregate `network` class itself. This virtual object class is defined using both a conjunctor and a projector: by using the conjunctor `trackRelatants (class: router, role: has-as-a-part)` and a projector which filters out the properties of the base `network` class itself, we will in effect obtain all the `router` objects which the `network` contains as components.

Suppose further that we wish to focus on a particular `router` object and determine which other `routers` are its adjacent neighbors in the `routerNetwork` topology. This is easy: for the selected `router` object in the `routerNetwork` class we can apply the function `trackRelatants (class: router, role: interconnects-to, depth: 1)`. Note that every relatant of the selected `router` via the `interconnects-to` role is also a `router` in the virtual class `routerNetwork`, even if this is not true in the actual class `network`. Since `trackRelatants()` takes a depth argument for transitive roles, specifying `depth: 1` ensures that only the routers which are adjacent in the `routerNetwork` topology are returned (even though they may not be adjacent in the actual `network` topology). If we wish to track every `router` which is reachable from the starting `router`, we may simply omit the `depth` argument.

What if a `router` in the network is not a stand-alone `networkDevice`, but a component of some other `networkDevice`? For example, a `router` may be a module which is inserted as a component into a `wiringHub` object. Thus, even though there may be an `interconnectivity` relationship between a stand-alone `router` and the `wiringHub` object, no such relationship has been defined between the stand-alone `router` and the `router` module *inside* the `wiringHub`. Fortunately, with virtual relationships, the solution to this problem is easy: we simply specify a distributive virtual relationship in which the `interconnects-to` role distributes ahead of the `has-as-a-part` role. Thus, if `router` A `interconnects-to` `wiringHub` B and `wiringHub` B `has-as-a-part` `router` C, then `router` A `interconnects-to` `router` C. Thus, `router` C will show up as reachable from `router` A when all of A's `router` relatants are tracked.

27.9. Network Simulation

The activity of *network simulation* involves exercising the network configurations created by the network synthesis tool from the object-oriented model. Simulation permits the network architect to test each proposed configuration for its behavior under various conditions of traffic load and refine the topology, device capacities, and link bandwidths until the design is satisfactory.

The benefit of network simulation is that the behavior of the synthesized network can be studied in terms of its model before the network is actually deployed. Hypothetical "what-if" scenarios can be explored and performance can be analyzed [Jain91]. Configurations can be refined, device capacities adjusted and link bandwidths redimensioned, depending on the behavior exhibited under simulation. Answers can be provided to questions such as what happens when devices are added or dropped, links are added or dropped, processing power and bandwidth are changed, protocol stacks are modified, and applications are upgraded. This results in predictability and significant cost savings during the deployment of the network [Shan92, Jeru92], since the activities of capacity planning, budget forecasting, equipment evaluation, growth management, and migration strategization are integrated with the activity of network architecture.

Simulation provides an opportunity to study network functionality under different kinds of traffic, without recording tedious physical data or performing complex mathematical analyses. This helps to identify where the network is overbuilt or underbuilt, consider possible restructuring, evaluate the impact of different protocols, and analyze the costs of supporting incremental traffic and workloads.

Parameters for Network Simulation

Many interesting parameters can be studied under simulation; some typical metrics include the following:

- *Performance Analysis*: Does the network deliver adequate end-to-end performance under normal conditions? Under exceptional conditions?

- *Capacity Utilization*: What percentage of the processing capacity of the devices and the link bandwidth is actually utilized? Is this within safety tolerances?

- *Throughput Analysis*: Is the total throughput of the network adequate? If not, how will changing the number and type of devices and links affect the throughput?

- *Congestion and Bottleneck Determination*: If throughput is not adequate, where are the bottlenecks? If those bottlenecks are removed, where will the new bottlenecks be?

- *Delay Profiles*: What are the average and extreme delays for network traffic, including queueing delay, processing delay, and transmission delay? Are they within tolerances?

- *Load Balancing*: Is the load adequately distributed over the resources available? If not, how can traffic be redistributed?

- *Device Substitution, Addition, and Removal*: What is the effect of substituting one device type with another? Of adding a new device? Of removing an existing device?

- *Link Substitution, Addition, and Removal*: What is the effect of substituting one link type with another? Of adding a new link? Of removing an existing link?

- *Blocking Probabilities*: What is the probability that a connection establishment request will be blocked?

- *Non-Delivery Probabilities*: What is the probability that a packet will fail to reach its destination?

- *Reconfiguration Response*: How does the network respond to reconfiguration, initiated either manually or automatically?

- *Failure Modes*: What are the modes in which the network can fail? What is the effect of device failure? Link failure? Subnetwork failure?

- *Failure Response*: How do local failures affect the performance and throughput? Do the backup devices have adequate capacity?

- *Failure Propagation*: Do failures propagate through the network? How are performance and throughput affected?

- *Degraded Operation*: Can the network continue to perform at a degraded level of operation under multiple failures? Can critical devices and links continue to function?

- *Stability*: Does the network exhibit the characteristics of a stable dynamical system under failure perturbation? Can it restabilize to a lower level of operation under exceptional situations? Under what conditions will it exhibit catastrophic outages?

27.10. Traffic Engineering

One of the key features of a simulation environment is *traffic generation*. This involves creating a traffic pattern in the simulation environment to approximate the traffic pattern that the network will experience in its actual environment. Naturally, the quality of this approximation will strongly influence the validity of the network design. With a good approximation for the traffic pattern, we can make accurate projections of the performance, throughput, delay, congestion, and many other parameters discussed in the previous section.

Queueing Systems

The analysis of network behavior under varying traffic conditions requires the in-depth application of *queueing theory* [Klei76]. Queueing theory models systems in which customers arrive at a certain rate and must wait for service from one or more servers. It applies to networks because the payload to be transmitted across the network (e.g., packets, calls) must generally compete for resources (e.g., switches, routers, token frames, shared-media access), and is often buffered ("queued") until the service is provided. Extensive work has been performed over the last several decades in the area of applying queueing theory to the design of communication networks.

Queueing systems are characterized by the notation $A/B/m$, where A is the probability density function for inter-arrival delays (sometimes called an *arrival rate*), B is the probability density function for service delays (*service rate*), and m is the number of servers. This notation assumes that no prioritization occurs, that is, service is always first-come first-served, and that buffer space in the queues is not a limiting factor.

Where both the inter-arrival delay probability density function and the service delay probability density function can be represented by an exponential distribution and there is only 1 server, the queueing system is known as an M/M/1 system (M standing for Markov). Such a system is analytically tractable; many interesting performance metrics (average number of packets in the queue, average response time, the probability that *n* packets are in the queue, etc.) can be obtained as closed-form analytical solutions. Such information can be used to size buffers and determine the optimum number of devices sharing a link. A system such as a D/D/m system assumes that both rates are constant. If both probability density functions have arbitrary distributions, the system is known as a G/G/m system, which in general has no analytical solution. Of course, it is possible to have systems such as M/G/m, and so on.

Different types of traffic have different inter-arrival probability density functions and service functions. For example, a protocol where the source produces cells at a constant clock rate (e.g., isochronous traffic in ATM cells), which are routed through a switching fabric with a near-constant switching time, may be well approximated as a D/D/1 system. On the other hand, bursty traffic such as packets originating on a LAN may have wide variance in their arrival rate distribution. In such situations, the M/D/1 distribution (exponential arrival rate and constant service rate) is often used as a starting point for many simulations; this assumption can be refined as more data becomes available.

Traffic Generation

To permit different types of traffic to be generated, we need a new object class in our synthesized network. We call this the trafficGenerator object class. This object class **specializes-into** many descendants which have the ability to generate different kinds of traffic (isochronous streams, fixed-length packets, variable-length frames, connection establishment requests, acknowledgements, etc.) The traffic generated by each trafficGenerator object is regulated by attributes such as meanPacketSize and packetSizeStandardDeviation. By setting these attributes to different values for different instances of trafficGenerator, we can generate different packet size distributions.

Aside from the traffic type, each trafficGenerator class further **specializes-into** descendants based on other attributes which control the arrival rate distributions. Each descendant of trafficGenerator can generate a different arrival rate distribution: for example, the exponentialTrafficGenerator class exhibits the behavior of an exponential probability density distribution. For each instance of this class, we may control the parameters of this behavior as we desire by setting the values of its attributes (such as lambda, the mean arrival rate). In a good simulation environment, each trafficGenerator object will permit us to independently vary parameters such as the mean and standard deviation of the resulting arrival rate distribution.

Of course, it is not sufficient to control just the arrival rate distributions — we must also control the service rate distributions. This means that we must have controllable implementations of `protocolEntity` objects in the simulation environment. If we have such implementations, then their FUNCTIONs such as `receivePacket`, `transmitPacket`, and `tableLookup` must have service rate distribution parameters controllable by the simulation environment. With these features, we can characterize the service rate distributions as we desire (e.g., constant, Poisson, Erlang, hyperexponential, hypoexponential, or other general phase distribution).

The simulation environment must permit multiple instances of `traffic-Generator` objects to be created and placed within the synthesized network, with each `trafficGenerator` possibly creating a different kind of traffic. We might also require some `trafficGenerators` to create mixed-mode traffic, such as would be required to simulate multimedia applications. Each `trafficGenerator` should also be capable of generating single-addressee messages, multicast messages, or broadcast messages, if the protocol being tested has these capabilities.

27.11. The Simulation Environment

A good simulation environment has many features which assist the simulation process. Some of these features include

- *User-definable traffic format*: This feature permits the network architect to control certain characteristics of the simulation traffic, for example, packet formats, packet sizes, and packet size distributions. A good simulation tool will also have a library of commonly used formats (both isochronous and non-isochronous) available for use.

- *User-definable traffic distribution*: This feature permits the network architect to select the arrival rate distributions of traffic on the network. Usually, traffic distributions are selected using some well-known statistical model, such as Erlang-B for connection establishment requests, or Poisson for packet arrival rates.

- *Parametric sensitivity analysis*: This feature permits the network architect to "unfix" a property of an object and make it a variable for the simulation, so as to determine how its variation influences overall network function. This property may be an attribute value, a function argument, a function result, a constraint, a rule precondition, and so on. By identifying critical properties and varying them independently, one at a time or in combination, we can study the complex interaction of parameters and the sensitivity of the network to each property.

- *Interactive parametric sensitivity*: This feature permits the network architect to perform parametric variation dynamically, so that the effect of the varied parameter is reflected immediately in the ongoing simulation. With this feature, if some particular simulation run goes obviously awry, it is no longer necessary to wait until it completes or to abort and restart from the beginning; it can be fixed interactively.

- *Interactive reconfiguration*: This feature permits the network architect to interactively reconfigure the network during the simulation. This can be used, for example, to simulate device or link failure during network operation, or device or link return-to-service. A good simulation tool will demonstrate whether traffic can dynamically adapt to such failures and restabilize, cause performance degradation, or trigger propagated outages.

- *Animation*: This feature displays aspects of the simulation as it proceeds. A good simulation tool permits the network architect to specify what parameters she wishes to monitor during the simulation (e.g., queue lengths and processing delays). The tool then presents dynamic graphs or charts with this information as the simulation executes. A good tool will permit the network architect to change the viewed information interactively during the simulation, and also to deactivate and reactivate the entire animation feature. (Running a simulation with animation turned off usually speeds up execution.)

- *Debugging*: This feature permits the network architect to track the detailed progress of a particular activity step by step. For example, a simulation tool supporting debugging will permit the network architect to generate just a single packet from a traffic generator and trace the route of the packet in a stepwise fashion from device to device and link to link, so that mis-routing and other problems can be investigated in a detailed manner.

- *Session recording and playback*: This feature permits the network architect to record a simulation session, so that it may be captured in some persistent medium (e.g., a disk file). The playback feature recreates the same run with the same input parameters. A good environment also permits the editing of recorded session files so that they may be played back in an abbreviated or expanded manner, or with some change in parameter values.

- *Captured live traffic insertion*: This feature permits the simulation to execute against an actual traffic stream captured from a live network (e.g., recorded via a protocol analyzer), instead of traffic generated by a statistical traffic generator. This is typically used when actual traffic data is available from an existing network, which needs to be simulated to test for reconfiguration or future growth.

- *Capture file editing*: This feature permits the network architect to edit the capture file containing the live traffic, so that it may be fed to the simulation model with uninteresting or undesirable aspects of the live traffic removed, and extraordinary events (e.g., broadcast storms) inserted within normal traffic for simulation testing.

- *Financial analysis*: A good simulation tool permits the network architect to attach "weights" (device costs and link tariffs) to elements of the proposed configuration and to perform a financial analysis of network operating costs. These weights should be editable on a case-by-case basis so that speculative "what-if" analysis can be performed. While the synthesis tool can estimate deployment cost (by adding the `cost` attributes of every instance in the proposed configuration), only the simulation tool can estimate operating cost (based on the traffic volume on each link during the simulation).

- *Time-scale information*: Very few simulation tools can perform in real time, since the large traffic volumes and high link bandwidths of real networks cannot be re-created in the simulation environment. Because of this, a simulation involving a few minutes' worth of traffic in an actual network may take several hours to execute on the simulation platform. A simulation tool with time-scale information provides an indication of this time-scale expansion, and also specifies how the expansion is influenced by other CPU-consuming features if they are simultaneously active (e.g., animation or session recording).

- *Scenario programming*: In the later phases of network development, where most of the early errors have been corrected, a network model must typically be exercised for longer periods of time before the next error is found. To speed up execution for long-running tests, a simulation tool supporting compiled simulation permits the network architect to program standard operational scenarios in a compilable "simulation language" for faster execution. This is especially useful if the network design is frequently regression-tested (e.g., under a policy that the impact of any configuration change must first be simulation-tested under prede-fined scenarios). Such a compilable language also gives the network architect detailed control over the scenarios she wishes to develop. (Note that this involves scenario programming, not programming for the traffic generation or service algorithms.)

- *Scenario scripting*: This feature is similar to scenario programming but enables the network architect to run the simulations involving previously developed scenarios simply by invoking them from a "scenario library". Thus, previous simulation runs may be "scripted" together in various combinations to create new runs.

- *Automatic scenario generation*: Besides scenario programming and scripting, a good simulation environment can also perform automatic scenario generation, based on its knowledge of the object-oriented model underlying the network configuration. Obvious scenarios which can be automatically generated from the model are the saturation of each `link`, the failure of each `link`, the return-to-service of that `link`, the saturation of each `networkDevice`, the failure of each `networkDevice`, the return-to-service of that `networkDevice`, the failure of component objects of `networkDevices`, various combinations of multiple failures, and so on. The network architect can then select any or all of the suggested scenarios she wishes to simulate.

- *Result postprocessor*: The recorded results of the simulation can be statistically analyzed with a postprocessor, so that aggregate parameters of interest can be reported. A postprocessor will compute the statistical information which the network architect requests (e.g., means, variances and distributions).

Results of Simulation

The result postprocessor can provide all the performance metrics of interest to the network architect. Some of these metrics might be available directly by directly reading values of network objects implemented for the simulation environment (e.g., counter attributes of protocol entities), while others might have to be explicitly computed from data recorded during the simulation (e.g., probability distributions). Typical metrics of interest are listed below.

For `link` objects in a circuit-switched environment:

- *Link statistics* (availability as a function of time, bandwidth saturation as a function of time, percentage utilization as a function of time, total load carried as Erlangs/cells/packets, etc.)

- *Connection load statistics* (connections attempted, connections blocked, connections disconnected, connections queued, distribution of connection durations, etc.)

- *Connection service statistics* (queue size distribution, queueing time distribution, blocking probability distribution, etc.)

For `link` objects in a packet-switched environment:

- *Packet load statistics* (packets offered, packets delivered, packets dropped, packet size distribution, etc.)

- *Packet service statistics* (packet queueing probability, queue size distribution, queueing time distribution, etc.)

For non-terminal `networkDevice` objects (e.g., routers, switches):

- *Device statistics* (availability as a function of time, percentage utilization as a function of time, total load switched, number of busy processors, etc.).

- *Packet load statistics* or *connection load statistics* for each terminated `link`

- *Packet service statistics* or *connection service statistics* for each terminated `link`

For terminal `networkDevice` objects:

- *Connection load statistics* (for connection-oriented terminals)

- *Packet load statistics* (for packet-oriented terminals)

For shared-medium `link` objects:

- *Link statistics*

- *Collision statistics* (number of collisions, number of backoffs, backoff delay distribution, backoff queue size distribution, etc.)

- *Token statistics* (token waiting time distribution, etc.)

27.12. Synthesis with Simulation

Synthesis and simulation go hand in hand — each supports the other. The results of the simulation must be fed back into the synthesis process so that the network configuration can be refined. Therefore, it is necessary for the simulation tool to have strong links with the synthesis tool; in particular, they must both work with reference to the same architecture information base. These links make it possible for the simulation tool to present the network architect immediately with new candidate reconfigurations and possible trade-offs as soon as it recognizes a problem in the simulation. By exploring architectural alternatives, evaluating performance and selecting trade-offs early in the design cycle, the network architect can verify correctness beforehand and obtain reasonable confidence in the deployed network.

Much network simulation has focused on micro-simulation, for example, simulation at the level of individual LAN protocols [Fros90, Erso92]. Macro-simulation, or network-wide simulation for complex data and voice networks, is not as widely performed due to its computational expense and the lack of sufficiently powerful modeling methodologies for large networks. With the development of modeling methodologies such as those of this book, and with the increasing affordability of processing power for large-scale simulation runs, this situation will doubtless improve.

The simulation tools of the future will not only be able to perform the simulation but analyze the results in an intelligent manner and suggest configuration changes to the architect. For example, a simulation tool may notice that the bandwidth saturation on a link is 90%, inspect the architecture information base, determine that the network-Devices terminating the link participate in the termination relationship with a relatant multiplicity greater than 1 (i.e., it is possible for the networkDevices to terminate multiple links) and suggest to the network architect that either another link be added, or the existing link be upgraded to a higher bandwidth. The architect can then select the best alternative from the possible solutions presented by the simulation tool for the problems that it has discovered.

27.13. Summary

Considerable benefit can be derived by applying an object-oriented modeling methodology to network architecture. Network synthesis can be performed with respect to an architecture information base. By using relationships as prescriptive construction rules, an algorithmic approach can be used to create network configurations which deliver the required services. Optimization techniques can be used to select the configurations which are best with respect to stated criteria.

The simulation of a network configuration created using an object-oriented model can help to further refine the proposed architecture. Simulation exercises the network configuration so that appropriate devices and links can be redimensioned to support the anticipated workload. With a systematic object-oriented approach to network synthesis and simulation, significant cost savings can result and the network can be deployed with confidence.

28. Modeling for Network Operations

> *"Not much good at anything. Consider promotion to standards rep."*
> — *in personnel review file of anonymous network architect.*

28.1. Introduction

In this chapter, the application of object-oriented network models to network operations is discussed. We introduce the concept of an operations information base for storing an object model of all the information necessary for the run-time operation of the network. The attributes and relationships which network devices can obtain from the operations information base are presented. The concepts of interoperability and interworkability are defined, and mechanisms for network devices to autodiscover these relationships among themselves are demonstrated. We conclude with a discussion of how object-oriented models might apply to the international Intelligent Network standards.

28.2. Network Operations

Network operations involves the proper functioning of a network. Once a network has been architected, validated, and deployed, the network must function as designed and deliver the services required of it. Although a network is architected with a particular configuration, during operations the configuration is unlikely to remain static for long periods of time. The reasons for this are many: routine and unplanned outages, link failures, device failures, workload increase, capacity saturation, equipment upgrades, equipment decommissioning, addition of terminal devices, interconnection with other networks, and so on. Some alterations might require simply "tinkering around the edges" of the old configuration; others might require major modifications. While all these changes are occurring, it is important to keep network operations running as smoothly as possible with minimal interruption and downtime.

Autoconfiguration Capability

The quality of network operations is greatly enhanced if any new interconnection or configuration change can be executed in as automated a fashion as possible. Minimal interruption to network operations can be assured if the devices added or interconnected to the existing network are, as far as possible, "plug-and-play". This means that the devices themselves have the capability — by referring to some object model — of determining how best to interoperate with other devices. The devices of the future, possessing sufficient intelligence to organize by themselves the interfaces they present to other devices, will be capable of *autoconfiguration*.

Autoconfiguration ability among network devices becomes increasingly important as their capabilities increase. As the cost of processing power decreases, the variety of functions that can be performed by any one device will increase. In the network of the future, devices will present multiple interfaces, support multiple protocols, and provide multiple services. Networks will be called upon to interconnect with other networks, either temporarily or permanently, and must provide this interconnection in a smooth, uninterrupted fashion. Telecommunications networks, enterprise networks, data internetworks, cable television networks, cellular networks, mobile data networks, and satellite-based networks must function together to deliver services. Devices within these networks, therefore, must be very versatile, as they will be called upon to interoperate with each other with as much flexibility of configuration as possible.

It is desirable to manufacture devices which possess sufficient intelligence to perform the required handshaking upon interconnection, and, if they support multiple protocol suites, select one for interoperating with each other. On being plugged into the network, they will be able to query each other's configuration and service capabilities, determine at what level they can interoperate, negotiate a communication protocol with applicable options and parameters, and automatically configure themselves for service.

To quote Perlman [Perl92]: "Tomorrow's networks must run themselves as much as possible. Ideally, naive users should be able to buy a piece of equipment from the local discount department store, plug it into a network, and be operational. They should not have to configure complex parameters. They should not need to find the address guru to be given an address. (The address guru will be on vacation or will eventually quit, and the envelope on which the address guru scrawled the address assignments will be lost.) They should not have to find the manager of other nodes in order to have information about their new node configured into databases."

The following extrapolation of this scenario to residential telecommunication services may seem fanciful but will soon be commonplace. In the near future, plugging in a terminal device into a residential outlet could cause the service provider's equipment in the central office to "know" whether the terminal is a plain old telephone terminal, a fax terminal, a standard television monitor, a digital HDTV terminal with interactive capabilities, a computer system with a full data stack, or one of the new consumer electronics devices of the future. The service provider's equipment can then determine the formats and protocols the terminal device can interpret and configure its own interfaces to provide the proper service. As the variety of terminal devices which can share a common physical interface increase, so will the variety of central-office equipment — the conventional distinction between "voice switches", "routers", and "CATV head-end systems" will lose currency. This example only illustrates autoconfiguration in the residential environment; autoconfiguration capabilities in enterprise networks, manufacturing networks, and other specialized networks will similarly cause vast benefits to accrue.

The Operations Information Base

An object-oriented modeling methodology is important to achieving autoconfiguration capability, for it is only with reference to a common object model that devices can determine how best to interoperate. By interrogating the object models of other devices, and by possessing the ability to interpret that object model, a device (or some external intelligence controlling the device) can decide how it can best interwork with other devices. By exposing its own object model for inspection by other devices, a device can advertise its availability for interconnection to other devices. Using such object models, each device can determine what the nature and type of the other device is, how it is configured, what its capacity is, what its throughput is, what its components are, what protocol stacks it supports, and what its access and security restrictions are. Based on this information, it can determine at what level it can interoperate with the other device.

The object model from which devices can obtain this information is termed an *operations information base*. An operations information base is a subset of the model information base, containing all *run-time* information which the functioning network will require. An operations information base can be interrogated by devices themselves, or by some external intelligence controlling the devices, so that all the information necessary about the object models of other devices can be obtained.

An operations information base is not necessarily a centralized data store with a database implementation. It may be a distributed data store — parts of the operations information base may be available in different places within the network. One network might decide to maintain its operations information base as a single, centralized data store, as illustrated in Figure 28-1. Another network might implement parts of the operations information base inside each device itself, as was illustrated in Figure 1-3. A high-end device might be capable of storing its own object model and making it available to other devices when requested. As long as the necessary information can be located and accessed, the actual implementation of an operations information base is architecturally unimportant.

Throughout this chapter, we will often speak of "a device being able to determine" or "a device being able to infer" certain information about the object model of other devices. While high-end devices may possess such determination capability internally, without loss of generality such anthropomorphism should be understood to apply to any external intelligence controlling the devices as well. Autoconfiguration for service delivery can be executed just as well by an agency controlling the devices, as long as it has access to the object-oriented model in the operations information base. The fundamental operative notion is that this happens in an automated fashion, without the intervention of any human agency to configure or provision each device; thus, the network may be considered to be *self-aware*, *self-adapting*, and *self-provisioning* [Berk91].

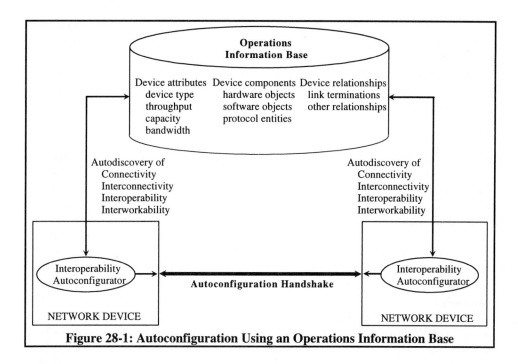

Figure 28-1: Autoconfiguration Using an Operations Information Base

28.3. Interoperability and Interworkability

It is important for devices to be able to determine their interoperability on-line, that is, through the run-time interrogation of an operations information base. In Chapter 27, we saw how `connectivity` and `interconnectivity` relationships between network devices may be inferred from the object model. Instances of these same relationships between network devices can also be determined in the operations information base. Connectivity and interconnectivity, however, only indicate whether a sequence of wire-line or wireless links exists between some pair of network devices; they do not indicate whether they can interoperate. To make an on-line determination of their ability to exchange data with each other, network devices must have ways of discovering *interoperability relationships* between themselves.

The devices seeking to make such mutual interoperability determinations may or may not be located across jurisdictional boundaries. Devices from each network jurisdiction can mutually query the operations information bases of devices from other network jurisdictions, to the extent that each jurisdiction makes such information available. If the operations information base exposes data about the components, protocol stacks, interfaces, and applications which each `networkDevice has-as-a-part`, and the relationship instances which that `networkDevice` has with other objects (e.g., `termination` relationship instances with `link` objects), then external devices can determine their capabilities and make appropriate decisions for interoperability. If a jurisdictional authority does not wish to allow external access to certain objects, it can ensure that they remain invisible to other networks in the operations information base.

Interoperability Relationships

We define interoperability only with respect to a particular layer of a particular reference model. Thus, it is not meaningful in our methodology to say "networkDevice A interoperates with networkDevice B". It is only meaningful to say "networkDevice A interoperates with networkDevice B *at the transport layer*" or "*at the application layer*".

Interoperability is relative to a particular layer because devices infer it by a *pairwise matching of protocol stacks* between themselves and another device. Starting from the lowest layer, a networkDevice compares its own protocolStack components with those of the other networkDevice. The highest layer to which the protocolStacks compare equal is the layer at which they can interoperate. Thus, we cannot define interoperability in the abstract; we can only define network-interoperability, transport-interoperability, application-interoperability, and so on. If two networkDevice objects contain full protocol stacks identical up to the application layer, then they are application-interoperable. If they are identical only up to the network layer, either because the transport layers are different, or because one of them does not contain a full stack (for example, it may be a router), then they are only network-interoperable.

Note that connectivity is a necessary condition for interoperability, although it is not a sufficient condition; mere connectivity does not guarantee interoperability. Nevertheless, two networkDevice objects cannot interoperate with each other unless they are also connected-to each other via a wireline or wireless link. For the time being, we shall work under this assumption; after we have developed some modeling concepts, we will expand it to show how devices need not be directly connected to interoperate but can also interoperate over a *sequence* of connections (that is, over inter-connectivity relationships).

The roles of any interoperability relationship are {X-interoperates-with, is-X-interoperable-with}, where X is a metavariable ranging over the layers of the reference model of interest. Examples of role-pairs are {network-interoperates-with, is-network-interoperable-with} for network-interoperability relationships, {transport-interoperates-with, is-transport-interoperable-with} for transport-interoperability relationships, and so forth. Note that X is not a relationship attribute of the interoperability relationship, since the interoperability relationship itself is virtual. Rather, for a reference model with *n* layers, there are *n* different possible interoperability role-pairs. Clearly, all these role-pairs are commutative.

Note, however, that interoperability relationships are not *transitive*. For example, if networkDevice A knows that it application-interoperates-with networkDevice B, and knows also that networkDevice B application-interoperates-with networkDevice C, then networkDevice A *cannot* infer that it too application-interoperates-with networkDevice C. This is because `networkDevice` B may be running two entirely different sets of full protocol stacks, one to communicate with `networkDevice` A and another with `network-Device` C. Figure 28-2 illustrates basic interoperability relationships.

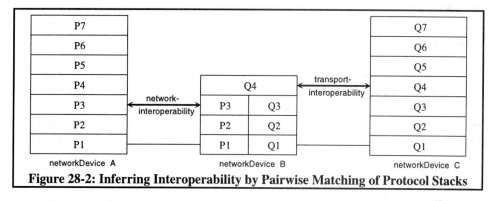

Figure 28-2: Inferring Interoperability by Pairwise Matching of Protocol Stacks

Such interoperability determinations can also apply to trivial single-layer "stacks" for isochronous communication: for example, a `videoConferenceRecorder` may infer that it interoperates with an `hdtvTerminal` if it can determine that they both `have-as-a-part` identical "protocol entity" objects (i.e., encoder/decoder chip sets) capable of interpreting the same format for isochronous video signal streams.

Interworkability Relationships

Interoperability is not necessarily a prerequisite for exchanging data, because of the possibility of protocol translation functions. For example, if a `desktopComputer` object runs only an OSI `protocolStack`, it cannot interoperate with an `ftpServer` object running only an Internet `protocolStack` at any layer higher than data link. Nevertheless, it might still be possible to exchange files between them. A third object, say a `protocolGateway`, may be `connected-to` both devices, functioning as a translator. Such a device might implement *both* an Internet and an OSI protocol stack, with an FTP-FTAM application gateway between them. Thus, the `ftpServer` and `desktop-Computer` objects can still exchange data through the translation function in the `protocolGateway` device. This does not, however, mean that they interoperate with each other, since by definition interoperability arises from pairwise matching of protocol stacks. In this network, the only interoperability relationships that exist are between the `ftpServer` device and the `protocolGateway` device, and between the `protocolGateway` device and the `desktopComputer` device.

We define the relationship where two `networkDevice` objects cannot interoperate at a given layer, but can still exchange information at that layer through the use of intermediate translators or gateways, as the *interworkability relationship*. Like interoperability relationships, interworkability relationships are also relative to particular layers: the roles of any interworkability relationship are {`X-interworks-with, is-X-in-terworkable-with`}, where `X` is a metavariable ranging over the layers of one or more reference models. In the case where interworking occurs across different reference models, X must stand for a layer which is analogous in both reference models.

The existence of interworkability relationships can also be inferentially derived by the devices themselves. For example, if `networkDevice` A knows that it `application-interoperates-with` `networkDevice` B, and also knows that `networkDevice` B `application-interoperates-with` `network-Device` C, and knows in addition that `networkDevice` B `has-as-a-part` a `protocolEntity` object with a translation function between the two applications, then `networkDevice` A can infer that it `application-interworks-with` `networkDevice` C. Figure 28-3 illustrates this situation.

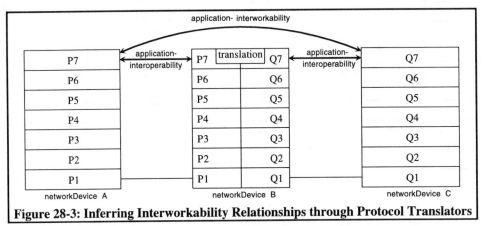

Figure 28-3: Inferring Interworkability Relationships through Protocol Translators

In general, the translation function which provides interworkability could be at any layer. Examples are LAN bridges (at the data link layer), transport bridges (at the transport layer [Rose90]), and application gateways (at the application layer).

Autodiscovering Interoperability and Interworkability

Earlier, we demonstrated how devices may infer interoperability relationships between themselves by pairwise matching of protocol stacks. There is a second way that interoperability relationships can be inferred, and that is from an *interworkability relationship in the layer below*. It is possible, for example, that `networkDevice` A `dataLink-interoperates-with` `networkDevice` B, and `networkDevice` B `dataLink-interoperates-with` `networkDevice` C. As explained earlier, interoperability is not transitive, so it does not necessarily follow that `networkDevice` A `dataLink-interoperates-with` `networkDevice` C. However, if `networkDevice` B `has-as-a-part` some `protocolEntity` with a translation function (e.g., a bridging function) at the data link layer, then, using the concepts of Figure 28-3 at the data link layer, it is possible that `networkDevice` A `dataLink-interworks-with` `networkDevice` C.

The existence of an *interworkability* relationship at a lower layer makes it possible to have *interoperability* relationships at higher layers. In the previous example, it is possible for `networkDevice` A to interoperate with `networkDevice` C at the network layer or higher, if they have the same `protocclEntity` objects at the network layer and up. Thus, `networkDevice` A can infer a `network-interoperability` relationship with `networkDevice` C *if* (a) they both have at least one common network-layer protocol entity, and (b) there is a `dataLink-interworkability` relationship between them. Thus, interoperability can also arise from a convolute virtual relationship. Figure 28-4 shows how interoperability in the layer above may be inferred by interworkability in the layer below.

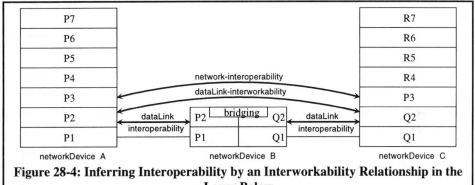

Figure 28-4: Inferring Interoperability by an Interworkability Relationship in the Layer Below

In the example of Figure 28-4, `networkDevice` B could be a `hetergeneousBridge` object with `networkDevices` A and C being end-stations on LAN segments of different types. Note that we have now relaxed the temporary assumption we had made earlier, namely that `connectivity` was a necessary condition for interoperability. As Figure 28-4 shows, interoperability can occur across multiple wireline or wireless links, and so the necessary condition for interoperability is not `connectivity` but `interconnectivity`.

Figure 28-4, however, represents the simple case with just one intermediate object. In the general case, there can be an arbitrarily long chain of interworkability relationships in the layer below. Thus, `networkDevice` objects must be able to infer interoperability in the layer above with other `networkDevice` objects across an arbitrary number of "hops", including across WANs; we need extended reasoning mechanisms in addition to the cascaded convolutions arising in Figure 28-4.

We make such reasoning possible for the devices in two ways. First, we specify in the operations information base that, for all layers, interworkability relationships are *transitive*. This means that, if `networkDevice` A `dataLink-interworks-with` `networkDevice` C, and `networkDevice` C `dataLink-interworks-with` `networkDevice` E, then `networkDevice` A `dataLink-interworks-with` `networkDevice` E. This contrasts with interoperability relationships, which are *not* transitive. Figure 28-5 illustrates the transitivity of interworkability relationships.

Second, we also specify in the operations information base that, at any given layer, interworkability *distributes over* interoperability, conditional to a translation func-

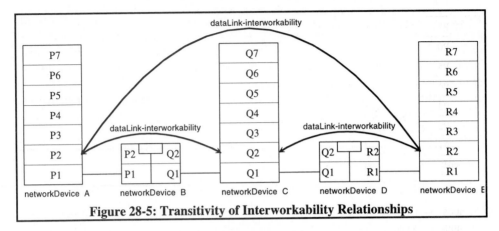

Figure 28-5: Transitivity of Interworkability Relationships

tion at that layer: if `networkDevice A dataLink-interworks-with` `networkDevice F`, and `networkDevice F dataLink-interoperates-with` `networkDevice G`, then `networkDevice A` also `dataLink-interworks-with networkDevice G`, *if* `networkDevice F` has a translation function (e.g., bridging) at the data link layer. Figure 28-6 illustrates the distribution of interworkability over interoperability.

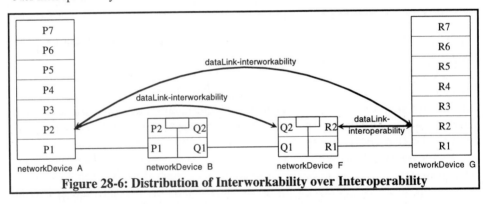

Figure 28-6: Distribution of Interworkability over Interoperability

Although all these figures draw upon examples at the data link layer, the transitivity of interworkability and the distribution of interworkability over interoperability apply at every layer. Further, if `networkDevice A` discovers interworkability with another network device at layer *n*, and if it can pairwise-match its protocol stacks with that network device at layers *n+1* and higher, then it is permitted to infer *interoperability* at the highest possible layer at which the protocol stacks match. This is similar to the convolution of Figure 28-4, except that this can now occur across multiple "hops". Figure 28-7 illustrates an example of this situation.

In Chapter 27, we developed precise definitions for the concepts of *connectivity* and *interconnectivity*; we now have precise definitions for the concepts of *interoperability* and *interworkability*. Together, all these definitions go a long way toward equipping

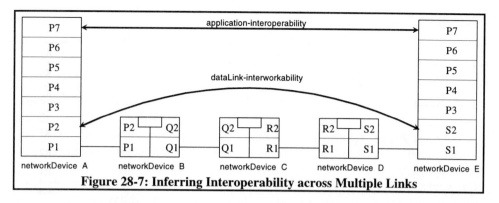

Figure 28-7: Inferring Interoperability across Multiple Links

devices with the intelligence to perform autoconfiguration. The only actual relationship instances which need to be available in the operations information base are for (a) the aggregation relationships between `networkDevice` objects and the `port` and `protocolStack` objects they `have-as-a-part` and (b) the `termination` relationships between `networkDevice` and `link` objects. From this information, network devices can discover for themselves the following:

- *Connectivity* relationships with other `networkDevices` can be autodiscovered by determining which `networkDevices` have `termination` relationships with the same `link` object they do;

- *Interconnectivity* relationships with other `networkDevices` can be autodiscovered by virtue of a chain of `connectivity` relationships (that is, by implication from `connectivity`, by distribution over `connectivity`, and by transitivity of `interconnectivity`).

- *Layer-n-interoperability* relationships can be autodiscovered from existing `connectivity` relationships between `networkDevices` which `have-as-a-part` a `protocolStack` or substack identical up to layer *n*;

- *Layer-n-interworkability* relationships with other `networkDevices` can be autodiscovered (a) from a layer-*n*-interoperability relationship with a common `networkDevice` object which `has-as-a-part` a protocol translation entity at layer *n*, or (b) by distribution over layer-*n*-interoperability, also conditional to a translation entity at layer *n*, or (c) by transitivity of layer-*n*-interworkability.

- *Layer-n+1-interoperability* relationships can be autodiscovered between `networkDevices` which have the same `protocolEntity` at layer *n*+1, and a layer-*n*-interworkability relationship in the layer below.

Reference Points

For conciseness, interoperability and interworkability relationships are often defined across *reference points*. A reference point is a hypothetical location, often given a name, across which protocol stacks can be pairwise-matched and message exchanges defined. We can model this as the fully abstract referencePoint object class, with no properties aside from a referencePointType attribute, and specify an optional relationship between it and the link object class. Thus, a link object may or may not mark a referencePoint. Reference points are not active functionaries in a network model; they are usually created to logically partition subnetworks or demarcate administrative or jurisdictional boundaries. For succinctness, a networkDevice may assume interoperability with another networkDevice if they both terminate a link which marks the same instance of referencePoint, the level of interoperability being predefined by the type of the reference point.

Using Autodiscovered Relationships in Autoconfiguration

The ability of network devices to autodiscover connectivity, interconnectivity, interoperability, and interworkability among themselves from an operations information base is a large part, but not all, of their autoconfiguration ability. It is important for each network device to determine other factors as well. For example, once networkDevice A has discovered interconnectivity and interoperability with networkDevice B, it may also wish to determine the objects which networkDevice B has-as-a-part. The components of interest may be hardware, software, or protocol entities; their presence or absence may provide networkDevice A with additional information about how best to interoperate with networkDevice B. Further, networkDevice A may also wish to read attribute values for networkDevice B, such as its capacity, throughput, bandwidth, or packet processing rate. All such information about networkDevice B can be obtained by networkDevice A by interrogating the operations information base.

Further, the ability to discover interoperability and interworkability relationships between network devices is not restricted to the operations information base; it can be used in the architecture information base as well. During network architecture, this ability allows the automated network synthesis tool to determine which networkDevice objects must be selected to provide the services required of the network. The automated synthesis tool only selects those sets of devices which have mutual interoperability relationships and can work together to meet the desired goals.

The notion of autoconfiguration need not necessarily be restricted to interfaces between network devices — it can be extended to higher-level objects as well. For example, an aggregate object such as a subnetwork object consisting of many networkDevice components may also be able to autoconfigure itself. If the network architecture process, through synthesis and simulation, has determined different optimum configurations for the subnetwork object based on workload, that information can be stored for run-time use in the operations information base and applied when required. An intelligent subnetwork consisting of multiple end-stations and a wiringHub with internal modules for bridging and segmentation might be able to automatically break or unbreak LAN segments as the number of end-stations it serves changes, to optimize the workload. Such autoconfiguration might be driven by information accessed by the `sub-network` from the operations information base describing the different configuration possibilities as a function of workload.

28.4. The Intelligent Network

Object-oriented methodologies for network operations and for the design of operations software can be beneficial in many networks. One internationally standardized network architecture where these methodologies can be used to advantage is the *Intelligent Network*. The Intelligent Network is a family of ITU standards defining the next generation of telecommunications networks for the delivery of advanced services [ITU-T Q.1200]. Many of the design principles used in the Intelligent Network for its architecture, during operations, and for its network management are similar (but not equivalent) to the object-oriented methodology of this book.

The goal of the Intelligent Network is to develop an architecture for providing advanced telecommunications services. Because business and residential subscribers demand increasingly sophisticated services beyond basic two-party call processing, it is necessary to have "intelligence" (software control on a call-by-call basis) within the network which can make advanced services possible. The Intelligent Network architecture incorporates information processing systems (programmable environments and database machines) to provide this intelligence. The architecture is designed to facilitate a flexible allocation of functions and services throughout the network, using modularity and reusability.

Intelligent Network Services

The types of services that can be provided by an Intelligent Network include [ITU-T Q.1211, ITU-T Q.1218]:

- *Freephone service*: Regional, national, or international "800" service

- *Universal personal telephone service* (UPT): The ability to receive calls at any terminal by programming it with a unique personal number

- *Virtual private network service* (VPN): Simulation of dedicated lines on public resources, including private numbering plans and abbreviated dialing

- *Flexible routing service*: Call routing based on called number, calling number, geographic origin, time of day, day of week, date of month, month of year, forward-on-busy, or other subscriber-defined routing preferences

- *Flexible charging service*: Call charging to calling party, called party, third party, credit card, split charging, premium charging, and so on.

- *Flexible user interaction*: Announcements and subscriber control of other services such as abbreviated dialing, service deactivation, routing preference lists, and call forwarding lists.

Each of the above services is created by assembling together a set of predefined building blocks. The set of services that can be provided by the Intelligent Network is potentially vast. Groups of services which can be deployed together are called *capability sets*. While the capability set described above deals mostly with services for connection-oriented voice traffic, future capability sets will define the ability for subscribers to access and configure multimedia and other kinds of services.

A supporting set of standards defines the environment for rapidly introducing Intelligent Network services. This is called the *service creation environment* and is designed so that new services can be conceptualized, prototyped, created, tested, implemented, and provisioned in an accelerated manner. In essence, the service creation environment is an *architecture information base*, since it defines all the components which are available for combination using known relationships (assembly rules) to create complete services. Service objects are assembled using an object-oriented design process, applying components and relationships which can easily be codified in an architecture information base. This eventually results in reliable models for software development and greatly reduced development cycles [Fuji91, Ande92, Hase92].

Intelligent Network Conceptual Model

We already introduced one view of the Intelligent Network in Chapter 8. We now describe a more complete view. The basic architecture of the Intelligent Network is defined as a *conceptual model* [ITU-T Q.1201]. This model is structured into four planes, each of which provides an increasing level of abstraction. The lowest plane is the *physical plane*; above this are, in order, the *distributed functional plane*, the *global functional plane*, and the *service plane*. Figure 28-8 illustrates this model.

The *physical plane* describes the physical architecture of the Intelligent Network, in terms of the network devices which constitute the network and the links between them [ITU-T Q.1205]. The topology of the network and geographical location information is available from this plane. In Intelligent Network terminology, the network devices are called *physical entities*, and the links between them are called *interfaces*. The physical entities contain *functional entities* which provide the basic units of network functionality.

The *distributed functional plane* takes a "distributed processing" view of the architecture. It describes the details of the functional entities and their interactions without regard to their physical mapping. This plane deals with the functions and information exchanges between the functional entities in the abstract, so that the same functional entities may be implemented differently in various networks. The details of each functional entity are defined in terms of a set of *functional entity actions*, and its information exchanges with other functional entities are defined as a set of *relationships*.

The *global functional plane* rises to a higher level of abstraction, from which the entire network is viewed as a single entity supplying various functions on demand. This level of abstraction makes it possible for the global functional plane to be used as the basis for creating and defining network services. It defines *service-independent building blocks* as the units of service functionality, much as the physical plane defines functional entities as the units of network functionality. These service functionality units are defined in a manner independent of where their supporting network functionality units are avail-

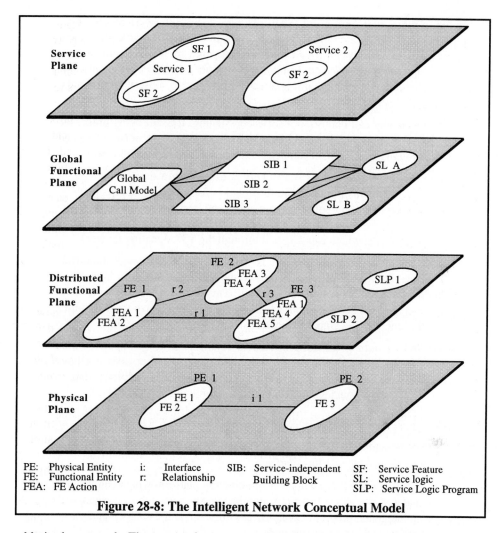

PE: Physical Entity   i: Interface   SIB: Service-independent   SF: Service Feature
FE: Functional Entity   r: Relationship   Building Block   SL: Service logic
FEA: FE Action   SLP: Service Logic Program

Figure 28-8: The Intelligent Network Conceptual Model

able in the network. The *service logic* — the high-level description of what the service-independent building blocks do — is also defined at this plane.

The *service plane* creates complete *services* by assembling various service-independent building blocks. It describes the *service features* of each service, that is, the capabilities that the service has from a subscriber's perspective, without regard to how the service is implemented or provisioned in the network.

Intelligent Network Physical Entities

Many of the entities of the physical plane of the Intelligent Network architecture were introduced in Figure 8-17. A brief description of the important physical entities is as follows [ITU-T Q.1201, ITU-T Q.1205, Dura92]:

- *Service switching point* (SSP): This is a switching system providing centralized switching of calls requiring Intelligent Network services. It determines how each call must be processed by invoking the service logic from a *service control point* or *adjunct processor*. It may also act as a call control agent if it is directly connected to subscriber terminals.

- *Network access point* (NAP): This is also a switching system but provides only call control, not service switching. If a call being processed at a NAP requires Intelligent Network services, it must be routed through an SSP which can determine the applicable service logic.

- *Service control point* (SCP): This is essentially a database computer which contains the rules and information for invoking various types of service logic and software to control and orchestrate the appropriate services requested by an SSP [Bowe91]. An SCP can be shared by many SSPs, which can access it through the SS7 signaling network.

- *Adjunct processor* (AD): This is equivalent to an SCP, with the difference that it is directly connected to the SSP by means of a high-speed interface and usually dedicated to it. This provides an SSP with faster access to the service logic, which otherwise would have to be obtained through the SS7 signaling network from an appropriate SCP.

- *Service data point* (SDP): This is also a database computer which stores additional processing information and rules but does not have the software to control service execution. It provides additional data to an SCP or adjunct and may be accessed through the SS7 network.

- *Intelligent peripheral* (IP): This is a database and voice-processing platform which provides for end-user interaction. Services such as voice mail, announcements, voice recognition, and speech processing can be provided on this platform.

- *Services node* (SN): This is a combination platform which can provide many of the above functions simultaneously; a switching system with an integrated program execution environment and database capabilities may be used as a services node.

The interaction of these physical entities and the functional entities which map to them are illustrated in Figure 28-9.

Intelligent Network Functional Entities

Depending on the platforms available, it is possible for particular instances of the physical entities of Figure 28-9 to implement both their required and optional functional entities. The functional entities of the Intelligent Network are

- The *service switching function* (SSF): This provides the ability to recognize and act upon calls that require special processing by the Intelligent Network. It can determine the applicable service logic from the *service control function*, and process the call accordingly.

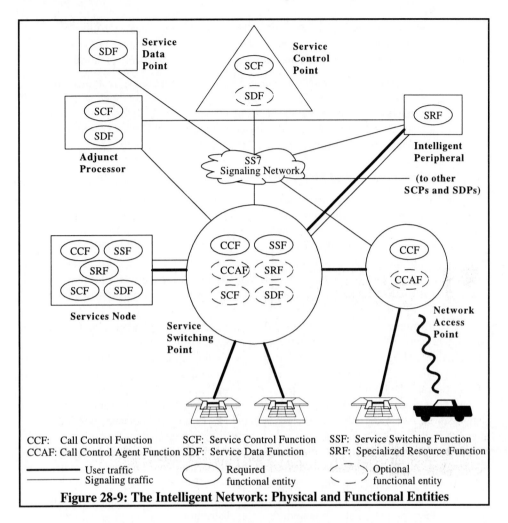

Figure 28-9: The Intelligent Network: Physical and Functional Entities

- The *call control function* (CCF): This constitutes the traditional ability to perform basic call processing, including connection establishment and tear-down.

- The *call control agent function* (CCAF): This interacts with subscribers to provide them with service access and acts as their agent with respect to the call control function.

- The *service control function* (SCF): This contains the "brains" of the Intelligent Network service; it provides all the logical analysis necessary for processing the call (e.g., translation, rerouting, screening, charging).

- The *service data function* (SDF): This contains the rules and information related to service data and network configuration which are necessary for the service logic and supplies this data to the SCF as required.

- The *specialized resource function* (SRF): This constitutes the ability to interact with the end-user to provide special resources, such as announcements, voice recognition, speech storage and forwarding, fax storage and forwarding, and digit collection for subscriber control of services (e.g., call forwarding, call screening, distribution lists).

Applying Object-Oriented Modeling

Although the Intelligent Network conceptual model is not defined in terms of the object-oriented methodologies of this book, the strong analogies are easily apparent. The modeling notions of flexible allocation of functions to physical entities and the composition of services using building blocks can, during high-level design and analysis, be easily brought within the realm of object-oriented modeling. Just as the service creation environment for Intelligent Network services acts as an architecture information base, so can the run-time model required for its operation be captured in an operations information base.

The interested reader may exploit this natural correspondence and recast the Intelligent Network conceptual model architecture in terms of object classes, inheritance hierarchies, aggregation, and other relationships. At the top level, four different branches can be created for the inheritance hierarchy corresponding to the four planes. Many relationships can be defined, both within a plane and across planes. Within the physical plane, we already attempted specifying aggregation relationships in Figure 8-18. Other aggregations can be defined across planes between physical entities and functional entities, and between services and service-independent building blocks. Relationships other than aggregation, such as service provision relationships, will also be required; a practitioner of this methodology can describe the Intelligent Network conceptual model as an object-oriented architecture with a modest amount of effort.

Since objects capture essential properties inside abstraction and encapsulation barriers, they provide natural boundaries for distribution. At its physical plane, the Intelligent Network is a system of network devices with various links to other devices. We already know how to model this as an object-oriented system. At its distributed functional plane, it is a distributed processing system in which functional entities have relationships with other functional entities; this too can be modeled with class relationships. The global functional plane and service plane deal largely with services, which are implemented as software entities; the advantages of having an object-oriented model as the basis for the development of software for distributed services have been widely recognized [Guen93].

The telecommunications architectures of tomorrow, which will provide access to information networking and support multimedia traffic [SR 2282, Nata92, Rubi94], can use object-oriented development principles to advantage. This will speed up the deployment of complex services through modularity and reusability, increase flexibility, assure interoperability across multiple jurisdictional boundaries, and handle the increased capabilities of end-user equipment [Barr93]. Emerging standards such as the *Telecommunications Information Networking Architecture*, (TINA) [Chap92, Appe93, Hall93] are attempting to bring object-oriented methodologies developed for the *Telecommunications Management Network* (TMN) within the purview of the Intelligent Network, so that an integrated methodology can be applied for both subscriber services and management services. We will explore the TMN architecture in greater detail in Chapter 29 and examine how its object-oriented information model brings flexibility to the services it can provide.

28.5. Distributed Computing Systems

A *distributed computing system* is an information processing system which consists of several nodes co-operating over a communications network. Usually, this terminology refers to computer systems and their peripherals in a private enterprise environment. A distributed computing system becomes necessary because general-purpose computer systems and their peripherals **specialize-into** classes such as desktopComputer, file-Server, transactionProcessingSystem, and highSpeedPrinter, instances of which may be located in geographically distant areas. These instances must communicate over local or wide-area networks in order to function co-operatively and deliver value to the enterprise.

While interworkability and interoperability relationships at all levels are clearly important in distributed computing systems, their architectures tend to focus largely on the upper layers. These architectures generally assume that reliable data transfer services are available from the lower layers, and that standard operating system services are also available in most nodes. Based on these assumptions, distributed computing architectures define objects at the application layer which can co-operate using common *Remote Procedure Call* (RPC) and other messaging mechanisms. The objects of a distributed computing system are generally all software objects.

A distributed computing architecture supports both *client-server* and *peer-to-peer* application-interoperability between application-layer objects. Naturally, the roles of "client", "server", and "peer" are not static. An object such as a highSpeedPrinter or databaseServer may almost always act as a server. Another object may be a client in one interaction, a server in another, and a peer in a third. The general object interaction mechanism works identically regardless of whether the client and server objects are local (co-hosted on the same node) or remote (on different nodes, including across WANs). The interacting objects always make the same interface calls, and it is up to the distributed computing system to determine whether the requested services are local or remote and arrange the communication accordingly. Thus, services are available in a *location-transparent* manner to the interacting objects, which might be arbitrarily distant in the distributed computing topology. Figure 28-10 illustrates the application view of a distributed computing system.

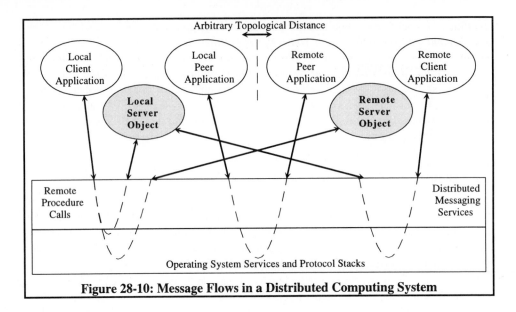

Figure 28-10: Message Flows in a Distributed Computing System

OSA / CORBA

There are many proprietary and standard distributed computing architectures. We describe here the *Object Service Architecture* (OSA) which has been standardized by the Object Management Group (OMG) industry consortium [OMG 92]. An important component of this framework is the *Common Object Request Broker Architecture* (CORBA) [OMG 90, OMG 91]. We describe this in some detail below; in Chapter 29, we will see how CORBA can be adapted for management of distributed computing systems.

In the CORBA architecture, since either interacting object may not know how to locate the other, the request passes through one or more *Object Request Brokers* (ORB). More than one ORB may exist in the network; the location of the ORBs is well known. Each interacting object knows how to contact at least one local ORB, using either advertisement by the ORB, solicitation by the object, preconfigured addresses, or some other mechanism. Each ORB can access a directory indicating the capabilities of various servers in the network and the optimal means of accessing them. ORBs only exist as a medium to facilitate ("broker") client-server interaction, and as such perform control-plane activities; they do not initiate client-like activities themselves with user-plane primitives.

Each ORB knows how to contact other ORBs and how to communicate with them using remote procedure call mechanisms (RPC). The subnetwork of ORBs may be considered to be a "software backplane" which allows relaying of messages. As an analogy to an internetworking environment, the system of ORBs is equivalent to a set of designated routers in multiple domains: each request out of a given domain goes through its ORB and is routed to the correct ORB which can relay it to its destination. In some distributed computing environments, brokers only execute the initial matchmaking between clients and servers (directory, location, and selection functions) but do not relay messages between them; such brokers are known as *traders* [Ansa92]. Figure 28-11 illustrates message passing between ORBs.

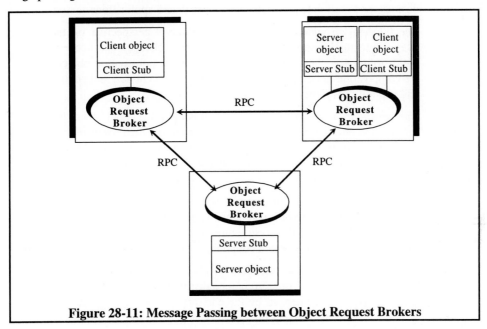

Figure 28-11: Message Passing between Object Request Brokers

DCE

Several other standard distributed computing architectures exist. Although not all are specified in the terminology of object-oriented modeling, many object-oriented design principles are used in their architecture. An important architecture is the *Distributed Computing Environment* (DCE) standardized by Open Software Foundation (OSF) industry consortium. DCE offers many lower-layer services used by application objects, such as a distributed file system, a distributed time service, name and directory services, remote procedure calls, and other "glue" interfaces for multivendor interoperability.

ODP

Other distributed computing architectures which are internationally standardized include ISO's *Open Distributed Processing* (ODP), which is aligned with ITU's *Distributed Application Framework* (DAF). The ODP architecture is object-oriented and has its own reference model, which is superordinated over the entire OSI reference model [Lini91, Scho91, IWODP 91, Schi93]. The ODP reference model is described in a five-part specification: an *overview*, a *descriptive model*, a *prescriptive model*, a *user model*, and *architectural semantics* [ITU-T X.901, ITU-T X.902, ITU-T X.903, ITU-T X.904]. Current developments in ODP include the effort to introduce a formal notation such as Object Z to specify semantics [ISO WG7/N372, Cusa91].

The ODP reference model can be viewed from a number of different viewpoints:

- The *enterprise viewpoint* describes applications from the perspective of the value delivered to the organization. It considers the influence of business and corporate requirements on distributed applications.

- The *information viewpoint* provides a high-level perspective on the overall information model, including the data exchanges that occur in the distributed application. Semantic modeling of information objects, the composition of complex objects, data types and classes, and control and visibility restrictions are considered at this stage.

- The *computation viewpoint* uses and builds upon the model from the information viewpoint. It describes a software-oriented view of distributed applications, identifying the different program components, their interface specifications, and the message flows between them.

- The *engineering viewpoint* is concerned with the configuration and control of distributed applications. It addresses the correct placement and distribution of software components, performance evaluation and tuning, and the technical infrastructure underlying the system, including the interface to the selected communication services.

- The *technology viewpoint* considers the choice of actual hardware and software components in order to build a distributed application system. This viewpoint is influenced by the enterprise viewpoint (which dictates the level of investment in new technology) and in turn influences the decisions made in the engineering viewpoint.

The ODP reference model provides a user's view of distributed computing and demonstrates how OSI's application service elements, in combination with new services, can be used to synthesize application systems such as transaction processing, remote database access, and store-and-forward communication. ODP does not focus on the communication architecture as OSI and other reference models do; it concentrates on distributed applications, preferring to leave the communication component as the "plumbing" for application-interoperability between ODP objects. A high-level comparison of ODP with other modeling approaches may be found in [Kilo93b].

28.6. Intelligent Networks versus Networked Intelligence

There are many commonalities between standard Intelligent Network architectures and standard distributed computing architectures. This is hardly surprising, because they both approach a common goal from two different perspectives:

- *Intelligent Network architectures add intelligence to communications facilities by incorporating and subsuming information processing systems within themselves.*

- *Distributed computing architectures add distribution to information processing systems by incorporating and subsuming communications facilities within themselves.*

As might be expected, Intelligent Network and distributed computing architectures complement and feed upon each other. The information processing systems inside an Intelligent Network can themselves use distributed computing architectures. The service control and service data functions of an Intelligent Network may be implemented on distributed computing architectures. As we shall see in Chapter 29, the Telecommunications Management Network also has a distributed computing architecture. To complement this, private distributed computing systems in an enterprise environment can themselves use communication facilities provided by an Intelligent Network. Figure 28-12 illustrates the interdependency of Intelligent Network and distributed computing architectures.

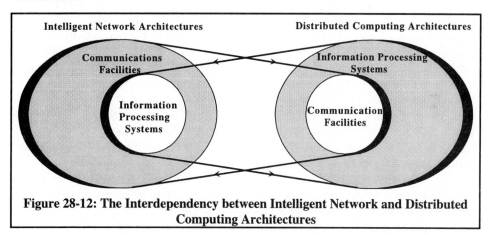

Figure 28-12: The Interdependency between Intelligent Network and Distributed Computing Architectures

In general, the common goals of both Intelligent Networks and distributed computing systems may be summarized as follows:

- A common "architectural substrate" is provided into which a variety of users and services can be "plugged in".

- This architectural substrate is scalable: new users and services can be added without affecting existing users and services.

- Service objects and formats can be defined, created, deployed, maintained, and evolved independently of their users, since they use a common interface to access the substrate.

- User objects and formats can be defined, created, deployed, maintained, and evolved independently of the services they access, since they use a common interface to access the substrate.

- Services are available to users in a location-transparent manner; the network itself determines the optimum location which can provide a requested service to a user.

- The network maintains naming and directory facilities to assist in service location, user authentication, and access authorization.

- The network maintains switching/routing/brokering entities which can connect users to different services and to each other.

- The network maintains switching/routing/brokering entities which use internal signaling/messaging mechanisms to contact other switching/routing/brokering entities to facilitate user-service and user-user interaction.

While this analogy is strong, it is, naturally, not perfect. The Service Control Points of an Intelligent Network tell the network itself how to route user calls; users do not directly access the service data (except for the specialized resource data in an Intelligent Peripheral). Further, the communication between Service Switching Points and Service Control Points (or other Service Switching Points) takes place over the Signaling System 7 network. The SS7 facilities are entirely dedicated to C-Plane activity, which is out-of-band with respect to U-Plane traffic. By contrast, user objects in the CORBA architecture directly access the service objects themselves. Object Request Brokers, in contacting each other, use the same RPC and messaging mechanisms that are used to transmit user data between client and server objects. As explained in Chapter 15, in non-isochronous data-only environments, it is traditional to use the same stacks for C-Plane and U-Plane activity because both types of traffic have similar requirements.

Figure 28-13 explores the parallels between adding intelligence to communication systems and adding communication to intelligent systems.

As Intelligent Networks interconnect to other Intelligent Networks using distributed computing systems, and as distributed computing systems interconnect to each other via Intelligent Networks, it is vital that they be configured for interoperability with each other — preferably in as automated a fashion as possible. In the next section, we will see how this can be achieved by using the operations information base as a platform for *shared conceptual schema*.

28.7. Shared Conceptual Schema

To automate interoperability determination in any communication network, autoconfigurability is an important consideration. As we have indicated, these determinations can be made with respect to an operations information base. The operations information base defines the schema — the classes and relationships — of the object model underlying the architecture of the network. When this knowledge is exchanged between different networks in a federation, it is sometimes referred to as the *shared conceptual schema*.

Each network in a federation has its own view of its universe of discourse. A network intended largely for wide-area data transport (such as a service provider network) might refer to all subscriber information systems as `computerSystem` objects and might not care about their specialization into subclasses such as `transactionProcessingSystem`, `databaseServer`, and `fileServer`. A network intended largely for private enterprise computing will certainly be concerned about these distinctions, but it might not care about the specialization of various objects in its WAN service provider's network. Each network thus has its own *conceptual schema*. If the two networks have to interoperate, each must obviously become knowledgeable about *some part*

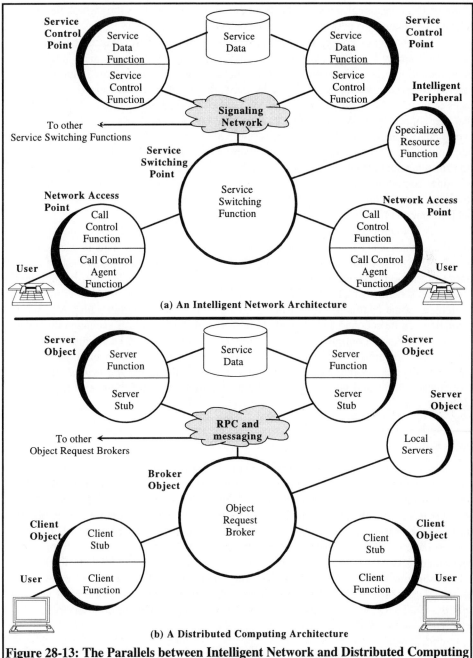

(a) An Intelligent Network Architecture

(b) A Distributed Computing Architecture

Figure 28-13: The Parallels between Intelligent Network and Distributed Computing Architectures

of the other's conceptual schema. The shared conceptual schema is the intersection of the schema which any two networks expose to each other.

The sharing of conceptual schema between multiple interconnected networks has been traditionally accomplished in various ways, mostly by having human intelligence interpret and translate the schema of a given network and determine how it applies to the other. Reference material is published by network providers which describes the interfaces of their network, which influences the nature and capabilities of the user equipment that can connect to it. Some of these schema definitions are de facto, due to historical evolutionary patterns in network engineering. Other schema definitions are created collaboratively by various standards bodies. Every standards document is in effect a definition for *some* conceptual schema which can be shared between different networks, even if it defines something as simple as an electrical/mechanical interface or a PDU format. As long as a participating network conforms to this definition, it is free to provide any internal implementation which supports that schema.

True interoperability requires sharing a more complex high-level schema definition than simply electrical/mechanical interfaces and PDU formats. This is where an object-oriented conceptual schema can help. By creating and maintaining an on-line operations information base, each network of the future can make some subset of its high-level conceptual schema available for automatic inspection and exchange with other networks. As long as some common format can be agreed upon *a priori* within which schema information can be couched and formatted, networks of the future can exchange this information on-line, and configure themselves for interoperability with each other. By reducing the need for human intervention in determining the extent of interoperability between various networks, operations information bases can facilitate the *automated* sharing of conceptual schema and greatly increase the autoconfiguration capabilities of heterogeneous networks.

28.8. Summary

It is important to invest network devices with the ability to determine how they can interoperate with other network devices, so that they can autoconfigure themselves for optimum operation. This is accomplished with the use of an operations information base, which stores all the object models necessary for the run-time operation of the network. By querying the object models of other devices, a network device can discover whether it is interoperable or interworkable with them. It can use such information to configure itself accordingly so that it may deliver advanced services. Interoperability and interworkability relationships arise from protocol compatibility, and can also be inferred in other ways. These relationships may also be used in an architecture information base by a network synthesis tool to create a network configuration for delivering the required services.

29. Modeling for Network Management

"I can use only 10% of my brain — the management
protocol takes up the rest."
— lament of anonymous network manager.

29.1. Introduction

We study in this chapter the utility of modeling for a special case of network operations called network management. We demonstrate the applicability of various modeling methodologies to network management protocols and to the creation of a management information base. Since many standard network management architectures are already widely deployed, we discuss the various methodologies in common use: we consider both the SNMP and OSI network modeling methodologies. We also present management architectures such as the TMN. Finally, we conclude with a look at possible future developments in the use of models in network management.

29.2. Network Management

A special case of an operations information base arises when one of the devices or subnetworks within the network is a *network management system*. A network management system is a single device or subnetwork with the characteristics of an *information processing system* (a program execution environment, a full-fledged operating system with filesystem support, a database platform, a set of communication protocols, and usually a user interface), which stores an operations information base containing the object model of the entire network (including possibly its own). This operations information base is given the special name *management information base*. As such, the network management system is one device (or subnetwork of devices) which can interoperate in the management plane with all the objects in the network whose model it "knows". Thus, the `networkManagementSystem` object has a `management` relationship with every

625

other object in the network, in which it plays the `manages` role, and in which each object reciprocates with `is-managed-by`.

The purpose of a network management system is to control and administer the network and ensure its proper functioning. The network management system is responsible for the monitoring, command, control, diagnostics, configuration, reconfiguration, service deployment, software download, performance analysis, and security of the network. The network management system may use the network itself to issue requests and receive responses from the devices, applications, protocols, and services in the network. The monitoring that the network management system performs may be *passive*, that is, it may simply wait for various network objects to report status information if they are capable of issuing unsolicited reports; or it may be *active*, that is, it may periodically poll various network objects for their status.

The traffic to and from a network management system is carried in a *network management protocol*. The network management protocol may be an ordinary user protocol which happens to carry network management data in its payload, or it may be a protocol designed specially for network management.

In-band and Out-of-band Management

The network management system may use the links of the network itself to control the objects in it, or it may be connected to the network using links which are dedicated only to network management. Using the definitions of Chapter 15, this means that network management may be *fully in-band*, *partially in-band* (up to a certain layer), or *fully out-of-band*. If the network management is fully out-of-band, a distinction is sometimes made between the links dedicated to network management, which are called the *management network*, and the links for normal user traffic, which are called the *managed network* or the *target network*. Fully out-of-band network management is more expensive to implement but is more reliable as there is a greater chance of continued availability in the event of the failure of links in the target network. Of course, it is possible to build a network management system which permits fully out-of-band access for critical devices (e.g., a separate dial-up port on designated routers), while remaining in-band for other devices.

Managers, Agents, and MIBs

Because the network management system must perform monitoring, configuration, and diagnostic activities on the network, it must be able to understand and interpret an object model of the target network. This object model is stored in a *management information base* (MIB). A management information base is a subset of the model information base and contains all the run-time information necessary for the network management system to function. Essentially, it defines that subset of the complete network object model which can be monitored, controlled, configured, and diagnosed by the network management system using a network management protocol. A MIB specification contains schema information; an implementation of a MIB also contains instance information.

Many network management architectures follow a *manager-agent* paradigm. The software in the network management system which initiates command and control procedures is called the *manager*. The software in the objects in the target network tasked with responding to the manager is called the *agent*. The manager and agent can only exchange information about that subset of the MIB which they both understand. An agent is essentially an "adapter": it represents the object in the target network to the manager and knows how to map management requests to the object's internal instrumentation. As such, it is only required to know the model of the object it represents, which usually is a small part of the MIB. Naturally, an object model is an abstraction; there may be characteristics of the object which are not captured inside the abstraction barrier. If so, those characteristics cannot be managed by the manager. The manager is generally responsible for managing multiple objects in the target network; therefore, it can usually interpret the models of many different kinds of objects.

A network management system is not necessarily implemented on a single computer connected to the target network. The network management system itself may be a distributed system; typically, if the target network is large, many network management stations may be required to control it. Naturally, since they control the same network, all these stations must use the same management information base. Figure 29-1 illustrates this view of a network management system.

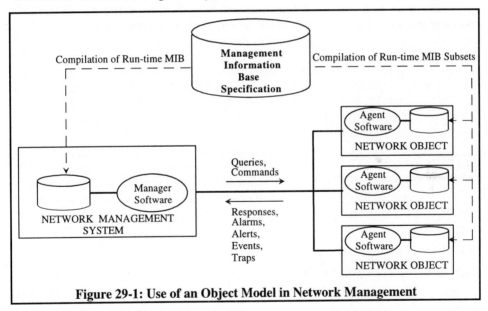

Figure 29-1: Use of an Object Model in Network Management

MIB Realization

The management information base itself is not necessarily a centralized data store with a database implementation. There are many ways to implement the MIB; the MIB can be implemented as a distributed data store, with some pieces of information located in the network management system, and others located in different places throughout the target network, retrieved as necessary. Information of a dynamic nature, such as counter attributes of protocol entities, is generally available from within the devices themselves.

Information of a relatively static nature, such as the current topology of the target network, is generally stored within the network management system. System-wide information, such as a directory of objects in the target network, inventory information, and historical records of network activity, is also generally stored within the network management system. Sometimes, reliability requirements dictate that even though MIB information is available from objects within the target network (such as the current configuration profile of a device), a replicated copy of it must still be stored within the network management system, as it may not be available from the target network in an unreliable situation.

The MIB information stored in the management system must be in persistent storage and is generally hosted on some database platform. The choices for this are many: a relational database, a hierarchical database, a network database, a flat-file database, an object-oriented database, or some proprietary database. The choice of a database platform for MIB implementation has been extensively studied [Bapa91a, Kler91, Yemi93a]; no one implementation is most optimal, and each network management system product must select an appropriate MIB platform pertinent to its own needs.

There are many proprietary and standard network management protocols which can carry the request and response traffic to and from a network management system. Generally, each protocol is tailored to carry the information specified in the object model for a particular MIB schema. Examples of standard network management protocols are SNMP (the *Simple Network Management Protocol*), an Internet standard [RFC 1441, RFC 1448], and CMIP (the *Common Management Information Protocol*), an OSI and ITU standard [ITU-T X.710, ITU-T X.711]. An older protocol — TL-1 (*Transaction Language 1* [TR 62, TR 831]) — is also used for the control of cross-connects and telecommunications equipment.

There are many excellent sources available for the description of network management protocols and architectures of network management systems [Stal93, Plev93, Rose93a]. Since the focus of this book is not the description of protocols but of object models, we shall restrict our discussion to object models. In the rest of the chapter, we shall explore the object models described in the various standards and compare them with the methodology of this book.

29.3. The SNMP Object Model

The object model used for network management by SNMP is defined by a standard called the *Structure of Management Information* (SMI [RFC 1442]). The formal notation used to define this model is the *ASN.1 macro definition notation*, a notation specified in an earlier version of ASN.1 which has since been made obsolete by information object classes. SNMP also uses the International Registration Hierarchy of Figure 9-3 to label its modeling constructs, creating branches below the label assigned to the Internet.

The intention and philosophy behind SNMP are to keep network management as simple as possible, an approach which has many advantages. In particular, one of the guiding principles behind this philosophy is to minimize the impact of adding manageability to any device in the target network. This implies that the overhead that the *agent* adds to the device must be minimal. This is an extremely important consideration in certain product markets: if an agent can be implemented in only a few kilobytes' worth of firmware, then the pricing of the product can remain competitive. Figure 29-2 illustrates the architecture for an SNMP-based management system.

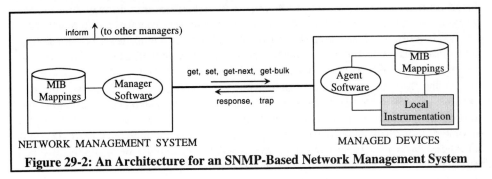

Figure 29-2: An Architecture for an SNMP-Based Network Management System

Object Types

There are two important consequences of a minimal-agent philosophy in network management. First, the protocol with which the agent communicates with the manager must be a low-overhead protocol, a role which SNMP fulfills ably. Second, and perhaps more important to our purpose, the object model which the protocol interprets and manipulates must be fairly simple. Thus, it is not advisable to have a complex object model in the agent from which it must extract much derivative information at run time. With this in mind, the SNMP SMI is designed to be relatively elementary, so that the subset of the MIB understood by each agent can be implemented as simply as possible.

In particular, the SNMP SMI does not define a class inheritance hierarchy, since inheritance resolution requires either traversing the class hierarchy at every lookup (run-time inheritance resolution), or increasing the size of the information base through hierarchy telescoping (compile-time inheritance resolution). Either of these approaches would make the agent too complex, too large, and too unwieldy. For this reason, the SNMP SMI defines individual *object types* rather than object classes. Because there is no inheritance, there is no specificational referencing involved between one object type and another. Thus, there is no mechanism for specification reuse. (One exception to this situation is the AUGMENTS clause, which we shall discuss in the section on conceptual tables). Even if two object types are semantically coupled, they must be specified independently. Consequently, although some claims have been made that the SNMP SMI has an "object-oriented expression" [Rose93a], its object-orientation is very rudimental (the AUGMENTS clause permits limited specification reuse with no specialization semantics). From Wegner's taxonomy of modeling paradigms in Figure 2-7 we see that, since the SNMP SMI supports neither classes nor inheritance, it is *object-based* rather than object-oriented. The advantage of being object-based is that we avoid the need for inheritance resolution in the agent altogether.

Although the SNMP SMI makes a distinction between object types and instances, it does not have a separate addressing scheme for instances. This is because the protocol is intended to manage protocol entities and low-end devices. Most of the object types defined in the SNMP SMI (e.g., datagram and segment counters) occur only once per protocol entity, and most of the protocol entities occur only once per managed device. Thus, the IP address of the device can itself serve as the identifier that distinguishes one instance of the object type from another, since each instance occurs in a different device. The ASN.1 object identifiers which register the object types themselves serve as labels of object instances; the context is assumed to be the device whose IP address is the destination of the protocol data unit carrying the SNMP request.

The OBJECT-TYPE macro defines the syntax of each object type and the permissions on it. The SYNTAX clause of the OBJECT-TYPE macro essentially represents its data type and is similar to a *type field* of an information object class. The SMI restricts all objects to a small subset of built-in ASN.1 types (and their subtypes). MIB specifiers may define their own objects with their own syntax, but they must eventually resolve to a simple or structured type involving the basic SMI types.

We will demonstrate the SNMP information model with respect to the hypothetical high-speed *transfer* protocol X of Figure 20-2, which combines in a single entity the traditional functions of both the network and transport layers. An example of an object type in this protocol is

```
xInboundPDUs OBJECT-TYPE
     SYNTAX          Counter32
     MAX-ACCESS      read-only
     STATUS          mandatory
     DESCRIPTION     "The total number of PDUs received"
     ::= { xLabel 1 }
```

This construct establishes xInboundPDUs as an object type whose syntax is Counter32. The type Counter32 is defined separately in the SMI as a type reference name:

```
Counter32 ::=
     [APPLICATION 1] IMPLICIT INTEGER (0..4294967295)
```

Essentially, this defines Counter32 as a non-negative INTEGER; the prefix terms are for creating ASN.1 tags so that the type is recognized uniquely in an ASN.1 PDU. As we see in the example above, the SMI also includes many implementation hints. It defines the status of this object type as mandatory, meaning that it is required in all implementations. It also defines its maximal access level as read-only because, while its value changes with the normal operation of the X protocol entity, *management* is only permitted to read it. This access level is maximal because, in general, a management implementation may lower it (e.g., make it not-accessible) but not raise it (e.g., make it read-write).

The final clause "`::= {xLabel 1}`" is the old way of assigning `OBJECT IDENTIFIER`s in the ASN.1 macro definition notation; it merely established a new label (assuming `xLabel` is already an `OBJECT IDENTIFIER` label) for the whole `xInboundPDUs` construct. This is no different from an ordinary ASN.1 value reference name, because the definition of the `OBJECT-TYPE` macro defines its instances to "ultimately" have a value of type `OBJECT IDENTIFIER`. From the viewpoint of the ASN.1 macro compiler, the entire definition of `xInboundPDUs` above is equivalent to

```
xInboundPDUs OBJECT IDENTIFIER ::= { xLabel 1 }
```

Here, the `OBJECT IDENTIFIER` value `{xLabel 1}` is called the *delivered value* of the macro, which is assigned to the `xInboundPDUs` value reference name. Consequently, the entire construct `xInboundPDUs` may be considered to have this registration label. To retrieve the current value of the `xInboundPDUs` counter from any device, an SNMP protocol request may be issued to that device asking for the value of the item registered as `xInboundPDUs.0`; this works because `xInboundPDUs` is a "scalar", that is, there is only one object of this object type in any X protocol entity.

The `OBJECT-TYPE` macro can have other optional clauses; these do not appear in the example above as they do not apply. The `UNITS` clause specifies a textual string defining the dimensions of the object type (e.g., "Mbps"), which permits application software in the manager to perform proper calculations with it. The `REFERENCE` clause is a textual clause containing a cross-reference to other ASN.1 modules, in the event that the object-type is being recast in the SNMP SMI after its semantics have already been defined using some other formal notation. Other clauses such as `INDEX` and `AUGMENTS` are only required if the object is a table entry.

Object Groups

There is only one structuring principle in the SNMP SMI, called an *object group*. An object group collects together related object types in a single collection. An object group is merely a set; object types within a group are unordered and have no aggregation semantics (part-whole relationships) or property assignment semantics (class-attribute associations) with the grouping construct.

As an example, consider the object group `xGroup` which creates a model for the X protocol entity:

```
xGroup OBJECT-GROUP
    OBJECTS {
        xInboundPDUs,          xInboundOverloadDiscards,
        xBadHeader,            xBadAddress,
        xBadChecksum,          xHopCountExceeded,
        xForwarded,            xVersionMismatch,
```

```
      . . .
      xMaxConnections,          xActiveConnections,
      xConnectionsInitiated,    xConnectionsResponded,
      xConnectWaitTimer,        xDisconnectWaitTimer
      xCurrentConnectionsTable,    . . .
            }
   DESCRIPTION
      "A collection of objects providing basic
       instrumentation of the X protocol entity."
   ::= { xObjects 1 }
```

This group consists of several scalar object types and at least one table, xCurrentConnectionsTable. (Although Figure 20-2 illustrates functionally dependent counters as well, we need not include them all here, because the Case Invariants reduce four degrees of freedom. The SNMP SMI cannot model constraints, and discourages but does not prohibit modeling functionally dependent object types.) Note that structuring all these objects in a group is not recognized by the SNMP protocol. That is, within an SNMP PDU, an object type does not have to be identified as a named object within a named group; the named object is itself sufficient. The value of the xGroup construct is simply {xObjects 1}, being the value delivered by the macro that defines it.

Conceptual Tables

In the situation where there are multiple instances of an object type in a given device, the SNMP SMI organizes them in a *conceptual table*. This table is conceptual only, in that the protocol which carries this information does not recognize tabular structures. The protocol addresses the fields within the rows of a table as if each were an individual object type; it is up to the manager requesting this information to "understand" and present this information as a tabular structure.

The table construct is itself modeled as an OBJECT-TYPE. However, since it is not recognized by the protocol, its MAX-ACCESS is always not-accessible. It is defined as follows:

```
   xCurrentConnectionTable OBJECT-TYPE
         SYNTAX          SEQUENCE OF XCurrentConnectionEntry
         MAX-ACCESS      not-accessible
         STATUS          mandatory
         DESCRIPTION     "A table containing X connection-
                          specific information."
         ::= { xLabel 40 }
```

The type of a table entry, corresponding to a row, is an ASN.1 type reference name defined as a `SEQUENCE` of other type reference names. As an example, the table `xCurrentConnectionsTable` represents all the currently active X connections. Each row corresponds to one connection and has seven fields: the local network-layer address, the local connection context key, the remote network-layer address, the remote connection context key, the state of the connection (from a state transition diagram from protocol entity X), the maximum transmission rate on the connection, and the maximum burst rate on the connection. Each table entry is also modeled as an `OBJECT-TYPE`:

```
xCurrentConnectionEntry OBJECT-TYPE
        SYNTAX          XCurrentConnectionEntry
        MAX-ACCESS      not-accessible
        STATUS          mandatory
        DESCRIPTION     "Information about a particular
                        current X connection."
        INDEX           { xConnLocalAddress,
                          xConnLocalContextKey,
                          xConnRemoteAddress,
                          xConnRemoteContextKey }
        ::= { xCurrentConnectionTable 1 }
```

Objects of this type are created and destroyed during the normal course of operation of the X entity, as its users set up and tear down connections across the network. Since network management cannot create or destroy a connection entry, the whole table entry construct is also `not-accessible`. The practical utility of the inaccessible `xCurrentConnectionEntry` object is to store the `OBJECT IDENTIFIER` value `{xCurrentConnectionTable 1}`, which can now be referenced elsewhere simply as `xCurrentConnectionEntry`. The utility of this value is that each of the columns of the table can now be registered "under" it in the registration tree. Each table also has a supporting type reference name defining the structure of a conceptual row:

```
XCurrentConnectionEntry ::= SEQUENCE
{
        xConnState                  INTEGER,
        xConnLocalAddress           OCTET STRING,
        xConnLocalContextKey        INTEGER,
        xConnRemoteAddress          OCTET STRING,
        xConnRemoteContextKey       INTEGER,
        xConnRate                   Counter64,
        xConnBurst                  Counter64
}
```

The construct XCurrentConnectionEntry above is not an object type (since it does not have a registration label assigned to it); it is merely a supporting type reference name, as it begins with an uppercase character. It defines the structure of a "row" of the conceptual table. In this table, the field xConnState is an INTEGER listing the possible states of an X transition diagram. (More correctly, it should be a subtype of INTEGER restricted only to a few values.) The fields xConnLocalAddress and xConnRemoteAddress are both of type OCTET STRING, each indicating a network-layer address; both are necessary to identify a connection since any device implementing X may in general have multiple network-layer addresses. The fields xLocalContext-Key and xRemoteContextKey are of type INTEGER; they identify, at each end, the upper protocols or client processes which are the users of the connection and also serve to index into the buffer caches allocated for that connection.

The field xConnRate identifies the maximum number of octets the receiver will accept in each one-second time period, while xConnBurst identifies the maximum number of octets per burst (the length of a burst being defined separately by an xBurst-Time scalar, which prevents the X entity from transmitting more than xConnBurst octets per xBurstTime). These are necessary because of the wide variation in processing speeds that may occur in devices on gigabit networks due to the coexistence of different implementations of X. These are per-connection fields because it is theoretically possible for two different connections between the same two devices to be established using different paths in the internetwork, with different link and router processing delays on each.

Each column of the conceptual table is separately defined in its own OBJECT-TYPE macro. The OBJECT-TYPEs for the column xConnState, xConn-LocalAddress, xConnLocalContextKey, xConnRemoteAddress, xConn-RemoteContextKey, xConnRate, and xConnBurst are assigned the values {xCurrentConnectionEntry 1} through {xCurrentConnectionEntry 7}. These labels may be thought of as representing "column heading" objects:

```
xConnState OBJECT-TYPE
      SYNTAX           INTEGER
      MAX-ACCESS       read-write
      STATUS           mandatory
      DESCRIPTION      "The state of this connection."
      ::= { xCurrentConnectionEntry 1 }


xConnLocalAddress OBJECT-TYPE
      SYNTAX           OCTET STRING
      MAX-ACCESS       read-only
      STATUS           mandatory
```

```
        DESCRIPTION     "Local Network Layer Address for
                         this connection."
        ::= { xCurrentConnectionEntry 2 }


xConnLocalContextKey OBJECT-TYPE
        SYNTAX          INTEGER
        MAX-ACCESS      read-only
        STATUS          mandatory
        DESCRIPTION     "The local context number for this
                         connection."
        ::= { xCurrentConnectionEntry 3 }


xConnRemoteAddress OBJECT-TYPE
        SYNTAX          OCTET STRING
        MAX-ACCESS      read-only
        STATUS          mandatory
        DESCRIPTION     "The remote address for this
                         connection."
        ::= { xCurrentConnectionEntry 4 }


xConnRemoteContextKey OBJECT-TYPE
        SYNTAX          INTEGER
        MAX-ACCESS      read-only
        STATUS          mandatory
        DESCRIPTION     "The remote context number for this
                         connection."
        ::= { xCurrentConnectionEntry 5 }


xConnRate OBJECT-TYPE
        SYNTAX          Counter64
        MAX-ACCESS      read-write
        STATUS          mandatory
        UNITS           "OctetsPerSecond"
        DESCRIPTION     "The maximum number of octets that
                         may be transmitted in 1 second on
                         this connection."
        ::= { xCurrentConnectionEntry 6 }
```

```
xConnBurst OBJECT-TYPE
     SYNTAX          Counter64
     MAX-ACCESS      read-write
     STATUS          mandatory
     UNITS           "OctetsPerBurstTime"
     DESCRIPTION     "The maximum number of octets that
                     may be transmitted in xBurstTime
                     seconds on this connection."
     ::= { xCurrentConnectionEntry 7 }
```

Addressing Table Data

Entries can be read from this table using a mechanism unique to SNMP. While each one of the column headings in the table above is registered using its own OBJECT IDENTIFIER, the rows are not; indeed, it is not known how many rows there are, since the number of rows could change as connections are opened and closed. The column heading objects themselves are not very useful; the interesting values are those in the rows under the column headings.

SNMP therefore implicitly assigns a temporary "registration label" to each value in each row, such that the *label depends on the current values of other fields of that row*. Thus, although each field of each row is not formally assigned a registration label *as a modeling construct*, it can be read by referencing it with a "temporary" OBJECT IDENTIFIER label, constructed by suffixing the (permanent) label of its column heading, with the (temporary) *values* of other fields of the row. Not all the other fields need be used for this purpose; only those defined as INDEX fields must. When the agent decodes this label to retrieve the value of some field of some row, it knows which column to go to by interpreting the first part of the label; it knows which row to go to by matching the values in the second part of the label with the values in the index columns of all rows of the table.

The SNMP standard defines how the temporary suffix to the permanent label of the column heading is added to create a full OBJECT IDENTIFIER in various cases: when the index column is integer-valued, when the index column is string-valued (fixed-length or variable), when the index column is an address (IP or NSAP), and when the index column is itself already an object identifier. Of course, it is possible to use more than one column simultaneously as an index, as in the xCurrentConnectionTable above. Values in index columns of different syntaxes are transformed into a temporary sequence of integers resembling an OBJECT IDENTIFIER; this sequence is then suffixed to the permanent OBJECT IDENTIFIER label of the column heading. While this may seem like a counter-intuitive and convoluted way of getting at a field of a row, it helps preserve SNMP's simplicity. By assigning an implicitly created label to every table value, it makes table values resemble ordinary object types; this makes it possible to apply the same protocol request regardless of whether the requested item is a scalar or a table value.

As an example, the `xCurrentConnectionTable` above requires four `INDEX` columns. We can derive this from functional dependency theory: in the relation scheme defined by the type `XCurrentConnectionTable`, the field `xConnState` must satisfy a functional dependency on the four fields `xConnLocalAddress`, `xConn-LocalContextKey`, `xConnRemoteAddress`, and `xConnRemoteContextKey` individually. Applying Armstrong's axioms of union and pseudotransitivity [Arms74], we can infer a minimal cover closed over these columns simultaneously; there is no other lossless decomposition for this dependency set in this relation scheme. To obtain a value of `xConnState` in some row, we must therefore specify the values of all four columns to uniquely identify that row. Thus, in a row where the value of `xConnLocalAddress` is `20`, `xConnLocalContextKey` is 1, `xConnRemoteAddress` is `30`, and `xConn-RemoteContextKey` is 2, the temporary label assigned to the `xConnState` field of that row is `xConnState.20.1.30.2`. By using this value in a protocol request, the value of `xConnState` in the desired row can be obtained. Figure 29-3 gives an example of a table.

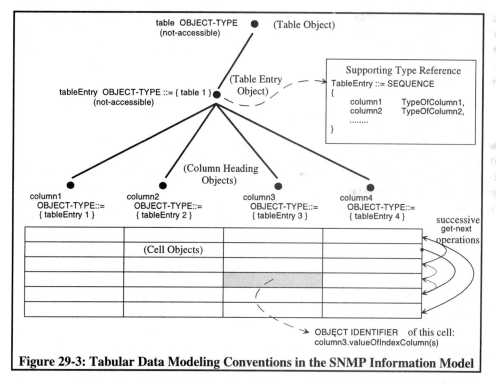

Figure 29-3: Tabular Data Modeling Conventions in the SNMP Information Model

Normally, columns of tables or entire tables are traversed using SNMP's get-next operator. Rows are returned according to the lexicographic ordering of the values of the index column. If a particular table needs an "external" index column solely for the purposes of indexing to a specific user-designated row, then such an `OBJECT-TYPE` must be explicitly created and defined to be a column of that table. When rows are created, known values (e.g., 1, 2, 3) can then be assigned to this special field, so that specific rows can be identified and retrieved using this field as an index. Since the protocol does not recognize arrays either, array-valued data must be modeled as a single-column "table".

Extending Tables

SNMP's AUGMENTS clause permits table entry objects to be defined in terms of a previously defined table entry object (called a *base conceptual row*), so that only the added columns need be specified in the new table entry object. The INDEX on the new table entry object remains the same as that on the base conceptual row. This is the only mechanism for specification reuse in SNMP; although it does permit extension (analogous to attribute addition), it permits no incremental refinement as it does not carry any specialization semantics. Only augmentation is permitted in this relation scheme; other relational operations (e.g., projections or Cartesian products with other table entry objects) are not permitted. The new relation scheme defined by such augmentation need not correspond to any particular normalization, so it is possible to define augmentations which map to columns of a base conceptual row via a functional dependency (e.g., to provide some statistical summarization of the data in other fields of the same row). Just as proprietary extensions can be added to MIBs by defining new scalars, proprietary extensions can be added to MIB tables by defining new columns.

29.4. Commentary: SNMP Information Model

The primary capability derived from using SNMP as a network management protocol is the ability to retrieve and set values via the agents embedded inside various network devices. Because of its simplicity, SNMP is particularly suitable as a standard protocol which can be deployed in devices that otherwise would be too expensive to manage: its low-overhead implementation makes it an apt vehicle for introducing standardized manageability in low-cost, low-end, and low-margin devices. Since the 1970s, many of these devices have been managed using other low-overhead protocols which also used the get-set paradigm, but these protocols were all proprietary. SNMP's strength has been to borrow this paradigm from the early proprietary management protocols, and couch within the open formalism of ASN.1 and standardize it in the Internet community.

Nevertheless, performing network management by using *only* the SNMP information model has some disadvantages as well. As we discussed in Chapter 1, there is always a trade-off between simplicity and economy of implementation on one hand, and sophistication and power on the other. Where the problem domain is complex, a modeling technique which is more powerful and semantically richer than SNMP's flat object-based modeling paradigm is required. For example, in large and complex systems such as telecommunication, satellite-based, or entertainment distribution networks, even if a simple information model were used to retrieve raw data using an efficient protocol, a modeling technique with structuring principles such as inheritance, aggregation, and domain partitioning would still be required in analysis and interpretation of the data [Sylo89, Slom89]. SNMP-based management systems are very effective in retrieving raw data objects from the managed devices and reporting their values, but they usually perform no additional reasoning with it since its modeling paradigm does not support any mechanisms for this purpose. SNMP leaves it up to the user to understand the significance of the values it reports, interpret them correctly, correlate them with other values, analyze this correlation, and take action as appropriate. If the significance of the values reported by SNMP is not understood by the user, the utility of SNMP-based network management is severely compromised.

It should be remembered that SNMP's user is not necessarily a human operator but is the *manager software* on the management station. Thus, the burden is on the manager software to correctly interpret SNMP-reported data. The modeling paradigm of the SNMP SMI is deliberately kept simple to reduce the implementation complexity of the *agent*. This does not mean that the *manager* must necessarily also be simple (although many developers of SNMP-based systems have inadvertently perpetuated this belief). It is possible that, once data has been retrieved using SNMP, the manager can perform extended reasoning with it, use correlations to draw logical inferences, recommend particular actions, or even execute operations in an automated fashion.

To quote Rose [Rose93a]: "....MIB modules are all geared towards instrumentation rather than problem solving. For example, look at the routing table in MIB-II or in the IP Forwarding Table MIB. Both provide a lot of information about the routes to a known device. But neither tells the implementor of a management station the kinds of problems that can be solved using this information, nor does either tell the implementor what algorithms to implement in order to solve those problems. So, the MIB module can be implemented in agent products, but the implementors of management stations are given little help in making use of this information. This may perhaps explain why most of today's management applications are either of the 'browser' or the 'flashing', but not the 'thinking' variety."

In order to perform SNMP-based management with "thinking" applications, it is possible and desirable to have a better-structured and semantically richer modeling technique for the *interpretation software* in the management station, even though the *protocol* itself works with the simpler information model. SNMP-gathered data can be translated so that it is couched within the semantically richer model. Rose further states [Rose93b] "...object-oriented concepts are realized solely at the management station, and are unnecessary either at the agent or between the management station and the agent. This is an important observation for two reasons. First, it does not unnecessarily burden the agent: the goal of an agent is to efficiently export management instrumentation. ...Second, by realizing these concepts at the management station, we are free to experiment with the framework, refine our understanding, and perhaps even learn something."

Once SNMP-generated data has been couched within a semantically richer framework in a management station, extended reasoning can be performed with it involving relational databases, expert systems, or deductive platforms within the management system. Parts of specialization theory, with object classes and relationships, can also be applied. This will make it possible to build intelligent applications which are able to perform detailed correlations, elaborate fault analysis, and automate network backup and restoral in the event of failure.

29.5. The OSI Management Object Model

An internationally standardized management environment has been created for use with the OSI Reference Model. This has been defined in several standards, collectively termed "OSI Management" [ITU-T X.701]. OSI Management specifies a set of management services, defined in the standard *Common Management Information Service Definition* (CMIS [ITU-T X.710]), which are provided by a network management protocol, defined in the standard *Common Management Information Protocol* (CMIP [ITU-T X.711]). Figure 29-4 illustrates the overall architecture of an OSI management system; as before, our concern is not with the protocol itself but with the object model underlying OSI management.

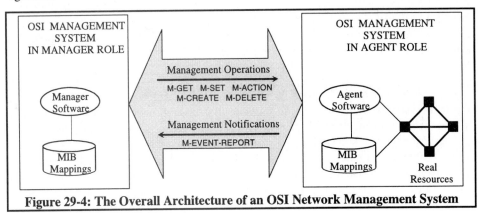

Figure 29-4: The Overall Architecture of an OSI Network Management System

The OSI management object model is defined in a standard also called the *Structure of Management Information* (SMI), which has three parts. The *Management Information Model* [ITU-T X.720] defines the modeling concepts underlying the OSI SMI. The *Definition of Management Information* (DMI [ITU-T X.721]) defines some basic managed objects commonly found in an OSI MIB; and the *Guidelines for the Definition of Managed Objects* (GDMO) [ITU-T X.722] defines a special-purpose notation using which the model is expressed. At its inception, OSI management also used ASN.1 macro notation but since has evolved to an independent notation using its own *templates*, within which its modeling semantics are expressed.

The OSI SMI uses many modeling concepts similar to those presented in this book. It uses object-oriented structuring principles for defining its managed objects. That is, managed objects are defined using an inheritance hierarchy, thus permitting specification reuse. It disallows refinement by cancellation, thereby enforcing monotonic inheritance (called *strict inheritance*). It also permits multiple inheritance. Excellent tutorial descriptions of the OSI information model and the protocol services it facilitates are available in [LaBa91, Kler93, Rama93, Yemi93b].

The chief distinction between the object-oriented methodology of the OSI SMI and specialization theory is that in the OSI information model, abstraction and encapsulation are performed *from the management perspective only*. This means that, for each object class, only those structural and behavioral characteristics important to network management are modeled. Any property or behavior which might be important for, say, network architecture or operations, may be considered irrelevant from the network management perspective. Research on extending GDMO to capture additional semantics is also largely management-oriented [Fisc93]. As we discuss the model, we will point out how the OSI Management information is suited especially well for comprehensive network management, whereas network models constructed using specialization theory are also suitable for network architecture.

Managed Object Classes

The class inheritance hierarchy of the OSI SMI is rooted at an artificial object class called `top`, whose properties are `objectClass` and `name`, and a few others we shall discuss later. Every object class is derived, directly or indirectly, from `top`. Since abstraction and encapsulation are performed only for management, the OSI SMI calls its classes *managed object classes*. An example of a managed object class is the `system` class, specified as follows:

```
system MANAGED OBJECT CLASS
DERIVED FROM top;
CHARACTERIZED BY
     systemPackage PACKAGE
          ATTRIBUTES
               systemID              GET,
               operationalState      GET,
               administrativeState   GET-REPLACE,
               managementState       GET;
          ATTRIBUTE GROUPS
               state,
               relationships;
          NOTIFICATIONS
               objectCreation,
               objectDeletion,
               objectNameChange,
               ...
               equipmentAlarm,
               environmentalAlarm;;
CONDITIONAL PACKAGES
     dailyScheduling PRESENT IF
               both the weekly scheduling and external
               scheduler packages are not present in an
               instance,
```

```
weeklyScheduling PRESENT IF
      ...,
repairStatus PACKAGE
      ATTRIBUTES
            repairStatus GET-REPLACE;; PRESENT IF
                  an instance supports it,
   ...
REGISTERED AS { smi2MObjectClass 14 };
```

In the GDMO template above, capitalized words are keywords. A MANAGED OBJECT CLASS is specified in terms of its *superclass* (using the DERIVED FROM clause) and the *packages* it contains. The REGISTERED AS clause assigns to the entire MANAGED OBJECT CLASS a registration label from the international registration hierarchy. The DERIVED FROM clause has the usual semantics of cascaded specification reuse from all its ancestral classes. The OSI SMI does not require a formal basis of specialization. Figure 29-5 illustrates part of the managed object class hierarchy from the Definition of Management Information standard (DMI [X.721]).

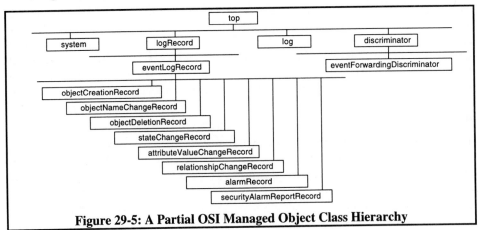

Figure 29-5: A Partial OSI Managed Object Class Hierarchy

Packages

Packages are collections of properties such as attributes and notifications. In the OSI SMI, attributes cannot occur as "free-standing" immediate properties of a managed object class; each attribute must occur in a package, and only packages can be immediate properties of a managed object class. Packages are rather like the *capsules* of specialization theory, in that they represent collections of properties which occur either together or not at all. Like capsules, packages are considered to be "absorbed" within the object that possesses them. Packages are specified using a PACKAGE template.

The GDMO language also permits *in situ definition*: if a package occurs only in one MANAGED OBJECT CLASS, then it need not be separately registered, and its full definition may be specified in-line nested within the MANAGED OBJECT CLASS definition itself. Examples of *in situ* package definitions are the systemPackage and repairStatus packages in the system MANAGED OBJECT CLASS above. Some packages may occur in more than one managed object class, and so must be separately defined and registered. An example of such a package is

```
dailyScheduling PACKAGE
        ATTRIBUTES
                intervalsOfDay  DEFAULT VALUE
                    Attribute-ASN1Module.defaultIntervalsOfDay
                GET ADD-REMOVE;
REGISTERED AS { smi2Package 1};
```

The packages that are mandatory (i.e., those that occur in every instance of that class) are defined in the CHARACTERIZED BY clause of the MANAGED OBJECT CLASS template. Others are conditional packages and are specified in the CONDITIONAL PACKAGES clause. A conditional package specification also has a PRESENT IF subclause, which provides a textual natural-language explanation of the circumstances in which the package is present in a given instance. Every managed object can be queried for the packages it actually possesses by inspecting the flag attribute packages. Since every managed object has this attribute, it is modeled as a property of top.

Attributes

The attributes which a package contains are also each separately defined in an ATTRIBUTE template. This template defines the syntax (i.e., data type) of each attribute, and indicates in the MATCHES FOR clause the comparators that may be applied to it. In the MANAGED OBJECT CLASS template, each attribute is qualified with a GET or a GET-REPLACE, indicating whether that attribute is read-only or read-write in that managed object class. An example of an ATTRIBUTE template is

```
operationalState ATTRIBUTE
        WITH ATTRIBUTE SYNTAX
                    Attribute-ASN1Module.OperationalState;
        MATCHES FOR Equality;
REGISTERED AS {smi2AttributeID 71};
```

The syntax of the attribute is defined using the ASN.1 type reference name OperationalState in the supporting ASN.1 module Attribute-ASN1Module. The MATCHES FOR clause indicates that only the equality comparator can be meaningfully applied to this attribute. The REGISTERED AS clause assigns an OBJECT

IDENTIFIER label to each ATTRIBUTE construct. While each attribute is specified using the ATTRIBUTE template in the special-purpose GDMO notation, the syntax of the attribute is specified in actual ASN.1. An example of such a definition is

```
OperationalState ::=
        ENUMERATED { disabled (0), enabled (1) }
```

The syntax of an attribute can be any arbitrarily complex type which can be expressed as an ASN.1 type reference name. For example, an entire table can be represented as a single attribute, whose type might be specified as SET OF SEQUENCE {TypeOf-Column1, TypeOfColumn2, ..., and so forth}. Unlike the SNMP information model which only uses restricted ASN.1 types, the full capability of ASN.1 type reference names is available in the OSI model.

Attribute Groups

Attributes may be assembled together in *attribute groups*, which are collections of attributes which occur either together or not at all. To save specification effort, a PACKAGE may simply specify the entire attribute group in its ATTRIBUTE GROUPS clause. The group itself is a minimal set: a managed object class (or a subclass thereof) may extend the group by adding attributes to it, unless the group is defined to be FIXED. An example of such a group is

```
state ATTRIBUTE GROUP
    GROUP ELEMENTS
            managementState,
            repairStatus,
            installationStatus,
            availabilityStatus,
            controlStatus;
    REGISTERED AS {smi2AttributeGroup 1};
```

Each one of the elements in the GROUP ELEMENTS clause of an attribute group is a separately specified attribute. The REGISTERED AS clause assigns an OBJECT IDENTIFIER label to each ATTRIBUTE GROUP construct. Since this attribute group specification does not contain the keyword FIXED, a managed object class which contains this attribute group (such as the system managed object class above) and its subclasses are free to extend it with object-specific state attributes if their specifier so chooses.

Behaviours, Actions, and Notifications

Other important templates in the OSI SMI are the BEHAVIOUR, ACTION, and NOTIFICATION templates. The BEHAVIOUR template is actually a supporting template, in that it is used to provide behavioral information which qualifies the characteristics of managed object classes, attributes, name bindings, actions, notifications, and parameters from the management perspective. This information is provided textually in a natural language. Because the BEHAVIOUR template always occurs in the context of another template, it is not registered as a separate construct.

The ACTION template specifies the actions which may be performed on a managed object by a management system. Such actions include any administrative or operational functions which the management system may wish to perform using the CMIS M-Action service. Each ACTION template specifies the syntax of the information associated with the action request, the syntax of the reply associated with it, and indicates whether or not it is a confirmed action. Each ACTION template is registered separately. Note that actions are specified only from a management perspective; messages sent to the object in its normal course of operation (for example, by other objects) are not modeled in the OSI SMI.

The NOTIFICATION template defines the notifications which the managed object can issue to the management system. It identifies the event reports which a managed object can emit using the CMIS M-Event-Report service. As with actions, notifications are only management-oriented; messages sent by an object for its normal operation (e.g., to another object) are not modeled. Each NOTIFICATION template specifies the syntax of the information associated with the notification, the syntax of the reply associated with it, and indicates whether or not it is confirmed. Each template is registered separately. An example is

```
equipmentAlarm   NOTIFICATION
BEHAVIOUR         equipmentAlarmBehaviour;
MODE              CONFIRMED AND NON-CONFIRMED;
WITH INFORMATION SYNTAX
                        Notification-ASN1Module.AlarmInfo
      AND ATTRIBUTE IDS
            probableCause        probableCause,
            specificProblems     specificProblems,
            perceivedSeverity    perceivedSeverity,
            . . .
REGISTERED AS {smi2Notification 4};
```

In this template, the field names in the AND ATTRIBUTE IDS clause list the attribute values which are the adjunct information reported along with this notification. To associate values with the correct attributes, the values are reported together with the OBJECT IDENTIFIER of the attribute. In specifying notifications, it is conventional to use the same identifier for the field name as the attribute name itself. The type reference name AlarmInfo is used to define, in actual ASN.1, the structure of the information associated with this notification. This is defined in the module Notification-ASN1-Module as

```
AlarmInfo :: = SEQUENCE
{
        probableCause           ProbableCause,
        specificProblems    [2] SpecificProblems
                                              OPTIONAL,

        perceivedSeverity   [3] PerceivedSeverity,
        ...                     -- many other fields

}
```

where each field in this SEQUENCE type has its own supporting type specification, such as

```
ProbableCause ::= OBJECT IDENTIFIER


SpecificProblems ::= SET OF OBJECT IDENTIFIER


PerceivedSeverity ::= ENUMERATED
{
        indeterminate (0),  critical (1),  major (2),
        minor (3),          warning (4),   clear (5)

}


    ...
```

Containment and Naming

Aside from specification of managed object classes and their properties, the OSI SMI specifies a *containment hierarchy*. The containment hierarchy is conceptually similar to the aggregation hierarchy of specialization theory. Containment specifies which managed object classes may be contained in other managed object classes and is defined using a construct known as a *name binding*. This somewhat non-intuitive term is used because, as we shall see, the containment hierarchy is also used to create names of object instances. A name binding establishes aggregation semantics (part/whole relationships) between two managed object classes. Containment is logical; besides "natural" containments such as physical aggregations of cards within devices, logical nestings (such as cities inside states, states inside countries) can also be modeled.

The NAME BINDING template specifies a contained object class, called a *subordinate* object class, which is a part of a containing object class, called a *superior* object class. Containment is orthogonal to inheritance, and it is important not to confuse the superior/subordinate relationship with the superclass/subclass "relationship". (In specialization theory, the superclass/subclass relationship would be called an *association* since it expresses a connotational semantic linkage rather than an operational one.) Every managed object can be queried for its name bindings by inspecting its `nameBindings` attribute. This attribute is modeled as a property of `top`, since it is possessed by every managed object.

In the OSI SMI, containment is also used as a *naming* mechanism, that is, the addressing scheme for managed objects arises out of their logical containment in other objects. Each managed object can be addressed using its *distinguished name*, which is a sequence of managed object names starting from the highest object in the containment hierarchy. In general, at each level of containment, the attribute used to name the managed object could be different; each name binding therefore specifies the attribute used by the superior managed object to name the subordinate managed object. This helps ensure uniqueness among multiple subordinate managed objects contained in the same superior managed object.

Since containment is both transitive and one-to-many, it is a *hierarchically structurable* relationship. The containment hierarchy describes the subordinate managed object instances contained within superior managed object instances. By following the naming attributes from the root of this hierarchy to any managed object within it, the complete distinguished name of the object can be constructed. Figure 29-6 shows an example of a containment hierarchy on managed object instances.

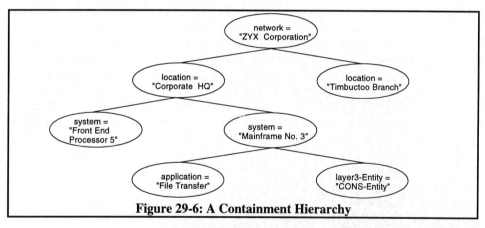

Figure 29-6: A Containment Hierarchy

A name binding also defines the qualifiers on the circumstances under which a subordinate managed object may be created or destroyed within a superior managed object. An optional *create-modifier* or *delete-modifier* may be specified in a name binding. When a subordinate managed object is created, a create-modifier specifies (a) whether it should be "cloned" from a similar prototype object, and (b) whether it should be named automatically. When a subordinate managed object is deleted, a delete-modifier specifies whether the deletion is permitted even if the deletand object has further contained managed objects within it. An example of a name binding is

```
logRecord-log NAME BINDING
     SUBORDINATE OBJECT CLASS          logRecord;
     NAMED BY
     SUPERIOR OBJECT CLASS             log;
     WITH ATTRIBUTE                    logRecordID;
     DELETE                only-if-no-contained-objects;
REGISTERED AS {smi2NameBinding 3};
```

In this name binding, each `logRecord` managed object, when contained in a `log` managed object, is uniquely identified using its `logRecordID`; further, it may only be deleted if it contains no other objects.

Allomorphism

The OSI SMI introduces a concept called *allomorphism*. Allomorphism is often compared to polymorphism but is not quite the same. (Statements such as "Allomorphism is polymorphic to polymorphism" have been inaccurately made in various discussions on OSI management.) In Chapter 3 we identified two forms of polymorphism used in standard object-oriented terminology: *function polymorphism*, in which functions with the same name do different things when applied to different objects, and *signature polymorphism* (also called overloading) in which functions with the same name do different things when invoked with a different set of arguments. Polymorphism is a property of the *functions* of an object class, and when it holds, it applies to all instances of the object class. By contrast, allomorphism is a property of individual managed *objects*: one object may exhibit allomorphic properties, but another of the same class may not.

Allomorphism is the ability of a managed object to present itself as if it were an object of a class other than its own. An object may "pretend to be" a member of another class *if it exhibits behavior compatible with the other class*. Allomorphism is a mechanism which permits managed objects and network management systems to evolve independently of each other, as it makes backward compatibility possible. For example, a management system may not know the model of the new version of some managed object. In this case, the new managed object can declare itself to be allomorphic to some old class already known to the management system, and thereby permit the management system to manage it in some limited fashion. Every managed object can be queried for the classes it is allomorphic to by inspecting its `allomorphs` attribute which, being present in every managed object, is modeled as a property of `top`.

There are two forms of allomorphism: *static allomorphism*, in which a managed object presents a consistent appearance of another class to all management systems, and *dynamic allomorphism*, in which a managed object simultaneously presents different appearances to different management systems. For example, an object which is a `bridge-Router`, possessing both `bridge` and `router` packages, may present itself to be a `bridgeDevice` object to a management system which can manage only bridges, and as a `routerDevice` object to a management system which can manage only routers. In general, dynamic allomorphism permits proprietary extensions to an object model to be managed by its vendor's proprietary management system, while permitting other management systems to manage it as an object of a standard class. Consequently, allomorphism permits a managed object to present only that *subset* or *projection* of the properties which constitute its *standardized* object model; vendor-specific and value-added extensions may be given restricted visibility if so desired.

The concept that is analogous to allomorphism in specialization theory is that of a *virtual object class*; by formally specifying a virtual object class with an appropriate selector and projector, objects of a set (selected as narrowly as we wish) can present a subset of their properties (projected as narrowly as we wish) to their users. Since an object can be a member of more than one virtual object class, specialization theory can in effect mimic both static and dynamic allomorphism. By exposing only the virtual object class as a standard class to other management systems, and keeping the proprietary extensions hidden in the private object model, virtual object classes can, like allomorphism, permit interoperability while protecting vendor privacy and competitiveness.

Relationships

The OSI information model defines *relationships* between managed objects. The original standard, *Attributes for Representing Relationships* [ITU-T X.732], defines only five specific relationships between managed objects: `service` relationships, `fallback` relationships, `backup` relationships, `group` relationships and `peer` relationships. This standard also defines *roles* for objects participating in these relationships: these are analogous to the roles we defined in Chapter 17 but are defined slightly differently. For example, the objects participating in a `service` relationship are termed the *provider* object and the *user* object. The roles of a `fallback` relationship are *primary* and *secondary* object; of a `backup` relationship, *backup* and *backed-up* object; of a `group` relationship, *owner* and *member* object; and of a `peer` relationship, both *peer* objects.

This standard uses *attributes* in managed object classes to model their relationships. Each managed object has a set of relationship attributes, which "point to" the object or objects to which it is related. Thus, each object can be queried for its related objects in various roles. The standard further categorizes relationships as *one-way* relationships (in which only one of the participating objects stores an attribute pointing to the other, usually on the "many" side of a one-to-many relationship) and *reciprocal* relationships (in which both participating objects store attributes pointing to each other). The five standard relationship types described earlier are all reciprocal relationships. Figure 29-7 illustrates attributes used as conjugate pointers in a reciprocal relationship.

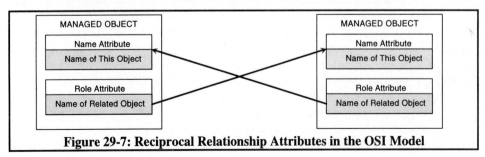

Figure 29-7: Reciprocal Relationship Attributes in the OSI Model

Relationships can be established, queried, modified, and terminated during the normal course of operation of a network, or explicitly by a management system. When relationships are so altered, an object may issue a *relationship change notification* to a management system. Ternary relationships are also permitted in the model. The "third object" involved in the relationship is sometimes a participant in one of its characterizing roles and sometimes is a *relationship co-ordinator* object responsible for managing the relationship and assuring its integrity. A co-ordinator object may manage more than one relationship, and all operations for managing the relationships must be directed through it. Figure 29-8 illustrates relationship co-ordination.

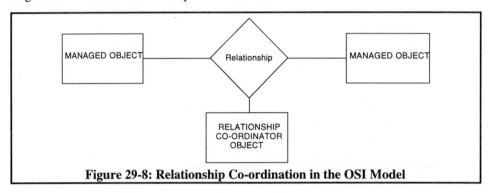

Figure 29-8: Relationship Co-ordination in the OSI Model

A later standard, the *General Relationship Model* (GRM) [ITU-T X.725], provides much more general and flexible relationship modeling mechanisms. It defines a relationship as a *manageable binding* between managed objects. It permits the modeling of general *n*-ary relationships between objects and suggests the use of Kilov diagrams to represent them graphically. An *n*-ary relationship can have *n* different roles, and each participant object must play at least one of those roles. Relationships are defined using a *relationship class* template. The GRM does not necessarily require mutual pointers as attributes in its participant managed objects to represent relationship participation; it permits an alternate realization of relationships using "relationship objects", or any other implementation mechanism.

In the GRM, the roles of a relationship can be *dynamic* or *static*. If a role is static, all managed objects playing that role must be bound in a relationship at the same time that the relationship is established and can only be unbound when the relationship is destroyed. If it is dynamic, a managed object may be bound in that role after the relationship is established or unbound before it is destroyed. This is referred to as *dynamic entry* and *dynamic departure*. Each role is specified using a *role cardinality*, which is always a (potentially unbounded) set of non-negative integers. If the role cardinality set includes the value 0, then the participant managed object for that role may be optionally absent. The role cardinality is used to specify the "semantic" or "natural" cardinality of that role.

For each implementation of a managed system, the GRM allows two subsets of the role cardinality set to be defined: a *permitted role cardinality set* and a *required role cardinality* set. The permitted role cardinality set indicates all the possible quantities of managed objects which the managed system is *allowed* to bind in that role, while the required role cardinality set indicates all the quantities of managed objects which the managed system *must* be capable of binding in that role. As might be expected, the required role cardinality must be a subset of the permitted role cardinality, which in turn must be a subset of the overall "natural" role cardinality. The required and permitted role cardinalities are roughly analogous to the minimum and maximum values of a multiplicity domain specification in specialization theory.

The collection of all similar relationships is defined to be a *relationship class*. A relationship class gives rise to *relationship objects*, each involving its participant managed objects. A relationship class is defined using the RELATIONSHIP CLASS template:

```
<relationship-class-label> RELATIONSHIP CLASS
     [DERIVED FROM      <relationship-class-label>
                        [, <relationship-class-label>]*;]
     [BEHAVIOUR         <behaviour-definition-label>
                        [, <behaviour-definition-label>]*;]
     [ROLE <role-label> roleproperties
           [REGISTERED AS object identifier];]*
     REGISTERED AS object identifier;
```

Each relationship class is registered using this template. As many roles as necessary may be defined for this relationship class, each also being registered using its own OBJECT IDENTIFIER. The properties of each role are specified in the supporting production roleproperties:

```
roleproperties ->
     [CHARACTERIZED BY   <package-label>
                         [, <package-label>]*];
     [CONDITIONAL PACKAGES <package-label>
                    PRESENT IF condition -definition
                         [,<package-label>
                    PRESENT IF condition -definition]*]
     [PERMITTED ROLE CARDINALITY SubtypeSpec]
     [REQUIRED  ROLE CARDINALITY SubtypeSpec]
     [DYNAMIC ENTRY [CREATE [<parameter-label>]*]]
     [DYNAMIC DEPARTURE
           [DELETE [<parameter-label>]*]
           [DELETES-ALL-IN-ROLES  <role-label>
                               [, <role-label>]*]
           [RELEASES-ALL-IN-ROLES <role-label>
                               [, <role-label>]*]
```

```
[ONLY-IF-NONE-IN-ROLES <role-label>
                   [, <role-label>]*]]
```

A role may possess packages, which are specified with the usual PACKAGE template. Thus, a role may be characterized by its own attributes, operations, and notifications. The cardinality of each role object is specified as a SubtypeSpec, which is an ASN.1 type reference name resolving to some subset of INTEGER(0..MAX), that is, a set of non-negative integers.

If a role permits dynamic departure, the template also describes what must happen during departure to the participant managed objects playing that role and to participant managed objects playing *other* roles, in order to preserve the semantic integrity of the relationship. When departure occurs, the managed system may simply release the participant managed objects playing that role (no qualifier), or release and simultaneously delete the participant managed objects playing that role (DELETE), or simultaneously trigger the release of *other* participant managed objects playing *other* identified roles (RELEASES-ALL-IN-ROLES), or release *and* simultaneously delete other participant managed objects playing some other identified roles (DELETES-ALL-IN-ROLES), or block the departure as long as some other participant managed object continues to play some other identified role (ONLY-IF-NONE-IN-ROLES).

Just as managed object classes are arranged in an inheritance hierarchy, so are relationship classes. Although this is conceptually a completely different generalization hierarchy involving only pure relationship classes, it is tied into the managed object class hierarchy. Thus, relationship classes are also MANAGED OBJECT CLASSes. The root of this hierarchy is called relationshipTop, which in turn DERIVES FROM the normal top for managed object classes.

A relationship subclass indicates its relationship superclass in the DERIVED FROM clause and inherits all its roles and its behavior. Multiple inheritance is also permitted, in which a relationship subclass may inherit roles from more than one relationship superclass. A relationship subclass may add new roles, add more packages to an inherited role, and extend inherited behavior. It may also extend the required role cardinality set for an inherited role, or restrict the permitted role cardinality set. This is somewhat analogous to multiplicity domain restriction, with the difference that in specialization theory it is the participant object classes that undergo specialization (not the relationship itself) and restrict their multiplicity domains.

A relationship class does not specify the managed object classes which can participate in the relationship; this is done independently of relationship classes in a *relationship binding* template. Specific groups of managed object classes which participate in a relationship are "bound together" in a relationship binding. A relationship class may engender more than one relationship binding. Thus, managed object classes A, B, and C might be bound together in a ternary relationship R in one relationship binding, managed object classes D, E, and F might be bound together in the same relationship R in a different relationship binding, while managed object classes B, C, and A may be bound together in the same relationship R — in different roles — in a third relationship binding. It is also possible to have (different instances of) A, A, and A participating in a relationship binding for R. This is similar to a name binding, which binds different pairs of managed object classes together in containment relationships. The format of a relationship binding template is

```
<relationship-binding-label> RELATIONSHIP BINDING
    RELATIONSHIP CLASS <relationship-class-label>;
    [BEHAVIOUR          <behaviour-definition-label>
                    [, <behaviour-definition-label>]*;
    [RELATIONSHIP OBJECT <class-label>
                    [AND SUBCLASSES];]
    ROLE <role-label> role-specifier;
    [ROLE <role-label> role-specifier;]*
REGISTERED AS object-identifier;


role-specifier ->
    RELATED CLASS <class-label> class-specifier
    [RELATED CLASS <class-label> class-specifier]*
    roleproperties


class-specifier ->
    [AND SUBCLASSES]
    [RESTRICTED ATTRIBUTES
            <attribute-label> [value-constraint]
        [,<attribute-label> [value-constraint]]*]
    [RESTRICTED ACTIONS
            <action-label> [argument-constraint]
        [,<action-label> [argument-constraint]]*]
```

The relationship binding template indicates which relationship class it pertains to in the RELATIONSHIP CLASS clause. If all relationships from a relationship binding are realized as mutual pointer attributes in its participant managed object classes, the RELATIONSHIP OBJECT clause is unnecessary. If, however, some relationships from this binding are realized as separate relationship objects, then the RELATIONSHIP OBJECT clause indicates the *managed object class* whose instances must be interpreted as being individual relationships of this relationship binding. This managed object class must be either relationshipTop or one of its subclasses. This permits relationships from a given relationship binding to be realized as instances of relationship classes other than the RELATIONSHIP CLASS of the relationship binding itself.

For each role, the ROLE construct specifies the managed object classes which may play that role in the relationship; each managed object class which may possibly participate in that role is specified using the RELATED CLASS clause. If [AND SUBCLASSES] is present for that participant class, its subclasses may also participate. For each participant class, the attribute value changes which are constrained or prohibited while it is a participant in that relationship are specified using the RESTRICTED ATTRIBUTES clause. The actions which are constrained or prohibited while it is a participant in that relationship are specified using the RESTRICTED ACTIONS clause.

The binding may further extend the role properties specified in the relationship class with the same supporting roleproperties production specified earlier. For example, a relationship binding may place additional constraints on role cardinalities of that relationship, by extending the required role cardinality set, restricting the permitted role cardinality set, or both.

Just as a relationship class is a MANAGED OBJECT CLASS, a role can also be realized as a MANAGED OBJECT CLASS. This is called the roleObject MANAGED OBJECT CLASS, and its subclasses are individual roles of relationship classes. The role object is considered to be contained in the relationship class by containment. Thus, a NAME BINDING is defined between relationshipTop (the superior managed object class) and roleObject (the subordinate managed object class). Other relationship bindings realizing relationships and roles as managed objects may define additional NAME BINDINGs between them.

The Metamodel

The OSI information model specifies its own *metamodel*. This is defined in a standard called *Management Knowledge Management* [ITU-T X.750]. As we discussed in Chapter 25, metamodel information is often necessary so that different networks can negotiate schemas on-line and determine at run time the classes and relationships supported in each other's operations information base. In OSI management, *management knowledge* is exchanged on-line between network management systems so that each may determine how best to interoperate with the other.

For managing management knowledge, a management system is permitted to acquire from another system the list of supported managed object classes, current object instances, supported relationship classes, current relationship instances, its naming scheme, and any knowledge of management policies. A complete "metamodel dump" also includes the constraints on object creation and deletion, the conditions for inclusion of conditional packages, and the list of allomorphic resemblances for each object.

To this end, the standard defines all its *modeling templates* as *managed object classes* for the metamodel. Thus, the MANAGED OBJECT CLASS template, the ATTRIBUTE template, the NAME BINDING template, the NOTIFICATION template, and many others, themselves become managed object classes. All of these are subclasses of a top-level template superclass. The managedObjectClassTemplate MANAGED OBJECT CLASS, for example, has as its attributes the derivedFrom clause, the characterizedBy clause, the conditionalPackages clause, and the registeredAs clause. As we have discussed on earlier occasions, the existence of such a metamodel permits the modeling methodology to "turn on itself" and become *reflective*, so that it may use itself to exchange information about its own schema.

29.6. Commentary: OSI Management Information Model

Before comparing the OSI management model with specialization-theoretic network models, we clarify some terminological differences:

- In OSI, the terms "superclass" and "subclass" apply to all managed object classes above and below a given managed object class in the inheritance hierarchy. In specialization theory, the terms "superclass" and "subclass" are restricted to immediate parent/child relationships; the set of all classes above and below an object class in the inheritance hierarchy are termed "ancestral" and "descendant" classes respectively.

- In most object-oriented methodologies, the term "is-a" represents the association a descendant class bears with its ancestors. In the OSI model, the term "is-a" stands for the "relationship" between an *instance* and its managed object class. (In specialization theory, the corresponding association is **is-an-instance-of**, with the complementary association being **has-as-an-instance**.)

- In the OSI model, the term "is-derived-from" is used between a subclass and its superclass. This is similar to our **derives-from**. In addition, we also use the association **specializes-from** between descendant and ancestral classes, the complementary association being **specializes-into**.

Relationships versus Associations

Perhaps the most important difference between the OSI information model and specialization theory is that specialization theory makes a distinction between *connotational linkages between modeling constructs* (which are called *associations*) and the *operational linkages between object classes* (which are called *relationships*). In the OSI model, this distinction is not made — everything is a "relationship". Thus, the connotational linkages **is-a** and **is-derived-from** have equal semantic weight as is-the-backup-of, is-the-peer-of, and other operational linkages. This makes it difficult to see the conceptual orthogonality of inheritance and relationships, making the derivation of relationship-based specialization principles non-intuitive. In specialization theory, principles such as relationship inheritance and relatant specialization follow quite naturally from the distinction between connotational semantics and operational semantics.

The OSI methodology does model the notions of composition and decomposition inheritance. The complete form of the NAME BINDING template is

```
<name-binding-label> NAME BINDING
SUBORDINATE OBJECT CLASS <class-label> [AND SUBCLASSES]
     NAMED BY
SUPERIOR OBJECT CLASS <class-label> [AND SUBCLASSES];
     WITH ATTRIBUTE <attribute-label>;
```

```
[BEHAVIOUR <behaviour-definition-label>
         [, <behaviour-definition-label>]*];
[CREATE [create-modifier [, create-modifier]]
                              [<parameter-label>]*;]
[DELETE [delete-modifier] [<parameter-label>]*;]
REGISTERED AS object-identifier;
```

The clause [AND SUBCLASSES] for both the subordinate and superior managed object classes causes the same name binding (and consequently, the containment relationship) to be inherited by their subclasses as well. However, this is not a well-defined notion of composition or decomposition inheritance, as it does not address whether every one of the (say *m*) subclasses of the subordinate is contained in each one of the (say *n*) subclasses of the superior, thereby creating *m×n* different inherited containment relationships. As we have seen from Chapter 7, this is not necessarily the case. Further, the optional nature of the [AND SUBCLASSES] clause permits a subclass of a superior class *not* to contain a subordinate class (or subclasses thereof) at will; in specialization theory, degenerate aggregation is only permitted if the component class includes 0 in its component multiplicity domain. Specialization principles such as component multiplicity restriction and component specialization help us formalize the notions of composition and decomposition inheritance very precisely.

In a similar manner, OSI's relationship binding template also models relationship inheritance using an [AND SUBCLASSES] clause for the participant classes specified in the class-specifier, but again, it is optional. In specialization theory, relationship inheritance is automatic, and relationship participation can be modified by descendant classes only in accordance with well-defined specialization principles. The OSI model does not address the precise interaction mechanisms between relationships and specialization. Thus, it does not model the accurate specification of mechanisms such as relatant multiplicity restriction, subject multiplicity regression, and relatant specialization.

Containment versus Relationships

In specialization theory, the analogue of containment — aggregation relationships — is considered equivalent to all other relationships and is modeled, treated, and registered exactly the same as any other operational coupling. All relationship-based specialization principles, such as relatant multiplicity restriction and relatant specialization, apply over aggregation exactly as they apply over every other relationship. In the OSI model, the containment relationship is specially singled out and given greater importance; it is modeled using a separate template, and the top managed object class has a special attribute to represent its nameBindings.

Since specialization theory treats aggregation as just another relationship, a meaningful multiplicity specification can be associated with it. By contrast, the OSI model specifies containment in a NAME BINDING template which does not indicate how many instances of the subordinate (component) may be contained in an instance of the superior (aggregate). Neither does it address inclusive composition (i.e., with sharable components). To work around the cardinality limitation, the OSI GRM suggests in a non-normative annex that a `generalComposition` RELATIONSHIP CLASS be defined, which can specify the cardinality with which a managed object playing the `component-Role` may be contained in a managed object playing the `compositeRole`. Even so, the OSI model does not recognize attribute-defined expressions and consequently does not model attribute-based cardinality specifications. In any case, to have two separate structures (a name binding and a relationship binding of the `generalComposition` relationship class) to model the same semantic concept appears to be an overkill.

In the OSI model, containment relationships have overloaded semantics — they not only specify part/whole relationships between managed object classes but also do double duty as a naming scheme. In specialization theory, a naming scheme can be independently created; it does not necessarily require that the naming scheme be linked to aggregation semantics *as a modeling concern*. Although it is certainly possible (and probably sensible) for an implementation to use the aggregation hierarchy for naming, specialization theory permits the use of alternative naming schemes if desired.

Relationship Classes

The notion of relationship classes in the OSI model is sufficiently flexible that it permits either an attribute-based realization using conjugate pointers, or a relationship-object-based realization. The notion of binding different groups of managed objects together in similar relationships provides additional flexibility. The RELATIONSHIP CLASS template of OSI is similar to the ROLE-PAIR template of Chapter 19 (in that they both only define the roles of a relationship) while the RELATIONSHIP BINDING template of OSI is similar to the RELATIONSHIP template (in that they both indicate which object classes participate in the relationship). In specialization theory, relationships between different pairs of object classes with the same role-pair are called *isomorphic* relationships; in OSI, they are considered different bindings of the same RELATIONSHIP CLASS.

OSI relationship classes permit more than two objects to participate in a relationship, which specialization theory does not. In practice, *n*-ary relationships with $n>2$ are rare and can often be decomposed into multiple binary relationships. Further, the arrangement of relationship classes in a generalization hierarchy is rarely useful, since in practice such hierarchies tend to be extremely shallow and extraordinarily broad. The depth of "specialization" of "relationship subtypes" from "relationship supertypes" rarely exceeds 1, if that. It is much more useful to model a flat, unstructured space of relationships between *object classes* which undergo specialization in accordance with defined principles. This approach has mathematical foundations in *category theory*, in which relationship roles can be viewed as *morphisms* (arrows) that map a mathematical *category* (subject instances) onto another (relatant instances). In category theory, morphisms themselves cannot be categories.

By not "objectizing" or "classizing" relationships, the specialization-theoretic model lends itself to interpreting relationship roles as *logical predicates* which are satisfied by particular pairs of subject and relatant instances. It is this logical-predicate view of relationship roles that gives rise to the extended reasoning mechanisms of virtual relationships. In addition, the simple "arrows-between-sets" approach to relationship modeling gives rise to relationship-based navigation mechanisms such as `trackRelatants()`, security mechanisms such as conjunct virtual classes, and richer modeling semantics such as spanning constraints and spanning rules operating between relatant objects. The OSI model does not perform any such extended reasoning because its relationships are encumbered with ternary participation, with relationship generalization hierarchies, and with complex packages as properties of roles.

The OSI GRM fixes many problems with the earlier [ITU-T X.732] standard. In the GRM, as in specialization theory, the relationships an object participates in are considered to be outside the scope of its intrinsic properties captured inside its encapsulation barrier. Thus, attributes that describe an object's relationships are not specified as properties of the object *as a modeling issue*. It is possible that an implementation may add attributes to an object to capture relationship information, or it may obtain relationship information from elsewhere (e.g., an external tabular data structure). As we have discussed in Chapter 17, the choice of representing relationship participation either as an attribute of the participant object, or as a separate object denoting the entire relationship instance, is an implementation choice; the specification of relationships *as modeling abstractions* need not be concerned with design-level issues. For this reason, the distinction that the earlier standard [ITU-T X.732] made between *one-way* and *reciprocal* relationships (depending on where relationship attributes are stored) is artificial and unnecessary. In specialization theory, all relationships are considered two-way from the modeling viewpoint since each role has a reciprocal, and it is in theory possible to track the relationship from either participant object to the other (although implementations may choose to perform such tracking externally, rather than from inside each object).

One of the more confusing and non-intuitive areas of the OSI GRM is the intertwining of relationship classes with managed object classes. While the motivation behind this is clear (it is tempting to be able to manage relationships with the same protocol used to manage objects), it leads to a rather involved mixture of both model and metamodel information. This causes confusion in any system: it is always best to keep the metamodel entirely separate from the model. While the relationship class `relationshipTop` (the "superclass" of all relationship classes) may be defined as a MANAGED OBJECT CLASS in the metamodel, it is not necessary to do so in the actual network model. It then becomes unclear whether its "subclasses" (actual relationship classes) are best defined as managed object classes, relationship classes, or both. It can also be argued that `relationshipTop` need not be a subclass of `top`. If relationships must be arranged in a generalization hierarchy, it is best to maintain two entirely separate trees in the model — one for actual participant managed object classes, and another for relationship classes. (Of course, these trees may be mixed in the metamodel.) This will avoid the necessity to create imprecise distinctions between "regular entities" and "relationship entities" which occur in some OSI examples. In addition, the modeling of a `roleObject` as a MANAGED OBJECT CLASS and its containment within its enclosing RELATIONSHIP CLASS by way of a NAME BINDING is a pure metamodel issue; it is not necessary in the network information model. (As it is, normal inheritance among normal object classes can sometimes be a difficult concept for the beginner to grasp and a programmer to implement.)

Other Differences

The OSI model requires the flag attribute `allomorphs` to be a property of the `top` managed object class, so that each object can list the managed object classes it is allomorphic to. In specialization theory, an object "does not know" which virtual object classes it is a member of *as a modeling issue*; its membership in a virtual object class can change as per the specification of the virtual object class and the current values of the object's properties. By simply creating or redefining a virtual object class definition with a new selector and projector, an object can be automatically included or excluded. Recall from Chapter 21 that the entire membership of a virtual object class is *in effect* re-evaluated every time it is queried. (An implementation, of course, may choose to perform eager evaluation of virtual object class memberships and store them within each object to speed up execution.) In the OSI model, if a new managed object class is created to which an existing object bears an allomorphic resemblance, an attribute update must be issued to explicitly *tell* the object so.

The OSI model does not require a formal basis of specialization. It is therefore possible to inadvertently create overlapping and disjoint subclasses without this being checkable by a compiler, should we desire to discourage such specialization. The OSI model does not formally model constraints on object classes, nor does it have any mechanisms for rules as properties of object classes which trigger functions based on structural changes.

Because of the ability of specialization theory to derive much intensional (inferred) information using mechanisms such as virtual attributes, virtual relationships, and virtual object classes, it is better suited to complex analysis and extended reasoning. In addition, because of the use of functions such as `trackRelatants()`, it can perform better relationship-based navigation.

It should be remembered that many of these differences are legitimate, because the two methodologies have different purposes. The OSI information modeling methodology is exclusively intended for network management, whereas our application of specialization theory is intended for network architecture and network operations, with only a subset of it applicable to network management. For example, we model all functions of an object class, including those it uses in normal operation, since we require them for architecture and simulation, as described in Chapter 27. OSI only models those actions and notifications which are of use to network management. Thus, the OSI information model is closely tied to the network management protocol and must specify what happens when objects and relationships are created, under what circumstances they may be deleted, and all concomitant preconditions and postconditions. OSI templates have many parameters associated with CRUD (Create, Read, Update, Delete) operations. Specialization theory does not address protocol-oriented considerations because that is not its focus.

29.7. The Telecommunications Management Network

The *Telecommunications Management Network* (TMN) is an architecture for the management and control of service provider networks. By standardizing the architectures and functions of various elements in a telecommunications network, service providers are assured of interoperability between management systems provided by different equipment vendors. The TMN is defined in a set of international standards [ITU-T M.3010, ITU-T M.3020, ITU-T M.3100, ITU-T M. 3200, ITU-T M.3400].

It is the responsibility of a telecommunications management network to provide the *Operations, Administration, Management, and Provisioning* (OAM&P) functions for the managed telecommunications network. OAM&P functions include network configuration, network provisioning, network testing, bandwidth management (static and dynamic), data collection and processing (for traffic analysis, performance monitoring, and billing functions), alarm collection and processing, fault location, fault sectionalization, network restoral, and software download to network elements. The TMN can be used to perform OAM&P functions on various kinds of networks at different layers, including SONET [ITU-T G.784, SR 2439, Kher91], B-ISDN/ATM [ITU-T I.610], ISDN [Sahi88], information networks [SR 2286, SR 2287], and Intelligent Networks [TR 1254, SR 1578, SR 2802, Buga91, Tana91, Pont93].

The TMN uses CMIS at its application layer to perform most of the functions above; in addition, it uses FTAM, an OSI standard for *File Transfer, Access, and Management* [ISO 8571], for software download. Because it uses the CMIS information modeling techniques to create the model for the telecommunications network it manages, its view of the world is object-oriented.

The physical architecture of the TMN consists of a number of *function blocks*:

- A set of *operations system* function blocks which process information and initiate activities for OAM&P;

- A set of *workstation* function blocks which present an operator interface to the TMN;

- A set of *data communications network* function blocks, internal to the TMN, which interconnect various function blocks;

- A set of *network element* function blocks which represent the real network resources to be managed;

- A set of *mediation* function blocks which relay information between network elements and operations systems by means of protocol conversion and routing.

Figure 29-9 illustrates a possible physical architecture for the TMN.

It is not necessary for the TMN to use only the Data Communications Network function block to interconnect to its managed network elements. It is possible for TMN messages to use the managed telecommunication network itself for transmission, thereby making the TMN function partially in-band. For example, the management of SONET networks uses the *Embedded Operations Channel* (EOC) within the SONET frame to convey OAM&P messages. Other signal formats (such as basic rate ISDN and DS-1 ESF) have their own embedded operations channels within which TMN signals can be carried.

If OAM&P messages are carried in-band within the telecommunications network, they may go through multiple network elements. To assist in addressing the correct network element, the devices within the telecommunications network may be categorized

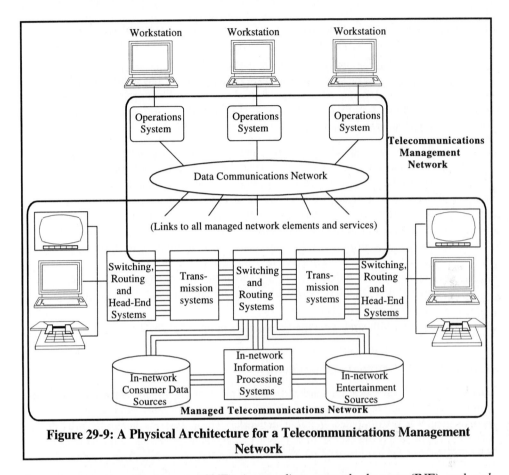

Figure 29-9: A Physical Architecture for a Telecommunications Management Network

into *gateway network elements* (GNE), *intermediate network elements* (INE), and *end network elements* (ENE). A GNE is the entry point at which the OAM&P message crosses over from the TMN into the managed network; an ENE is the device to which the message is addressed, and an INE is any element between the GNE and INE through which the message passes.

The interaction between the various function blocks of a TMN is defined in terms of *reference points*. A reference point represents a standardized interface across which interoperability between multi-vendor systems can occur. The important reference points of a TMN are

- *The **F** reference point*: This interface defines the interoperability, through the data communications network, between computer systems hosting the workstation function block and computer systems hosting the operations system or mediation function blocks.

- *The **X** reference point*: This interface defines the interoperability between multiple operations system function blocks across TMNs. This is usually application-interoperability, and so a full protocol stack must be supported by this interface.

- *The* **Q3** *reference point*. This interface defines the interoperability between operations systems and network elements, and thus must support all messages and functions of the application OAM&P functionality. Generally, the Q3 reference point requires a full protocol stack on either side of the interface.

- *The* **Qx** *reference point*: This interface defines the interoperability between function blocks that need only data-link interoperability; generally, the Qx interface only requires a short protocol stack up to the data link layer. If the network element is incapable of interpreting application OAM&P messages, then those messages are interpreted in the mediation device, which conveys them to the network element by means of a proprietary low-overhead network management protocol via a sequence of Qx links. However, if the network element is itself capable of supporting a full stack, then the Qx interface may be upgraded to a Q3 interface, regardless of the presence of a mediation device [ITU-T G.773].

Figure 29-10 illustrates the major reference points of a TMN.

29.8. Distributed Object Management

Just as the TMN provides standardized management of Intelligent Networks and telecommunications services, *distributed object management systems* provide standardized management for distributed computing networks. These systems generally provide an open platform, supporting standard network management protocols, with which almost any user-defined network configuration can be managed. However, these systems are not focused only on management of physical devices and protocol stacks; they can also be used to monitor and control software applications, file systems, access permissions, license authorizations, and many other *systems administration* aspects of distributed computing. Distributed object management technology is also sometimes referred to as *distributed systems management*.

As their name indicates, distributed object management systems view their universe of discourse in terms of abstracted and encapsulated objects. However, not all of them are object-oriented (in the Wegnerian sense of supporting both classes and inheritance); many are simply object-based. Some distributed object management systems support multiple paradigms, depending on the protocol used to manage their objects: if the protocol supports an object-oriented information model, then the standard applications provided generally also do the same.

Usually, a distributed object management system provides an *open platform*, with built-in core information processing functions such as database access, inter-process communication, user interface primitives, and communication protocols. On this platform, the user may specify the desired network configuration by compiling an appropriate

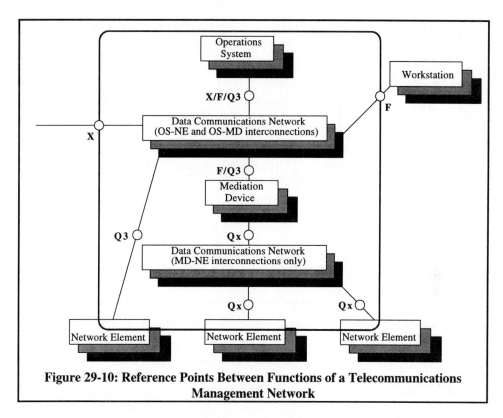

Figure 29-10: Reference Points Between Functions of a Telecommunications Management Network

MIB specification and providing instance information. This populates the database platform with instances and automatically generates the corresponding user interface representations for the specified objects. Management applications which generically apply to all objects are usually available in the open platform; besides these, the user may add any desired object-specific management applications into the open "slots" of the platform. Figure 29-11 describes a generic model for an open distributed object management platform.

A standardized open management platform which permits multiprotocol network management, called XOM (*X/Open Object Management*), has been developed by the X/Open consortium [XOpen C180]. This environment provides a common user interface which can relay requests to both SNMP-based and CMIP-based network management agents. Because the translation from the protocol-independent user interaction to the protocol-dependent device interaction is automatic, the actual network management protocol is transparent to the user [Serr93]. The common application programming interface (API) which performs this translation is called the *X/Open Management Protocol* (XMP) interface [XOpen P170]. By dispatching each user request to an appropriate protocol-dependent "package", XMP preserves the transparency of the real underlying protocols. Figure 29-12 shows the overall XMP architecture.

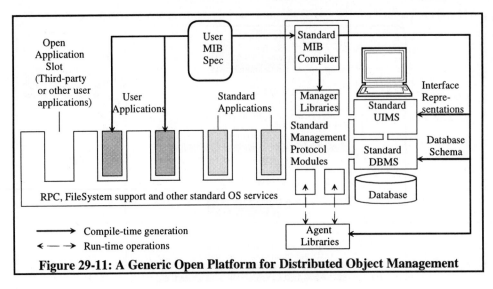

Figure 29-11: A Generic Open Platform for Distributed Object Management

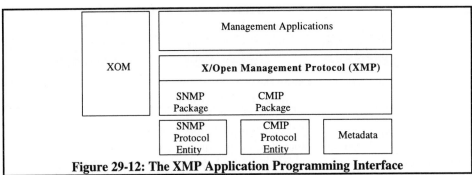

Figure 29-12: The XMP Application Programming Interface

Some open platforms (both proprietary and standardized) combine the CORBA distributed computing architecture, described in Chapter 28, and the XMP API together in a network management environment [Murr93]. Such platforms permit conventional network management using a manager-agent paradigm, client-server object interactions, peer-to-peer communication, and many other systems administration features for distributed systems management. Figure 29-13 illustrates a taxonomy of services available from an open platform.

In open management architectures, the Object Request Brokers which relay network management requests are often called *Management Request Brokers* (MRB). Like an ORB, an MRB conveys messages between management applications. When a message must be converted to a network management PDU to be issued to an actual network device, it is passed on to another specialized ORB, often called an *Instrumentation Request Broker* (IRB). The IRB interface is essentially the same as the XMP API of Figure 29-12. The IRB can access a directory which informs it as to the capabilities of the target network device and hence which actual network management protocol must carry the re-

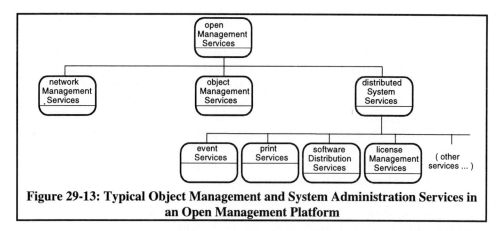

Figure 29-13: Typical Object Management and System Administration Services in an Open Management Platform

quest. The IRB then passes this request on to an appropriate package (SNMP or CMIP) which, after the necessary conversions, uses the underlying protocol entity to actually transmit the request to the network device. Figure 29-14 shows one such possible set of message flows in an open management system.

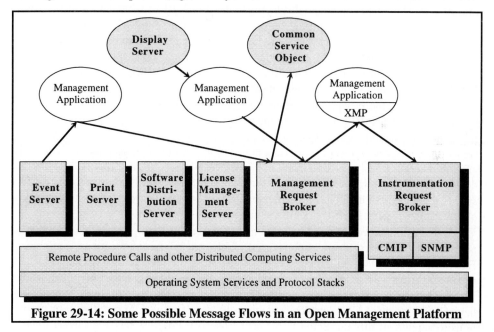

Figure 29-14: Some Possible Message Flows in an Open Management Platform

29.9. Multiple Information Models

It should be clear from the discussion in the last three chapters that no single information model of a communication network will suffice for all activities which require a network model. The activities of network architecture and planning, the activity of run-time network operations, and the activity of network management have different requirements; each focuses on a different aspect of the information model. As Figure 1-5 illustrates, an object-oriented framework provides much common ground for all these models, as there is much overlap in the information required for these activities. Nevertheless, each has some modeling constructs, classes, and relationships which are unique only to itself.

In the activity of network management alone, we have seen how different network management protocols work with different levels of modeling complexity, and as a consequence have achieved success in different markets. The conclusion we may draw from this situation is that multiple levels of complexity are required in information modeling, with each level of complexity having its own strengths and drawbacks.

As an example, SNMP is a widely deployable network management protocol because of its low impact and low implementation cost in almost any network device. Its peregrine ability arises as a result of the simple information model it uses, leading to many efficiencies in PDU processing and agent implementation. Unfortunately, many SNMP-based management system implementations incorrectly assume that the information model used in the protocol *is the only information model they can work with*. Thus, many SNMP systems use the same information model for user presentation and interaction as well. This often extends to displaying to the user MIB variable names from ASN.1 code and sometimes even requiring the user to enter long INTEGER sequences to construct the OBJECT IDENTIFIERs of desired objects. Since users are not generally skilled (nor need they be) in the art of MIB object design, registration hierarchies, and the sometimes non-intuitive indexing and traversal of tabular data, this makes many SNMP-based systems limited in their comprehensibility.

A perhaps more crippling assumption that many SNMP implementers make is that all processing of SNMP-gathered data must also be performed within the framework of the same information model used in the protocol. Since the information model is designed only for protocol and agent efficiency, and not to facilitate correlations, analyses, and inferences from device data, many implementers wrongly assume that nothing can be done with this data except report it and leave all interpretation to the user. Some SNMP system implementations do in fact generate remarkably good analyses and interpretations of data; unfortunately, these are not in the majority.

The OSI Management information model can capture complex semantics and thus permits the management of sophisticated, high-end telecommunications equipment. However, many OSI-based management systems make the reverse assumption, which is equally incorrect — that in order to use the model, the full protocol *must* be implemented in every managed device, or in some intermediate representative entity (e.g., a mediation device). The standard CMIP protocol requires the use of a full OSI stack with many options to support it; this raises the implementation cost. Progress has been made toward defining "slimmed-down" International Standardized Profiles [ISO ISP 11183, ISO ISP 12059, ISO ISP 12060], but even so the comparatively high overhead required still acts as an impediment to universal deployment.

Neither the OSI nor SNMP information models, however, have the capability to derive intensional information from gathered data and to use this information in extended reasoning and decision making. Neither model specifies rules to activate functions in the event of configuration change, which can automate network testing and restoral functions; neither specifies system-spanning constraints across network objects or performs relationship-based navigation. Specialization theory can do all those things, and more.

The differences highlighted are not intended to be a criticism of the information models; these differences are legitimate, as both OSI and SNMP are *protocol-oriented* models, intended to be encoded and transmitted over a communications link. Specialization theory creates *specification models* rather than *implementation models*; its methodology is not intended for use in a network management protocol or any other protocol. When applied to network management, specialization theory is most suited to creating a *database-oriented* model to support extended reasoning in a management system *database*. As such, it is protocol-independent; once appropriate translations are performed from any protocol-oriented information model, specialization theory can be used to apply "intelligence" and analyze the protocol-gathered data.

This may suggest that the network management systems of the future may work with *three* different projections of an information model in the same system, each with a different level of complexity and used for a different purpose, with appropriate run-time model translators between them. These information models are

- A *protocol-oriented information submodel*: A simple information submodel which can work with a low-overhead, universally deployable network management protocol;

- A *user-oriented information submodel*: A submodel of relatively moderate complexity which can hide from the user both the raw protocol-gathered data and any intricate constructs used in reasoning. (Unless specifically demanded, it should not be necessary to expose to the user either the MIB variable data or complex inheritance hierarchies.) This submodel can present summary information and the *results* of performing correlation, analysis, and reasoning.

- A *database-oriented information submodel*: A sophisticated submodel capable of capturing elaborate semantics in persistent storage, applying intelligent inferencing, and deriving as much intensional information from the data as possible. This submodel can facilitate applications for data correlation, data summarization, event analysis, extended reasoning, and automation of network management operations. Consequently, this submodel will be more complex than either of the two submodels above.

Figure 29-15 illustrates this situation.

29.10. Summary

Network management is an important application area which requires the use of an information model. This information model can be used to generate a management information base, which stores information about the schema and objects within an instantiated network. Each object which is managed by a network management system is repre-

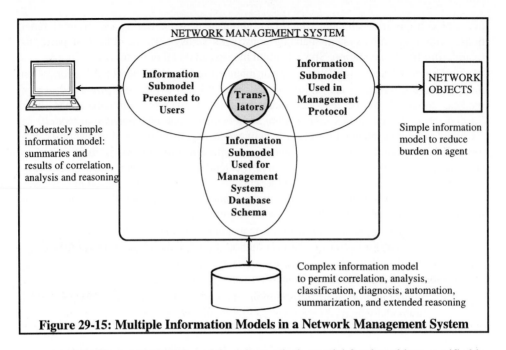

Figure 29-15: Multiple Information Models in a Network Management System

sented to the system by an agent, which understands the model for that object specified in the MIB. A network management protocol, designed to work with the information model, conveys messages between managers and agents.

Standardized information models used in network management include the SMIs for the SNMP and the OSI CMIP network management protocols, each of which has strengths and drawbacks. It is possible that future network management systems will work with multiple information models with run-time translators between them: one for usage with the network management protocol, one for user presentation, and one for facilitating extended reasoning in management information base implementations.

30. The Future of Network Modeling

"Now that I am networked to everybody everywhere in the world, I find I have nothing to say...."
— *anonymous Chief Executive Officer.*

30.1. Network Modeling

The object-oriented network modeling methodology introduced in this book has its foundations in specialization theory. Its objective has been to provide a precise, formal framework for

- Identifying and understanding the nature of the information needed for network architecture, operations, and management.

- Assisting the synthesis and evolution of new and existing networks.

- Facilitating the operation and maintenance of existing networks.

- Providing a mechanism to assess the suitability of networks to current and possible future business uses.

- Documenting operating rules and policies with sufficient accuracy that they can be automatically enforced by being incorporated into the network information model.

- Supporting resolution of problems encountered during the operation of networks.

- Ensuring that the development of additional network functions and services can easily build upon existing ones.

In our methodology, we have taken a declarative, specification-oriented approach for expressing network object abilities, their interoperability capabilities, their relationships with each other, their constraints, and operating rules. As a result, our methodology has the ability to deal with complex network structures and topologies.

30.2. Specification Models versus Implementation Models

The main focus of this book has been to introduce modeling constructs as formalisms for capturing the semantics of communication networks as precisely as possible. The modeling constructs collectively constitute a *specification model* rather than an *implementation model*. This means that the model is not intended to be directly executable as software in a networking device. The modeling constructs introduced in this book are optimized for semantic expressiveness, not for execution efficiency.

Although the modeling constructs are not an executable specification, they can serve as a basis for generating executable software. Because the methodology takes a comprehensive view of network architecture, it cannot as a whole be compiled into some intermediate executable form. Rather, as explained in Figure 26-2, different parts of the model can serve as input to specialized translators which will generate implementations suitable for execution in an appropriate environment, such as programming language representations, database representations, protocol representations, and logic programming representations.

By using an abstract specification language, we have ensured that our modeling technique has sufficient precision to be able to accommodate even the most minute details. The choice of specification language is irrelevant, as long as it is implementation-neutral and can provide constructs which are sufficiently rich in expressing the desired semantics.

30.3. Benefits of Formal Specification

Many specifications are written using natural languages, as they are easily understandable by humans. There are, however, many disadvantages to such specifications. Natural language specifications are sometimes inconsistent, and they cannot be validated automatically. They are not helpful in automatically deriving parts of the implementation, or parts of the test suite of an implementation.

Some formal specification languages are themselves executable. The advantage of these languages is that specifiers can use them as rapid prototypes to obtain immediate feedback about the specification itself. The disadvantage is that an executable specification language is usually more restricted in expressive power, because it must specify its functions in terms of computable statements. Many such languages, therefore, have an implementation bias.

If appropriate model validation tools are available, formal specifications should be automatically validated using these tools before implementation, as far as possible. For example, validation tools can automatically prove certain properties of formal protocol specifications before the protocol is implemented. Aside from proving correctness, it should be possible to derive large parts of implementation code from the formal specification.

In the ideal network architecture tool, a graphical front-end would provide a sufficient number of interface representations for the semantic constructs of our network modeling methodology (classes, instances, attributes, functions, relationships, and so on). With a complementary textual notation, such a graphical tool would be able to generate the syntactical representation of our model as the formal specification. By passing subsets of this formal specification through appropriate model compilers (e.g., an object-oriented application code generator producing C++, a relational database schema generator producing SQL, an Estelle compiler generating a protocol object implementation in C), it should be possible to derive large parts of the network implementation automatically.

By using a formal specification language which partially automates the network implementation and testing phases, development life cycles can be reduced. A formal specification language should have

1. A basis for *conveying knowledge* from the application domain, representing the underlying modeling methodology;

2. A basis for *formally expressing* domain concepts within the framework of a grammar, which is unambiguous, clear, precise, and concise;

3. A basis for analyzing the specification for *completeness* and *correctness*;

4. A basis for ensuring *conformance* of implementations to specifications;

5. A basis for determining *consistency* of specification modules with each other;

6. A basis for generating *tools* to create, maintain, analyze and simulate specifications;

7. A basis for *prototyping* and *simulating* the system without a complete implementation;

8. A basis for deriving *implementations* automatically from the specification itself.

With an appropriate understanding of the problem domain, the use of formal specifications in network design can become quite natural in the process of network architecture.

30.4. How Much Should We Specify?

Because the specification of a network is essentially the model of an imaginary network having the desired properties, all specifications are necessarily incomplete. We never *completely* know what the desired properties of the network are until after it has been deployed and in use for some time. It is impossible for specifiers to realistically anticipate all possible cases of use of the system. Therefore, either deliberately or inadvertently, parts of the system will be left unspecified. This can be an advantage, as it provides the implementers some leeway in making detailed decisions within the parameters of the high-level specification. Because specifications are developed iteratively and incrementally, the initial proposals for a formal specification will often undergo transformations before they stabilize sufficiently for use in a system.

The balance between specifying just enough and specifying too much is delicate — the boundary between specification and high-level design is admittedly fuzzy. As an example, in specialization theory we have argued for specifying relationships as abstract first-class constructs, while considering the presence of conjugate-pointer attributes inside each object a design-level issue. We have presented our arguments for this choice, but clearly other modeling methodologies may make other choices depending on their assessment of the specification/design boundary.

A sufficiently complete specification prevents the implementers from developing incorrect systems, but an overspecified system may tend to a given implementation bias. A specification has an implementation bias when it specifies externally unobservable structure or behavior. A specification that is sufficiently abstract (in the sense of specifying only externally observable characteristics) yet precise (in the sense of being detailed) provides an overview of the complex network but postpones tactical design-level decisions without excluding any valid manifestation of the implementation.

30.5. Prospects for Architecture Modeling

Network planning is becoming increasingly important as the complexity and cost of constructing communication networks go up. There will be growing demand for intelligent network architecture tools with both synthesis and simulation capabilities. These tools will work with large synthesis databases with thousands of configuration options and parameters. The simulation tools will become smarter, having the ability to predict problems based on the results of simulation, and automatically suggest solutions to those problems with reference to the synthesis database.

Network devices will become more complex and acquire richer functionality. For ongoing evolution and upgrading of existing networks, it will become necessary for customers to accurately predict and quantify the impact of new network devices before they are deployed within existing networks. The widespread availability of multimedia applications in commercial and residential environments will generate large traffic volumes, making proper bandwidth dimensioning and consequent financial analysis of link operating costs a prerequisite to deployment.

As such, it is possible that vendors of high-end networking hardware will in the future supply potential customers with a "simulation model" of their product first, so that customers may obtain confidence by running a device test with the simulation model of their existing network. The ability to "simulate-before-you-buy" will go a long way toward assuring customers about the suitability of new devices for their networks and assist them in planning their migration strategies and performing economic analyses. Eventually, this will lead to standardization of the simulation models of network objects, so that the structural and behavioral characteristics of different products from multiple vendors can be expressed in a common format to interwork together within a standardized simulation environment.

Figure 30-1 illustrates a possible future evolution of modeling methodologies for network architecture.

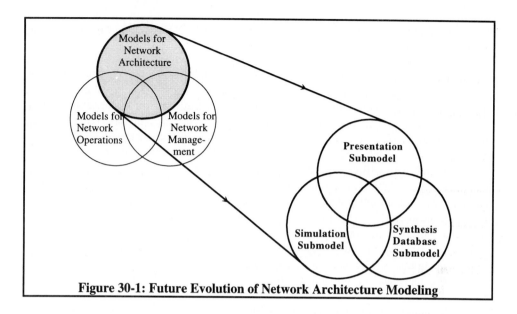

Figure 30-1: Future Evolution of Network Architecture Modeling

30.6. Prospects for Operations Modeling

For network operations, the focus of this book has been to arrive at a modeling methodology which can be used as the basis for creating a conceptual schema. This conceptual schema must be formalized so that different networks in a federation will be able to exchange schema information and perform autoconfiguration for interoperability.

Our focus has been to use specialization theory for the specification of network systems in the abstract, without regard to any specific implementation plans. Indeed, it is not envisioned that the capabilities described in the *specification* model will be literally translated to an *implementation* model for network operations. For example, the fact that the model of a `transparentBridge` object has its `helloTime` virtual attribute tracked into the `rootBridge` object of the spanning tree, does not mean that it will actually be dereferenced from the `rootBridge` object every time it is needed in an implementation. (In actuality, eager evaluation is performed for this virtual attribute by the network through a series of configuration PDUs, so that copies of this value exist in every bridge.) One will probably not encounter on the market anytime soon a LAN bridge with an embedded on-board expert system with a knowledge base of rules which make it self-aware, self-actualized, and self-enlightened. Indeed, such a state of Nirvana will never be achieved by most networking devices. In price-competitive markets for commoditized networking products, there will always be pressure to reduce costs and keep things simple; this will be counterbalanced by the pressure for product differentiation through increased functionality and added value. Nevertheless, it is instructive to note that transparent bridges *do* have the intelligence to perform a limited form of autoconfiguration within their universe of discourse (the set of all connected link-layer entities): they are able to learn the network topology and block certain ports in order to configure themselves into a spanning tree.

For federating entire networks, similar autoconfiguration abilities will be required, except at a higher level of complexity. To quote Bernstein [Bern93]: "We must view the network itself as the customer's database, and make sure it is self-diagnosing, self-healing, and intelligent." The future may well see dedicated information processing systems incorporated within networks for the purpose of interpreting and analyzing schema information from other networks and orchestrating the autoconfiguration of their own networks to achieve interoperability. These will be different from network management systems in that they will execute in an on-line, real-time, directly-connected, fully-automated, highly-available fashion without any human intervention. In some cases, these systems may even be integrated within high-end networking devices: for example, next-generation head-end systems may be able to configure the interfaces of the distribution units and subscriber terminals connected to them. In other cases, they may be general-purpose distributed computing systems programmed for network operations. These "operations brains" of the network will require their own network models to work with. Figure 30-2 speculates on possible future developments of modeling for network operations.

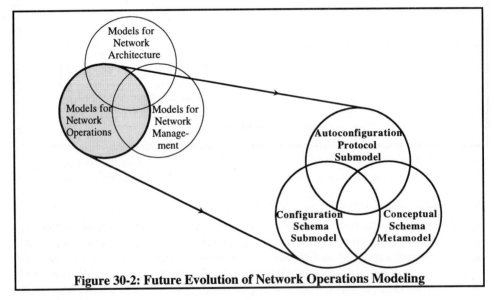

Figure 30-2: Future Evolution of Network Operations Modeling

30.7. Prospects for Management Modeling

As discussed in Chapter 29, network management is one area where the most effective use of network modeling has been made so far. The issues with respect to the "proper level of complexity" in creating management information models have led to much debate in the history of network management standards. This is only the first area in which deliberations about the "best" modeling paradigm have occurred; it is not unlikely that similar discussions will arise in the standardization of network architecture models and network operations models. Debate about a single "best" paradigm ensues because of the implicit (though incorrect) assumption that only one paradigm must be used: that the specification paradigm must be the same as the implementation paradigm, that it must be application-universal, and that it must be protocol-oriented. As we have seen in Figure 29-15, it is possible to have different submodels for protocol operations, user presentation, and database reasoning within the same network management system. Figure 30-3 illustrates this distinction.

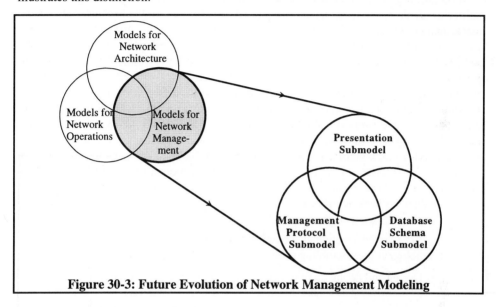

Figure 30-3: Future Evolution of Network Management Modeling

30.8. Future Challenges in Network Modeling

Next-generation networks will require cooperation among a wide variety of customers, providers, and vendors to provide a common substrate for exchanging financial, scientific, engineering, enterprise, commercial, and business information. This will require the interworking of telecommunication networks, information networks, entertainment networks, and wireless networks. Each interconnected network must have the ability to export some common subset of its operating model so that it may interoperate with other networks. Difficult problems await, not only in the area of defining network models with appropriately rich semantics but also in the area of massive scale-up and distribution of model data.

The processing of logical rules to derive inferential conclusions about network operation has traditionally been done off-line on "expert systems" dedicated for that purpose, sometimes with no direct connection to the network itself. Research is necessary as to how best to imbed this technology within network operations so that it can be availed of in an on-line, real-time manner. Tools will be necessary to validate and debug large collections of constraints and rules. These will first be introduced in provider networks; it will take some time for this technology to trickle down to customer-owned networking devices.

There is a requirement for model translation between the schema of different networks so that each network may export its model in an understandable form. This problem remains largely unsolved, as is the problem of the choice of an autoconfiguration protocol. Here, the advantage of a formal specification language is that it becomes possible to think of generating "model mappers" automatically. However, making such technology available dynamically in an on-line, real-time fashion for the exchange of conceptual schema is a formidable challenge.

As different networks are connected for interoperation, protocol interoperability and schema sharing will be just part of the problem. The larger problem is that of the operating policies of each pre-existing network in a federation. There will not be any single, global set of policies to which each network conforms. It is almost inevitable that the constraints, rules, and operating policies exported by each network will be in conflict with those of some other networks. We need research into mechanisms which will decompose rules into manageable subsets, analyze them for potential conflicts, and allow networks to resolve them through automated negotiation. The problems of propagating policies and constraints for enforcement across a federated network remain unsolved. Dramatic progress must be made in semantics: network models must include vastly more semantic information than has been attempted in this book.

Future generation networking technologies must address the following:

1. Accelerated creation of complex network structures and intricate topologies, by assembling pre-validated subnetworks and subtopologies.

2. Design and deployment of active, intelligent network components.

3. Rapid provisioning of new services.

4. Minimization of maintenance on an operating network.

5. Quick introduction of new and upgraded network components with minimal interruption and minimal human intervention.

6. Proactive prediction of prospective problems and preparation of programmed preventive procedures.

All of this must be achieved on a scale which seems daunting by today's standards. Current reasoning and analysis techniques are centered around individual event data; the reasoning mechanisms of the future must be massively scaled up, as they will have to work with summary data and aggregate, correlated information. Future challenges are quantitative as much as they are qualitative. Nevertheless, there is little doubt that network architects, engineers, managers, and other professionals in academia, industry, and government, working collaboratively and competitively, will be equal to the task.

Glossary:
Object-Oriented Modeling Terminology

Abelian ancestor: The *cognation ancestor* of all *participants* of *isomorphic commutative virtual relationships* which can be replaced with a single *involute relationship* on that *ancestor*.

Abstract class: An *object class* which cannot have *instances* and exists only for the purpose of *modeling* the common *properties* of its *descendant classes*. See *concrete class* and *fully abstract class*.

Abstraction: The activity of selecting the characteristics of an object which will be modeled as *properties* inside the *abstraction barrier* of the object.

Abstraction barrier: The conceptual boundary of an object which demarcates the *essential characteristics* of the object from *non-essential characteristics*.

Acquires-from: The *association* between a *virtual object class* and its *base class*, which has the effect of making *properties* of the base class (or its *relatants*) visible as *aspects* of the virtual class. The *complement* of *grants-to*; implied by *virtualizes-from*.

Actual attribute: An *attribute* with no dependency on any other *properties* and which must be independently specified. See *virtual attribute*.

Actual class: See *actual object class*.

Actual instance: An *instance* of an *actual object class*.

Actual object: See *actual instance*.

Actual object class: An *object class* which has a place in the *inheritance hierarchy* and *objects* can be *instantiated* as its *members*. See *virtual object class*.

Actual relationship: A *relationship* created by explicit *relationship assignment* between *participant* classes or their *ancestors*. See *virtual relationship*.

Actual relationship instance: A *relationship instance* of an *actual relationship*. See *virtual relationship instance*.

Aggregate addition: A *specialization principle* which permits a *descendant* of a *component class* to add a new *aggregate class*. See *component addition*.

Aggregate class: A *class* which may be *decomposed* into *component classes*. An *aggregate class* is a collection of *aggregate objects*. See *is-a-part-of* and *has-as-a-part*.

Aggregate object: An *object* which may be *decomposed* into *component objects*. An aggregate object *is-an-instance-of* an *aggregate class*. See *is-a-part-of* and *has-as-a-part*.

Aggregate specialization: A *specialization principle* which permits a *descendant* of a *component class* to restrict an inherited *aggregation relationship* to selected descendants of the *aggregate class*. See *component specialization*.

Aggregation: The identification of part-whole *relationships* between *objects*, useful for the construction of complex objects by assembling simpler objects together in meaningful configurations. See *aggregation relationship, aggregate class, component class, exclusive aggregation*, and *inclusive aggregation*.

Aggregation hierarchy: A hierarchy of *object classes* created by identifying a sequence of *aggregation relationships*.

Aggregation principle: A rule which states how an *aggregation relationship* interacts with *specialization*.

Aggregation relationship: A part-whole *relationship* between an *aggregate class* and a *component class*, whose *roles* are *is-a-part-of* and *has-as-a-part*.

Aggregation roles: The *role is-a-part-of* played by a *component class* with its *aggregate class* in an *aggregation relationship*, and the *role has-as-a-part* played by an *aggregate class* with a *component class* in an *aggregation relationship*. See *inclusion roles*.

Ancestor: See *ancestral class*.

Ancestral class: An *object class* which is *genealogically related* to a given *object class* by being above it in a branch of the *inheritance hierarchy*. See *descendant class*.

Anchoring class: A *class* which has a *spanning constraint* or *spanning rule* as its *property*.

Anchoring object: An *instance* of an *anchoring class*.

Application-specific language: A machine-processable language whose syntax is designed to support and capture the semantics of a specific *modeled system* which serves a particular application.

Argument: A *modeling construct* denoting an input parameter to a *function*.

Argument contravariance: A *specialization principle* which permits the *arguments* of a *function* of a *descendant class* to exhibit *contravariance*. See *result covariance*.

Aspect: A *property* of a *base class* visible in a *virtual object class*.

Aspect acquisition associations: The *associations acquires-from* and *grants-to* between a *base class* or its *relatants* and the *virtual object classes* supported by the base class. See *virtualization associations*.

Association: A *connotational coupling* between two *modeling constructs* created as a result of defining a model (as opposed to a *relationship* which is an *operational coupling* between two *object classes* created as a result of applying the defined *model* to a *modeled system*). An association always has a *complementary association* in the inverse direction. Examples of associations are *inheritance associations, instantiation associations, property assignment associations*, and so on.

Attribute: A *modeling construct* denoting a *property* of an *object class* indicative of its structural characteristics. An attribute has a *type*.

Attribute addition: A *specialization principle* which permits a *descendant class* to add an *attribute* as a new *property*.

Attribute domain restriction: A *specialization principle* which permits a *descendant class* to restrict the *domain* of an *attribute inherited-from* an *ancestral class*.

Attribute type: See *type*.

Attribute-defined expression: An expression generated by a grammar which permits mathematical and logical operators between values of *attributes* and *results* of *functions*.

Authentic class: A *referent class*. See *synthetic class*.

Autoclassification: The ability of the *members* of a *base class* to *classify* themselves among the *selected virtual classes* which *virtualize-from* the base class.

Base attribute: An *attribute* whose value is used to compute a *virtual attribute*.

Base class: See *base object class*.

Base object class: An *object class* which supports the definition of a *virtual object class*.

Base relationship: A *relationship* that gives rise to a *virtual relationship*.

Basis of generalization: A *structuring principle* which identifies the common *property* or properties of *sibling classes* that can unify them in the same *superclass*. See *basis of generalization*.

Basis of specialization: A *structuring principle* which identifies the *property* or properties that distinguish one *subclass* from another. See *basis of generalization* and *basis-free specialization*.

Basis of virtualization: A mechanism which is applied to a *base class* to create a *virtual object class*; it is either a *selector*, *projector*, or *conjunctor*, or some combination thereof.

Basis-free specialization: A *specialization* which occurs without an identified *basis of specialization*.

Belongs-to: The *association* between a *property* and its *object class*. The same as *is-a-property-of*.

Bequeaths-to: The *association* between an *ancestral class* and its *descendant class*, which acts as an *implicit property assignment* mechanism causing the descendant class to possess all the *properties* of its ancestral class. The *equivalent* of *specializes-into* and *generalizes-from*; the *complement* of *inherits-from*, *specializes-from*, and *generalizes-into*. See *inheritance associations*.

Capsule: A non-instantiable collection of *properties* which occur in an object class either collectively or not at all. See *mandatory capsule*, *optional capsule*, and *mixin class*.

Capsule addition: A *specialization principle* which permits a *descendant class* to add a *capsule* as a new *property*.

Capsule fixing: A *specialization principle* which permits a *descendant class* to make an *optional capsule inherited-from* an *ancestral class* a *mandatory capsule*.

Child class: See *subclass*.

Class: See *object class*.

Class hierarchy: See *inheritance hierarchy*.

Class hierarchy normalization: See *hierarchy normalization*.

Class relationship diagram: A diagram depicting *relationships* between *object classes* in an *object-oriented modeling paradigm*. See *entity-relationship diagram*.

Class-based modeling: The *modeling paradigm* which supports *objects* and *classes* and requires every object to *be-an-instance-of* a class. See *object-based modeling* and *object-oriented modeling*.

Class-hierarchy flattening: See *hierarchy telescoping*.

Class-hierarchy telescoping: See *hierarchy telescoping*.

Classification: The activity, during *modeling*, of categorizing *objects* sharing similar properties and fulfilling a similar purpose into *object classes*.

Closed-class relatant set: For any *subject instance*, the set of all *relatant objects* of one or more identified *object classes* generated by a *relatant-tracking* or a *relatant-counting function* (usually, with which it plays a specified *role*). See *open-class relatant set*.

Cognate classes: Any set of *classes* which are *genealogically related* to a common *ancestral class* other than genericObject. See *cognation ancestor*.

Cognation ancestor: The lowest common *ancestor* (other than genericObject) of any set of *cognate classes*.

Commutative role-pair: A *role-pair* in which the *forward role* implies its own *reciprocal role* and vice versa.

Commutative virtual relationship: A *virtual relationship* inferred from a *base relationship* with a *commutative role-pair*.

Complement: See *complementary association*.

Complementary association: The inverse direction of an *association*.

Complete specialization: A *specialization* which creates *subclasses* such that every existing or potential *member* of the *superclass* is a member of at least one subclass. See *incomplete specialization*.

Component addition: A *specialization principle* which permits a *descendant* of an *aggregate class* to add a new *component class*. See *aggregate addition*.

Component class: A *class* which *is-a-part-of* an *aggregate class*.

Component multiplicity: The *multiplicity* with which a *component class* participates in an *aggregation relationship*.

Component multiplicity inheritance: An *aggregation principle* which requires a *descendant* of an *aggregate class* to inherit the *component multiplicity* of an inherited *aggregation relationship*, which it may optionally restrict. See *component multiplicity restriction*.

Component multiplicity restriction: A *specialization principle* which permits a *descendant* of an *aggregate class* to restrict the *domain* of the *component multiplicity* of a *component class* in an inherited *aggregation relationship*. See *component multiplicity inheritance*.

Component object: An *object* which *is-a-part-of* an *aggregate object*.

Component specialization: A *specialization principle* which permits a *descendant* of an *aggregate class* to restrict an inherited *aggregation relationship* to selected descendants of the *component class*. See *aggregate specialization*.

Composition: The *role is-a-part-of* of an *aggregation relationship*.

Composition inheritance: An *aggregation principle* which requires a *descendant* of a *component class* to inherit the *composition relationships* of an *ancestral class* with an *aggregate class*. See *decomposition inheritance*.

Compound specialization: A *specialization* which simultaneously uses more than one *mode of specialization*. See *simple specialization*.

Concrete class: An *object class* (generally lower down in the *inheritance hierarchy*) which can be *instantiated*. See *abstract class* and *fully abstract class*.

Conditional virtual attribute: A *virtual attribute* whose specification uses different *attribute-defined expressions* depending on conditions imposed on its *base attributes*.

Conjunct virtual class: A *virtual object class* created by applying a *conjunctor* to its *base class*.

Conjunctor: A *basis of virtualization* indicating one or more *relatants* of the *base class* whose *properties* will also become *aspects granted-to* the *virtual object class*.

Connotational coupling: A semantic linkage between two *modeling constructs* designed to assist our understanding of the *modeled system*, which does not affect the operation of *objects* the system. See *operational coupling*, *association*, and *relationship*.

Constraint: A *property* of an *object class* which limits an *object's* structure and behavior. See *hard constraint*, *soft constraint*, *native constraint*, and *spanning constraint*.

Constraint addition: A *specialization principle* which permits a *descendant class* to add a *constraint* as a new *property*.

Constraint associations: The *associations* governs and is-governed-by between a *constraint* and the *properties* or *objects* it involves.

Constraint imposition: *Constraint addition* when applied to inherited rather than *original properties*.

Constraint restriction: A *specialization principle* which permits a *descendant class* to restrict an inherited *constraint*.

Contingent base attributes: The *base attributes* of a *tracked virtual attribute* which may be different depending on which *object class* they come from.

Contravariance: The phenomenon that a *property* or characteristic of an *object class* may legally expand its *domain* when the object class *specializes-into* a *descendant class*. See *covariance*.

Convolute role-pairs: A pair of *role-pairs* in which the first role-pair and the second role-pair together imply a third role-pair.

Convolute virtual relationship: A *virtual relationship* inferred from two *base relationships* with *convolute role-pairs*.

Core property: A *property* which is mandatory in every *instance* of an *object class*. See *variant property*, *mandatory capsule*, and *optional capsule*.

`countRelatants()`: See *relatant-counting function*.

Coupling: See *connotational coupling*, *operational coupling*, *association*, and *relationship*.

Covariance: The phenomenon that a *property* or characteristic of an *object class* may legally restrict its *domain* when the object class *specializes-into* a *descendant class*. See *contravariance*.

Data dictionary: A set of data structures describing the *schema* of a *model*, usually created by defining a *metamodel*.

Decomposition: The *role has-as-a-part* of an *aggregation relationship*.

Decomposition inheritance: An *aggregation principle* which requires a *descendant* of a *aggregate class* to inherit the *decomposition relationships* of an *ancestral class* with a *component class*. See *decomposition inheritance*.

Defined relationship: A *relationship* between two *object classes* which is created by explicit *relationship assignment*, or an *inherited relationship* whose defaults are explicitly modified using a legal *specialization principle*. See *implicit relationship*.

Degenerate aggregation: An *aggregation relationship* inherited by a *descendant class* in which the *component multiplicity* of an *optional component* is set to [0,0], using *component multiplicity restriction*.

Degenerate relationship: A *relationship* inherited by a *descendant class* in which the *relatant multiplicity* of an *optional relatant* is set to [0,0] using *relatant multiplicity restriction*. See *well-founded relationship*.

Delegation: The ability of an *object* to reuse the implementation of a *function* by referring it to a *prototype* object, which may not necessarily be an *instance* of its *superclass*.

Denotational semantics: A fundamental branch of computer science that deals with the specification of the "meaning" of a computer program by analyzing its execution using structural induction based on notational rules. It supplies the mathematical foundation for many *notational formal description techniques*. See *operational semantics*.

Dependent property: A *property* which has a *functional dependency* on other properties. See *orthogonal property*.

Derivation association: The association *derives-from* between a *subclass* and its *superclass*.

Derives-from: The *derivation association* between a *subclass* and its *superclass*. Implies *specializes-from, generalizes-into, inherits-from* and *is-a*.

Descendant: See *descendant class*.

Descendant class: An *object class* which is *genealogically related* to a given *object class* by being below it in a branch of the *inheritance hierarchy*. See *ancestral class*.

Disjoint specialization: A *specialization* which creates *subclasses* whose existing or potential *members* cannot form intersecting sets. See *overlapping specialization*.

Distributive role-pairs: A pair of *role-pairs* in which the first role-pair can be superimposed on (distributes over) the second role-pair.

Distributive virtual relationship: A *virtual relationship* inferred from two *base relationships* with *distributive role-pairs*.

Domain: The set of all values which a *property* may possess (usually an *attribute, multiplicity, function argument,* or *function result*).

Dominance priority: A priority assigned to every *original property* so that *multiple inheritance* conflicts can be resolved. See *precedence criterion, dominant property,* and *recessive property*.

Dominant property: A *property* which is selected to *belong-to* an *object class* in the resolution of a *multiple inheritance* conflict. See *recessive property* and *precedence criterion*.

Drives: The *association* of a *rule* with its *driving precondition*. The *complement* of *is-driven-by*.

Driving precondition: A structural condition which, when established, activates a *rule*, causing the invocation of its *triggered functions*.

Dynamic binding: The ability, in an *object-oriented programming environment*, of an *object* to select at run time the most appropriate implementation of a *function* invocation. See *signature polymorphism* and *static binding*.

Encapsulation: The activity of making only certain *properties* of the object visible at its *encapsulation barrier*. Also called *information hiding*.

Encapsulation barrier: The conceptual boundary of an object which demarcates the externally visible *properties* of an object from those not externally visible. This is a subset of (and often the same as) the *abstraction barrier*.

Entity: See *object*.

Entity-relationship diagram: A diagram depicting *relationships* between entities in the entity-relationship *modeling paradigm*. See *class relationship diagram*.

Entity-relationship modeling: A *modeling paradigm* which describes *entities* and the *relationships* between them.

Equality constraint: A *constraint* with an equality comparator, which can usually be turned into a definition for a *virtual attribute*. See inequality constraint.

Equivalent: See *equivalent association*.

Equivalent association: An *association* carrying the same semantics as another.

Essential characteristics: The characteristics of an object chosen to be modeled as *properties*.

Exclusive aggregation: An approach to modeling *aggregation relationships* which does not permit *component objects* to be shared among *aggregate objects*. See *inclusive aggregation*.

Exemplification: See *instantiation*.

Explicit-syntax virtual attribute: A *virtual attribute* whose *type* cannot be inferred from the *attribute-defined expression* in its definition (usually, a *conditional virtual attribute*) and so must be explicitly specified. See *implicit-syntax virtual attribute*.

Extension: The activity, during *modeling*, of *property assignment* to an *object class* such that it adds new characteristics as *properties*, in addition to those it *inherits-from* its *ancestral classes*. See *incremental refinement*.

Extent: The set of all *objects* which bear the *is-an-instance-of association* with a given *object class*, that is, the set of all *instances* of that object class. See *membership*.

Fellow instances: Any set of *objects* each of which *is-an-instance-of* the same *object class*. See *fellow members*.

Fellow members: Any set of *objects* each of which *is-a-member-of* the same *object class*. See *fellow instances*.

First-class construct: A *modeling construct* whose semantics cannot be inferred from other constructs.

Flag attribute: A Boolean-valued *attribute* which indicates the absence or presence of a *variant property*.

Forward role: The *role* played by the *subject* with the *relatant* in a *relationship*. See *reciprocal role*.

Free specialization: See *basis-free specialization*.

Fully abstract class: An *object class* which can have neither *instances* nor *members* and exists only for the purpose of *modeling* inter-class *relationships* used in the specification of other classes. See *abstract class* and *concrete class*.

Function: A *modeling construct* denoting a *property* of an *object class* indicative of its behavioral characteristics. A function has *arguments* and *results* and is either a *procedural function* or a *stream function*.

Function addition: A *specialization principle* which permits a *descendant class* to add a *function* as a new *property*.

Function extension: A *specialization principle* which permits a *descendant class* to extend the behavior of a *function inherited-from* an *ancestral class*.

Function polymorphism: The ability, in an *object-oriented programming environment*, of a *function* to perform different actions when applied to different *objects*. See *signature polymorphism* and *overloading*.

Functional dependency: An algorithm expressible as a mathematical function which maps the values of one *property* to those of another.

Functional dependency associations: The *associations is-functionally-dependent-on* and *functionally-determines* between a *virtual attribute* and its *base attributes*.

Functionally-determines: The *association* between a *base attribute* and any *virtual attribute* it supports. The *complement* of *is-functionally-dependent-on*.

Genealogical relation: The relation between two *object classes* which are nodes anywhere along the same branch of the *inheritance hierarchy*. See *ancestral class, descendant class, superclass,* and *subclass*.

Genealogy: The path from the root of the *inheritance hierarchy* to a given *object class*, consisting of an ordered list of the names of its *ancestral classes*.

Genealogy resolution: The determination of the *origin class* for every *property* of an *object class*.

Generalization: The activity, during *modeling*, of recognizing common *properties* of *object classes* and creating a new *superclass* for them. See *specialization*.

Generalization associations: The *association generalizes-from* between an *object class* and its *descendant classes*; and the *association generalizes-into* between an *object class* and its *ancestral classes*. See *inheritance associations, specialization associations, derives-from,* and *is-a*.

Generalizes-from: The *association* between an *object class* and all its *descendant classes*. The *equivalent* of *specializes-into* and *bequeaths-to*. The *complement* of *generalizes-into, specializes-from,* and *inherits-from*. See *generalization associations*.

Generalizes-into: The *association* between an *object class* and all its *ancestral classes*. The *equivalent* of *specializes-from, inherits-from,* implied by *derives-from,* and implies *is-a*. The *complement* of *generalizes-from, specializes-into,* and *bequeaths-to*. See *generalization associations*.

genericObject: The conceptual *abstract class* which serves as the root of the *inheritance hierarchy*, whose only properties are objectName and objectClass.

Governs: The *association* of a *constraint* with a *property* or an *object* it involves. The *complement* of *is-governed-by*.

Grants-to: The *association* between a *base class* and any *virtual object class* defined on it, which has the effect of making *properties* of the base class (or its *relatants*) visible as aspects of the virtual class. The *complement* of *acquires-from*; implied by *virtualizes-into*.

Hard constraint: A *constraint* which represents an immutable physical reality and can never be violated. See *soft constraint*.

Has-as-a-member: The *association* between an *object class* and an *instance* of any of its *concrete descendant classes*. Implied by the conjunction of *specializes-into* with *has-as-an-instance*. The *complement* of *is-a-member-of*. See *membership associations*.

Has-as-a-part: The *role* played by the *aggregate class* with the *component class* in an *aggregation relationship*. The *reciprocal* of *is-a-part-of*. See *aggregation roles*.

Has-as-a-property: The *association* between an *object class* and its *properties*. The *complement* of *is-a-property-of*. See *property assignment associations*.

Has-as-an-instance: The *association* between an *object class* and its *instances*. The *complement* of *is-an-instance-of*. See *instantiation associations*.

Hierarchically structurable relationship: A *relationship* which is both *transitive* and one-to-many.

Hierarchy flattening: See *hierarchy telescoping*.

Hierarchy normalization: The activity of adjusting the *classes* in an *inheritance hierarchy*, including possibly creating new intermediate classes, to eliminate undesirable features such as *selective inheritance* or *multiple inheritance*.

Hierarchy telescoping: The copying of *inherited properties* from all *ancestral classes* as direct properties into each *concrete class*. One method for performing *inheritance resolution*.

Horn-clause: A logical statement with one or more atomic conditions which together imply exactly one atomic conclusion.

Immutable inheritance: See *monotonic inheritance*.

Implicate virtual relationship: A *virtual relationship* inferred from a *base relationship* with an *implicating role-pair*.

Implicating role-pair: A *role-pair* which implies another role-pair, called an implicand role-pair.

Implicit property assignment: Indirect *property assignment* of a *property* to an *object class*, arising from a direct property assignment to some *ancestral class* of the object class.

Implicit relationship: An *inherited relationship* available to an *object class* accepting all defaults. If during *specialization* the object class explicitly modifies the inherited relationship by using a legal *specialization principle*, it is no longer an *implicit relationship* but remains a *defined relationship*.

Implicit-syntax virtual attribute: A *virtual attribute* whose *type* can be inferred from the *attribute-defined expression* in its definition. See *explicit-syntax virtual attribute*.

Imported virtual attribute: See *tracked virtual attribute*.

Inclusion: See *inclusive aggregation*.

Inclusion roles: The roles *includes* and *is-included-in* of an *inclusive aggregation relationship*. These are synonymous with the *aggregation roles* *has-as-a-part* and *is-a-part-of* but additionally indicate sharable components.

Inclusive aggregation: An approach to modeling *aggregation relationships* which permits a *component object* to be shared among multiple *aggregate objects*. Also called *inclusion*.

Incomplete specialization: A *specialization* which creates *subclasses* such that some existing or potential *member* of the *superclass* may not be a member of any subclass. See *complete specialization*.

Incremental refinement: The *property assignment* of new structural and behavioral *properties* to *object classes* by *extension* going down the *inheritance hierarchy*.

Independent property: See *orthogonal property*.

Inequality constraint: A *constraint* with an inequality comparator. See *equality constraint*.

Information hiding: See *encapsulation*.

Information resource dictionary system (IRDS): An ANSI standard for *data dictionaries*, useful for storing *schema* information and *metamodel* knowledge.

Inheritance: A second-order *structuring principle* which maps *object classes* onto other object classes to express the semantics of *extension, incremental refinement,* and *specialization.*

Inheritance associations: The *association inherits-from* between an *object class* and its *ancestral classes,* and the *association bequeaths-to* between an *object class* and its *descendant classes.* See *specialization associations, generalization associations, derives-from,* and *is-a.*

Inheritance hierarchy: A conceptual rooted and directed acyclic graph whose nodes are *object classes,* arising as a result of recursively applying *inheritance* to object classes to isolate their common *properties* into *superclasses.* Also called a *class hierarchy,* an *object class hierarchy,* or an *object inheritance hierarchy.*

Inheritance hierarchy normalization: See *hierarchy normalization.*

Inheritance resolution: The determination of the *inherited properties* of an *object class* by searching up the *inheritance hierarchy.* See *hierarchy telescoping.*

Inherited property: A *property* which a class *inherits-from* an *ancestral class.* See *original property.*

Inherited relationship: A *relationship* available to an *object class* through *relationship inheritance.*

Inherits-from: The *association* between a *descendant class* and its *ancestral class,* which acts as an *implicit property assignment* mechanism causing the descendant class to possess all the *properties* of its ancestral class. Implied by *derives-from,* the *equivalent* of *specializes-from, generalizes-into,* and implies *is-a;* the *complement* of *bequeaths-to, specializes-into,* and *generalizes-from.* See *inheritance associations.*

Instance: A *modeling construct* denoting a concrete *object* which is an example of its *object class.* See *instantiation associations.*

Instantiation: The activity, during the realization of a network *model,* of assigning or creating *objects* as *instances* of *object classes.* This activity creates the *associations is-an-instance-of* and *has-as-an-instance* between objects and their classes.

Instantiation associations: The *association is-an-instance-of* between an *instance* and its *object class,* and the *association has-as-an-instance* between an *object class* and any of its *instances.* See *membership associations.*

Involute relationship: A *relationship* which a *class* bears with itself.

Is-a: The *association* between an *object class* and all its *ancestral classes,* and the *association* of an *object class* with itself. Is implied by *specializes-from, derives-from,* and *inherits-from.*

Is-a-member-of: The *association* between an *object* and any of its *ancestral classes.* The *complement* of *has-as-a-member.* Implied by the conjunction of *is-an-instance-of* with *specializes-from.* See *membership associations.*

Is-a-part-of: The *role* played by the *component class* with the *aggregate class* in an *aggregation relationship.* The *reciprocal* of *has-as-a-part.* See *aggregation roles.*

Is-a-property-of: The *association* between a *property* and its *object class.* The *complement* of *has-as-a-property.* See *property assignment associations.*

Is-an-instance-of: The *association* between an *instance* and its *object class.* The *complement* of *has-as-an-instance.* See *instantiation associations.*

Is-driven-by: The *association* of a *driving precondition* with its *rule.* The *complement* of *drives.*

Is-functionally-dependent-on: The *association* between a *virtual attribute* and its supporting *base attributes.* The *complement* of *functionally-determines.*

Is-governed-by: The *association* between a *property* or an *object* and a *constraint* which involves it. The *complement* of *governs*.

Is-triggered-by: The *association* of a *triggered function* with its *rule*. The *complement* of *triggers*.

Isomorphic relationships: *Relationships* in which the *role-pair* is identical.

Kilov diagram: A graphical technique for representing the *associations* and *relationships* between *object classes*.

Leaf class: An *object class* which has no *descendant classes*. See *non-leaf class*.

Mandatory capsule: A *capsule* which must be present in every *instance* of an *object class*. See *optional capsule*, *core property*, and *variant property*.

Mandatory component: A *component object* of which at least one must be present in an *aggregate object*. See *optional component*.

Mandatory relatant: A *relatant* which participates in a *relationship* with the lower bound of the *domain* of its *relatant multiplicity* being greater than zero. See *optional relatant*.

Member: An *object* which is an example of one of its given *ancestral classes*. See *membership associations*.

Membership: The union of the *extents* of all the *concrete descendant classes* of a given *object class*, that is, the set of all *objects* which bear the *is-a-member-of association* with that object class.

Membership associations: The *association is-a-member-of* between a *member* and any of its *ancestral classes*, and the *association has-as-a-member* between an *object class* and any of its *members*. See *instantiation associations* and *specialization associations*.

Metamodel: A *model* of the modeling methodology itself in which *modeling constructs* are treated as *object classes*, and *associations* are treated as *relationships*. Metamodels are useful for designing and building tools to support the modeling methodology.

Mixin class: In an *object-oriented programming language*, the analogue of a *capsule*.

Mode of specialization: A legal way of creating a *subclass* as permitted by a *specialization principle*.

Model (noun): The abstract description of the structure and behavior of a *modeled system* in the *universe of discourse*.

Model (verb): The activity of systematically organizing and representing knowledge about the *universe of discourse* according to a *modeling paradigm* to create an approximation of reality.

Model information base: An information base which stores the *system model*.

Modeled system: An actual system in the *universe of discourse* which is subjected to the activity of *modeling*.

Modeling: The activity of creating a *model*.

Modeling construct: A feature of the modeling methodology formally describing some element of the *modeled system*. Examples of modeling constructs are *object, object class, attribute, function, relationship*, and so on.

Modeling paradigm: A perspective which gives rise to methodologies for creating *models*.

Monotonic aggregation inheritance: An *aggregation principle* which prohibits a *descendant class* from canceling any *aggregation relationship* defined for an *ancestral class*.

Monotonic inheritance: The requirement that no *descendant class* may drop or override the *properties* of an *ancestral class*. Also called *immutable inheritance* and *strict inheritance*. See *refinement by cancellation, overriding, selective inheritance,* and *spaghetti inheritance*.

Monotonic relationship inheritance: A *relationship principle* which prohibits a *descendant class* from canceling any *relationship* defined for an *ancestral class*.

Multiparadigmatic Modeling Methodology: A methodology which uses multiple *modeling paradigms*.

Multiple inheritance: The ability of a *subclass* to *derive-from* more than one *superclass*.

Multiplicity: A *modeling construct* which expresses the quantification and optionality of the number of *members* of an *object class* which must participate in a *relationship*.

Multiplicity interval: The interval bounded by the lower limit and the upper limit of a *multiplicity* value.

Naming attribute: An *attribute* which is used by an *aggregate object* to identify a *component object*.

Native constraint: A *constraint* which is a *property* of an *object class* and only *governs* other properties of the same object class. See *spanning constraint*.

Native rule: A *rule* whose *driving preconditions* and *triggered functions* are *properties* of its *anchoring class*.

Native virtual attribute: A *virtual attribute* all of whose supporting *base attributes* are *properties* of the same *object class*. See *tracked virtual attribute*.

Natural domain: The set of all values a *property* may possess as permitted by its syntactic specification, without consideration of any further restrictions arising from *modeling* semantics.

Nijssen information analysis methodology (NIAM): A *modeling paradigm* which decomposes the *universe of discourse* into an extremely elementary set of binary couplings.

Non-essential characteristics: The characteristics of an object not chosen to be modeled as *properties*.

Non-leaf class: An *object class* which has further *descendant classes*. See *leaf class*.

Non-referent class: An o*bject class* which, in an *object-oriented programming environment*, does not reflect an entity in the *modeled system* and is created only for the purpose of programming convenience. See *referent class*.

Normalization: See *hierarchy normalization* and *relationship normalization*.

Object: A *modeling construct* denoting an entity *abstracted* and *encapsulated* for the purposes of *modeling*. An object is an *instance* of an *object class*.

Object class: A *modeling construct* denoting a collection or set of *objects* having similar *properties* and fulfilling a similar purpose.

Object class hierarchy: See *inheritance hierarchy*.

Object inheritance hierarchy: See *inheritance hierarchy*.

Object instance: See *instance*.

Object persistence: The ability, in an *object-oriented programming environment*, of an *object* to retain its state and identity regardless of the lifetime of the software programs which create, read, or modify it.

Object-based modeling: The *modeling paradigm* which requires that every element in the *universe of discourse* be an *abstracted* and *encapsulated object*. See *class-based modeling* and *object-oriented modeling*.

Object-oriented modeling: The *modeling paradigm* which supports *objects*, *classes*, and *inheritance*, requires all objects to be *instances* of classes, and requires all classes to support inheritance. See *object-based modeling* and *class-based modeling*.

Object-oriented programming: The activity of creating a software program in an *object-oriented programming language*.

Object-oriented programming environment: An environment which supports the creation and execution of programs in an *object-oriented programming language*, generally also with support for editors, compilers, linkers, and debuggers, and optional support for object persistence, object version management, CASE tools, software configuration management tools, and documentation tools.

Object-oriented programming language: A programming language whose syntax supports *objects*, *classes*, and *inheritance*.

`objectClass`: An *attribute* which every *object class inherits-from* `genericObject` (and thus *is-a-property-of* every object class) whose value in every *object* indicates the name of its object class. This attribute compares equal to the name of each of its *ancestral classes*.

`objectName`: An *attribute* which every *object class inherits-from* `genericObject` (and thus *is-a-property-of* every object class) whose value in every *object* indicates the name of that *instance*.

Ontology: See *weak ontology* and *strong ontology*.

Open-class relatant set: For any *subject instance*, the set of all *relatant objects* of any *object class* enumerated by a *relatant-tracking* or a *relatant-counting function* (usually, with which it plays a specified *role*). See *closed-class relatant set*.

Operational coupling: A semantic linkage between two *object classes* describing how, in the actual *modeled system*, the operation of *instances* of one object class affects instances of the other. See *connotational coupling*, *association*, and *relationship*.

Operational semantics: A fundamental branch of computer science that deals with the specification of the "meaning" of computer program by analyzing its execution as a state induction based on operational rules, with reference to some particular actual or virtual machine. See *denotational semantics*.

Optional capsule: A *capsule* which may be optionally present in *instances* of an *object class*. See *mandatory capsule*, *core property*, and *variant property*.

Optional component: A *component object* which may be optionally present in an *aggregate object*. See *mandatory component*.

Optional relatant: A *relatant* which participates in a *relationship* with the lower bound of the *domain* of its *relatant multiplicity* being zero. See *mandatory relatant*.

Ordered relationship: A *relationship* with a *relatant multiplicity* greater than 1 in which, when requested by the *subject*, *instances* of the *relatant* are enumerated as ordered according to one or more of its *attributes*. See *ordering criterion* and *rank*.

Ordering criterion: An *attribute* of the *relatant* in an *ordered relationship* with a comparator used for sequencing *instances*. See *rank*.

Origin class: The *object class* in which a *property* is first defined, that is, the highest *object class* for which a *property* is not an *inherited property*.

Origin preservation: A technique of performing resolution of conflicting *properties* in *multiple inheritance*, by renaming all conflicting properties to be prefixed with the name of their *origin class*.

Original property: A *property* which is newly defined in a given *object class*, that is, one which is not *inherited-from* an *ancestral class*.

Orthogonal property: A *property* which does not have a *functional dependency* on any other property. See *dependent property*.

Overlapping specialization: A *specialization* which creates *subclasses* whose existing or potential *members* may form intersecting sets. See *disjoint specialization*.

Overloading: See *signature polymorphism*.

Overriding: The ability of a *descendant class* to change the *properties inherited-from* an *ancestral class*. See *monotonic inheritance* and *selective inheritance*.

Parametric polymorphism: See *signature polymorphism*.

Parent class: See *superclass*.

Partial specialization: See *incomplete specialization*.

Participant: Either of the two *classes* participating in a *relationship*. See *subject* and *relatant*.

Participant instance: Either of the two *objects* forming a *relationship instance*. See *subject instance* and *relatant instance*.

Participation constraint: A *constraint* which places an upper or lower limit on the total number of *relatant objects* from two or more non-*cognate classes* which can participate in *relationships* with a *subject*.

Persistence: See *object persistence*.

Polymorphism: See *function polymorphism*, *signature polymorphism*, and *overloading*.

Polythetic hierarchy: A *classification* hierarchy for *universes of discourse* in which the *objects* of a set have many characteristic *properties*, and each property is possessed by many objects, but every object does not possess every property. A polythetic hierarchy forms a directed graph which is connected but may not be rooted or acyclic; biological taxonomies are often polythetic.

Precedence criterion: A criterion which disambiguates between the *properties* of an *object class* which conflict in *multiple inheritance*. See *dominant property*, *recessive property*, and *dominance priority*.

Precondition: See *driving precondition*.

Precondition contravariance: A *specialization principle* which permits a *descendant class* to weaken a *driving precondition* of an inherited *rule*, if the rule has no else-clause.

Procedural function: A *function* whose *arguments* and *results* are structured data types. See *stream function*.

Projected virtual class: A *virtual object class* created by applying a *projector* to its *base class*.

Projector: A *basis of virtualization* indicating a list of properties of the *base class* which will be the *aspects granted-to* the *virtual object class*.

Property: A *modeling construct* denoting a characteristic (*attribute, function, capsule, constraint,* or *rule*) of an *object* or an *object class*.

Property assignment: The activity, during *modeling*, of allocating a *property* (an *attribute, function, capsule, constraint,* or *rule*) to an *object class*. This activity creates the *associations is-a-property-of* and *has-as-a-property* between the property and the object class.

Property assignment associations: The *association is-a-property-of* between a *property* and its *object class*, and its *complementary association has-as-a-property* between an *object class* and its *properties*.

Prototype: An *object* which serves as a reference for other objects for the implementation of a *function*. See *delegation*.

Qualitative basis of specialization: A *basis of specialization* which partitions the enumerated *domain* of a discrete-valued *attribute* of the *superclass*. See *quantitative basis of specialization*.

Quantitative basis of specialization: A *basis of specialization* which partitions the numerical *domain* of a continuous-valued *attribute* of the *superclass*. See *qualitative basis of specialization*.

Rank: The sequence number of each *relatant instance* enumerated according to an *ordering criterion* in an *ordered relationship*.

Recessive property: A *property* which is not selected to *belong-to* an *object class* in the resolution of a *multiple inheritance* conflict. See *dominant property* and *precedence criterion*.

Reciprocal role: The *role* played by the *relatant* with the *subject* in a *relationship*. See *forward role*.

Recursive: An activity which can be meaningfully applied to its own result.

Referent class: An *object class* which, in an *object-oriented programming environment*, reflects an entity in the *modeled system*. See *non-referent class*.

Refinement by cancellation: See *selective inheritance*.

Reflexive association: An *association* which a *class* may bear with itself (e.g., *is-a*).

Relatant: The *object class* which participates in a *relationship* with the *subject*.

Relatant attribute restriction: A *specialization principle* which permits a *descendant class* to restrict the *domain* of an *attribute* of a *relatant* in an inherited *relationship*.

Relatant instance: The *object* which forms a *relationship instance* with the *subject instance*.

Relatant multiplicity: The *multiplicity* of the *relatant* in a *relationship*. See *subject multiplicity*.

Relatant multiplicity inheritance: A *relationship principle* which requires a *descendant class* to inherit the *relatant multiplicity* of an inherited *relationship*, which it may restrict. See *subject multiplicity inheritance, relatant multiplicity restriction*, and *subject multiplicity regression*.

Relatant multiplicity restriction: A *specialization principle* which permits a *descendant class* to restrict the *domain* of the *relatant multiplicity* in an inherited *relationship*. See *subject multiplicity regression, subject multiplicity inheritance*, and *relatant multiplicity inheritance*.

Relatant specialization: A *specialization principle* which permits a *descendant class* to restrict an inherited *relationship* to selected descendants of the *relatant*. See *specialized relatant inheritance*.

Relatant virtualization: A *basis of virtualization* which creates a *selected virtual class* by selecting only those *members* of its *base class* which participate in *relationship instances* with those members of the *relatant class* which are also members of another *virtual object class* supported by the relatant.

Relatant-counting function: An environmental function available to each *member* of every *object class* which, given certain arguments, can count its *relatant objects*; called `countRelatants()` in our methodology. See *relatant-tracking function*.

Relatant-tracking function: An environmental function available to each *member* of every *object class* which, given certain arguments, can enumerate its *relatant objects*; called `trackRelatants()` in our methodology. See *relatant-counting function*.

Relationship: A *modeling construct* denoting an *operational coupling* between *object classes*.

Relationship addition: A *specialization principle* which permits a *descendant class* to add a new *relationship*.

Relationship assignment: The establishment of a *relationship* between two *object classes*.

Relationship attribute: An *attribute* of a *relationship*, which is different from the attributes of either the *subject* or the *relatant*.

Relationship attribute restriction: A *specialization principle* which permits a *descendant class* to restrict the *domain* of a *relationship attribute* of an inherited *relationship*.

Relationship inheritance: A *relationship principle* which requires a *descendant class* to inherit the *relationships* of an *ancestral class*.

Relationship instance: An *instance* of a *relationship* between two *object instances*.

Relationship instance: An *operational coupling* between *objects*.

Relationship instantiation: The establishment of a *relationship instance* between two *object instances*.

Relationship multiplicities: The *subject multiplicity* and *relatant multiplicity* of a *relationship*.

Relationship normalization: The determination of the best *object class* in the *inheritance hierarchy* to which a *relationship assignment* may be applied.

Relationship principle: A rule which states how a *relationship* interacts with *specialization*.

Result: A *modeling construct* denoting an output parameter of a *function*.

Result covariance: A *specialization principle* which permits the *results* of a *function* of a *descendant class* to exhibit *covariance*. See *argument contravariance*.

Reusability: The ability, in an *object-oriented programming environment*, to use *inherited properties* in a *descendant class* by reference to their implementation in an *ancestral class*; or, in an *object-oriented model*, to use inherited properties in a descendant class by reference to their specification in an ancestral class.

Role: A direction between the two *participant classes* of a *relationship*. See *forward role* and *reciprocal role*.

Role-pair: A pair of mutually reciprocal *roles*. See *forward role* and *reciprocal role*.

Root: In any tree-structured organization of items growing downward, the item which occurs highest. For example, `genericObject` is the root of the *inheritance hierarchy*.

Rule: A *modeling construct* which describes how a structural change causes certain behavior. See *driving precondition*, *triggered function*, *native rule*, and *spanning rule*.

Rule addition: A *specialization principle* which permits a *descendant class* to add a *rule* as a new *property*.

Rule function addition: A *specialization principle* which permits a *descendant class* to add a new *triggered function* to an inherited *rule*.

Rule precondition contravariance: See *precondition contravariance*.

Rule-based modeling: A *modeling paradigm* which infers facts about the *universe of discourse* given other facts.

Schema: The framework within which a *model* is organized in the *model information base*.

Selected virtual class: A *virtual object class* created by applying a *selector* to its *base class*.

Selective inheritance: The ability of a *descendant class* to drop or override the *properties* of an *ancestral class*. Also called *refinement by cancellation*. See *monotonic inheritance* and *overriding*.

Selector: A *basis of virtualization* expressing a logical condition which must be satisfied by *members* of the *base class* in order to qualify as members of the *virtual object class*.

Semiotic compiler: A compiler which translates a pictorial representation or graphical specification directly into an executable software program.

Sibling classes: *Object classes* which *derive-from* the same *superclass* as part of the same *specialization*.

Signature: The sequence and data types of the *arguments* of a *function*.

Signature polymorphism: The ability, in an *object-oriented programming environment*, of an object to invoke different implementations of a *function* depending on the syntax of the *signature* used for its invocation. Also called *overloading*. See *function polymorphism*.

Simple specialization: A *specialization* which uses one *mode of specialization*. See *compound specialization*.

Soft constraint: A *constraint* which represents a policy or desirable state but which may be occasionally violated. See *hard constraint*.

Spaghetti inheritance: A random behavior-sharing pattern in an *inheritance hierarchy* created by using *selective inheritance* merely for the sake of code reuse convenience, without regard for correct *taxonomy*. See *monotonic inheritance*.

Spanning constraint: A *constraint* which is a *property* of an *object class* and also *governs* properties of its *relatant classes*. See *native constraint*.

Spanning rule: A *rule* whose *driving preconditions* and *triggered functions* may be *properties* of *relatants* of its *anchoring class*.

Specialization: The activity, during *modeling*, of creating a new *subclass* to express *extension* and *incremental refinement* of an existing *object class*. Each specialization usually has a *basis of specialization*. See *generalization*.

Specialization associations: The *association specializes-from* between an *object class* and its *ancestral classes*, and the *association specializes-into* between an *object class* and its *descendant classes*. See *inheritance associations*, *generalization associations*, *derives-from*, and *is-a*.

Specialization mode: See *mode of specialization*.

Specialization principle: A rule which states how a *descendant class* may legally *specialize-from* an *ancestral class*.

Specialization theory: A rigorous *object-oriented modeling* methodology, an important feature of which is the construction of *inheritance hierarchies* based only on certain *specialization principles*.

Specialized aggregate inheritance: An *aggregation principle* which requires a *descendant* of a *component class* to *be-a-part-of* at least one descendant of the *aggregate class*, if any *specialization* of the *aggregate class* is *complete*. See *specialized component inheritance* and *aggregate specialization*.

Specialized component inheritance: An *aggregation principle* which requires a *descendant* of an *aggregate class* to *have-as-a-part* at least one descendant of a *mandatory component* *class*, if any *specialization* of the *component class* is *complete*. See *specialized aggregate inheritance* and *component specialization*.

Specialized relatant inheritance: A *relationship principle* which requires a *descendant class* to participate in an inherited *relationship* with at least one descendant of a *mandatory relatant*, if any *specialization* of the *relatant class* is *complete*. See *relatant specialization*.

Specializes-from: The *association* between an *object class* and all its *ancestral classes*. The *equivalent* of *generalizes-into*, *inherits-from*, implied by *derives-from*, and implies *is-a*. The *complement* of *specializes-into*, *generalizes-from*, and *bequeaths-to*. See *specialization associations*.

Specializes-into: The *association* between an *object class* and all its *descendant classes*. The *equivalent* of *generalizes-from* and *bequeaths-to*. The *complement* of *specializes-from*, *generalizes-into*, and *inherits-from*. See *specialization associations*.

Static binding: The requirement, in an *object-oriented programming environment*, that the most appropriate implementation of a *function* invocation must be selected by an *object* at compile-time. See *signature polymorphism* and *dynamic binding*.

Stream function: A *function* at least one of whose *arguments* or *results* is an unstructured continuous analog or digital stream. See *procedural function*.

Strict inheritance: See *monotonic inheritance*.

Strong ontology: An approach, in *modeling*, which considers that an object *is-an-instance-of* all its *ancestral classes*. See *weak ontology*.

Structuring principle: A notion used to impose an organization on an unordered collection of facts, objects, or elements. An example of a structuring principle is a *basis of specialization* used for classifying objects.

Subclass: The *object class* immediately below a given object class in the *inheritance hierarchy*. See *superclass*.

Subject: The *object class* in a *relationship* on which we choose to focus. See *relatant*.

Subject instance: The *object* in a *relationship instance* on which we choose to focus. See *relatant instance*.

Subject multiplicity: The *multiplicity* of the *subject* in a *relationship*. See *relatant multiplicity*.

Subject multiplicity inheritance: A *relationship principle* which requires a *descendant class* to inherit the *subject multiplicity* of an inherited *relationship* with its lower bound regressed to zero by default, which it may override, and its upper bound unchanged by default, which it may regress to a non-zero value. See *relatant multiplicity inheritance*, *relatant multiplicity restriction*, and *subject multiplicity regression*.

Subject multiplicity regression: A *specialization principle* which permits a *descendant class* to regress the *domain* of the *subject multiplicity* in an inherited *relationship*. See *zero regression*, *relatant multiplicity restriction*, *subject multiplicity inheritance*, and *relatant multiplicity inheritance*.

Subtype: A data type created by modifying its *supertype* in permissible ways, and is fully substitutable in all situations for the supertype.

Superclass: The *object class* immediately above a given object class in the *inheritance hierarchy*. See *subclass*.

Supertype: A data type which serves as the basis for creating *subtypes*.

Synonymous virtual relationship: An *implicate virtual relationship* in which the implicating and implicand *role-pairs* are synonyms for each other.

Synthetic class: A *non-referent class*. See *authentic class*.

System architecture: A method of describing the organization of the *modeled system*, identifying its major components and their interaction.

System model: See *model*.

System operation: The monitoring and manipulation of the digital representation of the *system model*, which has the effect of executing actions on the actual *modeled system*.

Taxonomy: An organization of the elements of the *universe of discourse* in accordance with chosen *structuring principles*. *Classification* of *object classes* in an *inheritance hierarchy* is an example of a taxonomy.

Top-level class: An *object class* which is an immediate *subclass* of the *root* of the *inheritance hierarchy*.

Total specialization: See *complete specialization*.

Tracked virtual attribute: A *virtual attribute* at least one of whose supporting *base attributes* is a *property* of *relatant class*. See *native virtual attribute*.

Tracked virtual function: A *function* which appears to execute in one *object instance* but may actually execute in one or more of its *relatant instances*. See *tracked virtual attribute*.

`trackRelatants()`: See *relatant-tracking function*.

Transitive closure: The set of all *object classes* which are reachable from a given object class using either a *transitive association* or a *transitive role*.

Transitive role-pair: A *role-pair* in which, for either *role*, a sequence of links of that role implies a single link.

Transitive virtual relationship: A *virtual relationship* inferred from a *base relationship* with a *transitive role-pair*.

Transitivity: A feature of an *association*, *relationship*, or *role* which enables it to preserve its semantics across a chain of links consisting of itself.

Triggered function: A *function* which is invoked when a *rule* is activated by the establishment of its *driving precondition*.

Triggers: The *association* of a *rule* with its *triggered functions*. The *complement* of *is-triggered-by*.

Type: The data type of any *modeling construct*; for example, of an *attribute*, of the *argument* to a *function*, or the *result* of a *function*.

Type knowledge: The ability of every *object* to know its *class*.

Universe of discourse: The body of knowledge which we deem sufficiently interesting to *model*.

Variant property: A *property* which is optional in *instances* of an *object class*. See *core property*, *mandatory capsule*, and *optional capsule*.

Venn diagram: A diagram which uses circles to represent inclusion, exclusion, and intersection of sets or *classes*.

Virtual attribute: An *attribute* which is *functionally dependent* on other attributes or *function results*, specified using an *attribute-defined expression* defining this functional dependency. See *actual attribute*, *base attribute*, *native virtual attribute*, and *tracked virtual attribute*.

Virtual attribute domain restriction: A *specialization principle* which permits a *descendant class* to apply *attribute domain restriction* on a *virtual attribute*.

Virtual class: See *virtual object class*.

Virtual instance: An *instance* of a *virtual object class*.

Virtual object: See *virtual instance*.

Virtual object class: An *object class* whose *members* are determined by certain criteria satisfied by the members of another object class. A virtual object class has no *instantiated* members and no place in the *inheritance hierarchy*. See *actual object class*, *base class*, *selected virtual class*, *projected virtual class*, and *conjunct virtual class*.

Virtual relationship: A *relationship* whose existence can be inferred from other relationships. See *actual relationship* and *base relationship*. See also *commutative virtual relationship*, *transitive virtual relationship*, *distributive virtual relationship*, *convolute virtual relationship*, and *implicate virtual relationship*.

Virtual relationship instance: A *relationship instance* of a *virtual relationship*. See *actual relationship instance*.

Virtualization: The activity of creating a *virtual object class*.

Virtualization associations: The *associations virtualizes-from* and *virtualizes-into* between a *virtual object class* and its *base class*. See *property acquisition associations*.

Virtualizes-from: The *association* between a *virtual object class* and its *base class*; the *complement* of *virtualizes-into*.

Virtualizes-into: The *association* between a *base class* and any *virtual object class* defined on it; the *complement* of *virtualizes-from*.

Visibility control: The ability of an *ancestral class* to choose which of the *properties* it *bequeaths-to* its *descendant classes* are visible in the descendants.

Weak ontology: An approach, in *modeling*, which considers that an *object is-an-instance-of* only one *class* and *is-a-member-of* all its *ancestral classes*. See *strong ontology*.

Well-founded relationship: A *relationship* which is created by explicit *relationship assignment*, or is inherited by a *descendant class* without becoming a *degenerate relationship*, or is a legal *virtual relationship*.

Zero-regression: The phenomenon that the lower bound of the *subject multiplicity* in a *relationship* drops to zero when that relationship is inherited by a *subclass* of the *subject*.

Glossary:
Communications Terminology

Add-drop multiplexer (ADM): A *multiplexer*, usually at some intermediate point, which has the capability of dropping some substream of its composite signal and inserting a new substream in its place.

Address resolution protocol (ARP): A protocol of the *Internet reference model* used to dynamically resolve an IP address to a physical hardware address on a network which supports broadcast. See *ES-IS*.

Adjunct processor (AD): A functional analogue of a *service control point* which is directly connected and dedicated to a *service switching point* by means of a high-speed interface, instead of through the *SS7* network. Contains the service control function and the service data function.

Advanced intelligent network (AIN): One architecture for implementing an *intelligent network*, created by Bellcore for use by its client companies.

Advanced peer-to-peer networking (APPN): A networking architecture created by IBM to permit heterogeneous equipment to internetwork with distributed routing control, as opposed to mainframe-centric hierarchical networking.

APPN network node: A *network device* which acts as a *router* for *APPN* traffic.

Architecture information base: A subset of the *model information base* which supports the activity of *network architecture*. See *operations information base* and *management information base*.

Asynchronous transfer mode (ATM): A high-speed communication protocol for *broadband ISDN* consisting of fixed-length 53-octet cells whose payload may contain data or digitized voice, image, or video.

ATM adaptation layer (AAL): The layer in the *broadband ISDN reference model* which resides above *ATM* and adapts upper-layer traffic for transmission as ATM cells.

Autoconfiguration: The capability of a device, protocol, or application to interrogate the parameters of other devices, protocols, or applications and determine how best to configure itself for interoperation.

Automatic call distributor (ACD): A network service or a computer system which distributes inbound calls among a local or distributed bank of terminals, depending on their availability and other load allocation criteria.

Automatic number identification (ANI): The activity of supplying the calling number to the called number in a telephone network, either on-line or subsequently.

Bandedness: For *control plane* and *management plane* data, the characteristic of being carried in the same *protocol stack* as *user plane* data. See *in-band* and *out-of-band*.

Bandwidth-on-demand: A capability of any *network device* to adjust the bandwidth available from the *service provider* network in response to changes in demand in the subscriber network.

Bridge: A *network device* used to connect, forward, and filter traffic between two or more LAN segments. See *transparent bridge*, *source-routing bridge*, and *source-routing transparent bridge*.

Bridge-router: A *network device* which acts as a *bridge* but can also act as a *router* if it recognizes a routable network-layer protocol.

Broadband integrated services digital network (B-ISDN): A family of ITU standards intended to provide advanced high-speed communication, using *ATM* as its infrastructure.

Broker: See *Object request broker*.

Brouter: See *bridge-router*.

Case diagram: A *graphical formal description technique* which describes the counter *attributes* affected by the processing of *PDUs* in a *protocol entity*. See *Case invariant*.

Case invariant: A mathematical equation that defines one counter *attribute* in a *protocol entity* as a linear combination of other counter attributes. See *Case diagram*.

CCITT High-level language (CHILL): A *notational formal description technique* for specifying the behavior of a concurrent, real-time *network device* such as a *switching system*.

Central office: A *switching system*, usually in a public telephone network; (informally) the location of such a system.

Central-office equipment: A *network device* co-located with a *central office*.

Centrex: A *network service*, provided by a *switching system*, offering an internal subscriber extension many features typically available in a *PBX*.

Channel port: The *port* of a *network device* which supplies a low-speed signal stream as input to some multiplexing function. See *composite port*.

Channel service unit (CSU): A *network device* installed at a subscriber site which terminates a *service provider*'s channel and furnishes the service provider with protective and diagnostic capabilities.

Circuit switching: A mode of communication in which a connection path through the network is established between the end-stations prior to communication, along which information flows continuously and at a constant rate. See *packet switching*.

Client-server computing: An information processing paradigm in a *distributed computing system* in which one *object* acts as the requester and another the provider of certain services. See *peer-to-peer computing*.

Collapsed-backbone hub: A *wiring hub* with a high-bandwidth backplane which, if used to concentrate all premises LANs, eliminates the need for an external high-speed backbone.

Common carrier: A telecommunications company or public authority providing wireless or wireline facilities to carry traffic between end-users or between end-users and *information service providers*. Also *service provider*.

Common channel signaling: The consolidation of all *signaling* activity for different end-user connections on a common physical facility in a dedicated signaling network. See *SS7*.

Common management information protocol (CMIP): A protocol of the *OSI reference model* used for *network management*. See *CMIS, SNMP, OSI management,* and *Internet management*.

Common management information service (CMIS): The set of *network management* services for *OSI management* provided by *CMIP*.

Common object request broker architecture (CORBA): A *distributed computing system* architecture standardized by the Object Management Group. See *Object services architecture, Object request broker,* and *Distributed computing environment*.

Composite port: The *port* of a *network device* producing the combined output signal after multiplexing its input signals in some fashion (e.g., a *multiplexer*). See *channel port*.

Connectionless network protocol (CLNP): An *OSI* network-layer protocol which conveys *PDUs* between end-systems without requiring connection establishment prior to communication. See *IP* and *TP-4*.

Connectivity: The *relationship* between *network devices* which are topologically adjacent by virtue of having a termination relationship with the same *link* object. See *interconnectivity*.

Constant bit rate traffic (CBR): A communication signal stream whose source generates bits at a constant rate. See *variable bit rate traffic*.

Continuous bitstream organization (CBO): See *constant bit rate traffic*.

Control plane: In any *network device*, the set of *protocol stacks* which carry *routing* and *signaling PDUs*. See *user plane* and *management plane*.

Cross-connect: A *network device*, often used as *central-office equipment*, to provide permanent and semi-permanent connections between lines and trunks. A cross-connect demarcates *transmission equipment* from *switching systems* and may also provide traffic consolidation, traffic segregation, network restoration, and protection switching.

Customer premises equipment (CPE): Any *network device* which interfaces with a *service provider*'s network and is located on the subscriber premises beyond the demarcation point terminating the service provider's channel (e.g., *PBXs, multiplexers, modems, routers, wiring hubs,* etc.).

Data flow diagram: A *graphical formal description technique* which describes behavior as data flows between processes and data stores.

Datagram: A *protocol data unit* generated by a connectionless (usually network-layer) *protocol entity*.

Dedicated circuit: A connection path supplied by a *service provider* for permanently connecting two or more locations and reserved for the subscriber's sole use.

Designated router: In a data network with hierarchical routing domains, the distinguished *router* selected in a lower-level domain to route datagrams to the next higher-level domain.

Dial modem: A *modem* for use with a connection established over a switched telephone network.

Digital cross-connect: A *cross-connect* which is controlled digitally, providing automation of provisioning and many other programmable features (e.g., time-of-day rearrangement of trunk group assignments).

Digital loop carrier (DLC): A *network device* in the subscriber loop which provides pair-gain and transmission of multiplexed subscriber lines to *central-office equipment*.

Digital service unit (DSU): A *network device* converting a customer's digital data stream into a bipolar format suitable for transmission over a *service provider*'s digital circuit.

Digital signal-*n* (DS-1, DS-3, etc.): Nominal signal rates and multiplex levels in the North American Time-Division Multiplexing hierarchy.

Direct inward dialing (DID): A *network service*, provided by a *switching system*, facilitating the ability to directly dial an internal subscriber extension as a public telephone number. See *Centrex* and *PBX*.

Distributed application framework (DAF): A *distributed computing system* architecture standardized by the ITU and aligned with ISO's *Open distributed processing*.

Distributed computing environment (DCE): A *distributed computing system* architecture standardized by the Open Software Foundation. See *Common object request broker architecture*.

Distributed computing system: An information processing system consisting of a collection of computers and peripherals functioning co-operatively over a set of communications facilities. See *Common object request broker architecture, Distributed computing environment, Open distributed processing,* and *Distributed application framework*.

Distributed file system: A single file system, generally a part of a *distributed computing system*, deployed over multiple computer systems which may be geographically separated.

Distributed object management: A system for performing *network management* and systems administration of a *distributed computing system*.

E-1, E-3, etc.: Multiplex levels in the ITU Time Division Multiplexing hierarchy (at 2.048 and 34.368 Mbps respectively). See *T-1, T-3, etc.*

E-1 multiplexer: A *multiplexer* whose *composite port* produces an *E-1* data stream.

Eight hundred service: A *network service* providing automatic called-party billing.

End-System-to-Intermediate-System (ES-IS): A protocol of the *OSI reference model* used to dynamically resolve an OSI address to a physical hardware address on a network which supports broadcast. See *ARP*.

Estelle: A *notational formal description technique* which describes behavior as transitions between the states of an *object*. See *state transition diagram*.

Ethernet: A popular LAN protocol running over a variety of media, implementing the physical and data-link layers of a protocol stack. Ethernet usually has a nominal data rate of 10 Mbps, uses a broadcast carrier-sense multiple-access with collision-detection mechanism, and is similar to the IEEE 802.3 standard.

Federated network: A network of interoperating devices, protocols, and applications, which belong to different administrative, jurisdictional, regulatory, or service-providing agencies.

Fiber distributed data interface (FDDI): An ANSI standard originally intended for high-speed communication over optical fiber but now run over a variety of non-fiber media. FDDI has a nominal data rate of 100 Mbps, uses a dual counter-rotating ring topology and an access control mechanism similar to *token-ring*.

Formal description technique: A specification technique which describes behavior precisely and formally. See *graphical formal description technique* and *notational formal description technique*.

Format and protocol language (FAPL): A proprietary IBM *notational formal description technique*, based on PL/1 for describing the behavior of a *protocol entity* as a set of state transitions.

Fractional T-1: A nominal data rate equal to one of the defined sub-rates of *T-1*.

Frame relay: A high-speed connection-oriented *packet-switching* protocol of the *ISDN reference model*, similar to *X.25* but eliminating some layers of protocol processing at intermediate nodes.

General relationship model (GRM): An *OSI SMI* standard describing *relationships* between managed object classes.

Graphical formal description technique: A formal description technique which is pictorial. See *state transition diagram, data flow diagram, timing sequence diagram*, and *Case diagram*.

Guidelines for the definition of managed objects (GDMO): A template notation used for defining *SMI* constructs in *OSI management*.

High-speed serial interface (HSSI): A high-speed protocol with a nominal data rate of 50 Mbps for dedicated connections between computer systems over short distances.

In-band: Any *control plane* or *management plane* data carried in the same *protocol stack* as *user plane* data. See *bandedness* and *out-of-band*.

Information service provider: A provider of an end-user information service which produces data for consumption by a subscriber over a *common carrier* network. An information service provider may or may not be the same agency as a common carrier.

Information superhighway: A *federated network* providing a combination of telecommunication, information, commercial, and entertainment services over a variety of wireline and wireless media.

Integrated services digital network (ISDN): A family of ITU standards intended to provide integrated telecommunications and data communications. See *broadband ISDN*.

Intelligent network (IN): A network that follows the set of ITU Intelligent Network (IN) standards, whose physical plane consists of *service switching points, network access points, service control points, intelligent peripherals, adjunct processors, service data points*, and *services nodes*, generally supported by other equipment such as *signal transfer points, service management systems*, and *operations support systems*.

Intelligent peripheral (IP): A computer system providing the special resource function for end-user interaction in an *intelligent network*, such as voice synthesis, announcements, digit collection, and speech recognition.

Interconnectivity: The *relationship* between *network devices* which are topologically reachable from each other by virtue of a chain of *connectivity* relationships.

Interface substack: A partial *protocol stack* which is a dedicated *component* of a *port*.

Intermediate session routing (ISR): A routing protocol of the *APPN* protocol family used in *APPN network nodes* to route APPN traffic.

Intermediate-System-to-Intermediate-System (IS-IS): A protocol of the *OSI reference model* used between routers to communicate routing and topology information. See *OSPF*.

International registration hierarchy: The universal *registration hierarchy* administered by ISO and the ITU for assigning *registration labels* to the items of subscribing countries and agencies.

Internet management: A collective reference to the set of Internet standards for network management, including *SNMP*, its *SMI*, and related aspects defined in RFCs 1441-1452. See *OSI management*.

Internet protocol (IP): An internet-layer protocol of the *Internet reference model* which conveys connectionless *datagrams* across an internetwork. See *TCP* and *CLNP*.

Internet reference model: A family of Internet standards for the transmission of packet data over a connectionless internetwork, including popular protocols such as *TCP*, *IP*, *UDP*, and *SNMP*.

Interoperability: A *relationship* between *network devices* which have the same *protocol stack* up to a given layer, or which have the same *protocol entity* at a given layer with an *interworkability* relationship in the layer below.

Interworkability: A *relationship* between *network devices* which can exchange data at a layer at which they do not have an *interoperability* relationship, via some translator or gateway device.

Inverse layering: A *protocol layering* in which a *protocol entity* which would normally layer below another protocol entity is layered above it.

Isochronous traffic: A communication signal stream which is invalidated unless there is a timing relationship between its source and destination terminals. See *non-isochronous traffic*.

Larch: A *notational formal description technique* for specifying the behavior of software *functions*.

Leased-line: A line supplied by a *service provider* for permanently connecting two or more locations and dedicated for the subscriber's sole use.

Leased-line modem: A *modem* for use with a *leased-line*.

Link: An *object* which has a termination *relationship* with one or more *network devices*. The link *object class* may *specialize-into* wireless links, wireline links, circuits, LAN segments, and so on.

LOTOS: A *notational formal description technique* which describes behavior as parallel interactions between processes.

Management information base (MIB): A subset of the *model information base* which supports the activity of *network management*. See *architecture information base* and *operations information base*.

Management plane: In any *network device*, the set of *protocol stacks* which carry *network management PDUs*. See *user plane* and *management plane*.

Message transfer agent (MTA): A process which co-operates with similar processes to convey messages throughout an *OSI* X.400 message handling system.

Modem: A *network device* which converts a digital signal for transmission over an analog line, and vice versa. See *leased-line modem* and *dial modem*.

Motion picture experts group (MPEG): An ISO standard for the compression of full-motion digital video signal streams.

Multiplexer: A *network device* capable of combining multiple signals into a composite signal for transmission over common facilities and (usually) also capable of reversing the process.

National information infrastructure: A network of *information superhighways*, created, co-ordinated, regulated, and operated by a combination of private and public organizations.

Network access point: A *switching system* in an *intelligent network* which provides call control and call control agent functions but not service switching.

Network architecture: The activity of designing a communications network by mapping the re-quirements of the network to a *system model* which can fulfill those requirements. See *net-work design automation*.

Network design automation: A way of creating a *network architecture* by automating the design of a communication network, including automation of the activities of *network syn-thesis* and *network simulation*.

Network device: An *object* with a physical (hardware) embodiment which is a functionary in a network. A network device may perform intermediate functions (such as switching or rout-ing) or may be a terminal device (an ultimate producer or consumer of data).

Network management: The activity of performing tasks for the monitoring, command, control, diagnostics, configuration, reconfiguration, service deployment, software download, per-formance analysis, and security of a communication network. See *OAM&P*.

Network management system: A *distributed computing system* responsible for *network man-agement*. See *TMN*.

Network operations: The run-time functioning and maintenance of a communication network.

Network service: A service offered by a *service provider* to a subscriber.

Network simulation: The activity of testing the digital *model* of a proposed network configura-tion created by *network synthesis* against various operational scenarios to determine its ac-ceptability. See *network architecture* and *network design automation*.

Network synthesis: The activity of creating a digital *model* for a proposed configuration of a communication network by assembling devices, protocols, and applications from a standard model library following the correct assembly rules; generally followed by the activity of *net-work simulation*. See *network architecture* and *network design automation*.

Network-network interface (NNI): The interface between two *network devices* within a *service provider's* network, at which *signaling* and *routing* protocols such as *SS7*, *OSPF*, and *IS-IS* are used. See *user-network interface*.

Non-isochronous traffic: A communication signal stream which remains valid regardless of any timing relationship between its source and destination terminals. See *isochronous traffic*.

Numbering plan: A *registration hierarchy* representing the unique assignment *registration labels* to items of interest, usually telephone lines.

Object request broker (ORB): In the *Common object request broker architecture*, the entity which provides distributed object location, naming, and messaging facilities. See *trader*.

Object services architecture (OSA): A *distributed computing system* architecture standardized by the Object Management Group, which includes the *Common object request broker archi-tecture*.

Open distributed processing (ODP): A *distributed computing system* architecture standardized by ISO and aligned with ITU's *Distributed application framework*.

Open shortest path first (OSPF): A protocol of the *Internet reference model* used between routers to communicate routing and topology information. See *IS-IS*.

Open systems interconnection (OSI): A family of international data communication standards, including a *reference model, service definitions,* and protocol specifications, defined by the ISO.

Operations, administration, maintenance, and provisioning (OAM&P): The functional analogue of *network management* in a telecommunications network.

Operations information base: A subset of the *model information base* which supports the activity of *network operations.* See *architecture information base* and *management information base.*

Operations support system (OSS): A stand-alone or distributed computer system responsible for supporting the *network operations* of a telecommunications network, typically including many functions of a *network management system.*

Optical carrier-*n* (OC-1, OC-3, etc.): The nominal optical signal rates and multiplex levels in the *SONET* digital hierarchy (at 51.84 and 155.52 Mbps respectively).

Origin-based routing service: A *network service* which directs calls according their originating geographical area.

OSI management: A collective reference to the set of *OSI* standards for *network management,* including *CMIS, CMIP,* the *OSI SMI,* and related aspects defined in the ITU-T X.700 series. See *Internet management.*

Out-of-band: Any *control plane* or *management plane* data carried in a different *protocol stack* than *user plane* data. See *bandedness* and *in-band.*

Packet: See *protocol data unit.*

Packet switching: A mode of communication in which information is divided into individual packets which are forwarded from *network device* to network device. See *circuit switching.*

Peer-to-peer computing: An information processing paradigm in a *distributed computing system* in which both *objects* mutually request and provide reciprocal services to each other. See *client-server computing.*

Permanent virtual circuit: A *virtual circuit* which is established at service provisioning time as if it were a *dedicated circuit.* See *switched virtual circuit.*

Plug-and-play capability: The capability of a device, protocol, or application to *autoconfigure* itself for operation as soon as it is connected to the network.

Port: A *component* of a *network device,* containing at least a physical-layer *protocol entity,* for external communication.

Private branch exchange (PBX): A *network device,* usually *customer premises equipment,* which provides switching between private telecommunication terminals (telephones, fax machines, paging devices, etc.) and usually includes access to a *service provider*'s network.

Protocol data unit (PDU): A sequence of bits constituting a single unit generated by a *protocol entity,* including a protocol header, payload data, and (optionally) a protocol trailer.

Protocol entity: Any entity having a hardware, firmware, or software implementation capable of encoding and decoding a communication protocol.

Protocol layering: A rule which permits a *protocol entity* to be layered above another protocol entity.

Protocol stack: A path which a *protocol data unit* may take through a *network device.*

Q.931: A protocol used in *ISDN* to perform *signaling* at the *user-network interface* (generically, the entire stack of protocols below Q.931 which performs this function).

Queueing system: A mathematical system characterized by the notation A/B/m, where A is the probability density function for inter-arrival delays, B is the probability density function for service delays, and m is the number of servers.

Reference model: An architecture for layering *protocol entities* so that functionality is divided among the layers, with each layer using and building upon the services provided by the layer below.

Reference point: A hypothetical location on a link which defines some specified *interoperability* relationship for *network devices* on either side and may also demarcate an administrative boundary.

Registration: The assignment of a *registration label* to a *modeling construct* in the *model information base*.

Registration authority: The authority in charge of issuing unique *registration labels*.

Registration hierarchy: A data structure representing an arrangement of *registration labels*.

Registration label: A sequence of integers used to identify any item of interest (e.g., a *modeling construct*).

Router: A *network device* capable of decoding a connectionless network-layer protocol and routing *datagrams* to appropriate interfaces. See *routing*.

Routing: The activity of determining at each node the path which a *PDU* will take in a connectionless internetwork. See *signaling*.

Segmentation: The activity of dividing a broadcast LAN into multiple segments, usually with *bridges*, to reduce the traffic volume in each segment.

Service control point (SCP): A fault-tolerant transaction-processing database computer system providing call handling information in response to network queries in an *intelligent network*. Contains the service control function and the service data function.

Service creation environment: An environment for conceptualizing, prototyping, creating, testing, implementing, and provisioning services rapidly in an *intelligent network*.

Service data point (SDP): A fault-tolerant transaction-processing database computer that stores information, or service data function, required for the service control function of an *intelligent network*. See *service control point*.

Service definition: A precise, implementation-independent description of the capabilities offered by a *protocol entity* to its user.

Service logic execution environment (SLEE): The run-time software system which handles the logic required for providing a service in an *intelligent network*.

Service management system (SMS): An *operations support system* for managing an *intelligent network* service, typically including the storage and update of customer records.

Service provider: See *common carrier*.

Service switching point (SSP): A *switching system* in an *intelligent network* capable of *SS7 signaling*. It contains the capability to identify calls requiring special handling, determining their handling information from a *service control point*, and providing the special handling. Contains the call control function and the service switching function.

Services node (SN): A node in an *intelligent network* that can provide a service switching function, a call control function, a special resource function, a service control function, and a service data function. See *service switching point*, *service control point*, and *intelligent peripheral*.

Shared conceptual schema: The network model knowledge consisting of *object classes, relationships,* and other *modeling constructs,* which is exchanged between two networks to facilitate *autoconfiguration* and interoperability.

Signal transfer point (STP): A high-capacity high-availability packet switch to transfer *signaling* messages between the nodes of an *intelligent network* (e.g., between *service switching points*).

Signaling: The activity of communicating information required for call setup, call routing, and call tear-down of connections in a telecommunications network. See *routing* and *SS7.*

Signaling system 7 (SS7): A layered set of protocols intended to communicate *signaling* information between network nodes in *broadband ISDN* and *intelligent networks.*

Simple network management protocol (SNMP): A protocol of the *Internet reference model* used for *network management.* See *CMIP, Internet management,* and *OSI management.*

Source-routing bridge: A *bridge* which requires its end-stations to supply the routing information for each frame. See *transparent bridge* and *source-routing transparent bridge.*

Source-routing transparent bridge: A *bridge* capable of performing transparent bridging and processing source-routed frames. See *transparent bridge* and *source-routing bridge.*

Specification and description language (SDL): A *notational* and *graphical formal description technique* for specifying the behavior of a real-time, interactive *network device* such as a *switching system.*

State transition diagram: A *graphical formal description technique* which describes behavior as transitions between the states of an *object.*

Structure of management information (SMI): The organization and format of the constructs of interest for *network management.*

Switched circuit: A connection path established through the switched public network.

Switched multimegabit data service (SMDS): A high-speed internetworking protocol for carrying connectionless *datagrams* over a public packet network belonging to one or more *service providers.*

Switched virtual circuit: A *virtual circuit* which is established as needed on a per-call basis. See *permanent virtual circuit.*

Switching fabric: The hardware modules within a *switching system* or a *wiring hub* which provide the ability to switch connections (or cells) between their external interfaces.

Switching system: A stored-program control switch supporting call control functions and providing interconnection of lines to trunks and to each other.

Synchronous data link control (SDLC): An IBM protocol for dedicated communication at the data link layer between computer systems.

Synchronous digital hierarchy (SDH): The international version of *SONET,* defined by the ITU.

Synchronous optical network (SONET): A family of ANSI telecommunications standards for high-speed synchronous communication over optical facilities. See *synchronous digital hierarchy.*

Synchronous transport signal-*n* (STS-1, STS-3, etc.): The electrical counterparts of the optical carrier signal levels *OC-1, OC-3, etc.*

T-1, T-3, etc.: Transmission media in the North American T-carrier hierarchy, corresponding to the *DS-n* signal rates of the TDM hierarchy (at 1.544 and 44.736 Mbps respectively). See *E-1, E-3, etc.*

T-1 multiplexer: A *multiplexer* whose *composite port* produces a *T-1* data stream.

T-3 multiplexer: A *multiplexer* whose *composite port* produces a *T-3* data stream.

Telecommunications management network (TMN): A distributed set of computer systems for performing *OAM&P* functions for a telecommunications network, defined by a set of ITU standards. See *network management system.*

Timing sequence diagram: A *graphical formal description technique* which describes the exchange of messages between objects as a function of time.

Token ring: A popular LAN protocol running over a variety of media, implementing the physical and data-link layers of a protocol stack. Token ring uses a broadcast mechanism with transmit permission controlled by possession of a token which circulates among stations in a ring topology. Token ring is defined by the IEEE 802.5 standard.

TR-303: The Bellcore standard for a *SONET digital loop carrier*, defining its interfaces to a *switching system* and its *network management* aspects.

Trader: In a *distributed computing system*, an entity which performs directory and location functions between clients and servers but does not relay messages between them. See *Object request broker.*

Traffic generator: An *object* which, in a *network simulation* environment, generates traffic of a specified type with a specified distribution to exercise a proposed network configuration in software.

Transmission control protocol (TCP): A transport-layer protocol of the *Internet reference model* which provides reliable data transmission with sophisticated error detection and correction. See *IP* and *TP-4.*

Transmission equipment: Equipment and facilities such as channels, circuits, interoffice trunks, tie lines, feeder cables, distribution cables, and so on, designed to convey signals between multiple *switching systems* or between *customer premises equipment* and switching systems.

Transparent bridge: A *bridge* which functions transparently with respect to its end-stations by learning the topology of the network and performing frame forwarding and filtering automatically. See *source-routing bridge* and *source-routing transparent bridge.*

Transport protocol 4 (TP-4): One of the transport-layer protocols of *OSI*, providing reliable data communication with sophisticated error detection and correction. See *CLNP* and *TCP.*

Tree and tabular combined notation (TTCN): A *notational formal description technique* for specifying the behavior of a *protocol entity* in the design of a test suite for validation.

Tunneling: See *inverse layering.*

User datagram protocol (UDP): A protocol of the *Internet reference model* which permits application processes to generate datagrams for delivery across an internetwork via *IP.*

User plane: In any *network device*, the set of *protocol stacks* which carry *PDUs* or *isochronous traffic* for user applications. See *control plane* and *management plane.*

User-network interface (UNI): The interface between a user's *network devices* and a *service provider's* network devices, at which *signaling* and *routing* protocols such as *Q.931*, *ARP*, and *ES-IS* are used. See *network-network interface.*

Variable bit rate traffic (VBR): A communication signal stream whose source generates bits at a variable rate. See *constant bit rate traffic.*

Variable bitstream organization (VBO): See *variable bit rate traffic*.

VHSIC Hardware description language (VHDL): A *notational formal description technique* for specifying the behavior of hardware *functions*. VHDL is an IEEE standard for electronic design automation, defining a formal language for specifying electronic components.

Vienna development method (VDM): A *notational formal description technique* for specifying the behavior of software *functions*.

Virtual circuit: In a *packet-switching* network, a path established ahead of time to emulate a connection, so that all packets follow the same route, arrive in sequence, need not carry full address information, and have bounded delay. See *switched virtual circuit* and *permanent virtual circuit*.

Virtual private network service: A *network service* provisioned over *switched circuits* to give the appearance of *dedicated circuits* to its subscriber.

Wireless communication: Communication whose sole physical medium is one or more frequencies of the electromagnetic spectrum. See *wireline communication*.

Wireline communication: Communication whose physical medium is an electrical cable or optical fiber. See *wireless communication*.

Wiring hub: A *network device* which provides structured wiring for LAN concentration, and optionally provides repeater functions, internal *segmentation*, *bridging*, *routing*, and WAN connectivity.

X.25: A suite of protocols, defined by the ITU, for packet switched public data networks; more precisely, the layer-3 packet-switching protocol for data transfer between data terminal equipment (e.g., a computer terminal) and data communications equipment (e.g., a *modem*).

Z: A *notational formal description technique* for specifying the behavior of software *functions*.

Glossary:
ASN.1 Terminology

Abstract syntax: A precise and formal specification language. See *concrete syntax*.

Abstract syntax notation one (ASN.1): An OSI and ITU standard which specifies (a) a notation for a formal syntax, used for specifying data types, *values*, and information objects; and (b) a set of encoding rules for transmission of *values*.

Associated table: A conceptual table generated by a defined *information object set* considering the *fields* of its *information object class* as columns and the *values* of the fields in the *information objects* in that set as rows.

At-notation: A notation to create a *component relation constraint*.

Choice: A structuring construct which creates a *type* resolving to any one of its component types.

Component relation constraint: A *table constraint* which requires two or more components of a particular construct to possess *values* from the same row of an *associated table*.

Concrete syntax: An implementation language compilable to executable programs or value encodings. See *abstract syntax*.

Constrained type: A *type* whose permissible *values* are restricted in some fashion. See *constraint specification*.

Constraint specification: A notation which permits the creation of *constrained types*. See *table constraint*, *subtype constraint*, and *size constraint*.

Delivered value: In the *macro definition notation*, the *value* that is ultimately assigned to the *value reference name* created by the macro (obsolete).

Field: A component of an *information object class*. See *type field*, *fixed-type value field*, *variable-type value field*, *fixed-type value set field*, *variable-type value set field*, *object field*, and *object set field*.

Field name: An identifier which denotes a *field* of an *information object class*. Must begin with an "&".

Fixed-type value field: A *field* of an *information object class* denoting a *value* of a specified *type*.

Fixed-type value set field: A *field* of an *information object class* denoting a *value set* of a specified *type*.

Identifier field: A *fixed-type value field* of an *information object class* selected to be the distinguishing characteristic of all *information objects* of that information object class. See *unique*.

Information from objects: See *value from object*, *value set from objects*, *object from object*, *object set from objects*, and *type from object*.

Information object: A collection of *values*, *types*, and information objects packaged as specified in an *information object class*.

Information object assignment: A notation which creates an *information object* of a particular *information object class*.

Information object class: A mechanism to package together *values*, *types*, and information object classes as a template to create *information objects*.

Information object class assignment: A notation which creates an *information object class*.

Information object class reference: An identifier which denotes an *information object class*. Must be all upper-case.

Information object reference: An identifier which denotes an *information object*. Must begin with a lower-case initial.

Information object set: A set of *information objects*.

Information object set assignment: A notation which creates an *information object set*.

Information object set reference: An identifier denoting an *information object set*. Must begin with an upper-case initial.

Macro definition notation: A notation for creating *value reference names* with additional syntactic information (obsolete).

Object class field type: A mechanism which extracts the *type* of a *field* of an *information object class* by suffixing the *information object class reference* with the *field name* (e.g., INFO-OBJECT-CLASS-NAME.&fieldName). An *object class field type* can be used as a *type*.

Object field: A *field* of an *information object class* denoting an *information object* of a specified information object class.

Object from object: A mechanism to extract an *information object* from an *object field* of another information object by suffixing the *information object reference* with the *field name* (e.g., infoObjectName.&objectFieldName). See *information from objects*.

Object identifier: A built-in *type* denoting a sequence of integers representing an arc in a *registration hierarchy*.

Object set field: A *field* of an *information object class* denoting an *information object set* of a specified information object class.

Object set from objects: A mechanism which extracts an *object set field* from an *information object* (e.g., infoObjectName.&ObjectSetFieldName). An *object set from objects* is also obtained by extracting an *object field* (or *object set field*) from a defined *information object set* by suffixing the *information object set reference* with the *field name* (e.g., {InfoObjectSetName}.&objectFieldName   or   {InfoObjectSet-Name}.&ObjectSetFieldName). See *information from objects*.

Open type: A *type* that represents any *value*. (The result of extracting the *object class field type* of a *type field*.)

Parameter: A *value, value set, information object, information object set, type,* or *information object class* which may be "passed in" to a *parameterized assignment*. A parameter requires a *parameter governor* unless it is a type or an information object class.

Parameter governor: The *type* of a *value* or *value set,* or the *information object class* of an *information object* or *information object set,* which is required to prefix the *parameter* with a ":" separator.

Parameterized assignment: A notation which creates a parameterized type, parameterized value, parameterized value set, parameterized information object class, parameterized information object, or parameterized information object set by accepting a *parameter* which is "passed in" to an appropriate *type assignment, value assignment, value set type assignment, information object class assignment, information object assignment,* or *information object set assignment,* respectively.

Parameterized type: See *parameterized assignment*.

Sequence: A structuring construct which creates a *type* which is of an ordered list of its component types.

Sequence of: A structuring construct which creates a *type* which is an ordered list of a given type.

Set: A structuring construct which creates a *type* which is of an unordered list of its component types.

Set of: A structuring construct which creates a *type* which is an unordered list of a given type.

Simple table constraint: A *table constraint* which requires a component of a particular construct to possess *values* from a certain column of an *associated table*.

Simple type: A built-in or primitive *type*. See *structured type*.

Size constraint: A mechanism which applies a size restriction to a *type*.

Structured type: A *type* which is created by using one of the structuring constructs. See *simple type*. See also *set, set of, sequence, sequence of,* and *choice*.

Subtype constraint: A mechanism which applies a constraint to a *type* to indicate a subset of its possible *values*.

Table constraint: A *constraint specification* which uses an *associated table*. See *simple table constraint* and *component relation constraint*.

Type: A data type.

Type assignment: A notation which creates a *type*.

Type field: A *field* of an *information object class* which is a *type reference name*.

Type from object: A mechanism which extracts a *type field* from an *information object* by suffixing the *information object reference* with the *field name* (e.g., `infoObject-Name.&TypeFieldName`). A *type from object* can be used as a *type*. See *information from objects*.

Type reference name: An identifier which denotes a *type*. Must begin with an upper-case initial.

Unique: A notation for indicating the *identifier field* of an *information object class*.

Value: A concrete quantity which is an example of a *type*.

Value assignment: A notation which creates a *value* of a particular *type*.

Value from object: A mechanism which extracts the *value* of a *fixed-type value field* or a *variable-type value field* from an *information object* by suffixing the *information object reference* with the *field name* (e.g., `infoObjectName.&fixedTypeValueFieldName` or `infoObjectName.&variableTypeValueFieldName`). See *information from objects*.

Value reference name: An identifier which denotes a *value*. Must begin with a lower-case initial.

Value set: A set of *values*.

Value set type assignment: A notation which creates a *type* as a subtype of an existing type, restricted to an identified *value set*.

Value set from objects: A mechanism which extracts a *fixed-type value set field* or a *variable-type value set field* from an *information object* by suffixing the *information object reference* with the *field name* (e.g., `infoObjectName.&FixedTypeValueSetFieldName` or `infoObjectName.&VariableTypeValueSetFieldName`). A *value set from objects* is also obtained by extracting a *fixed-type value field* or *fixed-type value set field* from an *information object set* by suffixing the *information object set reference* with the *field name* (e.g., `{InfoObjectSetName}.&fixedTypeValueFieldName` or `{InfoObjectSetName}.&FixedTypeValueSetFieldName`). A *value set from objects* can be used as a *type*. See *information from objects*.

Variable-type value field: A *field* of an *information object class* denoting a *value* of a variable *type*, determined by the contents of a *type field*.

Variable-type value set field: A *field* of an *information object class* denoting a *value set* of a variable *type*, determined by the contents of a *type field*.

With-syntax: A notation in an *information object class assignment* which permits the creation of *information objects* of that class in a user-definable syntax.

References

Journal Title Abbreviations

CNIS	*Computer Networks and ISDN Systems*
JACM	*Journal of the ACM*
JNSM	*Journal of Network and Systems Management*
JOOP	*Journal of Object-Oriented Programming*
JSAC	*IEEE Journal of Selected Areas in Communications*
IRE	*Internetworking Research and Experience*
LNCS	*Springer Lecture Notes on Computer Science*
SIGMOD Rec.	*Record of the ACM Special Interest Group on the Management of Data*
TODS	*ACM Transactions on Database Systems*
TOPLAS	*ACM Transactions on Programming Languages and Systems*
Trans. Comm.	*IEEE Transactions on Communications*
Trans. KDE	*IEEE Transactions on Knowledge and Data Engineering*
Trans. Net.	*IEEE/ACM Transactions on Networking*

Conference Title Abbreviations

CAMAD	*IEEE International Workshop on Computer-Aided Modeling, Analysis and Design of Communication Links and Networks*
DOOD	*International Conference on Deductive and Object-Oriented Databases*
DSOM	*IFIP/IEEE International Workshop on Distributed Systems Operations and Management*
ECOOP	*European Conference on Object-Oriented Programming*
EDS	*International Conference on Expert Database Systems*
FORTE	*IFIP TC-6/WG-6.1 International Conference on Formal Description Techniques*
Globecom	*IEEE Global Telecommunications Conference*
ICCC	*International Conference on Computer Communications*
ICDE	*IEEE International Conference on Data Engineering*

ICERA	*International Conference on Entity-Relationship Approach*
IJCAI	*International Joint Conference on Artificial Intelligence*
Infocom	*IEEE Conference on Computer Communications*
ISINM	*IFIP TC-6/WG-6.6 International Symposium on Integrated Network Management*
IWODP	*IFIP TC-6/WG-6.4 International Workshop on Open Distributed Processing*
NMCW	*IEEE Network Management and Control Workshop*
NOMS	*IEEE Network Operations and Management Symposium*
OOPSLA	*ACM Conference on Object-Oriented Programming Systems, Languages, and Applications*
PKRR	*International Conference on the Principles of Knowledge Representation and Reasoning*
POPL	*ACM Symposium on the Principles of Programming Languages*
PSTV	*IFIP TC-6/WG-6.1 International Symposium on Protocol Specification, Testing and Verification*
SIGCOMM	*Communication Architectures and Protocols: Conference of the ACM Special Interest Group on Communications*
SIGMOD	*International Conference on the Management of Data: Conference of the ACM Special Interest Group on Management of Data*
TINA	*Telecommunications Information Networking Architecture Workshop*
TOOLS	*International Conference on Technology of Object-Oriented Languages and Systems*
VLDB	*International Conference on Very Large Data Bases*

References

[Abit91]   Abiteboul, Serge, and Bonner, Anthony, "Objects and Views", *Proc. SIGMOD 91*, pp. 238-247, 1991.

[Abit93]   Abiteboul, Serge; Lausen, George; Uphoff, Heinz; and Waller, Emmanuel, "Methods and Rules", *Proc. SIGMOD 93*, pp. 32-41, 1993.

[Abra91]   Abrahams, Paul, "Subject: Objectivism", *Communications of the ACM*, Jan 1991, pp. 15-16.

[Agra87]   Agrawal, R., and Jagadish, H.V., "Direct Algorithms for Computing the Transitive Closure of Database Relations", *Proc. VLDB 87*, pp. 255-266, 1987.

[Agra89]   Agrawal, R., and Gehani, N.H., "Ode (Object Database and Environment): The Language and the Data Model", *Proc. SIGMOD 89*, pp. 36-45, 1989.

[Aho74]   Aho, A.V.; Hopcroft, J.E.; and Ullman, J.D., *The Design and Analysis of Computer Algorithms*, Addison-Wesley, Reading, Massachusetts, 1974.

[Aho86]   Aho, A.V.; Sethi, R.; and Ullman, J.D., *Compilers: Principles, Techniques and Tools*, Addison-Wesley, Reading, Massachusetts, 1986.

[Ande92]   Anderson, David G., and Pennington, William C., "Service Creation and the AIN", *Telephony*, May 18, 1992, pp. 29-32.

[Ansa92]   Architecture Projects Management, Ltd., "ANSA: An Engineer's Introduction to the Architecture", APM, Cambridge, United Kingdom, May 1992.

[ANSI X3-138] "Information Resource Dictionary System (IRDS)", ANSI X3-138, 1988.

[ANSI X3-183] "High-Performance Parallel Interface: Mechanical, Electrical and Signaling Protocol Specification (HIPPI-PH)", ANSI X3-183, 1991.

[ANSI X3-ODM]"Object Data Management Reference Model", Accredited Standards Committee X3, Database Systems Study Group/Object-Oriented Database Systems Task Group (DBSSG/OODBTG) Final Report, ANSI, Sep 1991.

[ANSI X3S3] "Intermediate System-to-Intermediate System Inter-Domain Routing Information Exchange Protocol", ANSI X3S3.3/90-132, 1990.

[ANSI X3T9] "FiberChannel: Physical and Signaling Interface", ANSI X3T9.3/92-007, Jan 1992.

[Anwa93] Anwar, E.; Maugis, L.; and Chakravarthy, S., "A New Perspective on Rule Support for Object-Oriented Databases", *Proc. SIGMOD 93*, pp. 99-108, 1993.

[Aoya93] Aoyama, Tomonori; Tokizawa, Ikuo; and Sato, Ken-ichi, "ATM Virtual-Path-Based Broadband Networks for Multimedia Services", *IEEE Communications*, Apr 1993, pp. 30-39.

[Appe93] Appeldorn, Menso; Kung, Roberto; and Saracco, Roberto, "TMN + IN = TINA", *IEEE Communications*, Mar 1993, pp. 78-85.

[Arms74] Armstrong, W.W., "Dependency Structures of Database Relationships", *Proc. 1974 IFIP Congress*, pp. 580-583, North-Holland, Amsterdam, The Netherlands, 1974.

[Aspe91] Asperti, Andrea, and Longo, Giuseppe, *Categories, Types and Structures*, MIT Press, Cambridge, Massachusetts, 1991.

[Atki89] Atkinson, Michael; Bancilhon, Francis; DeWitt, David; Dittrich, Klaus; Maier, David; and Zdonik, Stanley, "The Object-Oriented Database System Manifesto", *Proc. 1st DOOD*, 1989.

[Atwo91] Atwood, Thomas, "The Case for Object-Oriented Databases", *IEEE Spectrum*, Feb 1991, pp.44-47.

[Banc90] Bancilhon, Francis, and Kim, Won, "Object-Oriented Database Systems: In Transition", *SIGMOD Rec.*, 19(4), Dec 1990, pp. 49-53.

[Bane87] Banerjee, J.; Kim, W.; and Korth, H.F., "Semantics and Implementation of Schema Evolution in Object-Oriented Databases", *Proc. SIGMOD 87*, pp. 311-322, 1987.

[Bapa91a] Bapat, Subodh, "OSI Management Information Base Implementation", *Proc. 2nd ISINM 91*, pp. 817-831, 1991.

[Bapa91b] Bapat, Subodh, "Mapping C++ Objects to SQL Relational Schema", *Proc. 1991 C++ At Work Conference*, Santa Clara, California, Nov 1991.

[Bapa92] Bapat, Subodh, "Optimizing OSI Management System Performance", *Proc. NOMS 92*, 1992.

[Bapa93a] Bapat, Subodh, "Richer Modeling Semantics for Management Information", *Proc. 3rd ISINM 93*, pp.15-28, 1993.

[Bapa93b] Bapat, Subodh, "Factors in Performance Optimization of OSI Management Systems", *Proc. 2nd NMCW 93*, Sep 1993.

[Bapa93c] Bapat, Subodh, "Toward Richer Relationship Modeling Semantics", *JSAC*, Dec 1993, pp. 1373-1384.

[Barl91] Barletta, R., "An Introduction to Case-based Reasoning", *AI Expert*, Aug 1991, pp. 43-49.

[Barr93] Barr, William J.; Boyd, Trevor; and Inoue, Yuji, "The TINA Initiative", *IEEE Communications*, Mar 1993, pp. 70-76.

[Bars91] Barsalou, T.; Siambela, S.; Keller, A.M.; and Wiederhold, G., "Updating Relational Databases through Object-Based Views", *Proc. SIGMOD 91*, pp. 248-258, 1991.

[Batc68] Batcher, K.E., "Sorting Networks and Their Applications", *Proc. 1968 AFIPS Spring Joint Computer Conference*, pp. 307-314, 1968.

[Baza77]   Bazaraa, M.S., and Jarvis, J.J., *Linear Programming and Network Flows*, John Wiley, New York, New York, 1977.

[Baza79]   Bazaraa, M.S. and Shetty, C.M., *Nonlinear Programming: Theory and Algorithms*, John Wiley, New York, New York, 1979.

[Beli89]   Belina, Ferenc, and Hogrefe, Dieter, "The CCITT Specification and Description Language SDL", *CNIS*, Vol. 16, pp. 311-341, 1989.

[Bell91]   Bellamy, John, *Digital Telephony*, 2nd Edition, John Wiley, New York, New York, 1991.

[Benn89]   Bennett, Larry, and Chou, Wushow, "An Expert System for Diagnosing Performance Problems in SNA Networks", *Proc. 1st NMCW 89*, pp.221-247, Sep 1989.

[Benz93]   Benz, Christoph, and Leischner, Martin, "A High-Level Specification Technique for Modeling Networks and Their Environments including Semantic Aspects", *Proc. 3rd ISINM 93*, pp. 29-43, 1993.

[Berk91]   Berkowitz, Gary; Fuhrer, Philip; Gray, Blaine Jr.; Johnston, Alan; and McElvany, Gary, "A Nodal Operations Manager for SONET OAM&P", *Proc. 2nd ISINM 91*, pp. 403-411, 1991.

[Berm92]   Berman, Roger K., and Brewster, John H., "Perspectives on the AIN Architecture", *IEEE Communications*, Feb 1992.

[Bern76]   Bernstein, Philip A., "Synthesizing 3rd Normal Form Relations from Functional Dependencies", *TODS*, 1(4), pp. 277-298, 1976.

[Bern87]   Bernstein, Philip A.; Hadzilacos, Vassos; and Goodman, Nathan, *Concurrency Control and Recovery in Database Systems*, Addison-Wesley, Reading, Massachusetts, 1987.

[Bern93]   Bernstein, Lawrence, and Yuhas, C.M., "Managing Telecommunications Networks", *IEEE Network*, Nov 1993, pp. 12-14.

[Bert89]   Bertino, Elisa, et al., "Integration of Heterogeneous Applications Through an Object-Oriented Interface", *Information Systems*, Pergammon Press, 14(5), pp. 407-420, 1989.

[Bert91]   Bertino, E., and Martino, L., "Object-Oriented Database Management Systems: Concepts and Issues", *IEEE Computer*, Apr 1991, pp. 33-47.

[Bhar89]   Bharath, Ramchandran, *Prolog: Sophisticated Applications in Artificial Intelligence*, Windcrest Books, Blue Ridge Summit, Pennsylvania, 1989.

[Bhar91]   Bhargava, Amit, ed., *Integrated Broadband Networks*, Artech House, Norwood, Massachusetts, 1991.

[Blah88]   Blaha, Michael; Premerlani, William; and Rumbaugh, James, "Relational Database Design Using an Object-Oriented Methodology", *Communications of the ACM*, Apr 1988, pp. 414-427.

[Bobr83]   Bobrow, D.G., and Stefik, M., *The LOOPS Manual*, Xerox PARC, Palo Alto, California, 1983.

[Boch90a]   Von Bochmann, Gregor, "Protocol Specification for OSI", *CNIS*, Vol. 18, pp. 167-184, 1989-90.

[Boch90b]   Von Bochmann, Gregor, "Specification of a Simplified Transport Protocol Using Different Formal Description Techniques", *CNIS*, Vol. 18, pp. 335-377, 1989-90.

[Boch91]   Von Bochman, Gregor; Mondain-Monval, Pierre; and Lecomte, Louis, "Formal Description of Network Management Issues", *Proc. 2nd ISINM 91*, pp. 77-92, 1991.

[Bolo87]   Bolognesi, Tommaso, and Brinksma, Ed, "Introduction to the ISO Specification Language LOTOS", *CNIS*, Vol. 14, pp. 25-59, 1987.

[Booc94]   Booch, Grady, *Object-Oriented Analysis and Design with Applications*, Benjamin Cummings, Redwood City, California, 1994.

[Bowe91]   Bowen, Tom; Gopal, Gita; Herman, Gary; and Mansfield, William, Jr., "A Scale Database Architecture for Network Services", *IEEE Communications*, Jan 1991.

[Brac92]   Brachman, Ronald; Levesque, Hector; and Reiter, Raymond, eds., *Knowledge Representation: Proc. 1st PKRR*, MIT Press, Cambridge, Massachusetts, 1992.

[Brea00]   Breal, Michael, *Semantics: Studies in the Science of Meaning*, Henry Holt and Co., New York, New York, 1900.

[Bren92]   Brendler, Joseph, "Tactical Military Communications", *IEEE Communications*, Jan 1992, pp 62-72.

[Brin86]   Brinskma, Ed, "A Tutorial on LOTOS", *Proc. 6th PSTV 86*, pp. 171-194, North-Holland, Amsterdam, The Netherlands, 1986.

[Brow84]   Brownston, L.; Farrell, R.; Kant, E.; and Martin, N., *Programming Expert Systems in OPS5*, Addison-Wesley, Reading, Massachusetts, 1984.

[Bruc93]   Bruce, Kim, et al., "Safe and Decidable Type Checking in an Object-Oriented Language", *Proc. OOPSLA 93*, pp. 29-45, 1993.

[Brui87]   Bruijning, Jeroen, "Evaluation and Integration of Specification Languages", *CNIS*, Vol. 13, pp. 75-89, 1987.

[Buch91]   Buchholz, Dave; Odlyzko, Paul; Taylor, Mark; and White, Richard, "Wireless In-Building Network: Architecture and Protocols", *IEEE Network*, Nov 1991.

[Budk87]   Budkowski, Stanislaw, and Dembinski, Piotr, "An Introduction to Estelle: A Specification Language for Distributed Systems", *CNIS*, Vol. 14, pp. 3-23, 1987.

[Buga91]   Buga, Wladyslaw, "Management of Telecommunications Services Provided by Multiple Carriers", *Proc. 2nd ISINM 91*, pp. 343-355, 1991.

[Cant71]   Cantor, D.B., "On Non-Blocking Switching Networks", *Networks*, Vol. 1, 1971, pp.367-377.

[Carg92]   Cargill, Tom, *C++ Programming Style*, Addison-Wesley, Reading, Massachusetts, 1992.

[Carr89]   Carrington, D., et al., "Object Z: An Object-Oriented Extension to Z", *Proc. FORTE 89*, 1989.

[Case91]   Caseau, Yves, and Hoffoss, Diane, "The LAURE Language Documentation", Version 2.0, Bellcore, Piscataway, New Jersey, 1991.

[Chap89]   Chappell, David, "Abstract Syntax Notation One (ASN.1)", *Journal of Data and Computer Communications*, Spring 1989.

[Chap90]   Chapuis, Robert J., and Joel, Amos E., *Electronic Computers and Telephone Switching: A Book of Technological History* in *Volume 2: 1960-1985 of "100 Years of Telephone Switching"*, North-Holland Series in Telecommunications, Vol. 13, North-Holland Elsevier, Amsterdam, The Netherlands, pp. 274-279, 1990.

[Chap92]   Chapman, M.; Tonnby, I.; and Schoo, P., "Suggestions for Object-Oriented Modeling from ROSA", *Proc. TINA 92*, Narita, Japan, Jan 1992.

[Chen76]   Chen, P., "The Entity-Relationship Model — Toward a Unified View of Data", *TODS*, 1(1), 1976.

[Cher89]   Cheriton, D. R., "VMTP as the Transport Layer for High-Performance Distributed Systems", *IEEE Communications*, Jun 1989.

[Ches89]   Chesson, G., "XTP Protocol Definition", Protocol Engines Inc., 1989.

[Chip92]   Chipalkatti, R.; Zhang, Z.; and Acampora, A.S., "High-Speed Communication Protocols for Optical Star Network Using WDM", *Proc. Infocom 92*, 1992.

[Chor90]   Chorafas, D., and Steinman, H., *Intelligent Networks: Telecommunications Solutions for the 1990s*, CRC Press, Boca Raton, Florida, 1990.

[Clar90]   Clark, David, "Policy Routing in Internetworks", *IRE*, Vol. 1, pp. 35-52, 1990.

[Coad90]   Coad, Peter, and Yourdon, Edward, *Object-Oriented Analysis*, Yourdon Press, Englewood Cliffs, New Jersey, 1990.

[Codd70]   Codd, Edgar F., "A Relational Model for Large Shared Data Banks", *Communications of the ACM*, 13(6), pp. 377-387, Jun 1970.

[Codd72]   Codd, Edgar F., "Relational Completeness of Database Sublanguages", pp. 33-64, in *Data Base Systems*, Rustin, R., ed., Prentice Hall, Englewood Cliffs, New Jersey, 1972.

[Codd90]   Codd, E.F., *The Relational Model for Database Management, Version 2*, Addison-Wesley, Reading, Massachusetts, 1990.

[Coel89]   Coelho, David R., *The VHDL Handbook*, Kluwer Academic Publishers, Hingham, Massachusetts, 1990.

[Come91]   Comer, Douglas, *Internetworking with TCP/IP, Volume I: Principles, Protocols, and Architecture*, Prentice Hall, Englewood Cliffs, New Jersey, 1991.

[Cone88]   Conery, John S., "Logical Objects", *Proc. 1988 International Conference on Logic Programming*, pp. 404-419, 1988.

[Cons93]   Consens, Mariano P., and Hasan, Masum Z., "Supporting Network Management through Declaratively Specified Data Visualizations", *Proc. 3rd ISINM 93*, pp.725-738, 1993.

[Cour88]   Courtiat, J.P., "Estelle* : A Powerful Dialect of Estelle for OSI Protocol Description", *Proc. PSTV 88*, Atlantic City, New Jersey, 1988.

[Cron88]   Cronk, Robert H.; Callahan, Paul, H.; and Bernstein, Lawrence, "Rule-Based Expert Systems for Network Management and Operations: An Introduction", *IEEE Network*, Sep 1988, pp. 7-21.

[Cusa91]   Cusack, E., "Object-oriented Modeling in Z for Open Distributed Processing", *Proc. IWODP 91*, 1991.

[Date85]   Date, C.J., *An Introduction to Database Systems*, Addison-Wesley, Reading, Massachusetts, 1985.

[Dawe91]   Dawes, J., *The VDM-SL Reference Guide*, Pitman, New York, New York, 1991.

[Day91]   Day, Andrew, "International Standardization of B-ISDN", *IEEE LTS (Lightwave Transmission Systems)*, Aug 1991, pp. 13-20.

[Dema79]   DeMarco, Tom, *Structured Analysis and System Specification*, Prentice Hall, Englewood Cliffs, New Jersey, 1979.

[DePr91]   DePrycker, Martin, *Asynchronous Transfer Mode: Solution for B-ISDN*, Ellis-Horwood, New York, New York, 1991.

[DePr93]   DePrycker, Martin; Peschi, Robert; and Van Landegem, Thierry, "B-ISDN and the OSI Protocol Reference Model", *IEEE Network*, Mar 1993.

[Deva91]   Devanbu, Premkumar; Brachman, Ronald J.; Selfridge, Peter, G.; and Ballard, Bruce W., "Lassie: A Knowledge-Based Software Information System", *Communications of the ACM*, May 1991.

[Diaz89]   Diaz, Michel, and Vissers, Chris, "SEDOS: Designing Open Distributed Systems", *IEEE Software*, Nov 1989, pp. 24-32.

[Diaz91]   Diaz, O.; Paton, N.; and Gray, P., "Rule Management in Object-Oriented Databases: A Unified Approach", *Proc. VLDB 91*, 1991.

[Ditt91]   Dittrich, Andreas, "Composite Managed Objects", *Proc. 2nd ISINM 91*, pp.789-799, 1991.

[Doss93]   Dossogne, Florence, and Dupont, Marie-Pascale, "A Software Architecture for Management Information Model Definition, Implementation, and Validation", *Proc. 3rd ISINM 93*, pp. 593-604, 1993.

[Duke90]   Duke, David, and Duke, Roger, "Towards a Semantics for Object Z", *Proc. VDM 90: VDM and Z!, LNCS*, 1990.

[Duke91]   Duke, R.; King, P.; Rose, G.; and Smith, G., *The Object Z Specification Language, Version 1*, Technical Report 91-1, The University of Queensland, Queensland, Australia, Jan 1991.

[Dupu91]   Dupuy, Alexander; Sengupta, Soumtira; Wolfson, Ouri; and Yemini, Yechiam, "Netmate: A Network Management Environment", *IEEE Network*, Mar 1991; also in *Proc. 2nd ISINM 91*, pp. 639-650, 1991.

[Dura92]   Duran, Jose M., and Visser, John, "International Standards for Intelligent Networks", *IEEE Communications*, Feb 1992, pp. 34-42.

[Eame91]   Eames, T.R., and Hawley, G.T., "The Synchronous Optical Network and Fiber in the Loop", *IEEE LTS (Lightwave Transmission Systems)*, Nov 1991.

[Elma88]   Elamsri, R.; Weeldreyer, J.; and Hevner, A., "The Category Concept: An Extension to the Entity-Relationship Model", *Data and Knowledge Engineering*, 1985.

[Elma89]   Elmasri, Ramez, and Navathe, Shamkant, *Fundamentals of Database Systems*, Benjamin Cummings, Redwood City, California, 1989.

[Erfa89]   Erfani, Shervin; Malek, Manu; and Sachar, Harvi, "An Expert System-Based Approach to Capacity Allocation in a Multiservice Application Environment", *Proc. Globecom 89*, pp. 24.6.1-24.6.6, 1989; also in *IEEE Network*, May 1991, pp. 7-12.

[Eric89]   Ericson, E.; Ericson, L.; and Minoli, D.; eds., *Expert Systems Applications to Integrated Network Management*, Artech House, Norwood, Massachusetts, 1990.

[ERL90]   Electronics Research Laboratory Report, *Third-Generation Database System Manifesto*, College of Engineering, The University of California at Berkeley, Berkeley, California, 1990.

[Erso92]   Ersoy, Cem, and Panwar, Shivendra, "Topological Design of Interconnected LAN-MAN Networks", *Proc. Infocom 92*, 1992.

[Estr90]   Estrin, Deborah, and Breslau, Lee, "Design of Inter-Administrative Domain Routing Protocols", *Proc. SIGCOMM 90*, pp. 231-241, 1990.

[Estr93]   Estrin, Deborah; Steenstrup, Martha; and Tsudik, Gene, "A Protocol for Route Establishment and Packet Forwarding Across Multidomain Internets", *Trans. Net.*, Feb 1993, pp. 56-70.

[Faci91]   Faci, Mohammed; Logrippo, Luigi; and Stepien, Bernard, "Formal Specification of Telephone Systems in LOTOS: The Constraint-Oriented Style Approach", *CNIS*, Vol 21, pp. 53-67, 1991.

[Fagi82]   Fagin, R., "Horn Clauses and Database Dependencies", *JACM*, 4(29), pp. 952-985, 1982.

[Fan66]   Fan, L.T., *The Continuous Maximum Principle: A Study of Complex Systems Optimization*, John Wiley, New York, New York, 1966.

[Feij92]   Feijs, L.M.G., and Jonkers, H.B.M., *Formal Specification and Design*, Cambridge University Press, Cambridge, England, 1992.

[Feri91]   Feridun, Metin, "Diagnosis of Connectivity Problems in the Internet", *Proc. 2nd ISINM 91*, pp. 691-701, 1991.

[Fest93]   Festor, Oliver, and Zorntlein, George, "Formal Description of Managed Object Behavior: A Rule-Based Approach", *Proc. 3rd ISINM 93*, pp.45-57, 1993.

[Fink92]   Finkelstein, Richard, "UniSQL Merges Relational and Object-Oriented Models", An Independent Study, Performance Computing Inc., Chicago, Illinois, Jan 1992.

[Fink93]   Finkelstein, Richard, "Breaking the Mold", *Database Programming and Design*, Feb 1993.

[Fisc93]   Fischer, Axel; Herpers, Martine; Holden, David; and Sievert, Stephan, "The DOMAINS Management Language", *Proc. 3rd ISINM 93*, pp. 181-192, 1993.

[Fong90]   Fong, Elizabeth, ed., "The Convergence of Open Systems Interconnection and Data Management Standards", *Proc. 2nd Joint CBEMA/ANSI-X3 Meeting 1990, Orlando, Florida*, pp. 34-35, 1990.

[Fros90]   Frost, Victor S., "A Tool for Local Area Network Modeling and Analysis", *Simulation*, Nov 1990, pp. 283-297.

[Fuji91]   Fujioka, Masanobu; Yagi, Hikaru; and Ikeda, Yoshikazu, "Universal Service Creation and Provision Environment for Intelligent Network", *IEEE Communications*, Jan 1991, pp. 44-51.

[Fuku86]   Fukunaga, Koichi, and Hirose, Shin-ichi, "An Experience with a Prolog-Based Object-Oriented Language", *Proc. OOPSLA 86*, pp. 224-231, 1986.

[Gadr87]   Gadre, Sharad H., "Building an Enterprise and Information Model", *Database Programming and Design*, Nov 1987 (Premier Issue), pp. 48-58.

[Gadr93]   Gadre, Sharad H., "Conceptual Schema: Unexplored Potential", Parts I and II, *Database Programming and Design*, Jun and Jul 1993.

[Gane78]   Gane, Chris, and Sarson, Trish, *Structured Systems Analysis: Tools and Techniques*, Prentice Hall, Englewood Cliffs, New Jersey, 1978.

[Garr93]   Garrahan, James R.; Russo, Peter A.; Kitami, Kenichi; and Kung, Roberto, "Intelligent Network Overview", *IEEE Communications*, Mar 1993, pp. 30-36.

[Geha91]   Gehani, N.H., and Jagadish, H.V., "Ode as an Active Database: Constraints and Triggers", *Proc. VLDB 91*, pp. 327-336, 1991.

[Geha92]   Gehani, N.H.; Jagadish, H.V.; and Shmueli, O., "Event Specification in an Active Object-Oriented Database", *Proc. SIGMOD 92*, pp. 81-90, 1992.

[Getc92]   Getchell, David, and Rupert, Paul, "Fiber Channel in the Local Area Network", *IEEE LTS (Lightwave Transmission Systems)*, May 1992.

[Ghos92]   Ghosh, Suvankar, "Designing Integrated Corporate Networks", *Telecommunications*, Oct 1992, pp. 28-36.

[Giac91]   Giacopelli et al., "Sunshine: A High-Performance Self-Routing Broadband Packet Network", *JSAC*, Oct 1991, pp.1289-1298.

[Gode30]   Godel, Kurt, "The Completeness of the Axioms of the Functional Calculus of Logic", 1930, reprinted in *From Frege to Godel*, ed. J. van Heijenoort, Harvard University Press, Cambridge, Massachusetts, 1967.

[Gode31]   Godel, Kurt, "On Formally Undecidable Propositions in *Principia Mathematica* and Related Systems", 1931, reprinted in *On Formally Undecidable Propositions*, Basic Books, New York, New York, 1962.

[Gogu87]   Goguen, J., and Meseguer, J., "Unifying Functional, Object-Oriented and Relational Programming with Logical Semantics", in *Research Directions in Object-Oriented Programming*, Shriver, Bruce, and Wegner, Peter, eds., MIT Press, Cambridge, Massachusetts, 1987.

[Gold83]   Goldberg, Adele, and D. Robson, *Smalltalk 80: The Language and its Implementation*, Addison-Wesley, Reading, Massachusetts, 1983.

[Gold93]   Goldszmidt, German, and Yemini, Yechaim, "Evaluating Management Decisions via Delegation", *Proc. 3rd ISINM 93*, pp. 247-257, 1993.

[Good91]   Goodman, R.M., and Latin, H., "Automated Knowledge Acquisition from Network Management Databases", *Proc. 2nd ISINM 91*, pp. 541-546, 1991.

[GOSIP 92]   "Internet 2000: A Protocol Framework to Achieve A Single Worldwide TCP/IP/OSI/CLNP Internet by Year 2000", White Paper, Version 2.2, The GOSIP Institute, Fairfax, Virginia, 1992.

[Goya88]   Goyal, Shri, and Worrest, Ralph, "Expert Systems Applications to Network Management", in *Expert Systems Applications to Telecommunications*, ed. J. Liebowitz, John Wiley, New York, New York, 1988.

[Goya91]   Goyal, Shri, "Knowledge Techniques for Evolving Networks", *Proc. 2nd ISINM 91*, pp. 439-461, 1991.

[Gran92]   Grant, John, and Minker, Jack, "The Impact of Logic Programming on Databases", *Communications of the ACM*, Mar 1992, pp. 67-81.

[Grie82]   Van Griethuysen, J.J., ed., "Concepts and Terminology for the Conceptual Schema and Information Base", ISO TC/97/SC5/WG3, Committee Report N.695, 1982.

[Guen93]   Guenther, Wolfgang, and Wackerbarth, Gerd, "Object-Oriented Design of ISDN Call-Processing Software", *IEEE Communications*, Apr 1993, pp. 40-45.

[Gunt92]   Gunter, Carl, *Semantics of Programming Languages*, MIT Press, Cambridge, Massachusetts, 1992.

[Gunt94]   Gunter, Carl, and Mitchell, John C., eds., *Theoretical Aspects of Object-Oriented Programming: Types, Semantics, and Language Design*, MIT Press, Cambridge, Massachusetts, 1994.

[Gupt91]   Gupta, Rajiv, and Horowitz, Ellis, eds., *Object-Oriented Databases with Applications to CASE, Networks, and VLSI CAD*, Prentice Hall, Englewood Cliffs, New Jersey, 1991.

[Gupt93]   Gupta, Ashish, and Widom, Jennifer, "Local Verification of Global Integrity Constraints in Distributed Databases", *Proc. SIGMOD 93*, pp. 49-58, 1993.

[Gutt85]   Guttag, J.V., Horning, J.J., and Wing, J.M., *Larch in Five Easy Pieces*, Technical Report 5, DEC Systems Research Center, Jul 1985.

[Gutt93]   Guttag, J.V.; Horning, J.J.; Garland, S.J.; Jones, K.D.; Modet, A.; and Wing, J.M., *Larch: Languages and Tools for Formal Specification*, Springer-Verlag, New York, New York, 1993.

[Haas91]   Haas, Zygmunt, "A Protocol Structure for High-Speed Communication over Broadband ISDN", *IEEE Network*, Jan 1991, pp. 64-68.

[Hall93]   Hall, Jane, and Magedanz, Thomas, "Uniform Modelling of Management and Telecommunications Services in Future Telecommunication Environments based on the ROSA Approach", *Proc. 3rd ISINM 93*, pp.739-750, 1993.

[Hare87]   Harel, David, "Statecharts: A Visual Formalism for Complex Systems", *Science of Computer Programming*, Vol. 8, pp. 231-274, 1987.

[Harr91]   Harris, Warren, "Contravariance For The Rest Of Us", *JOOP*, Nov-Dec 1991, pp. 10-18.

[Hase92]   Haselton, E. Fletcher, "Service-Creation Environments for Intelligent Networks", *IEEE Communications*, Feb 1992, pp. 78-82.

[Haye91]   Hayes, Fiona, and Coleman, Derek, "Coherent Models for Object-Oriented Analysis", *Proc. OOPSLA 91*, pp. 171-183, 1991.

[Hazz89]   Hazzah, Ali, "Data Dictionaries: Paths to a Standard", *Database Programming and Design*, Aug 1989.

[Hege88]   Hegering, Heinz-Gerd, and Valta, Robert, "Describing an OSI Network Configuration — Problems and Possible Solutions", *Proc. ICCC 88*, Tel Aviv, Israel, Oct 1988.

[Heil92]   Heilmeier, George H., "Global Begins At Home", *IEEE Communications*, Oct 1992, pp. 50-56.

[Helm90]   Helm, Richard; Holland, Ian; and Gangopadhyay, Dipayan, "Contracts: Specifying Behavioral Compositions in Object-Oriented Systems", *Proc. OOPSLA 90*, pp. 169-180, 1990.

[Hens88]   Henshall, John and Shaw, Sandy, *OSI Explained*, Ellis Horwood, Chichester, England, 1988.

[Herb94]   Herbert, Andrew, "An ANSA Overview", *IEEE Communications*, Jan 1994, pp. 18-23.

[Heyd79]   Heydweiller, John C., and Fan, L.T., "A Random-to-Pattern Search Procedure for Global Minimization of Constrained Problems", *Proc. 1979 Annual AIChE Meeting*, AIChE, San Francisco, California, 1979.

[Higa92]   Higa, Kunihiko; Morrison, Mike; Morrison, Joline; and Sheng, Olivia, "Object-Oriented Methodology for Knowledge Base/Database Coupling", *Communications of the ACM*, Mar 1992, pp. 99-113.

[Hoar85]   Hoare, C.A.R., *Communication Sequential Processes*, Prentice Hall, Englewood Cliffs, New Jersey, 1985.

[Hogr88]   Hogrefe, Dieter, *Protocol and Service Specification with SDL: A Case Study*, FBI Report, University of Hamburg, Germany, 1988.

[Hugh91]   Hughes, John G., *Object-Oriented Databases*, Prentice Hall International, Hemel Hempstead, United Kingdom, 1991.

[Ibra90]   Ibrahim, Mamdouh H., and Cummins, Fred A., "KSL/Logic: Integration of Logic with Objects", *Proc. 1990 IEEE International Conference on Computer Languages*, pp. 228-235, 1990.

[IEEE 1076] "VHDL: VHSIC Hardware Description Language Reference Guide", IEEE Standard 1076.

[Ioan86]   Ioannidis, Y.E. "On the Computation of Transitive Closure of Relational Operators", *Proc. VLDB 86*, pp. 403-411, 1986.

[Ioan88]   Ioannidis, Y.E., and Ramakrishnan, R., *Efficient Transitive Closure Algorithms*, Technical Report-765, Department of Computer Science, University of Wisconsin, Madison, Wisconsin, 1988.

[ISINM 89] Meandzija, Branislav, and Westcott, Jil, eds., *Integrated Network Management I: Proceedings of the IFIP TC-6/ WG-6.6 International Symposium on Integrated Network Management, Boston, Massachusetts, May 1989*, North-Holland, Amsterdam, The Netherlands, 1991.

[ISINM 91] Krishnan, Iyengar, and Zimmer, Wolfgang, eds., *Integrated Network Management II: Proceedings of the IFIP TC-6/ WG-6.6 International Symposium on Integrated Network Management, Washington, DC, April 1991*, North-Holland, Amsterdam, The Netherlands, 1991.

[ISINM 93] Hegering, Heinz-Gerd, and Yemini, Yechiam, eds., *Integrated Network Management III: Proceedings of the IFIP TC-6/ WG-6.6 International Symposium on Integrated Network Management, San Francisco, California, April 1993*, North-Holland, Amsterdam, The Netherlands, 1993.

[ISO 7498] "OSI Basic Reference Model", ISO 7498-1, 1992. Also ITU-T Rec. X.200.

[ISO 8073] "Connection-Oriented Transport Protocol Specification", ISO 8073, 1992. Also ITU-T Rec. X.224.

[ISO 8348] "Network Service Definition", ISO 8348, 1993. Also ITU-T Rec. X.213.

[ISO 8473] "Protocol for Providing the Connectionless Network Service, Part 1: Protocol Specification", ISO 8473-1, 1993. Also ITU-T Rec. 233.

[ISO 8571] "File Transfer, Access and Management", ISO 8571, 1988.

[ISO 8807] "LOTOS — A Formal Description Technique Based on the Temporal Ordering of Observational Behavior", ISO 8807, 1989.

[ISO 8824]   See [ITU-T X.680], [ITU-T X.681], [ITU-T X.682], and [ITU-T X.683].

[ISO 8825]   See [ITU-T X.690].

[ISO 8879]   "Standard Generalized Markup Language", ISO 8879, 1986.

[ISO 9007]   "Concepts and Terminology for the Conceptual Schema and the Information Base", ISO 9007, 1987.

[ISO 9074]   "Estelle — A Formal Description Technique Based on an Extended State Transition Model", ISO 9074, 1989.

[ISO 9542]   "End-System to Intermediate-System (ES-IS) Routing Information Exchange Protocol for Use in Conjunction with the Protocol for the Provision of Connectionless-mode Network Service", ISO 9542, 1988.

[ISO 9595]   "Common Management Information Service (CMIS) Definition", ISO 9595, 1991. Also ITU-T Rec. X.710.

[ISO 9596]   "Common Management Information Protocol, Part 1: Specification", ISO 9596, 1991. Also ITU-T Rec. X.711.

[ISO 9646-3]   "OSI Conformance Methodology and Framework, Part 3: The Tree and Tabular Combined Notation (TTCN)", ISO 9646-3, 1992.

[ISO 9834]   "Procedures for the Operation of OSI Registration Authorities", ISO 9834, 1992. Also ITU-T Rec. X.660.

[ISO 10027]   "Information Resource Dictionary System (IRDS) Framework", ISO 10027.

[ISO 10040]   "Systems Management Overview", ISO 10040, 1992. Also ITU-T Rec. X.701.

[ISO 10164-3]   "Systems Management — Part 3: Attributes for Representing Relationships", ISO 10164-3 1992. Also ITU-T Rec. X.732.

[ISO 10164-16] "Systems Management — Part 16: Management Knowledge Management", ISO 10164-16, 1992. Also ITU-T Rec. X.750.

[ISO 10165-1]   "Management Information Services — Structure of Management Information — Part 1: Management Information Model", ISO 10165-1, 1992. Also ITU-T Rec. X.720.

[ISO 10165-2]   "Management Information Services — Structure of Management Information — Part 2: Definition of Management Information", ISO 10165-2, 1992. Also ITU-T Rec. X.721.

[ISO 10165-4]   "Management Information Services — Structure of Management Information — Part 4: Guidelines for the Definition of Managed Objects", ISO 10165-4, 1992. Also ITU-T Rec. X.722.

[ISO 10165-7]   "Management Information Services — Structure of Management Information — Part 7: General Relationship Model", ISO 10165-7, 1994. Also ITU-T Rec. X.725.

[ISO 10589]   "Intermediate-System to Intermediate-System (IS-IS) Routing Information Exchange Protocol for Use in Conjunction with ISO 8473", ISO 10589, 1992.

[ISO 10746-1]   "Basic Reference Model for Open Distributed Processing, Part 1: Overview and Guide to Use", ISO 10746-1, 1994. Also ITU-T Rec. X.901.

[ISO 10746-2]   "Basic Reference Model for Open Distributed Processing, Part 2: Descriptive Model", ISO 10746-2, 1994. Also ITU-T Rec. X.902.

[ISO 10746-3]   "Basic Reference Model for Open Distributed Processing, Part 3: Prescriptive Model", ISO 10746-3, 1994. Also ITU-T Rec. X.903.

[ISO 10746-4]   "Basic Reference Model for Open Distributed Processing, Part 4: Architectural Semantics", ISO 10746-4, 1994. Also ITU-T Rec. X.904.

[ISO ISP 11183] "International Standardized Profiles AOMnn — Management Communication Protocols", Parts 1-3, ISO ISP 11183, 1992.

[ISO ISP 12059] "International Standardized Profiles — Management Functions — Common Information for Management Functions", Parts 0-6, ISO ISP 12059, 1993.

[ISO ISP 12060]   "International Standardized Profiles AOMnnn — OSI Management — Management Functions", Parts 1-5, ISO ISP 12060, 1993.

[ISO TR 10000]   "Framework and Taxonomy of International Standardized Profiles, Parts 1 and 2", ISO Technical Report 10000, 1990.

[ISO WG7/N6089] "Z and Object-Oriented Z", Working Document N6089, ISO-IEC JTC1/SC21/WG7 and ITU-T SGVII/Q19, 1992.

[ISO WG7/N372]   "Z and Object Z for Use in ODP", Working Document N372, ISO-IEC JTC1/SC21/WG7 and ITU-T SGVII/Q19, 1991.

[ITU-T E.163]   "The Numbering Plan for the International Telephone Service", ITU-T Rec. E.163, 1984; also "Proposed Revision to E.163", 1988.

[ITU-T E.164]   "The Numbering Plan for the ISDN Era", ITU-T Rec. E.164, 1984; Revised Rec. E.164, 1988.

[ITU-T G.773]   "Synchronous Digital Hierarchy — Functions and Protocols for TMN Interfaces", ITU-T Rec. G.773, 1992.

[ITU-T G.784]   "Synchronous Digital Hierarchy — Management Aspects", ITU-T Rec. G.784, 1992.

[ITU-T I.150]   "Broadband ISDN ATM Functional Characteristics", ITU-T Rec. I.150, 1992.

[ITU-T I.211]   "Broadband ISDN Service Aspects", ITU-T Rec. I.211, 1990.

[ITU-T I.320]   "ISDN Protocol Reference Model", ITU-T Rec. I.320, 1988.

[ITU-T I.321]   "B-ISDN Protocol Reference Model and its Application", ITU-T Rec. I.321, 1991.

[ITU-T I.361]   "B-ISDN ATM Layer Specification", ITU-T Rec. I.361, 1992.

[ITU-T I.362]   "B-ISDN ATM Adaptation Layer (AAL) Functional Description", ITU-T Rec. I.362, 1992.

[ITU-T I.363]   "B-ISDN ATM Adaptation Layer (AAL) Specification", ITU-T Rec. I.363, 1992.

[ITU-T I.364]   "Support of Broadband Connectionless Data Service on B-ISDN", ITU-T Rec. I.364, 1992.

[ITU-T I.610]   "OAM Principles and Functions for B-ISDN", ITU-T Rec. I.610, 1992.

[ITU-T M.3010]   "Principles for a Telecommunications Management Network", ITU-T Rec. M.3010, 1992.

[ITU-T M.3020]   "TMN Interface Specification Methodology", ITU-T Rec. M.3020, 1992.

[ITU-T M.3100]   "Generic Network Information Model", ITU-T Rec. 3100, 1992.

[ITU-T M.3200]   "TMN Management Services: Overview", ITU-T Rec. M.3200, 1992.

[ITU-T M.3400]   "TMN Management Functions", ITU-T Rec. M.3400, 1992.

[ITU-T Q.700]   "Introduction to Signaling System No. 7", ITU-T Rec. Q.700, 1989.

[ITU-T Q.931]   "ISDN User-Network Interface: Layer 3 Specification", ITU-T Rec. Q.931, 1989.

[ITU-T Q.93B]   "Broadband ISDN User-Network Interface", ITU-T Rec. Q.93B, 1993.

[ITU-T Q.1200]   "Intelligent Networks", ITU-T Rec. Q.1200, 1992.

[ITU-T Q.1201]   "Intelligent Network Conceptual Model", ITU-T Rec. Q.1201, 1992.

[ITU-T Q.1205]   "Intelligent Network Physical Plane Architecture", ITU-T Rec. Q.1205, 1992.

[ITU-T Q.1211]   "Intelligent Network Capability Set 1", ITU-T Rec. Q.1211.

[ITU-T Q.1218]   "Interface Recommendation for Intelligent Network Capability Set 1", ITU-T Rec. Q.1218, 1992.

[ITU-T T.411]   "Text and Office Systems — Office Document Architecture and Interchange Format", ITU-T Rec. T.411, 1989. Also ISO 8613.

[ITU-T X.25]   "Interface Between Data Terminal Equipment and Data Circuit Terminating Equipment for Terminals Operating in the Packet Mode on Public Data Networks", ITU-T Rec. X.25, 1980.

[ITU-T X.121] "International Numbering Plan for Public Data Networks", ITU-T Revised Rec. X.121, 1988.

[ITU-T X.210] "OSI Service Conventions", ITU-T Rec. X.210, 1987. Also ISO Technical Report 8509.

[ITU-T X.400] "Message-Oriented Text Interchange System (MOTIS)", ITU-T Rec. X.400, 1990. Also ISO 10021.

[ITU-T X.407] "Abstract Service Definition Conventions", ITU-T Rec. X.407, 1990. Also ISO 10021-3.

[ITU-T X.500] "The Directory", ITU-T Rec. X.500, 1990. Also ISO 9594.

[ITU-T X.660] See [ISO 9834].

[ITU-T X.680] "Information Technology — Abstract Syntax Notation One (ASN.1) — Specification of Basic Notation", ITU-T Rec. X.680, 1994. Also ISO 8824, Part 1.

[ITU-T X.681] "Information Technology — Abstract Syntax Notation One (ASN.1) — Information Object Specification", ITU-T Rec. X.681, 1994. Also ISO 8824, Part 2.

[ITU-T X.682] "Information Technology — Abstract Syntax Notation One (ASN.1) — Constraint Specification", ITU-T Rec. X.682, 1994. Also ISO 8824, Part 3.

[ITU-T X.683] "Information Technology — Abstract Syntax Notation One (ASN.1) — Parameterization of ASN.1 Specifications", ITU-T Rec. X.683, 1994. Also ISO 8824, Part 4.

[ITU-T X.690] "Information Technology — ASN.1 Encoding Rules — Specification of Basic Encoding Rules (BER), Canonical Encoding Rules (CER) and Distinguished Encoding Rules (DER)", ITU-T Rec. X.690, 1994. Also ISO 8825.

[ITU-T X.701] See [ISO 10040].

[ITU-T X.710] See [ISO 9595].

[ITU-T X.711] See [ISO 9596].

[ITU-T X.720] See [ISO 10165-1].

[ITU-T X.721] See [ISO 10165-2].

[ITU-T X.722] See [ISO 10165-4].

[ITU-T X.725] See [ISO 10165-7].

[ITU-T X.732] See [ISO 10164-3].

[ITU-T X.750] See [ISO 10164-16].

[ITU-T X.901] See [ISO 10746-1].

[ITU-T X.902] See [ISO 10746-2].

[ITU-T X.903] See [ISO 10746-3].

[ITU-T X.904] See [ISO 10746-4].

[ITU-T Z.100] "Specification and Description Language SDL", ITU-T Rec. Z.100, 1988.

[ITU-T Z.200] "CCITT High-Level Language (CHILL)", ITU-T Rec. Z.200, 1988. Also ISO 9496, 1989.

[IWODP 91] De Meer, J.; Heymer, V.; and Roth, R., eds., *Open Distributed Processing: Proceedings of the IFIP TC-6/ WG-6.4 International Workshop on Open Distributed Processing, Berlin, Germany, October 1991*, North-Holland, Amsterdam, The Netherlands, 1991.

[Jack83] Jackson, Michael, *System Development*, Prentice Hall, Englewood Cliffs, New Jersey, 1983.

[Jaga87] Jagadish, H.V.; Agrawal, R.; and Ness, L., "A Study of Transitive Closure as a Recursion Mechanism", *Proc. SIGMOD 87*, pp. 331-344, 1987.

[Jaga92] Jagadish, H.V., and Qian, X., "Integrity Maintenance in an Object-Oriented Database", *Proc. VLDB 92*, 1992.

[Jain91]   Jain, Raj, *The Art of Computer Systems Performance Analysis*, John Wiley, New York, New York, 1991.

[Jals94]   Jalsberg, Jens, and Schwartzbach, Micheal, *Object-Oriented Type Systems*, John Wiley, New York, New York, 1994.

[Jeru92]   Jeruchim, Michael C.; Balaban, Philip; and Shanmugan, K. Sam, *Simulation of Communication Systems*, Plenum Press, 1992.

[Jone90]   Jones, C.B., *Systematic Software Development Using VDM*, 2nd Edition, Prentice Hall, Englewood Cliffs, New Jersey, 1990.

[Kahn86]   Kahn, K.; Tribble, E.D.; Miller, M.S.; and Bobrow, D.G., "Objects in Concurrent Programming Languages", *Proc. OOPSLA 86*, pp. 242-257, 1986.

[Kaza88]   Kazar, Michael, "Synchronization and Caching Issues in the Andrew File System", *Proc. 1988 Usenix Winter Technical Conference*, Dallas, Texas, 1988.

[Kemn91]   Kemnitz, Greg, and Stonebraker, Michael, *The POSTGRES Reference Manual*, Electronics Research Laboratory, University of California at Berkeley, Berkeley, California, Feb 1991.

[Kers89]   Kerschberg, Larry, ed., *Expert Database Systems: Proceedings from the 2nd International Conference on Expert Database Systems, Vienna, 1988*, Benjamin Cummings, Redwood City, California, 1989.

[Kers93]   Kershenbaum, Aaron, *Telecommunications Network Design Algorithms*, McGraw-Hill, New York, New York, 1993.

[Kher91]   Kheradpir, Sheygan; Stinson, William; and Sundstrom, Gunilla, "A Network Management Architecture for SONET-based Multi-Service Networks", *Proc. 2nd ISINM 91*, pp. 371-382, 1991.

[Kilo90]   Kilov, Haim, "From Semantic to Object-Oriented Data Modeling", *Systems Integration 90: Proc. 1st International Conference on Systems Integration*, IEEE Computer Society Press, pp 385-393, 1990.

[Kilo91a]   Kilov, Haim, "Generic Information Modeling Concepts: A Reusable Component Library", *Proc. 4th TOOLS 91*, Paris, France, Mar 1991.

[Kilo91b]   Kilov, Haim, "Conventional and Convenient in Entity-Relationship Modeling", *ACM SIGSOFT Software Engineering Notes*, Apr 1991.

[Kilo92]   Kilov, Haim, "Two Approaches to Information Modeling Standardization: Managed Objects for the OSI Management Information Service and Object Data Management Reference Model", *Computer Standards & Interfaces*, Vol. 14, pp. 231-238, 1992.

[Kilo93a]   Kilov, Haim, "Information Modeling and Object Z: Specifying Generic Reusable Associations", *Proc. International Workshop on Next Generation Information Technologies and Systems*, ed. Etzion, Opher, and Segev, Arie; Haifa, Israel, Jun 1993.

[Kilo93b]   Kilov, Haim, and Redmann, Laura S., "Specifying Joint Behavior of Objects: Formalization and Standardization", *Proc. IEEE-CS Software Engineering Standards Symposium*, 1993.

[Kilo94a]   Kilov, Haim, and Ross, James, "Generic Concepts for Specifying Relationships", *Proc. NOMS 94*, 1994.

[Kilo94b]   Kilov, Haim, and Ross, James, *Information Modeling: An Object-Oriented Approach*, Prentice Hall, Englewood Cliffs, New Jersey, 1994.

[Kim87]   Kim, W.; Banejee, J.; Chou, H.; Garza, J.F.; and Woelk, D., "Composite Object Support in an Object-Oriented Database System", *Proc. OOPSLA 87*, pp. 118-125, 1987.

[Kim88]   Kim, Won, et al., "Integrating an Object-Oriented Programming System with an Object-Oriented Database System", *Proc. OOPSLA 88*, pp. 142-152, 1988.

[Kim89]   Kim, Won, and Lochavsky, Frederick, eds., *Object-Oriented Concepts, Databases and Applications*, Addison-Wesley/ACM Press, Reading, Massachusetts, 1989.

[Kim90a]   Kim, Won, *Introduction to Object-Oriented Database Systems*, MIT Press, Cambridge, Massachusetts, 1990.

[Kim90b]   Kim, Won, "Architectural Issues in Object-Oriented Databases", *JOOP*, Mar/Apr 1990, pp. 29-38.

[Kim90c]   Kim, Won, ed., "Special Issue: Directions for Future Database Research and Development", *SIGMOD Rec.*, 19(4), Dec 1990.

[Klee56]   Kleene, S.C. "Representation of Events in Nerve Nets and Finite Automata", in *Automata Studies*, Shannon, C.E. and McCarthy. J., eds., Princeton University Press, Princeton, New Jersey, pp. 3-40, 1956.

[Klei76]   Kleinrock, Leonard, *Queueing Systems: Vol. I: Theory* and *Vol. II: Computer Applications*, John Wiley, New York, New York, 1974 and 1976.

[Klem91]   Klemba, Keith, and Kosarchyn, M., "A Model for Object Relationship Management", *Proc. 2nd ISINM 91*, pp. 801-812, 1991.

[Kler91]   Klerer, S. Mark, and Cohen, Roberta, "Distribution of Managed Object Fragments and Managed Object Replication", *Proc. 2nd ISINM 91*, pp.763-774, 1991.

[Kler93]   Klerer, S. Mark, "System Management Information Modeling", *IEEE Communications*, May 1993, pp. 38-44.

[Knut68]   Knuth, Donald, "Semantics of Context-Free Languages", *Mathematical Systems Theory*, 2(2), Jun 1968, pp. 95-96.

[Kolo93]   Kolodner, Janet, *Case-Based Reasoning*, Morgan Kaufman, San Francisco, California, 1993.

[Kosc88]   Koschman, Timothy, and Evans, Martha W., "Bridging the Gap Between Object-Oriented Programming and Logic Programming", *IEEE Software*, Jul 1988, pp. 36-42.

[Kouy91]   Kouyzer, A.J., and Van Den Boogaart, A.K., "The LOTOS Framework for OSI Systems Management", *Proc. 2nd ISINM 91*, pp. 147-156, 1991.

[Kowa79]   Kowalski, R.A., *Logic for Problem Solving*, 1979.

[LaBa91]   LaBarre, Lee, "Management by Exception: OSI Event Generation, Reporting and Logging", *Proc. 2nd ISINM 91*, pp. 227-242, 1991.

[Lafo91]   Lafontaine, Christine; Ledru, Yves; and Schobbens, Pierre-Yves; "An Experiment in Formal Software Development Using the B Theorem Prover on a VDM Case Study", *Communications of the ACM*, May 1991, pp. 63-87.

[Lamp83]   Lamport, L., "Specifying Concurrent Programming Modules", *TOPLAS*, 5(2), Apr 1983, pp. 190-222.

[Lea91]   Lea, Doug, and D'Souza, Desmond, "Type Safe Programming in C++", Conference Tutorial Notes, *The C++ At Work Conference*, Santa Clara, California, Nov 1991.

[Lee90]   Lee, T.T., "A Modular Architecture for Very Large Packet Switches", *Trans. Comm.*, Jul 1990, pp.1097-1106.

[Lern90]   Lerner, Barbara, and Habermann, A. Nico, "Beyond Schema Evolution to Database Reorganization", *Proc. OOPSLA 90*, pp 67-76, 1990.

[Lewi93a]   Lewis, Lundy, and Dreo, Gabi, "Extending Trouble Ticket Systems to Fault Diagnostics", *IEEE Network*, Nov 1993, pp. 44-51.

[Lewi93b]   Lewis, Lundy, "A Fuzzy Logic Representation of Knowledge for Detecting/Correcting Network Performance Deficiencies", *Proc. 2nd NMCW 93*, Sep 1993.

[Lini91]   Linington, P.F., "Open Distributed Processing and Open Management", *Proc. 2nd ISINM 91*, pp. 553-562, 1991.

[Linn88]   Linn, Richard, "The Features and Facilities of Estelle", *Open Systems Data Transfer*, No. 37, Omnicom Inc., Vienna, Virginia, Dec 1988.

[Lipp91]   Lippis, Nick, and Herman, James, "The Internetworking Decade", *Data Communications*, Jan 1991.

[Lisk93]   Liskov, Barbara, and Wing, Jeanette, "Specifications and Their Use in Defining Subtypes", *Proc. OOPSLA 93*, pp. 16-28, 1993.

[Liu92]   Liu, Hong, "Models for T-1 Problem", *Proc. 4th CAMAD 92*, 1992.

[Lloy87]   Lloyd, J.W., *Foundations of Logic Programming*, Springer-Verlag, New York, New York, 1987.

[Logr90]   Logrippo, Luigi; Melanchuk, Tim; and Du Wors, Robert, "The Algebraic Specification Language LOTOS: An Industrial Experience", *Proc. ACM SIGSOFT International Workshop on Formal Methods in Software Development*, 1990.

[Lohm91]   Lohman, Guy; Lindsay, Bruce; Pirahesh, Hamid; and Schiefer, K. Bernhard, "Extensions to Starburst: Objects, Types, Functions and Rules", *Communications of the ACM*, Oct 1991, pp. 94-109.

[MacK90]   MacKinnon, Dennis A.; McCrum, William A.; and Sheppard, Donald A., *An Introduction to OSI: Open Systems Interconnection*, Computer Science Press, Rockville, Maryland, 1990.

[Maie83]   Maier, David, *The Theory of Relational Databases*, Computer Science Press, Rockville, Maryland, 1983.

[Mala91]   Malamud, Carl, *Stacks: Interoperability in Today's Computer Networks*, Prentice Hall, Englewood Cliffs, New Jersey, 1991.

[Malp87]   Malpas, J., *Prolog: A Relational Language and its Applications*, Prentice Hall, Englewood Cliffs, New Jersey, 1987.

[Maru91]   Maruyama, K.; Watanabe, N.; Koyanagi, K.; Kai, T.; and Tomita, S.; "A Concurrent Object-Oriented Switching Program in CHILL", *IEEE Communications*, Jan 1991, pp. 60-68.

[Mats89]   Matsubara, Mark, "Evolution of CCITT Numbering Plans and Network Interworking", *CNIS*, Vol. 17, pp.47-57, 1989.

[Mazu89]   Mazumdar, Subrata, and Lazar, Aurel, "Knowledge-Based Monitoring of Integrated Networks", *Proc. 1st ISINM 89*, pp. 235-241, 1989.

[McCa89]   McCarthy, D.R., and Dayal, U., "The Architecture of an Active Database Management System", *Proc. SIGMOD 89*, pp. 215-224, 1989.

[McQu90]   McQuillan, John M., "Broadband Networks: The End of Distance?", *Data Communications*, Jun 1990, pp. 48-55.

[Mese92]   Meseguer, Jose, "Multiparadigm Logic Programming", in *Proc. 3rd International Conference in Algebraic and Logic Programming, LNCS*, pp. 158-200, H. Kirchner and G. Levi, eds., Springer-Verlag, New York, New York, 1992.

[Mese93]   Meseguer, Jose, and Qian, Xiaolei, "A Logical Semantics for Object-Oriented Databases", *Proc. SIGMOD 93*, pp. 89-98, 1993.

[Meye88]   Meyer, Bertrand, *Object-Oriented Software Construction*, Prentice Hall, Englewood Cliffs, New Jersey, 1988.

[Meye92]   Meyer, Bertrand, "Applying Design by Contract", *IEEE Computer*, Oct 1992, pp. 28-51.

[Mier91]   Van-Mierop, Dono, "The Next Generation Hub — An Architecture That Simplifies the Data Network", *3Tech: The 3Com Technical Journal*, 3Com Corporation, Santa Clara, California, Summer 1991.

[Miln80]   Milner, R., "A Calculus of Communicating Systems", *LNCS,* Vol. 92, Springer-Verlag, New York, New York, 1980.

[Mink82]   Minker, Jack, "On Indefinite Databases and the Closed-World Assumption", *Proc. Sixth Conference on Automated Deduction*, Loveland, D., ed., Springer-Verlag, New York, New York, 1982.

[Mink88]   Minker, Jack, *Foundations of Deductive Databases and Logic Programming*, Morgan Kaufman, San Francisco, California, 1988.

[Mitr91]   Mitra, Nilo, and Usiskin, Suzanne, "Relationship of the Signaling System No. 7 Protocol Architecture to the OSI Reference Model", *IEEE Network*, Jan 1991, pp. 26-37.

[Mody92]   Mody, R.P., "Functional Programming is not Self-Modifying Code", *ACM SIGPLAN Notices*, Nov 1992, pp. 13-14.

[Moor89]   Moore, Deborah, and Calvert, Jonathan, "NORA: An Intelligent Advisor for Traffic Management", *Proc. 1st NMCW 89*, pp. 263-274, Sep 1989.

[Mulm87]   Mulmuley, Ketan, *Full Abstraction and Semantic Equivalence*, MIT Press, Cambridge, Massachusetts, 1987.

[Murr93]   Murrill, Bruce, "OMNIPoint: An Implementation Guide to Integrated Networked Information Systems Management", *Proc. 3rd ISINM 93*, pp. 405-416, 1993.

[Naka91]   Nakai, Shoichori; Kiriha, Yoshiki; Ihara, Yoshiko; and Hasegawa, Satoshi, "A Development Environment for OSI Systems Management", *Proc. 2nd ISINM 91*, pp. 157-168, 1991.

[Nata92]   Natarajan, N., and Slawsky, G.M., "A Framework Architecture for Multimedia Information Networks", *IEEE Communications*, Feb 1992, pp. 97-104.

[Need75]   Needham, Rodney, "Polythetic Classification: Convergence and Consequences", *Man*, 10(3), pp. 349-369, Sep 1975.

[Neuh91]   Neuhold, E.J., and Paul, M., *Formal Description of Programming Concepts*, Springer-Verlag, New York, New York, 1991.

[Newm92]   Newman, Peter, "ATM Technology for Corporate Networks", *IEEE Communications*, Apr 1992, pp. 90-101.

[Nier93]   Nierstrasz, Oscar, "Regular Types for Active Objects", *Proc. OOPSLA 93*, pp. 1-15, 1993.

[Nijs89]   Nijssen, G.M., and Halpern, T.A., *Conceptual Schema and Relational Database Design*, Prentice Hall, Englewood Cliffs, New Jersey, 1989.

[NMCW 89]   Kershenbaum, Aaron; Malek, Manu; and Wall, Mark, eds., *Network Management and Control: Proceedings of the 1st IEEE Network Management and Control Workshop, Tarrytown, New York, September 1989*, Plenum Press, New York, New York, 1990.

[Norm92a]   Van Norman, Harrell, *LAN/WAN Optimization Techniques*, Artech House, Norwood, Massachusetts, 1992.

[Norm92b]   Van Norman, Harrell, "The Case for Simulation and Modeling in the Internetwork Environment: Parts I and II", *Telecommunications*, Aug and Sep 1992.

[ODMG 93]   Cattell, R.G.G., ed., *The Object Database Standard: ODMG-93*, Morgan Kaufman, San Francisco, California, 1993.

[Olde91]   Olderog, E.-R., *Nets, Terms and Formulas: Three Views of Concurrent Processes and their Relationship*, Cambridge University Press, Cambridge, England, 1991.

[OMG 90]   Soley, Richard, ed., *Object Management Architecture Guide*, Version 1.0, Object Management Group, Framingham, Massachusetts, Nov 1990.

[OMG 91]   "The Common Object Request Broker: Architecture and Specification", Object Management Group, Framingham, Massachusetts, Dec 1991.

[OMG 92]   "Object Services Architecture", Rev. 6.0, Object Management Group, Framingham, Massachusetts, 1992.

[Onvu94]   Onvural, Raif, *Asynchronous Transfer Mode Networks: Performance Issues*, Artech House, Norwood, Massachusetts, 1994.

[Ozsu91]   Ozsu, Tamer, and Valduriez, Patrick, *Principles of Distributed Database Systems*, Prentice Hall, Englewood Cliffs, New Jersey, 1991.

[Ozsu93]   Ozsu, Tamer; Dayal, Umeshwar; and Valduriez, Patrick, eds., *Distributed Object Management*, Morgan Kaufman, San Francisco, California, 1993.

[Paep93]   Paepke, Andreas, *Object-Oriented Programming: The CLOS Perspective*, MIT Press, Cambridge, Massachusetts, 1993.

[Pars90]   Parsaye, Kamran; Chignell, Mark; Khoshafian, Setrag; and Wong, Harry, *Intelligent Databases: Object-Oriented, Deductive and Hypermedia Technologies*, John Wiley, New York, New York, 1990.

[Penn87]   Penney, J., and Stein, J., "Class Modification in the GemStone Object-Oriented DBMS", *Proc. OOPSLA 87*, 1987.

[Perl91]   Perlman, Radia, "A Comparison Between Two Routing Protocols: OSPF and IS-IS", *IEEE Network*, Sep 1991.

[Perl92]   Perlman, Radia, *Interconnections: Bridges and Routers*, Addison-Wesley, Reading, Massachusetts, 1992.

[Perr91a]   Perry, Tekla, "Special Report: Air Traffic Control", *IEEE Spectrum*, Feb 1991, pp. 22-36.

[Perr91b]   Perry, Douglas, *VHDL*, McGraw-Hill, New York, New York, 1991.

[Pfen92]   Pfenning, Frank, ed., *Types in Logic Programming*, MIT Press, Cambridge, Massachusetts, 1992.

[Phip91]   Phipps, Geoffrey; Derr, Marcia; and Ross, Kenneth; "Glue-Nail: A Deductive Database System", *Proc. SIGMOD 91*, pp. 308-317, 1991.

[Piat89]   Piatesky-Shapiro, Gregory; and Frawley, William, eds., *Knowledge Discovery in Databases: Workshop* in *Proc. IJCAI 89*, AAAI Press, Cambridge, Massachusetts, 1989.

[Piat91]   Piatesky-Shapiro, Gregory; and Frawley, William, eds., *Knowledge Discovery in Databases*, AAAI Press, Cambridge, Massachusetts, 1991.

[Pier92]   Pierce, Benjamin, "Bounded Quantification is Undecidable", *Proc. POPL 92*, pp. 305-315, 1992.

[Plat92]   Plat, Nico, and Larsen, Peter, "An Overview of the ISO VDM-SL Standard", *ACM SIGPLAN Notices*, Aug 1992, pp. 76-82.

[Plev93]   Plevyak, Tom, ed., *Network Management into the 21st Century*, IEEE Press, Piscataway, New Jersey, 1993.

[Pneu86]   Pneuli, A., "Applications of Temporal Logic to the Specification and Verification of Reactive Systems: A Survey of Current Trends", in *Current Trends in Concurrency: Overviews and Tutorials*, LNCS, Vol. 224, pp. 510-584, Springer-Verlag, New York, New York, 1986.

[Pont93]   Pontailler, Catherine, "TMN and New Network Architectures", *IEEE Communications*, Apr 1993, pp. 84-88.

[Pool90]   De Sola Pool, Ithiel, *Technology Without Boundaries: On Telecommunications in a Global Age*, Harvard University Press, Cambridge, Massachusetts, 1990.

[Rabi89]   Rabih, Sameh, "Applications of Expert Systems to Network Surveillance", *Proc. 1st NMCW 89*, pp.249-262, Sep 1989.

[Raha91]   Rahali, Ilham, and Gaiti, Dominique, "A Multi-agent System for Network Management", *Proc. 2nd ISINM 91*, pp. 469-479, 1991.

[Rama93]   Raman, Lakshmi, "CMISE Functions and Services", *IEEE Communications*, May 1993, pp. 46-51.

[Reit78]   Reiter, R, "On Closed World Databases", in *Logic and Databases*, Gallaire, H. and Minker, J., eds., Plenum Press, New York, New York, 1978.

[RFC 768]   "User Datagram Protocol", Internet Society, Aug 1980.

[RFC 791]   "Internet Protocol", Internet Society, Sep 1981.

[RFC 792]   "Internet Control Message Protocol", Internet Society, Sep 1981.

[RFC 793]   "Transmission Control Protocol", Internet Society, Sep 1981.

[RFC 821]   Postel, Jonathan, "Simple Message Transfer Protocol", Internet Society, Aug 1982.

[RFC 826]   Plummer, D.C., "Ethernet Address Resolution Protocol: Or Converting Network Protocol Addresses to 48-bit Ethernet Addresses for Transmission on Ethernet Hardware", Internet Society, Nov 1982.

[RFC 998]   Clark, D.D.; Lambert, M.L., and Zhang, L., "NETBLT: A Bulk Data Transfer Protocol", Internet Society, Mar 1987.

[RFC 1045]   Cheriton, D. R., "VMTP: Versatile Message Transaction Protocol: Protocol Specification", Internet Society, Feb 1988.

[RFC 1060]   Reynolds, J.K., and Postel, J.B., "Assigned Numbers", Internet Society, Mar 1990.

[RFC 1117]   Romano, S.; Stahl, M.K., and Recker, M., "Internet Numbers", Internet Society, Aug 1989.

[RFC 1125]   Estrin, Deborah, "Policy Requirements for Inter-Administrative Domain Routing", Internet Society, 1989.

[RFC 1190]   Topolic, C., ed., "Experimental Internet Stream Protocol, Version 2 (ST-II)", Internet Society, Oct 1990.

[RFC 1213]   McCloghrie, Keith, and Rose, Marshall, "Management Information Base for TCP/IP-based Internets: MIB-II", Internet Society, Mar 1991.

[RFC 1271]   Waldbusser, Steve, et al., "Remote Network Monitoring Management Information Base (RMON-MIB)", Internet Society, Nov 1991.

[RFC 1247]   Moy, John, "Open Shortest Path 1st Protocol, Version 2", Internet Society, Jul 1991.

[RFC 1441]   Case, Jeffrey D.; McCloghrie, Keith; Rose, Marshall T.; and Waldbusser, Steve, "Introduction to Version 2 of the Simple Network Management Protocol", Internet Society, Jul 1993.

[RFC 1442]   Case, Jeffrey D.; McCloghrie, Keith; Rose, Marshall T.; and Waldbusser, Steve, "Structure of Management Information for Version 2 of the Simple Network Management Protocol", Internet Society, Jul 1993.

[RFC 1448]   Case, Jeffrey D.; McCloghrie, Keith; Rose, Marshall T.; and Waldbusser, Steve, "Protocol Operations for Version 2 of the Simple Network Management Protocol", Internet Society, Jul 1993.

[RFC 1483]   "Encapsulation of IP datagrams in AAL Type 5", Internet Society, Jul 1993.

[Rech91]   Rechtin, Eberhardt, *Systems Architecture: Creating and Building Complex Systems*, Prentice Hall, Englewood Cliffs, New Jersey, 1991.

[Robi92]   Robinson, J. Alan, "Logic and Logic Programming", *Communications of the ACM*, Mar 1992, pp. 41-64.

[Robr91]   Robrock, Richard B., "The Intelligent Network — Changing the Face of Telecommunications", *Proceedings of the IEEE*, 79(1), Jan 1991, pp. 7-20.

[Rose90]   Rose, Marshall, *The Open Book: A Practical Perspective on OSI*, Prentice Hall, Englewood Cliffs, New Jersey, 1990.

[Rose92]   Rose, G.A., "Object Z", *Object-Orientation in Z: Workshops in Computing*, ed. Stepney, S.; Barden, R.; and Cooper, D., Springer-Verlag, 1992, New York, New York, pp. 59-77.

[Rose93a]   Rose, Marshall, *The Simple Book: An Introduction to the Management of TCP/IP-based Internets,* 2nd Edition, Prentice Hall, Englewood Cliffs, New Jersey, 1993.

[Rose93b]   Rose, Marshall, "Challenges in Network Management", *IEEE Network*, Nov 1993, pp. 16-19.

[Rubi94]   Rubin, Harvey, and Natarajan, N., "A Distributed Software Architecture for Telecommunication Networks", *IEEE Communications*, Jan 94, pp. 8-17.

[Rumb87]   Rumbaugh, James, "Relations as Semantic Constraints in an Object-Oriented Language", *Proc. OOPSLA 87*, pp. 466-481, 1987.

[Rumb91a]   Rumbaugh, James; Blaha, Michael; Premerlani, William; Eddy, Frederick, and Lorensen, William, *Object-Oriented Modeling and Design*, Prentice Hall, Englewood Cliffs, New Jersey, 1991.

[Rumb91b]   Rumbaugh, James, "Object-Oriented Methodology", *American Programmer*, Oct 1991, pp 6-10.

[Russ13]   Russell, Bertrand, and Whitehead, Alfred North, *Principia Mathematica*, Cambridge University Press, Cambridge, England, 1913.

[Sahi88]   Sahin, V.; Omidyar, C.G.; and Baumann, T., "Telecommunications Management Network Architecture and Interworking Designs", *JSAC*, May 1988, pp. 685-696.

[Sara87]   Saracco, R., and Tilanus, P.A.J., "CCITT SDL: Overview of the Language and its Applications", *CNIS*, 13 (1987) pp. 65-74.

[Scha86]   Schaffert, C., et al., "An Introduction to Trellis/Owl", *Proc. OOPSLA 86*, 1986.

[Sche90]   Scheuermann, Peter, and Yu, Clement, "Report on the Workshop on Heterogeneous Database Systems", *SIGMOD Rec.*, Dec 1990, pp. 23-31.

[Schi93]   Schill, Alexander, and Zitterbart, Martina, "A System Framework for Open Distributed Processing", *JNSM*, Mar 1993, pp. 71-93.

[Scho91]   Schoo, P., and Tonnby, I., "The ROSA Object Model", *Proc. IWODP 91*, pp. 291-300.

[Schr88]   Schrefl, M., and Neuhold, E., "Object Class Definition by Generalization Using Upward Inheritance", *Proc. ICDE 88*, pp. 4-13, 1988.

[Schu92]   Schulzrinne, H., "Issues in Designing a Transport Protocol for Audio and Video Conferences and other Multiparticipant Real-Time Applications", Internet Draft, Internet Society, Dec 1992.

[Scot90]   Scott, Bancroft, "OSS ASN.1 Tools: General Information", Open Systems Solutions, Princeton, New Jersey, 1990.

[Serr93]   Serre, Jean-Marc; Lewis, Pierre; and Rosenfeld, Ken, "Implementing OSI-Based Interfaces for Network Management", *IEEE Communications*, May 1993, pp. 76-81.

[Shan92]   Shanmugan, K. Sam; Frost, Victor S.; and LaRue, William, "A Block-Oriented Network Simulator", *Simulation*, Feb 1992, pp. 83-94.

[Shet91]   Sheth, Amit, ed., "Semantic Issues in Multidatabase Systems: Special Issue", *SIGMOD Rec.*, 20(4), Dec 1991.

[Shla88]   Shlaer, Sally, and Mellor, Stephen, *Object-Oriented Systems Analysis: Modeling the World in Data*, Yourdon Press, Englewood Cliffs, New Jersey, 1988.

[Sidh90]   Sidhu, Deepinder, and Blumer, Thomas, "Semi-Automatic Implementation of OSI Protocols", *CNIS*, Vol. 18, pp. 221-238, 1989-90.

[Silb91]   Silberschatz, Avi; Stonebraker, Michael; and Ullman, Jeff; "Next-Generation Database Systems: Achievements and Opportunities", *Communications of the ACM*, Oct 1991, pp. 110-120.

[Simp90]   Simpson, P.K., *Artificial Neural Systems: Foundations, Paradigms, Applications and Implementations*, Pergammon Press, New York, New York, 1990.

[Skor92]   Skorupa, Joseph S., "Smart Hubs: A Guide to Applications and Capabilities", *InteNet*, Sep 1992, pp. 44-46.

[Slom89]   Sloman, Morris, and Swift, Jonathan, "Domain Management for Distributed Systems", *Proc. 1st ISINM 89*, pp. 505-516, 1989.

[Smit93]   Smith, Kenneth, and Jones, Larry, "Efficient Consistency Maintenance of Derived Data", *Journal of Computer and Software Engineering*, 1(1), Spring 1993.

[Smit93b]   Smith, Gail, "Planning for Migration to ATM", *Business Communications Review*, May 1993.

[Sowa91]   Sowa, John, ed., *Principles of Semantic Networks: Explorations in the Representation of Knowledge*, Morgan Kaufman, San Francisco, California, 1991.

[Spec85]   Spector, Alfred, et al., "The ITC Distributed File System: Principles and Design", *Proc. 10th ACM Symposium on Distributed System Principles*, Dec 1985.

[Spiv88]   Spivey, J.M., *Understanding Z: A Specification Language and its Formal Semantics*, Cambridge University Press, Cambridge, England, 1988.

[Spiv89]   Spivey, J.M., *The Z Notation: A Reference Manual*, Prentice Hall International, Hemel Hempstead, United Kingdom, 1989.

[Spiv90]   Spivey, J.M., "Specifying a Real-Time Kernel", *IEEE Software*, Sep 1990, pp. 21-27.

[SR 1578]   Bellcore Special Report, "OPS/INE to Network Element Generic TL-1/X.25 Interface Support", SR-OPT-001578, Issue 3, Sep 1993.

[SR 1623]   Bellcore Special Report, "Advanced Intelligent Network: Release 1 Network and Operations Plan", SR-NPL-001623, Issue 1, Jun 1990.

[SR 1826]   Bellcore Special Report, "Information Modeling Concepts and Guidelines", SR-OPT-001826, Issue 1, Jan 1991.

[SR 2008]   Bellcore Special Report, "The Framework: A Disciplined Approach to Analysis", SR-OPT-002008, Issue 1, May 1992.

[SR 2010]   Bellcore Special Report, "The Materials: A Generic Object Class Library for Analysis", SR-OPT-002010, Issue 1, Oct 1992.

[SR 2247]   Bellcore Special Report, "Advanced Intelligent Network Release 1 Update", SR-NWT-002247, Issue 1, Dec 1992.

[SR 2268]   Bellcore Special Report, "Specifications for Information Networking Architecture", SR-NWT-002268, Issue 2, Apr 1993.

[SR 2282]   Bellcore Special Report, "INA Cycle 1 Framework Architecture", SR-NWT-002282, Issue 1, Apr 1993.

[SR 2286]   Bellcore Special Report, "INA Cycle 1 Network Management Functional Architecture", SR-NWT-002286, Issue 2, Apr 1993.

[SR 2287]   Bellcore Special Report, "INA Cycle 1 Management Information Model", SR-NWT-002287, Issue 2, Apr 1993.

[SR 2344]   Bellcore Special Report, "TR-303 Integrated Digital Loop Carrier Network and Operations Plan", SR-OPT-002344, Issue 1, Nov 1992.

[SR 2439]   Bellcore Special Report, "Interface Functions and Information Model for Initial Support of SONET Operations Using OSI Tools", SR-NWT-002439, Issue 1, Dec 1992.

[SR 2723]   Bellcore Special Report, "Applicable TL-1 Messages for SONET Network Elements", SR-NWT-002723, Issue 1, Jun 1993.

[SR 2802]   Bellcore Special Report, "Operations Systems Interfaces to Existing STPs and SCPs", SR-NWT-002802, Issue 1, Sep 1993.

[Stal93]   Stallings, William, *SNMP, SNMPv2 and CMIP*, Addison-Wesley, Reading, Massachusetts, 1993.

[Stee90]   Steedman, Douglas, *ASN.1: The Tutorial and Reference*, Technology Appraisals, The Camelot Press, Trowbridge, Wiltshire, United Kingdom, 1990.

[Stef86]   Stefik, M., and Bobrow, D.G., "Object-Oriented Programming: Themes and Variations", *AI Magazine*, 6(4), pp. 40-62, 1986.

[Ster86]   Sterling, L., and Shapiro, E., *The Art of Prolog*, MIT Press, Cambridge, Massachusetts, 1986.

[Ston89]   Stonebraker, Michael, "Future Trends in Database Systems", *Trans. KDE*, Mar 1989, pp. 33-44.

[Ston91]   Stonebraker, Michael, and Kemnitz, Greg; "The Postgres Next-Generation Database Management System", *Communications of the ACM*, Oct 1991, pp. 78-92.

[Stro90]   Stroustrup, Bjarne, *The Annotated C++ Reference Manual*, Addison Wesley, Reading, Massachusetts, 1990.

[Stro91]   Stroustrup, Bjarne, *The C++ Programming Language*, 2nd Edition, Addison Wesley, Reading, Massachusetts, 1991.

[Sylo89]   Sylor, Mark, "Guidelines for Structuring Manageable Entities", *Proc. 1st ISINM 89*, pp. 169-183, 1989.

[TR 29]   Bellcore Technical Reference, "Service Control Point Node Generic Requirements for IN/1", TA-TSY-000029, Issue 1, Sep 1990.

[TR 57]   Bellcore Technical Reference, "Functional Criteria for Digital Loop Carrier Systems", TA-NWT-000057, Issue 2, Feb 1993.

[TR 62]   Bellcore Technical Reference, "Protocol and Language for OS/NTE Interfaces: LAPB, X.25/PVC and X.25/SVC Cases", TR-TSY-000062, Jun 1986.

[TR 93]   Bellcore Technical Reference, "Telephone Area Code Directory (TACD)", TR-EOP-000093 Issue 8, Dec 1992.

[TR 170]   Bellcore Technical Reference, "Digital Cross-Connect System Generic Requirements and Objectives", TR-NWT-000170, Issue 2, Jan 1993.

[TR 253]   Bellcore Technical Reference, "Synchronous Optical Network (SONET): Common Generic Criteria", TR-NWT-000253, Issue 2, Dec 1991.

[TR 303]   Bellcore Technical Reference, "Integrated Digital Loop Carrier System Generic Requirements, Objectives, and Interface", TR-NWT-000303, Issue 2, Dec 1992.

[TR 772]   Bellcore Technical Reference, "Generic System Requirements in Support of Switched Multimegabit Data Service (SMDS)", TR-TSV-000772, Issue 1, May 1991.

[TR 831]   Bellcore Technical Reference, "Operations Technology Generic Requirements: Operations Application Messages — Language for Operations and Application Messages", TR-TSY-000831, Issue 2, Feb 1988.

[TR 915]   Bellcore Technical Advisory, "The Bellcore OSCA Architecture", TR-STS-000915, Issue 1, Jul 1992.

[TR 1062]   Bellcore Technical Reference, "Generic Requirements for Phase 1 SMDS Customer Network Management Service", TR-TSV-1062, Issue 1, Apr 1993.

[TR 1064]   Bellcore Technical Reference, "SMDS Generic Criteria on Operations Interfaces — SMDS Information Model and Usage", TR-TSV-001064, Issue 1, Dec 1992.

[TR 1093]   Bellcore Technical Reference, "Generic State Requirements for Managing Network Elements", TR-NWT-001093, Issue 1, Sep 1993.

[TA 1123]   Bellcore Technical Advisory, "Advanced Intelligent Network (AIN) Release 1 Switching Systems Generic Requirements", TA-NWT-001123, Issue 1, May 1991.

[TA 1126]   Bellcore Technical Advisory, "Advanced Intelligent Network (AIN) Release 1 Switch-Service Control Point (SCP)/Adjunct Application Protocol Interface Generic Requirements", TA-NWT-001126, Issue 1, May 1991.

[TR 1127]   Bellcore Technical Advisory, "Advanced Intelligent Network (AIN) Release 1 Adjunct Framework Generic Requirements", TR-NWT-001127, Issue 1, Feb 1993.

[TA 1129]   Bellcore Technical Advisory, "Advanced Intelligent Network (AIN) Release 1 Intelligent Peripheral (IP) Generic Requirements", TA-NWT-001129, Issue 1, Sep 1991.

[TR 1254]   Bellcore Technical Reference, "Advanced Intelligent Network (AIN): OS/Adjunct Generic Requirements", TR-NWT-001254, Issue 2, Feb 1993.

[TA 1280]   Bellcore Technical Advisory, "Advanced Intelligent Network (AIN) Service Control Point Generic Requirements", TA-NWT-001280, Issue 1, May 1993.

[Tana91]   Tanaka, A.; Matsumoto, N.; and Morino, K., "An Application of OSI Systems Management to Intelligent Network Services", *Proc. 2nd ISINM 91*, pp. 45-55, 1991.

[Tann88]   Tannenbaum, Andrew, *Computer Networks*, 2nd Edition, Prentice Hall, Englewood Cliffs, New Jersey, 1988.

[Tarj81]   Tarjan, Robert E., "A Unified Approach to Path Problems", *JACM*, 28(3), pp. 577-593, 1981.

[Tars41]   Tarski, Alfred, "On the Calculus of Relations", *The Journal of Symbolic Logic*, 6(3), pp. 73-89, 1941.

[Teor94]   Teorey, Toby J., *Database Modeling and Design*, 2nd Edition, Morgan Kaufman, San Francisco, California, 1994.

[Tolm92]   Tolmie, Dan, "Gigabit Networking", *IEEE LTS (Lightwave Transmission Systems)*, May 1992.

[Turi37]   Turing, Alan, "On Computable Numbers, with an Application to the Entscheidungsproblem", Proc. London Mathematical Society, 1937, reprinted in *The Undecidable: Basic Papers on Undecidable Propositions, Unsolvable Problems, and Computable Functions*, ed. M. Davis, Raven Press, New York, New York, 1965.

[Turn88]   Turner, Jonathan, "Design of a Broadcast Packet Network", *Trans. Comm.*, Jul 1988, pp. 734-743.

[Turn93]   Turner, K., ed., *Using Formal Description Techniques: An Introduction to Estelle, Lotos and SDL*, John Wiley, New York, New York, 1993.

[Ullm88]   Ullman, Jeffrey, *Principles of Database and Knowledge-Base Systems, Vols. I and II*, Computer Science Press, Rockville, Maryland, 1988.

[Ullm90]   Ullman, Jeffrey, and Zaniolo, Carlo, "Deductive Databases: Achievements and Future Directions", *SIGMOD Rec.*, 19(4), Dec 1990, pp. 75-82.

[Unla89]   Unland, R., and Schlageter, G., "An Object-Oriented Programming Environment for Advanced Database Applications", *JOOP*, May/Jun 1989, pp. 7-20.

[Vaha93]   Vahalia, Uresh, "UNIX Internals", Conference Tutorial Notes, *UniForum 93*, San Francisco, California, Jan 1993.

[Vald88]   Valduriez, P., and Koshafian, S., "Transitive Closure of Transitively Closed Relations", *Proc. 2nd EDS 89*, 1989.

[Valt91]   Valta, Robert, "Design Concepts for a Global Network Management Database", *Proc. 2nd ISINM 91*, pp.777-788, 1991.

[Ward86]   Ward, Paul, and Mellor, Steve, *Structured Development for Real-Time Systems*, Yourdon Press, Englewood Cliffs, New Jersey, 1986.

[Wegn88]   Wegner, Peter, and Zdonik, Stanley, "Inheritance as an Incremental Modification Mechanism", *Proc. ECOOP 88*, *LNCS*, Vol. 322, pp. 55-77, Springer-Verlag, New York, New York, 1988.

[Wegn90]   Wegner, Peter, "Concepts and Paradigms of Object-Oriented Programming", *ACM SIGPLAN OOPS Messenger*, 1(1), Aug 1990.

[Whit89]   White, James E., "ASN.1 and ROS: The Impact of X.400 on OSI", *JSAC*, 7(7), Sep 1989, pp. 1060-1072.

[Wido90]   Widom, Jennifer, and Finkelstein, Sheldon, "Set-oriented Production Rules in Relational Database Systems", *Proc. SIGMOD 90*, pp. 259-270, 1990.

[Wido94]   Widom, Jennifer, and Dayal, Umeshwar, eds., *A Guide to Active Databases*, Morgan Kaufman, San Francisco, California, 1994.

[Wing90]   Wing, Jeanette M., "A Specifier's Introduction to Formal Methods", *IEEE Computer*, Sep 1990, pp. 10-22.

[Wink92]   Winkler, Jurgen, "Objectivism: Class Considered Harmful", *Communications of the ACM*, Aug 1992, pp. 128-130.

[Wins93]   Winskel, Glynn, *The Formal Semantics of Programming Languages: An Introduction*, MIT Press, Cambridge, Massachusetts, 1993.

[Witt22]   Wittgenstein, Ludwig, *Tractatus Logico-Philosophicus*, New York Books, New York, New York, 1922.

[Witt93]   Wittig, Marcus, and Pfeiler, Martin, "A Tool Supporting the Management Information Modeling Process", *Proc. 3rd ISINM 93*, pp.739-750, 1993.

[Wu90]   Wu, Stephen, and Kaiser, Gail, "Network Management with Consistently Managed Objects", *Proc. Globecom 90*, pp. 304.7.1-304.7.6, 1990.

[Wu91]   Wu, Shaun-inn, "Integrating Logic and Object-Oriented Programming", *ACM SIGPLAN OOPS Messenger*, 2(1), Jan 1991, pp. 28-37.

[XOpen C180] "OSI Abstract Data Manipulation API (XOM)", X/Open CAE Specification C180, Nov 1991.

[XOpen P170] "Systems Management: Management Protocols API (XMP)", X/Open Preliminary Specification P170, Jul 1992.

[Yell92]   Yelland, Philip, "Experimental Classification Facilities for Smalltalk", *Proc. OOPSLA 92*, pp. 235-246, 1992.

[Yemi93a]   Yemini, Yechaim, and Betser, Joseph, "Network Management Platform Technologies", Conference Tutorial Notes, *3rd ISINM 93*, San Francisco, California, 1993.

[Yemi93b]   Yemini, Yechaim, "The OSI Network Management Model", *IEEE Communications*, May 1993, pp. 20-29.

[Your79]   Yourdon, Edward, and Constantine, Larry, *Structured Design*, Yourdon Press, Englewood Cliffs, New Jersey, 1979.

[Your89]   Yourdon, Edward, *Modern Structured Analysis*, Yourdon Press, Englewood Cliffs, New Jersey, 1989.

[Zani84]   Zaniolo, C., "Object-Oriented Programming in Prolog", *Proc. 1984 IEEE Conference on Logic Programming*, pp. 265-270, 1984.

[Zani89]   Zaniolo, Carlo, "Object Identity and Inheritance in Deductive Databases: An Evolutionary Approach", *Proc. 1st DOOD 89*, 1989.

[Zegu93]   Zegura, Ellen Witte, "Architectures for ATM Switching Systems", *IEEE Communications*, Feb 1993, pp. 28-37.

[Zeil92]   Zeile, Mike, "Expanding the Enterprise by Collapsing the Backbone", *Data Communications*, Nov 21, 1992, pp. 71-80.

[Zitt91]   Zitterbart, Martina, "High-Speed Transport Components", *IEEE Network*, Jan 1991.

[Zolf91]   Zolfaghari, Ali; Ikuenobe, Tom; and Chum, Stanley, "A Model and Tool for Integrated Network Planning and Management", *Proc. 2nd ISINM 91*, pp. 413-424, 1991.

Abbreviations

AAL	ATM Adaptation Layer	CCS	Common Channel Signaling
ACD	Automatic Call Distributor	CCS	Calculus of Communicating Systems
AD	Adjunct Processor		
ADM	Add-Drop Multiplexer	CDMA	Code-Division Multiple Access
AIN	Advanced Intelligent Network	CDPD	Cellular Digital Packet Data
ANI	Automatic Number Identification	CHILL	CCITT High-level Language
		CLNP	Connectionless Network Protocol
ANSI	American National Standards Institute	CLNS	Connectionless Network Service
API	Application Programming Interface	CLOS	Common Lisp Object System
APPN	Advanced Peer-to-Peer Networking	CMIP	Common Management Information Protocol
ARP	Address Resolution Protocol	CMIS	Common Management Information Service
ASN.1	Abstract Syntax Notation One		
ATM	Asynchronous Transfer Mode	CMISE	Common Management Information Service Element
B-ISDN	Broadband ISDN		
BERT	Bit Error Rate Tester	CONP	Connection-Oriented Network Protocol
Bps	Bits Per Second		
BRI	Basic Rate Interface	CONS	Connection-Oriented Network Service
CASE	Computer-Assisted Software Engineering		
		CORBA	Common Object Request Broker Architecture
CATV	Community Access Television		
CBO	Continuous Bitstream Organization	CPE	Customer Premises Equipment
		CPU	Central Processing Unit
CBR	Constant Bit Rate	CSP	Communicating Sequential Processes
CCAF	Call Control Agent Function		
CCF	Call Control Function	CSU	Channel Service Unit
CCITT	International Telegraph and Telephone Consultative Committee	DAF	Distributed Application Framework
		DBMS	Database Management System

738

DCC	Data Communications Channel	IRDS	Information Resource Dictionary System
DCE	Distributed Computing Environment	IS-IS	Intermediate System-to-Intermediate System
DCE	Data Communications Equipment	ISDN	Integrated Services Digital Network
DFS	Distributed File System		
DID	Direct Inward Dialing	ISO	International Organization for Standardization
DLC	Digital Loop Carrier		
DLCI	Data Link Connection Identifier	ISP	International Standardized Profile
DMI	Definition of Management Information	ISR	Intermediate Session Routing
DS-n	Digital Signal-n	ITU-T	International Telecommunication Union, Telecommunication Standardization Sector
DSU	Digital Service Unit		
DTE	Data Terminal Equipment		
DTMF	Dual-Tone Multi-Frequency		
EDA	Electronics Design Automation	Kbps	Kilobits Per Second
ENE	End Network Element	LAN	Local Area Network
EOC	Embedded Operations Channel	LAPD	Link Access Procedure D
ER	Entity-Relationship	LLC	Logical Link Control
ES-IS	End System-to-Intermediate System	LOTOS	Language of Temporal Ordering Specifications
ESF	Extended Superframe	MAC	Medium Access Control
FAPL	Format and Protocols Language	Mbps	Megabits Per Second
FC	FiberChannel	MIB	Management Information Base
FDDI	Fiber Distributed Data Interface	MIS	Management Information System
FEP	Front-End Processor		
FIFO	First In First Out	MMM	Multiparadigmatic Modeling Methodology
FTAM	File Transfer, Access and Management	MPEG	Motion Picture Experts' Group
GDMO	Guidelines for the Definition of Managed Objects	MRB	Management Request Broker
		MTA	Message Transfer Agent
GNE	Gateway Network Element	NANP	North American Numbering Plan
GOSIP	Government OSI Profile		
GRM	General Relationship Model	NAP	Network Access Point
HDLC	High-level Data Link Control	NETBLT	Network Block Transfer Protocol
HDTV	High-Definition Television		
HIPPI	High-Performance Parallel Interface	NFS	Network File System
		NIAM	Nijssen Information Analysis Methodology
HSSI	High-Speed Serial Interface		
ICMP	Internet Control Message Protocol	N-ISDN	Narrowband ISDN
		NNI	Network-Network Interface
IDRP	Inter-Domain Routing Protocol	NP-hard	Non-Polynomially hard
IEEE	Institute of Electrical and Electronics Engineers	NSAP	Network Service Access Point
		OAM&P	Operations, Administration, Maintenance and Provisioning
IN	Intelligent Network		
INA	Information Networking Architecture	OC-n	Optical Carrier-n
		ODM	Object Data Management
INE	Intermediate Network Element	ODP	Open Distributed Processing
IP	Internet Protocol	OMG	Object Management Group
IRB	Instrumentation Request Broker	OOP	Object-Oriented Programming

ORB	Object Request Broker		SS7	Signaling System Number 7
OSA	Object Services Architecture		SSF	Service Switching Function
OSF	Open Software Foundation		SSP	Service Switching Point
OSI	Open Systems Interconnection		ST-II	Streams-II Protocol
OSPF	Open Shortest Path First Protocol		STP	Signal Transfer Point
			STP	Shielded Twisted Pair
PBX	Private Branch Exchange		STS-n	Synchronous Transport Signal-n
PDU	Protocol Data Unit		SVC	Switched Virtual Circuit
PLCP	Physical-Layer Convergence Protocol		TA	(Bellcore) Technical Advisory
			TCP	Transmission Control Protocol
PRI	Primary Rate Interface		TDM	Time-Division Multiplexer
PVC	Permanent Virtual Circuit		TDMA	Time-Division Multiple Access
QOS	Quality Of Service		TFTP	Trivial File Transfer Protocol
RFC	Request For Comments		TINA	Telecommunications
RIP	Routing Information Protocol			Information Networking
RISC	Reduced Instruction Set Architecture			Architecture
			TL-1	Transaction Language-1
RJ-n	Remote Jack-n		TMN	Telecommunications
RMON	Remote Network Monitoring			Management Network
RPC	Remote Procedure Call		TP-n	Transport Protocol-n
RTP	Real-Time Transport Protocol		TR	(Bellcore) Technical Reference
SCF	Service Control Function		TTCN	Tree and Tabular Combined
SCP	Service Control Point			Notation
SDF	Service Data Function		UDP	User Datagram Protocol
SDH	Synchronous Digital Hierarchy		UIMS	User Interface Management
SDL	Specification and Description Language			System
			UNI	User Network Interface
SDLC	Synchronous Data Link Control		UPT	Universal Personal Telephone
SDP	Service Data Point			Service
SLEE	Service Logic Execution Environment		UTP	Unshielded Twisted Pair
			UUCP	Unix-to-Unix Copy Program
SMDS	Switched Multimegabit Data Service		VBO	Variable Bitstream Organization
SMI	Structure of Management Information		VBR	Variable Bit Rate
			VDM	Vienna Development Method
SMS	Service Management System		VHDL	VHSIC Hardware Description
SMTP	Simple Mail Transfer Protocol			Language
SN	Services Node		VHSIC	Very High Speed Integrated
SNA	Systems Network Architecture			Circuit
SNMP	Simple Network Management Protocol		VLSI	Very Large Scale Integration
			VMTP	Versatile Message Transfer
SNPA	Sub-Network Point of Attachment			Protocol
			VPN	Virtual Private Network Service
SONET	Synchronous Optical Network		VT-n	Virtual Tributary-n
SQL	Structured Query Language		WAN	Wide Area Network
SR	Source Routing		XDR	External Data Representation
SR	(Bellcore) Special Report		XMP	X/Open Management Protocol
SRF	Specialized Resource Function		XOM	X/Open Object Management
SRT	Source-Routing Transparent		XTP	Express Transfer Protocol

Index

~ Denotes the enclosing top-level entry.
* Denotes ASN.1 items.